Computer Graphics

An Object-Oriented Approach
to the Art and Science

Cornel Pokorny

California Polytechnic State University,
San Luis Obispo

FRANKLIN, BEEDLE & ASSOCIATES, INCORPORATED
8536 SW St. Helens Drive, Suite D
Wilsonville, Oregon 97070
(503) 682-7668

Publisher	Jim Leisy
Developmental Editor	Samantha Soma
Manuscript Editor	Eve Kushner
Art and Production	Bill DeRouchey
Additional Production	Lisa Cannon
Proofreader	Tom Sumner
Cover Image	"Pier" by Kyle Campbell
Manufacturing	Hart Graphics, Austin, Texas

Rights and Permissions
Franklin, Beedle and Associates Incorporated
8536 SW St. Helens Drive, Suite D
Wilsonville, Oregon 97070

Library of Congress Cataloging-in-Publication Data

Pokorny, Cornel K.,
    Computer graphics: an object-oriented approach to the art and
science / Cornel Pokorny.
        p.   cm.
    Includes index.
    ISBN 0-938661-55-8
    1. Computer graphics. 2. C++ (Computer program language)
I. Title.
T385.P653 1994
006.6'6--dc20   94-2872
                                                             CIP

PREFACE

This book is written for students majoring in computer science, engineering, or mathematics, and developers of computer graphics systems. It presents the principles behind the art and science within an object-oriented context. Prerequisites for the material covered include both college-level mathematics and a modicum of the C++ programming language.

Computer-generated graphics are used in such diverse areas as displaying the results of engineering and scientific computations, producing television commercials, illuminating statistical data, generating the images for space movies, showing word processing documents as they will appear on paper, and computer-aided design. Consequently, the subject matter of this book is broad and combines elements of computer hardware and software, mathematics and numerical methods, complex data structures, and art.

This book covers these topics in detail, presents and compares multiple algorithms for generating images, and provides all C++ source code on diskette. Rather than discussing hardware separately, hardware is treated throughout the book where appropriate to the discussion of a graphics operation.

The source code follows an object-oriented design based on class hierarchies and polymorphic functions. This design makes the source code easy to change, adapt, or augment—changing functionality simply involves redefining member functions or deriving classes for new graphics objects.

Mastering object-oriented programming techniques increases the productivity of software developers; therefore this book presents computer graphics within the object-oriented programming paradigm. The object-oriented principles used in the design and development of the source code are emphasized in order to elucidate and justify their use.

There is more in this book than can be covered in a one-term course. The book's first half can serve to cover an introductory computer graphics course. The second half can be used for an advanced computer graphics course. Certainly, the instructor can pick some topics from the second half (like polygon meshes and backface removal) and leave out some of the first half (like parametric curves) in an introductory course, and vice versa. In a semester system the coverage might simply be more thorough throughout than in a quarter system.

ACKNOWLEDGMENTS

Thanks go to Curtis Gerald, for his patient and thorough help in writing the basic text for the first edition of this book. Thanks go to Jim Leisy and the staff at Franklin, Beedle and Associates for giving me the opportunity to write this book and for their encouragement all along the way—in particular to production manager Bill DeRouchey for the beautiful and neat figures.

Special thanks go to Number Nine Computer Corporation for donating a #9GXi 32-bit true color board, allowing me to do a significant part of the graphics work at home. Working with this fantastic graphics board gave me the first real true-color experience—it was and still is a very enjoyable one.

Thanks go to my colleague at California Polytechnic State University, Dr. Clinton Staley, for the lookup table manager, `colormap.c`, which is an absolute necessity for high-quality color work in any non true-color environment. It is a valuable help in all our graphics classes that work on 8-bit machines.

Thanks go to many of my students at Cal Poly: to Mike Cancilla for Xglib, the user friendly interface to the X Window graphics routines, a life saver in all our Computer Graphics classes; to Josh Lober for significant help in the procurement of hardware; to Todd Sprague for the raytracing scene-file preprocessor; to Tuyet-Nhi Luu for the depth sorting code; to Jane Young for testing the mouse routines; to Dave Meny for making photographic prints and slides of the pictures; and to all those who have contributed their raytracing pictures made in my last Computer Graphics class.

Heartfelt thanks go to my wife, Betty, my son, Peter, and my daughter, Vanessa, for making my life great.

In addition, thanks go to the following people whose constructive reviews of the manuscript improved the book:

Brian Barsky	*University of California, Berkeley*
Steve Cunningham	*California State University at Stanislaus*
William Kubitz	*University of Illinois*
Jim Murphy	*California State University at Chico*
Charles Williams	*Georgia State University*
Roni Yagel	*Ohio State University*

and also to the following people who helped to provide color images:

Adrienne Biggs	*Industrial Light & Magic*
Tim Bohn	actor, Schick commercial
Donna Clark	*J. Walter Thompson Company*
Bruce Fox	*Evans and Sutherland*
Googy Gress	actor, Schick commercial
Sue Mascer	*Photo Research*
J.R. McGrail	*J. Walter Thompson Company*
Benny Quan	actor, Schick commercial
Rick Shiiki	*Shiiki & Sichler*
Scott Sichler	*Shiiki & Sichler*

TABLE OF CONTENTS

1

INTRODUCTION

1

Each chapter of this book begins with a short overview to help prepare you for the material.

Chapter 1 gives an overview of the book, tells why computer graphics is important, discusses a number of its applications, talks about the C++ code, and concludes by summarizing the mathematics knowledge we expect you to have. The chapter is divided into five major sections.

1.0   **Overview of the Book** lists each chapter's major topics to show the progression of ideas.

1.1   **Graphical User Interfaces** discusses the importance of interfacing graphically with the computer and some developments in computer hardware that made it feasible to display information pictorially.

1.2   **Computer Graphics Applications** gives an overview of several applications, including paint systems, word processing, desktop publishing, presentation graphics, computer-aided design, and flight simulation. One of the earliest widespread applications was in computer games. The section ends with a definition of graphics primitives.

1.3   **The C++ Code** explains the design principles and the programming conventions used to produce the code that accompanies the book.

1.4   **Mathematics Background** summarizes the mathematical topics we expect you to know. If you feel weak in any of these areas, check the appendix, which provides a tutorial.

1.0   OVERVIEW OF THE BOOK

Computer graphics has become such a diverse and complex discipline that it cannot be mastered in a quarter or semester. This book will introduce you to the essentials of computer graphics knowledge: a mathematical background, various algorithms, examples of code, and some of the concepts behind the special hardware of graphics. A computer scientist is expected not only to use a graphics system, but also to design the systems of the future.

We intend this book to be a textbook, rather than an encyclopedia. We have written it for computer graphics students, not teachers. Instead of presenting the complete field of computer graphics, we have chosen essential topics, based on their importance (they are necessary in many image creation methods), simplicity (beginning computer graphics students can understand them), popularity (they are used in several important areas), and affordability (they do not require expensive hardware). We have made an effort to present topics in detail, including basic, established algorithms. We cover alternative methods more sketchily because a book with detailed descriptions of the entire field would be enormous and expensive.

We have excluded some methods because they are based on difficult mathematics or because of the book's limited volume. Those methods are β-splines (Barsky), some of the newer shading and reflectance models (Blinn, Cook, Torrance, etc.), certain methods for fractal generation (Voss), scan line algorithms for curved surfaces (Blinn, Lane, Whitted, etc.), ray tracing of free-form B-spline surfaces (Sweeney & Bartels), and radiosity methods.

In every scientific discipline, several solutions often exist for a particular problem, and computer graphics is no exception. Thus, several algorithms usually exist to produce a given graphic image. The various algorithms each have strengths and weaknesses. In a particular problem, one algorithm may be more efficient than another, even though both can do the job.

In some chapters, we present more than one method to solve a common problem. For example, in the chapters about scan conversion, there are four procedures for drawing a straight line, four for making circles, and several more for ellipses and polygons. This can create problems for the reader. You may wish to obtain an overview of them all and then choose to learn just one. However, if you are willing to make the effort to learn all of them, you will acquire a more thorough understanding.

While hardware is very important in computer graphics and some hardware items are built expressly for graphic output, you will not find a separate chapter on hardware. The reason for this is that hardware and software are so intertwined in computer graphics that we cannot consider either alone. Whenever you require a knowledge of hardware to understand certain functions or algorithms, we will present the details in the context of the discussion, sometimes in sidebars.

Each chapter begins with a description of its contents. Exercises at the end of the chapters will solidify your understanding.

Chapter 1 contains general information and introduces the notion of a graphics primitive, the first and most basic thing to learn in computer graphics. It discusses some design and coding principles for the C++ code and summarizes the mathematics used later in the book.

Chapter 2 covers scan conversion for straight lines and polygons. Scan conversion refers to displaying the graphics primitive on a raster display. Through this process, two important graphics primitives—straight lines and polygons—can become visible on a raster CRT.

Chapter 3 continues the discussion of scan conversion to include circular and elliptical arcs. While most curved lines in computer graphics are constructed as a sequence of connected, short, straight lines, these curves are used frequently and are simple enough to be drawn directly.

Chapter 4 is about windowing, clipping, and two-dimensional (2D) transformations, which are fundamental even for simple computer graphics. It introduces the concept of "world" coordinates versus absolute device coordinates and the transformations required to relate these. Then it introduces the concept of a window, and some algorithms that clip an image to a window. Finally, it explains how to change an object's orientation via 2D transformations.

Chapter 5 leads into three-dimensional (3D) space. We learn how to work with 3D vectors and matrices. Realizing that some students may lack a strong mathematical background in vectors and matrices, we have introduced this subject, not only in this chapter, but also in the appendix. The chapter deals with projections, 3D transformations, and 3D windowing and clipping using extensions of algorithms discussed in Chapter 4. We must use projections to display 3D objects on a 2D medium. A projection flattens a volume onto the two-dimensional display surface, analogous to the shadow that an object casts on a wall, except that the projections retain colors and other characteristics.

Chapter 6 introduces techniques for drawing plane curves. We present these as parameterized equations. In this chapter we explain how to draw B-spline curves, Catmull-Rom curves, and Bezier curves.

Chapter 7 explains how to construct curved surfaces, corresponding to the various types of plane curves. Also, it introduces the Oslo Algorithm.

Chapter 8 introduces color and light. Up to now, all the topics we have discussed can be handled on a black-and-white screen. This chapter adds color to displayed pictures. We explore the properties of light, present several color models, and explain the geometry for computing illuminations.

Chapter 9 introduces fractals. These have become important in recent years in many fields besides computer graphics. In graphics they help in drawing natural-looking scenes. We first explore the basic characteristics of fractals. We then treat them without using difficult mathematics. Finally, we give examples of ways to generate and render fractals.

Chapter 10 introduces techniques for hidden surface and line removal. We introduce the data structure of the polygon mesh. Beginning with the simplest algorithm, backface removal, we move to more complex ones; these sort the polygons that make up surfaces on their distance from the viewer.

Chapter 11 explains how to find which surfaces and parts of surfaces are hidden by other objects in a scene. We develop methods of general application, which are more time-consuming to compute.

Chapter 12 concludes the discussion of methods for hidden line and surface removal by considering two special cases with applications for displaying mathematical surfaces.

Chapter 13 explains some of the rendering techniques that have been developed in the quest for visual realism. Rendering simulates what we perceive when we look at objects in the real world. There are many different models for rendering; we avoid those with a difficult mathematical background. However, some ingenious and simple models give surprisingly good results. Phong shading fits this description and is widely used. This chapter compares Lambert and Gouraud shading to Phong shading and presents data structures useful in these methods.

Chapter 14 covers the principles of ray casting. It introduces a ray caster that can make more than just spheres. It defines three solid primitives and explains how to combine them to create almost any shape (this is also called Constructive Solid Geometry).

Chapter 15 extends the techniques introduced in Chapter 14 for recursive ray tracing by explaining reflection and transparency. It also talks about a speed-up method and the principles of distributed ray tracing.

Chapter 16 explains how to generate planar and solid textures. This is a modern technique in computer graphics that goes well with ray tracing. Chapters 14, 15, and 16 collectively present a method of photorealistic rendering. It is popular, powerful, and unsurpassed for creating scenes with objects that cast shadows onto each other, are transparent, or reflect other parts of the scene.

Chapter 17 explains why animation works and how to make animation in computer graphics. It explains real-time animation and conventional animation, which one does through a sequence of still pictures.

Chapter 18 categorizes the different applications and defines some computer graphics standards. We also describe various printers.

1.1 GRAPHICAL USER INTERFACES

We human beings are visually oriented creatures. Our highly developed and extremely powerful visual perceptors allow us to take in information pictorially. This makes a graphic interface with computers attractive. It took hardware advances to make a graphics interface commonplace. No longer must we communicate with the computer by typing cryptic commands and receiving cryptic messages in return. The Apple Macintosh exemplifies this user-friendly interface. Its windowing environment, drop-down menus and icons, and, significantly, its mouse-driven cursor have set the pattern for the two-dimensional graphics interface in most computers today. Using the mouse to interact with the computer hinges on optical feedback and the visual perception of motion, operating very much as a human hand grabs something. It is far superior to typing commands into a computer.

The user's needs are an integral part of any design, whether software or hardware. It is difficult to gear every design decision and all development details to the user's convenience. However, such considerations are vital, especially in interactive systems.

INTERFACING WITH THE OPERATING SYSTEM

An operating system has several functions, its major purpose being to help the user control the hardware. A large part of this relates to file handling: retrieving, storing, copying, deleting, and rearranging files on secondary storage media. The operating system also accepts user requests from a number of input devices and provides a data stream to output devices. Systems more sophisticated than a single-user microcomputer operating system must keep track of multiple functions when several people are using the system simultaneously. We will not discuss most of this because we want to concentrate on the user-machine interface and the role that graphics can play in the interaction.

With early computers, the user talked to the system with cards and a job control language (JCL). Learning to use JCL effectively was harder than learning a programming language. Part of the trouble was that the manuals certainly did not have the naive user in mind! Memorizing the cryptic and not very mnemonic commands proved arduous. To make matters worse, every machine's JCL was different, so that moving to a new computer was a major undertaking. After the demise (thank goodness) of card input, JCL's heritage continued, but not for long. Newer computer systems adopted better ways for the user to communicate. Micro-based personal computers led the way toward this improved communication. The breakthrough to the graphics-oriented user interface came with the Macintosh. This revolutionized the way the user issued commands. Now they could point to pictures instead of typing a command line.

The development of the personal computer was accompanied by drastically lower hardware prices. With inexpensive memory, a low-cost but powerful processor, and cheap peripheral chips, the personal computer has given us more capabilities than a mainframe of that time. In addition, it sits on a desktop! The personal computer's hardware environment has put computer graphics within everyone's reach. However, the user still cannot interact effectively through a graphics interface, nor can users create pictures in a truly "friendly" way. In two-dimensional graphics, present-day paint systems are setting a de facto standard, but for three-dimensional work, everything is still rudimentary. It depends on the development of graphics software. That is what this book is all about.

EXAMPLE: THE MACINTOSH INTERFACE

Actually, the Macintosh did not initiate the pictorial interface. Some years earlier at Xerox's Palo Alto Research Center, experimental graphics terminals and graphics-oriented operating systems interfaces showed that a mouse was a versatile pointing device and that pictures ("icons") were more descriptive than words and letters on the screen. Apple Computer obviously borrowed heavily from the concept pioneered by a competitor. You may wonder why Xerox does not receive more credit for leading the way. Well, so does the author. Much of the reason is the system's lack of commercial success, largely due to its high price. Desktop publishing is another Xerox innovation that will probably never receive proper acknowledgment. We hope you will forgive us if we also call something a Macintosh feature when the credit really lies elsewhere. Certainly Apple should receive applause for popularizing the "desktop" metaphor.

Figure 1.1 shows a typical Macintosh screen. The concept of working at a desk is suggested by a gray pattern on the screen that resembles a desk blotter. The Trash (a garbage can icon) is at the lower right. Icons representing each drive on the system are displayed at the right side with labeled pictures of the floppy disks they contain. At the top are headings for pull-down menus. They appear as if on a roller shade when you touch them with the mouse button depressed. Pushing the button while moving the mouse down (*dragging*) highlights each selection on the menu. Releasing the button activates the highlighted selection. The menu disappears and the highlighted function is performed.

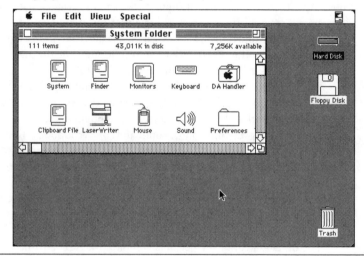

Figure 1.1   Macintosh desktop

You can bring a disk directory to the screen by clicking on its icon (a labeled picture), which will then be highlighted, and selecting Open from the File menu. This double action displays the directory in a window. Because doing two things is slow, the more experienced user double-clicks on the disk icon to bring up the directory more quickly. You can use the same technique to open a file. Click on its icon and select Open from the File menu. Again, double-clicking on the icon is faster. Files may be displayed by icons (labeled pictures) or by file names.

You can move windows on the screen by dragging them with their title bar. (Windows in this sense are different from the windows of Chapter 4. Here, they are rectangular "display sheets" for icons and other information.) You can enlarge or shrink windows by dragging the double square at the lower right. If you cannot fit all the file icons within the window, you can scroll vertically or horizontally by dragging the *slider box* within the right or bottom border. Alternatively, you can scroll more slowly by clicking on arrows at the ends of the borders.

You can copy files by dragging their icon to the desired destination, whether to another disk or to a folder. (A *folder* is another name for a subdirectory, but is perhaps more descriptive to someone with little computer experience.) Similarly, you can copy entire disks by dragging their icons. Delete files by "throwing them away" into the trash can (as you drag the mouse, the icon follows). In the Macintosh system, you can retrieve a discarded file by opening the Trash and spilling its contents onto the desk, just as one might dig into the wastebasket to get a discarded paper. However, you can do this only if you have not highlighted the Empty Trash command.

There is much more to explain, of course, but we only want to give you the flavor of a graphical user interface (GUI). What are the programming techniques behind such actions? We need to discuss how the system knows that a mouse has been moved and a button pressed. If there are two or three buttons, as on some mice, how does it know which one was pressed? Is it a routine matter for the system to display a menu and then remove it? How does highlighting work? How does the system store and edit icons?

The hard part of learning to write a Macintosh application is understanding what these routines do, how to write programs that use them, and the order in which to place commands. The tools are there, but require explanation and practice. Apple provides developers with a toolbox and certain standards for using them.

Of course, providing the developer with a toolbox is not unique to the Macintosh. Similar routines are available in GEM (Graphics Environment Manager), which runs on IBM PCs and many other computers. Other routines include Windows, another developer's package and, more recently, OS/2 for Intel-based PCs. These all provide user-oriented graphical features similar to those described above, plus other nongraphical features, such as task switching.

1.2   COMPUTER GRAPHICS APPLICATIONS

Computer graphics is applications-oriented. From its beginnings, developers have used computer graphics to solve problems that require more than just words as output. The first application may seem trivial, but is not; it permitted the user to draw on the screen. Ivan Sutherland's Sketchpad, SUTH63, showed that people could use computers interactively to produce graphic output on a CRT display. This early use of graphics has grown into elaborate systems that allow amateurs as well as professionals to become artists. The terms we now use for such interactive programs are *paint systems* and *draw systems*.

1.2.1   PRESENTATION GRAPHICS

The contrast between a picture and a "thousand words" may be most dramatic in the business world. Whether it be for individual analysis, making a point to associates, impressing a potential client, or catching the public's attention through an advertisement, presentation graphics is an important adjunct to managing, marketing, and sales. Computer-generated graphics can assist the process in several ways, though more is required than just a good computer and software. No program by itself can provide the artistic touch that good presentation graphics requires.

Business people rely on many types of charts and graphs. These include the familiar pie and bar charts, as well as line graphs. Specialized versions—high-low-close charts for stock prices, Gantt charts for project planning, and connected boxes for organization charts—are also common. Figure 1.2 shows two simple examples.

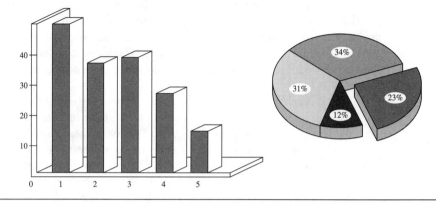

Figure 1.2   Bar chart and pie chart

The basic styles vary considerably. A pie chart may have one slice moved out from the center ("exploded"). Bar charts can be stacked, aligned horizontally or vertically, presented in perspective, shaded to provide a three-dimensional appearance, and so forth. Line graphs can use various styles for the data points or can hide the points. Several graphs drawn together can be distinguished by line type or color and can be shaded to look three-dimensional. When any of these charts and graphs has color, it becomes more dramatic and its message has more impact. The correct scaling is important. Captions and legends contribute as well, and good business graphics applications offer several type styles, sizes, and fonts.

One graphic can combine several features, for example, showing sales by state as stacked bars superimposed on a map. The vertical bar can be subdivided into colors to show the relative importance of separate customer groups, giving a vivid visual impression of the most significant groups in each state. On a CRT display, animation can add emphasis to parts of the graphic, for instance, by moving one slice of pie in and out of the pie. Displayed text can further explain an idea. Sound can be coordinated with images. The combination of these different media is called *multimedia.*

Graphics applications also enhance scientific presentations, education, publishing, or anything intended to inform, teach, impress, or sell. The average business person needs a simple package. A standard personal computer can easily display a chart on the screen. Putting the output into final form, usually as a slide or a printout, is another matter.

There are three phases in producing a business graphic. First, one must accumulate the data, then one must design and produce the graphic, and finally, one must put it into final presentation form. A spreadsheet program is often the source of data, but many applications can accept ASCII files in a variety of formats. For example, the spreadsheet program accumulates and organizes the data statistically, and then relates data to each other (sorting on various groups, etc.)

One option for the second step is to use a spreadsheet program with built-in graphics capabilities. Most spreadsheet programs include this feature, but they usually reduce one's flexibility. Nearly all independent programs can interface with standard spreadsheets and use data from standard files. They often provide a library of prepared images (*clip art*) that can be added to the final output. Several colors are available, but these depend on the graphics hardware. Many presentation graphics programs can use any of the standard graphics boards and monitors.

The third step in producing presentation graphics involves hardware. Normally, people want output to take the form of a color slide. The simplest way to obtain this is to photograph the CRT directly. Specialized camera arrangements do most of the work for you. A more professional product results from special film recorders that use the computer's frame buffer or, better still, accept commands to duplicate the picture in higher resolution. While a standard 35mm slide cannot really utilize more resolution than about 2000 lines vertically, some film recorders produce images with up to 10,000 vertical lines. (These are valuable in making sharp images on larger format film.) Film recorders, especially those that give high resolution, are expensive and may have to be operated by trained technicians, so one option is to employ a service bureau that specializes in producing slides from the data.

An alternative to producing slides is to display the graphic directly on a CRT, either on a slightly larger than normal computer screen, or on a TV screen. (Here, a change in the output signal may be required to give the NTSC [National Television System Committee] signal, as we explain in Chapter 17.) One advantage of this kind of output is the ease with which one can include animation and sound.

1.2.2   PAINT SYSTEMS

Graphics-oriented interfaces are the hallmark of the new desktop computers and a major milestone in personal computing. However, making the basic communication between human and computer more pictorial is just one example of computer graphics applications. Another is the wide variety of paint systems available for the home computer. These programs allow the user to produce simple pictures that resemble ones drawn with pencil on paper, but in many respects surpass the potential one has with hand-drawn images.

MacPaint, used on the Apple Macintosh, was one of the early paint programs, but was soon followed by many others: Degas and DegasElite on the Atari ST, and others for the Amiga and IBM-type PCs. Remarkably, these paint systems required no upgrade to the hardware; they literally ran on the computer as it came from the box. This was possible because the computers had enough memory to use a *bitmapped* display method. (We will explain this term in Chapter 2.) The original IBM PC did not have such a large memory, and its user interface was not graphic. As a consequence, it could accommodate a paint system only with added hardware. The newer IBM PS/2 units have an enlarged memory space and use bitmapped graphics, joining the other brands in providing the hardware for excellent user-friendly graphics. IBM's move underscores the importance of graphics capabilities.

1.2.3   WORD PROCESSING

Word processing has long been an important computer function, especially on desktop machines. Here too, graphics has made a contribution, allowing people to incorporate pictures into the document. No longer must we cut out pictures and paste them into every new printout. The newer systems resemble something between word processors and desktop publishing systems.

1.2.4   DESKTOP AND COMMERCIAL PUBLISHING

Desktop publishing is mostly a personal computer phenomenon. The term refers to composing a professional-looking publication without taking conventional paths to making books and brochures. To do this requires merging text and images, using a variety of fonts and type styles, arranging the material properly into pages, and having hardware that can print the product with nearly commercial quality or provide camera-ready copy for commercial printing. Such systems also display the entire page on the screen or even several pages side by side.

A desktop publishing program lets you set up columns for entering text. You can combine these in any desired way to direct the text flow, moving whole text columns or changing their shape. The program will then automatically rearrange the text in the columns to fit the new size. You can change the style and size of the text at any time. The text runs horizontally, except when more powerful systems allow you to change the text direction. Also, you can mix graphics into the text. This is possible because the system treats text as a graphics object, knowing the precise position coordinates, rotation, size, and style of every letter.

The system can read images from files as bit maps, crop, scale, or rotate them. This corresponds to commercial publishing systems' capability of dealing with high resolution color bit maps scanned in from photographs. These systems have more memory and higher processing speeds.

What makes desktop publishing possible is the laser printer and the Page Description Languages (PDLs). Here, Apple did make a contribution by marketing an affordable laser printer in early 1985. It was more than just moderately priced; it included a PostScript interpreter that generated characters in the professionally designed fonts that distinguish computer printing from commercial printing.

The idea of doing much of the publishing operation on a computer is not new. Commercial publishers have been using computers, often specially designed systems, in many phases of their work. Even so, commercial printing remains labor-intensive. Pictures and photographs are still cut and pasted by hand (stripped) onto the transparencies that are used to make the actual printing plates.

This is changing today. The tendency now is to do all prepress work on a computer. This requires fully merging line art (represented by paint systems), type art (text and fonts handling), and images (scanned bit maps) in one computer system. Commercial color prepress systems require a high resolution WYSIWYG (What You See Is What You Get) display with full color capability (a frame buffer with 24 to 48 bits per pixel), a high resolution scanner, and a laser film recorder. Today, these are available with the software.

A desktop publishing program is precisely such software. Because it runs on a desktop computer, it works much more slowly than a commercial prepress system. The screen display is not as accurate because it must cope with a lower screen resolution. The displayed colors are unable to reflect the colors on the final product precisely. Its output goes to paper through a laser printer, instead of to film through a laser film recorder.

What the ordinary user is unaware of is that camera-ready output, or output on printing films, must have all gray levels *screened* (see Chapter 18, PostScript). A desktop or a commercial publishing program does not do any screening because one cannot display screens on a CRT. On the CRT, they display the fill color or gray level of graphics primitives or letters as well as possible. No matter how good this display is, the gray level or color is stored only as numbers, which the laser printer will later transform into screens.

A desktop publishing program, similar to a commercial prepress system, transforms the document's internal description (position coordinates, rotation, font, style, and size of each letter; style, thickness of lines, arcs, and curves; fill color of polygons, letters, graphics primitives) into a PDL program, usually PostScript. The PDL interpreter on the laser printer then produces camera-ready or commercial quality output, including screening. Gray levels become screens and the high-quality letter fonts in the interpreter (not the ones in the computer) will be used to create the type. The printer's PDL interpreter will produce hard copy, whose resolution depends only on the printer's quality, not the computer on which the document was created. The same applies if the output is to a laser film recorder. There is only a difference of degree, not of principle, between desktop and commercial publishing.

On commercial quality color prepress systems, color printout is produced by decomposing the RGB-colors (red, green, and blue) in the computer document into the four printing primaries (cyan, magenta, yellow, and black) and creating a separate PDL description for each. This makes four different films, called *color separations*. With these, one can create printing plates for each of the four inks.

1.2.5 COMPUTER-AIDED DESIGN

One of the most important commercial applications of computer graphics is computer-aided design (CAD). CAD systems allow for speedy, simple design of buildings, mechanical systems, floor plans, electronic circuit boards, or engineering drawings, in both two and three dimensions. CAD systems save time and energy, especially when you revise the original design. You might use such a program if, for example, you were planning to rearrange your furniture, do some landscaping, or add a covered patio to your residence. Such simple projects are not hard for a professional to draw, but are difficult for the rest of us. The computer makes the output look professional, even if the user is not.

CAD has been a driving force in several computer hardware developments. However, large-scale CAD requires expensive hardware and software. The underlying computer graphics theory is more complicated and of a different nature than that used in paint systems or desktop publishing systems because it involves portraying objects in three dimensions. Several CAD systems for personal computers rival large-scale CAD systems' capabilities.

CAD systems aim to be "user-friendly"; one need not know algorithms or programming, but one still must thoroughly understand the geometric and mathematical essentials that underlie objects' design and the special commands that manipulate drawings. The system's very power creates considerable complexity in the user interface; one can master a CAD system only after considerable learning. The underlying system, however, is even more complex.

CAD's development is a good example of the interplay between hardware and software in computer graphics. The notion that a line is the basic element of pictures led to the early creation of vector scan devices. These, in turn, initiated algorithms for hidden line removal, still important for plotters, which are also vector devices. Vector scan technology was later surpassed by raster scan technology, which is in many respects more powerful. Raster scanning permits solid modeling, which is becoming essential in CAD systems. This book will explain raster scan hardware and the algorithms underlying solids modeling in detail.

For companies that design and lay out complex projects, computer-based design and drafting systems help cut costs, obtain results more rapidly, utilize libraries of previously created parts, and optimize the design. Such systems help people test and compare alternative designs, modify drawings or items from the library, and create customer presentations. They also store designs and their specifications compactly as magnetic files, rather than on bulky paper, and provide better organization and faster retrieval times. However, the major advantage is probably not cost savings, but improved designs.

Advanced systems do much more than replace draftspeople. Once someone specifies an object, the program can compute its properties, such as areas, volumes, cross sections, and so forth. Color output can discriminate between portions of the design with different functions, for example, differentiating fire protection lines from ordinary water lines, the hot water system from cold, and so on. The different portions of a complex wiring diagram in a control system can be set apart by color, or each can be drawn on a separate layer with the various layers overlaid to produce the whole.

Fields of application include aerospace (airplanes and space vehicles), automotive (bodies, drive train, control systems, springs, brakes), mechanical (machines, parts, plastic objects, molds and fixtures), civil (roads, bridges, dams, structures), electronic and electrical (circuit boards, integrated circuits, wiring diagrams, motors, electrical supply systems), architecture (buildings, landscaping, room layout), and the list goes on and on. You can sense something of the field's importance from hearing which companies are active vendors of hardware and software: IBM, GE/Calma, Hewlett-Packard, Lockheed, Boeing, Digital Equipment, and more specialized firms, such as Computervision and Applicon.

Perhaps the greatest economic advantages come not just from CAD itself, but from its integration with other steps in the manufacturing process. For example, the production of the masks used in manufacturing integrated circuits is now largely automated with CAD. Another example is CAD/CAM, an acronym for CAD plus computer-aided manufacturing. The concept is to use the design specifications and dimensions created in the design phase for input to automated manufacturing. Modern production tools can be controlled through computerization to produce mechanical parts more precisely than ever before with little human intervention. Such NC (numerically controlled) machines can receive input from the CAD system, a step toward the ideal of paperless manufacture, where hard-copy drawings are never required.

Another extension of CAD with great potential is CAE (computer-assisted engineering). Computing an object's properties (areas, volumes) is only the beginning. One application is to create the intermediate cross sections of an airplane wing from a few key sections made by the engineer, similar to the in-betweening described in Chapter 17. Another important application of CAE is using the finite element method (FEM) to calculate a part's behavior while still in the design stage (even before a sample has been manufactured).

CAD programs must maintain an internal record of objects' geometry and hierarchy, albeit not for graphics purposes. It is therefore not optimal to write a CAD application in a retained mode package, such as PHIGS (see Chapter 18). With little additional effort, the application can use its own data structures to do display traversal, pick correlation, etc. and use only the package's bare graphics primitives. Here, a retained mode graphics package means duplication.

1.2.6 FLIGHT SIMULATION

Another major computer graphics application is in flight simulation. While flight simulation is valuable only to a special class of users, it is so important for training pilots that a broad market is unnecessary. It offers great savings in fuel and aircraft, provides a safe learning environment, and can give the neophyte pilot experience in landing at many airports without leaving the ground. This application has led to the development of specialized hardware and software, with a strong emphasis on animation techniques. Custom electronic chips and highly parallel processing achieve the speeds needed for real-time simulation. However, these systems cost millions of dollars.

Even though many of the computations for flight simulation are done in hardware, the algorithmic principles are the same as those described in this book. Realistic flight simulation is available for personal computers, though this application is more of a game. Figure 1.3 shows a simplified example; when presented in color and with landscape changes that simulate a plane's actual approach to the runway, the result is most dramatic. You can learn more about flight simulation in Chapter 17.

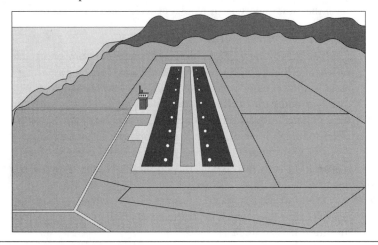

Figure 1.3   Runway approach in flight simulation

1.2.7 COMPUTER GAMES

Computer arcade games such as Pac-Man, Donkey Kong, and others have contributed considerably to the popularity of computer graphics. The early ones produced only flat, two-dimensional graphics, but later versions have excellent renditions of three-dimensional objects. Animation is a standard component. Custom-built hardware and sprites help achieve the speed necessary for their spectacular effects. Remarkably, these games do not use sophisticated graphics algorithms. They are interesting mainly from the standpoint of the digital electronic engineering. Almost all of them use color raster displays. Similar games that run on home computers are usually not as fast because they lack the hardware support of the arcade games. However, some of the newer home computers have programmable sprites that can speed up certain kinds of two-dimensional animation. We will discuss this in more detail in Chapter 18.

1.2.8 "PURE" COMPUTER GRAPHICS

The area we call "pure" computer graphics is where computer graphics is pushed to its limits. Algorithms and models are being developed to allow new rendering and shading techniques and new color effects. As people set more challenging tasks, they design and test new hardware. Here, the graphics artist must understand the mathematical background, master algorithmic details, be able to program everything to the last semicolon, and cope with and understand the special hardware. No graphics package or system can help create the picture that resides in the mind of this advanced graphics artist.

This is the area in which the most beautiful and breathtaking displays are produced, the area in which complicated computations are performed and high-speed computers run for hours to produce a single frame. Here, the graphics primitive is just a single pixel. Here, fractal landscapes of strange beauty are created, or fragile-looking glass objects float in space, penetrating and circling each other, reflecting and refracting the scene on their shiny surfaces. In this arena, artists can create animated scenes that one cannot observe in reality. Pure computer graphics also has an application in the field of TV commercials and space movies. We will cover the most important principles of such "pure" graphics.

GRAPHICS PRIMITIVES

This great variety of graphics applications does not mean that there is a similarly great variety of elements with which to create them. In fact, everything is constructed from three basic "atoms" of computer graphics. We call these elemental structures *graphics primitives*.

The most basic of all is the *pixel*, short for picture element. A pixel is a point of light on the computer's display screen, essentially a very small dot. Plotters and other output devices often do things differently, but they all can print or plot a dot.

The next important graphics primitive is the *line*. On a raster device, it is created by a sequence of closely spaced dots. It is a primitive because we need to perceive it as an indivisible unit.

The third and last graphics primitive is the *polygon*, a plane figure of more than two sides. We will define the polygon in greater detail in Chapter 2, but it, too, is a primitive because we must treat it as an single entity.

From these three graphics primitives, single pixels, lines, and polygons, we can construct all computer graphics images. Only the pixel is strongly hardware-based. We will assume that the system has a command, probably at the lowest level of system design, that sets a pixel at a given location on the screen. In our codes we use two different commands to do this, depending on whether we work in the X Window System or on the #9GXi graphics board. In the X Window System, the command

```
setpix(x,y)
```

sets the pixel at (x y) to the current drawing color. On the #9GXi board, the command

```
put_pixel(col,x,y)
```

sets the pixel at (x y) to the 32-bit color *col*.

1.3 THE C++ CODE

We use C++ for all coding because it is one of the most versatile and powerful programming languages today. We expect the reader to have some familiarity with C++. Almost all the topics we present come with C++ code, which is available on a diskette. You should use this code as a learning and teaching tool. Feel free to experiment with it and to make changes, additions, or deletions. The code focuses on the bare essentials. This means that sometimes the user interface could be more user-friendly or a class specification could be more general or more powerful. Whoever feels that way is welcome to add his or her ideas to the code.

Although codes are the final result of graphic algorithms, we cannot present them all in the text. Doing so would make this book too long and the reading difficult. On the other hand, explaining code that we have not included can be futile. We have tried to resolve this dilemma by including only class specifications, describing their behaviors, and explaining their data structures and function prototypes. Fortunately, implementation details are usually not important. In C++, specification and implementation are separable. When an implementation is short and instructive, we often include it in the text. We show the class hierarchies with class diagrams.

C++ is an extension of the C language and embodies all its features. C became the language of choice for most commercial and professional software developers because of its extreme flexibility, its concise way of expressing complicated detail, and its powerful pointer and dereferencing mechanism. Whether the C language is cryptic or not depends only on one's familiarity with it.

C++ far surpasses the powers of C. Its overloadable functions and operators make programming even more convenient and the code less distracting. It is possible to express the

sum of two vectors by:	`vec1 + vec2`
the dot product by:	`vec1 * vec2`
the product with a scalar *s* by:	`s * vec1`
the sum of two matrices by:	`mat1 + mat2`
the product of two matrices by:	`mat1 * mat2`

and whatever else the programmer chooses. Undoubtedly, the expression

```
mat1 * mat2
```

is easier to read and less distracting than

```
matmult(mat1,mat2)
```

There is no limit to the complexity that you can master with the powerful, abstract data types that you can define in C++. In this respect C++, with its inheritance mechanism and run-time binding capabilities, goes beyond Ada's capabilities.

When programming graphics algorithms and applications, there is ample opportunity to use all C++ features. You can express even simple, short algorithms in a more concise and familiar way with overloaded operators. However, the benefits of data hiding and inaccessibility of private members become clear only in the developmental stage of large systems that need many classes and complex class hierarchies. The codes in this book constitute a moderately large software system. Even so, we make extensive use of object-oriented design and programming principles (OOD and OOP), including inheritance and polymorphism.

However, we do not use these principles to excess, only when they help solve problems. If, for example, the problem space does not warrant using inheritance or polymorphism, we do not use them. We do not believe in squeezing these into a solution design that does not really need them; you will not find inheritance in a simple straight line DDA. Several paradigms justify using C++; inheritance and polymorphism are only two of them. Even without these, C++ is a superior programming language in several areas, including computer graphics. Other true OOP languages, such as Eiffel, CLOS, Object Pascal, and Smalltalk, cannot compare, due to their slower object code (run-time type checking), unavailability, or low popularity.

SOME DESIGN ISSUES

Conforming to modern software production style, we provide the code in the form of class specifications and implementations, and group them into several files. The files for a particular group of algorithms are collected in one directory, which bears a characterizing name.

All important abstract data types in this book are defined by two files. The first is a header file that contains the class specification—the class data members and the member function prototypes. These header files always have the file extension .h. The second file is the class implementation, which contains the member function bodies and sometimes additional functions or classes. (We consider such additional functions and classes "hidden" in the implementation.) The implementation #includes the specification. For example, the class sphere_t used in ray tracing is defined (specified) in sphere.h and implemented in sphere.c.

To prevent header file clashes (for example, repeated inclusion of the same class specification) each header file is preceded by the preprocessor directives #ifndef and #define and followed by #endif. The code for sphere.h is arranged as shown:

```
#ifndef SPHERE_T    // we use the class name in uppercase
#define SPHERE_T
// specification of class sphere_t
// only data members and function prototypes
// ....
#endif
```

The file sphere.c #includes the file sphere.h and all header files used here for class specifications. It contains the implementations of all member functions of the class sphere_t and, if applicable, other functions that are not part of the class interface, but are hidden in the implementation.

Because a class is a type in C++, we adopt the method of appending each class identifier with an _t (underscore t). This avoids confusion between variable identifiers and type identifiers, making code easier to read. (Other common methods not used in this text involve starting all type identifiers with uppercase letters or appending an uppercase T to them.)

We adhere to the design principle that logical units should be identical to syntactical units (files). As a result, syntactical units can be large (with several logically related member functions grouped in one file) or very small. All member functions and free functions remain small and logically independent from each other. Within the same implementation (that is, inside the same `.c` file), we do not always avoid global variables. Whenever it seems natural to communicate through a few shared globals among logically related functions inside the same `.c` file, we use globals and make them invisible from outside this file. If used properly, this not only makes the code easier to read, but also faster.

SOME PROGRAMMING RULES

The rules that we follow throughout are:

1. Constants specified in `#defines` are capitalized.
2. Variables and functions are in lowercase; only the first letter can be uppercase.
3. Each indentation level is three spaces.
4. Class and type definitions end with `_t` to mark them clearly as such. For example, the class representing a point in 3D space is declared as

```
class point3_t
{
    ....
} ;
```

5. In declarations of variables, commas or semicolons are separated from the variable by at least one space and are aligned as much as possible, to increase legibility, as in:

```
double high ,
       low  ,
       i    ;
```

6. Pairs of matching braces are positioned in the same column. They align with the first word of the control structure that necessitates them. The statements in the braces are indented by three spaces, as in:

```
for (i = 0; i < n; i++)
{
   x[i] = cos(2*pi*i/n);
   y[i] = sin(2*pi*i/n);
}
```

One exception is the `switch` statement, in which we do not indent on the first level. The other exceptions are occasional, short pieces of code in which we align only the closing brace, as in:

```
if (next) {
   foo(next); bar(next);
}
```

7. We distinguish between declarations with or without initializations and all other statements by the placing of the terminating semicolon; we insert one or more blank spaces before a semicolon on declarations and none in all other statements.

HARDWARE DEPENDENCIES

Because graphics must be written to match hardware, no code can run on all machines. However, the hardware dependencies can be limited to very few items. Two of those include the dimensions of the raster display, the width DWID and the height DHEI. All algorithms that run on a particular display share them. The reader might define a particular display's dimensions as:

```
#define DWID 640              // display width in pixels
#define DHEI 400              // display height in pixels
```

in the include file const.h. and include them wherever needed. In our code, the file const.h is included in the class specification win_view.h and therefore does not need to be included in .c files that use the window class.

The provided code runs on three different platforms: Xwin8, Xwin24, and Tiga. Xwin8 is the X Window System in UNIX with an 8-bit deep frame buffer and a lookup table. Xwin24 is the X Window System in UNIX with 24-bit true color but no lookup table. Tiga is Texas Instruments Graphics Architecture in DOS using the #9GXi 32-bit true color board and no lookup table.

Programs that produce graphics need two function calls in the main driver: one for initializing and one for ending the graphics environment. These, as well as all other platform-dependent function calls in the code are conditioned by #ifdef and #endif preprocessor directives. We sometimes include other graphics commands inside these directives, such as lookup table settings or current drawing color settings. The user has to define the platform on which the code is to run in the file opsys.h. This file is included wherever there is platform-dependent code. It consists of only three #defines, two of which should be commented out. Users of the X Window System on UNIX should consider that the platform to be defined (Xwin8 or Xwin24) is the one on which the graphics is displayed, *not* the one on which the code is running.

A reader who has neither of these platforms available will need to make changes in the platform-dependent parts of the code. In particular, the following graphics primitives should be available:

1. void move(int x, int y) ;
   move current location to (x y)
2. void draw(int x, int y) ;
   draw straight line from current location to (x y), update current location to (x y)
3. void setpix(int x, int y) ;
   set pixel (x y) to current drawing color
4. void setfr(int c) ;
   set whole display to color c in 8-bit color, or
   void setfr(int r, int g, int b) ;
   the same, but in 24-bit color
5. void col(int c) ;
   set current drawing color to c in 8-bit color, or
   void col(int r, int g, int b) ;
   the same, but in 24-bit color

6. `void setlook(int r, int g, int b, int loc) ;`
   only in 8-bit color:
   set lookup table entry *loc* to the values *r* (red), *g* (green), *b* (blue)

Not all of those are absolutely necessary. For example, move and draw can be implemented from setpix with one of the straight line DDAs. Functions setpix and col are basic, and we expect the reader to have at least these available. A reader who has hardware with 24-bit color does not need setlook.

The functions may be available in different concepts. Instead of move(x1,y1) and draw(x2,y2) there may be only one function, draw(x1,y1,x2,y2), which draws a straight line from $(x_1 \ y_1)$ to $(x_2 \ y_2)$. Instead of col(r,g,b) and setpix(x,y) there may be only one function, setpix(x,y,rgb), which sets the pixel at $(x \ y)$ to the 24-bit color *rgb*. All this is acceptable.

1.4 MATHEMATICS BACKGROUND

The mathematics used in computer graphics is not difficult; you have probably studied all you need to know in previous courses. At the same time, it is easy to forget. The following summary will refresh your memory. In addition, we will point out which topics are useful to us. The appendix contains a tutorial on these topics; refer to it if you need a fuller explanation.

COORDINATE SYSTEMS

We will normally use Cartesian coordinates to represent a point. We write them as number pairs or number triples with separating spaces (not commas). The point $(x \ y)$ is at distances *x* and *y* from two perpendicular axes. The reason for this departure from the usual (x,y) notation will become clear when we discuss vectors below. The $(x \ y)$-plane in which the coordinate axes lie can be divided into parts. The quarter between the two positive axes is the first quadrant. Drawing diagonal lines through the origin creates octants. In the first quadrant, the lower triangle is the first octant.

In three dimensions, the $(x \ y \ z)$ coordinates are measured from three mutually perpendicular axes. In 3D, if the thumb, index, and middle fingers of the left hand align with the *x*-, *y*-, and *z*-axes, we have a left-handed system (LHS). When the *z*-axis points in the opposite direction, we have a right-handed system (RHS).

The distance between two points is:

$$d = \sqrt{(x_2 - x_1)^2 + (y_2 - y_1)^2 + (z_2 - z_1)^2}$$

If we work in 2D, we drop the *z*-terms.

The use of coordinates pervades in computer graphics in describing the objects we display as well as their images on the screen. In fact, the essential problem of computer graphics is to compute points on the screen that correspond to points on the real object.

One operation that we will want to do is to rotate points by a given angle about the origin. Rotating a point by the angle ϕ is equivalent to rotating the axes by $-\phi$. After rotation, the point's coordinates are:

$$x_r = x\cos\phi - y\sin\phi \qquad\qquad y_r = x\sin\phi + y\cos\phi$$

ANALYTIC GEOMETRY

The relation $y = f(x)$ represents a curve in the $(x\ y)$-plane. If the curve is a straight line, there are several ways to express the relation. Most often we use the general form:

$$Ax + By - C = 0$$

where A and B are not both zero.

The distance of the point $(x_1\ y_1)$ from the line $Ax + By - C = 0$ is:

$$d = \frac{\left|Ax_1 + By_1 - C\right|}{\sqrt{A^2 + B^2}}$$

where the vertical bars mean absolute magnitude.

The general form of a plane in space is:

$$Ax + By + Cz - D = 0$$

where A, B, and C are not all zero.

The distance of the point $(x_1\ y_1\ z_1)$ from the plane $Ax + By + Cz - D = 0$ is:

$$d = \frac{\left|Ax_1 + By_1 + Cz_1 - D\right|}{\sqrt{A^2 + B^2 + C^2}}$$

Please refer to the sections on matrices and vectors for more information on planes.

PARAMETRIC DESCRIPTIONS

The relation $y = f(x)$ can be put into parametric form, where u is the parameter:

$$x = X(u) \qquad\qquad y = Y(u)$$

For a straight line between $(x_1\ y_1)$ and $(x_2\ y_2)$,

$$x = x_1 + u(x_2 - x_1) \qquad\qquad y = y_1 + u(y_2 - y_1)$$

As u varies from 0 to 1, $(x\ y)$ moves from $(x_1\ y_1)$ to $(x_2\ y_2)$ along the line.

A circle is described parametrically with θ as the parameter, by:

$$x = r\cos\theta \qquad\qquad y = r\sin\theta$$

Conic sections are described by quadratic equations. In the plane the equation:

$$Ax^2 + Bxy + Cy^2 + Dx + Ey + F = 0$$

where A, B, and C are not all zero, describes a circle, ellipse, parabola, or hyperbola.

Conics in space (*quadrics*) are described by quadratic equations with three variables.

We will mostly use points, lines, and planes to describe objects and their positions. The images will generally be formed from pixels, straight lines, and polygons. Lines in parameterized form are useful when computing projections and when intersecting rays with various objects in space.

ALGEBRA

We will solve quadratic equations, where $ax^2 + bx + c = 0$, with the formula:

$$x = \frac{-b \pm \sqrt{b^2 - 4ac}}{2a}$$

We solve cubic equations with Cardano's formula and quartic equations. These are explained in more detail in Appendix B.

Newton's method solves equations iteratively. If $f(x) = 0$, an approximate solution can usually be obtained by repeating the computation:

$$x_{n+1} = x_n - \frac{f(x_n)}{f'(x_n)}$$

$n = 0, 1, \ldots$ choosing x_0 suitably. We use it in ray tracing to improve the solution of a cubic equation obtained with Cardano's formula.

Cramer's rule solves two or more simultaneous linear equations using determinants.

VECTORS

A *vector* is an entity with both magnitude and direction; this means that a vector can be represented by a directed line segment. Two vectors are equal if they have the same magnitude and direction, so the point $(x\ y)$ is equivalent to the vector in the $(x\ y)$-plane from the origin to the point; x and y are called the components of the vector. Because a point and a vector are equivalent, we use $(x\ y)$ to represent a point, rather than (x,y).

A vector can have more than two components; $(x\ y\ z)$ is a three-component vector equivalent to a point in space. We will use four-component vectors such as $(x\ y\ z\ 1)$ in Chapter 5. A vector is represented symbolically by a boldface lowercase $\mathbf{v}$.

A vector is a special case of a matrix (see below). When a vector is considered as a matrix, there are two forms. A *row vector* exhibits its components in a row and is written $(x\ y\ z\ \ldots)$. When we need to consider the vector as components in a column, it is written as $(x\ y\ z\ \ldots)^T$ where the superscript T stands for transpose. Such a vector is called a *column vector*.

We can add and subtract vectors (here we use two-dimensional row vectors):

$$\mathbf{v}_1 + \mathbf{v}_2 = (x_1\ y_1) + (x_2\ y_2) = (x_1 + x_2\ y_1 + y_2)$$
$$\mathbf{v}_1 - \mathbf{v}_2 = (x_1\ y_1) - (x_2\ y_2) = (x_1 - x_2\ y_1 - y_2)$$

If a vector is multiplied by a scalar we have:

$$c \cdot \mathbf{v} = (cx\ cy)$$

The magnitude of a vector is its length:

$$|\mathbf{v}| = \sqrt{x^2 + y^2}$$

A vector is normalized by dividing each component by the length, producing a vector of magnitude 1.

In three-dimensional space, we will use two kinds of vector products:

Dot product: $\quad \mathbf{v}_1 \cdot \mathbf{v}_2 = x_1 x_2 + y_1 y_2 + z_1 z_2$

Cross product: $\mathbf{v}_1 \times \mathbf{v}_2 = \left(y_1 z_2 - z_1 y_2 \quad z_1 x_2 - x_1 z_2 \quad x_1 y_2 - y_1 x_2 \right)$

The *dot product* is a scalar quantity and the *cross product* is a vector. The latter vector is perpendicular to $\mathbf{v}_1$ and $\mathbf{v}_2$. When two vectors are perpendicular, their dot product is zero; when they are parallel, their cross product is zero.

The cross product of two vectors that lie in a plane is the best way to describe the plane's orientation, because this defines a normal vector for the plane. By forming the cross product of vectors drawn through three points and taken in counter-clockwise order, we define a vector that points to the positive side of the plane.

MATRICES

A *matrix* is a rectangular array of values, where the position and value are important. The matrix's size is given by the number of rows, r, and columns, c. The elements of a matrix are often represented by a subscripted lowercase variable, while the matrix itself is the same variable in bold uppercase or the general element enclosed in brackets:

$$\mathbf{A} = \begin{pmatrix} a_{11} & a_{12} & a_{13} \\ a_{21} & a_{22} & a_{23} \\ a_{31} & a_{32} & a_{33} \end{pmatrix} = \begin{bmatrix} a_{ij} \end{bmatrix}$$

Matrices can be added, subtracted, multiplied by a scalar, and multiplied with each other. You can learn more about this in the appendix.

To transpose a matrix, write the rows as columns. This is indicated with a superscript T:

$$\text{if } \mathbf{M} = \begin{pmatrix} 1 & 3 & 7 & 2 \\ -2 & 4 & 0 & -3 \end{pmatrix}, \text{ then } \mathbf{M}^T = \begin{pmatrix} 1 & -2 \\ 3 & 4 \\ 7 & 0 \\ 2 & -3 \end{pmatrix}$$

A vector is a special kind of matrix. A matrix with only one row is a row vector. With one column, it is a column vector. Using the notation for matrix multiplication and transposition, the dot product of two vectors is $\mathbf{v} \cdot \mathbf{w}^T$.

Square matrices have special properties. In the *identity matrix*, which we will use at times, all diagonal elements are 1 and all others are 0. Thus:

$$\mathbf{I} \cdot \mathbf{A} = \mathbf{A} \cdot \mathbf{I} = \mathbf{A}$$

A square matrix has a *determinant*, represented by magnitude bars. You can expand the determinant in terms of minors in any row or column. Expansion from row 1 of a 3×3 matrix gives:

$$|\mathbf{A}| = \det \mathbf{A} = a_{11} \begin{vmatrix} a_{22} & a_{23} \\ a_{32} & a_{33} \end{vmatrix} - a_{12} \begin{vmatrix} a_{21} & a_{23} \\ a_{31} & a_{33} \end{vmatrix} + a_{13} \begin{vmatrix} a_{21} & a_{22} \\ a_{31} & a_{32} \end{vmatrix}$$

$$= a_{11}(a_{22}a_{33} - a_{23}a_{32}) - a_{12}(a_{21}a_{33} - a_{23}a_{31}) + a_{13}(a_{21}a_{32} - a_{22}a_{31})$$

Using the formalism of a determinant, we obtain a concise expression for the equation of a line through points $(x_1 \ y_1)$ and $(x_2 \ y_2)$:

$$\begin{vmatrix} x & y & 1 \\ x_1 & y_1 & 1 \\ x_2 & y_2 & 1 \end{vmatrix} = 0$$

Matrices are widely used in graphics in transforming an image. This might include translating, scaling, and rotating the image, as well as performing geometric operations in space, as in ray tracing. Another application of matrix and vector notation is describing a general conic in space (sphere, ellipsoid, cylinder, cone, or hyperboloid). The general conic in space with the center (0 0 0) is represented by a *quadratic form*:

$$(x \quad y \quad z) \begin{pmatrix} m_{11} & m_{12} & m_{13} \\ m_{21} & m_{22} & m_{23} \\ m_{31} & m_{32} & m_{33} \end{pmatrix} \begin{pmatrix} x \\ y \\ z \end{pmatrix} = 1 \text{ or } 0 \text{ or } -1$$

DERIVATIVES

The following assumes $x = x(u)$, $y = y(u)$ and uses the notation $dx/du = x'$, $dy/du = y'$.

$$\frac{d(x+y)}{du} = x' + y'$$

$$\frac{dy}{dx} = \frac{dy}{du} \cdot \frac{du}{dx} = \frac{dy}{du} \div \frac{dx}{du} = \frac{y'}{x'}$$

$$\frac{dx^n}{du} = n \cdot x^{n-1} x'$$

$$\frac{d(\sin x)}{du} = (\cos x) x'$$

$$\frac{d(\cos x)}{du} = (-\sin x) x'$$

Differential equations describe some important objects of computer graphics:

A line: dy/dx = constant.
A circle: $dy/dx = -x/y$ (center is at the origin).

Derivatives help us express the slope of a curve.

COMPLEX NUMBERS

Complex numbers are composed of a real part and an imaginary part, $z = a + ib$. Because they resemble two-component vectors in their makeup, an alternate representation is $z = (a \quad b)$. This is a point or a vector in the complex plane, which has two perpendicular axes. Such a representation is called an Argand diagram.

Addition and subtraction are isomorphic to vectors. In vector representation, multiplication and division are:

$$z_1 = \left(a_1 \ \ b_1 \right) \qquad z_2 = \left(a_2 \ \ b_2 \right)$$

$$z_1 z_2 = \left(a_1 a_2 - b_1 b_2 \ \ a_1 b_2 + a_2 b_1 \right)$$

$$\frac{z_1}{z_2} = \frac{\left(a_1 a_2 + b_1 b_2 \ \ a_1 b_2 - a_2 b_1 \right)}{a_2{}^2 + b_2{}^2}$$

The magnitude of a complex number is:

$$|z| = \sqrt{a^2 + b^2}$$

We will use complex numbers in describing some fractals.

BINARY NUMBERS

Computer memories are composed of bistable (can assume only two different values) elements, so all values must be stored in binary. A *binary number* uses place values that are powers of 2. For example, (1 0 1 1 0 1) as a base 2 number

$$= 1(2^5) + 0(2^4) + 1(2^3) + 1(2^2) + 0(2^1) + 1(2^0)$$
$$= 32 + 0 + 8 + 4 + 0 + 1 = 45 \text{ as a base 10 number.}$$

The AND and OR of two binary numbers is computed by ANDing or ORing the corresponding bits. Another operation is XOR, exclusive OR. The results of each are given by:

AND	0	1
0	0	0
1	0	1

OR	0	1
0	0	1
1	1	1

XOR	0	1
0	0	1
1	1	0

RANDOM NUMBERS

Drawing from an infinite pool of noncorrelated values produces random numbers. However, computers must determine them by other means, so they are not really random, but pseudorandom. In effect, a set of numbers is random if the value of any of them is not known in advance. We will use random numbers in computing some fractals and in simulating some solid textures.

ABSTRACT DATA TYPES

C++ is one of the most powerful languages to implement abstract data types. An abstract data type (ADT) is a construct of simple or other abstract data types together with an interface that describes its behavior and its interaction with other ADTs or pieces of code. We will use several abstract data types, depending on the problem to which they relate. In C++ they are usually implemented through classes. Aside from ADTs, we will also use traditional aggregate types, such as arrays, structures and linked lists.

Arrays: The successive values of the set are referenced through a subscripted variable. For example, $x[0]$, $x[5]$, $x[99]$ are the first, sixth, and one-hundredth members of the set. Double subscripts allow us to reference a table or matrix of values. All elements of an array must be of the same type.

Structures: The members of the set are elements that are not necessarily alike (floats, integers, strings, etc. can be combined). Structures are the precursors of classes in C++. Classes differ from structures in that their members can be not only data, but also functions.

Linked lists: We can link structures together by including pointers to (addresses of) other structures as elements of each structure. The address of the list's first structure is called head pointer. A null pointer in the last structure indicates the end of the list.

SUGGESTED READINGS

More about various computer graphics applications can be found in MIEL91 and in the reference manuals for the diverse products like Publishing Partner for the Atari or Versacad for the PC. A good introduction to C++ is LIPP91. As an introduction to OO thinking, BARD93 is recommended.

EXERCISES

SECTION 1.2

1. Make a list of all the computer systems at your school or organization that have graphics capabilities. Which of these are accessible to you and which are restricted to a set of special users? Do all provide color displays or are some equipped only with monochrome displays? Are any what you would call *special purpose* installations?

2. In the card catalogue of your library, look up titles of books under the heading "Computer Graphics." How many are there? List those in some specialized field of interest to you.

3. Computer graphics probably began with an important study by Ivan Sutherland at the Massachusetts Institute of Technology that developed Sketchpad. Do some literature research to find references to this system and write a brief report that summarizes its capabilities.

4. Most of today's personal or desktop computers have graphics capabilities. Help a prospective purchaser decide between two brands of small computers by writing a report to compare their features.

2

STRAIGHT LINES AND POLYGONS

Straight lines and polygons, basic elements in computer graphics, form the subject matter of Chapter 2. There are four major sections.

2.0   **Introduction** explains why lines and polygons are important, how the spacing of pixels affects the problem of setting the proper pixels, and what criteria a good line-drawing algorithm should meet. Since polygon edges are straight lines, these considerations apply to them as well.

2.1   **Straight Lines** can be developed in two different ways. A structural method determines which pixels to set before drawing the line. A conditional method tests certain conditions to find which pixel to set next.

2.2   **Polygons** are drawn with straight lines as their edges. One must carefully consider how to store the data that describes the polygon. We examine this problem in some detail.

2.3   **Polygon Filling** normally occurs once the polygon is defined. It is filled either with a constant color, a pattern, or with crosshatches. We explain these techniques in this section.

2.0   INTRODUCTION

Lines, especially straight lines, constitute an important building block of computer images. They are used in line graphs, bar and pie charts, two- and three-dimensional graphs of mathematical functions, engineering drawings, and architectural plans. Their importance becomes even clearer when we consider that curved lines are often approximated by a sequence of short, straight lines in computer graphics. Efficient methods of drawing straight lines are quite valuable. The algorithms to draw straight lines are similar conceptually to those of curved lines, such as circular and elliptical arcs. Because the latter are so common in computers and are mathematically simple, we should consider special algorithms for them, rather than always approximating them with short, straight lines. We will do this in Chapter 3.

In computer graphics the straight line is so basic in creating an image that we call it a graphics primitive. In raster displays (see below), the pixel is another basic building block. Calling one tiny dot on the display a graphics primitive is not entirely correct, because it has no structure. However, this is not really important. The third basic building block we consider to be a graphics primitive is the polygon; we will introduce it later in this chapter.

Actually, there is no generally accepted definition of a graphics primitive. Throughout this book, we will define it as a graphics object used so often that it is essential to creating images. These primitives can help construct the most complex images.

When we use these primitives, we must specify certain parameters. With `setpix()`, which sets a single pixel, we give the screen coordinates of the pixel that is to be set. (With a color display, we add a third parameter for the color.) The straight line primitive requires that we specify the coordinates of the line's beginning and end.

We have said that a pixel is the most basic graphic building block in pictures generated by computers on raster displays. In the next several pages we explain what pixels are and how we work with them. To do this, we must first explain the hardware for raster graphics.

THE CATHODE RAY TUBE

The *CRT* (*cathode ray tube*) is the most important display device for computer graphics. We will describe the basic principle of the black-and-white CRT, which is used in black-and-white TVs and computer displays. Figure 2.1 shows a cross section.

At the narrow end of a sealed conical glass tube is an electron gun that emits a high-velocity, finely focused beam of electrons. The other end, the CRT's face, is slightly curved and is coated inside with phosphor, which glows with a certain color when the electron beam strikes it. The beam's energy can be controlled so as to vary the intensity of light output and, when necessary, to cut off the light altogether. A system of electromagnetic coils mounted outside the tube at the base of the neck can deflect the electron beam to different parts of the tube face. This system of coils is called the *yoke*.

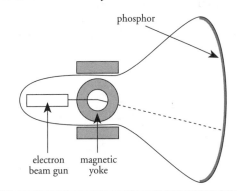

Figure 2.1   Cross section of a cathode ray tube

The phosphors used in a graphic display are chosen for their color and persistence. The color is conventionally green, but in newer tubes it is amber, or preferably white, particularly for applications where dark information appears on a light background. Persistence is the time it takes for the brightness to drop to one-tenth of its initial value after the electron beam stops exciting the phosphor. Ideally, it should last about 100 milliseconds or less, allowing refresh at 30 Hz rates (Hertz = cycles per second) without noticeable lingering as the image is changed.

You can produce a picture on the screen by tracing it out with the electron beam. There are two different methods of doing this. The most common one is the raster scan, where the electron beam sweeps in a fixed path and with fixed speed over the entire screen surface. Two oscillators produce sawtooth-like curves of voltages, which, after amplification, are applied to the deflector coils in the yoke. One of the oscillators deflects the beam in a left-right direction with a frequency between about 12 and 32 Khz, sometimes higher. The other deflects it up and down with a frequency of about 60 Hz. The movement to the left (horizontal retrace) is much faster than that to the right (raster line). See Figure 2.2.

Similarly, the movement up (vertical retrace) is much faster than the movement down (downward sweep). See Figure 2.3.

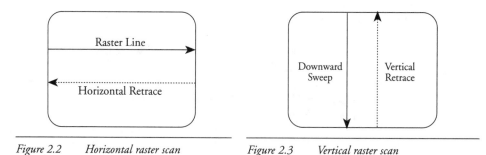

Figure 2.2   *Horizontal raster scan*   Figure 2.3   *Vertical raster scan*

The combination of these two oscillations makes the beam sweep the screen surface in parallel, almost horizontal lines. Figure 2.4 shows the path of the beam during a downward sweep, while Figure 2.5 demonstrates the path during a vertical retrace. A downward sweep is called a *field*. Covering the whole screen surface with scan lines is called a *frame*. Here, a field is identical to a frame.

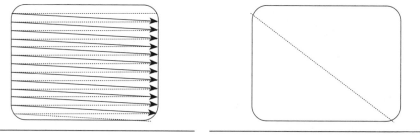
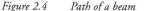

Figure 2.4   *Path of a beam*   Figure 2.5   *Vertical retrace*

The heavy lines from left to right in Figure 2.4 are the only part of the path during which the beam can be turned on to a writing intensity. During the movement from right to left the beam is always turned off. This path is idealized. In practice, there is a slight overscan on the left, right, and bottom that is not shown here. The lines are much denser, about 500 per sweep, sometimes over 1000, depending on the tube model and driving circuitry. This makes the lines almost horizontal. The path of the vertical retrace is idealized, too. In some CRTs, when the beam is not jerked up fast enough, it zigzags a few times on the way up, because the horizontal oscillation does not stop during the vertical retrace.

NONINTERLACED VERSUS INTERLACED METHODS

Graphics CRT displays can work with as few as 200 and as many as 1000 scan lines. However, in our explanation of the difference between these two techniques, we assume a display of 400 scan lines.

If the horizontal frequency is about 400 cycles for each vertical cycle (vertical frequency 60 Hz), the beam will scan all 400 scan lines per field. Each field produces an entire frame. Our horizontal frequency needs to be approximately 24 Khz. We say "about 400 cycles" and "approximately 24 Khz," because some horizontal scans will be done during the vertical retrace and so will be lost in the scan line count, but these details are not important for your understanding of this simplified model. This straightforward scanning method, called *noninterlaced*, corresponds directly to Figures 2.4 and 2.5. It is the highest quality CRT display method, and CRTs of this type are becoming more popular.

Lower quality CRT monitors (and other related hardware) cannot work with such a high horizontal frequency; they apply the *interlaced* display technique. This technique allows (in our example) the production of 400 scan lines on the screen, while working with only half the horizontal frequency; with just 12 Khz, the beam's left-right movement will be half as fast. Consequently, only 200 horizontal lines will be drawn for one vertical sweep, and they will be farther apart from each other. How, then, do we obtain the 400 scan lines we need for a frame? Through interlacing.

Interlacing results from making a slight change in the ratio between horizontal and vertical frequencies. If we choose a nonintegral number of horizontal lines for each vertical retrace, say 200½ instead of 200 lines, the first line will fit entirely on the screen, but only half of the lowest scan line appears on the screen. See Figure 2.6 (an *odd field*). In the next field, after the vertical retrace, half of the first scan line will be drawn on the screen. By the end of this field, however, the last scan line will fit entirely on the screen. See Figure 2.7 (an *even field*).

Therefore, all the second field's scan lines will be drawn precisely in between the first field's scan lines. We can verify this by superimposing these two figures.

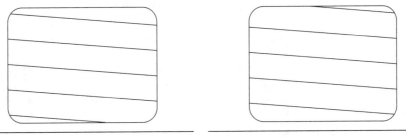

Figure 2.6   Odd field   *Figure 2.7   Even field*

In the third field, the first scan line will again fit entirely on the screen, so this field will be identical to the first. Thus, an odd and even field alternate. Two consecutive fields together put 400 scan lines on the screen, thereby producing one frame. However, now a frame takes two vertical cycles and therefore 1/30 of a second. This technique is developed to perfection in TV monitors and is adopted in many CRT displays. Good graphics monitors, however, work noninterlaced.

DISPLAYING A PICTURE

A picture is displayed by turning the beam on or off at certain points during its sweep over the screen. These points are called *pixels*. A fixed number of pixels divides each scan line. This number does not depend on the CRT's hardware, only on the frequency with which the beam can be switched on and off, or the *pixel rate*.

The number of pixels per scan line is fixed for each display setup. Continuing with our example, we assume that a scan line has 640 pixels. Accordingly, the whole screen is covered with a rectangular raster of $640 \times 400 = 256,000$ pixels. The more pixels there are, the finer the display's resolution becomes. By turning on the proper pixels, we display pictures, but only within the limits of this finite resolution. The horizontal distance between pixel centers depends on the pixel rate; the vertical distance is identical to the scan line distance and depends on the horizontal frequency. Pixels, therefore, are not always square. Pixels are turned on in response to bits in a frame buffer. We explain this process below.

Figure 2.8 shows the raster display of a pie divided into six equal parts. The pie is very small in relation to the pixel raster to exaggerate the effects of this display. In reality, adjacent pixels touch or even overlap one another. This makes the picture a little smoother.

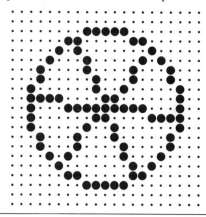

Figure 2.8   Raster display

The beam's movement is independent of the displayed picture; even if nothing is displayed, the beam still sweeps across the screen. As the beam travels through its scan lines, it is turned on or off at the proper positions. Figure 2.9 shows the uppermost three scan lines of the pie above and the sequence in which the beam hits the pixels that will be turned on in noninterlaced display mode.

Figure 2.9   Sequence of pixel illumination

To produce a steady display the whole field must be redrawn at least 30 times per second. The information about which pixels will be turned on is stored in the computer memory in a *frame buffer*. For a simple black-and-white display, each pixel needs only one bit. In our example of 640×400 pixels, the frame buffer needs 32 Kbytes. A 1 bit means "pixel on" and a 0 bit means "pixel off." It is now the computer's duty to send the frame buffer information at precisely the same speed at which the monitor scans the screen and to send a "set" signal whenever it meets a 1 bit. A CRT controller usually performs this task.

An alternative to raster display is the vector scan CRT. Instead of displaying pixels, the electron beam can be moved anywhere on the screen to draw curves directly. The raster scan has many advantages, so we concentrate on this more widely used output device.

OPERATION OF THE CRT CONTROLLER

Every time the computer is booted up, the operating system prepares the CRT controller for its task by setting the display parameters. The most important parameters are the number of bytes per scan line, the number of scan lines per field, whether the operation is interlaced or noninterlaced, and the length of the monitor's horizontal and vertical retraces.

To match the speeds of these two processes precisely (the electron beam's scanning of the screen and the CRT controller's scanning of the frame buffer), the CRT controller sends out horizontal and vertical synchronization signals to the monitor circuitry. It sends a horizontal sync whenever one line has been scanned (judging by the number of bytes sent). The controller sends a vertical sync whenever one field has been scanned (judging by the number of horizontal sync signals sent). These sync signals are able to correct for moderate deviations in the monitor circuitry's speed.

Here is how the process works in the simple case of a black-and-white display without gray levels. In the frame buffer, one byte contains information for eight consecutive pixels on the screen. When the CRT controller accesses the byte, its eight bits are moved in parallel into a shift register. From there, they are shifted out serially to the monitor circuitry. See Figure 2.10. In that figure, the byte containing the first eight bits in the first scan line has just been addressed and has moved into the shift register. The first five bits have been shifted out and appear on the screen.

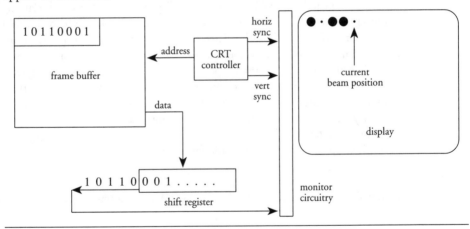

Figure 2.10   Schematic of the CRT controller's operation

Here, the controller accesses one byte at a time, the data bus is eight bits wide, and the shift register holds eight bits. It shifts bits out at the pixel rate (approximately 15 Mhz for the noninterlaced display in our example). The frame buffer must be accessed once for each eight pixels. This results in a contention for frame buffer accesses with the main processor setting the proper bits in the frame buffer to create pictures. If, for example, 256 bits could be shifted in parallel into a correspondingly long shift register, the contention problems would be reduced drastically. This has led to the development of *video RAM chips*, which have long shift registers and are used for high-resolution graphic CRT displays (see, for example, the Texas Instruments TMS4161 description). The display technique in which one or more bits of memory represent each pixel is called *bit-mapping*, because the bits in video memory are "mapped" onto pixels on the screen.

GRAY LEVELS

The electron beam's intensity can be not only on or off, but also in intermediate states. The light that the phosphor emits will then have intermediate intensities. This is how one can achieve gray levels. To store the several possible gray levels of a pixel, we need more than one bit per pixel. With four bits, we can store 16 different gray levels. The 640×400 pixel display then needs a frame buffer of 128 Kbytes.

We will not go into details about the hardware architecture of such frame buffers, reading the information, shifting it out, and so on. Instead, we will imagine four of the above setups working in parallel, called *bit planes*. All four bit planes have the same addresses, and the data are shifted out in parallel. The four bits coming out of the bit planes are fed together into a *D/A* (*digital to analog*) converter. From there, the analog intensity goes to the monitor. However, the luminosity of the pixels displayed is not exactly proportional to this voltage (see sidebar on gamma correction).

Gamma Correction

A characteristic problem with CRT displays is the nonlinear relation of input to output. More precisely, the voltage applied to the CRT monitor to control the electron beam's intensity is not linearly related to the intensity of the phosphor's luminous output. For example, doubling the voltage of the input signal does not double the pixels' luminosity. The luminosity is less than expected at low voltages and more at higher voltages.

The input normally varies from 0 volts to about 5 volts, but this varies widely from monitor to monitor. We can account for this variation by normalizing the range of the display signal inputs, considering the lowest input as 0 and the highest input as 1. Let us do the same for the phosphors' luminosity output. Then, we can express the nonlinear relationship approximately with the formula:

$$(display\ signal\ input)^{gamma} = luminous\ output$$

in which *gamma* does not equal 1. Figure 2.A shows a typical nonlinear relationship.

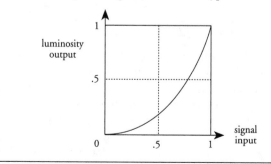

Figure 2.A   *Nonlinear relation between input and output on a CRT*

Even though monitors differ, the basic shape of this curve is about the same. The curve is well-approximated by the above relation, with gamma-values ranging from 2 to 2.8. While the gamma-values differ in monitors, the international convention is to assume a gamma-value of 2.2. This means that applying 50 percent of full-scale input voltage will result in 22 percent of full-scale luminous output.

The value of gamma reflects the nonlinear relationship between output and input; a gamma-value of 1 would demonstrate a linear relation. For television signals, the gamma nonlinearity is corrected at the source of the signal, the TV camera, by reversing the above relation. The signal output is raised to the power $1/2.2 = 0.454$ by analog circuitry. The overall relation from source to CRT monitor will then be linear.

With a computer graphics monitor, there are several ways to handle this nonlinearity. One way is to have built-in analog circuitry that corrects the display signal that the D/A converter generates before it applies this signal to the monitor. Another way is to correct all intensity values by software. In a monochrome display with gray levels, one could correct all intensities before entering them in the frame buffer. In a color display, intensity values are stored in the lookup tables (see Chapter 8) and must be corrected there for all three primary colors (red, green, and blue). The correction consists of raising the fractional intensity value to the power 0.454.

For example, assume an intensity of 100 in a range of 0 to 255. The fractional value is $100/255 = 0.392$. Since $0.392^{0.454} = 0.654$, the corresponding intensity of 167 (0.654×255) is entered instead of 100.

Designers of graphics systems must know whether their monitors have built-in gamma correction, so as to compensate if necessary. However, we sometimes just ignore this and accept the nonlinearity as an inherent characteristic of the system.

SCAN CONVERSION

Scan conversion is the process of creating the pattern of dots to match the object to be displayed. In this chapter we will develop techniques for scan conversion of straight arcs and polygons; we will consider circular arcs and elliptical arcs in Chapter 3. While it is possible to build scan conversion algorithms for all sorts of algebraic curves, including parabolas and hyperbolas, we will usually not need them, so we will not develop algorithms for them. Another reason why we can ignore these other curves is that any algebraic curve can be so closely approximated by a sequence of short straight lines that it is impossible for a human observer to tell the difference. Finally, the raster of dots that are used to display everything forces an optical digitization; therefore, virtually everything on such a display is only an approximation of the real-world object.

PIXEL RATIO

The horizontal and vertical distances between pixel centers depend on the characteristics of the display monitor and the setting of the CRT controller; the programmer cannot normally influence them. Sometimes, especially on older systems, pixels are more closely spaced horizontally than vertically. We define the pixel ratio as the horizontal distance between adjacent pixels divided by the vertical distance. Raster displays with pixel ratios other than 1 have all but disappeared. We will therefore assume a pixel ratio of 1 in all scan conversion algorithms. Pixels are not always round; they can also have the shape of an ellipse. The definition of a pixel on a color CRT is more complicated, so we will discuss it later.

BASIC PROBLEMS

Several basic problems arise when converting a line to pixels on a raster display. (A vector display brings a different set of problems.) Circular arcs have the same problems as straight lines; we will only discuss the situation for straight lines.

To create the image of a line, certain pixels on the screen must be turned on. This set of pixels is often called a *digital arc* or *digital line*. For the same straight line, many different combinations of pixels can be set to give essentially the same impression; see Figures 2.11 and 2.12.

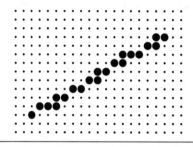

Figure 2.11   Raster image of a straight line

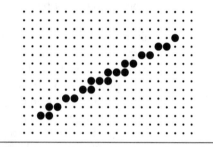

Figure 2.12   Another raster image of a straight line

Let us consider what criteria are appropriate for drawing a line by setting pixels on the screen.

1. The line should not look too thick, as in Figure 2.13. Do not set more pixels than necessary when constructing a line.

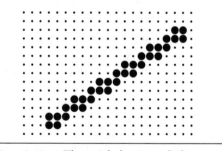

Figure 2.13   The straight line is too thick

2. The line should not look too thin, as in Figure 2.14. Set enough pixels to have a coherent sequence of adjacent pixels. There should be no gaps.

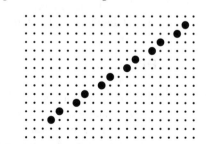

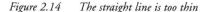

Figure 2.14   The straight line is too thin

3. The line should have constant density, or equal thickness, not unevenness, as in the line in Figure 2.15.

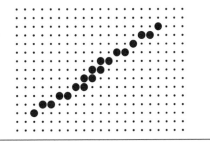

Figure 2.15   The straight line is uneven

We will not attempt to postulate a necessary minimum requirement for creating a straight line, because this depends on many factors, including the user's judgment. For example, when are pixels adjacent? We could find a simple mathematical formula for our rectangular grid of pixels, but we prefer not to give many mathematical definitions at this point. We will quantify some of these concepts later in this chapter.

As we have seen, the picture that appears on the screen represents the contents of the frame buffer. Every pixel on the display corresponds to a certain location in the frame buffer. In order to set a particular pixel, we must set the corresponding location in the frame buffer to a certain value. In a simple black-and-white display, the corresponding location in the frame buffer consists of a single bit. We must set this bit to 1 to express white and 0 to express black (or the reverse, if that is the way the hardware was designed). In a color display, the frame buffer locations consist of several bits in order to express the particular color choice for each pixel. Regardless of the pixel's color, the line-drawing algorithm must determine the proper locations. This problem is identical to the geometrical problem of determining which pixels best fit the theoretical line to be drawn.

Line-generating algorithms need to be fast because straight lines are frequently used. They are usually written in machine language and are machine-dependent. Special graphics chips are steadily becoming more popular; these perform algorithms in microcode. The C++ programs below show only the algorithmic principle. The compiled code will be machine-dependent, for reasons related to the bitmap's hardware architecture and how it is associated with the pixel grid, and in some cases to the pixel ratio mentioned above.

Hardware Developments in This Area

Scan conversion algorithms are so important that several of them have already been implemented in hardware. In 1982, Nippon Electric Company and Intel produced a graphics coprocessor (NEC 7220 or Intel 82720) whose hardware could draw straight lines in all directions, as well as circular arcs and rectangles, and also could fill rectangular areas with user-specified patterns. In 1985, Hitachi released an even faster and much more advanced graphics coprocessor with the modest name Advanced CRT Controller (HD63484-8). A newer development is Texas Instruments' TI34020.

These chips produce straight lines by executing line generators, such as the Bresenham algorithm described below. This is not achieved by executing machine code stored in

(continued)

memory, but instead by executing microcode in silicon, thereby attaining very high speeds. This approach is also faster because once a command for line drawing (or some other graphics primitive) has been sent to the graphics coprocessor, the main processor is no longer involved and can perform other calculations. Both chips work for some time in parallel.

Drawing with the Hitachi Advanced CRT Controller or with the TI34020 is simple. To draw a straight line, the user need only send a command and enter the x- and y-coordinates of the point to which the line should be drawn. Furthermore, these coprocessors can create a significant number of graphics primitives, including filling simple polygons.

These devices represent only the beginning of the development in dedicated graphics chips. More and more functions will be implemented in hardware, and dedicated chips will play an increasingly important role in all computer graphics techniques.

2.1   STRAIGHT LINES

All straight-line generating algorithms need only the starting and ending points in the pixel grid in order to draw the line. The ideal straight line that connects these two grid points usually does not go through other grid points.

2.1.1   STRUCTURAL METHODS

With a *structural method* for drawing a line, one generates all the line's pixel addresses (its *structure*) before setting any of the pixels. One develops the structure as a whole, usually by starting with a coarse approximation, and then gradually refining it. In contrast, with the *conditional method*, one sets each pixel before determining where the next point will be. This method is conditional because setting the position of each pixel depends on conditions that one checks while creating the line. Conditional methods are preferable because a structural method is currently more useful in theory then in reality.

As we discuss these algorithms, you will find precise definitions for *adjacent, digital line,* and *straightness*. The theory behind structural methods shows relations to number theory, linguistic methods, and automata theory. We will present the *best-fit structural method*.

CHAIN CODING

To quantify the notions *coherent* and *adjacent*, we first explain *eight-connected-ness*. Two pixels in a grid are eight-connected if they are vertically, horizontally, or diagonally adjacent. A pixel therefore has eight eight-connected neighbors (see Figure 2.16).

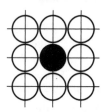

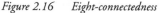

Figure 2.16   Eight-connectedness

The thinnest coherent line of pixels in a grid represents a line on a raster display. It can be expressed as a sequence of eight-connected pixels.

Freeman's chain coding scheme (FREE70) can describe such a line. Let a pixel's eight different directions to its eight neighbors be numbered as in Figure 2.17.

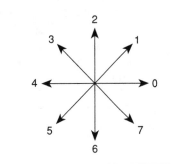

A *chain* is a sequence of numbers that indicates the location of successive pixels on the screen. The Freeman chain can represent any digital arc by a string with symbols 0, 1, 2, ..., 7, where the values show the relative direction to the next pixel. The word *arc* here means any connected set of raster points, whether in a straight, circular, or any predefined pattern. We will restrict ourselves to straight lines in the following discussion. The chain for the straight line from A to B in Figure 2.18 is the string 454545454.

Figure 2.17   Numbering of a pixel's neighbors

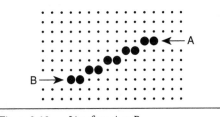

Figure 2.18   Line from A to B

STRAIGHTNESS OF A DIGITAL ARC

One recent addition to the theory of digital arcs was discovered by Hung and Kasvand, HUKA84. They state that a digital arc represents a straight line if and only if its chain contains no uneven subchains. (Two equally long subchains of a chain are uneven if the sums of the values of the two subchain elements differ by more than 1.) We list three interesting consequences without proving them. (Proof is of a number theoretical nature and not interesting here.)

1. A chain has at most two different symbols which can differ by at most 1 modulo 8.
2. The less frequent symbol only occurs isolated.
3. The more frequent symbol occurs in runs that differ by at most 1 in length.

We can restrict ourselves to considering straight lines with slopes between 0 and 45 degrees. One can derive every other straight line with symmetry. For such lines in the first octant, the chain is extremely simple, consisting only of 0s and 1s. (0 means that the next point lies to the right; 1 means that it lies above and to the right.) A horizontal line will have a chain of all 0s, a 45-degree line will have a chain of all 1s. Lines with a slope between 0 and 45 degrees have a mixture of 0s and 1s.

THE BEST-FIT METHOD

The best-fit method was developed by Castle and Pitteway, CAPI85. This elegant method is conceptually simple. It uses Euclid's algorithm to generate the chain for a straight line in the first octant, not including 0-degree and 45-degree lines. (In these cases one does not need the algorithm.)

INFORMAL DESCRIPTION

We will demonstrate the generation of a chain with an example. We need two substrings, *sub1* and *sub2*, which are originally loaded with the symbols 0 and 1. We also need the coordinates of the end point $(x\ y)$, assuming the line starts at $(0\ 0)$. The inverse of a string will be denoted by $(s)^{-1}$, so $(11101)^{-1} = 10111$, and concatenation will be denoted by +, so $1110 + 10 = 111010$.

Here is the pseudocode to do it:

```
x is assigned x-y
start:
    x is compared to y and, depending on the outcome:
        if x > y: then sub2 = (sub2)⁻¹+ sub1 and
            y is subtracted from x
        if x = y:  we are done and the final chain is produced
            (see below)
        if x < y: then sub1 = (sub1)⁻¹+ sub2 and
            x is subtracted from y
go to start
```

Here are the successive values for a line from $(0\ 0)$ to $(41\ 25)$. Starting values are:

$$x = 16 \quad y = 25 \quad sub1 = 0 \quad sub2 = 1$$

Table 2.1 shows how values develop.

x	y	*sub1*	*sub2*
41	25	0	1
16	25	01	1
16	9	01	101
7	9	10101	101
7	2	10101	10110101
5	2	10101	1010110110101
3	2	10101	101011011010110101
1	2	10101101011011010110101	101011011010110101
1	1	$x = y$ so output final chain:	
		1010110101101101011010110101101011011010110101	

Table 2.1   Generation of the substrings in the best-fit method

The final chain is obtained by concatenating $(sub2)^{-1} + sub1$ or $(sub1)^{-1} + sub2$ (these will be identical) and repeating the resulting string x or y times (x and y are equal at the conclusion). The ending values for x and y will be 1, unless the starting values have a common divisor. Observe that the resulting chain is symmetric with respect to the center, unless all the long runs are an odd number long. Even so, this method produces the best-fit line.

Other chain coding methods, for example Brons's method, which we do not demonstrate, BRON74, BRON85, may be faster than the best-fit method, but are algorithmically more complicated. We show a worst case, in which the best-fit method does the maximum number of string reversals and concatenations.

Consider a line from (0 0) to (40 1). The first generated substring will be 01. With every step this substring will be reversed, a single 0 will be appended to the left of it, and *x* will be decremented by 1. The substring will grow in length by one only in every step and will assume the following values:

$$10$$
$$010$$
$$0100$$
$$00100$$
$$001000$$
$$0001000$$

until it has the length 40. The continuing reversal results in having the single 1 in the middle of the whole string. Forty reversals of the substring are necessary, making the algorithm slow. Brons's method does not have this problem.

CODED ALGORITHM

To implement the best-fit method, we first declare a class `string_t`, which does essentially the same as the string functions in the C library. However, the class allows you to define constructors and operators for strings that make coding the algorithm easy. It is not a general purpose string class. The function `bestfit()` in `Shape2d/bestfit.c` demonstrates the algorithm and allows the reader to produce chains on the command line—it does not draw a line!

```
//*********************** File bestfit.h ************************

#ifndef STRING_T
#define STRING_T


class string_t
{
public:
   string_t(int) ;
   string_t(const char*) ;
   string_t(const string_t&) ;
  ~string_t() ;

   string_t operator += (const string_t&) ; // augment this by string
   string_t operator * (int) ;              // replicate this int times
   string_t& invert() ;

   void print() ;

private:
   char* s ;
   int len ;
```

```
} ;

#endif

//*******************************************************************
```

Structural methods are worth considering, even if the algorithms presented here are slow and look more complicated than the conditional methods presented next. The string manipulations, which are time consuming to perform in software, serve only to demonstrate the algorithm. A hardware-close implementation would not use any strings. Because only two kinds of symbols can occur, a single bit would represent a symbol, so bit patterns would be used instead of strings. It has been suggested that concatenating and reversing substrings could be done in long shift registers. Shifting one register into another can reverse a string quickly, as shown in Figure 2.19. Even more operations could be performed "in silicon." Then the structural methods would generate straight lines very rapidly.

Figure 2.19   *Reversing a string through shifting*

Shifting register 1 into register 2 (indicated by the arrow) reverses a string, CAPI85. The registers would have to be as long as the number of pixels horizontally on the screen. *Barrel shifters* can achieve very fast shifts. This special hardware development is used, for example, in video RAMs.

2.1.2   CONDITIONAL METHODS

There are many different conditional methods for generating straight lines. A conditional method sets each pixel without knowing where the next pixel will be, a significant difference from the structural methods. After setting one pixel, we check certain conditions to determine the position of the next. We generate a line by stepping forward pixel by pixel until we reach the end point.

We could precisely calculate the next grid point closest to the theoretical line and set a pixel there, but that would be very slow. As lines are among the most frequently used graphics primitives, it is essential to draw them very rapidly. We must therefore use only methods that require few computations. The incremental methods that we explain below are very fast. We introduce the topic with several examples.

INCREMENTAL METHODS

Suppose we want a line from the grid point (0 0) to the grid point (10 0). There is an increment of 10 in x, but no increment in y. We move from (0 0) to (10 0) by incrementing x at every step, never incrementing y, and setting pixels along the way. We stop as soon as we reach (10 0) (see Figure 2.20). Observe that the slope of the line is 0.

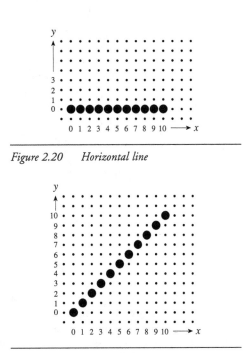

Figure 2.20   Horizontal line

Now consider the case of a line from (0 0) to (10 10). Here, too, the incremental method is easy. We start at (0 0) and increment both x and y at each step, set pixels along the way, and stop at the end point (see Figure 2.21). Observe that the slope of the line is 1.

Figure 2.21   Line with slope 1

In the next example, we create a straight line from (0 0) to (10 5). It is easy to see that y must be incremented half as often as x in order to reach the end point. We achieve this by incrementing x at each step and y every second step. The resulting line is shown in Figure 2.22. Observe that the slope of the line is 0.5.

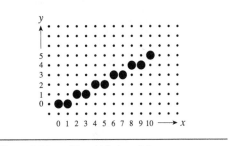

Figure 2.22   Line with slope 0.5

DDA ALGORITHMS

The above examples show that we increment y, relative to incrementing x, according to the slope of the line. Basically, incremental algorithms do only two things. They test whether to increment a variable, and they count how many pixels they set using the start point and end point coordinates.

A *digital differential analyzer* (DDA) is such an incremental method. You can design DDAs for circular arcs, other curves, and straight lines. In fact, they can draw any curve whose differential equation is given. The differential equation of a straight line is:

$$\frac{dy}{dx} = c$$

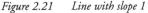

where c is a constant. This relation remains true if we replace the slope dy/dx with the quotient Dy/Dx, where Dx and Dy are both finite differences. The quotient of the increments must be equal to the slope of the line (its derivative).

Given the start point and end point, we can draw a line by doing the following. We calculate the slope and choose incremental values Dx and Dy in the proper ratio. The start point is the first point on the line. We increment the x-value by Dx and the y-value by Dy. The result, in most cases, will not correspond to a pixel location, so we round it to the nearest integers, giving us the location of the closest grid point. We display a pixel at this location.

To reach the next point, we must add Dx and Dy to the nonrounded results of the previous step. The nonrounded results will correspond exactly to points on the ideal line and the rounded numbers give the closest grid point location for pixels. The internal iteration process is:

$$x_{n+1} = x_n + Dx$$
$$y_{n+1} = y_n + Dy$$
$$\texttt{setpix(round}(x_{n+1})\texttt{,round}(y_{n+1})\texttt{)}$$

Each step is computed with just two floating point additions and two rounding operations.

The choice of values for Dx and Dy is important. If the values we choose are too small, then after rounding we could get the same pixel address again; this could happen several times before we really advance to a new pixel. If we make the incremental values too large, then we could jump over pixels that should be set. Figures 2.23 and 2.24 show these two situations. The arrows point to the actual pixels which are obtained by rounding the x- and y-values.

In Figure 2.23 the incremental values are too small, so some pixels are computed and set several times.

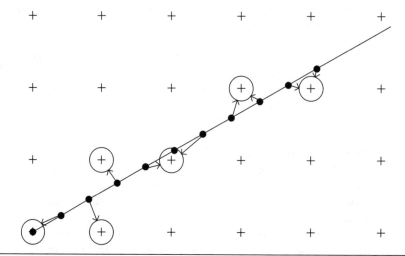

Figure 2.23   Incremental values are too small

In Figure 2.24 the incremental values are too large and the line has gaps.

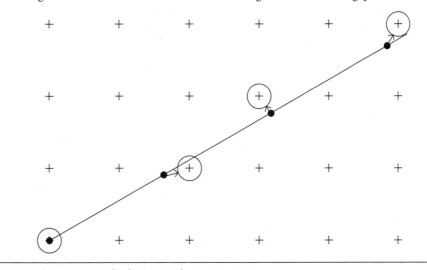

Figure 2.24   Incremental values are too large

The proper choice of increments should lead to a new pixel at each step, but should not be so large that the resulting pixel sequence is not eight-connected, as in Figure 2.14. We can solve this problem by computing the incremental values so that the larger has magnitude 1. The simple straight line DDA presented below does exactly that.

THE SIMPLE STRAIGHT LINE DDA

This DDA first calculates the required number of incrementing steps. It sets $distx = abs(x_{start} - x_{end})$ and $disty = abs(y_{start} - y_{end})$ and computes:

$$nstep = \text{number of steps} = max(distx, disty)$$

If we take $Dx = distx/nstep$ and $Dy = disty/nstep$, it follows that either Dx or Dy equals 1. A true division is needed only to compute the smaller increment. Comparing $distx$ to $disty$ can determine which one this is. We speed up the incrementing process by replacing one of the floating point adders with a simple counter. This algorithm draws exactly $nstep$ pixels, one for each step.

The code below specifies the logic of this DDA without implementing all possible further improvements. By finding whether Dx or Dy has magnitude 1 and considering their signs, each step needs only one rounding operation and one floating point addition. One should consider this when programming the algorithm in assembly; the floating point operations should be done by floating point hardware.

We do not include an implementation of this algorithm in C++. The reader should keep in mind that a graphics application would certainly not call either of these two functions, but probably an assembly coded or siliconized version of Bresenham's straight line DDA.

CODED ALGORITHM

```
void float_dda(int x1,int y1,int x2,int y2)
{
   double Dx = 0 ,
          Dy = 0 ,
          x = x1 ,
          y = y1 ;
   int    i ,
          nstep = abs(x1 - x2) ;

   if (abs(y1 - y2) > nstep)
      nstep = abs(y1 - y2);
   if (nstep > 0)
   {
      Dx = (double)(x2 - x1)/nstep;
      Dy = (double)(y2 - y1)/nstep;
   }
   for (i = 0; i <= nstep; i++)
   {
      setpix((int)(x+0.5),(int)(y+0.5));      // rounding to
      x += Dx;                                // nearest pixel
      y += Dy;
   }
}
```

BRESENHAM'S STRAIGHT LINE ALGORITHM

We will take a heuristic approach to Bresenham's straight line algorithm. We limit our consideration to lines from (0 0) to any point within the first octant; these lines are between 0 and 45 degrees. Every other line is algorithmically identical, except for simple symmetry considerations.

We will draw a line from (0 0) to (19 4). Imagine the precise, straight line in the pixel grid from (0 0) to (19 4) as shown in Figure 2.25.

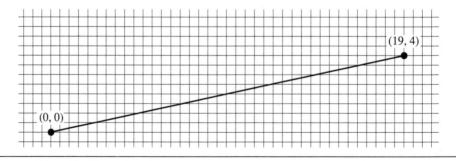

Figure 2.25   Ideal line and pixel grid

The line intersects the vertical grid lines at 18 positions between the x-values of 0 and 19. In our given case (and also in general) these intersections are in between, not on, pixel locations. We set the pixel that is closer to the intersection. The line's start point and end point lie exactly on grid points.

Figure 2.26 shows the beginning of the ideal line and the first few intersections.

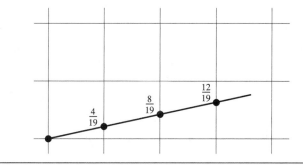

Figure 2.26   Intersection values at grid lines

The height at which the ideal line intersects the vertical grid line is 4/19 for the first intersection, 8/19 for the second, 12/19 for the third, and so on. Because the value for the first intersection is below 0.5, we choose the pixel at height 0, corresponding to a horizontal step. The second intersection also is below 0.5, so again the we choose pixel at height 0, which is another horizontal step. At the third intersection we have 12/19, which is greater than 0.5, so we choose the pixel at height 1, corresponding to a horizontal and a vertical step. From now on, we will never choose the pixel at height 0; we will decide between the pixels at height 1 and height 2. We will compare the height to the number 1.5, instead of 0.5.

Thus, we always take a horizontal step. We take a vertical step, as well, whenever the line would intersect above the halfway point. If the intersection is exactly at the halfway point, we can choose the pixel arbitrarily.

Perhaps we should summarize this using some special terms. *Elevation* is the y-value on the ideal line. *Midpoint* is the y-value to which we compare the elevation when deciding whether to move vertically when setting a pixel. We set a pixel at (0 0) and make the elevation value 0. We then add 4/19 to it and compare it to a midpoint value of 0.5. If the y-value is smaller than 0.5, we only make a horizontal step; if the y-value is greater, we make a horizontal and a vertical step. We repeat this for all 19 steps, adjusting the elevation and midpoint values when appropriate.

This algorithm can be demonstrated through a schematic in which we write the numbers themselves at the places where the pixels are to be set. The starting elevation is 0. It is increased by 4/19 with each step and a comparison is made to the midpoint of 0.5 = 9.5/19. As long as the elevation is smaller, we write it to the right of the current elevation value. If the elevation is larger than 9.5/19, we take a horizontal plus a vertical step; that is, we write the next number at 45 degrees above the last number. From now on, we will compare the elevation to 1.5 = 28.5/19. We write the midpoint values to the left of the corresponding row. The schematic is not executed to completion; there will actually be 19 steps.

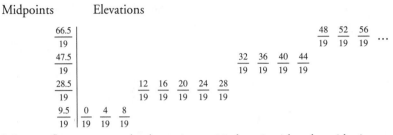

It is superfluous to carry the denominator 19 along in either the midpoints or the elevations. Below is the schematic without the denominator:

Midpoints   Elevations

```
66.5 │                                        48 52 56 ...

47.5 │                            32 36 40 44

28.5 │              12 16 20 24 28

 9.5 │ 0  4  8
```

With no denominators, we can easily see that the midpoint values increase by 19. The elevation increases by 4. Instead of increasing the midpoint values by 19 and having to calculate 1.5×19, or 2.5×19, we can subtract 19 from the elevation after each vertical step and always compare to 9.5. This gives the following schematic:

```
                                              −8 −4  0

                                    −9 −5 −1  3  7

                          −6 −2  2  6

             −7 −3  1  5  9

  0  4  8
 ─────────────────────────────────────────────────────
      −19              −19             −19             −19
```

Whenever the elevation becomes larger than 9.5, we take a vertical step and subtract 19. The −19 below the line indicates when this has been done. It is no coincidence that we end up with 0 after 19 steps. Altogether, we have added 4 a total of 19 times and we have subtracted 19 a total of 4 times. Therefore, we must have exactly 0 after the 19 horizontal steps.

We can now make two more major improvements. The first consists of doubling all numbers. This does not change the schematic and leads to pure integer arithmetic, not only in our example, but in all cases. The reason is that the comparison to 9.5 resulted from the original comparison to 1/2, or 3/2, and so forth, in setting the grid point. This brought the denominator 2 into play. We eliminate this denominator by doubling all numbers.

```
                                              -16  -8   0
                                    -18 -10  -2   6  14
                          -12  -4   4  12
                -14  -6   2  10  18
         0   8  16
```
-38	-38	-38	-38

Now we add 8, subtract 38, and compare to 19. The second improvement consists of comparing the elevations to 0 instead of to 19. We can achieve this easily; the schematic will not change if we start out with -19 instead of 0 and compare to 0 instead of 19. This will just decrease all numbers in the schematic by 19. Machine code works faster by comparing numbers to 0, rather than to any other number. Also, to avoid having everything negative, we change all signs. Thus, we start with 19, subtract 8, add 38; we still compare to 0. We now have:

```
                                              35  27  19
                                    37  29  21  13   5
                          31  23  15   7
                33  25  17   9   1
         19  11   3
```

This is Bresenham's straight line algorithm for a line from (0 0) to (x y). We can summarize it as: Set first pixel and start the number with x, subtract 2y; if the number is positive, do a horizontal step; if negative, do a diagonal step and add 2x to the number. Continue until you perform x steps. If the number equals 0, go either horizontally or diagonally, just be consistent. Figure 2.27 shows the resulting line in the pixel grid.

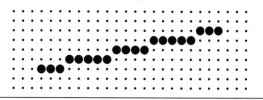

Figure 2.27   Line drawn with Bresenham's algorithm

CODED ALGORITHM

We have not used strict mathematical reasoning in developing Bresenham's algorithm; the heuristic understanding is enough for our purposes. The code below reflects precisely the method we have explained. However, this code draws lines only in the first octant. To make it complete, the reader would have to add almost identical code segments for the remaining 7 octants and would need to test into which octant a line belonged. It would slow down the algorithm if we made the case distinctions during the line drawing process. We can derive the logic from the case presented with symmetry.

```
//              Only for lines between 0 and 45 degrees

void bresline(int x1,int y1,int x2,int y2)
{
   int x   = x1          ,
       y   = y1          ,
       sum = x2 - x1     ,
       Dx  = 2*(x2-x1)   ,
       Dy  = 2*(y2-y1)   ;

   for (int i = 0; i <= x2-x1; i++)
   {
      setpix(x,y);
      x++;
      sum -= Dy;
      if (sum < 0)                         // check for sign change
         y++ , sum += Dx;
   }
}
```

The code above differs from the example in that the code does not require the line to start at the point (0 0); the line can start at any grid point. The starting pixel is always set, so drawing a line from a point to itself sets just one pixel. The code does no multiplications and no divisions; doubling Dx and Dy is not a multiplication. The processor simply shifts the number's bit pattern by one bit to the left.

Bresenham's algorithm is the fastest straight-line drawing algorithm and is well suited for implementation on raster graphics systems. Similar to the simple straight line DDA, it never sets a pixel more than once. Some graphics processors have it implemented in silicon.

THE OO DESIGN FOR 2D GRAPHICS

Before we continue with polygons, we want to present our OO design for 2D graphics. This design involves certain concepts that we have not yet introduced, but it would be counterproductive to present the design after we have explained all the concepts. It is certainly possible to grasp the basic design ideas at this stage.

The user can create a two-dimensional scene by adding any number of graphics primitives, such as lines, circles, or polygons to the scene. An individual primitive can be drawn, rotated, scaled, or whatever operation the user wishes to implement. Users can also manipulate the entire scene in these ways by sending the appropriate message to the scene that contains them. We therefore introduce a class scene_t, which is a container for graphics primitives. The scene deals only with objects of type prim_t from which all actual primitives are derived.

For example, we can draw the whole scene with a member function scene_t::draw(), which simply walks through the scene's list of primitives and invokes each primitive's draw function. Since the primitive's draw function is virtual, run-time binding occurs and the actual primitive's draw functions will be executed.

To do the design correctly, we must realize at this stage that all graphics primitives will be treated in world coordinates (Chapter 4). All primitives in a scene are stored and handled with the same user-defined coordinate system, called a "window-viewport system" (Chapter 4). This does not prevent the user from defining several scenes with different window-viewport systems in the same program. However, the scene has another member—a reference to a window-viewport system—that pertains to all its primitives.

Not knowing enough about a window-viewport system is no obstacle at this point. Specifying a default window-viewport system will set the coordinates such that the primitives seem to be specified and treated in device coordinates.

CLASS SPECIFICATIONS

Here we introduce the above-mentioned classes. The class `scene_t` has a pointer to a primitive and a reference to a window-viewport system. It is constructed with those two parameters. It has an overloaded operator +=, which adds another primitive to the scene. A whole scene can be drawn, filled with a solid color, hatches, or a pattern, and then rotated or translated (the individual primitive decides for itself whether such a request makes sense). Rotating a scene means revolving all of its primitives about their individual centroids. Translating a scene translates all primitives by the same amount.

```
//*********************** File scene.h **************************

#ifndef SCENE_T
#define SCENE_T

#include "../Shape2d/win_view.h"
#include "../Shape2d/pattern.h"
#include "../Shape2d/prim.h"

class scene_t
{
public:
   scene_t(const win_view_t& wv) : wv(wv) , prim(0) {}
   ~scene_t() { delete prim; }

   void operator += (const prim_t&) ;
   virtual void draw() const ;
   virtual void solid() const ;
   void hatch(int) const ;
   void pattern(const pattern_t&) const ;
   scene_t& rot(double) ;                                // 2D rotation
   scene_t& translate(const point_t&) ;

   prim_t* givprim() const { return prim; }
   const win_view_t& givwv() const { return wv; }

protected:
   prim_t* prim ;
   const win_view_t& wv ;
} ;

#endif
//***************************************************************
```

The class `point_t` represents an arbitrary point in a 2D Cartesian coordinate system. We give it operator functions for adding and subtracting points, multiplying with a scalar, and so on. To obtain a point object's x- and y-components, we send it the message `givx()` or `givy()`. We also provide it with a virtual member function `givz()`, which returns 0 for a 2D point. We will see later why this is necessary. Another virtual function, `set()`, allows us to set both coordinates.

```cpp
//************************* File point.h *************************

#ifndef POINT_T
#define POINT_T


class point_t                                            // point in 2D space
{
public:
   point_t() ;
   point_t(double,double) ;
   point_t(const point_t&) ;

   point_t  operator + (const point_t&) const ;
   point_t  operator - (const point_t&) const ;
   point_t  operator * (double) const ;
   point_t  operator / (double) const ;
   point_t& operator+= (const point_t&) ;
   point_t& operator-= (const point_t&) ;
   point_t  operator - () const ;

   double givx() const { return x;}
   double givy() const { return y;}
   virtual double givz() const { return 0; }
   virtual void set(const point_t& p) { x = p.x; y = p.y; }
   void setx(double x) { point_t::x = x;}
   void sety(double y) { point_t::y = y;}

protected:
   double x , y ;
} ;

point_t operator *(double,const point_t&) ;

#endif

//*****************************************************************
```

The class `prim_t` serves as the base class for all our drawable shapes. It contains only one member, `prim_t* next`, which allows us to link graphics primitives into a list. This class is basically a collection of virtual member functions that can be invoked against objects of classes derived from the class `prim_t`. These functions include copying itself, drawing itself, rotating itself about the centroid in 2D, rotating itself about the x-, y-, or z-axis in 3D, or translating itself in 2D or 3D. The functions `givnext()` and `setnext()` obtain or set the link. The functions `solid()`, `hatch()`, and `pattern()` make sense when invoked against a polygon type or whatever is derived from it.

```
//************************* File prim.h ************************

#ifndef PRIM_T
#define PRIM_T

#include "../Shape2d/pattern.h"
#include "../Shape2d/point.h"

class scene_t ;

class prim_t
{
public:
    prim_t(prim_t* next = 0) : next(next) {}
    virtual ~prim_t() { delete next; }

    virtual prim_t* copy() const { return 0; }
    virtual void draw(const scene_t*) const {}
    virtual void solid(const scene_t*) const {}
    virtual void hatch(const scene_t*,int) const {}
    virtual void pattern(const scene_t*,const pattern_t&) const {}
    virtual prim_t& rot (double) { return *this; }
    virtual prim_t& rotx(double) { return *this; }
    virtual prim_t& roty(double) { return *this; }
    virtual prim_t& rotz(double) { return *this; }
    virtual prim_t& translate(const point_t&) { return *this; }
    virtual prim_t& viewtrans(
        const point_t&,const point_t&,const point_t&) { return *this; }
    prim_t* givnext() { return next; }
    void    setnext(prim_t* p) { next = p; }

protected:
    prim_t* next ;
} ;

#endif

//*****************************************************************
```

The class `line_t` is the first "concrete" graphics primitive derived from `prim_t`. It represents a straight line. Observe that its end points are of type `point_t`, rather than the addresses of pixels in the pixel grid. We draw a line by rounding its end points to the nearest pixel locations and executing a DDA for those locations (if they are within the range of the device coordinates). We do this because we treat all primitives in world coordinates.

We can construct a line with four doubles, two `point_t`, or the mouse. In the last case, the user must enter the two end points using the mouse cursor and a button click. Like all classes derived from `prim_t`, `line_t` must have a function `copy()` that creates a copy of itself. This function is needed for adding the line to a scene.

The implementation of `line_t` in `Shape2d/line.c` uses the device-dependent graphics library functions `move()` and `draw()`, which exist in every graphics library, rather than the simple straight line DDA or Bresenham's straight line DDA. Using these as an implementation of `line_t::draw()` is possible, but means a significant sacrifice in speed, as they are not written in assembly language and do not take advantage of specific hardware features.

```
//************************* File line.h *************************

#ifndef LINE_T
#define LINE_T

#include "../Shape2d/prim.h"
#include "../Shape2d/point.h"
#include "../Shape2d/scene.h"
#include "../Shape2d/mouse.h"

class line_t : public prim_t                              // 2D line
{
public:
   line_t() ;                                             // constructors
   line_t(double,double,double,double) ;
   line_t(const point_t&,const point_t&) ;
   line_t(mouse_t&) ;
   line_t(const line_t&) ;

   prim_t* copy() const ;
   void draw(const scene_t*) const ;
   prim_t& rot(double) ;
   prim_t& translate(const point_t&) ;
   point_t giva() const { return a; }
   point_t givb() const { return b; }

private:
   point_t a , b ;                                        // line end points
   point_t cen ;                                          // centroid
} ;

#endif

//*****************************************************************
```

We specified the class `mouse_t` simply for the convenience of entering graphics primitives with the mouse. It is initialized with a window-viewport parameter because it transforms the clicked-in points immediately to world coordinates.

```
//************************* File mouse.h *************************

#ifndef MOUSE_T
#define MOUSE_T

class point_t ;
class win_view_t ;

class mouse_t
{
public:
   mouse_t(const win_view_t&) ;
  ~mouse_t() ;
   int wait_button_down(point_t&) ;
   void wait_button_click(void) ;

private:
   short x , y;
   short x1 , y1 , x2 , y2 ;
   const win_view_t& wv ;
   void test_button(int,int,int,int,short&) ;
} ;

#endif

//*********************************************************************
```

2.2 POLYGONS

We consider a polygon a graphics primitive because we often want to treat it as a single entity. Polygons are important in representing objects from the real world. In this chapter we address only 2D polygons.

We must understand polygons very broadly as any area of an image bounded by straight or curved lines and filled with one solid color. Since images are two-dimensional, a polygon is a closed planar figure. Accepting curved lines as boundaries poses no problem because it is easy to approximate a curved outline with a sequence of straight lines. When we do this, our image is no further from reality than if we used an outline defined by mathematical curves, because neither curves nor straight lines are real; both are abstractions in our mind. Our visual system readily perceives a straight line sequence as a smooth curve. This justifies our including figures bounded by smooth outlines as polygons.

We will relax the requirement that the area be filled with one solid color when displayed on a color monitor. Areas in which gradual color changes occur constitute one polygon. Such color variations occur naturally, due to differences in light reflection from surfaces. An abrupt color change indicates a boundary of the polygon. It is almost impossible to define how abrupt a change must be to qualify as a boundary, but we do not need such a definition. We can declare a polygon boundary wherever we desire. We will always decompose a scene from the real world into a collection of polygons of simple shapes.

Based on this general concept of a polygon, we can build every picture from filled polygons. Of course, what we get from this is only an approximation of the scene, but that is all we can hope to do. Actually, neither straight lines nor polygons precisely describe a real-world scene; such scenes actually seem to be of a fractal nature. We will study fractals in Chapter 9.

2.2.1   INTERNAL REPRESENTATION OF POLYGONS

The above paragraphs assume that polygons are in two-dimensional space, the plane of the display screen. We will consider the real-world objects that we recreate on the screen as also having surfaces composed of polygons, but these polygons are three-dimensional. Thinking of objects as bounded by polygons is somewhat artificial, and limited, just as thinking of images as being composed only of polygons has constraints. For example, when an object's smooth, curved surface is represented by many flat polygons joined together, the result is not smooth. However, techniques have been developed to make the representation appear smoothly curved, with invisible connections between the polygons. We study such methods in Chapter 13.

The reason for using polygonal surfaces is that we must project every three-dimensional scene onto the two-dimensional display screen. For display purposes, we turn three-dimensional polygons that comprise surfaces into two-dimensional polygons.

A polygon consists of a finite, ordered set of straight boundaries, called edges. Alternately, we can define the polygon as a sequence of vertices—its corners. By connecting adjacent vertices, we obtain the polygon's edges. We close the polygon by connecting the last vertex to the first.

If we need only a polygon's boundary, we can produce it with a sequence of line draw commands. However, we need to be able to do more with a polygon than just draw its boundary. Because we make a polygon a graphics primitive represented by an abstract data type, the system can distinguish between a sequence of unrelated line draw commands and a sequence of edges that belong to a polygon. We can represent polygons in various ways, depending on the types of data structures the programming language supports. One technique puts the sequence of edges (or vertices) into a linked list. Another technique stores the sequence of vertices in arrays.

The graphics system needs the stored polygon information to derive other information necessary for various algorithms. For example, it can fill a polygon only in 2D space. This process consists of setting pixels and, as such, is part of producing an image, so it is done in image space. In 2D or in 3D space, the system can clip the polygon to a given window. In 3D space, the system can find the plane in which a polygon lies or can divide a polygon into smaller polygons for depth sorting.

CLASS SPECIFICATIONS

We use a linked list of vertices to store a polygon. A vertex is derived from `point_t` and adds only one member—a link to the next vertex. Its base class `point_t` is virtual, because we will later use multiple inheritance with the shared base class `point_t`. Below we show the class `vertex_t`. A vertex can make a copy of itself with the command `copy()`. A vertex can construct an edge with `make_edge()`. This is important for polygon filling. When a polygon is filled, a list of its edges is created. These edges contain the necessary fill information, as shown below in Section 2.3. This feature gives you flexibility in implementing the diverse filling algorithms. For example, a 3D vertex will construct a different type of edge than will a 2D vertex, and a 3D polygon will therefore be filled in a different manner (see Z-buffer or Phong shading).

```cpp
//************************* File vertex.h *************************

#ifndef VERTEX_T
#define VERTEX_T

#include "../Shape2d/point.h"
class edge_t ;

class vertex_t : virtual public point_t
{
public:
    vertex_t() ;
    vertex_t(double,double,vertex_t* = 0) ;
    vertex_t(const point_t&) ;
    virtual ~vertex_t() ;

    virtual   edge_t*    make_edge(const vertex_t&) const ;
    virtual   vertex_t*  copy() const ;
    vertex_t* givnext() const { return next; }
    void      setnext(vertex_t* v) { next = v; }

protected:
    vertex_t* next ;
} ;

#endif

//*******************************************************************
```

We use the class `edge_t` in polygon filling. It is constructed from two 2D points. We explain the use of this class below.

```cpp
//************************* File edge.h *************************

#ifndef EDGE_T
#define EDGE_T

class point_t ;

class edge_t                                        // polygon edge
{
public:
    edge_t(const point_t&,const point_t&) ;
    virtual ~edge_t() {}                     // edges must be deleted singly

    double    givymax()        { return ymax; }
    double    givymin()        { return ymin; }
```

```
    double    givx()            { return x; }
    edge_t*   givnext()         { return next; }
    void      setnext(edge_t* e) { next = e; }
    edge_t**  givaddrnext()     { return &next; }
    virtual  void update       ()    ;
    virtual  void solidscan    (double) ;
    virtual  void hatchscan    (double) ;
    virtual  void patternscan  (double) ;

protected:
    double   ymax  ,                    // larger of the edge's y-values
             ymin  ,                    // smaller of the edge's y-values
             dx    ,              // negative inverse slope of the edge
             x     ;        // intersection x-value of edge and scan line
    edge_t* next  ;
} ;

#endif

//***************************************************************
```

The class `convex_t` represents a convex polygon. It is our second "concrete" primitive derived from `prim_t`. From `convex_t`, we derive several other shapes that we can view as convex polygons, including circles, ellipses, rectangles, and triangles. To describe filled shapes with smooth outlines, one simply uses a polygon with many vertices. We also derive the more complicated shape of a general polygon, which can be convex and can overcross itself. The reason for this distinction is that filling a convex polygon is much simpler than filling a general one. Furthermore, all polygons that bound 3D shapes are triangles or convex quadrangles (quadrangle is just another word for quadrilateral). Their filling routines (Gouraud, Phong, Z-buffer) inherit the basic fill algorithms from `convex_t`.

Convex_t has a member operator +=, through which vertices are added to the polygon. It redefines the basic filling function `solid()`, `hatch()`, and `pattern()`, the 2D rotation `rot()`, and the translation `translate()`. It has a virtual member function `make_elist()` that builds the list of edges used for filling.

```
//********************** File convex.h **********************

#ifndef CONVEX_T
#define CONVEX_T

#include "../Shape2d/vertex.h"
#include "../Shape2d/pattern.h"
#include "../Shape2d/prim.h"
#include "../Shape2d/mouse.h"
#include "../Shape2d/scene.h"
#include "../Shape2d/elist.h"


class convex_t : public prim_t // convex polygon is a container class
```

```
{
public:
    convex_t() ;
    convex_t(const mouse_t&) ;
    convex_t(const convex_t&) ;
    virtual ~convex_t() ;

    virtual void draw(const scene_t*) const ;
    void operator = (const convex_t&);
    void operator+=(const vertex_t&) ;
    virtual void solid(const scene_t*) const ;          // solid fill
    virtual void hatch(const scene_t*,int) const ;   // crosshatch fill
    virtual void pattern(const scene_t*,const pattern_t&) const ;
    prim_t& rot(double) ;                      // 2D rotation about centroid
    prim_t& translate(const point_t&) ;
    prim_t* copy() const ;

protected:
    vertex_t* v ;
    int vernum ;
    point_t cen ;                                        // 2D centroid

private:
    virtual elist_t* make_elist(vertex_t*) const ;     // make edgelist
} ;

#endif

//*********************************************************************
```

The class polygon_t is derived from convex_t and inherits all its routines and members. It redefines only the virtual function make_elist(), to create a different sort of edge list than in convex_t.

```
//************************* File  polygon.h ************************

#ifndef POLYGON_T
#define POLYGON_T

#include "../Shape2d/pattern.h"
#include "../Shape2d/convex.h"
#include "../Shape2d/mouse.h"
#include "../Shape2d/scene.h"
#include "../Shape2d/elist.h"


class polygon_t : public convex_t     // polygon is a container class
{
public:
    polygon_t() ;
    polygon_t(const mouse_t&) ;
```

```
    polygon_t(const polygon_t&) ;
    ~polygon_t() ;

    prim_t* copy() const ;

private:
    elist_t* make_elist(vertex_t*) const ;
} ;

#endif

//*************************************************************************
```

2.2.2   DRAWING A POLYGON

To draw a polygon, we simply draw its edges. We move to the first vertex and then draw to the successive vertices. Then we draw the connecting line to the first. The implementation in `Shape2d/convex.c` also clips the polygon against the window of the scene in which it is contained. Drawing a general polygon is identical to drawing a convex one, so `draw()` is a member function of `convex_t` and is inherited by `polygon_t`.

2.3   POLYGON FILLING

An infinitely long horizontal line in the same plane as the polygon will intersect the boundaries of the polygon a certain number of times. This number can range from zero up to the number of polygon edges. For now, we restrict our consideration to horizontal lines because, when working on a raster display, the whole screen is filled by horizontal scan lines. These scan lines are the basis for filling a polygon. We could also fill a polygon with vertical or slanted lines, but the limitations of hardware and display technology make this much slower. Filling with slanted lines would not work if solid filling is desired, because slanted lines are stairstepped; if the lines are at other than 45°, holes may appear in the fill.

Figure 2.28 shows some possible situations when a horizontal line intersects the polygon boundaries. An odd number of intersections can occur only if the line goes through a vertex. In all other cases, the number of intersections must be even.

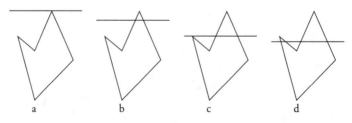

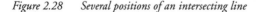

a   b   c   d

Figure 2.28   Several positions of an intersecting line

We fill the polygon by setting all pixels within or on the polygon boundary to the fill color. It is theoretically possible but impractical to decide whether each pixel on the screen is inside or outside a given polygon by using an inside-outside test. We do not define the notions *inside* and *outside* precisely. There is no need, because inside-outside tests are expensive and because we can avoid them.

Recall that pixels have fixed locations on the screen and are arranged in scan lines. We will use scan lines as the horizontal lines intersecting with the polygon.

Suppose we want to fill a polygon with a certain color. We could move down the whole screen starting with the uppermost scan line, traversing each scan line from left to right. When we reach or cross a polygon boundary, we set the pixel and all following pixels to the fill color, stopping when we again reach or traverse a boundary. We leave pixels in their unset state until we again reach or cross a boundary or until we reach the edge of the screen. Crossing polygon boundaries acts like a switch that determines if the pixels should be set or left alone.

Figure 2.29 shows two edges of a polygon and three scan lines with pixel positions. We traverse scan lines in the direction of the arrow. The circles are set pixels; the dots are unchanged pixels. The solid lines are the polygon edges.

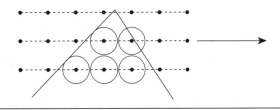

Figure 2.29   Setting pixels inside a polygon

This method is simple. It works if the switch is always in the off position before we begin a scan and if no polygon extends beyond the screen boundaries. This requirement can be met by filling only polygons that have been *clipped*, meaning that parts beyond the screen are clipped off and replaced by a line at the screen's boundary. In a clipped polygon, the first and last pixel of a scan line will be either outside or on a polygon edge. When the scan line hits a polygon vertex, we have to check whether the two edges emanating from it extend to the same side of the scan line or to different sides. In the first case, the scan line does not cross an edge, in the second it does.

We can improve this process. It is not necessary to traverse those scan lines above the polygon's highest vertex, nor those below the lowest vertex. Therefore, we should find the highest y-coordinate and the lowest y-coordinate of all vertices and restrict the scanning process to scan lines within this range.

While traversing a scan line, we do not have to check for edge intersections at the leftmost pixel and continue to test throughout the whole scan line. Instead, we can compute in advance all points at which the edges will intersect with this scan line. In general, these intersections will not be integer values, so we round them to the closest integer values. This will always give us an even number of integer-valued intersections. They will be at most half a pixel off the true intersections; this is the best we can do. To fill the polygon, we move to the leftmost intersection, draw horizontally to the next intersection, move to the next intersection, draw to the next, and so on until all intersection pairs are used up.

The above two paragraphs describe the essence of the polygon-filling algorithm. We will now implement it. The main implementation problem is to find an economical way of computing the intersection points for each scan line. We discuss this below.

In Figure 2.30, only an even number of polygon edges intersect with a scan line. The polygon has six edges and five different scan lines are shown. Only edges of the polygon with a greater *y*-value above and a smaller *y*-value below the scan line value intersect with the scan line.

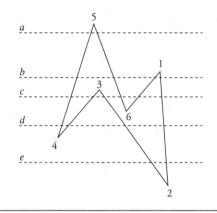

Figure 2.30   Intersection of scan lines with polygon edges

Scan line *a* intersects with two edges: 4–5 and 5–6.
Scan line *b* intersects with four edges: 4–5, 5–6, 6–1, and 1–2.
Scan line *c* intersects with six edges: 4–5, 3–4, 2–3, 5–6, 6–1, and 1–2; and so on.
Edges 1–2, 6–1, 3–4, and 2–3 are not cut by scan line *a*.
Edges 5–6 and 6–1 are not cut by scan line *d*; and so on.

For a given scan line, we can go through all edges of the polygon and check the *y*-values of the two vertices for each edge. We call the larger *y*-coordinate of each edge *ymax* and the smaller *y*-coordinate *ymin*. If *ymin* < *scan* ≤ *ymax*, the edge will intersect with the scan line and we compute the intersection. As soon as we have all intersections, we draw horizontal lines between the intersection pairs as described above. This method would give correct results, but is not economical. For example, once the scan line goes lower than vertex 6, the two edges 5–6 and 6–1 can never be cut. It would be a waste to check all succeeding scan line values against *ymin* and *ymax* of these two edges.

INFORMAL DESCRIPTION OF THE ALGORITHM

We avoid the above inefficiency by using a data structure that indicates only those edges that the current scan line will cut. We call these the *cutting edges*. When we lower the scan line, some of the cutting edges may not be cut anymore; some previously uncut edges may now be cut. We must update the data structure by excluding edges that have just been passed and including edges that the lowering scan line has just met. We will organize the data structure so that once an edge is excluded, it will not be tested again for inclusion. This minimizes the checking.

The scan begins just below the greatest *y*-value and continuously sweeps over the polygon from top to bottom, decreasing in steps of one after each scan. An edge is included in the data structure only if its *ymax* is greater than or equal to the current scan line, so we must check just the edge structure's *ymax* components. An edge is excluded only if its *ymin* is greater than or equal to the current scan line, so just the *ymin* component must be checked. Furthermore, only the cutting edges must be checked for exclusion. All this considerably decreases the amount of checking required.

If we sort the edges of the polygon of Figure 2.30 by their *ymax* values, the arrangement of edges looks like this:

$$4\text{–}5 \quad 5\text{–}6 \quad 6\text{–}1 \quad 1\text{–}2 \quad 3\text{–}4 \quad 2\text{–}3$$

We will insert these edges in this order in a linked list created solely for filling the polygon. If we begin with the highest scan line value that intersects with polygon edges, then the edges with the highest *ymax* value (the two leftmost in the above list) will certainly be among the cutting edges. This means that at the beginning of the algorithm, the cutting edges extend from the leftmost in the list to an edge further to the right in the list. Therefore we can use a single pointer, *rite*, to indicate the rightmost cutting edge. It simplifies the programming technique to let *rite* point to the edge *after* the rightmost cutting edge.

For scan line *a* we have:

4–5   5–6   6–1   1–2   3–4   2–3
                ↑
               rite

For scan line *b* we have:

4–5   5–6   6–1   1–2   3–4   2–3
                              ↑
                            rite

For scan line *c* we have:

4–5   5–6   6–1   1–2   3–4   2–3
                                        (*rite* = NULL)

To determine which edges must be included among the cutting edges after lowering the scan line, we need to test the edges, starting with the one to which *rite* points. We perform the test by comparing *scan* to *ymax*. If *ymax* ≥ *scan* for an edge, we include that edge. We mark inclusion by advancing *rite* to the next edge. Once a comparison results in *ymax* < *scan*, no more comparisons are necessary, because we have sorted the *ymax* values.

We determine which edges to exclude from the cutting edges by checking all cutting edges' *ymin* values against *scan*. If *ymin* ≥ *scan* for an edge, we exclude that edge by simply deleting it from the list. Handling exclusions in this way ensures that the cutting edges include the first edge in the list up to, but not including, the edge to which *rite* points.

The *x*-values of the cutting edges' intersection with the scan lines need not be listed in a left-to-right order. The algorithm must sort the cutting edges to obtain this.

Now that we know how to maintain a list of the cutting edges, we consider computing the intersection points. Not much computation is necessary because polygons are bounded by straight lines. The scan decreases in units of 1, so the intersection points of scan lines with a given edge will change by a constant amount (see Figure 2.31).

Figure 2.31 shows several scan lines intersecting part of the edge 4–5 from the Figure 2.30 polygon. The x-value of the intersection point changes by the constant amount dx for each new scan line. This quantity must be added to the old intersection value to obtain the new one (dx in this case is negative). The constant dx value for each edge will be computed before the scanning process begins and will be stored in the edge structure.

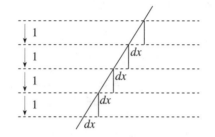

Figure 2.31   Intersection with scan line changes by constant amount dx

For each edge, we also store the x-value of the intersection with the scan line. (See below for more about these values.) For each new scan line, these values will be updated by adding the dx for each cutting edge to its old x-value for the intersection.

We now present the final structure used for the filling process. It is a linked list with as many elements as there are edges in the polygon. Each edge has four entries. Observe that this edge structure is used solely for the filling process and is abandoned once the polygon is filled. (The linked list is implemented below in the classes `elist_t` and `glist_t`.)

The four entries are:

ymax	the maximum y-coordinate of the edge
ymin	the minimum y-coordinate of the edge
dx	the change in x-value for this edge per scan
x	the x-value of the intersection with the scan

Let $(x_1\ y_1)$ and $(x_2\ y_2)$ be the vertices of this edge. Then dx is computed as:

$$dx = -\frac{x_1 - x_2}{y_1 - y_2}$$

This is the negative inverse slope of the edge. We know how to obtain the x-value for the next intersection from the previous one, by adding dx. But what value should we assign the initial x? Assume that s is the scan line value just above *ymax* (s has only integer values), see Figure 2.32. The distance from s down to *ymax* is ($s - ymax$). So the x-value where the edge intersects with the scan line s is the x-value associated with *ymax* minus $dx(s - ymax)$. If we initialize x with this value, the value of x after adding the first dx will be precisely the x for the first intersection with the scan line s–1.

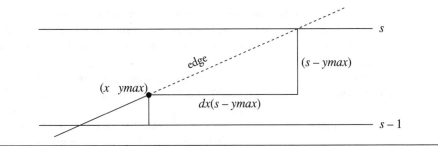

Figure 2.32   *Computing intersection of edge with scanline s*

To show the initialization of the list and operation of the algorithm, consider the polygon in Figure 2.33.

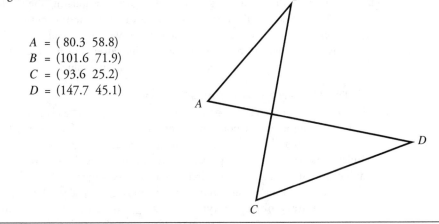

A = (80.3 58.8)
B = (101.6 71.9)
C = (93.6 25.2)
D = (147.7 45.1)

Figure 2.33   *Sample polygon*

The contents of the four elements of the linked list are shown below. The edge for that list element is indicated on the left. We see the *ymax* and *ymin* entries, the *dx* values, and the starting *x*-values for the computation of the edge and scan-line intersection. The expressions on the right show how we obtain the starting *x*-values.

edge	*ymax*	*ymin*	*dx*	*x*	*x* obtained as
1: *BC*:	71.9	25.2	−0.17	101.61	101.6 + 0.17∗0.1
2: *AB*:	71.9	58.8	−1.63	101.76	101.6 + 1.63∗0.1
3: *AD*:	58.8	45.1	4.91	79.32	80.3 − 4.91∗0.2
4: *CD*:	45.1	25.2	−2.71	150.12	147.7 + 2.71∗0.9

After the first decrement, *scan* will have the value 71. This will cause the edges *BC* and *AB* to be included, as their *ymax* is greater than *scan*. *Rite* will point to element 3. Elements 1 and 2 will be the cutting edges. After we update the *x*-values of these two edges, their values will be 101.44 and 100.13 respectively. We see that they are not in increasing order. Therefore, the cutting edges must be sorted on their *x*-values before fill lines are drawn between the pairs of *x*-values. Here, a horizontal line will be drawn from round(100.13) to round(101.44), that is, from 100 to 101. (A rounding function may be needed here.) We will explain the sorting of the *x*-values later.

The next *scan* value is 70. No inclusions or exclusions are required and the line is drawn from round(98.5) to round(101.27), that is, from 99 to 101. The fill line will start sooner and end sooner for every new *scan* value.

The first major change occurs when *scan* reaches the value 58. Then *scan* will be less than *ymin* of edge *AB*, so *AB* will be excluded; *ymax* of *AD* will be greater than *scan*, so *AD* will be included.

From now on, the starting value of the fill line grows by 4.91 for every new scan line and the point is soon reached where the two edges cross over. The starting value of the fill line is then greater than the terminating value. This shows that updating the *x*-values by adding the respective *dx* can change their order. We also saw that the starting entries in the table did not automatically put the *x*-values in increasing order. We must obtain this ordering by sorting.

This tells us that we have to sort the cutting edges (but not the others) on *x* after we update the *x*-values, which means for every new scan line value.

OO DESIGN AND CODED ALGORITHM

We introduce the classes `elist_t` and `glist_t`. The class `elist_t` is the list of edges for filling a convex polygon in the most basic way. The class `glist_t` is derived from `elist_t` and is intended for filling a general polygon. Filling a convex polygon is simpler, because there are always exactly two cutting edges. Also, most polygons in computer graphics are convex (for example, circles, triangles, rectangles, and polygons in 3D that bound solid objects), so it makes sense not to use the most general algorithm all the time.

A temporary object of type `elist_t` is created in the member function `convex_t::solid()`. The argument for its constructor is a pointer to the first vertex in the convex polygon. The edges are then created through the virtual function `vertex_t::make_edge()` and linked in. This provides a high amount of flexibility and code reusability; if the polygon consists of a certain type of vertices, for example 3D vertices, then the `elist_t` will be constructed with the type of edges that pertain to that type of vertex, such as 3D edges. These edges contain all the information necessary to fill that sort of polygon.

We explain the basic member functions in `elist_t` for filling a convex polygon. You will notice that these functions reflect what was explained in the algorithm above.

> `void insert_edge(vertex_t&,vertex_t&)` constructs an edge from two vertices and inserts it into the edge list, which is ordered on the *ymax* values.
>
> `void include()` includes an edge in the cutting edges when *scan* has passed its *ymax* value.
>
> `void exclude()` excludes an edge from the cutting edges when *scan* has passed its *ymin* value.
>
> `virtual void swap()` exchanges the two cutting edges to sort them by their *x*-values.
>
> A convex polygon always has exactly two cutting edges, so no real sorting is neces-

sary. Swap() is virtual and will be redefined in polygon, where there can be more than two cutting edges and it becomes necessary to really sort them by their *x*-values.

virtual void update() updates the two cutting edges. In a basic convex polygon, this consists of simply adding *dx* to their *x*-values. In a general polygon, there can be more than two cutting edges and, depending on the type of edge, updating can consist of doing considerably more than here (see Z-buffer fill and Phong shading).

virtual void fill() performs the filling by scanning the polygon and calling the other functions. It has an argument of type "pointer to member function of class edge_t." The function pointed to is also virtual and draws the scan lines. (The edge object has the information about what sort of scan line to draw, depending on the type of polygon being filled, so different edge-types will have different versions of scan-line functions.) Giving solidscan() as an argument fills the polygon solid, hatchscan() crosshatches it and patternscan() fills it with a pattern. In a convex polygon, fill() draws only one scan line segment. In a general polygon it will be redefined to draw an arbitrary number of scan line segments.

The members of elist_t are as follows: head, a pointer to the beginning of the edge list; rite, a pointer to the rightmost cutting edge; scan, the current scan line value; and scan_decrement, which is 1 in normal cases, but will later assume other values, too. Scan is of type double to allow non-integer scan line advances and code reuse.

```
//*********************** File elist.h ***********************

#ifndef ELIST_T
#define ELIST_T

#include "../Shape2d/vertex.h"
#include "../Shape2d/edge.h"


class elist_t                       // edge list for filling convex polygon
{
public:
    elist_t(vertex_t *) ;
    elist_t() ;
    ~elist_t() {}
    virtual void fill(void (edge_t::*)(double)) ;

protected:
    void insert_edge(vertex_t&,vertex_t&) ;
    void include()                      ;
    void exclude()                      ;
    virtual void swap()                 ;
    virtual void update()               ;

    edge_t* head ;                          // beginning of edge list
    edge_t* rite ;                  // points beyond rightmost cutting edge
    double scan ;
    double scan_decrement ;
```

```
} ;

#endif

//****************************************************************
```

The class `glist_t` is derived from `elist` and fills general polygons. It redefines the virtual member functions `swap()`, `update()`, and `fill()` as explained above.

```
//*********************** File glist.h ***********************

#ifndef GLIST_T
#define GLIST_T

#include "../Shape2d/elist.h"


class glist_t : public elist_t //edge list for filling general polygon
{
public:
   glist_t(vertex_t*) ;
   ~glist_t() ;
   void fill(void (edge_t::*)(double))  ;              // is redefined
protected:
   void swap()   ;                                     // is redefined
   void update() ;                                     // is redefined
} ;

#endif

//****************************************************************
```

APPLICATIONS OF THE FILL ALGORITHM

The basic purpose of the fill algorithm is to traverse all pixels within a polygon defined by its vertices. In doing this, it is possible to fill a polygon with solid lines, a pattern, or crosshatch, as we will soon explain.

However, we can use a traversing algorithm for much more. Several other algorithms traverse a polygon's pixels in image space (that is, on the screen) in performing computations or setting individual pixel illuminations. These algorithms use the above traversing operation, but do not draw solid lines between x-value pairs.

We will use the fill algorithm when we discuss three-dimensional objects. Z-buffer methods, as well as other ones, use this algorithm. Z-buffer methods perform a depth computation for each pixel in the polygon. Then, by comparing this computation with a given depth buffer, they determine whether to set that pixel.

Shading methods do something similar. They compute the illumination of individual pixels within the two-dimensional projection of a polygon, depending on information derived from the three-dimensional polygon description, light source directions, and other factors.

We now consider simple two-dimensional applications of our routines. These are solid fill, pattern fill, and crosshatching.

2.3.1   SOLID FILL

First, we show solid fill. We can draw a single horizontal fill line using a general DDA algorithm, but that is inefficient. Drawing a horizontal line is very simple and will be much faster using a special machine-dependent implementation. Such a routine is called `sline()` in this code. It needs only three arguments: starting *x*-value, ending *x*-value, and *y*-value. The sidebar on drawing horizontal lines explains this.

In the case of a convex polygon, a fill line consists of only one part; in the general case, it can consist of several parts. We make fill lines by taking consecutive pairs of *x*-values from among the current edges and drawing a horizontal line between each pair. We first show the convex case, implemented in `clist_t::fill()`.

```
void clist_t::fill(void (edge_t::*f)(double))
{
    while (scan--      ,
           include()  ,
           exclude()  ,
           update()   ,
           swap()     ,
           head       )                 // stop when edge list empty
        (head->*f)(scan);
}
```

The general case is implemented in `elist_t::fill()`.

```
void elist_t::fill(void (edge_t::*f)(double))
{
    while (scan--      ,
           include()  ,
           exclude()  ,
           update()   ,
           swap()     ,
           head       )                 // stop when edge list empty
        for (edge_t* p = head; p != rite; p = p->givnext()->givnext())
            (p->*f)(scan);
}
```

Drawing Horizontal Lines

A fill line is always horizontal and coincides with a scan line of the raster display. Because the state of each pixel on the screen depends on values in the portion of memory that comprises the frame buffer or bit map, to draw any line requires access to corresponding memory cells. For a raster scan device, horizontally aligned pixels correspond to memory cells in adjacent memory locations. This means that the address-decoding logic of a linearly organized RAM, which associates each memory address with a group of eight bits (a byte) or, sometimes, 16 bits (a word), must only increment the address and fetch the byte or word. A dumb chip, perhaps a DMA chip, can do this very rapidly and need

(continued)

not involve the main processor. No computations are needed, in contrast to the many computations required for a general straight line. We do have to compute the start of each fill line and how many pixels should be set for each fill line, but that is all.

Keep in mind that the correspondence between bits in the bit map and pixels on the screen depends on how memory is organized. The exact relationship may vary, but it is always simpler for horizontally adjacent pixels than for any other. This means that we can always draw horizontal lines more rapidly than other lines. We should not use a DDA algorithm to fill a polygon. If not already available in hardware, adding a short machine-language segment will make operations more efficient.

2.3.2   PATTERN FILLING

Moving from filling with a solid color to filling with a pattern is easy. All we must provide is a fill line that fills with a pattern instead of with a constant color. Figure 2.34 shows a pattern and a polygon filled with that pattern.

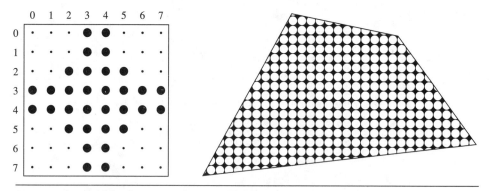

Figure 2.34   Predefined pattern and pattern-filled polygon.

If the frame buffer has a depth of eight (eight bit planes), then each pixel in the pattern is represented by one byte. If the frame buffer is 24 bits deep, we need three bytes for each pixel in the pattern. We show two variations of the pattern class specification, the 8-bit pattern is for Xwin8, the 24-bit pattern is for Xwin24 and for Tiga; see page 18.

```
//********************** File pattern.h **************************
#ifndef PATTERN_T
#define PATTERN_T
#include "../opsys.h"

#ifdef Tiga
class pattern_t
{
public:
    pattern_t(int,int,unsigned long*) ;
    pattern_t() : p(0) {}
    ~pattern_t() ;
    unsigned long* operator [] (int i) { return p + i*c; }
```

```
      void operator = (const pattern_t&) ;
      unsigned long
         item(int r,int c) { return (*this)[r%this->r][c%this->c]; }
   private:
      unsigned long* p ;
      int r ;                                    // number of rows
      int c ;                                    // number of columns
   } ;
   #endif

   #ifdef Xwin24
   class pattern_t
   {
   public:
      pattern_t(int,int,unsigned long*) ;
      pattern_t() : p(0) {}
      ~pattern_t() ;
      unsigned long* operator [] (int i) { return p + i*c; }
      void operator = (const pattern_t&) ;
      unsigned long
         item(int r,int c) { return (*this)[r%this->r][c%this->c]; }
   private:
      unsigned long* p ;
      int r ;                                    // number of rows
      int c ;                                    // number of columns
   } ;
   #endif

   #ifdef  Xwin8
   class pattern_t
   {
   public:
      pattern_t(int,int,unsigned char*) ;
      pattern_t() : p(0) {}
      ~pattern_t() ;
      unsigned char* operator [] (int i) { return p + i*c; }
      void operator = (const pattern_t&) ;
      char item(int r,int c) { return (*this)[r%this->r][c%this->c]; }
   private:
      unsigned char* p ;
      int r ;                                    // number of rows
      int c ;                                    // number of columns
   } ;

   #endif
   #endif
   //****************************************************************
```

The pattern is a two-dimensional array of unsigned characters or unsigned longs, which is allocated dynamically. The numbers of rows and columns are data members. Copying in some hardcoded pattern at run time initializes the pattern with its dimensions.

For our explanations we assume an array with 8×8 characters. The fill algorithm copies this array into the polygon so that row 0 of the pattern will go into rows 0, 8, and 16, and so on, in the frame buffer. Row 1 of the pattern will go into rows 1, 9, and 17, and so on. The same is true of the columns. This is easy to achieve through modulo arithmetic. When a fill line is to be drawn from x_1 to x_2 at the scan height, we compute the column pointer as x_1 mod 8 and the row pointer as *scan* mod 8. Whatever the size of the pattern, the principle is to assign the color of pattern element [i%row_number] [j%column_number] to the pixel (i,j) for any values of i and j.

The pattern can have any size and values and is passed as an argument to the function `prim_t::pattern()`. The implementation details of `edge_t::patternscan()` should be taken from the enclosed source codes.

To do pattern fill effectively, we must pay particular attention to the specific hardware being used. Fast pattern-fill algorithms are programmed in assembly, but follow the same basic idea. In assembly, there would be no subscript arithmetic, and certain bits would be masked out, making modulo 8 arithmetic very fast.

When we fill a polygon with a special pattern, we can achieve something similar to crosshatching. Figure 2.35 shows two patterns. Both would produce a crosshatch, with only a slight difference in the way the lines cross. The resulting filled polygons would look almost identical. An 8×8 pattern can do crosshatches only with a hatch line distance of 4. For a different distance, we would use a different size of pattern and a different modulo arithmetic.

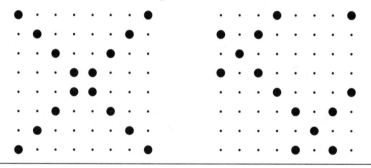

Figure 2.35   Two crosshatch patterns

2.3.3   CROSSHATCHING

One way of crosshatching a polygon in a raster display is to compute only the positions where pixels are to be set, ignoring all other pixel positions. This is not a special form of pattern filling. You can specify any desired distance between the hatch lines. The basic process is identical to that of solid filling, except for replacing the function `edge_t::solidscan()` with `edge_t::hatchscan()`.

The algorithm is a bit tricky. Observe that in a 45° crosshatch, the distances between the intersections of the scan line with the hatch lines are constant between every other intersection. (When two hatch lines intersect a scan line at the same position, they count as two intersections.) The distances between succeeding intersections toggle between only two values. The position of the first pixel is computed and the pixel is set, then the step to the next pixel is computed. After this, the step size is varied between two values that depend on the value of *scan*. In the presented algorithm, the hatch lines intersect at 90 degrees. The details should be taken from the enclosed source codes.

Another way of crosshatching a polygon is to actually draw slanted, solid fill lines. Such a method is required if a polygon is to be crosshatched on a plotter. This is the topic of one of the following exercises.

SUGGESTED READINGS

More about the fundamental algorithms can be found in EARN85, which contains a collection of articles from many authors about these subjects. An approach to polygon filling similar to ours is described in FVFH90.

EXERCISES

SECTION 2.0

1. Try to determine the resolution (number of pixels on the screen) of the graphics monitor on which you are working. You can do this with a trial-and-error method. The only graphics primitive you need is the straight line with absolute screen coordinates as start and end points.

2. You might use a graphics workstation that provides for a default user coordinate system with a very high resolution, such as 4000×3000. Such a system will probably let you specify graphics primitives only within this coordinate system. Try to find out whether this user coordinate system really corresponds to the physical resolution of the monitor. Hint: draw a straight line, for example from (0,100) to (3500,101). You should obtain precisely one stair step in the middle of that line. If you do not, the physical resolution is lower.

3. How much memory is needed for the frame buffer to store a 640×400 display with 16 gray levels?

4. Consider a raster display with 1024×1024 pixels, noninterlaced display mode, and a screen width of 35 cm. Estimate the average speed of the electron beam across the screen surface.

5. The horizontal oscillation frequency, also called scan rate, is expressed in Hertz (Hz), which is oscillations per second. Assume that the vertical retrace time is 10 percent of the vertical sweep time. Assume a 640×400 frame buffer and a refresh frequency of 60 frames per second. What scan rate is needed to display this frame buffer in noninterlaced mode?

6. Repeat Exercise 5 using an interlaced display.

7. On your graphics device, implement a graphics primitive called `setpix(x,y)`, which sets a single pixel at the absolute device address (*x y*). Color or gray level is unimportant.

8. Distinguish between pixel ratio and the frequently encountered term *aspect ratio*. Aspect ratio is the physical height to width ratio of a display, for example, of a CRT. What is the

aspect ratio of a 12" × 16" display?

9. Workstations often have large size CRTs with high resolution, which are useful in computer-aided design. Look up this topic in recent computer journals to see what the maximum limits are for output devices of this type that are on the market (not specialized research devices).

SECTION 2.1.1

10. Draw the arc corresponding to the chain 44344344344344.

11. Does the chain 3233233223223323 represent a straight line? If not, why not? Can this be seen directly from the chain?

12. Write a program to test two chains for unevenness. The program should sum the symbols of all substring pairs of equal length and compare them.

13. Find a digital arc that looks almost straight but is not. Find the two uneven substrings in its chain.

14. One of the three consequences of Hung and Kasvand's straight line theorem is that the less frequent symbol only occurs isolated. Using an example, show that evenness is violated in a chain that does not fulfill this.

15. Using the best-fit method, produce by hand the chain for the line from (0 0) to (13 5).

SECTION 2.1.2

16. Implement a straight line DDA according to the formula given in Section 2.1.2. Produce lines with very small and very big values for Dx and Dy. Observe how the line develops gaps when the steps are too big and becomes thicker when the steps are too small.

17. Use the graphics primitive `setpix()` developed in Exercise 7 to implement the simple straight line DDA in C++.

18. Increase the speed of the DDA algorithm of Exercise 17 by realizing that because one of the increments always equals 1, one of the additions can be done in integer arithmetic. Compare the speeds of the unimproved and the improved versions.

19. Modify the simple straight line DDA to draw either solid, dashed, or dotted lines.

20. Modify the simple straight line DDA to draw lines of three different widths: normal (thinnest eight-connected line), approximately two pixels thick, and approximately three pixels thick.

21. Execute Bresenham's straight line algorithm by hand as shown in the text to produce a line from (0 0) to (17 12).

22. Implement Bresenham's straight line algorithm in C++, making case distinctions to enable lines to be drawn in all directions. You can reduce the number of cases from eight to four by drawing only lines whose end points' x-values are equal to or higher than the start point. Test the given end points for this condition and swap them if necessary.

23. Compare the speed of Bresenham's straight line algorithm to the speeds of the DDA algorithms in Exercises 19 and 20.

24. Implement Bresenham's straight line algorithm in assembly language to achieve a fast execution time. For example, avoid calling the graphics primitive `setpix()` with the two arguments x and y, because each call involves complicated overhead.

SECTION 2.2

25. Implement the member function `polygon_t::draw()` by walking through the vertex list, taking two successive vertices, constructing a `line_t` with its coordinates, and then calling `line_t::draw()`. This has some disadvantages in terms of speed. Discuss those.

26. Discuss the cases in which `vertex_t::make_edge()` does not create an edge. Does this guarantee that there is always an even number of cutting edges?

SECTION 2.3

Use the following information on crosshatching polygons for Exercises 28 to 32.

Crosshatching a polygon with the methods shown in the text will work only for raster displays, not on a line plotter. To crosshatch a polygon on a line plotter, you must literally draw the crosshatch lines. We now explain how to do this.

This method crosshatches a polygon with two sets of lines. The lines of one set are slanted at 45° and the lines of the other are slanted at −45°. The distance between the lines should be enough to make them individually recognizable.

The basic steps in the algorithm above—sorting the edges by *ymax*, drawing horizontal fill lines, and so on—would have to undergo major changes if we really fill the given polygon with slanted lines. We can avoid these complications if instead of drawing slanted lines into the given polygon, we rotate the polygon by −45° and compute the horizontal fill lines. These lines will have the proper position in relation to the polygon, but before we draw these lines, we rotate them by 45°, so they will have the proper position in the unrotated polygon. We never really draw the rotated polygon—we need only its vertices in memory. Therefore, we can apply rotations just around the origin.

We rotate the point $(x\ y)$ by −45° into $(xr\ yr)$ by transforming:

$$xr = 0.707107*(x + y)$$
$$yr = 0.707107*(-x + y)$$

We do this to all vertices of the given polygon, then we fill it with horizontal lines. We change the fill algorithm by changing the scan line decrement and *dx*. Let *dist* be the vertical distance between the crosshatch lines measured in pixels. We draw the first fill line at *dist*/2 below the highest *ymax*. We change *dx* to

```
-dist*(v1.x-v2.x)/(v1.y-v2.y) ;
```

where v_1 and v_2 are the two end points of the edge.

The most significant change occurs in function `solidscan()`. The end points of a horizontal fill line are $(x_1, scan)$ and $(x_2, scan)$. We have to rotate these points by 45° and then draw a straight nonhorizontal line between the rotated points. We replace

```
move(x1,scan);
draw(x2,scan);
```

with

```
xr = 0.707107*(x1-scan);
yr = 0.707107*(x1+scan);
move(int(xr+0.5),int(yr+0.5));
xr = 0.707107*(x2-scan);
yr = 0.707107*(x2+scan);
draw(int(xr+0.5),int(yr+0.5));
```

This gives us one set of hatch lines. We must produce the other set analogously.

27. Use OO programming to implement the crosshatching method described above. It is essential that you use existing code without touching it. Implement only additions and changes to existing code. Here are some hints:

Derive `hpolygon_t` from `polygon_t` and give it all necessary constructors, a destructor, and the copy function. Redefine only the function `polygon_t::hatch()`. We outline this function below—compare to `convex_t::hatch()`:

```
{
    // do nothing if less than 3 vertices
    // clip against window - then 'clipped' points to clipped list
    // window-device transformation on whole clipped list
    // rotate whole clipped list by 45°
    hlist_t(clipped).fill(&hedge_t::hatchup);
    // rotate whole clipped list by -90°
    hlist_t(clipped).fill(&hedge_t::hatchdown);
    delete clipped;
}
```

You need to derive class `hlist_t` from `glist_t`. It differs from `glist_t` only in its constructor. The constructor initializes `scan_decrement` to the hatch line distance *dist* and the starting value of *scan* to the smallest integer multiple of *dist* which is larger than the largest *ymax*.

Also, you need to derive class `hedge_t` from `edge_t` and give it the member functions `hatchup()` which rotates a scanline by −45° before drawing it and `hatchdown()` which rotates a scanline by 45° before drawing it. Through this derivation it is possible to call `hlist_t::fill()` with pointers to `hatchup()` or `hatchdown()` as arguments.

To crosshatch a polygon with this method it must be constructed as an `hpolygon_t` and its member function `hatch` called. An `hpolygon_t` can also be filled in any way defined before.

28. Write an algorithm that hatches a polygon with one set of lines at an arbitrary angle α and a distance *dist*.

29. Why do we always fill polygons with horizontal lines? Can we do it with vertical lines?

30. Is filling with vertical lines slower than filling with horizontal lines?

31. Can a polygon be solidly filled with slanted lines? Why or why not? An angle of 45° is an exception; explain why.

3

CIRCLES AND ELLIPSES

Circles and ellipses are important enough that we devote this chapter to methods for drawing them. There are three major sections in the chapter.

3.0   **Introduction** tells why you should know about methods that generate circular and elliptical figures.

3.1   **Circles** summarizes some useful properties of circles and describes three ways to set the pixels in the image of a circle. The most important are DDA methods that use equations for the slope to find which pixel to set next.

3.2   **Ellipses** does the same for ellipses. The algorithms for drawing an ellipse are similar to those for circles because a circle is a special case of an ellipse.

3.0   INTRODUCTION

As we mentioned in Chapter 2, curves in computer graphics are usually generated as sequences of many short, straight lines. But some curves, in particular circles and ellipses, are so common that we should develop DDA and other specialized algorithms for them. A specialized algorithm is much faster than approximation by many straight lines. However, such an algorithm will have a speed advantage only if programmed in assembly language or provided in silicon.

The *pixel ratio* of a raster display is the quotient of the distance between the centers of two horizontally adjacent pixels over the distance between the centers of two vertically adjacent pixels. Practically all raster displays now used in computer graphics have a pixel ratio of 1 (*square pixel ratio*). We will therefore not adapt our circle generators to nonsquare pixel ratios.

The Liquid Crystal Display (LCD)

Many substances can be in a state between crystallized and liquid, or a *mesostate*. This means that the molecules have more freedom of motion than in the solid state, but not as much as in a liquid. Chemists seek substances that exhibit these properties at room temperature. Liquid crystal technology is an area of intensive research.

We distinguish among three types of liquid crystal substances. One is called *smectic*. In such a substance, the molecules are arranged in layers with their long axes perpendicular to the plane of the layers. Within a layer, the molecules usually are regularly spaced with respect to each other, but the layers can easily slide over each other.

Another type is called *nematic*. In this substance, the molecules can move freely in all spatial directions, but can rotate only around their own long axes, so they stay parallel to each other.

The third type is called *cholesteric*. In this type, the molecules are arranged in thin parallel layers with their long axes parallel to the plane of layers. The diameter of the thin layers is about one molecule. Several hundred thin layers make up a thick layer. The thin layers are not geometrically independent of each other. The long axis of a molecule in one thin layer is slightly and systematically rotated with respect to the axis of molecules in the layers above and below. This results in a helical structure through one thick layer. Such substances have great optical activity because the diameter of the thick layers is about the wavelength of visible light.

The forces that maintain a certain order of the liquid crystal molecules in the mesostate are usually very weak. Electric or magnetic fields, temperature, or pressure can easily influence, change, or destroy the order. Figure 3.A shows unordered molecules in a liquid.

Figure 3.A   *Molecules in random orientations*

A single optical liquid crystal element basically consists of a substance in a liquid crystal state enclosed between two transparent electrical conductors. If a voltage is applied across these two conductors, it creates an electric field, which reorders the molecules in between. Figure 3.B shows one possible arrangement of molecules in a smectic substance.

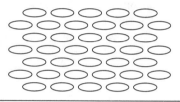

Figure 3.B   *Molecules in a certain arrangement*

Figure 3.C shows the same substance with a different molecule arrangement. When the electric field is switched off, the molecules return to their former arrangement.

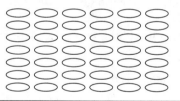

Figure 3.C   *Molecules in another arrangement*

In one of the arrangements, light can penetrate, while in the other it is blocked. Precisely how this works is complicated. Sometimes the oscillating direction (polarization) of polarized light waves is rotated when they pass through the helix of a cholesteric substance and is not rotated when an electric field disturbs the helix. A polarizing filter then blocks the rotated light and lets unrotated light pass. Sometimes dye molecules are mixed into the liquid crystal substance, whose molecules force the dye molecules into certain arrangements. The optical activity of liquid crystal substances can switch individual LCD cells on and off in many different ways.

(continued)

Liquid crystals can even store information. Certain smectic substances tend to align their molecules at one of two possible angles with the enclosing wall, say 45° or 135°. Interestingly, they then stay this way as if they were in a crystalline state. Applying a certain electric field can change the alignment angle; applying a different field changes it back. The arrangement can also be read out, which makes it possible to construct storage media with a density of 10^{12} bits per square inch (U.S. patent 3,775,757).

The optical properties of liquid crystals are often used in displays for small calculators and digital watches. Only a few coarsely shaped elements can form the few digits. To produce raster displays is a major technological challenge because the individual LCD pixels need to be very small and dense. Addressing the pixels individually in order to switch them requires a complicated wiring mechanism. It is difficult to change the molecule arrangement as quickly as desired. Research often focuses on finding fast switching substances. Many of these difficulties have been overcome today. LC raster displays, often with color capabilities, are being increasingly used in laptop computers.

Little energy is needed to maintain the electric field and thus a certain molecule arrangement, because hardly any electricity is actually flowing. LCD's almost zero energy consumption is one of their big advantages, as is the display's essential flatness and absence of flicker. This makes liquid crystal raster displays more and more valuable for microcomputers. They may one day be used to provide a thin screen TV display.

3.1   CIRCLES

We can create circles with methods derived from differential equations. On most raster displays, a regular polygon with 60 sides would look like a circle, even though it consists of a sequence of short, straight lines that we can create with repeated invocations of a straight line DDA. Such a method is much slower than using a special circle-generating DDA designed to attain speed. This section describes both DDA and non-DDA methods for circles. Before we describe the algorithms for generating circles, we cover some features of images of circular objects.

CENTRAL SYMMETRY

As a preliminary to circle generation, we consider how to use a circle's symmetry. If the center is at the origin and a pixel $(x\ y)$ lies on the circle's circumference, then we can easily calculate seven more pixels on this circle. Figure 3.1 shows the given pixel in black, and the derived pixels as open circles.

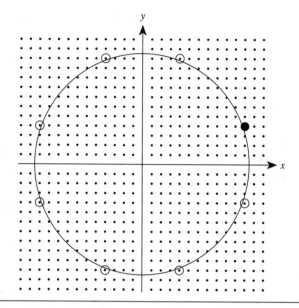

Figure 3.1   Using symmetry in a circle

Whenever we compute a circle's individual pixels with a DDA method, we can use this symmetry. We will present such DDA methods below. The function `eight_octs()` shows how to use this symmetry.

```
void eight_octs(int x,int y)                    // set 8 pixels by
{                                               // symmetry around center
    setpix( x+xcen, y+ycen);
    setpix(-x+xcen, y+ycen);
    setpix( x+xcen,-y+ycen);
    setpix(-x+xcen,-y+ycen);
    setpix( y+xcen, x+ycen);
    setpix(-y+xcen, x+ycen);
    setpix( y+xcen,-x+ycen);
    setpix(-y+xcen,-x+ycen);
}
```

CIRCLE GENERATORS

Let us now study various algorithms for drawing circles. We discuss four circle generators. Two are non-DDAs and two are DDAs. They all need to generate only one-eighth of a circle, as the symmetry function above does the rest. They generate a circle with the origin at the center. Generating a circle with a different center is no problem; it involves only adding the center coordinates to every generated pixel which is left to the symmetry algorithm. The algorithms below therefore call `eight_octs()`.

The Plasma Display

The main problems with the CRT as a display device are the very high voltages it requires, its bulkiness, and its weight. The plasma display solves some of these problems.

Figure 3.D demonstrates the principle of the plasma display. Two sheets of glass with thin, closely spaced gold electrodes attached to the inner faces are covered with a dielectric material. Each set of electrodes consists of a set of closely spaced parallel wires. The two sets of electrodes cross at a right angle. The two sheets of glass are spaced a few thousandths of a millimeter apart, and the intervening space is filled with a special gas and sealed. By applying voltages between the electrodes, we make the gas within the panel behave as if it were divided into tiny cells, each one independent of its neighbors. In other words, when we apply a voltage between two electrodes, we create an electric field at the place where the two electrodes are closest to each other. This electric field turns the gas into a plasma. Plasma is a gas in an electricity-conducting state. It also usually emits light.

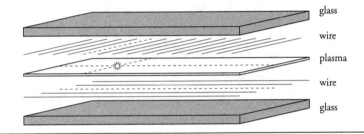

Figure 3.D   *Exploded view of a plasma display*

When certain cells glow, a picture is generated. We can make a cell glow by placing a firing voltage across it by means of the electrodes. The gas within begins to discharge; this develops very rapidly into a glow. We can sustain the glow by maintaining a high-frequency alternating voltage across the cell. If we have chosen the signal amplitude correctly, cells that have not been fired will not be affected. In other words, each cell has two stable states. We call an element with two stable states *bistable*.

Cells can be switched on by momentarily increasing the voltage above the sustaining level. We can do this selectively by modifying the signal in the two conductors that intersect at the desired cell. Similarly, if we lower the sustaining signal, the glow disappears. Thus, the plasma panel allows both selective writing and selective erasing at speeds of about 20 microseconds per cell. We can increase this speed by writing or erasing several cells in parallel. A cell stays lit or unlit until changed, so the plasma display "remembers" the picture.

The plasma display produces a very steady image, totally free of flicker, and is a less bulky device than a CRT of comparable screen size. Its main disadvantages are its relatively poor resolution, about 60 dots per inch, and its complex addressing and wiring requirements. Its inherent memory is useful, but is not as flexible as a frame buffer memory; besides, memory prices have come down quite a bit in recent years and will continue to do so. Plasma displays can be of value in portable microcomputers because of their flatness and low energy requirements.

3.1.1   PARAMETER METHOD

The first circle generator we discuss is not a DDA. It consists of calculating:

$$x = r \cos u$$

$$y = r \sin u$$

and increasing u in small steps. If u goes from 0 to 2π, we obtain an entire circle around the origin with radius r. This method always produces the best possible circle, but it is slow because it involves the repeated evaluation of the sin and cos functions. If the increase in u is $\leq 1/r$ (length of r expressed in pixels), we advance by approximately one pixel with every step. After computing x and y and rounding them to integers, we can set 8 pixels at the symmetry locations of $(x\ y)$ by calling `eight_octs`; u goes only from 0 to $\pi/4$.

We can also make larger steps and connect consecutive points with straight lines. The created points advance in steps of four degrees, which seems to be a good compromise. To take advantage of the symmetry, the step size must be such that an integer number of steps covers 1/8 of the circle. Each line is then drawn at eight symmetric locations.

3.1.2   ROTATION METHOD

Another non-DDA method that generates an exact circle consists of rotating a point in two dimensions about the origin.

$$x_{rot} = x \cos u - y \sin u$$

$$y_{rot} = x \sin u + y \cos u$$

We compute a succession of rotated points, starting with $(x_0\ y_0) = (r\ 0)$:

$$x_{n+1} = x_n \cos u - y_n \sin u$$

$$y_{n+1} = x_n \sin u + y_n \cos u$$

This generates points on a circle around the origin in a counterclockwise direction. We have to compute sin u and cos u only once. If we choose $u \leq 1/r$, we obtain approximately one pixel increase with every step. The larger the radius, the smaller u must be. This circle generation involves four multiplications and two additions for every pixel, and is therefore faster than the previous one. The computed x_n and y_n values must be rounded to the nearest pixel location before calling `eight_octs()`. We let the iteration go for only one octant.

If the step size is larger than one pixel, we connect the computed points by straight lines, as in the code below. The code does not take advantage of symmetry, but it is as easy to do as in the last generator and is left as an exercise.

This code serves only to explain the algorithmic principle of the rotation method.

```
void draw()                                    // rotation method
{
    double x1 = r , y1 = 0 ,
           x2 , y2 ,
           su = sin(2*3.14159265/90) ,
           cu = cos(2*3.14159265/90) ;
```

```
    for (int i = 0; i < 90; i++)              // steps of 4 degrees
    {
        x2 = x1*cu - y1*su;
        y2 = x1*su + y1*cu;
        line_t(x1+cenx,y1+ceny,x2+cenx,y2+ceny).draw();
        x1 = x2;
        y1 = y2;
    }
}
```

DDA METHODS

Because they are faster in execution, we usually prefer DDA methods for calculating which pixels to set to draw a circle. The differential equation for a circle centered at the origin is:

$$\frac{dy}{dx} = \frac{-x}{y}$$

where $(x\ \ y)$ is any point on the circle. The radius does not occur in this equation because the equation expresses all circles around the origin. The equation is true only when x and y have the same scale in Cartesian coordinates. The derivative dy/dx is the slope of the tangent line at $(x\ \ y)$.

3.1.3　THE "SPIRAL" CIRCLE GENERATOR

We expect the equation to express something close enough to a circle if dy and dx are replaced by small, though not infinitesimal, values Dx and Dy. This gives:

$$\frac{Dy}{Dx} = \frac{-x_n}{y_n}$$

in which $(x_n\ \ y_n)$ is the nth point that the DDA generates. It follows that there is some value ε such that $Dy = \varepsilon * x_n$ and $Dx = -\varepsilon * y_n$. This leads to a formula for calculating the n+1st point on the circle given the nth point:

$$x_{n+1} = x_n + Dx = x_n - \varepsilon * y_n$$
$$y_{n+1} = y_n + Dy = y_n + \varepsilon * x_n$$

We expect a deviation from the true circle because the continuously changing derivative has been replaced by a quotient, which changes in steps as n increases. If $(x\ \ y)$ is a point in the iteration, the next point is $(x - \varepsilon * y\ \ \ y + \varepsilon * x)$. The lengths of the vectors (radii to the two points) are not identical:

$$\left| (x - \varepsilon * y\ \ \ y + \varepsilon * x) \right| = \left| (x\ \ y) \right| * \sqrt{1 + \varepsilon^2}\ ^\dagger$$

This means that every consecutive point in the iteration becomes farther from the origin by this constant factor. The deviation is such that the points lie on a curve that spirals outwards. The choice of a small ε makes the spiraling effect small and perhaps tolerable. We do not show code for the spiral method.

$\dagger$ You can verify the truth of this by expanding both sides. Recall that $\left| (x\ \ y) \right| = \sqrt{x^2 + y^2}$.

3.1.4 THE "ELLIPSE" CIRCLE GENERATOR

Modifying the iterations removes the continuing spiraling effect without increasing the number of operations. We use the already computed x_{n+1} in computing y_{n+1}:

$$x_{n+1} = x_n - \varepsilon * y_n$$
$$y_{n+1} = y_n + \varepsilon * x_{n+1}$$

The reason this works is that the under- or over-adjustments to the y-values in one octant are compensated by over- or under-adjustments in the next. The curve thus created is still not a circle. The proof is as follows. We can express one iteration step as a matrix multiplication:

$$\begin{pmatrix} x_{n+1} & y_{n+1} \end{pmatrix} = \begin{pmatrix} x_n & y_n \end{pmatrix} * \mathbf{A}$$

$$\text{where } \mathbf{A} = \begin{pmatrix} 1 & \varepsilon \\ -\varepsilon & 1 - \varepsilon^2 \end{pmatrix}$$

We should not think, just because $\det(\mathbf{A}) = 1$, that the length of $(x\ y)*\mathbf{A}$ is the same as the length of $(x\ y)$, and therefore all iterated points lie on a circle. They do not.[†]

If we take any starting point other than $(0\ 0)$, the iterated points lie on an ellipse with center at $(0\ 0)$, axes $2r/\sqrt{2+\varepsilon}$ and $2r/\sqrt{2-\varepsilon}$, and a tilt of $45°$. The equation of this ellipse is:

$$x^2 - \varepsilon xy + y^2 - 2r^2 = 0$$

where r is a scaling factor depending on the starting point. This method is just a special case ($\alpha = \beta = \varepsilon$) of the general ellipse DDA that we give in Section 3.2.1.

The "spiral" and the "ellipse" methods both recalculate the increments to x_n and y_n with every step and produce a sequence of real number pairs that lie approximately on a circle. While these real values must be kept internally for the next iteration, they are rounded to the closest grid position, where a pixel is set.

We start the circle by choosing a starting point $(x_0\ y_0)$ on the intended circumference and computing succeeding points $(x_n\ y_n)$ until some end condition is fulfilled. The criterion could be that x and y are equal, if only one octant is to be generated.

Both methods require two floating multiplications, two floating additions (or subtractions), and two rounding operations for every step. Because floating arithmetic is more time-consuming than simple integer arithmetic, DDA algorithms have been designed to do everything in integer arithmetic (Bresenham's circle generation of Section 3.1.5 is an example).

This situation is changing. Modern dedicated processors have floating point arithmetic built into their hardware and execute such arithmetic much faster than before. The tendency to put more and more into hardware will continue. Eventually, floating point arithmetic may be almost as fast as integer arithmetic. Fast floating point hardware will reduce the advantage of the integer-arithmetic DDAs considerably, although these will always be faster if programmed properly. An advantage of the above two circle generators is that they have a straightforward

---

[†] The vector $(x\ y)*\mathbf{A}$ can be longer than $(x\ y)$. Indeed, taking $(1\ 0)$ as the starting point, the next point is $(1\ \varepsilon)$, with $|(1\ 0)| = 1$ and $|(1\ \varepsilon)| > 1$. Therefore, the iterated points do not lie on a circle.

testing plays an essential part. Although the condition there is very simple (just a sign flag test), it puts a conditional jump in the Bresenham assembly program, slowing it down.

When starting a circle of radius r on the positive x-axis at $(r\ 0)$, we could simply make ε equal to $1/r$. Because ε is a small number, a further improvement might be to choose a negative power of 2 for ε. Then ε should equal 2^{-n} where $2^{-n-1} \le r < 2^{-n}$. In this case, the multiplications reduce to a subtraction in the exponent part of the real number representation of x or y, increasing the speed. This last improvement is normally insignificant.

We must also consider precision. Neither the spiral nor the ellipse method produces mathematically exact circles. How good are they for practical purposes? You can find an answer to this in the exercises.

The code below serves to explain the algorithmic principle of the "ellipse method." The generated x_n and y_n values are rounded to the nearest pixel, while calling `eight_octs()`. The DDA produces only one octant; the rest is done by symmetry. The ending condition for the DDA is $x_n \le y_n$.

```
void draw()                                         // "ellipse" method
{
   double eps = 1.0/r ,
          x   = r     ,
          y   = 0     ;

   while (x > y)
   {
      eight_octs((int)(x+0.5),(int)(y+0.5));
      x -= eps*y;
      y += eps*x;
   }
}
```

3.1.5   BRESENHAM'S CIRCLE GENERATOR

This generator does only integer arithmetic, BRES77, which makes it considerably faster than any of the above methods if a processor has no hardware to perform floating point arithmetic.

The version presented here creates only one octant (one-eighth) of the circle, or more precisely, the arc from 90° to 45° in a clockwise fashion (see Figure 3.2). We derive the other seven octants of the circle by symmetry. The circle is generated with the center at the origin and with an integer-valued radius r.

The algorithm calculates one new pixel per step. From any point $(x_n\ y_n)$ on the circle, the next point $(x_{n+1}\ y_{n+1})$ must be one to the right or one to the right and one down from the current point because of the octant in which we are working. If P_n with the coordinates $(x_n\ y_n)$ is the current point, then the next

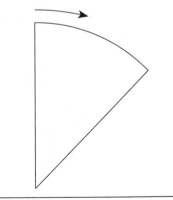

Figure 3.2   *Direction of pixel generation in Bresenham's circle DDA*

point can be either A or B, whose coordinates are $(x_{n+1} \ y_n)$ or $(x_{n+1} \ y_{n-1})$ respectively. Figure 3.3 demonstrates this.

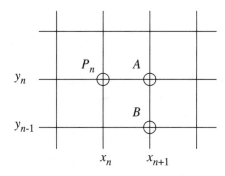

Figure 3.3   *Choosing the successor pixel of P_n*

We choose one of these pixels based on a test. To do this, we observe that the function $f(x,y) = x^2 + y^2 - r^2$ determines a circle with radius r around the origin in the following way:

> all points $(x \ y)$ for which $f(x,y) = 0$ lie on the circle
> all points $(x \ y)$ for which $f(x,y) > 0$ lie outside the circle
> all points $(x \ y)$ for which $f(x,y) < 0$ lie inside the circle

The sketches in Figure 3.4 show the point P_n, the two possible successors A and B, and five positions for the circular arc. In cases a, b, d, and e, P_n can only be in the indicated place, relative to the arc, but in case c, the arc can pass below, through, or above P_n.

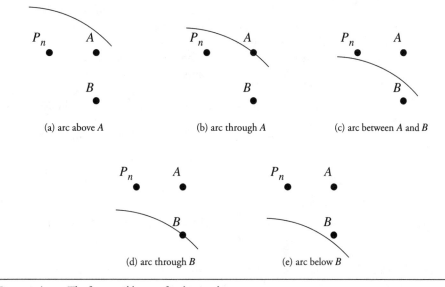

Figure 3.4   *The five possible cases for the circular arc*

Functions that determine how the pixels A and B lie with respect to the circle are:

$$f(A) = (x_n + 1)^2 + y_n^2 - r^2$$

$$f(B) = (x_n + 1)^2 + (y_n - 1)^2 - r^2$$

Table 3.1 shows the signs of these expressions and the sign of their sum, $s = f(A) + f(B)$, for the five possible positions of the circle relative to the points A and B. In case a, the pixels A and B both lie inside the circle. A is certainly closer to the circle, so we choose it.

	a	b	c	d	e
f(A)	−	0	+	+	+
f(B)	−	−	−	0	+
f(A) + f(B) (sum,s)	−	−	−,0,+	+	+

Table 3.1   *The functions used in finding the successor pixel*

In case b, the pixel A lies precisely on the circle and is chosen.

In case c, the pixel A lies outside and the pixel B lies inside the circle. The sum $f(A)+f(B)$ in this case always consists of a positive and a negative term. If the sum is negative or zero, then pixel A is closer to the circle (measured along a normal to the circle through the pixel center) and is chosen. If it is positive, then pixel A may be closer to the circle than pixel B. Even so, the algorithm in this case chooses pixel B because it is computationally expensive to calculate the actual distance. There is a slight tendency to choose the pixel inside the circle, but this does not significantly change the appearance of the resulting image.

In case d, the pixel B lies precisely on the circle and is chosen.

In case e, both pixels A and B lie outside the circle. B is certainly closer to the circle and is chosen.

All that we need to make a choice between pixels A and B is the sign of the sum $f(A)+f(B)$. It is not necessary to calculate both formulas and the sum for every step.

The starting pixel P_0 is taken as $(x_0 \ y_0) = (0 \ r)$. We obtain:

$$f(A) = (0+1)^2 + r^2 - r^2 = 1$$

$$f(B) = (0+1)^2 + (r-1)^2 - r^2 = 2 - 2r$$

It follows that $s = 3 - 2r$.

Depending on whether s is greater than, equal to, or less than zero, we choose A or B as the next pixel P_1. We can express the next s going from P_1 to P_2 very simply in terms of the old s value.

We will show this for the general case P_n with coordinates $(x_n \ y_n)$. Consider how we choose the next two pixels. The expression for s is:

$$s = (x_n + 1)^2 + y_n{}^2 - r^2 + (x_n + 1)^2 + (y_n - 1)^2 - r^2$$

For $s < 0$, we continue with pixel P_{n+1} with coordinates $(x_{n+1} \ \ y_n)$, as shown in Figure 3.5. (We consider $s = 0$ and $s > 0$ below.)

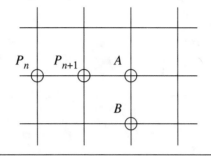

Figure 3.5   Choosing the successor pixel of P_{n+1}, first case

In order to go from here to the next pixel P_{n+2} (which can be A or B in Figure 3.5), we must compute the value of the sum again. We will call it s_{new} and express it using the coordinates of P_n:

$$s_{new} = (x_n + 2)^2 + y_n{}^2 - r^2 + (x_n + 2)^2 + (y_n - 1)^2 - r^2$$

An algebraic transformation shows that:

$$s_{new} - s = 4x_n + 6, \text{ hence } s_{new} = s + 4x_n + 6$$

For $s \geq 0$, we continue with pixel P_{n+1} with coordinates $(x_{n+1} \ \ y_{n-1})$, as shown in Figure 3.6.

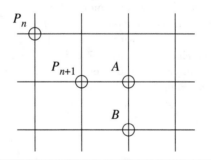

Figure 3.6   Choosing the successor pixel of P_{n+1}, second case

In order to go from here to the next pixel, P_{n+2} (which can be A or B in Figure 3.6), we must compute the value of the sum again:

$$s_{new} = (x_n + 2)^2 + (y_n - 1)^2 - r^2 + (x_n + 2)^2 + (y_n - 2)^2 - r^2$$

An algebraic transformation shows that:

$$s_{new} - s = 4(x_n - y_n) + 10, \text{ hence } s_{new} = s + 4(x_n - y_n) + 10$$

This shows that calculating s_{new} from the former s is very simple in both cases. It uses only a multiplication by 4 (this is a left shift by two bits), an addition, and sometimes a subtraction. We use only the sign of s in deciding about the next pixel. C++ permits us to perform the test and the computations on one line, shown in the code below. This code serves only to explain the algorithmic principle.

```
void draw()                              // Bresenham's circle DDA
{
   int x = 0 ,
       y = radius ,
       s = 3 - 2*radius ;

   while (x <= y)
   {
      eight_octs(x,y);
      s += s <= 0 ? 4*x++ + 6 : 4*(x++ - y--) + 10;
   }
}
```

This code generates an entire circle by calling `eight_octs()`. It works directly with the pixel addresses, needing no rounding to the pixel grid.

CLASS SPECIFICATION

We derive the class `circle_t` from `convex_t`, meaning we consider the circle a special type of convex polygon.

The class `circle_t` has a center and a radius. Its center is identical to the centroid of `convex_t`, so it inherits the member `cen`. We can construct the circle with center and radius, or interactively with the mouse. It needs its own copy function, so we can add it to a scene. We redefine the functions `draw()` and `rot()`; drawing a circle like a polygon would close the clipped-off parts with lines along the window boundary, but we think it more natural to draw it like a line (see Figures 3.7 and 3.8). Rotation becomes a null body, because rotating a circle about its center requires no action. All fill functions are inherited from `convex_t` and require no coding.

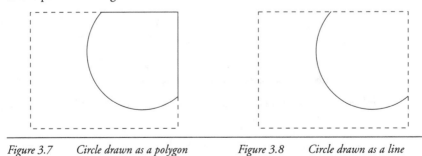

Figure 3.7   Circle drawn as a polygon   *Figure 3.8   Circle drawn as a line*

When creating a circle, the constructor computes 90 vertices along the perimeter, basically creating a convex polygon. The method used is the one explained in Section 3.1.2 without the symmetry—here, we are not concerned with speed.

```
//************************** File circle.h ***************************

#ifndef CIRCLE_T
#define CIRCLE_T

#include "../Shape2d/convex.h"
#include "../Shape2d/scene.h"


class circle_t : public convex_t
{                                       // center is the convex's centroid
public:
    circle_t(point_t,double) ;                      // center and radius
    circle_t(const circle_t&) ;
    circle_t(mouse_t& m);

    prim_t* copy() const ;
    void draw(const scene_t*) const ;   // circle is drawn like a line
    prim_t& rot(double) { return *this; }
private:
    double r ;                                           // radius
} ;

#endif

//*******************************************************************
```

3.2 ELLIPSES

We describe only ellipses parallel to the coordinate axes. An ellipse is defined by its center and its semiaxes. For axis-parallel ellipses, we have a similar situation as for circles; for any point on the circumference (except points on the coordinate axes), we can derive three more points with symmetry. We define a function four_quads(), which sets the four symmetric pixels.

```
void four_quads(int x,int y)                    // symmetry for ellipses
{
    setpix( x+xcen, y+ycen);
    setpix(-x+xcen, y+ycen);
    setpix(-x+xcen,-y+ycen);
    setpix( x+xcen,-y+ycen);
}
```

We now present several ellipse generators, some of which are DDAs and some not.

3.2.1 PARAMETER METHOD

This is a non-DDA method. It is identical to that for a circle, except that the coordinates $(x\ y)$ are multiplied by the semiaxes a and b respectively, instead of by r.

```
void draw()                                    // parameter method
{
    double fac = 2*3.14159265/90 ;             // 1/90 of a full circle
    double x1 = xcen + x , y1 = ycen ;
    double x2 , y2 ;

    for (int i = 1; i <= 90; i++)              // steps of 4 degrees
    {
        x2 = xcen + a*cos(fac*i);
        y2 = ycen + b*sin(fac*i);
        line_t(x1,y1,x2,y2).draw();
        x1 = x2;
        y1 = y2;
    }
}
```

3.2.2   A DDA ELLIPSE GENERATOR

We can produce an ellipse by choosing two small real numbers, α and β, with $0 < \alpha*\beta < 4$, and a starting point $(x_0 \; y_0) \neq (0 \; 0)$. We perform the following iteration:

$$x_{n+1} = x_n - \alpha * y_n$$
$$y_{n+1} = y_n + \beta * x_{n+1}.$$

To prove this assertion, express the iteration step as a matrix multiplication:

$$\left(x_{n+1} \quad y_{n+1} \right) = (x_n \quad y_n) * \mathbf{A} \text{ where } \mathbf{A} = \begin{pmatrix} 1 & \beta \\ -\alpha & 1 - \alpha\beta \end{pmatrix}$$

The iteration process consists of repeatedly multiplying the starting vector $(x \; y)$ by the matrix $\mathbf{A}$. This causes the point to rotate about the origin to create an ellipse.[†]

Using this method creates a curve that looks like an ellipse with center $(0 \; 0)$, but we should prove that it really is an ellipse. To do this, we begin with the general equation for a conic with center at the origin:

$$ax^2 + 2bxy + cy^2 - 1 = 0$$

This equation is determined by the three coefficients: a, b, and c. We can find the values of these constants by solving the system of equations that results when we substitute the coordinates $(x \; y)$ of three points through which the curve passes. (We solve the resulting system for the unknowns a, b, and c.)

We will do this with the initial point $\neq (0 \; 0)$ and two iterated points. To make the calculation easy, we start at $(1 \; 0)$. The two following points are $(1 \; \beta)$ and $(1-\alpha\beta \; 2\beta-\alpha\beta^2)$. The equations become:

[†] The eigenvalues of $\mathbf{A}$ are $\left(2 - \alpha\beta \pm \sqrt{\alpha\beta(\alpha\beta - 4)} \right) / 2$. When $0 < \alpha\beta < 4$, the expression under the root is negative and yields complex eigenvalues. For such values of $\alpha\beta$, a real valued starting vector can never converge to an eigenvector of $\mathbf{A}$ with the repeated multiplications. In other words, such a starting vector will always be rotated around the origin; the multiplication cannot just stretch it without rotation. This is why the iteration works only for $0 < \alpha\beta < 4$.

$$a - 1 = 0 \quad \text{from which} \, a = 1$$

$$2b\beta + c\beta^2 = 0 \quad \text{giving } 2b = -c\beta$$

$$(1 - \alpha\beta)^2 + 2b\beta(1 - \alpha\beta)(2 - \alpha\beta) - 2b\beta(2 - \alpha\beta)^2 - 1 = 0 \quad \text{giving } 2b = -\alpha$$

We find the unknowns to be $a = 1$, $2b = -a$, and $c = a/b$. Putting these into our general equation for a conic and multiplying by b we have:

$$\beta x^2 - \alpha\beta xy + \alpha y^2 - \beta = 0$$

as the equation of the conic with a starting point of $(1 \;\; 0)$. As the constant term in the equation has only a scaling effect, we can replace it with r and thus obtain the general form of this conic through some starting point $(q \;\; 0)$ and two succeeding points:

$$\beta x^2 - \alpha\beta xy + \alpha y^2 - r = 0$$

in which r depends on the starting point.

The discriminant equals $(\alpha\beta)^2 - 4(\alpha\beta)$. For $0 < \alpha\beta < 4$, this is negative; from analytic geometry, we know the figure must be an ellipse.

The above proves that the curve through the first three points is indeed an ellipse, but we should also prove that all points of the iteration lie on this ellipse. We have to show that for any point on the ellipse, its successor from the iteration also lies on the ellipse.

If we start with a point $(x \;\; y)$ on the ellipse, it fulfills $\beta x^2 - \alpha\beta xy + \alpha y^2 - r = 0$. The successor point is $(x - \alpha y \quad \beta x + y - \alpha\beta y)$. If we put this point into the equation and the equation equals zero, then we have proved the assumption correct. This is true, but will be an exercise.

For our ellipse, the slant angle of the major axis is δ, where $\tan 2\delta = \alpha\beta/(\alpha - \beta)$. For $\alpha/\beta > 1$, $-\pi/4 < \delta < \pi/4$ (ellipse is more horizontal); for $\alpha/\beta < 1$, $\pi/4 < \delta < 3\pi/4$ (ellipse is more vertical).[†]

Figure 3.9 shows the ellipse corresponding to an iteration with $\alpha = 1.2$, $\beta = 0.7$, and a starting point $(2 \;\; 0)$. Its major axis lies at an angle of 29.6°. The purpose of this figure is to make the development clearer. Do not get the impression that we use this method to create slanted ellipses. In practice, the method is used with very small values for α and β, so the ellipses will be practically parallel to the coordinate axes.

[†] The relation $\tan 2\delta = \alpha\beta/(\alpha - \beta)$ tells us which ellipse the iterated points approach in the limit, when α and β both go to 0 with a constant ratio $\alpha/\beta \neq 1$. The product $\alpha\beta$ has a higher order approach to 0 than does $\alpha - \beta$; therefore $\alpha\beta/(\alpha - \beta)$ goes to 0. In the case $\alpha/\beta > 1$, the major axis is more horizontal, so we must take the value closer to 0 of $\tan^{-1}(\alpha\beta/(\alpha - \beta))$; it follows that 2δ approaches 0. In other words, the smaller α and β, the closer to 0 the slant angle of the major axis will be. In the case of $\alpha/\beta < 1$, analogous reasoning shows that the slant angle of the major axis approaches $\pi/2$.

For very small α and β, the axes of the ellipse will be practically parallel to the coordinate axes, so we call them a and b and we have (approximately): $a/b = \sqrt{\alpha}/\sqrt{\beta}$

The iteration formula shows the changes for x and for y that occur in one step. When the steps are parallel to a coordinate axis, either x or y is nearly 0. At the x-axis, y is changed by $\beta * x$ (x equals a); at the y-axis, x is changed by $\alpha * y$ (y equals b). From this, together with the length ratio for the axes, we find that the ratio of the step length in the x-direction to the step length in the y-direction equals a/b.

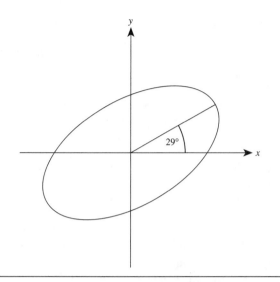

Figure 3.9   The theoretical ellipse corresponding to large values of α and β

When we use this method, we must choose values for α and β small enough to set adjacent pixels. If $a > b$, then we should set $\alpha = 1/b$ and $\beta = b/a^2$. If $b > a$, then we should set $\beta = 1/a$ and $\alpha = a/b^2$. This guarantees that the largest step will never exceed the distance between two pixels. However, we will take smaller steps in places. This implies setting some superfluous pixels (some pixels are set twice). This effect increases with the ellipse's eccentricity. Therefore the method is not good for very eccentric ellipses.

The method generates a sequence of real number pairs $(x_i\ y_i)$, which must be rounded to integers, while calling four_quads(). Each iteration step requires two multiplications, two additions (or subtractions), and two rounding operations. If floating point arithmetic can be done in hardware, this method still is adequately fast. The algorithm is amazingly simple.

```
void draw()                      // DDA ellipse generator
{
   double alfa = 1/b , beta = 1/a ;
   if (a > b)
      beta *= beta*b;
   else
      alfa *= alfa*a;

   double x = a , y = 0 ;
   while (x > -1)
   {

      four_quads((int)(x+0.5),(int)(y+0.5),xcen,ycen);
      x -= alfa*y;
      y += beta*x;
   }
}
```

3.2.3   KAPPEL'S ELLIPSE GENERATOR

There are some close algorithmic analogies between Bresenham's circle and Kappel's ellipse generator, KAPP85, but the step from one to the other is not trivial. The basic difference is that Bresenham's circle algorithm, as we have presented it, evaluates the circle function at both points from which we choose, while Kappel's ellipse algorithm evaluates the ellipse function at only one point, which lies between the two points from which we choose.

The following equation expresses an ellipse around the origin:

$$\left(\frac{x}{a}\right)^2 + \left(\frac{y}{b}\right)^2 - 1 = 0$$

in which a and b are the semi-axes of the ellipse. Although this formula is strongly related to the circle formula, we cannot modify Bresenham's algorithm to generate elliptical shapes by using the ellipse equation instead of the circle equation. If we were to parallel Bresenham's method, we would need a formula for the sum of the function values at the two pixels between which we are deciding. But this sum will contain a term involving the quotient b^2/a^2. To calculate the next sum value from the previous one involves multiplying by this quotient. We cannot use the simple integer arithmetic that is fundamental in Bresenham's circle algorithm.

We use a different approach to explain Kappel's ellipse generator. The function $f(x,y) = b^2x^2 + a^2y^2 - a^2b^2$ determines an ellipse in the following way:

all points $(x \ y)$ for which $f(x,y) = 0$ lie on the ellipse
all points $(x \ y)$ for which $f(x,y) > 0$ lie outside the ellipse
all points $(x \ y)$ for which $f(x,y) < 0$ lie inside the ellipse

This ellipse is centered at $(0 \ 0)$ and its axes are parallel to the coordinate axes. The ellipse intersects the x-axis at a and $-a$ and the y-axis at b and $-b$. In calculating the pixels that correspond to the ellipse, we can restrict our consideration to the first quadrant. We can obtain all other pixels of the ellipse with symmetry around the origin. We can use this algorithm to obtain ellipses not centered at the origin but with axes parallel to the coordinate axes by translating the results, which requires two additions per pixel. This algorithm cannot produce truly general ellipses whose axes are at an angle to the coordinate axes.

In the first quadrant, the algorithm creates the pixels starting at the point $(a \ 0)$ and moves in a counter-clockwise direction along the curve. It will go through two different phases. As long as the slope of the ellipse is smaller than -1, the algorithm is in its first phase. It obtains the next pixel by always increasing y and possibly decreasing x. Here, the essential work of the algorithm is to determine whether or not to decrease x.

There is a point s on the ellipse where the slope is exactly -1 (see Figure 3.10). After crossing this point, the algorithm enters the second phase. In this phase it obtains the next pixel by always decreasing x and possibly increasing y. Here, the essential work of the algorithm is to determine whether or not to increase y.

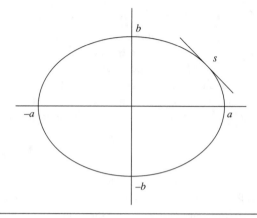

Figure 3.10   At point s the slope is −1

Kappel's algorithm uses the *midpoint method*. B. K. P. Horn (HORN76) first used this method to generate the raster points for a circle. At each step in the process, one must decide between two possible pixels. The decision is based on the value of $f(x,y)$ at the midpoint between the two possible pixels.

FIRST PHASE

Until we reach point s, we will choose between two horizontally adjacent pixels, A and B. The figures below reflect this situation. The choice of pixel A or pixel B depends on the value of $f(x,y)$ at the midpoint $M1$, which lies halfway between A and B. We need to consider only two cases. In the first case, shown in Figure 3.11, $f(M1) < 0$. The midpoint lies inside the ellipse, so A is closer to the curve and is chosen.

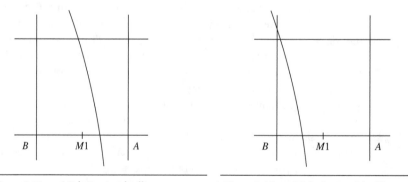

Figure 3.11   Midpoint inside ellipse   *Figure 3.12   Midpoint outside ellipse*

In the second case, shown in Figure 3.12, $f(M1) > 0$. The midpoint lies outside the ellipse, so B is closer to the curve and is chosen. When $f(M1) = 0$, we can choose either point and include it in either of the cases presented in Figures 3.11 and 3.12.

The algorithm's main novelty lies in the technique it uses to calculate the values of $f(x,y)$ for the midpoints. We will now demonstrate this, again considering two cases.

Suppose we choose pixel A. We must then decide between pixels C and D. (Bear in mind that the slope of the curve is smaller than -1.) If A's coordinates are $(x\ \ y)$ and B's are $(x{-}1\ \ y)$, then $M1 = (x{-}\frac{1}{2}\ \ y)$, and from this:

$$f(M1) = b^2 (x - \tfrac{1}{2})^2 + a^2 y^2 - a^2 b^2$$

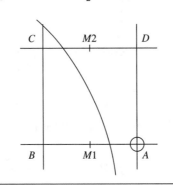

Figure 3.13   Choosing between C and D

The next midpoint lies between C and D and has the coordinates $M2 = (x{+}\frac{1}{2}\ \ y{+}1)$ (see Figure 3.13). From this:

$$f(M2) = b^2 (x - \tfrac{1}{2})^2 + a^2 (y+1)^2 - a^2 b^2$$

The difference between the function values at $M1$ and $M2$ is: $f(M2) - f(M1) = 2a^2 y + a^2$. This value is not constant (it depends on y), but it is easy to calculate. At the curve's starting point, where y is 0, this difference is just a^2, and then it becomes $2a^2{+}a^2$, $4a^2{+}a^2$, $6a^2{+}a^2$, and so on; it grows by $2a^2$ with every increase in y. The algorithm therefore uses a variable, *yslope*, which represents the value by which it grows. We can obtain the function value at the midpoint $M2$ by taking $f(M1)$, adding the variable *yslope*, and adding the constant a^2 whenever we choose A as:

$$f(M2) = f(M1) + yslope + a^2$$

If we choose pixel B, we must then choose between pixels C and E (see Figure 3.14). This is true even if the ellipse passes between pixels C and D (we will not consider pixel D, because its x-coordinates cannot increase). Assuming B has the coordinates $(x\ \ y)$, we have $M1 = (x{+}\frac{1}{2}\ \ y)$ and from this:

$$f(M1) = b^2 (x + \tfrac{1}{2})^2 + a^2 y^2 - a^2 b^2$$

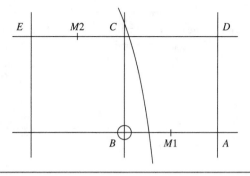

Figure 3.14   Choosing between C and E

The midpoint between E and C has the coordinates $M2 = (x - \frac{1}{2}\ y+1)$. From this we obtain:

$$f(M2) = b^2 (x - \tfrac{1}{2})^2 + a^2 (y+1)^2 - a^2 b^2$$

The difference between the function values of $M1$ and $M2$ is:

$$f(M2) - f(M1) = -2b^2 x + 2a^2 y + a^2$$

This difference depends on x and y, but its calculation is easy. It increases by $2b^2$ whenever x is decreased and increases by $2a^2$ whenever y is increased. The algorithm therefore has another variable, *xslope*, with the value $2b^2 x$. It starts with $2b^2 a$, because x's starting value is a, and is decreased by $2b^2$ with every decrease in x. We obtain the function value at the midpoint $M2$ by taking $f(M1)$, subtracting the variable *xslope*, adding the variable *yslope*, and adding the constant a^2 whenever we choose B:

$$f(M2) = f(M1) - xslope + yslope + a^2$$

This shows that in the first phase, we can obtain a midpoint's function value by simple additions from the former midpoint's function value. The algorithm will represent this value with the variable *fmid*, which the algorithm will check in deciding between the two pixels.

Since x and y represent pixel addresses, they must be integers. As a is float, x's starting value will be the nearest integer. The first pixel to set will always be (round(a) 0). The first pixel's x-coordinate depends on whether the rounding is up or down, but in either case, the algorithm will increase y and will choose between pixels (x–1 1) and (x 1) (see Figures 3.15 and 3.16).

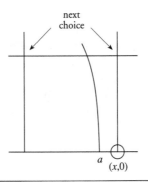

Figure 3.15   Rounding up

If a is rounded down, we will need the function value at the midpoint $(x-\frac{1}{2}\ 1)$. The starting value of *fmid* will therefore be:

$$fmid = b^2(x - \tfrac{1}{2})^2 + a^2 - a^2 b^2$$

Observe that this is not an integer expression.

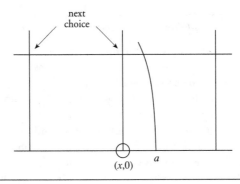

Figure 3.16   Rounding down

The slope of a curve defined by $f(x,y) = 0$ is:

$$\frac{dy}{dx} = -\frac{f_x}{f_y}$$

where f_x and f_y are the partial derivatives of $f(x,y)$ with respect to x and y. We find that $-f_x = -2b^2x$ and $f_y = 2a^2y$, which are the values of *xslope* and *yslope*—hence their names. The algorithm works in its first phase (below the point s), where the slope dy/dx is smaller than -1. The algorithm also checks the slope of the ellipse at every step to determine whether it is still in the first phase. However, the quotient $-2b^2x/2a^2y$ only expresses the slope of the ellipse at the point $(x\ y)$ if $(x\ y)$ lies precisely on the ellipse. During the algorithmic evaluation this is not the case. In the expression, we use x- and y-values from the last pixel set. What we check is just an approximation of the slope, because this pixel misses the true curve. Thus, there is a potential error of one pixel for extremely narrow ellipses. (You can find a more detailed explanation in KAPP85.)

SECOND PHASE

As soon as $dy/dx \geq -1$, the algorithm enters its second phase in which x always decreases with every new pixel calculation and y possibly increases. In the second phase, the midpoint is defined differently.

We choose between two vertically adjacent pixels A and B according to the function value at the midpoint $M1$ between the two. Figures 3.17 and 3.18 reflect this situation. When $f(M1) < 0$, the midpoint lies inside the ellipse, so A is closer to the curve and is therefore chosen (see Figure 3.17).

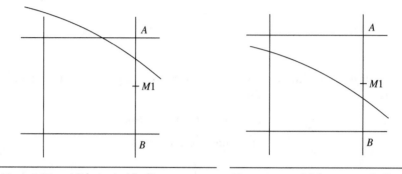

Figure 3.17   *Midpoint inside ellipse*   Figure 3.18   *Midpoint outside ellipse*

When $f(M1) > 0$, the midpoint lies outside the ellipse, so B is closer to the curve and is therefore chosen (see Figure 3.18). For the case $f(M1) = 0$, we can choose either A or B and include our choice in either of the cases.

The development is analogous to the algorithm's first phase, so we do not repeat it. We describe only the computation of *fmid* for the second phase.

The starting value of *fmid* for the second phase is not equal to the value of *fmid* upon completion of the first phase. We leave the first phase when *xslope* $\leq$ *yslope*. When we do this check, the algorithm has already calculated the new value of *fmid* as being between two horizontally adjacent pixels, as if it were still in the first phase. Because we have begun the second phase, we must instead decide between two vertically adjacent pixels, so we must correct *fmid*.

The new midpoint is always one-half pixel to the left and one-half pixel down from the old midpoint. Figure 3.19 shows the last chosen pixel, the projected midpoint $M2$ at the end of the first phase, the corrected midpoint Mc, and two possible positions of the ellipse.

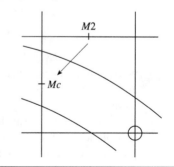

Figure 3.19   *Correction of midpoint*

We can derive the corrected *fmid* in the following way. Upon leaving the first phase, the function value of $M2$ is:

$$f(x-\tfrac{1}{2}, y+1) = b^2(x^2 - x + \tfrac{1}{4}) + a^2(y^2 + 2y + 1) - a^2 b^2$$

The function value of Mc is:

$$f(x-1, y+\tfrac{1}{2}) = b^2(x^2 - 2x + 1) + a^2(y^2 + y + \tfrac{1}{4}) - a^2 b^2$$

The difference between these two function values is:

$$b^2(-x+\tfrac{3}{4}) + a^2(-y-\tfrac{3}{4})$$

Observe that this is not an integer expression. We will add this to *fmid* as soon as the first phase is completed and it will produce a proper starting value for the second phase. The second phase of the algorithm ends as soon as the first quadrant is filled, that is, as soon as x becomes negative. Except for the two floating point computations mentioned above, the algorithm works entirely in integer arithmetic. Its code is in `Shape2d/kappell.c`.

Figure 3.20 shows the first quadrant of an elliptical arc with $a = 15$ and $b = 10$, drawn by Kappell's algorithm. To draw a whole ellipse, use symmetry.

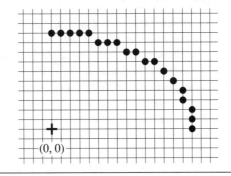

Figure 3.20   *Elliptic arc produced by kappell.c*

ERROR CONSIDERATIONS

It is certainly not possible to set all pixels precisely on the ellipse—they can only be approximations to the curve. How far off the true curve will they be in the worst case? The error of a pixel (its distance from the curve) can be defined in several ways. The most natural definition says a pixel's error is the distance from its center to the nearest point on the ellipse (see Figure 3.21).

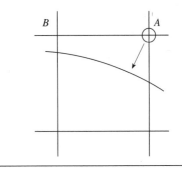

Figure 3.21   *Normal error definition for a pixel*

We must measure this distance along the line that is normal to the ellipse and that passes through the pixel center. However, it is time-consuming to compute this distance. Therefore, the ellipse algorithm and practically all other curve generators do not use this error definition. Instead, they define the error at a pixel as the distance from the pixel center to the ellipse, measured in a direction parallel to the x-axis in phase 1 and parallel to the y-axis in phase 2 (see Figures 3.22 and 3.23).

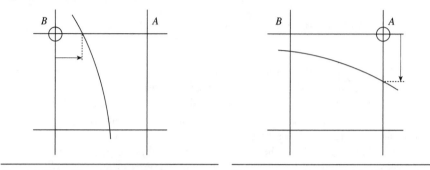

Figure 3.22   Error definition in phase 1   *Figure 3.23   Error definition in phase 2*

Using this second definition, the error at a pixel never exceeds 0.5. The line along which we measure this distance is generally not normal to the ellipse. The distance measured along a line normal to the ellipse through the same pixel center does not exceed this, so the normal definition also bounds the pixel error by 0.5. However, the algorithm does not always choose the pixel closest (by the normal definition) to the curve. A pixel may be chosen, even though a closer pixel (closer in terms of the normal definition) is adjacent to it. The pixel errors are bounded by 0.5, but are not optimal.

Figure 3.24 shows such a case. The true elliptical arc crosses the line between A and B somewhat closer to A and with a slope less than -1. The distance from the intersection point to A is less than 0.5; therefore A is chosen. However, the arc then bends to the left enough so that B is actually closer than A, according to the normal error definition. B would have been a better choice. This sort of situation may occur only at the transition point.

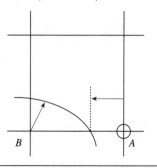

Figure 3.24   Choice not always optimal

We do not provide a class specification for ellipses. But one can easily specify a class `ellipse_t` and implement it in analogy to `circle_t`. It should be derived from `convex_t` to inherit all filling functions. `Ellipse_t::draw()` could be implemented with Kappel's algorithm.

SUGGESTED READINGS

Scan-converting techniques can produce many other curves. These references describe some of them: hyperbolas, PITT67; conics in general, COHE69; and other nonparametric curves, JOLH73. They are useful only in special cases because a specific algorithm is faster than a general algorithm. But it is not practical to have a special algorithm for each possible curve. Very fast straight line, circle, and ellipse generators suffice as does approximating the wide variety of other curves with a sequence of short, straight lines.

EXERCISES

SECTION 3.0

1. List some advantages of an LCD over a CRT display.
2. List some advantages of a CRT display over an LCD.
3. What are the three main types of liquid crystals and what are their essential characteristics?

SECTION 3.1

4. What advantage do LCD and plasma displays share over the CRT?
5. Implement the parameter method for a circle. Assume that you have only the graphics primitive `setpix()`; that is, you cannot connect points on the circle perimeter with straight lines. Experiment with bigger and smaller step sizes for u.
6. Implement the choice of an optimal step size for u, that is, a step size small enough to set adjacent pixels, but not smaller than necessary. Hint: For $u_0 = 0$ and radius $= r$, set the first pixel to $(r\ 0)$; r should not be too small. For the next parameter value, $u = u_1$. We want to set the pixel $(r\ 1)$, so we need $x = r*\cos(u_1) \approx r$ and $y = r*\sin(u_1) \approx 1$, from which it follows that $\sin(u_1) \approx 1/r$. Therefore $u_1 \approx \arcsin(1/r)$.
7. Implement the parameter method for a circle and take advantage of the 8-symmetry.
8. Implement the rotation method for a circle and take advantage of the 8-symmetry.

Exercises 9 through 11 assume that straight lines connect the computed points.

9. Using the parameter method when connecting computed points with straight lines is the easiest circle generation to implement. By changing the expressions for x and y in the parameter equations, we can obtain all sorts of nice-looking curves, called *Lissajous curves*. For example:

$$x = r\cos(3u)$$
$$y = r\sin(2u)$$

gives the curve shown in Figure 3.25. The factors for the parameter u are integers, but are not equal. Implement this method and experiment with other integer factors.

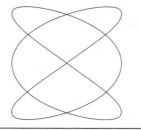

Figure 3.25   A Lissajous curve

10. Another degree of variation involves adding a certain constant to the parameter, as in:

$$x = r\cos(3u+1)$$
$$y = r\sin(2u)$$

This results in the curve shown in Figure 3.26. Experiment with other constants and integer factors.

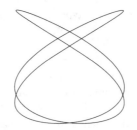

Figure 3.26   Another Lissajous curve

11. Multiplying the parameter with noninteger factors and letting it go from 0 to 2π results in a curve that does not close back to the starting point. We can obtain a closed curve by letting the parameter go to multiples of 2π. If the equations are

$$x = r\cos(3u)$$
$$y = r\sin(2.2u)$$

how many multiples of 2π does the parameter need to go through to obtain a closed curve? Draw this curve.

Exercises 12 through 15 deal with the "spiral" and the "ellipse" methods for circle generation. With these methods, you must choose a small step size and set the computed points as individual pixels, unconnected by straight lines. Choose ε to be $1/r$, as the text suggests.

12. If we use the spiral method to generate one octant of a circle with a radius of 200 pixels, how much is the generated curve off the true circle in the worst case? *Hint:* Find out roughly how many pixels you need for one octant with radius 200. This number of pixels is the number of steps performed.

13. If we use the ellipse method to generate one octant of a circle with center (0 0) starting at pixel (100 0), how much is the generated curve off the true circle? *Hint:* Point (100 0) lies on the ellipse, therefore from the ellipse equation we have $100^2 - 2r^2 = 0$, which gives $2r = 100\sqrt{2}$. Compute the longer and the shorter axis and the ε that you need to choose.

14. Implement the ellipse method without taking advantage of symmetry considerations and choose a rather big ε, for example, $\varepsilon = 0.5$ or $\varepsilon = 1$. Set only individual pixels, iterate for about 200 steps, and observe the resulting slanted ellipse.

15. One can make the deviation from the true circle arbitrarily small by choosing a very small ε. What is the reason for not doing this? That is, why does one work with $\varepsilon = 1/r$ and cope with the resulting error?

In Exercises 16 and 17 on Bresenham's circle generation, only individual pixels are set.

16. Assume that the sum s in Bresenham's circle generator is exactly 0. Show that, in this case, pixel A is closer to the ideal circular arc than pixel B, with the distance measured along radials from the center to those pixels.

17. Assume that the sum s in Bresenham's circle generator is exactly 0. This does not imply that the ideal circular arc intersects the line between the two pixels at the midpoint. Show that the arc intersects at a point that is always a little closer to pixel A. *Hint:* $s = 0$. That is,

$$x^2 + y^2 - r^2 + x^2 + (y-1)^2 - r^2 = 0$$

which can be compressed to:

I: $x^2 + y^2 - y + \frac{1}{2} - r^2 = 0$

Also, we have:

$$x^2 + (y-1+d)^2 - r^2 = 0$$

which can be expanded to:

II: $x^2 + y^2 + d^2 + 1 + 2dy - 2d - 2y - r^2 = 0$

Subtracting II from I gives a relation in d and y alone. Isolate d from that relation and show that the resulting expression in y is greater than $1/2$ for every positive y-value.

18. Use the parameter method for a circle and the function `polygon_t::solid()` to implement a program that draws a pie chart. The program produces the pie chart interactively. It asks the user for the number of sections, n, then for the amounts of the sections. The program converts the amounts to percentages, assuming their sum to be 100%. The program draws the pie sections by connecting the center to the proper points on the perimeter.

SECTION 3.2

19. Specify a class `ellipse_t : public convex_t {}` as explained in the text.
20. Write a member function

    ```
    void ellipse_t::drawtype(int type) const
    ```

    that uses the parameter method to draw an ellipse with axes a and b, center at ($xcen$ $ycen$), and linetype specified by type: 1 = normal; 2 = dashed; 3 = dotted.
21. Draw one quadrant of a circle of given radius with the methods of Exercises 14 and 15 and find out if they differ in some pixels.
22. What is the value of r in the ellipse equation, if the starting point is (c 0)?
23. When using the DDA ellipse generator we iterate a point (x_n y_n) $\approx$ 0 with $x_{n+1} = x_n - \alpha * y_n$ and $y_{n+1} = y_n + \beta * x_{n+1}$. Show that the points so iterated lie on the ellipse $\beta x^2 - \alpha\beta xy + \alpha y^2 - r = 0$. Show that if a point ($x$ y) fulfills the ellipse equation, the next point in the iteration: $x_1 = x - \alpha y$, and $y_1 = \beta x + y - \alpha\beta y$ also fulfills the equation. Insert (x_1 y_1) into the equation, simplify, and use $\beta x^2 - \alpha\beta xy + \alpha y^2 - r = 0$.
24. Assume you have the straight line primitive. Implement an ellipse generation using the equation:

$$\frac{(x - xcenter)^2}{a^2} + \frac{(y - ycenter)^2}{b^2} = 1$$

    In this equation, ($xcenter$ $ycenter$) is the center of the ellipse, a is the length of the horizontal axis, and b is the length of the vertical axis. Using this equation, compute points on the circumference and connect them with straight lines. Is this an efficient method? Why or why not?
25. Generate an ellipse slanted by α degrees. An ellipse with the center at the origin, slanted by α degrees, with axes a and b, is expressed parametrically by the formulas:

$$x = a\cos(u) - b\sin(u + \alpha)$$
$$y = b\sin(u) + a\cos(u + \alpha)$$

    Generate an ellipse slanted by 15° with long axis 50 pixels and short axis 30 pixels. Compute points on the perimeter of the ellipse and connect them with straight lines.
26. Repeat Exercise 23, but do not use the straight line primitive; set only single pixels. You have to work with a very small step size, one small enough to set adjacent pixels, but not smaller than necessary.

Exercises 27 and 28 let you draw other curves. Use straight lines to connect individual points along the curves.

27. Draw the sine curve, expressed parametrically by:

$$x = u$$
$$y = \sin(u)$$

28. Draw the curve:

$$x = u$$
$$y = \sin(u) + \sin(2u) + \sin(3u)$$

4

WINDOWING AND CLIPPING

Chapter 4 defines the terms window and viewport as applied to computer graphics and describes how to clip away portions of a two-dimensional picture so as to fit it within a window. There are four sections.

4.0 **Introduction** sets the background by defining window and clipping.
4.1 **The Two-Dimensional Window Concept**, a rectangular portion of the scene, is mapped onto a rectangular portion of the computer screen, the viewport. This mapping requires a transformation between coordinate systems.
4.2 **Clipping Algorithms** are systematic procedures for "not drawing" the parts of lines that lie outside the window. We describe two algorithms in detail. We extend these to clipping polygons. We also overview the different processes for clipping text.
4.3 **Two-Dimensional Transformations** gives the mathematics behind translating, scaling, and rotating two-dimensional objects using homogeneous coordinates.

4.0 INTRODUCTION

A window is very familiar to all of us. It is an opening through which we see a portion of the world that exists outside. Its frame cuts off part of that outside world from view, but what we do not see still exists. In effect, we limit the view with an artificial device. There does not have to be an actual window to limit what we want to see. We have all noticed photographers make a "window" with their hands in order to visualize what will appear in the final photograph. If we concentrate hard enough on a portion of the real world, we can mentally block out extraneous details.

In computer graphics, the idea of a window is important. The word has a somewhat different meaning, however. This chapter first describes the general concept and purpose of a two-dimensional window in computer graphics. We then explain problems that arise when we create windows.

We cannot limit what we see on the computer screen just by drawing a window frame. Instead, we must "not draw" those parts of the total image that we wish to suppress. Determining which portions to omit is called clipping. We will need to consider the clipping of lines, polygons, and text separately. We will discuss two different algorithms for clipping lines, which differ in complexity and in the number of computations they require. Since clipping polygons is quite an involved process, we present only one algorithm for this procedure. Our treatment of text clipping will be less detailed.

Clipping images is also important for three-dimensional objects. Windowing and clipping in three dimensions are extensions of the two-dimensional concepts. The algorithms are similar. Chapter 5 deals with these topics.

4.1 THE TWO-DIMENSIONAL WINDOW CONCEPT

Most windows in the real world are rectangular. We can also think of a window as a rectangular frame that goes around a picture, limiting what we see. In computer graphics, it is also natural to use a rectangular window, because the display areas (screen, plotter, etc.) are rectangular.

A *window* in computer graphics is a rectangular range of a Cartesian, two-dimensional, real-world, coordinate system (see Figure 4.1). Some graphics packages allow specifying a window and, through it, a so-called *world coordinate system*. When we specify a window, it implies a coordinate system, which we use to describe all objects (points, lines, circles, polygons, etc.). By specifying a window, the user can choose any coordinate system that is meaningful for the particular application. One might use "millimeter" as the coordinate unit in describing a circuit board, "centimeter" in describing a piece of furniture, "foot" in describing a floor, and so on.

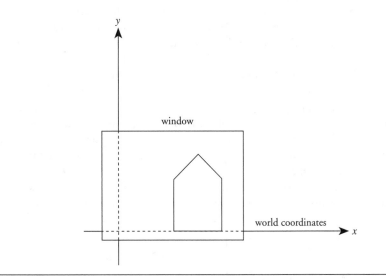

Figure 4.1   A window is a rectangular subrange of a coordinate system

We can always express the window range with four numbers: the left, right, bottom and top boundaries. Left and right determine the range in *x*, bottom and top the range in *y*. The range lies over a rectangular portion of the real world or an imagined set of objects. Using the world coordinate system, we can relate each point inside and outside that range to the window.

For example, we can imagine the window in Figure 4.1 to range from –5 to 25 in *x* and from –2 to 20 in *y*. Figure 4.2 shows that same window just by itself. We have now indicated the window range and the coordinates of the house.

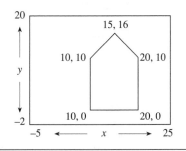

Figure 4.2   A window determines a coordinate system

Inside in a computer graphics system, one must describe the objects with a set of numbers. These numbers relate to the world coordinate system that the window specifies. For example, when relating the Cartesian coordinates (15 16) to the window in Figure 4.2, we obtain the point located at the house's gable.

Whenever a window is specified, it is assumed that this window is displayed on the graphics output device (usually a CRT screen, but it could be, for example, a plotter). In this chapter, *screen* means not only a CRT screen, but also any appropriate display device.

We assume that, by default, the window is displayed on the whole screen. It is often advantageous to use only a rectangular portion of the screen to display the window. This rectangular part of the screen where the window is displayed is called a *viewport*. Lacking a viewport specification, we consider the entire screen to be the *default viewport*. A viewport is that area of the graphic output device onto which the window is mapped. (The term "window" is sometimes used differently. For example, the phrases "windowing environment," "Microsoft Windows," and "X Windows" are really references to viewports.)

The coordinates for specifying a viewport must be independent of the window coordinates. Therefore, one uses normalized device coordinates (NDC). The display device is considered to have a coordinate range from 0 to 1 in x and from 0 to 1 in y, no matter what the height-to-width ratio of the device really is. In this case, the same graphics software can output to different graphics devices.

Figure 4.3 shows a window into a landscape. Figure 4.4 shows that same window mapped onto a viewport on a display device. Observe that lines outside the window have been clipped.

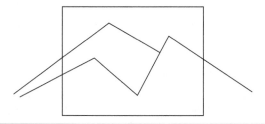

Figure 4.3   *Window into a landscape*

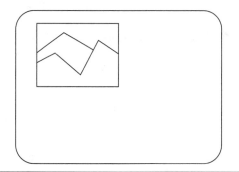

Figure 4.4   *Mapped window*

We can map a window onto a specified viewport by using the window-viewport transformation. When using a window, it is common to give the user the freedom to define the object in any way desired. Then, the user need not ensure that all the points specifing the object lie inside the given window range, because the object is clipped. Figure 4.4 shows the effect of this. We have indicated the viewport with a rectangle so you can see its extent. Usually, the viewport boundaries are not displayed. In Figure 4.4 the viewport's NDC are from 0.1 to 0.5 in x and from 0.5 to 0.9 in y.

It is helpful for the beginning student to define an object by a set of points ((x y)-values), place the object inside some rectangular area, and then find the window coordinates so that the rectangular area (the window) is the coordinate range.

If we define a viewport in which to display the window of Figure 4.1, then we could obtain a display as in Figure 4.5 (without the viewport border). The viewport boundaries on this display go from approximately 0.6 to 1.0 horizontally and 0.5 to 1.0 vertically. Notice that the house has been distorted slightly, because the height-to-width ratio of the window is not the same as that of the viewport.

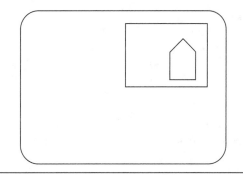

Figure 4.5   *Mapped window*

Below, we show the formula for the window-viewport transformation. For this, we introduce the variables *w.l*, *w.r*, *w.b*, and *w.t* to indicate the window boundaries left, right, bottom, and top. The same is true for the viewport: *v.l*, *v.r*, *v.b*, and *v.t*. See Figure 4.6.

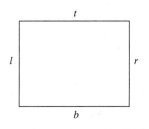

Figure 4.6   *Window and viewport*

Any point in world coordinates (x_w y_w) is transformed to NDC coordinates (x_{NDC} y_{NDC}). The formula is just a combination of simple translation and scaling, with no elaboration:

$$x_{NDC} = (x_w - w.l)/(w.r - w.l) * (v.r - v.l) + v.l$$

$$y_{NDC} = (y_w - w.b)/(w.t - w.b) * (v.t - v.b) + v.b$$

Every line defined in world coordinates must ultimately be drawn in absolute device coordinates, so we still have to transform the NDC to absolute device coordinates. This is easy: x_{NDC} is multiplied by *DWID* and $(1 - y_{NDC})$ by *DHEI*. The latter transformation is an exchange in the up-down direction. This is necessary on almost all CRT displays because the absolute device coordinates start with 0 at the screen top and go to the highest value at the bottom. The entire transformation from window to device coordinates is implemented by the member function `win_dev()` in the window-viewport system. We also implement the inverse, `dev_win()`.

$$x_{dev} = ((x_w - w.l)/(w.r - w.l) * (v.r - v.l) + v.l) * DWID$$

$$y_{dev} = (1 - (y_w - w.b)/(w.t - w.b) * (v.t - v.b) - v.b) * DHEI$$

$$x_w = (x_{dev}/DWID - v.l)/(v.r - v.l) * (w.r - w.l) + w.l$$

$$y_w = (1 - y_{dev}/DHEI - v.b)/(v.t - v.b) * (w.t - w.b) + w.b$$

Since window and viewport go together, we define a class `win_view_t`. By default, the window viewport system is initialized with (0, *DWID* – 1, 0, *DHEI* – 1) for the window and (0, 1, 0, 1) for the viewport. The first two numbers are the *x*-extent; the last two, the *y*-extent. This default window means that, by not specifying a window, the user prefers to work in absolute device coordinates. The default viewport is the whole display. The user must supply the constants *DWID* and *DHEI*.

We can construct a window-viewport system with any other numbers, as well. The user can construct window-viewport systems, but not windows or viewports alone. A window-viewport system contains the two above-mentioned member functions, `win_dev()` and `dev_win()`.

The window-viewport system consists of a class `window_t`, a class `viewport_t`, and a class `win_view_t` that inherits from both. The class `window_t` has four data members that describe its boundary. It has four clipping functions, one for each of its boundaries, which work internally to clip polygons. It has a clipping function that takes a vertex list (of a polygon) and returns the clipped vertex list. Another of its clipping functions takes a line and returns a pointer to the clipped line.

The class `viewport_t` also has its four boundary members, but no member functions. The class `win_view_t` represents the whole window-viewport system.

```
//*********************** File win_view.h ***********************

#ifndef WINVIEW_T
#define WINVIEW_T

#include "../Shape2d/const.h"
#include "../Shape2d/vertex.h"

class line_t ;
```

```
class window_t
{
public:
   window_t(double=0,double=DWID-1,double=0,double=DHEI-1) ;
   virtual vertex_t* clipvl(vertex_t*)       const ; // clip vertex list
   virtual line_t* clipln(const line_t&) const ; // clip straight line

protected:
   double l , r , b , t ;                         // world coordinates

private:
   void cltop(double,double) const ;
   void clbot(double,double) const ;
   void clrit(double,double) const ;
   void cllef(double,double) const ;
   char reg_code(double,double) const ;
} ;


class viewport_t
{
public:
   viewport_t(double=0,double=1,double=0,double=1) ;
protected:
   double l , r , b , t ;              // normalized device coordinates
} ;


class win_view_t : virtual public window_t , public viewport_t
{
public:
   win_view_t() ;
   win_view_t(const window_t&) ;
   win_view_t(const viewport_t&) ;
   win_view_t(const window_t&,const viewport_t&) ;

   point_t dev_win(const point_t&) const ;
   virtual void win_dev(point_t&) const ;
   virtual double givd() const { return 0; }
   virtual point_t givcen() const { return point_t(0,0); }
} ;

#endif

//*****************************************************************
```

The win_view_t definition for Figure 4.5 would be:

```
win_view_t(window_t(-5, 25, -2, 22) , viewport_t(0.6,1.0,0.5,1.0)) ;
```

When we specify several window-viewport systems that differ only in their viewports, we can display the same object several times in different screen locations. If we do allow overlapping viewports, we should associate priorities with each so that objects in higher priority viewports cover those in lower ones. There are several strategies, some of which are implemented in graphics software.

AVOIDING DISTORTIONS

The window-to-device transformation unavoidably distorts displayed shapes, unless the following is true for the ratios of window, viewport, and device dimensions:

$$\frac{(w.r - w.l)*(v.t - v.b)}{(w.t - w.b)*(v.r - v.l)} = \frac{DWID}{DHEI}$$

A distortion usually goes undetected if the displayed shapes are already irregular. However, distortion becomes obvious when we expect a familiar outcome, such as a circle (it will look like an ellipse) or a square (it will look like a rectangle or a diamond).

LEAVING THE WINDOW BOUNDARIES

If we perform the window-viewport transformation on a point outside the window, we produce a point outside the viewport which could be outside the absolute device coordinate range. A primitive draw function such as setpix() does not check for this. Most often, the frame buffers are memory mapped areas in the computer's general working memory. Setting a pixel at an address outside the frame buffer corrupts the memory. This can cause a program crash or other undesirable effects. A pixel address outside the frame buffer's absolute address range could still indicate a location inside the frame buffer, due to the internal address decoding mechanism. This can cause the picture to wrap around, so that lines leave the screen on the left and come back in from the right. If the viewport is smaller than the total display area, parts of the image will be drawn outside the viewport.

Therefore, every window implementation provides clipping. When this is done, we are free to specify objects that are partially or totally outside the window; the clipping takes place before the window-to-device transformation is performed. We now look at clipping algorithms.

4.2   CLIPPING ALGORITHMS

Clipping is easy for the human visual system, even with an imaginary window. We just do not see (or mentally block out) those parts of the world that lie outside the boundaries of the window. For a computer, it is much more complex. The computer must display in the viewport only those parts of the image that are inside the window boundary. Images may be lines, polygons, or text.

Let us speculate a little about how clipping might be done. With bitmapped graphics, "low-level clipping" is feasible. This is something very closely related to the particular system's hardware. Suppose we have a raster CRT, a window, and a viewport. As we have already seen, everything drawn on the screen must be written into the frame buffer with a pixel-by-pixel correspondence. The software that does this could be either a DDA algorithm, an algorithm that fills the interior of outlines, or possibly a microcode-implemented, fast line-drawing routine. The routines that set individual pixels in the frame buffer could check each pixel's address and do nothing if this address is outside the window. The hardware that does the fast line drawing could do the same. This would certainly slow the drawing processes, but it would perform the clipping properly.

Newer Graphics Processors

Some of the newer processors that emphasize graphics do clipping in microcode at the hardware level. The window boundaries are mapped internally to absolute device coordinates corresponding to the specified viewport and held in registers. A linear-to-xy-address conversion routine is also implemented in hardware. Whenever an operation requires pixels to be set and a window has been specified, each setpix command is preceded by a test of the xy-address against the window boundaries. If the address is outside, no pixel is set and, optionally, an interrupt can be generated. This permits an interrupt-servicing routine to cancel invalid pixel-setting operations. If the processor is drawing a line, the algorithm can be terminated immediately. A good example of this is the TMS34010 processor (TEXA86).

Clipping by hardware is not just a recent phenomenon. For vector scan displays, very low-level (practically in hardware) clipping devices were developed many years ago. The first one was the "clipping divider" from Sproull and Sutherland (SPSU68). It is based on the midpoint subdivision algorithm. (This is essentially a binary search to find the point on the line that corresponds to the edge of the viewport.) Besides doing clipping, the hardware also performed divisions for perspective transformations. More recently, J. H. Clark's "geometry processor" (CLAR80) implements Cohen-Sutherland line-clipping (discussed in the next section) against six clipping planes in space in floating point arithmetic. It also includes 4×4 matrix multiplication and viewing transformations, all in hardware.

4.2.1 LINE CLIPPING

It is simplest to clip a straight line. Figure 4.7 shows several positions of a line in relation to the window.

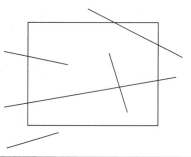

Figure 4.7   *Straight lines in relation to a window*

COHEN-SUTHERLAND CLIPPING

One well-known way to clip lines is with the Cohen-Sutherland algorithm. This algorithm divides the whole 2D plane into nine regions, as shown in Figure 4.8. Each region is assigned a "region code." The innermost area in the diagram is the window.

1001	0001	0101
1000	0000	0100
1010	0010	0110

Figure 4.8   The nine regions for Cohen-Sutherland clipping

The region code of a point in the 2D plane is a four bit pattern. We number the bits in the order 3 2 1 0.

- ❑ Bit 3 indicates the left boundary and is 1 if the point is to the left of the left boundary.
- ❑ Bit 2 indicates the right boundary and is 1 if the point is to the right of the right boundary.
- ❑ Bit 1 indicates the bottom boundary and is 1 if the point is below the bottom boundary.
- ❑ Bit 0 indicates the top boundary and is 1 if the point is above the top boundary.
- ❑ Otherwise, if all bits are 0, the point is within the window. Note that this includes points precisely on the edges of the window.

Clipping a line works as follows. The line's two end points are each assigned their appropriate region codes. Then, the two region codes are logically ORed. If the result is 0000, both end points lie within the window and no clipping is necessary; the line is trivially accepted (accepted without clipping).

If the first result is not 0000, the two region-codes are logically ANDed. If this result is not precisely 0000, that is, if it contains at least one 1, then the line lies completely outside the window. For example, if the ANDed result is 1000, bit 3 must be equal to 1 in both end point region codes. Thus, both end points lie to the left of the window, which means the line lies entirely to the left as well. A 1 in any other position implies a similar situation. Such a line does not need to be clipped because it will not be displayed at all. The line is trivially rejected (rejected without clipping).

There remain the nontrivial cases, where the line may or may not cross the window. This can be discovered only during the clipping process, which we now explain through an example. The line in Figure 4.9 is neither rejected nor accepted trivially, so it must cross some boundary of the window. Both end points are outside different boundaries and at least one of the region codes contains 1-bits.

The algorithm will not know automatically which region code this is. Therefore, it first tests the region code of one end point; if it is 0000, then the algorithm uses the other one. The region code is tested bitwise in the order 3 2 1 0 for a bit that is 1. This tells which boundary the end point lies outside. The line's intersection with that boundary is then computed with a simple mathematical formula. This particular end point will be replaced by the point of intersection.

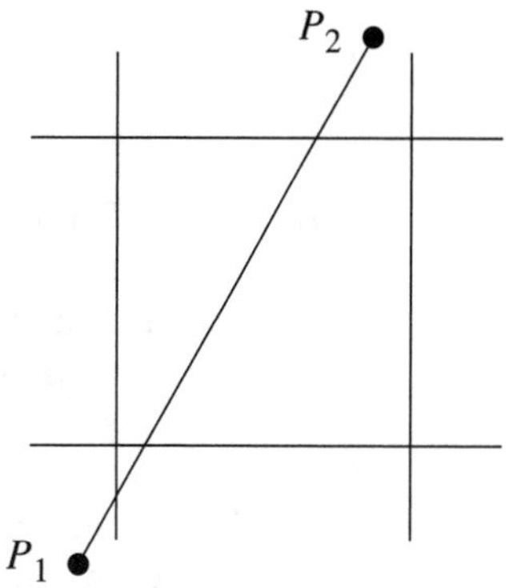

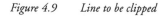

Figure 4.9   Line to be clipped

Suppose that the algorithm first tests the region code of point P_1. Testing the bits in the order 3 2 1 0, it finds that P_1 lies left of the left boundary. Therefore, it must compute the intersection of the line with the left boundary. Let the intersection point be called A. Point P_1 is no longer of interest and is clipped away. Point A is in some way closer to the window than P_1 (see Figure 4.10).

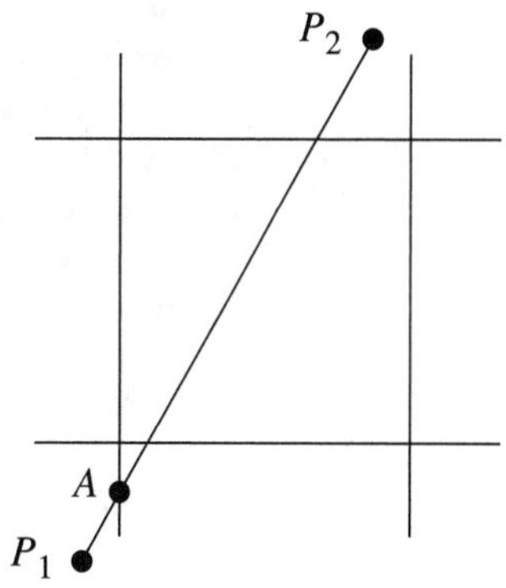

Figure 4.10   Line after the first clipping

The algorithm now calculates the region code of point A and repeats the clipping process with the line from A to P_2.

Again, the line A–P_2 is not trivially accepted or rejected. Testing the bits of region code A in the order 3 2 1 0 (left-right-bottom-top), the algorithm finds that A lies below the bottom boundary. Therefore it computes the intersection of the line with the bottom boundary, giving the intersection point B (see Figure 4.11).

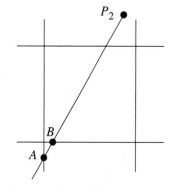

Figure 4.11   Line after the second clipping

It now calculates the region-code of point B and repeats the whole clipping process with the line from B to P_2.

Once more, it does not trivially accept or reject the line. Testing the bits of region code B in the order 3 2 1 0, the algorithm finds no 1-bits. Therefore, the algorithm swaps points B and P_2 and tests region code P_2. It finds P_2 to lie above the top boundary, so it calculates the intersection of the line with the top boundary, giving the intersection point C in Figure 4.12.

The algorithm now calculates the region code of point C (it is (0 0 0 0)) and repeats the whole clipping process with the line from B to C. This time, the line will be trivially accepted, because both region codes are 0000.

In the worst case, we must repeat the clipping process four times. Which line constitutes the worst case depends on the order in which the algorithm checks "out of bounds" for a given point. For checking in the order left-right-bottom-top, as in the above example, there are two worst-case lines (see Figure 4.13).

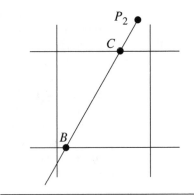

Figure 4.12   Line after the third clipping

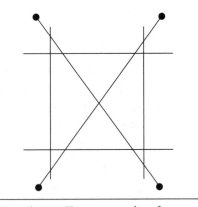

Figure 4.13   Two worst case lines for clipping order l-r-b-t

OO DESIGN

We do not make `clip` a member function of any of our graphics primitives, because such a clip function would never be called from outside the implementation of that primitive. We only need clipping when drawing a primitive. Instead, clipping is a member function of the class `window_t`.

We need only two different types of clipping in 2D—clipping a single straight line and clipping a linked list of vertices. In the second case, the object in question is a polygon, and clipping must produce a new linked list of vertices, whether longer or shorter than the original one.

Accordingly, we provide the class `window_t` with two member functions for clipping: `window_t::clipln()` clips a straight line and `window_t::clipvl()` clips a vertex list. Whenever a graphics primitive is to be drawn, the drawing algorithm first clips it inside and then draws the result.

All our graphics primitives are members of a scene that is initialized with a window-viewport system. When we call the primitive's individual draw functions in the scene, the window against which they are to be clipped is available.

An advantage of this design is that these two clipping functions are virtual. When another type of window-viewport system is derived from the present one, it will redefine them. Then, the code in a draw or fill function that invokes the clipping of a 2D line or polygon against a 2D window will also clip a 3D line or polygon against a 3D window.

Be sure that you recognize that the region code of a point on the window boundary is 0000; such a point is considered to be inside the window. Although this algorithm uses floating point arithmetic, it is very fast and efficient when it can be done in specialized hardware, such as the VLSI-based floating point clipper described in CLAR80.

In assembly language, the region codes can be determined even more readily by doing subtractions in registers and building the region code from the sign flags:

$x - l$: sign flag gives bit 3 of region code
$r - x$: sign flag gives bit 2
$y - b$: sign flag gives bit 1
$t - y$: sign flag gives bit 0

We do not present the implementation of the Cohen-Sutherland line clipper in the text. It is implemented as the member function `window_t::clipln()` in `Shape2d/win_view.c`.

LIANG-BARSKY LINE-CLIPPING ALGORITHM

The clipping method of Liang and Barsky (LIBA84) uses a parameterized representation of the line. Remember, if $P_1 = (x_1\ y_1)$ and $P_2 = (x_2\ y_2)$ are two points in the plane, then we can express a line from P_1 to P_2 as two equations in the parameter u:

$$x = x_1 + (x_2 - x_1)u$$
$$y = y_1 + (y_2 - y_1)u$$

These equations express both the coordinates x and y as functions of the common parameter u, which is the only independent variable in these equations. As u goes from 0 to 1, the point $(x\ y)$ moves along the straight line from P_1 to P_2 (see Figure 4.14).

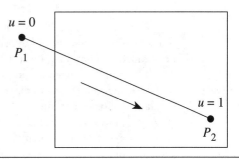

Figure 4.14   Line as function of parameter u

If we set $Dx = (x_2 - x_1)$ and $Dy = (y_2 - y_1)$, the equations are:

$$x = x_1 + Dx*u \qquad y = y_1 + Dy*u$$

Any point $(x\ y)$ is inside the window if:

$$l \leq x \leq r \quad \text{and} \quad b \leq y \leq t$$

where l, r, b, and t are the window boundaries.

A point on the line is inside the window if the four inequalities

$$l \le x_1 + Dx*u \le r$$
$$b \le y_1 + Dy*u \le t$$

are fulfilled for a value of u between 0 and 1. If the inequalities can be fulfilled only for values of u less than 0 or greater than 1, then just the extension of the straight line passes through the window.

By writing the inequalities in a different way, we have:

$$-Dx*u \le x_1 - l \qquad (1)$$
$$Dx*u \le r - x_1 \qquad (2)$$
$$-Dy*u \le y_1 - b \qquad (3)$$
$$Dy*u \le t - y_1 \qquad (4)$$

A value of u which fulfills (1) specifies a point on the line to the right of the left window boundary. In the same way, inequality (2) relates to the right window boundary, (3) to the bottom, and (4) to the top boundary. We will put this into a more general notation by letting C_k stand for the coefficients of u (the Dx's or Dy's) and letting q_k stand for the right-hand sides. This gives the general shorthand notation:

$$C_k*u \le q_k \qquad \text{for } k = 1, ..., 4$$

In other words:

$$C_1 = x_1 - x_2 \qquad\qquad q_1 = x_1 - l$$
$$C_2 = x_2 - x_1 \qquad\qquad q_2 = r - x_1$$
$$C_3 = y_1 - y_2 \qquad\qquad q_3 = y_1 - b$$
$$C_4 = y_2 - y_1 \qquad\qquad q_4 = t - y_1$$

When $k = 1$ or 2, it relates to x-values (left, right) and when $k = 3$ or 4, it relates to y-values (bottom, top). In the discussion below, "line" means the infinite extension of the line segment determined by P_1 and P_2; it is the line through these points.

If $C_k > 0$, the line goes from the inside to the outside with respect to that particular window boundary. This means that a point $(x\ y)$ that moves along the line as t increases crosses that particular boundary from its inside to its outside (but not necessarily from inside the window to outside the window, because the crossing may lie outside another boundary). Consider the point P_2 and the line in Figure 4.15.

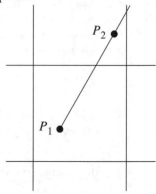

Figure 4.15   Extension of line crosses boundary

We have $x_2 - x_1 = C_2 > 0$. Therefore, as u increases, the corresponding point $(x \ y)$ on the line moves from left to right. With respect to the right window boundary, left is inside and right is outside, so the point moves from inside to outside. This does not indicate where the intersection with the boundary will take place; it may very well be outside the window and outside the finite line segment from P_1 to P_2, as in this case.

The meaning of inside and outside for all the other boundaries should be obvious. (For the left boundary, outside is the area to its left and inside is the area to its right, and so on for all the others.) You should verify the statements below about how the sign of C_k tells how the point moves with respect to each boundary as u increases.

If $C_k < 0$, the line goes from the outside to the inside with respect to that window boundary. This case is symmetric to the case above.

$C_k = 0$ is a special case. The line does not cross that particular boundary; it is parallel to it. However, the line can still go through the window if it is on the proper side of the boundary. It will not do so if the corresponding $q_k < 0$. If that is true, we can eliminate the line from further consideration.

The definition of C_k shows that C_1 always equals $-C_2$ and that C_3 always equals $-C_4$. In other words, for nonzero C_k, there is always a boundary for which the line goes from inside to outside and another boundary for which it does the opposite.

For a nonzero C_k, the value of u corresponding to the intersection point is very simply:

$$u = \frac{q_k}{C_k}$$

From the value of u alone, the algorithm can derive information about the intersection without having to calculate the intersection point. This is an important advantage over the Cohen-Sutherland clipping method because it requires only one division and two subtractions to compute q and C. Computing the intersection points requires one division, one multiplication, two subtractions, and one addition. We discuss below the conditions under which a line is rejected.

In Figure 4.16, $C_3 < 0$, so the line crosses the bottom boundary from the outside as u increases. We can then say that the value of the parameter u that corresponds to the intersection point is an "entry value" for the line. If this value for u is calculated and found to be 1.3, this entry point of the line is already beyond the end point, P_2. Whenever an entry value is greater than 1, the line is rejected.

Be sure to distinguish between entry to a boundary and entry to the window itself. Also, remember that in this parameterized representation, the starting point of the line P_1 corresponds to $u = 0$ and its end point P_2 corresponds to $u = 1$. This implies, in cases where $u = 1$, that the line is entirely outside the bottom boundary and therefore outside the window, so it will be rejected.

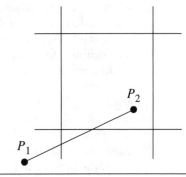

Figure 4.16   Bottom boundary is crossed as an "entry"

If $C_k > 0$, we calculate u values that can be interpreted as "exit values" of the line with respect to that boundary. If an exit value is smaller than 0, the line segment is outside the window and will be rejected. Figure 4.17 shows such a case.

In Figure 4.17, $C_4 > 0$ so the line crosses the top boundary from the inside out as u increases. We can call the value of u that corresponds to the intersection an exit value for the line. If this value is -0.1 (as in the figure), the exit point comes before the starting point of the segment, P_1. Whenever an exit value is less than 0, the line is rejected.

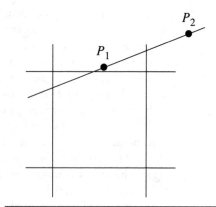

Figure 4.17 *Exit value with top boundary is smaller than 0*

A third situation where a line will be rejected is when an entry value is greater than an exit value. Lines that miss the window but have both end points outside the same boundary are rejected in this case (see Figure 4.18).

Remember that the "line" is more than just the segment between the end points. The line may well cross two boundaries before it enters the window. In fact, we may calculate entry values for two different boundaries and still not know if the line actually goes into the window.

The algorithm will calculate at most two entry values and two exit values for u. (The line cannot cross more than two boundaries before it enters the window, nor can it cross more than two boundaries on leaving.) This will involve at most four divisions.

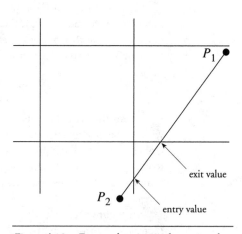

Figure 4.18 *Entry value greater than exit value*

Consider now the portion (if any) of the line segment that is inside the window. Only nonnegative entry values make sense, because points are not between P_1 and P_2 for negative u. By the same reasoning, the only exit values that make sense are ≤ 1. Let us use the symbol u_1 for the largest entry value from the set that consists of 0 and the two values of q_k/C_k for negative C_k. We use u_2 for the smallest exit value from the set comprised of 1 and the two values of q_k/C_k for positive C_k. During its execution, the algorithm can stop and reject the line as soon as the entry value > 1, the exit value < 0, or the entry value $>$ the exit value. The algorithm calculates intersection coordinates only if $u_1 > 0$ or if $u_2 < 1$.

It will help you to follow this reasoning if you look at some concrete examples. Table 4.1 gives six numerical examples. The window boundaries are kept fixed for all examples:

$$l = 10, \quad r = 20, \quad b = 3, \quad t = 11,$$

but the end points of the lines vary as shown in the table. The algorithm starts by computing C_1, q_1, and $u = q_1/C_1$, and checks whether to discard the line. If not, it continues to compute C_2, q_2, and $u = q_2/C_2$, checks again, and so on. Each computed u-value is subscripted with n or x, depending on whether it is an entry or an exit value. (If the corresponding $C < 0$, then u is an entry value; if it > 0, then u is an exit value.) All lines in these examples are discarded and the examples feature several different reasons for discarding. (See Figures 4.19 through 4.24.)

#	x_1	x_2	y_1	y_2	C_1	q_1	u	C_2	q_2	u	C_3	q_3	u	C_4	q_4	u
1	3	9	13.8	5.2	−6	−7	1.17_n	dis								
2	21.2	27	4.1	14	−5.8	11.2	-1.93_n	5.8	−1.2	-0.21_x	dis					
3	6.7	18	−2.9	0	−11.3	−3.3	0.29_n	11.3	13.3	1.18_x	−2.9	−5.5	1.90_n	dis		
4	16.6	12.4	12.5	22.2	4.2	6.6	1.57_x	−4.2	3.4	-0.81_n	−9.7	9.5	-0.98_n	9.7	−1.5	-0.15_x	dis
5	26.5	16	7	−3.4	10.5	16.5	1.57_x	−10.5	−6.5	0.62_n	10.4	4	0.38_x	dis		
6	25	7.5	8.3	20.5	17.5	15	0.86_x	−17.5	−5	0.28_n	−12.2	5.3	-0.43_n	12.2	2.7	0.22_x	dis

Table 4.1   Number values for the following examples

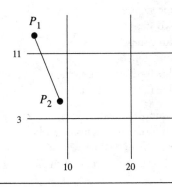

Figure 4.19   Example 1

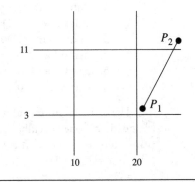

Figure 4.20   Example 2

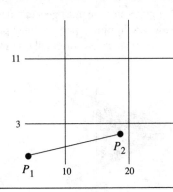

Figure 4.21   Example 3

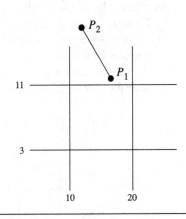

Figure 4.22   Example 4

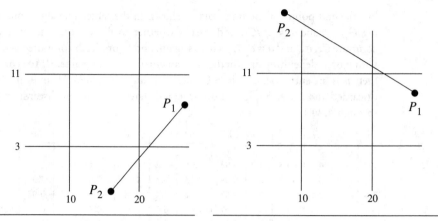

Figure 4.23   Example 5   *Figure 4.24   Example 6*

Reasons for discarding:

1. entry value   1.17 > 1 after one step
2. exit value   −0.21 < 0 after two steps
3. entry value   1.90 > 1 after three steps
4. exit value   −0.15 < 0 after four steps
5. exit value   0.38 < entry value 0.62 after three steps
6. exit value   0.22 < entry value 0.28 after four steps

The basic algorithmic idea consists of at most four consecutive checks against the window boundaries. If one check has a negative result, the others need not be performed. This algorithm, too, is coded as the member function of `window_t::clipln()` in the file `Shape2d/win_view.c` (the user must comment out one of them).

4.2.2   POLYGON CLIPPING

The method presented here (see Figures 4.25 through 4.27) is a version of the Sutherland-Hodgman polygon clipping, which does not need extra storage. We cannot just use a line-clipping algorithm on each edge of the polygon because we must generate new edges along the window boundaries and clip the original edges. Clipping a polygon may produce a polygon with fewer vertices or one with more vertices than it had originally. It may even produce several unconnected polygons.

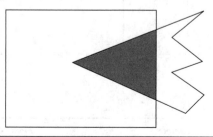

Figure 4.25   Seven vertices before and three vertices after clipping

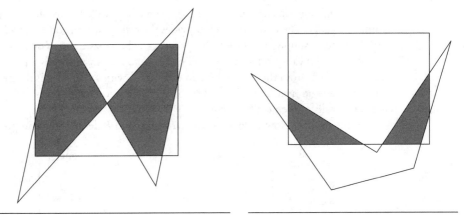

Figure 4.26   Four vertices before and ten vertices
after clipping

Figure 4.27   Two unconnected polygons
after clipping

A polygon consists of an ordered sequence of vertices. One draws a polygon's edge by connecting each successive pair of consecutive vertices with straight lines. The clipping algorithm will process the edges in the order of the vertices.

The clipping algorithm is called once for each polygon edge. An edge consists of a start vertex and an end vertex (the next vertex in the polygon). For each call, the algorithm returns either no vertex at all, or the end vertex without change, or one or more new vertices.

We can best understand the algorithm by imagining that it repeatedly executes what we call a basic clip against each of the four window boundaries. (Here, *boundary* means the infinite extension of the boundary line.) We describe the basic clip as independent of the boundary to which it is applied. Keep in mind that inside and outside relate to a boundary of the window, not to the window itself, and that a point on a boundary is considered inside. Inside for the left boundary is everything on or to the right of that boundary; inside for the right boundary is everything on or to the left of that boundary; inside for the bottom boundary is everything on or above that boundary; and inside for the top boundary is everything on or below that boundary, even if it is not within the window.

Although in principle there is only one basic clip, no matter to which boundary we apply it, for convenience we talk of four basic clips: the left clip is the one applied to the left boundary, the right clip is applied to the right, and so on. We must subject each polygon edge to all four basic clips. The algorithm works not by calling all four clips for the edge, but by calling only the left clip. The left clip then calls the right, the right calls the bottom, and the bottom calls the top. This sequence is arbitrary and forms what we call the *clipping pipe*.

A basic clip works with two points, one considered the start, and the other the end of an edge. (We say "considered" because during the algorithm, polygon vertices may change, so neither one of the two points may be a vertex of the original polygon.) The algorithm first determines whether or not this "edge" crosses the boundary. If it does not, the edge is either entirely inside or entirely outside. If it crosses, the crossing can be from inside to out or from outside to in. Consequently, there are four possible cases, illustrated in Figures 4.28 through 4.31.

Although a basic clip works with two points, it is called with only one point—the end point of an edge. The basic clip itself provides the start point, the one with which it was called the last time. It simply remembers this point, called the basic clip's *last point.*

A basic clip can produce zero, one, or two *outputs.* An output is a point on the edge (it may be different from the start point and end point) with which it calls the next basic clip. No output means no next basic clip will be called. One output means one call and two outputs mean two calls of the next basic clip.

In the figures below, S denotes the start point and P denotes the end point.

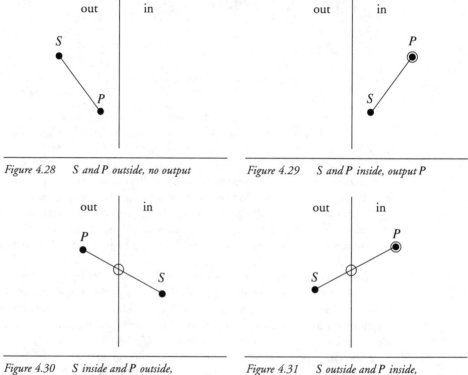

Figure 4.28   *S and P outside, no output*

Figure 4.29   *S and P inside, output P*

Figure 4.30   *S inside and P outside, output intersection*

Figure 4.31   *S outside and P inside, output intersection and P*

To perform a basic clip requires knowing the points S and P and the boundary against which the edge is to be processed. We could write an algorithm for the basic clip whose arguments include this boundary, but it is clearer and easier to understand if we write four different basic clips, one for each boundary.

The clipping pipe for a specific edge of the polygon consists of putting the end point of this edge through these four basic clips. (Do not be confused by the coincidence that there are four basic clips and four "in-out" cases within each clip.) The basic clip's output against one boundary is used as input for the basic clip against the next boundary, until all four boundaries have been considered. Only then do we have an output of the pipe. Only an edge's end point, not the start point, is given to the basic clip. How then does it know the start point? The start point is simply the point with which the basic clip was called the last time. We will soon see that the very first initialization of these "last points" is a problem. The names of the basic clips are: cllef(), clrit(), clbot(), and cltop().

Each polygon vertex goes through the pipeline of the four basic clips as the end point of some edge. In passing through the pipe, it may be killed altogether, it may come out unchanged, it may come out changed (clipped to a boundary), or it may branch out into several different points (these will all be on the window boundaries).

You will understand the code more if you first practice passing vertices through the "clipping pipe" by hand. In doing this, you will need to keep these rules handy:

CASE			OUTPUT
S outside	$\rightarrow$	P outside	None
S inside	$\rightarrow$	P inside	P
S inside	$\rightarrow$	P outside	Intersection
S outside	$\rightarrow$	P inside	Intersection plus P

We first do a general example, then a specific one.

We write the four letters $L\ R\ B\ T$ with some space between them. These represent the four basic clips in the order in which they are applied—left, right, bottom, top:

$$L \qquad R \qquad B \qquad T$$

The vertices of the polygon are numbered from P_1 through P_n. Each clip must know the last point with which it was called. However, at the start, there are no such "last points." We therefore initialize the last points for all four clips with the value of P_n (the last vertex of the definition of the original polygon). See below for further discussion of this.

To help us remember the "last point," we write it on a line above and to the left of the corresponding clip. Doing this, our starting arrangement is:

$$P_n \qquad P_n \qquad P_n \qquad P_n$$
$$L \qquad\quad R \qquad\quad B \qquad\quad T$$

We begin by putting the vertex P_1 into the left basic clip, L. We indicate this by writing it down at the left of the L:

$$P_n \qquad\quad P_n \qquad\quad P_n \qquad\quad P_n$$
$$P_1 \quad L \qquad\quad R \qquad\quad B \qquad\quad T$$
$$\rightarrow$$

The arrow emphasizes that P_1 is entering the pipe. We will not use it after this first example.

To the left of the letter L, we now have the vertex P_n and below it P_1. Read this as: The edge from P_n to P_1 is submitted to the left clip. We now determine the output from L (with P_n as the last point). The output from L could be nothing, the point P_1, a clipped point, or two points (a clipped point and P_1). If there is no output, then clipping P_1 is over. If the output is one point, we write it after L and before R. Thus, it becomes input for the basic clip R. Here, we assume that the output is a clipped point a:

$$
\begin{array}{llllllll}
P_n & & P_n & & P_n & & P_n & \\
P_1 & L & a & R & & B & & T \\
& & \rightarrow & & & & &
\end{array}
$$

If there are two outputs, we write the second output below the first, as a reminder that the pipe has split and that we must process it as soon as we have finished with the current branch. When processing the second branch, we write the remaining basic clips as letters. Here, we assume that the first branch of the pipe terminates with the output a from the top basic clip:

$$
\begin{array}{lllllllll}
P_n & & P_n & & P_n & & P_n & & \\
P_1 & L & a & R & a & B & a & T & a \\
\rightarrow & & \rightarrow & & \rightarrow & & \rightarrow & & \\
& & P_1 & R & & B & & T & \\
& & \rightarrow & & & & & &
\end{array}
$$

You see the second branch indicated by a P_1 before the letter R. As there is an "a" above P_1, read this as: the edge from a to P_1 is submitted to the right clip. This clip produces no output in our example, so the second branch ends here.

In this way, we send all vertices of the polygon through the pipe. For each vertex, we write a new pipe. As we write the new pipe, we update a drawing that shows the polygon being clipped.

Now we will give a specific example. We will no longer include the arrows.

Given the polygon in Figure 4.32, L is called with P_1; we use P_3 as its "last point" (we have just begun the process), so this is the case out-in. L will therefore produce two outputs to the next basic clip, the first with the intersection a, the next with P_1. Thus, the pipe branches, giving us:

$$
\begin{array}{llllllll}
P_3 & & P_3 & & P_3 & & P_3 & \\
P_1 & L & a & R & & B & & T \\
& & P_1 & R & & B & & T
\end{array}
$$

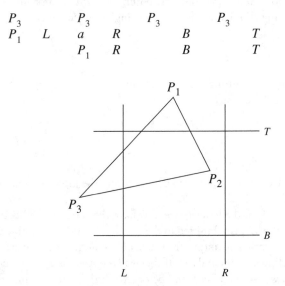

Figure 4.32   Polygon to be clipped

Following the upper branch, R is called with a; its last point is P_3. This is the case in-in, so R produces a, giving us:

P_3		P_3		P_3		P_3		
P_1	L	a	R	a	B		T	
		P_1	R		B		T	

B is called with a; its last point is P_3. From P_3 to a is the case in-in for B, so B produces a and we have:

P_3		P_3		P_3		P_3		
P_1	L	a	R	a	B	a	T	
		P_1	R		B		T	

T is called with a; its last point is P_3. From P_3 to a is the case in-in for T, so T produces a and we have:

P_3		P_3		P_3		P_3		
P_1	L	a	R	a	B	a	T	a
		P_1	R		B		T	

The first pipe is finished. Now we must follow the lower branching. R is called with P_1; its last point is a, which we can see in the line above. From a to P_1 is the case in-in for R, so R produces P_1, giving us:

P_3		P_3		P_3		P_3		
P_1	L	a	R	a	B	a	T	a
		P_1	R	P_1	B		T	

B is called with P_1; its last point is a. From a to P_1 is the case in-in for B, so B produces P_1 and we have:

P_3		P_3		P_3		P_3		
P_1	L	a	R	a	B	a	T	a
		P_1	R	P_1	B	P_1	T	

T is called with P_1 as Figure 4.33 shows. Its last point is a. From a to P_1 is the case in-out for T, so T produces the intersection point b, giving us:

P_3		P_3		P_3		P_3		
P_1	L	a	R	a	B	a	T	a
		P_1	R	P_1	B	P_1	T	b

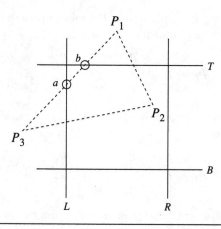

Figure 4.33   *Pipe output for edge P_3P_1*

We have seen that putting the first point through the pipe gives two output points (a and b); both are intersections. We now continue the pipe with P_2:

$$
\begin{array}{ccccccc}
P_1 & & P_1 & & P_1 & & P_1 \\
P_2 & L & & R & & B & & T
\end{array}
$$

L is called with P_2; its last point is P_1, which we can see in the last diagram. From P_1 to P_2 is the case in-in for L, so L produces P_1 and we have:

$$
\begin{array}{ccccccc}
P_1 & & P_1 & & P_1 & & P_1 \\
P_2 & L & P_2 & R & & B & & T
\end{array}
$$

R is called with P_2; its last point is P_1. From P_1 to P_2 is the case in-in for R, so R produces P_2 and we have:

$$
\begin{array}{ccccccc}
P_1 & & P_1 & & P_1 & & P_1 \\
P_2 & L & P_2 & R & P_2 & B & & T
\end{array}
$$

B is called with P_2; its last point is P_1. From P_1 to P_2 is the case in-in for B, so B produces P_2, giving us:

$$
\begin{array}{ccccccc}
P_1 & & P_1 & & P_1 & & P_1 \\
P_2 & L & P_2 & R & P_2 & B & P_2 & T
\end{array}
$$

T is called with P_2, as Figure 4.34 shows. Its last point is P_1 (the last point with which a basic clip is called is important, not the point it produces). From P_1 to P_2 is the case out-in for T, so T produces the intersection point c and the point P_2. The pipe branches and we have:

$$
\begin{array}{cccccccccc}
P_1 & & P_1 & & P_1 & & P_1 \\
P_2 & L & P_2 & R & P_2 & B & P_2 & T & c \\
& & & & & & & & P_2
\end{array}
$$

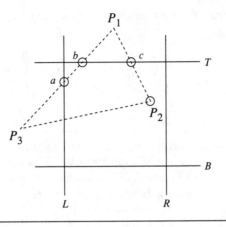

Figure 4.34   Pipe output for edge P_1P_2

This pipe also produces two points as output. Only P_3 remains to be put through the pipe, so L is called with P_3; its last point is P_2. From P_2 to P_3 is the case in-out for L, so L produces the intersection point d, giving us:

$$
\begin{array}{ccccccc}
P_2 & & P_2 & & P_2 & & P_2 \\
P_3 & L & d & R & & B & & T
\end{array}
$$

$R, B,$ and T produce d as well and we have:

$$
\begin{array}{ccccccccc}
P_2 & & P_2 & & P_2 & & P_2 \\
P_3 & L & d & R & d & B & d & T & d
\end{array}
$$

Now we have obtained all the vertices of the clipped polygon. They are a, b, c, P_2, and d (see Figure 4.35).

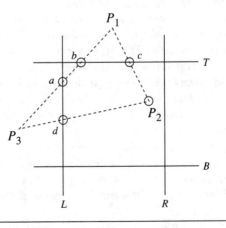

Figure 4.35   Pipe output for edge P_2P_3

To summarize the example, we repeat the entire schematic here:

P_3		P_3		P_3		P_3		
P_1	L	a	R	a	B	a	T	a
		P_1	R	P_1	B	P_1	T	b
P_2	L	P_2	R	P_2	B	P_2	T	c
								P_2
P_3	L	d	R	d	B	d	T	d

The output is a, b, c, P_2, and d. (These are always the last column of the schematic.)

Unfortunately, not all cases are as simple as this example. When clipping the polygon shown in Figure 4.36, the algorithm produces the points indicated in the drawing. Two points are even outside the window. The result is wrong.

The reason for this is the way we initialize the last points. When `clbot()` is called the first time (passing P_1 through the pipe), its last point is P_3, which is outside the window. This point could never actually be a last point resulting from a call to its preceding clipper, `clrit()`. The problem occurs from artificially setting the last points to P_3 initially.

We can consider each clip as a filter for the points with which it is called; whatever is passed on from `cllef()` must be to the right of or equal to the left boundary. `Clrit()` acts as another filter; whatever passes on from it is to the left of or equal to the right boundary. The points

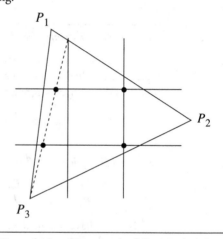

Figure 4.36   Wrong result of clipping algorithm

become more and more narrowed as they pass through the pipe. After passing all clips, a point must be inside or on the window boundary. Each clip accepts only points that have been filtered by the clip before. The sole exception is `cllef()`. If we could also provide `cllef()` only with points that have passed through a previous clip, the problem indicated in Figure 4.36 would disappear. This suggests that we can use a first pass of the vertices through the pipeline to generate a set of correct "last points" for a second pass.

This is simple and effective, though less efficient. In most cases, a full run through the polygon to set up the last points is not necessary; a partial run would be adequate. While it is possible to see with the naked eye how much partial run one needs, this depends on the specific polygon. Introducing such analysis into the algorithm would complicate it unduly. The advantage of two runs, however, is that there is freedom in initializing the last points; any values will work. We set them simply to zero by declaring them as static locals in each basic clipper.

Our solution is to run through the polygon twice: first to perform a "fake" clip. This generates correct initial last points for the second "real" clip. The included code reflects this idea precisely.

It is fairly easy to learn and master the algorithmic process from the above discussion. However, most students have trouble understanding why this indeed clips a polygon to the window. What might help is to imagine a thread laid around the polygon vertices. Whenever a vertex is outside a boundary, that particular clip snips off its edges and pulls the thread somewhat closer to this one boundary. The shortened vertex might still be outside the window with respect to another boundary and can be rectified only when that clip's turn comes. If that clip's turn is already over, another pass is needed. This explains why the same polygon might correctly clip in one pass for a particular clip sequence, but not for another. However, every polygon will clip correctly in two passes.

This algorithm has the advantage of not needing any extra storage, but one pays for its terseness and elegance with its conceptual difficulty.

It is implemented as the member function `window_t::clipvl()` in the file `Shape2d/win_view.c`. Let us explain the function a little: It uses two global pointers to `vertex_t`. We repeat here what we mentioned in the introduction. If a few functions in a small file need to share a few common variables, it is legal to have those as globals with file scope. We do this for the sake of speed by limiting the number of parameters passed back and forth between or through the various functions so that we can read the code more easily.

In an individual basic clip, the conditions are set to produce the outputs, as we explained in Figures 4.28 through 4.31. In particular, if start and end points both lie on the boundary, only the end point must be produced as output. The second condition provides for this. All basic clips are called only by the end point of the edge they clip. The last clip puts its result into a new list of vertices. A pointer to the first list element is returned. The parameter of `window_t::clipvl()` is the pointer to the first vertex in the polygon.

Whenever a new vertex is put into the linked list representing the clipped polygon, it is created using the virtual member function `vertex_t::copy()`. This ensures that the clipped list consists of vertices of the same type, although the function `window_t::clipvl()` works only with `vertex_t` pointers. This is essential for reusability of the clipping code.

When the clipping of a polygon creates two disjointed parts, two coinciding lines along the window boundary will connect them. This represents a part of the polygon with area 0. A polygon that surrounds the window several times, perhaps never having an edge penetrate into the window, may be clipped into multiple coincident lines along the whole window boundary, which would also represent a polygon of area 0. These degenerate, clipped polygons pose no problems for other applications. Whether or not you display such polygons of area 0 when filling them is a matter of personal taste.

The provided codes contain a function `Shape2d/main.c` that demonstrates how to use the classes introduced so far.

4.2.3   TEXT CLIPPING

When text is displayed within a window (remember that the entire screen can be a window), there are three levels of complexity to consider. There are also three basic ways to generate characters. The method that we use to clip text to fit within the window depends on both of these factors.

We will first describe the three levels of complexity as applied to the bitmap character generator, a method of generating characters.

BITMAP CHARACTER GENERATOR

A common way to produce characters on a graphics display is to copy a bitmap from a character generator (often in ROM) into the area where the character is to be displayed. The character generator contains one bitmap for every possible character. The bitmaps can be of different sizes; however, many character generators use the same size for all characters, such as 9 pixels wide by 14 pixels high (some of the vertical space is for descenders, as on the letters *p* and *y*).

There are three strategies for clipping characters generated through bitmaps. These differ, depending on whether we clip individual characters or work with sets of characters, namely, a *string*. String in this context means at most one line of text.

The first method is the "all-or-none string-clipping" strategy. The method consists of checking whether the entire text string is inside the window boundary. If it is not, we discard the whole string. We consider the string to cross a window boundary if any of the string's bitmaps cross it (see Figure 4.37). The string being clipped is **CLIP**. To carry this out, we must add all the widths of the bitmaps of the characters composing this string. The height of the bitmaps is usually the same for all characters. Using the sum of the widths and the height, we have a bounding rectangle for the string. This sum plus the string's starting position tell us if the string would cross a window boundary. If so, we display none of the string.

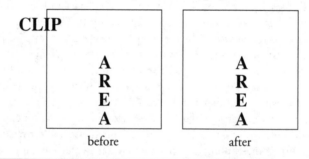

Figure 4.37   *All-or-none string-clipping*

Another method is the "all-or-none character-clipping" strategy. This consists of displaying only individual characters that fit entirely within the window. If a bitmap is completely or partly outside a window boundary, that character will not be copied onto the screen. Figure 4.38 shows this. We must check each individual character bitmap. The starting point together with the width and height of the individual bitmap can tell us whether it crosses a window boundary. After checking one character, we must update the starting point by the width or height of that character, continuing this until we have processed the entire string, character by character.

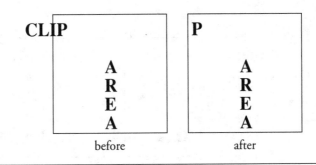

Figure 4.38   All-or-none character-clipping

The third method is the "individual character-clipping" strategy. Characters whose bitmaps are fully inside the window are copied onto the screen; those completely outside are ignored. Characters whose bitmaps are partly within the window are partially displayed (see Figure 4.39). From a bitmap's width and height, we can calculate which pixels are within the window. Only these are displayed. This is a much more elaborate process than the other strategies.

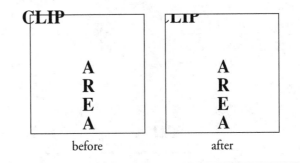

Figure 4.39   Individual character-clipping

VECTOR CHARACTER GENERATOR

In contrast to the bitmap technique, we can actually draw characters as a series of lines. This is called vector character generation. To accomplish this, a sequence of commands defines the start points and end points of straight lines (vectors), which will produce the character. Such character generators can easily produce slanted script or characters of different width and height. Vector character generation applies to plotters, as well as to raster scan and vector scan CRTs, because most plotters draw in vector mode.

We can apply the same three types of clipping strategies. First, we consider the "all-or-none string-clipping" strategy. We must compute the size of the rectangle that bounds the string and then check whether it lies completely inside the screen boundary. This involves knowing or computing the dimensions of bounding rectangles for each character. If the rectangle that bounds the entire string does not fall within the window, no part of the string will be displayed, as in Figure 4.40.

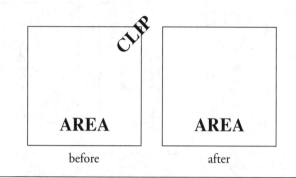

Figure 4.40   All-or-none string-clipping

In the "all-or-none character-clipping" strategy, we must check how each individual character fits into the window. This means that we must know or calculate the size of a rectangle that can just contain the vectors of the character being generated. If this rectangle is not completely inside the window, no part of the character is displayed. Figure 4.41 illustrates this.

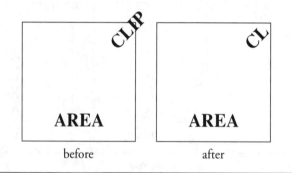

Figure 4.41   All-or-none character-clipping

Using "individual character clipping" with vector-generated characters is more complicated than with a bitmap character generator. To save computing time, it pays to check the bounding rectangle for the character against the display boundaries first. We can obtain information about this containing rectangle from the description of the character. If the rectangle is completely inside or completely outside the display, no clipping is necessary; the character is either fully displayed or not. If the bounding rectangle crosses a window boundary, then we must apply a straight line-clipping algorithm, such as Cohen-Sutherland, to each line of the character (see Figure 4.42).

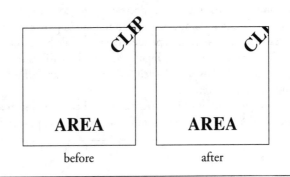

before   after

Figure 4.42   Individual character-clipping

TYPOGRAPHY CHARACTER GENERATOR

A third type of character generator produces typography-quality characters. We mention those here only to be thorough, not in the context of clipping. This type of generator is becoming increasingly important with the advent of the laser printer. The character generation in itself is an art and a science and is very complex. These characters are not stored as bitmaps, but as functions that produce a character of a certain font in any desired size in the laser printer's frame buffer. The outline of the character is produced using straight lines, circular arcs, and Bezier curves. Then, it is filled with any desired "screen." You can find a little more about this in books on PostScript. However, the precise method of generation is almost a trade secret. Companies such as Mergenthaler, Adobe, and Bitstream produce character generators for laser printers.

4.3   TWO-DIMENSIONAL TRANSFORMATIONS

A graphics system must allow the user to change the way objects appear. In the real world, we frequently rearrange objects or look at them from different angles. The computer should let us do the same with images on the screen. Objects in the real world move; our displays should be able to reflect such movement.

We want to be able to change the size of an object, its position on the screen, or its orientation. When we define a two-dimensional object, we describe its shape in only one basic way. It is impractical to produce many different sizes, positions, or orientations of the same object, just because we might want to view it differently later. It is much more sensible to make changes later to the object's original basic description. Implementing such a change is called a *transformation.*

What display changes are we most likely to want? Although there are several, only a few really help effect the changes an object may undergo in the real world. These are *translation* (moving the object), *scaling* (changing its size), and *rotation* (turning it on an axis).

Translations occur constantly in the real world because either objects move or we move, making objects appear as if they have moved. Scaling is also common; as we approach an object or when it moves closer to us, it increases in size. Scaling in computer graphics actually does more than just increase or decrease an object's size. We can stretch an object's length or height in ways that do not correspond to natural phenomena, because we can manipulate an object's two dimensions independently. If we scale both dimensions by the same amount, we achieve a simple size change. Figures 4.43 and 4.44 illustrate changing position and size. The original object is drawn in dashed lines and the transformed object in solid lines. The screen frame serves as a reference.

Figure 4.43 shows a pure translation. The image is shifted to the right and upward. The object's size and orientation are not changed; it remains parallel to its first position.

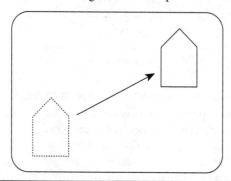

Figure 4.43   Translation

Figure 4.44 shows scaling. Both the *x*- and *y*-dimensions are multiplied by approximately 1.5. This results in a size change accompanied by a change of position. The orientation does not change; the object remains parallel to its first position. The house is scaled relative to a point, which is indicated in the picture. This means that each scaled vertex of the house lies on the line through that point and the original vertex.

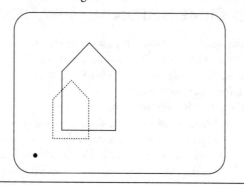

Figure 4.44   Scaling

Figure 4.45 shows a rotation of a smaller object, a chair. We most often notice that small objects are rotated in the real world. Strictly speaking, houses and mountains also rotate when we tilt our heads to look at them. Because they are not rotated in relation to the surrounding environment, however, we do not have the feeling that they rotate. Observe that the chair is rotated around a reference point in the lower left corner.

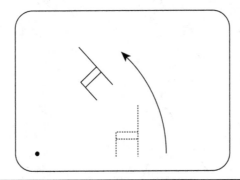

Figure 4.45   Rotation

Other transformations are sometimes found in graphics packages, for example, several types of shears and reflections. These have no equivalent in reality and are mostly used for special effects. They are not as common as the three described above, so we will not deal with them.

The transformations described above transform straight lines into straight lines. We call this property *geometric linearity* or simply *linearity.*[†]

Thus, if an object consists of vertices connected by straight lines, we can transform it by changing only the vertices and later connecting them with straight lines.

4.3.1   TRANSLATION

This transformation consists of shifting the object parallel to its first position in any direction in the $(x \ y)$-plane. We can accomplish such a shift by moving in the x-direction (horizontally) and in the y-direction (vertically). The mathematical description is simple. We call the amount of x-shift T_x and the amount of y-shift T_y. The translation of the point $(x \ y)$ into the point $(x_T \ y_T)$ is expressed with the formulas:

$$x_T = x + T_x$$

$$y_T = y + T_y$$

Translation is the only transformation that has no relation to a reference point. As an example, consider translating the triangle defined by the vertices (10 0), (40 0), (30 30) 10 units to the right and 15 units upward ($T_x = 10$, $T_y = 15$). You must apply the formulas to every vertex of the triangle. The translated vertices are (20 15), (50 15), (40 45) (see Figure 4.46). Connecting these points yields the translated triangle.

The translation is implemented as the member function `prim_t& translate()` of every graphic primitive derived from `prim_t`.

[†]This is not the same as *functional linearity.* A function $f(x)$ is linear if $f(\alpha x + \beta y) = \alpha f(x) + \beta f(y)$. What we are interested in is whether straight lines are transformed into straight lines (and planes into planes). All points on a straight line through the points $(x_1 \ y_1)$ and $(x_2 \ y_2)$ are expressed by $(\alpha * x_1 + \beta * x_2 \ \ \alpha * y_1 + \beta * y_2)$ with any α and β, such that $\alpha + \beta = 1$. The reader can easily verify that the three transformations fulfill this condition. This means that any point on a straight line through two given points is transformed into a point on the straight line through the transformations of the two points.

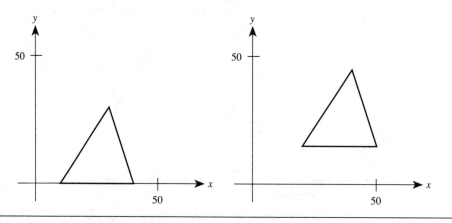

Figure 4.46   Example of translation

4.3.2 SCALING

Scaling consists of elongating or shrinking the object in the x-direction and in the y-direction by two independent factors, S_x and S_y. If $S_x = S_y$, this simply changes the object's size. Otherwise, this elongates or shrinks the object in either the x- or y-direction. The scaling of the point $(x \ y)$ into the point $(x_S \ y_S)$ is expressed with the formulas:

$$x_s = x * S_x$$
$$y_s = y * S_y$$

As an example, take the same triangle as above and make it wider by a factor of 1.5 and taller by a factor of 1.2 ($S_x = 1.5$, $S_y = 1.2$). Applying the formulas to every vertex yields (15 0), (60 0), (45 36). Connecting these yields a scaled triangle (see Figure 4.47). We can see that all points move away from the origin; the enlargement is relative to (0 0).

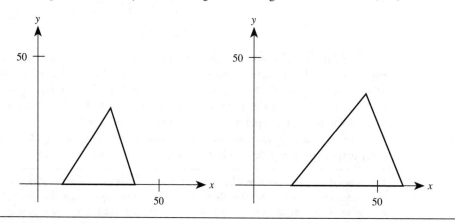

Figure 4.47   Example of scaling

If the scale factor is less than 1.0, scaling shrinks the image. Scaling with negative numbers results in various types of reflections or mirror images. For example, scaling with $S_x = -1$, $S_y = 1$ produces a mirror image of the object with respect to the y-axis.

Scaling is not implemented in the provided codes, but it is very simple, and the reader is invited to add the member function `prim_t& scale()` to all primitives derived from `prim_t`. Scaling should be done about the centroid of the primitive.

4.3.3 ROTATION

Rotation consists of turning the object around the point (0 0). When subjected to this transformation, the points of a picture rotate around (0 0) just as the stars in the sky rotate around the polar star. The rotation depends on only one number: the rotation angle ϕ. The rotation of the point $(x\ y)$ into the point $(x_R\ y_R)$ is expressed with the formulas:

$$x_R = x \cos\phi - y \sin\phi$$

$$y_R = x \sin\phi + y \cos\phi$$

Rotation is the only transformation in which each coordinate of the transformed point depends on both coordinates of the original point. Therefore, its mathematics is more difficult. The rotation goes from the positive x-axis to the positive y-axis by an angle of ϕ. Observe that the rotation is counterclockwise (ccw). If we rotate the above triangle by 25°, the rotated vertices are at (9.06 4.22), (36.24 16.88), (14.52 39.84). We connect those points with straight lines (see Figure 4.48).

Rotation is implemented as the member function `prim_t& rot()` in every primitive derived from `prim_t`. The rotation is always done about the centroid of the primitive (see Section 4.3.4).

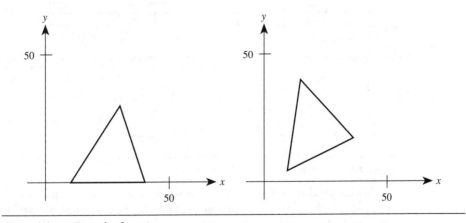

Figure 4.48   Example of rotation

4.3.4   CONCATENATION OF TRANSFORMATIONS

Translation is the only transformation not done in relation to a reference point. We did the above scaling and rotation relative to the point (0 0). These are the fundamental forms of these transformations, but we can also do them relative to any other point in the plane. We now demonstrate how to scale and rotate relative to any arbitrary reference point. In both cases, we use the same strategy. We translate the object along with the reference point, so that the reference point is at (0 0). We then apply the fundamental transformation, finally translating back the transformed image so that the reference point is restored to its original position. If the arbitrary reference point is (x y), the order of transformations will be:

1. translate (T_{-x},T_{-y})
2. rotate or scale
3. translate (T_x,T_y)

We show in Figures 4.49 and 4.50 the three stages of these generalized transformations. In both cases, the reference point is a point inside the house and the origin is near the lower left corner of the frame.

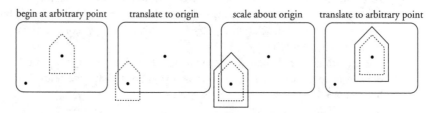

Figure 4.49   Scaling about an arbitrary point

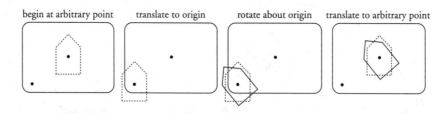

Figure 4.50   Rotating about an arbitrary point

We cannot alter the order in which we make successive transformations—any other order will produce a different result. The example below has just a rotation and a translation. Figures 4.51 and 4.52 show the results when we apply the same translation and the same rotation in a different order. The dot in the lower left corner of the screen is the origin.

Concatenating more than two transformations is order-dependent as well. There are some exceptions, such as concatenating several transformations of the same kind.

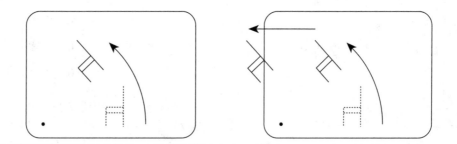

Figure 4.51   First rotation, then translation

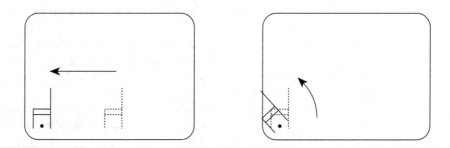

Figure 4.52   First translation, then rotation

4.3.5   HOMOGENEOUS COORDINATES AND MATRICES

The above formulas for computing two-dimensional transformations can be represented in a uniform way with 3×3 matrices. Although they map two-dimensional space into two-dimensional space, 2×2 matrices cannot describe all three transformations; translation is impossible through a 2×2 matrix. We can get a uniform matrix formalism if we define *homogeneous coordinates*. (Although it is possible to attach some geometric meaning to homogeneous coordinates, it is sufficient to consider them simply as a formalism that does the job.)

We can represent a point with a Cartesian description as $(x\ y)$, or we can use homogenous coordinates to represent it as $(x\ y\ 1)$ (note the 1 at the end). We consider all homogeneous coordinates $(w*x\ w*y\ w)$ for every value of $w \neq 0$ as identical to $(x\ y\ 1)$. (Note that we have normalized this last vector by dividing by w.)

Using normalized homogeneous coordinates and matrices, the transformation equations become:

$$\text{Translation by } (T_x, T_y): \qquad \begin{pmatrix} x_T & y_T & 1 \end{pmatrix} = \begin{pmatrix} x & y & 1 \end{pmatrix} \begin{pmatrix} 1 & 0 & 0 \\ 0 & 1 & 0 \\ T_x & T_y & 1 \end{pmatrix}$$

Scaling by (S_x, S_y): $(x_S \quad y_S \quad 1) = (x \quad y \quad 1) \begin{pmatrix} S_x & 0 & 0 \\ 0 & S_y & 0 \\ 0 & 0 & 1 \end{pmatrix}$

Rotation by ϕ: $(x_R \quad y_R \quad 1) = (x \quad y \quad 1) \begin{pmatrix} \cos\phi & \sin\phi & 0 \\ -\sin\phi & \cos\phi & 0 \\ 0 & 0 & 1 \end{pmatrix}$

Multiplying a normalized, homogeneous vector by any of the matrices shown will always yield a normalized, homogeneous vector; that is, a vector with a 1 at the end. We can discard the 1 from the result.

We concatenate transformations by multiplying the corresponding matrices in the order in which we want the transformations to occur. The resulting matrix expresses the overall transformation. This formalism has some advantage, no matter how many 3×3 matrices we multiply with each other, the result is always a 3×3 matrix.

Suppose we have an object consisting of 200 vertices, which we will rotate around a point other than the origin, then translate, then scale about its center, then rotate about some other point, and so on. If we first express all transformations by homogeneous matrices and multiply them into the overall matrix, we can then simply subject each vertex to one multiplication with this matrix and save computation time. Multiplying a vertex by the overall matrix requires roughly the same amount of computation as multiplying the vertex by any one of the simple transformation matrices. If we do not use our matrix formalism, we must do many more computations.

Our matrix formalism is very efficient. No matter how many matrices of the form

$$\begin{pmatrix} a & b & 0 \\ c & d & 0 \\ e & f & 1 \end{pmatrix}$$

we multiply, the resulting matrix will always have the vector $(0 \quad 0 \quad 1)^T$ in its rightmost column. Multiplying a point $(x \quad y \quad 1)$ by this matrix will require a maximum of four multiplications and four additions.

The column $(0 \quad 0 \quad 1)$ on the right is redundant and can be left out when specifying such a matrix. For example, in the PostScript language, transformations are specified by six numbers which represent the first two columns of the transformation matrix.

The noncommutativity of the transformation order corresponds to the noncommutativity of matrix multiplication.

SUGGESTED READINGS

Windowing and clipping, including nonrectangular windows, are described in great detail in FVFH90. Articles on individual subjects are NILN87 (an improvement of the Cohen-Sutherland algorithm), LIBA83 (a parametric polygon clipping algorithm), and WEIL80 (an algorithm for clipping arbitrary polygons against other arbitrary polygons).

EXERCISES

SECTION 4.2.1

1. Draw by hand two different lines that produce a worst case window crossing for the checking order left-top-right-bottom.
2. Repeat Exercise 1, but use the checking order right-top-bottom-left.

SECTION 4.2.2

Use Figures 4.53 through 4.58 for Exercises 3 through 8. Clip the given polygons against the window boundaries in the order $L R B T$ by applying the clipping pipe as shown in the text. First, run the clipping pipe and use the generated valid "last points"; then run it a second time. In simple cases, two runs do not seem necessary, but in complicated cases a single run will not be enough. Can you tell in advance when two runs will be required?

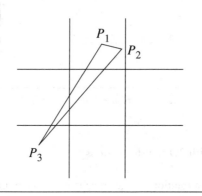

Figure 4.53   Exercise 3

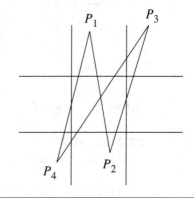

Figure 4.54   Exercise 4

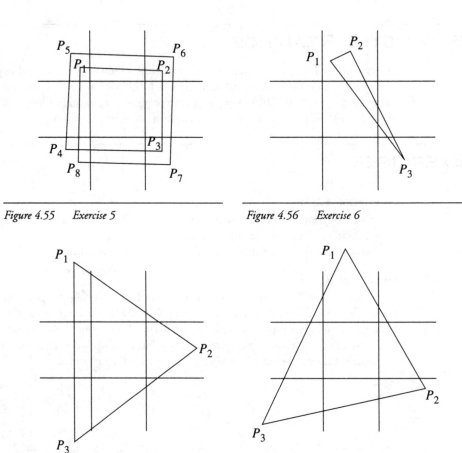

Figure 4.55   Exercise 5

Figure 4.56   Exercise 6

Figure 4.57   Exercise 7

Figure 4.58   Exercise 8

SECTION 4.3

Exercises 9 through 26 deal with 2D transformations.

9. Find the matrix that expresses a rotation by the angle ϕ about the point $(c_x \ c_y)$.
10. Find the matrix that expresses scaling by (S_x, S_y) relative to the point $(c_x \ c_y)$.
11. Find the matrix that magnifies the triangle $A = (1 \ 1)$, $B = (2 \ 2)$, $C = (4 \ -1)$ by the factor 2, while keeping the vertex B fixed.
12. Find the matrix for reflection about the x-axis.
13. Find the matrix for reflection about the y-axis.
14. Compose the reflection about an arbitrary line from translation, rotation, and reflection about the x-axis or y-axis. Let the arbitrary line have an angle θ with the x-axis and intersect the y-axis at $(0 \ b)$.
15. Find the numerical (not in general form) matrix for reflection about the line $y = 0.8x + 2$.

16. Show that the matrix expressing the concatenation of rotation by α followed by a second rotation by β equals the matrix for the rotation by $\alpha + \beta$.

17. Prove that the transformation of the straight line from point P_1 to point P_2 is identical to the straight line between the transformations of P_1 and P_2.

In Exercises 18 through 24, use homogeneous matrices.

18. Compute the composite transformation matrix for the following transformations in the given order:

> translate by (–2,1)
> rotate by 70°
> translate by (2,3)

19. Write the functions
```
void acc_translate(double tx,double ty) ;
void acc_rotate(double alpha) ;
void acc_scale(double sx,double sy) ;
```
that accumulate the specified two-dimensional transformations into a global matrix `tmatrix`.

20. Instead of performing each transformation separately, we compute a composite matrix and use that. What is the advantage?

21. Show analytically that translation followed by scaling is different from scaling followed by translation. Show it by multiplying a general scaling matrix and a general translation matrix in different orders to obtain different results.

22. Show analytically through matrix multiplication that when only translations are performed, their order is insignificant.

23. Repeat Exercise 22 for scaling.

24. Repeat Exercise 22 for rotation.

25. The essential characteristic of a nonlinear transformation is that straight lines are not necessarily transformed into straight lines. Draw the house front specified by the following five points:

> (–0.40 –0.4)
> (0.70 –0.4)
> (0.70   0.2)
> (0.15   1.0)
> (–0.40   0.2)

Then transform with:

$$x_t = \frac{x}{2} + \frac{x*x}{1.8} + \frac{y}{5} + 0.3$$

$$y_t = \frac{y}{2} + \frac{y*x}{1.7} + 0.3$$

If we perform this transformation on the five vertices only and connect the transformed vertices with straight lines, we do not obtain the correct transformation of the whole object. We must transform the lines connecting the vertices individually by transforming as many individual points on them as possible and connecting these with straight lines. This only approximates the transformation, but we do not need to be more precise than the pixel resolution. Write code that transforms and draws the given house. Observe that the transformed lines are not straight.

26. Implement the member function `virtual prim_t& scale(const point_t&)` for all 2D primitives derived from `prim_t`. You have to add a virtual prototype to the class `prim_t`.

5

THREE-
DIMENSIONAL
TECHNIQUES

Chapter 5 introduces a three-dimensional coordinate system, covers transformations of 3D objects, the display of 3D objects on a 2D screen, and 3D windowing and clipping.

5.0   **Introduction** introduces a three-dimensional coordinate system.

5.1   **Three-Dimensional Transformations** uses homogenous coordinates to extend the 2D formulas to the 3D case.

5.2   **Projections** shows that there are several ways to project an object's points onto the screen.

5.3   **The View Transformation** permits the display of a 3D object as it would appear when viewed from an arbitrary point in space. This requires the graphics system to do transformations before projecting.

5.4   **Three-Dimensional Windowing and Clipping** extends the concepts of Chapter 4 to three dimensions. This permits the projection of a portion of a 3D scene onto a 2D viewport. As you might expect, this is more complex.

5.0   INTRODUCTION

In this chapter we introduce a three-dimensional Cartesian coordinate system. It uses the three coordinate axes x, y, and z. In computer graphics we align the $(x\ y)$-plane with the screen. Now it is important to recognize that there are two different orientations for the z-coordinate axis. A right-handed system (rhs) has the z-axis pointing toward the viewer. A left-handed system (lhs) has the z-axis pointing away from the viewer. In this book, if we do not explicitly state otherwise, we will use lhs, because it is more natural; it makes objects that are farther away have larger positive z-coordinates. (We will make emphatically clear the few times that we depart from this.) Not all textbooks agree to use a left-handed system.

Figure 5.1 explains why we call it a left-handed system. You can orient your left hand as shown, but, try as you will, you cannot align the fingers of your right hand with your thumb pointing toward +x, your forefinger pointing toward +y, and your middle finger pointing toward +z. You can align the fingers of your right hand in this order only with a right-handed system.

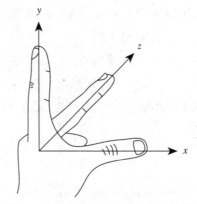

Figure 5.1   *Alignment of the left-hand thumb and fingers in a left-handed system*

5.1   THREE-DIMENSIONAL TRANSFORMATIONS

We consider five transformations of an object in space. The first two, translation and scaling, are simple extensions of the two-dimensional transformations. The other three transformations are rotations in space, one for each coordinate axis. They have no real counterpart in two dimensions, but they are not conceptually difficult. It is somewhat more difficult to combine these three rotations to obtain a rotation about an arbitrary axis in space.

The only object in space which we shall transform is a point. Of course, in any application, entire objects are transformed. However, if an object has a polygonal surface (it consists of points connected by straight lines), we can transform it by transforming all its vertices and connecting them with straight lines. The property that allows us to transform an object in this way is the transformation's linearity, as we explained in Section 4.3. All the spatial transformations considered here have this property. Nonlinear transformations are seldom used in computer graphics.

5.1.1   TRANSLATION

Translation in space is similar to translation in the plane, except now there is one more direction, the one parallel to the z-axis. Translating shifts a point by any amount in space and shifts an object parallel to its first position by a given amount. The shift can be considered as a composite of shifts in the x-direction, y-direction, and z-direction. We use T_x, T_y, and T_z to represent these separate shifts. The translation of the point $(x \;\; y \;\; z)$ into the point $(x_T \;\; y_T \;\; z_T)$ is expressed with the formulas:

$$x_T = x + T_x$$
$$y_T = y + T_y$$
$$z_T = z + T_z$$

Translation is the only transformation that does not depend on any reference point.

In matrix notation, using normalized homogeneous coordinates, we translate with:

$$(x_T \;\; y_T \;\; z_T \;\; 1) = (x \;\; y \;\; z \;\; 1) \begin{pmatrix} 1 & 0 & 0 & 0 \\ 0 & 1 & 0 & 0 \\ 0 & 0 & 1 & 0 \\ T_x & T_y & T_z & 1 \end{pmatrix}$$

The translation is implemented as the member function `prim_t& translate()` in every 3D primitive derived from `prim_t` (in particular: tmeshes and other polygon meshes).

5.1.2   SCALING

Scaling in space is essentially identical to scaling in the plane; the formulas are the same with one more coordinate added. The scaling transformation relocates a point with relation to the origin. When we scale an entire object, it shrinks or enlarges in its x-, y-, or z-dimension. We use S_x, S_y, and S_z to represent the scaling factors for the three dimensions. If $S_x = S_y = S_z$, the object simply changes size. Factors < 1 shrink the object, while factors > 1 enlarge it. We scale a point (x y z) by computing:

$$x_s = x*S_x \qquad y_s = y*S_y \qquad z_s = z*S_z$$

Using matrix notation and homogeneous coordinates:

$$(x_s \quad y_s \quad z_s \quad 1) = (x \quad y \quad z \quad 1) \begin{pmatrix} S_x & 0 & 0 & 0 \\ 0 & S_y & 0 & 0 \\ 0 & 0 & S_z & 0 \\ 0 & 0 & 0 & 1 \end{pmatrix}$$

The formulas above are for scaling with reference to the origin. When we scale an object, its distance from the origin changes. For example, enlarging an object by a factor of 2 in all coordinates will also double its distance from the origin.

The most frequent application of scaling is to change an object's size. In this case, we scale with $S_x = S_y = S_z$. More importantly, we must consider the reference point for scaling, or else the movement away from its original place may surprise us. To change only the size and not the location, we must make three transformations: a translation that puts the object's center at the origin, the scaling, and then a translation to relocate the center at its former location. The "center" of an object is hard to define formally, but we must specify it. What we mean by the center (to which scaling is relative) is a point in the object that does not move when the object grows or shrinks. After all, if an object changes in size, all points but one (the center) must move, and these moves are relative to that center.

This idea will become clearer as the discussion continues.

If the center of the object is (c_x c_y c_z), we change the size by performing the transformations in this order:

> translate ($T_{-cx}, T_{-cy}, T_{-cz}$)
> scale (S_x, S_y, S_z)
> translate (T_{cx}, T_{cy}, T_{cz})

Scaling is not implemented in the provided codes, but is very simple and the reader is invited to add the function `prim_t& scale()` to all 3D primitives derived from `prim_t`. Scaling should be done about the centroid of the primitive.

5.1.3   ROTATION

Rotation in space is essentially different from rotation in two dimensions, because it takes three numbers to specify an arbitrary spatial rotation. First, let us specify rotations about the coordinate axes.

The rotations about the x-axis, the y-axis, and the z-axis are each independent of the others. However, we can combine these three to obtain rotation about any arbitrary line in space. (We say "line" instead of "axis" to avoid confusion with the coordinate axes.) For more about this, refer to EKPE93.

When we think of rotation, it is always about an axis, and it can be in either of two directions—counterclockwise (ccw) or clockwise (cw). For rotation in the plane, the axis of rotation is an imaginary one, perpendicular to the plane and through the origin. This rotation axis could correspond to a z-axis that points toward us, giving a right-handed system (rhs). The rotation from positive x-axis to positive y-axis would be ccw.

ROTATION ABOUT THE X-AXIS

With our lhs convention, rotating a point clockwise (cw) by the angle ϕ about the x-axis (looking from the positive x-axis toward the origin) will move a point on the positive y-axis in an arc toward the positive z-axis. For any point, the new coordinates become:

$$x_{Rx} = x$$
$$y_{Rx} = y\cos\phi - z\sin\phi$$
$$z_{Rx} = y\sin\phi + z\cos\phi$$

In matrix notation with homogeneous coordinates:

$$\begin{pmatrix} x_{Rx} & y_{Rx} & z_{Rx} & 1 \end{pmatrix} = \begin{pmatrix} x & y & z & 1 \end{pmatrix} \begin{pmatrix} 1 & 0 & 0 & 0 \\ 0 & \cos\phi & \sin\phi & 0 \\ 0 & -\sin\phi & \cos\phi & 0 \\ 0 & 0 & 0 & 1 \end{pmatrix}$$

ROTATION ABOUT THE Y-AXIS

Rotating a point on the x-axis ccw by the angle ϕ about the y-axis (looking from the positive y-axis toward the origin) will move the point in an arc toward the positive z-axis. Note carefully that the sense of the rotation is ccw instead of cw, which we used for x-axis rotation. For any point, the new coordinates become:

$$x_{Ry} = x\cos\phi - z\sin\phi$$
$$y_{Ry} = y$$
$$z_{Ry} = x\sin\phi + z\cos\phi$$

In matrix notation with homogeneous coordinates:

$$\begin{pmatrix} x_{Ry} & y_{Ry} & z_{Ry} & 1 \end{pmatrix} = \begin{pmatrix} x & y & z & 1 \end{pmatrix} \begin{pmatrix} \cos\phi & 0 & \sin\phi & 0 \\ 0 & 1 & 0 & 0 \\ -\sin\phi & 0 & \cos\phi & 0 \\ 0 & 0 & 0 & 1 \end{pmatrix}$$

ROTATION ABOUT THE Z-AXIS

The cw rotation of a point on the positive x-axis by the angle ϕ about the z-axis (when we look from the positive z-axis toward the origin) will move the point in an arc toward the positive y-axis. (Remember that we are using a left-handed system!) For any point, the new coordinates become:

$$x_{Rz} = x\cos\phi - y\sin\phi$$

$$y_{Rz} = x\sin\phi + y\cos\phi$$

$$z_{Rz} = z$$

In matrix notation with homogeneous coordinates:

$$\begin{pmatrix} x_{Rz} & y_{Rz} & z_{Rz} & 1 \end{pmatrix} = \begin{pmatrix} x & y & z & 1 \end{pmatrix} \begin{pmatrix} \cos\phi & \sin\phi & 0 & 0 \\ -\sin\phi & \cos\phi & 0 & 0 \\ 0 & 0 & 1 & 0 \\ 0 & 0 & 0 & 1 \end{pmatrix}$$

If you do any of these rotations in the opposite direction—clockwise rather than counter-clockwise, or vice versa—then you must swap the minus sign between the $\sin\phi$ terms, from the lower left $\sin\phi$ to the upper right $\sin\phi$. Also, if we specify the sense of the rotation while looking toward the origin from the negative end of the axis of rotation, then the meaning of cw and ccw reverses. Changing the direction of the z-axis to make the system right-handed also reverses the meaning of cw and ccw.

All rotations are implemented as the member functions `prim_t& rotx()`, `prim_t& roty()`, and `prim_t& rotz()` in all 3D primitives derived from `prim_t`.

A TRICK FOR SPATIAL ROTATIONS

Because the sense of the three rotations is not the same, it is easy to become confused. However, one little trick can help. We can reduce the above rotation matrices to

$$\begin{pmatrix} \cos\phi & \sin\phi \\ -\sin\phi & \cos\phi \end{pmatrix}$$

by chopping out the rows and columns with a 1 in the diagonal. The *axis* of rotation is x or y or z, depending on whether we have removed the first, second, or third row and column. We obtain the *direction* of rotation by writing down $x+ y+ z+$ in this order and then removing the letter corresponding to the rotation axis. The remaining two letters specify the direction the first positive axis turns into the second. For example:

$$\begin{pmatrix} 1 & 0 & 0 & 0 \\ 0 & \cos\phi & \sin\phi & 0 \\ 0 & -\sin\phi & \cos\phi & 0 \\ 0 & 0 & 0 & 1 \end{pmatrix}$$

is reduced by chopping out row and column of the *x*-axis (and the "homogeneous" row and column). Removing x from the letters $x+ y+ z+$ gives $y+ z+$, so the rotation direction is from the positive *y*-axis to the positive *z*-axis on the shortest way. Watch the minus sign of the sin function. It must be at the lower left. If it is on the upper right, the direction is reversed.

This lets us find the direction independent of left-handed or right-handed systems, independent of clockwise or counterclockwise, and independent of the end from which we look along the rotation axis.

We can use the reverse of this rule for writing down a homogeneous 4×4 rotation matrix, which rotates about a given axis in a certain direction. For example, we obtain the rotation about y from $x+$ to $z+$ by starting with the 2×2 schematic of sin and cos values and inserting a third row and column of all zeroes, except for a 1 where they cross. We also insert the "homogeneous" row and column to obtain:

$$\begin{pmatrix} \cos\phi & 0 & \sin\phi & 0 \\ 0 & 1 & 0 & 0 \\ -\sin\phi & 0 & \cos\phi & 0 \\ 0 & 0 & 0 & 1 \end{pmatrix}$$

5.2 PROJECTIONS

All graphic display media are two-dimensional: a CRT screen, the plot from a plotter, or the printout from a printer. We will base our explanations on a CRT, as there is really no difference in any of them. When we display a three-dimensional object, we have to *project* it, or flatten the three-dimensional representation onto the two-dimensional medium.

A projection can be compared to the shadow an object casts onto a wall. The mathematical model we use to calculate these projections is simpler than what actually happens with shadows. In computer graphics, both the "object" and the "wall" where it casts a shadow are imaginary. We calculate the projections of all the object's points, some of which would be invisible in a real shadow cast by the object. While we might be surpassing nature, removing these extraneous points would give us great trouble.

Let us distinguish between object space and image space. *Object space* is the three-dimensional space in which the object is defined; we can think of this space as the real world. *Image space* is a two-dimensional space onto which the object is projected; we could conceive of this space as the wall, but it is better to think of it as the display screen.

Strictly speaking, an object is projected by projecting each of its points. As there are infinitely many points in an object, we cannot produce a projection in this way. However, straight lines in all the projections we will consider are projected into straight lines. This has many benefits. The most important is that we can project a straight line by projecting the line's two end points in object space, and then connect the two projected points with a straight line in image space.

We will consider parallel projection, perspective projection, and perspective depth transformation.

5.2.1 PARALLEL PROJECTION

Parallel projection simulates the shadow cast onto a flat wall by a light source that is infinitely far away. (The sun is far enough away to approximate this.) We obtain the parallel projection of a point $(x \; y \; z)$ in object space by drawing a line through this point with a certain direction $(x_p \; y_p \; z_p)$ in space. (By "direction" we mean lines parallel to the vector $(x_p \; y_p \; z_p)$). This line is called the *projection vector*. The point where this line intersects the plane $z = 0$ is the parallel projection of the given point; it has the coordinates (x_{pl} y_{pl} 0). The angle of the projection vector within the coordinate system determines where the projection lies on the screen, which is the (x y)-plane.

We represent the line (the projection vector) in parametric form:

$$x_u = x + u * x_p \qquad y_u = y + u * y_p \qquad z_u = z + u * z_p$$

In these equations (x_u y_u z_u) is any point on the projection vector determined by the value of u. For $u = 0$, we have the point (x y z) itself, so the line does go through the point. All points in the (x y)-plane have a z-coordinate of 0, so by setting z_u equal to 0 we obtain $0 = z + u * z_p$. From this it follows that $u = -z/z_p$ at the intersection point. The coordinates of the intersection point are then:

$$x_{pl} = x - \frac{z}{z_p} x_p$$

$$y_{pl} = y - \frac{z}{z_p} y_p$$

$$z_{pl} = 0$$

These general formulas give the coordinates for projected points for any angle of the projection vector. When that angle is specified, we know x_p, y_p, and z_p and we can solve for the unknown x- and y-coordinates of the projected point.

If the projection vector is normal to the projection plane, the projection is called *orthographic*. As we use the (x y)-plane where $z = 0$ as the projection plane, the projection is orthographic if the projection vector is parallel to the z-axis. That means that the projection vector is (0 0 −1); its x- and y-components are 0. The value for the z-coordinate means that it points towards us. The length is arbitrary, of course; here we let it be 1.

The formulas yield:

$$x_{ort} = x \qquad y_{ort} = y \qquad z_{ort} = 0$$

We obtain this projection by setting the z-coordinate to 0 so no calculations are necessary. In many cases, this projection is a good approximation of the actual projections that the human eye makes in the real world.

Three separate orthographic projections are often used in engineering drawings to produce the front, side, and top views of an object. The front and side views are called *elevations*; the top view is called the *plan*. Our discussion below considers only projections onto the (x y)-plane.

While orthographic projections do not change the length of lines parallel to the projection plane, other lines are projected with a reduced length.

Figure 5.2 shows the orthographic projection of a house onto the plane $z = 0$, which is represented by the screen. Points in the object space with the same x- and y-coordinates are projected onto the same point on the screen. The projection lines are shown parallel to the z-axis.

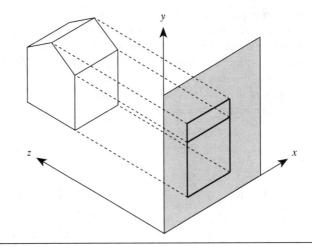

Figure 5.2   Orthographic projection

If the projection vector is not parallel to the z-axis, we have an *oblique projection*. Such a projection appears in nature when sunlight casts shadows on the ground. We use this projection to draw shadows in pictures, but not to display the objects themselves (except in special applications—see below) because it produces unnatural-looking distortions. Some distortions are not unnatural, but this one is, because it does not correspond to the way objects in the real world are projected into the human eye.

Formally, a parallel projection onto the $(x\ y)$-plane is oblique if the projection vector has nonzero x- and y-components. For the projected point, the above general formulas yield:

$$x_{obl} = x - \frac{z}{z_p} x_p$$

$$y_{obl} = y - \frac{z}{z_p} y_p$$

$$z_{obl} = 0$$

Two conditions must be specified before we know the direction of the projection vector. One is the angle it makes with the z-axis. The projection of a line parallel to the z-axis will be at some angle α with the horizontal on the projection plane. We can determine this from $\tan\alpha = y_p/x_p$. This angle is the second condition that we use to obtain the projection vector, as we will see below.

A special case of oblique projection is called *cavalier projection*. This occurs when the projection vector forms an angle of 45° with the z-axis. This means that:

$$\frac{x_p^2 + y_p^2}{z_p^2} = 1$$

A cavalier projection projects lines parallel to the z-axis with unaltered length.

We still must use the second condition to specify the direction of the projection vector fully.

As an example, let us find the projection vector for a cavalier projection of a cube so that the edges parallel to the z-axis create lines at an angle of 45° with the horizontal. We set $z_p = -1$ arbitrarily. From tan 45° = 1, it follows that $x_p = y_p$. We have $x_p^2 + y_p^2 = 1$, so we get (.707 .707 −1) for the projection vector. The sketch at the left in Figure 5.3 shows the cube looking down the y-axis toward the origin in a left-handed system. The sketch at the right is its projection onto the plane $z = 0$ with this projection vector (hidden lines are not shown). There is a distortion, making the cube look like an elongated parallelepiped.

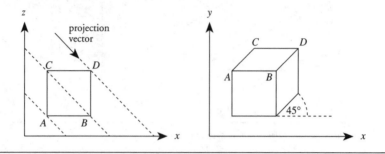

Figure 5.3   *Cavalier projection*

Another special case is called *cabinet projection*. It uses a projection vector that forms an angle of approximately 26.6° with the z-axis, or:

$$\frac{x_p^2 + y_p^2}{z_p^2} = \frac{1}{4}$$

A cabinet projection projects lines parallel to the z-axis with one-half their original length.

For the same cube as in the previous example, we will find the projection vector for a cabinet projection so that the edges parallel to the z-axis result in lines at an angle of 30° with the horizontal. We set $z_p = -1$; we also have tan 30° = 0.577. It follows that $0.577x_p = y_p$ or $0.333x_p^2 = y_p^2$, and we have $x_p^2 + y_p^2 = 1/4$, so $1.333x_p^2 = 0.25$. From this, we have $x_p = 0.433$. The projection vector is (.433 .25 −1).

The left drawing in Figure 5.4 shows our view of the cube as we look down the y-axis toward the origin in a left-handed system. On the right is its projection onto the plane $z = 0$ with this projection vector (hidden lines are not shown). This projection produces a much more realistic-looking image than the cavalier projection.

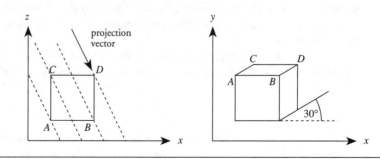

Figure 5.4   *Cabinet projection*

5.2.2   PERSPECTIVE PROJECTION

Perspective projection is the preferred method because it comes closest to the way real-world objects are projected into the human eye. This projection technique is important, not only in computer graphics, but also in most pictures and drawings. In the real world, objects that are farther away appear smaller. Perspective projection preserves this property. First, we need a center of projection. In the real world, this center is the human eye. In computer graphics, it is basically the same.

In what follows, the word "center" stands for the center of projection. We compute the projection for some assumed position of the center, a point in front of the screen. This point will be specified in the same coordinate system that we use in object space to describe the object. It has no relation to the user's real physical distance from the screen. We assume the screen itself to be in the plane $z = 0$ of the coordinate system. The distance of the center of projection from the plane $z = 0$ (the screen) is called d (and this will be specified as a positive value). We assume that the coordinates of the center of projection are $(0\ \ 0\ \ -d)$, where $d > 0$; that is, the center lies on the negative z-axis. With these assumptions, the computations are simple.

The *projection* of a point is the intersection of the straight line from that point to the center with the plane $z = 0$. Figure 5.5 shows the side view of the projection of the point $(x\ \ y\ \ z)$, which gives the point $(x_{ps}\ \ y_{ps})$. Through similar triangles we obtain $y_{ps} = d*y/(d + z)$ and $x_{ps} = d*x/(d + z)$. The coordinates of the projection are:

$$x_{ps} = \frac{d*x}{d + z}$$

$$y_{ps} = \frac{d*y}{d + z}$$

$$z_{ps} = 0$$

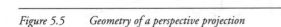

Figure 5.5   Geometry of a perspective projection

The assumptions that the center is on the z-axis and that the plane of projection is at $z = 0$ are not restricting, because we can obtain the formulas for a perspective projection with another center and onto another plane by adding a translation. It is essential, however, that the plane onto which we project be normal to the z-axis so that we have simple formulas.

Figure 5.6 shows a prism, the projection plane, the center, and the projection of the prism. This is a visual explanation of the process.

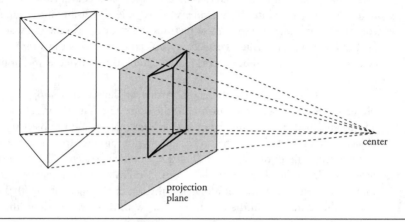

Figure 5.6   Spatial view of a perspective projection

We consider the screen to be a part of the projection plane. The rectangular region of the screen within which we want to display an image is a viewport. If we want to know which part of the object space we can project into the viewport, we have to draw lines from the center of projection through the four corners of the viewport. These lines will become the edges of the so-called *viewing pyramid.* The projection center is the top vertex of this pyramid. Everything within the viewing pyramid will be visible (unless depth clipping is performed) and everything outside will be invisible. The viewing pyramid is also called the *view volume* in the case of a perspective projection. Figure 5.7 shows a viewing pyramid. The rectangle in the figure is the viewport (usually the screen). The coordinate origin is the center of the rectangle.

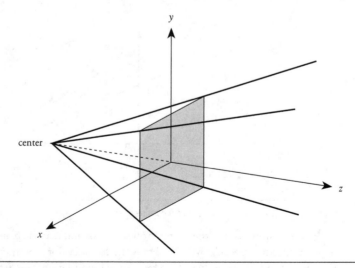

Figure 5.7   Viewing pyramid

5.2.3   PERSPECTIVE DEPTH TRANSFORMATION

Sometimes we need to do more than just project perspectively. A *perspective depth transformation* not only does a perspective projection, but also preserves depth information. It transforms every point in object space into a point in image space, but we now understand image space to be three-dimensional. This seems to be a contradiction in terms and there really is something artificial about it. However, it is very useful for algorithms that require not only an object point's projection, but also its distance from the projection plane. Some algorithms that use it include Warnock's algorithm, Z-buffer, and depth-sorting methods.

In this projection, the image space is augmented to a three-dimensional space. The x_{ps} and y_{ps} coordinates of a transformed point specify the location of a perspective projection of this point into a two-dimensional image space, exactly as above. The transformation also calculates a z_{ps} coordinate, which is not set to 0. The interpretation of the x_{ps} and y_{ps} coordinates does not change. The purpose of all this is to save the depth information of the original object point. The perspective projection of a point, then, is obtained by ignoring the z_{ps} coordinate.

If we chose $x_{ps} = d*x/(d + z)$, $y_{ps} = d*y/(d + z)$, and simply $z_{ps} = z$, we would keep the depth information. However, this is a bad choice because such a transformation does not transform straight lines into straight lines!

Therefore, algorithms that obtain their depth information from the image space coordinates would be incorrect. Objects are usually described by vertices in space connected by either straight lines or planar polygons. A nonlinear transformation does not allow us to change such an object by transforming all its vertices into image space and connecting the new transformed vertices with straight lines or polygons.

Figure 5.8 shows what can happen when we set z_{ps} equal to z. A point or small object B is behind a planar surface, which is shown in cross section; A and C are points in that surface. The transformed points are A', B', and C'. To determine if B' is in front of or behind the surface $A'C'$, the algorithm computes the depth of the surface at the point $(x\ y)$ on the screen onto which B is projected. Since it computes this depth as if $A'C'$ were a plane (which is not true), it obtains a wrong value. Observe that the relative depths of the projected points put B' on the wrong side of the surface if the original z-values are used.

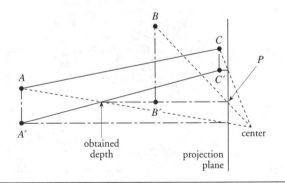

Figure 5.8   *Effect of a nonlinear depth transformation*

The explanation for the error is that the transformed surface $A'C'$ is not planar, but curved. It actually passes between B' and the projection plane, but this is not apparent from the original z-values.

The correct definition of z_{ps} is $z_{ps} = z/(z + d)$ (for further analysis see NESP79, p. 356). If $ps(P)$ denotes the transformation of a point P, and α and β are constants, then

$$ps(\alpha P_1 + \beta P_2) \neq \alpha ps(P_1) + \beta ps(P_2)$$

That is, we do not have functional linearity, but we have geometric linearity as described in Section 4.3. To show this requires lengthy calculations, which we will not do, although the exercises hint at how to prove this.

A correct perspective depth transformation consists of:

$$x_{ps} = \frac{d*x}{d+z}$$

$$y_{ps} = \frac{d*y}{d+z}$$

$$z_{ps} = \frac{z}{d+z}$$

This preserves the relative depth of points in the object. By this, we mean that even though the depth values in image and object space change, their relative order will be preserved. We can easily show this. If $z_1 < z_2$, it follows that $z_1/(z_1 + d) < z_2/(z_2 + d)$. In other words, a point with larger z-coordinate in object space will have a larger z-coordinate in image space.

Let us look at some properties of this transformation. If we have a left-handed system and assume all objects to be "behind" the screen (in the area of positive z-coordinates), then the

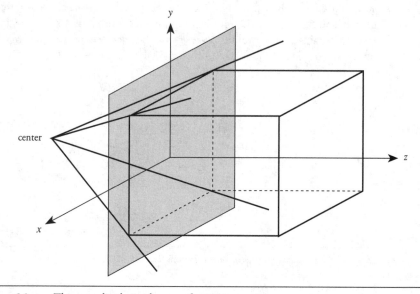

Figure 5.9   The normalized view box transformation

z-coordinates of transformed points are all between 0 and 1. (We could choose a different formula for obtaining z_{ps} in order to give the z_{ps} values a range different from 0–1, but this one is the most convenient.) All points in object space that lie on a ray emanating from the projection center are transformed onto a line parallel to the z-axis and bounded by 0 and 1, because of the definition of z_{ps}. It follows that the viewing pyramid behind the screen is transformed into a rectangular box, called the *view box*, which is bounded by the viewport on the projection plane and whose depth is 1 (see Figure 5.9). All objects in the viewing pyramid will be transformed into that box. We can obtain their perspective projections by performing an orthographic projection from the box onto the projection plane. This perspective depth transformation is often called a *normalized view box transformation* (normalized because of the 0–1 range of the z_{ps} coordinate).

5.3   THE VIEW TRANSFORMATION

Once an object has been been specified in space, the graphics system should be able to produce any view of it. If we want to see it from the side or from behind, the system should be able to compute how the object would look from such a viewpoint and display the appropriate image. We will explain the mathematics necessary for these computations later in this section.

Let us first think about the interaction with the system needed to achieve such transformations. To see an object from the side, we could rotate it around the y-axis by 90 degrees; this is easy to imagine. To see it from a point to the side and somewhat above the object, we could first rotate it about the y-axis by 90 degrees and then about the x-axis by a few degrees. Alternately, we could first rotate it around the z-axis by a few degrees and then around the y-axis by 90 degrees. In a more general case, however, it would be quite hard to imagine the angles, rotation sequences, and directions necessary to produce the desired view. The point of this discussion is to show that specifying rotation angles is not a user-friendly approach.

The most natural way of specifying a view is to define the point in space from which the object should be viewed and let the system automatically derive all parameters for the transformations. We develop this below by slightly modifying the approach that Steve Cunningham presented in CUNN90.

The point in space from which we want to see the object is the eyepoint E. Imagine that we place ourselves at the *eyepoint* and put a screen in front of us, aiming it toward the object as if it were a camera. The precise point at which we aim our view is the *view reference point*, R, which we have also specified. We sit directly in front of this screen and look through it at the object. The center of the screen is called O (origin). The direction in which we look at the object, or our *viewing direction*, is the vector N, which is derived as $R - E$ or $R - O$. The screen must be normal to N (see Figure 5.10). (The difference between this approach and the one in GGEM90 is that the viewing direction N points toward R, rather than toward our eye; we think this is more natural.)

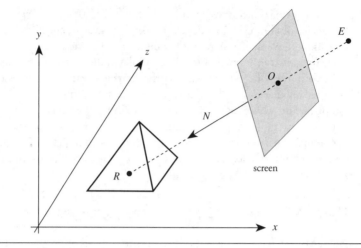

Figure 5.10   The parameters for a view transformation

Imagine a coordinate system with its origin in the center of the screen at O, its x-axis pointing to the right in the screen, its y-axis pointing up in the screen, and its z-axis identical with the viewing direction N. The $(x\ y)$-plane of this system, where $z = 0$, is the view plane. The viewing direction N is normal to the view plane. We can think of the screen as being embedded in the view plane. From now on, we will talk of the view plane, rather than the screen.

Whether we let the user specify the point O or the point E is immaterial because the points E, O, and R are collinear; one can easily derive O from E and vice versa. The transformation algorithm can be designed in either way. The distance from O to E is the perspective projection distance and should be kept constant, no matter where one places O (or E). In our system, the user specifies the point O. The algorithm will find E, provided we give a certain perspective distance. (The distance OE is insignificant for the view plane transformation. It influences only the perspective projection.)

The two points O and R cannot uniquely specify the new coordinate system; they only fix its z-axis. One of the other two axes must be fixed to have an unambiguous specification of the view plane system. Therefore, we let the user specify a *view-up* direction in order to fix the y-axis. However, the user should not have to tell the direction of the new y-axis precisely. This would require finding a vector normal to N, so it would be difficult and not user-friendly. We do it differently.

The view-up direction is specified in relation to the object with a vector. (This vector tells where "up" on the object is; this is easy to determine.) The algorithm then uses the projection of this vector onto the view plane as the up direction, which is the y-axis, in the new system. With the y-axis fixed, the view plane system is determined.

Users can specify whatever view-up direction they want. But if they choose the view-up vector parallel to the viewing direction, the new system remains ambiguous. In such a case, our code exits with an error message. Most naturally, the view-up vector should point in the same direction as the top of the user's head.

The transformation that makes an object look as if one sees it from the specified point is called the *view transformation*. We now explain the mathematics behind this.

The user specifies the origin point, the view reference point, and the view-up direction:

$(O_x\ O_y\ O_z)$	view plane origin	(point)
$(R_x\ R_y\ R_z)$	view reference point	(point)
$(V_x\ V_y\ V_z)$	view-up direction	(vector)

First we compute the vector $\mathbf{N} = \mathbf{R} - \mathbf{O}$. Then we normalize it and obtain $\mathbf{Z}$. Then we take the view-up direction $\mathbf{V}$ and tilt it so that it becomes normal to $\mathbf{Z}$. Infinitely many vectors are normal to $\mathbf{Z}$, but we want the one in the plane formed by $\mathbf{Z}$ and $\mathbf{V}$. We obtain this easily with vector addition (see Figure 5.11). It is not necessary to normalize $\mathbf{V}$ for this process. If we draw a vertical to $\mathbf{Z}$ through the end point of $\mathbf{V}$, then the length l of the projection is simply $\mathbf{V}*\cos(\phi)$. (In our example, where $\phi > \pi/2$, l is a negative quantity, so $\mathbf{Z}{\cdot}l$ points in the opposite direction from $\mathbf{Z}$.) If we now multiply $\mathbf{Z}$ by $-l$, we get the vector shown in dark. This vector is added to $\mathbf{V}$ to yield $\mathbf{V}'$, which is normal to $\mathbf{Z}$ in the same plane. We then normalize $\mathbf{V}'$ and obtain $\mathbf{Y}$.

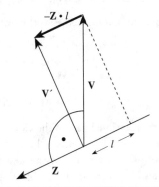

Figure 5.11   Obtaining $\mathbf{V}'$ *from* $\mathbf{V}$ *and* $\mathbf{Z}$

Then we produce the vector $\mathbf{X}$, normal to $\mathbf{Y}$ and $\mathbf{Z}$, by computing the cross product: $\mathbf{X} = \mathbf{Y} \times \mathbf{Z}$. This cross product points to the right in the view plane. (See the cross product explanation in the appendix.)

The three vectors $\mathbf{X}$, $\mathbf{Y}$, and $\mathbf{Z}$ are mutually orthogonal unit vectors, which form an orthonormal basis. They can be interpreted as the x-, y-, and z-axes of the new coordinate system (see Figure 5.12).

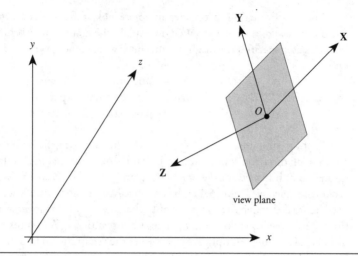

Figure 5.12   The new coordinate system (**X Y Z**)

If we arrange them in a matrix **M** as shown:

$$\mathbf{M} = \begin{pmatrix} X_x & Y_x & Z_x & 0 \\ X_y & Y_y & Z_y & 0 \\ X_z & Y_z & Z_z & 0 \\ 0 & 0 & 0 & 1 \end{pmatrix}$$

then **M** expresses the rotational part of the view transformation from old coordinates into new coordinates, provided that the origins of both systems coincide.

Therefore, we must first translate the new origin O into the origin of the old $(x\ y\ z)$ system. We must also translate all of an object's points in order not to change its position in relation to the new system.

The translation matrix is:

$$\mathbf{T} = \begin{pmatrix} 1 & 0 & 0 & 0 \\ 0 & 1 & 0 & 0 \\ 0 & 0 & 1 & 0 \\ -O_x & -O_y & -O_z & 1 \end{pmatrix}$$

The view transformation matrix **VMAT** is obtained by multiplying **T** by **M**:

$$\mathbf{VMAT} = \mathbf{T} * \mathbf{M}$$

VMAT is interpreted as follows. If we multiply a point $(x\ y\ z)$ in our original coordinate system by **VMAT**, we obtain $(x'\ y'\ z')$:

$$(x\ \ y\ \ z) * \mathbf{VMAT} = (x'\ \ y'\ \ z')$$

Then, $(x'\ y'\ z')$ are the coordinates in the new system of the same point, $(x\ y\ z)$. In other words, $(x\ y\ z)$ expressed in the old system and $(x'\ y'\ z')$ expressed in the new system are physically the same point in space. However, if we display the point $(x'\ y'\ z')$ in our original coordinate system, it will look as we see it in the new system from the new viewpoint! That is precisely what we want.

As we mentioned above, the code exits when the view-up vector is parallel to the viewing direction **N**. When the algorithm attempts to make it orthogonal to **N** it will become 0. Consequently, it cannot be normalized and the normalization routine exits.

OO DESIGN AND CLASS SPECIFICATIONS

Since objects are now specified by three-dimensional coordinates, we introduce the class `point3_t`, derived from the class `point_t`. It has member operators to add, subtract and multiply two 3D points, reusing as much existing code as possible. It has member functions for rotating a point about the x-, y-, or z-axis, translating and normalizing it.

```cpp
//*********************** File point3.h *********************

#ifndef POINT3_T
#define POINT3_T

#include <fstream.h>
#include "../Shape2d/point.h"


class point3_t : virtual public point_t
{
public:
   point3_t() ;
   point3_t(double,double,double) ;
   point3_t(const point_t&,double) ;
   point3_t(const point_t&) ;
   point3_t(const point3_t&) ;

   double givz() const { return z; }
   void   set(const point_t& p) { point_t::set(p); z = p.givz(); }
   void   setz(double z) { this->z = z; }

   point3_t operator +  (const point3_t&) const ;
   point3_t operator += (const point3_t&) ;
   point3_t operator -  (const point3_t&) const ;
   point3_t operator -= (const point3_t&) ;
   double   operator *  (const point3_t&) const ;
   point3_t operator *  (double) const ;
   point3_t operator ^  (const point3_t&) const ;    // cross product
   point3_t operator -  () const ;
   point3_t operator /  (double) const ;
   point3_t operator /= (double) ;
   void     operator =  (const point3_t&) ;
```

```
      virtual void rotx(double) ;
      virtual void roty(double) ;
      virtual void rotz(double) ;
      void translate(const point3_t&) ;
      point3_t normalize() ;

protected:
      double z ;
} ;


point3_t operator *(double,point3_t) ;
void operator >> (ifstream&,point3_t&) ;

#endif

//********************************************************************
```

To represent any 4×4 homogeneous matrix, we specify the class mat43_t. Its only data members are 12 doubles; we do not need to store the fourth column because it is always (0 0 0 1). A default constructor is provided and one which constructs the matrix from 12 doubles. We give it two operators for multiplying the matrix with a point3_t and with a plane_t.

```
//************************* File mat43.h *************************

#ifndef MAT43_T
#define MAT43_T

#include "../Shape3d/point3.h"
#include "../Shape3d/plane.h"


class mat43_t
{
public:
      mat43_t() ;
      mat43_t(double,double,double,
              double,double,double,
              double,double,double,
              double,double,double) ;
      double& operator [] (int i) { return m[i]; }

private:
      double m[12] ;
} ;

point3_t operator * (const point3_t&,mat43_t&) ;
plane_t operator * (const plane_t&,mat43_t&) ;

#endif

//********************************************************************
```

Another class that we specify in this chapter is plane_t, which represents a plane in 3D. We can construct it directly with its four coefficients or from three point3_t in space. We explain this fully in Chapter 10.

```
//************************** File plane.h **************************

#ifndef PLANE_T
#define PLANE_T

#include "../Shape3d/point3.h"


class plane_t
{
public:
    plane_t() ;
    plane_t(const plane_t&) ;
    plane_t(double,double,double,double) ;
    plane_t(const point3_t&,double) ;
    plane_t(const point3_t&,const point3_t&,const point3_t&) ;

    double giva() const { return a; }
    double givb() const { return b; }
    double givc() const { return c; }
    double givd() const { return d; }
    point3_t givnorm() const { return point3_t(a,b,c); }
    int frontface(const point3_t& p) const ; //true if frontface for p
    void rotx(double) ;
    void roty(double) ;
    void rotz(double) ;
    void translate(const point3_t&) ;

protected:
    double a , b , c , d;          // coefficients of the plane equation
} ;

#endif

//****************************************************************
```

5.4 THREE-DIMENSIONAL WINDOWING AND CLIPPING

A 3D window is an extension of a 2D window. Since a 2D window is a rectangular area of our visual perception of the real world, we extend this notion to three dimensions by defining a 3D window in the simplest case as a rectangular box in space. This extension is not very natural, because what we perceive from the real world is always a two-dimensional projection. Our visual system can add the feeling of depth through stereo vision and complicated internal processing, but we do not think in 3D windows.

Our perception of the real world is bounded at the left, right, bottom, and top. Objects can be outside these areas, but then we do not see them. Our perception is bounded at the front only by the physical presence of our perception mechanism; objects can be no closer than 0 units from our eyes. We must consider an object behind us as being outside the left, right, bottom, or top boundary, because we must turn our head to see it. Is not physically possible for an object to be outside the front boundary.

Our perception of distant objects is unbounded. While distant objects may appear too small to make out any details, they are still in our field of view. Hence, there are no bounds to our perception from front to back in the same sense as for left, right, bottom, and top.

For these reasons, a 3D bounding concept is artificial and is not a true generalization of the 2D window concept. We will call a 3D window a *view volume*. View volumes are useful in some computer graphics applications, for example, when we want to display part of a scene that has been defined in 3D space, omitting objects closer than a certain distance or farther away than some other distance.

5.4.1   THREE-DIMENSIONAL WINDOWS AND VIEW VOLUMES

The rectangular view volume must be associated with numbers in certain ranges. We can consider the left-right range as the extent of the x-coordinates, the up-down range as the extent of the y-coordinates, and the front-back range as the extent of the z-coordinates. We require the front plane to be parallel to the view plane, which normally coincides with the screen. (We will use the words *screen* and *view plane* interchangeably.) The view volume's contents will be projected onto the screen, which acts as a 2D window.

Only in the the the simplest case—orthographic projection—is the view volume a rectangular box. The different types of projections create different shapes of view volumes.

ORTHOGRAPHIC PROJECTION

In this case, the view volume is a rectangular box whose front plane is parallel to or coincident with the view plane. Objects within the box are visible when projected orthographically onto the view plane. Figure 5.13 shows an orthographic view volume in spatial view and top view.

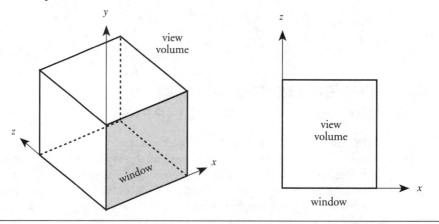

Figure 5.13   Orthographic view volume

OBLIQUE PROJECTION

In this case, the view volume is a slanted parallelepiped. Objects within the view volume are visible when projected obliquely onto the view plane. Figure 5.14 shows an oblique view volume in spatial view and top view.

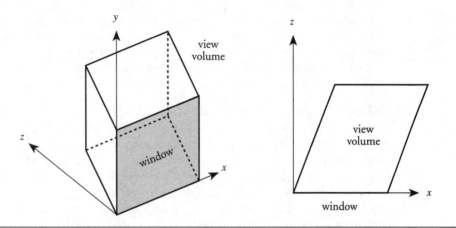

Figure 5.14   Oblique view volume

PERSPECTIVE PROJECTION

We do not deal further with orthographic and oblique view volumes, but only with perspective ones. In this case, the view volume is a truncated pyramid called a *frustum*. The pyramid's apex is the center of projection. The near plane is parallel to the view plane $z = 0$, but must be in front of the center of projection. Objects within the frustum are visible when projected perspectively onto the view plane. The frustum intersects with the view plane at the window. Figure 5.15 shows a perspective view volume in spatial view and top view.

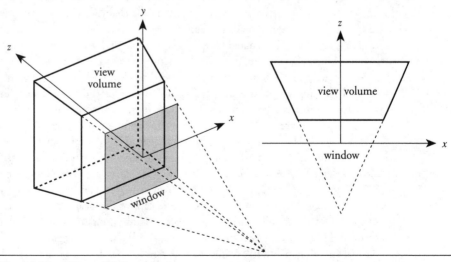

Figure 5.15   Perspective view volume

View volumes are bounded by six planes—the four sides and the near and far planes. In the figures above, the "near" plane is parallel to the view plane and the "far" plane is the other parallel plane. We can define *unbounded view volumes* in which unbounded applies in practical terms only to the far plane. The viewing pyramid of Figure 5.7 is an example. However, unbounded view volumes are not very useful.

The slopes of the sides of a perspective view volume depend on the location of the center of projection. Therefore, we need this information to uniquely determine a perspective view volume. We assume that the center is located at a distance of d from the view plane. Its coordinates are therefore $((l + r)/2 \ \ (b + t)/2 \ \ -d)$. The number d will be an additional parameter in specifying a perspective view volume.

OO DESIGN AND CLASS SPECIFICATIONS

Below is the class `win_view3_t`, which specifies a three-dimensional window-viewport system. It consists of a perspective view volume and a viewport. The perspective view volume consists of a 2D window, plus the data for the near plane, the far plane, and the distance of the frustum tip from the view plane. The viewport member has the same meaning as in Chapter 4. Using this system, three-dimensional lines, polygons, and polygon meshes can be defined in user coordinates, clipped, projected, and drawn or filled on the screen in the area that the viewport specifies.

While we have set the two-dimensional default window as the absolute screen coordinates, we do not do this for a 3D window. When drawing on the screen in two dimensions, it is common to use device coordinates directly. However, the 3D space is conceptually not a drawing plane, and there is no useful association between it and the screen coordinates. We therefore set the default window of the 3D system from -1 to 1 in x and in y. We set the near plane at -5, the far plane at $+5$, and the center of projection at $(0 \ \ 0 \ \ -10)$.

From `window_t`, we derive the class `window3_t` by adding a near plane, a far plane, and the distance of the center of projection. This class specifies a 3D window. (There are no 3D viewports.) We derive a 3D window-viewport system from `window3_t` and from `win_view_t`. This turns out to be more efficient than deriving it from `window3_t` and `viewport_t` because it allows a standard conversion from `win_view3_t` to `win_view_t`. The class `window_t` is a shared base in this class hierarchy, as shown in the class diagrams.

In `window_t`, the virtual member functions `clipln()` (clipping a straight line) and `clipvl()` (clipping a vertex list) are redefined to clip 3D lines or 3D vertex lists. The first one should be implemented using the 3D Cohen-Sutherland straight line clipper, which we have left as an exercise. For clipping 3D vertex lists, six inaccessible member functions have been added, representing the clippers in the 3D clipping pipe, as we explain below.

In `win_view3_t`, the virtual function `win_dev()` that transforms from window to device coordinates now transforms 3D points to device coordinates. It makes a perspective projection onto the view plane and then uses `win_dev()` of the 2D window to scale those points to screen coordinates. The argument of `win_view3_t::win_dev()` must be a `point_t`. According to the C++ syntax, one cannot cast the `point_t` to `point3_t` in order to obtain the member z of that object, because the derivation path contains a virtual derivation. Thus, the only way to obtain the z-coordinate of the argument `point_t` is to call its virtual function `givz()`, which returns z in a `point3_t` object. This is why we have defined the virtual member function `givz()` in the class `point_t` in Chapter 2.

```
//*********************** File win_vie3.h ***************************

#ifndef WIN_VIEW3_T
#define WIN_VIEW3_T

#include "../Shape2d/win_view.h"
#include "../Shape3d/vertex3.h"


class window3_t : public virtual window_t
{
public:
   window3_t() ;
   window3_t(const window_t&,double,double,double) ;
   window3_t(const window3_t&) ;
   line_t*   clipln(const line_t&) const ;        // clip straight line
   vertex_t* clipvl(vertex_t*)     const ;        // clip vertex list

protected:
   double  n , f , d ;                 // near , far , eyepoint distance
   point_t cen ;

   void clfar(double,double,double) const ;
   void clnea(double,double,double) const ;
   void cltop(double,double,double) const ;
   void clbot(double,double,double) const ;
   void clrit(double,double,double) const ;
   void cllef(double,double,double) const ;
} ;


class win_view3_t : public window3_t, public win_view_t
{
public:
   win_view3_t() ;
   win_view3_t(const window3_t&) ;
   win_view3_t(const window3_t&,const viewport_t&) ;

   void win_dev(point_t&) const ;
   double givd() const { return d; }
   point_t givcen() const { return cen; }
} ;

#endif

//*********************************************************************
```

Now that we have defined 3D window-viewport systems, we introduce 3D polygons. These are so simple that we do not even need a class for such polygons. The classes convex_t and polygon_t that we introduced in Chapter 2 serve as simple container classes that can contain all sorts of vertices. If we want a 3D polygon, we need only to define 3D vertices and add those to the container.

The class hierarchy leading to `vertex3_t` beautifully demonstrates the usefulness of multiple inheritance in C++. While we derive `point3_t` from `point_t` by adding a z-coordinate, we derive `vertex_t` from `point_t` by adding a link. Essentially, a `vertex3_t` is either a 2D vertex with a z-coordinate or a 3D point with a link. From which class should we derive `vertex3_t`? Whatever decision one makes, the resulting `vertex3_t` is either the first or the second but not both. The simplest and most natural solution is to derive `vertex3_t` from both classes by adding nothing!

All actions that a `convex_t` does with its vertices also pertain to `vertex3_t`, such as adding new ones to `convex_t` or copying a `convex_t`. Even drawing or filling a `convex_t` with 3D vertices will work; clipping will happen in 3D and the window-to-device transformation will automatically do a perspective projection. Creating an edge list works with `vertex_t`, as well as with `vertex3_t`, by simply ignoring the z-coordinates. Essential in our design is that a new vertex is always created by using the vertex's copy function. This ensures that vertices of the same type are created.

We can and will go further and respecify the member function `create_edge()` for `vertex3_t`, in order to create a new type of edge more specifically suited to 3D filling. We will exploit this later in Z-buffer filling and Phong shading.

```
//*********************** File vertex3.h ***************************

#ifndef VERTEX3_T
#define VERTEX3_T

#include "../Shape2d/vertex.h"
#include "../Shape3d/point3.h"


class vertex3_t : public point3_t , public vertex_t
{
public:
  ~vertex3_t() {}
    vertex3_t() ;
    vertex3_t(double,double,double,vertex_t* = 0) ;
    vertex3_t(const vertex3_t&) ;

    vertex_t* copy() const ;
    void operator = (const point3_t&) ;
} ;

#endif

//*******************************************************************
```

5.4.2   THREE-DIMENSIONAL CLIPPING

Bounded view volumes are used to perform depth clipping. Depth clipping removes those parts of a three-dimensional scene that are closer than the near plane or farther away than the far plane. (Actually, clipping is performed against all bounding planes of the volume and is therefore called 3D clipping, but depth clipping is the "new" feature.) The bounded view volumes are often called *clipping volumes*. In the real world, nothing can be closer than the near plane (the near plane being our eyes), but in computer graphics this is possible. Clipping parts of such a scene can be necessary because the projection algorithms do not distinguish between objects at greater and lesser depth and therefore project everything in the scene, even objects behind us. We do not see an object behind us, so that is a good reason to clip it. Also, in perspective projection, an object in front of the near plane and very close to the center of projection would have a projection so large that it could obscure the whole picture.

Interesting effects can be obtained with depth clipping, interesting because they do not exist in the real world. We can, for example, walk through scenes, houses, walls, and other objects. In walking forward, we also push the near and far planes forward. When the near plane intersects an object, the part closer than the near plane is removed and we are able to see into the object or at least produce images of such an effect.

The sequence in Figure 5.16 shows a scene consisting of a wall with an open door, a table, and a chair. On the left is a side view of the perspective view volume and on the right side the display. Heavy lines depict the wall and the objects. A realistic display (a solid model with removed hidden surfaces) shows only the front wall and the parts of the objects visible through the open door (see Figure 5.16a). When the view volume is moved forward, the objects become larger, but the front wall is still not clipped (see Figure 5.16b). In Figure 5.16c, the near plane has penetrated behind the front wall, the front wall has been clipped, and the objects behind it have become visible. If we had not clipped the wall, it would still hide parts of the objects.

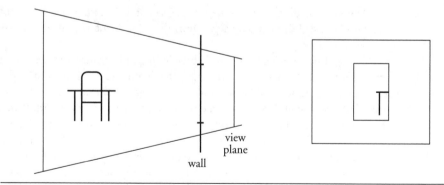

Figure 5.16a   The wall obscures parts of the objects

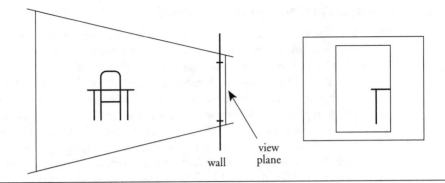

Figure 5.16b   The near plane is closer to the wall

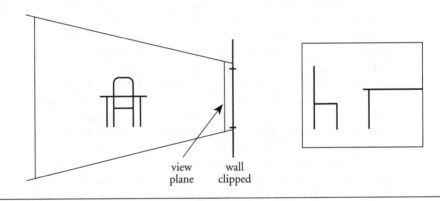

Figure 5.16c   The wall is clipped against the near plane

Depth clipping is the most important aspect of 3D windowing. We perform depth clipping with extended 2D clipping algorithms that clip the objects against all six planes of the given view volume.

We could perform depth clipping by clipping only against the near and far planes and ignoring the other planes. After projecting the depth-clipped objects onto the view plane, a 2D clipping algorithm would clip against the left, right, bottom, and top. Consequently, many parts of the scene would be projected only to be clipped away afterward. If we clip against all six planes in space before we project, then no superfluous projections will be performed. On the other hand, clipping in space is conceptually more difficult, although it does not require more intensive computations. It is hard to decide which approach is better.

We must clip against the near and far plane in any case, so we might as well perform the entire 3D clipping through an extended 2D clipping algorithm. In the 2D plane, we could clip a single straight line or a polygon. The latter was more complicated because new edges and vertices had to be created. We have a similar situation here. We can either clip a single straight line or a polygon against all six planes of the view volume. We first consider clipping a single straight line.

CLIPPING A SINGLE STRAIGHT LINE

We will develop this only for an orthographic view volume; later, we will present the more general polygon-clipping algorithm for a frustum. The extension of the 2D Cohen-Sutherland algorithm to the 3D case is straightforward for an orthographic view volume. The region code of a point $(x \ y \ z)$ now consists of six bits. We number the bits in the order 5 4 3 2 1 0.

$$\text{bit } 5 = 1 \text{ if } x < \text{left} \qquad (= l)$$
$$\text{bit } 4 = 1 \text{ if } x > \text{right} \qquad (= r)$$
$$\text{bit } 3 = 1 \text{ if } y < \text{bottom} \qquad (= b)$$
$$\text{bit } 2 = 1 \text{ if } y > \text{top} \qquad (= t)$$
$$\text{bit } 1 = 1 \text{ if } z < \text{near} \qquad (= n)$$
$$\text{bit } 0 = 1 \text{ if } z > \text{far} \qquad (= f)$$

Otherwise, all bits are zero.

We compute the region codes of both end points of the line. Then we test. If the logic OR of the two codes is 0, the line is completely inside the view volume and is trivially accepted. If the logic AND of the two codes is $\neq 0$, the line is completely outside the volume and is trivially rejected. In all other cases, the line intersects at least once with a boundary. We compute the intersection and trim the line by replacing the proper end point with the intersection. The line becomes shorter and shorter until it is completely contained in the volume. The algorithm is analogous to the two-dimensional case and is not repeated.

There is one major difference between the 2D and 3D applications; we need the intersection of a line with a plane. We have defined the six numbers l, r, b, t, n, and f above. Let $P_1 = (x_1 \ y_1 \ z_1)$ and $P_2 = (x_2 \ y_2 \ z_2)$ be the end points of the line to be clipped.

The line through the two points is expressed parametrically by:

$$x = x_1 + s(x_2 - x_1)$$
$$y = y_1 + s(y_2 - y_1)$$
$$z = z_1 + s(z_2 - z_1)$$

To find the intersection with the near plane where $z = n$, we obtain the s value of the intersection point from $n = z_1 + s(z_2 - z_1)$, which gives:

$$s = \frac{n - z_1}{z_2 - z_1}$$

Inserting this into the above equations gives the intersection point:

$$x = x_1 + \frac{n - z_1}{z_2 - z_1}(x_2 - x_1)$$

$$y = y_1 + \frac{n - z_1}{z_2 - z_1}(y_2 - y_1)$$

$$z = n$$

We obtain all the other line-plane intersections as easily.

CLIPPING A POLYGON

We will extend the 2D polygon-clipping algorithm to our 3D case. When we clip a polygon against a rectangle, we produce another polygon. Clipping the triangle in Figure 5.17 against the window's upper right corner creates a pentagon, as shown in heavy lines. We do not just clip the individual lines, because that would leave the polygon open. We insert vertices and edges to close the "wound."

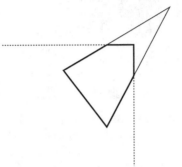

Figure 5.17   *Closing a clipped polygon*

What we consider now is clipping 3D objects against a given view volume. When a volume is clipped against another volume, the result should be a third volume. Three-dimensional clipping clips some solid object against the view volume. This is the true analogy to the two-dimensional polygon clipping. It is demonstrated in Figure 5.18.

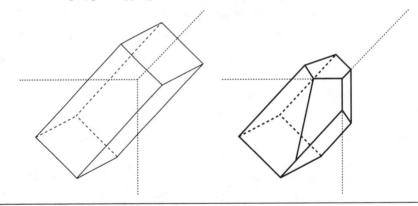

Figure 5.18   *Clipping a volume against another volume*

Figure 5.18 shows 3D clipping of a solid object. The front upper right corner of the view volume appears in dotted lines. The object is a four-sided prism. Clipping it against the corner produces the object shown on the right, in which the visible lines are heavy and the hidden lines are dashed. To achieve this result, when we clip off parts of the polygons that constitute this object, we add new polygons to heal the wound. The algorithm can do this only if it knows which adjacent vertices form polygons and which adjacent polygons form the surface. The analogy to the 2D case is obvious. In that case, the algorithm needed information about the order of the vertices that formed the edges of the polygon, because a polygon is more than just a set of edges or vertices.

However, we do not present such a general solid clipping algorithm—it would be very complicated. We gave the above explanation only to make the situation clear. Our algorithm is not a true extension of 2D polygon clipping; it will clip only individual 3D polygons against the view volume. This fact alone makes our algorithm demanding, but your familiarity with 2D polygon clipping will help you to understand it.

The volume against which we clip is a perspective frustum. Clipping against a rectangular box is a simplification of that case. We consider only the clipping of a single planar 3D polygon. We execute a clipping pipe in much the same way as in a 2D case. The six clippers repeat four basic clips. A basic clip acts exactly as we explained in Section 4.2.2, only now it clips a line against a plane. The basic clip must know the two end points of the line and the plane against which the clip is made. It will find out on which sides of the plane the end points lie. This is more complicated because the planes are not necessarily parallel to the coordinate axes.

We explain the algorithm with an example. We will not go into as much detail as in Section 4.2.2, but this should help you to understand the code. Our example clips a triangle whose vertices are all outside the view volume, but which intersects the top-right-far corner of the view volume. Figure 5.19 shows this. Since the other planes of the view volume are not involved in this particular example, we avoid drawing superfluous lines. Hidden lines are removed to increase the spatial impression. The dotted line from e to b represents the intersection line between the triangle plane and the right plane of the view volume. The other dotted lines mark similar intersections: c–f with the top plane and g–h with the far plane.

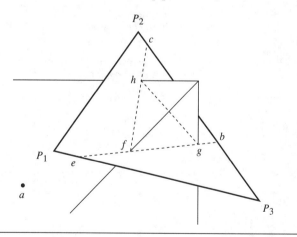

Figure 5.19   Spatial view of the clipping process

While this spatial view helps our imagination, it does not explain the process. We need two drawings that show edge-on views of all planes involved. Figures 5.20 and 5.21 serve this purpose. No two planes in a frustum necessarily intersect at right angles, but a view along the intersection line between two planes will show these two planes as lines. With a top view and a front view, we can position all points of the polygon and all generated intersection points unmistakably in relation to the planes. With one spatial view, this is not possible.

The clipping pipe is written down in the order:

Left Right Bottom Top Near Far

which indicates the six planes of the view volume. All clippers are initialized ("last points") with the left lower near corner of the view volume, which we call O. If a clipper produces no output, we put a cross (+) behind it to indicate that the point died in the pipe. If a clipper produces two outputs, we write the second output in the next line under the first; thus, the pipe branches. Whenever a point is produced, we show it in both edge-on views. We also enter it in the spatial view to help visualize the process. (Follow the steps in Figures 5.19, 5.20, and 5.21. The lowercase letters show the points we generate.)

We must put the polygon through the pipe twice; the first time, the output serves only to obtain valid last points.

Figure 5.20 is a front view, which shows the top plane and the right plane edge-on.

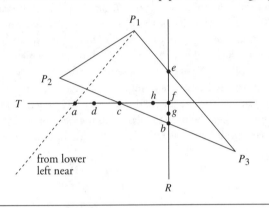

Figure 5.20   Intersection of top plane and right plane

Figure 5.21 is a top view. It shows the far plane and the right plane edge-on.

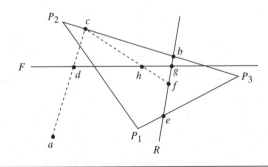

Figure 5.21   Intersection of far plane and right plane

The pipes are now processed, giving these results:

First run:

O		O		O		O		O		O	
P_1	L	P_1	R	P_1	B	P_1	T	a	N	a	F	a
P_2	L	P_2	R	P_2	B	P_2	T	$+$	N		F	
P_3	L	P_3	R	b	B	b	T	c	N	c	F	d
								b	N	b	F	$+$

Second run:

P_1	L	P_1	R	e	B	e	T	f	N	f	F	g
				P_1	B	P_1	T	$+$				f
P_2	L	P_2	R	P_2	B	P_2	T	$+$	N		F	
P_3	L	P_3	R	b	B	b	T	c	N	c	F	h
								b	N	b	F	$+$

This schematic condenses the whole clipping process. The second run produces the correct three vertices of the clipped triangle. A few explanations will be helpful.

First, the left clipper is called with the line from O to P_1, so it produces P_1. The same occurs with the right and the bottom clipper. The top clipper then produces the intersection point a. To visualize it, we construct a pipe from Figure 5.20 and enter it in Figure 5.19 and 5.21 at the approximate positions. The pipe outputs an a. Point P_2 dies in the pipe. Point P_3 will lead to an intersection b with the right plane, but that point is still outside the view volume. Visually, we construct it in Figure 5.20 and also enter it in the other drawings. This point will lead to a branch through the top clipper; we obtain c and b, constructed in Figure 5.20. The far clipper will produce point d, which is the intersection of line ac with the far plane. As a and c lie in the top plane, d also lies there. As d lies in the far plane, it must lie on the edge between the top and far edges. Figure 5.19 does not show d—it is hidden below the triangle. Points a and d are the whole output of the first run, but our purpose was to obtain correct last points for the second run. These are P_3, P_3, b, b, b, and b for the successive clips.

In the second run, P_1 leads to point e through the right clipper. It lies on the line from P_3 to P_1 and is therefore in the triangle. It also lies in the right plane, so it lies on the intersection line of the triangle plane with the right plane, as does point b. The top clipper then produces point f, where the line from b to e intersects the top plane. Point f therefore lies in the right plane, top plane, and in the triangle. This is one of the points at which the triangle intersects with the view volume. The far clipper produces the second intersection point, g. Point P_2 dies in the pipe. Point P_3 leads to the third intersection point, h.

MATHEMATICS OF THREE-DIMENSIONAL CLIPPING

We will develop the mathematics for a perspective view volume whose frustum appears in Figure 5.22. We make several assumptions. The coordinate system is left-handed; the center of projection is in the middle of the window at a distance of d from the window; the window is in the plane $z = 0$, because most projections are made to the plane $z = 0$. The view plane (the window) does not coincide with the near plane. The center of perspective projection is

$((l + r)/2 \;\; (b + t)/2 \;\; -d)$. The window of the frustum (its intersection with the view plane) is bounded by the values l, r, b, and t.

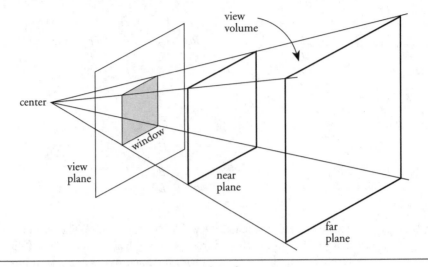

Figure 5.22   General perspective view volume and window

We need four constants to express the equations of the four side planes. These are the slopes of the planes in relation to the z-axis. Figure 5.23 shows a vertical cross section through the frustum, which will help determine the slopes for the top and bottom planes. A similar situation exists for the left and right planes.

slope of the left plane: $s_L = -\tfrac{1}{2}(r - l)/d$
slope of the right plane: $s_R = \tfrac{1}{2}(r - l)/d$
slope of the bottom plane: $s_B = -\tfrac{1}{2}(t - b)/d$
slope of the top plane: $s_T = \tfrac{1}{2}(t - b)/d$

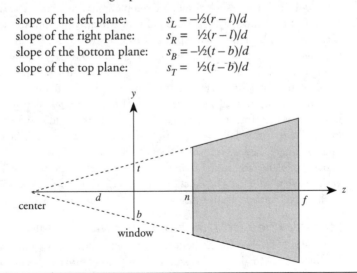

Figure 5.23   Cross section through the view volume

With these constants, the equations of the planes are:

$$
\begin{array}{ll}
L: & x = l + s_L z \\
R: & x = r + s_R z \\
B: & y = b + s_B z \\
T: & y = t + s_T z \\
N: & z = n \\
F: & z = f
\end{array}
$$

The near and far planes have especially simple equations. The others are simpler than general plane equations because they are parallel either to the x-axis or the y-axis.

The intersections of a line from $(x_1 \ y_1 \ z_1)$ to $(x_2 \ y_2 \ z_2)$ with these six planes are found as follows. First, we compute six u-values for the six planes:

$$
u_L = \frac{x_1 - l - s_L z_1}{x_1 - x_2 + s_L(z_2 - z_1)} \qquad u_R = \frac{x_1 - r - s_R z_1}{x_1 - x_2 + s_R(z_2 - z_1)}
$$

$$
u_B = \frac{y_1 - b - s_B z_1}{y_1 - y_2 + s_B(z_2 - z_1)} \qquad u_T = \frac{y_1 - t - s_T z_1}{y_1 - y_2 + s_T(z_2 - z_1)}
$$

$$
u_N = \frac{z_1 - n}{z_1 - z_2} \qquad u_F = \frac{z_1 - f}{z_1 - z_2}
$$

The intersection point $(x \ y \ z)$ with any of the planes is obtained by inserting the appropriate u-value into the parameterized line representation:

$$
\begin{aligned}
x &= x_1 + u(x_2 - x_1) \\
y &= y_1 + u(y_2 - y_1) \\
z &= z_1 + u(z_2 - z_1)
\end{aligned}
$$

A point $(x \ y \ z)$ is inside the view volume in relation to any of these planes if the corresponding condition is true:

$$
\begin{array}{ll}
\text{for the left plane} & x \geq l + s_L z \\
\text{for the right plane} & x \leq r + s_R z \\
\text{for the bottom plane} & y \geq b + s_B z \\
\text{for the top plane} & y \leq t + s_T z \\
\text{for the near plane} & z \geq n \\
\text{for the far plane} & z \leq f
\end{array}
$$

The code for clipping a 3D vertex list against a view volume is an adaptation of the 2D clipping code in Section 4.2.2. We have retained the variable names and types as much as possible to emphasize the similarities and to make the code easier to understand. A vertex list representing the clipped polygon is created and returned. As in two dimensions, we need two runs through the vertex list to obtain the correct result. We do not include the code in the text.

SUGGESTED READINGS

You can find very detailed descriptions of a variety of projection techniques in FVFH90. For 3D rotation about an arbitrary line in space, consult EKPE93. A stepwise development from a simple to a general view transformation is presented in WATT89.

EXERCISES

SECTION 5.1

Exercises 1 through 4 deal with three-dimensional transformations.

1. Compute the composite transformation matrix for the following transformations in three dimensions:

    translate by (3,2,4)
    rotate about x by 60°
    scale by (1.5,–2,2)
    rotate about y by 25°

2. Write a function

    ```
    void acc_trafo(trafo_t trafo) ;
    ```

    in C++ that accumulates the three-dimensional transformations specified in `trafo` into a global matrix tmatrix. The type `trafo_t` is:

    ```
    struct trafo_t
    {
        double tx , ty , tz ;        // translation
        double sx , sy , sz ;        // scaling
        double rx , ry , rz ;        // rotation
    } ;
    ```

    Use homogeneous points and matrices.

3. The five transformations presented in the text are linear. What is the practical consequence of this?

4. Implement the member function `virtual prim_t& scale (const point_t&)` for all 3D primitives derived from `prim_t`. Observe that the parameter is a two-dimensional `point_t`. You can still get its z-coordinate by using the function `point_t::getz()`, provided that the actual argument is a 3D point.

SECTION 5.2

5. Write a function that computes the parallel projection of any given point $(x\ y\ z)$ in a left-handed system for any given projection vector $(x_p\ y_p\ z_p)$.

6. Write a function that computes the perspective projection of any given point $(x\ y\ z)$ with $z > 0$ in a left-handed system for any given center of projection $(x_p\ y_p\ z_p)$ with $z_p < 0$. The projection axis is parallel to the z-axis and the projection is onto the $(x\ y)$ plane.

7. Let an object be defined in three-dimensional user coordinates. The left-right extent of the object is from -1 to $+1$ and the up-down extent is from $+0.8$ to -0.8 in user coordinates. It is at a distance of 3 from the view plane. Assume absolute screen coordinates $DWID = 640$ and $DHEI = 400$. Define a 3D window-viewport system, so that on the screen the left-right extent of the object's projection covers approximately 300 pixels.

8. In perspective depth transformation, a point $(x\ y\ z)$ is transformed into $ps(x\ y\ z)$ by:

$$x_{ps} = \frac{xd}{z+d} \qquad\qquad y_{ps} = \frac{yd}{z+d} \qquad\qquad z_{ps} = \frac{z}{z+d}$$

This transforms straight lines into straight lines. To demonstrate this, it suffices to use a two-dimensional line in $(x\ z)$-coordinates; the y-coordinates have the same transformation rule as the x-coordinates. We can express the transformation of the line as a parameterized straight line of the individual transformations. For the x-coordinate, this gives:

$$\frac{\left(x_1 + t(x_2 - x_1)\right)d}{z_1 + t(z_2 - z_1) + d} = \frac{x_1 d}{z_1 + d} + \alpha_x \left(\frac{x_2 d}{z_2 + d} - \frac{x_1 d}{z_1 + d} \right)$$

For the z-coordinate, this produces:

$$\frac{z_1 + t(z_2 - z_1)}{z_1 + t(z_2 - z_1) + d} = \frac{z_1}{z_1 + d} + \alpha_z \left(\frac{z_2}{z_2 + d} - \frac{z_1}{z_1 + d} \right)$$

a. Show that from the first expression we obtain:

$$\alpha_x = t \left(\frac{d + z_2}{d + z_1 + t(z_2 - z_1)} \right)$$

b. Show that from the second expression we have:

$$\alpha_z = t \left(\frac{d + z_2}{d + z_1 + t(z_2 - z_1)} \right)$$

c. What would we have for α_y?

d. Why does this mean that the transformed line is straight?

9. The perspective depth transformation changes planes into planes. If P is a plane in object space and $ps(P)$ is its image (the set of all image points of points from P), then $ps(P)$ also is a plane. Prove this by showing that there is a contradiction if the assertion is not true.

SECTION 5.4

10. Write the class specification `line3_t` that defines a straight line in space by its two end points. Do as much as possible in analogy to the class `Shape2d/line_t`, but do not inherit from `prim_t`, because there are not enough commonalities to warrant this. Use the type `point3_t` for the end points. Put the class specification in the file `Shape3d/line3.h`.

11. Write the class implementation for `line3_t`. Implement `line3_t::draw()` with a `win_view3_t` parameter, project, and then use `line_t::draw()`.

12. Write the 3D version of the Cohen-Sutherland line clipper for a perspective frustum. Use the inequalities presented in 3D polygon clipping to determine the region codes. Implement this as the member function `line3_t::clip()`.

PARAMETRIC
CURVES

While the images that we have drawn so far on the computer screen are composed of straight lines, we may need to compute points along a curve whose equation is defined by a set of points called control points. In Chapter 6, we describe several ways to do this.

6.0   **Introduction** explains the application of curves in computer graphics, the value of parametric forms in constructing curves, how interpolation differs from approximation, and why splines are a preferred type of curve.

6.1   **The Natural Cubic Spline** is widely used because it often does the job. These can be calculated either directly or by combining basic cubic splines.

6.2   **Uniform B-Spline Curves** avoid the problem of global influence by the control points, but are approximating rather than interpolating curves. We discuss both cubic and quadratic forms of these curves.

6.3   **Nonuniform B-Spline Curves** are a superset of which the uniform B-splines are a special case. While the uniform curves are usually adequate for graphics applications, you may also need these more general curves.

6.4   **Catmull-Rom Curves** are built up from basic curves, much as B-splines are built. They are able to interpolate by relaxing certain conditions. By generalizing them, we produce curves that look as if they are under more or less tension.

6.5   **Bezier Curves** are another type of approximating curves useful in computer graphics.

6.0   INTRODUCTION

Curves are important in many areas of computer graphics. One example is in animation. The animator draws key frames which must be linked together by many in-between frames; the computer can automatically generate these in-between frames. If points in these in-between frames that connect corresponding points of the key frames lie on a straight line, the motion will be jerky and unnatural. One creates a smooth curve that interpolates between the points on the key frames, and places the points of the in-between frames on that curve.

Another application of curves is to smooth an approximate outline given by a few points. In this case the curve itself is what we desire. One usually creates it with an interactive process of specifying control points that shape the curve. If one can change these control points interactively and rapidly display the resulting curve, one can actually mold the curve to fit a desired outline. Such interactive modeling, done in real time on the screen, is easy and natural. This process is used in computer-aided design and manufacturing (CAD/CAM).

Still another application of curves is to create surfaces. One usually achieves this by specifying discrete points on an object's surface, which are then connected by interpolating or approximating surfaces. Curves are involved because all surfaces are ultimately derived from curves and exhibit the same characteristics of smoothness or roughness.

We start the chapter by introducing parametric representations. This is not an issue that should be dismissed in a single paragraph, but a full understanding would be too difficult to explain here and is not necessary. As you need some degree of understanding before discussing the curves that are useful in computer graphics, we will cover the basics. The reader should understand that the curves we create behave in certain ways because of the parameterization, not due to properties of the individual component functions (see below). The importance of parametric representation is that it allows us to derive curves for the 2D plane; we can then transfer these without conceptual difficulties or any change in formalism to curves in three dimensions. A further conceptual step is necessary, however, to change 3D curves to 3D surfaces, which we will do in Chapter 7.

We also need to understand the difference between interpolation and approximation. Once we have clarified this, we will discuss the most important parametric curves—B-spline curves, Catmull-Rom curves, and Bezier curves.

PARAMETRIC REPRESENTATIONS

A curve in the 2D plane can be represented by the relationship between two variables. There are basically two ways to do this. One can make either y or x the independent variable:

$$y = f(x)$$
$$x = g(y)$$

Such representations lead to difficulties when there are infinite slopes and loops in the curve that give repeated points. There is lack of symmetry in such representations because one variable must be designated as independent and the other as dependent. Writing in parametric form avoids these difficulties. We use a single new independent variable, u, called the *parameter*, to write equations for both x and y:

$$x = X(u)$$
$$y = Y(u)$$

From now on, we will call $X(u)$ and $Y(u)$ the *component functions* or *component curves* whenever we refer to them. The combination of $x = X(u)$ and $y = Y(u)$ for the same value of u, will be called the *combined curve* whenever our terminology becomes confusing. Observe that there is now symmetry. The combined curve can loop and have infinite slopes in terms of x and y, without having to have infinite slopes for the component curves. Do not underestimate this important property. Without it, it would be literally impossible to draw the majority of curves on the computer screen.

Another advantage is the ease with which one can deal with only a finite portion of the combined curve by limiting the range of u. Figures 6.1a to 6.1c will help you visualize this. The two parameter curves are $x = \cos(u)$ and $y = \sin(u)$. The range of u is limited to $-\pi/4$ to $\pi/4$. The combined curve is the quarter-circle from $-45°$ to $45°$. The point $(1\ \ 0)$ on the combined curve corresponds to $u = 0$; the combined curve has an infinite slope at that point.

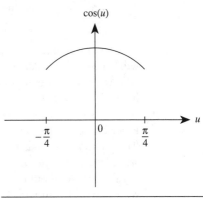

Figure 6.1a   x = cos(u)

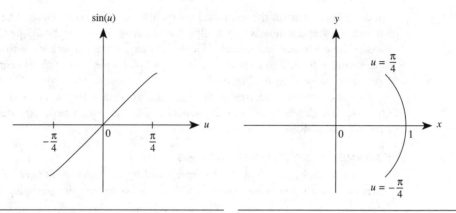

Figure 6.1b   y = sin(u)   *Figure 6.1c   Combined curve is a quarter circle*

A nonparametric description of the quarter circle could be $y = \pm\sqrt{1-x^2}$, with x limited to 0.707 to 1. Drawing the curve by a sequence of short straight lines from this description is awkward because of the double sign. However, this is a simpler case than most; in complicated cases with several y-values for a given x-value, it becomes practically impossible (see Exercises 1 through 4).

There is a lot about parametrics that is by no means obvious. For example, if the two component curves for x and y are both cubic polynomials, is the combined curve also a cubic polynomial? The answer is no; usually it is very difficult to express the combined curve implicitly. If the two component curves are both perfectly smooth, will the combined curve also be perfectly smooth? No; it can have sharp corners. See Exercises 5 and 6. You can find more about this in FVFH90 or BARS88.

Everything we have said about 2D curves in terms of x and y translates directly into 3D space. We much prefer not to use two relations to define the curve, such as

$$y = f(x) \qquad z = g(x)$$

Rather, we will use the parametric form:

$$x = X(u) \qquad y = Y(u) \qquad z = Z(u)$$

This gives us the same advantages as in the 2D situation. Because of these advantages, we will henceforth consider only parametric representations of curves and surfaces. An exception is in ray tracing, where implicit representations are used. However, that usage helps to find intersections with a ray, not to display the surfaces.

We will do all the mathematical developments and construction processes below in a generic way. There is no need to consider whether the x-, y-, or z-coordinate is being interpolated or approximated, as this is identical in all three cases. This must also be considered an advantage of parametric representations.

The reader should develop some familiarity with parametric representations by starting with Exercises 1 through 4 and trying 5 and 6.

INTERPOLATION AND APPROXIMATION

In areas more mathematically oriented than computer graphics, the problems of interpolation and approximation usually arise from the need to replace an analytically complicated function, or one known only at certain points, with a simple, well-defined curve. In computer graphics, we are primarily concerned with how the curve appears to a human observer and not with its mathematical properties. Our goal is not to replace one curve with another, worrying about error estimates and other matters, as is done in mathematics. Rather, we just want to create a curve that has a smooth look and satisfies our visual sense. The interpolation and approximation methods developed mainly in numerical analysis have proven to be good tools for this. The notions of interpolation and approximation may have a slightly different meaning in computer graphics; we will now define these meanings precisely enough to avoid later confusion.

The usual graphics problem is to connect a sequence of points in a plane or in space with a smooth curve. We can do this with interpolation and approximation.

In *interpolation*, the curve goes precisely through the points, as shown in Figure 6.2a.

Figure 6.2a   Interpolating curve

In *approximation*, the curve does not necessarily go through the points; it approximates them (see Figure 6.2b). Remember this distinction.

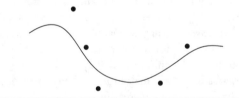

Figure 6.2b   Approximating curve

SPLINE CURVES

If we try to fit a curve to a given number of points with interpolation, we often find that doing so with a single polynomial of higher degree gives an unacceptable curve. This is because polynomials have a tendency that we call the "Polynomial Wiggle Problem." If the points $P_0, \ldots, P_n$ do not already lie on a polynomial (and this is rare in computer graphics), then making a polynomial go through them may create oscillations between some of the successive points. These oscillations (wiggles) become larger as the degree of the polynomial increases (MARO82, p. 203). Figure 6.3 shows a sixth degree polynomial fitted to the seven data points:

x	0	.04	.14	.21	1.22	1.5	1.93
y	−1	−.151	.894	.986	.895	.5	−.306

It develops strong wiggles in areas where the data points are sparse.

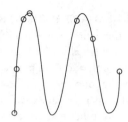

Figure 6.3   Interpolating polynomial

A high-degree polynomial that wiggles wildly, even though it matches all the data points, does not satisfy our desire for a smooth and "simplifying" curve. The best remedy is to use polynomials of low degree, but a single, low-degree polynomial cannot match the entire set. The solution is to separate the group of points into subsets and approximate the first three or four consecutive points with a low-degree polynomial, then the next three or four points with another polynomial, continuing like this until the whole group has been covered. It is also possible to use only part of each of these polynomials and allow the subsets to overlap. The joints must be smoothed where the separate polynomials meet. Several techniques have been developed to put these pieces of polynomials together so that the whole curve looks more or less smooth. The most popular of these techniques is a spline curve.

The term "spline" comes from the draftsman's spline, which is a flexible rod. By bending the flexible rod so that it fits at each of the given points, we can draw a smooth curve that interpolates the points. The main mathematical characteristic of splines is that no one equation describes them throughout their range of definition; they are certainly not a single polynomial. Instead they are "pieced together" from several other curves. Usually these individual pieces are themselves low-degree polynomials. The degree of the polynomials and other conditions imposed in the construction process determine the type of spline that results.

A more formal definition is that spline functions approximate or interpolate a set of points piecewise by polynomials of rather low degree, at the same time maintaining the continuity of the function values and one or more derivatives at the joints.

We will first consider the natural cubic spline, because this spline has historical importance. In computer graphics it is not used as much as other types of splines that we consider later. We also look at natural cubic splines to give a good understanding of the topic and to show why the newer developments are better suited for graphics purposes.

6.1   THE NATURAL CUBIC SPLINE

The *natural cubic spline* is an interpolating curve, called "natural" for several reasons. One is that it offers a good compromise between flexibility, smoothness, and ease of computation. "Flexibility" here means how well the curve can bend to fit a certain outline. This concept is similar to how readily a natural elastic object can bend to fit a certain outline without forcing or breaking; if the draftsman's spline bends around pegs, it assumes a form that can be called natural. The natural cubic spline also resembles the actual elastic object, in that it is a straight line outside the interpolation interval where there are no bending forces. Natural flexibility comes from using third-degree polynomials; this prevents the polynomials from making sharp bends. In computer graphics, the usual objective is not so much to make a curve go through the given points as to use the points to control the course of the curve. With degree three, the natural cubic spline is still flexible enough that it can approximate a desired outline satisfactorily.

Figure 6.4 shows a natural cubic spline using the same control points as in Figure 6.3. The difference in the two curves is obvious.

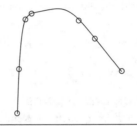

Figure 6.4   Interpolating cubic spline

The spline's flexibility can be increased by using polynomials of higher degree. The resulting curve will still look smooth and graceful, but more calculations will be required to obtain the spline. All in all, the cubic spline seems to be the best compromise to achieve a smooth, natural-looking interpolation of data points without too much calculation.

One property of natural splines is undesirable in computer graphics—their global nature. By this, we mean that it is not possible to change the course of the curve locally without affecting it in all other parts. Changing one of the points changes the curve throughout its length. You should consult MARO82 or GEWH89 for additional information.

DIRECT CALCULATION METHOD

We want to construct an interpolating natural cubic spline, given $n+1$ points $P_0, \ldots, P_n$. We need some notation. The interval $[0\ n]$ is the range of the parameter u. We divide the interval into n subintervals. (If the intervals are of equal lengths, the mathematical development is simpler, but this is not essential.) The n subintervals will be $[u_0\ u_1], \ldots, [u_{n-1}\ u_n]$. We wish to interpolate the $n+1$ given points P_i by a curve $C(u)$, which consists of a polynomial of degree three in each subinterval. Let the polynomial in $[u_{i-1}\ u_i]$ be called $q_i(u)$; then $C(u) = q_i(u)$ in the interval $[u_{i-1}\ u_i]$. The points u_i are also called *knots*, because the polynomials are pieced together there to form the spline. The following conditions must be met:

$$q_i(u_{i-1}) = p_{i-1} \text{ and } q_i(u_i) = p_i \qquad \text{for } i = 1, \ldots, n$$
$$q_i{}'(u_i) = q_{i+1}{}'(u_i) \qquad\qquad\qquad \text{for } i = 1, \ldots, n-1$$
$$q_i{}''(u_i) = q_{i+1}{}''(u_i) \qquad\qquad\qquad \text{for } i = 1, \ldots, n-1$$
$$q_1{}''(u_0) = 0 \text{ and } q_n{}''(u_n) = 0$$

The first pair of conditions requires that the ends of each cubic connect the two adjacent points. The next two say that the joins are smooth; thus, both the first and second derivatives must be the same where two cubics connect. The last two restrictions are *end conditions* because they define properties of the spline at the ends of the interpolation interval. The above end conditions define a natural cubic spline. Many other conditions can be used at the ends, for example, setting $q'(u_0) = c_0$ and $q'(u_n) = c_1$, where c_0 and c_1 are constants.

By setting, rearranging, and preprocessing these conditions in a certain way, we can arrive at an $(n-1) \times (n-1)$ linear system in which the system matrix is tridiagonal and well conditioned, making the system easy to solve. We do not explore this further, because it would detract from our main goal: B-spline curves, Catmull-Rom curves, and Bezier curves.

The natural cubic spline curve is the smoothest possible curve that goes through all control points when we define "smoothest" as minimizing the integral

$$\int_0^n [C''(u)]^2 \, du$$

over the range of control points.

USING BASIC, GLOBAL SPLINES

One could use a different method to construct an interpolating cubic spline. One builds it from a set of basic splines combined as a linear sum. This is the approach used to obtain an interpolating polynomial in the Lagrange form (see GEWH89).

We start with $n+1$ points P_0 to P_n defined through the parameter u on the interval $[0 \ \ n]$. We subdivide into n subintervals with $u_0 = 0$, $u_1 = 1$, ..., $u_n = n$. We construct $n+1$ basic spline functions $b_i(u)$, such that $b_i(u_i) = 1$ and $b_i(u_j) = 0$ for $j \neq i$. (This is a spline of degree three that equals 0 at each knot, except knot i where it is 1.) We assume as natural end conditions that $b_i''(0) = 0$ and $b_i''(1) = 0$.

Figure 6.5 shows the basic spline b_2 in an example where $n = 7$.

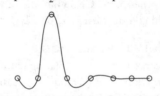

Figure 6.5   Basic cubic spline

The interval $[0 \ \ n]$ on which we define the basic splines has nothing to do with the domain in space or the plane in which the created curve will ultimately appear. It just represents the range of values for the parameter u as we move along the curve from P_0 to P_n. It is sufficient to work only with this interval of parameter values.

An arbitrary spline $C(u)$ that interpolates through $p_0, \dots, p_n$ is obtained by forming:

$$C(u) = \sum_{i=0}^n p_i * b_i(u)$$

If a linear sum of basic functions multiplied by the corresponding coordinates constructs a curve, you can think of the points as weighting factors applied to these basic functions; the weighted sum is the resulting curve.

The spline curve as we have defined it will pass through each of the given points. As all the b_i are natural cubic splines, the linear combination will also be a natural cubic spline with the desired function values $C(u_i) = p_i$. The spline so obtained is identical to the one we obtained by solving a linear system of equations. Although it is possible to calculate a natural cubic spline with a linear combination, one does not do that in practical applications. We use this example only to prepare you for the theory of B-splines.

Figure 6.5 shows that the b_i oscillate from one knot to the next, the oscillations becoming smaller but never 0. The basic function b_i represents the influence or control that the point P_i has on the resulting interpolating curve throughout the domain. Point P_i completely influences the spline curve C at the point P_i, so C goes through this point. At all the other points, P_i has no influence, but in the intervals between these points it pulses in and out, weakening with growing distance. This further shows that changing a single point P_i influences the course of the whole spline.

TOWARD LOCAL CONTROL

When constructing a curve through (or almost through) a series of given points in computer graphics, we want the points to exert only local control over the curve. Changing one of the points that determine the curve's course should change the curve only in a limited neighborhood about this point and should not influence the curve outside this neighborhood. This is called *local control.*

How can we achieve such locality? We find the answer to this question by examining the above approach where basic splines constructed a global interpolating spline. What makes the points have global influence is that these basic splines are not zero between the knots. Suppose we could force each b_i curve to be zero outside a certain distance from the point u_i (where it must equal 1). This would still make the curve $C(u)$ go through the points P_i; the points retain full control over the curve at their specific locations, but, at the same time, this control is limited to the region where the respective $b_i \neq 0$.

When we postulate all these conditions, we find that we end up with an overdetermined system that has no solutions. Does this mean that we cannot obtain the desirable local control of the points P_i? Yes and no. We can obtain the locality by dropping certain requirements, for example, that the curve go through the points P_i. Dropping this requirement leads to the cubic B-splines that we discuss below. Another way is to drop the requirement of second-order continuity, as this implies only a slight change in the resulting curve's visual appearance. This leads to the Catmull-Rom curves.

6.2   UNIFORM B-SPLINE CURVES

In 1947, Curry and Schoenberg originally introduced the functions that later became known as B-splines (CUSC47). In 1967, Schoenberg gave the functions this name (SCHO67). To make the approach to the B-spline methods easier, we will begin with uniform B-splines. After we have explained their properties and applications and you have become familiar with them, we will present the general (nonuniform) B-splines.

The letter B in the word B-spline stems from "basis." Therefore, B-splines are often called *basic splines* or *bases.* They are spline functions that form a basis for constructing curves from a set of control points. We do the construction by forming a linear combination of the basic splines.

Very often the curve we obtain with the B-spline method is itself called a B-spline. We will not use this terminology; instead, using Schoenberg's terminology, the word B-spline will refer only to the basic splines from which we obtain the approximating curve (DEBO78, p. 114). This resulting curve is denoted by C, and is called the *B-spline curve*. (Note that the word "curve" is appended.) Keep in mind that we will draw curves through parameterizations. From this it follows that the combined curve might have properties (such as sharp corners) that are absent in the component curve for a single coordinate.

B-splines can be defined for any degree. We will focus on the cubic (order 4) and will mention the quadratic (order 3) B-splines.

We have seen that it is desirable to construct a curve that is only locally controlled by the points it interpolates or approximates. We want the basic functions used in forming the curve to be nonzero on as small an interval as possible. The B-spline functions fulfill this, as they are nonzero only in a finite interval.

6.2.1   UNIFORM CUBIC B-SPLINES

We introduce the *uniform cubic B-spline* and explain some of its properties that are important for computer graphics. (The terms "periodic" or "canonical" B-spline, which occur in the literature, mean the same as uniform B-spline.) If we want to define a cubic spline on equally spaced knots, one which is nonzero on the smallest possible interval, there is only one solution: the uniform cubic B-spline. The mathematical proof is beyond the scope of this book.

No matter how great the range of the parameter u, the basic uniform cubic B-spline b stretches only over five consecutive knots and is equal to 0 outside this range. It is composed of cubic polynomials, as described below. The distances between the knots are all equal to 1. We choose the middle of the five knots as 0 in order to achieve symmetry in the formal description:

$$b(u) = 0 \qquad\qquad\qquad\qquad \text{for } u \leq -2$$
$$b(u) = \tfrac{1}{6}(2+u)^3 \qquad\qquad\qquad \text{for } -2 \leq u \leq -1$$
$$b(u) = \tfrac{1}{6}(2+u)^3 - \tfrac{2}{3}(1+u)^3 \qquad \text{for } -1 \leq u \leq 0$$
$$b(u) = -\tfrac{2}{3}(1-u)^3 + \tfrac{1}{6}(2-u)^3 \qquad \text{for } 0 \leq u \leq 1$$
$$b(u) = \tfrac{1}{6}(2-u)^3 \qquad\qquad\qquad \text{for } 1 \leq u \leq 2$$
$$b(u) = 0 \qquad\qquad\qquad\qquad \text{for } 2 \leq u$$

The term "order" expresses the fact that the B-spline stretches over four knot intervals and is composed of four different polynomials. (The order of B-splines is one higher than the degree of the composing polynomials.) The above shows that b consists of four different cubic polynomials between −2 and +2, and of a straight line outside this range. However, these different polynomials fit together so nicely that the whole of b looks like one smooth curve (see Figure 6.6). Keep in mind, though, that it is a patchwork of different curves.

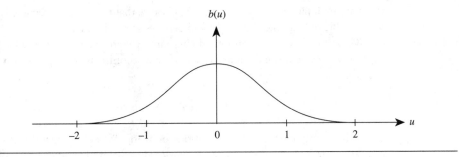

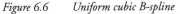

Figure 6.6   Uniform cubic B-spline

Some values are:

$$b(\pm 2) = 0 \qquad\qquad b'(\pm 2) = 0 \qquad\qquad b''(\pm 2) = 0$$
$$b(\pm 1) = \tfrac{1}{6} \qquad\qquad b'(\pm 1) = \pm\tfrac{1}{2}$$
$$b(0) = \tfrac{2}{3}$$

The function b, although a patchwork of different curves, is continuous up to its second derivative, which the definition confirms. It is essential that you distinguish between the uniformly spaced knots on which $b(u)$ is defined and the points P_i, which the curve will eventually approximate. The fact that the knots are equally spaced does not imply that the points are. This important but subtle point will be clarified as the development proceeds.

CONSTRUCTION OF A UNIFORM CUBIC B-SPLINE CURVE

If we need to draw a curve to n points P_0 to P_{n-1}, then we first define n uniform basic splines $b_0(u)$ to $b_{n-1}(u)$. We obtain each of these by simply shifting the curve $b(u)$ by an integer amount to the right with the transformation:

$$b_i(u) = b(u-i) \qquad\qquad \text{for } i = 0, \dots, n-1$$

Then we multiply P_0 by $b_0(u)$, P_1 by $b_1(u)$, and so on, and sum these terms for the subscripts 0 to $n-1$. This gives us the desired B-spline curve.

Here, a more detailed explanation is in order. By multiplying the curve $b_i(u)$ by P_i, we are multiplying the curve by the x-, y-, or z-coordinates of P_i. When we use the x-coordinates, we obtain the component curve for the x-coordinate in which u is the single argument:

$$C_x(u) = \sum_{i=0}^{n-1} x_i b_i(u) \dots \quad (1)$$

We obtain the component curve for the y- or z-coordinate by using the y- or z-coordinates, respectively. Therefore, the combined curve $C(u)$, called the B-spline curve, is then the set of points:

$$C(u) = \big(C_x(u) \ \ C_y(u) \ \ C_z(u) \big)$$

which approximates the control points P_i. (Realize that this combined curve is not a composition of cubic polynomials but looks and behaves as one in most ways.)

We simply express the combined curve in a generic way with the same formalism as in (1), but we leave out the reference to a particular coordinate; there is no subscript for C and instead of x_i, y_i, or z_i, we write p_i:

$$C(u) = \sum_{i=0}^{n-1} p_i b_i(u)$$

It is very important to understand the following. When we draw this curve, we let u run only from 1 to n-2. We do this because for u-values below 1 or above n–2, the curve is controlled not only by the control points, but also by the origin (0 0).

The example of Figure 6.7 will help to clarify this. It shows the five uniform B-splines b_0, ..., b_4 over several equidistant knot values on the interval [–2 6]. Only the knots 0, 1, 2, 3, and 4 are indicated. You can see that at every u-value between the knots 1, 2, and 3 there are four $b_i(u)$ greater than 0. Precisely at those knots, there are three $b_i(u)$ greater than 0. If you were to add the unweighted $b_i(u)$ values together, you would obtain a sum of 1 for every u-value from 1 to 3. But as soon as you move below 1 or above 3, the sum would drop below 1. Further out, it would equal 0. The geometric consequence of this is that the B-spline curve for u-values outside [1 3] bends toward the origin and eventually runs into the origin in a straight line. In other words, the control of the points P_i over the curve weakens and eventually disappears altogether.

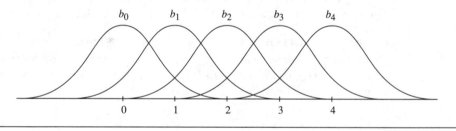

Figure 6.7   Five uniform cubic B-splines

We resolve this by drawing the B-spline curve only in the range in which it is solely controlled by the P_i. This is the parameter range [1 3].

A part of the interval from one knot value to the next is called a subinterval.

PROPERTIES OF THE CURVE

Some properties of the curve C result from properties of the B-splines; others result from the parameterization. The value of $C(u)$ is always a weighted sum of the three or four closest control points. At the parameter value u_i, $C(u_i)$ is a weighted sum of the three immediately adjacent points P_{i-1}, P_i, and P_{i+1}. The weights are the values of $b_{i-1}(u)$, $b_i(u)$, and $b_{i+1}(u)$ at the knot u_i. Respectively, these are $\frac{1}{6}$, $\frac{2}{3}$, and $\frac{1}{6}$, so we have:

$$C(u_i) = \tfrac{1}{6} p_{i-1} + \tfrac{2}{3} p_i + \tfrac{1}{6} p_{i+1}$$

This shows that $C(u)$ does not interpolate through the points P_i, but is rather an approximating curve. (If the three points are collinear and equispaced, the curve does pass through the middle point.) At a point on the curve corresponding to a parameter value u between u_{i-1} and u_i, $C(u)$ is a weighted sum of the four control points P_{i-2}, P_{i-1}, P_i, and P_{i+1}.

Figure 6.8 shows a curve $C(u)$ constructed from B-splines using five control points. Observe that it does not pass through any of the five control points, P_0, ..., P_4. The displayed curve portion corresponds to the parameter range [1 3]. The slope at the end near P_1 is parallel to the line from P_0 to P_2, at the end near P_3; it is parallel to the line from P_2 to P_4.

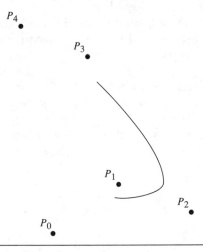

Figure 6.8   Uniform cubic B-spline to five control points

DOUBLE AND TRIPLE CONTROL POINTS

The control points for a curve are given in the sequence in which the curve will approximate them. Accordingly, we number the control points P_0, P_1, P_2, and so on. In the example above, the B-spline curve to five control points exhibits a certain shape. If we had used the same point positions in the plane, but numbered the points differently, we would have obtained a different curve. The user uniquely determines the sequence. The sequence has nothing to do with the positions of the control points in the plane or in space. P_i could be very far away from P_{i+1}, although these two are neighbors in the sequence. The order in which the control points are specified is called the *control point sequence* or the *control point vector*.

Two or more successive control points may have the same coordinates. We call this *repetition of control points*. To be mathematically correct, we should not think of a repeated control point, but instead of two or three successive control points that just happen to have the same coordinates. (The usual terminology is imprecise.) If successive control points have coinciding coordinates, the influence on the curve shape is significant. It assumes behaviors that result solely from the parameterization, such as the development of sharp corners.

Keep in mind that each control point is associated with a B-spline in the construction process, no matter whether or not some other control point has the same coordinates. Repeated control points imply a correspondingly increased number of B-splines and knots for the construction. Do not be misled by the fact that there are fewer *different* control points present.

Let us now explain how coinciding control points influence the curve. If two successive control points coincide, the curve is pulled closer to "this point" (actually to these two points). The curve has a steeper bend there, but is still smooth. If three successive control points coincide, the curve is forced through "this point" in a sharp corner. More than three coinciding points will not produce any further change. The curve will be the same as with only a triple control point. Thus, two specifications produce a slight change, three specifications a stronger change, and four or more produce no further change. With B-splines of higher degree, these numbers are correspondingly larger.

Do not confuse control points with knots! (Remember that control points are the P_i values—the given points that can be repeatedly specified—while knots are specific values of u in the parameter range.) While coinciding control points are very common when constructing B-spline curves, coinciding knots do not occur with uniform B-splines. (It is possible to specify coinciding knots when constructing B-spline curves, but this leads to nonuniform B-splines, which we briefly discuss later.) It is precisely because all knots are equispaced that we have uniform B-splines.

Figure 6.9 shows the effect of a "double" control point on the shape of the curve. The curve comes close to this point. The figure also shows how the curve would look if there were only one control point at P_j.

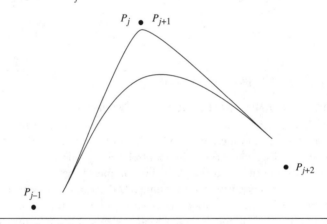

Figure 6.9   Two coinciding control points

Figure 6.10 shows the part of a B-spline curve in which three control points coincide: $P_j = P_{j+1} = P_{j+2}$. The curve passes through the triple point where it exhibits a sharp corner. The slope on the left of P_{j+1} is identical to the slope of the line connecting P_{j+1} to P_{j-1}. On the right of P_{j+1}, the analog is true with respect to point P_{j+3}.

To avoid giving too much detail, we do not mathematically prove this. The different left- and right-sided slopes mean that C has a sharp corner at the point P_{j+1}, in spite of the fact that the individual component curves—$C_x(u)$, $C_y(u)$, (and $C_z(u)$ if in space)—are perfectly smooth, piecewise, cubic polynomials!

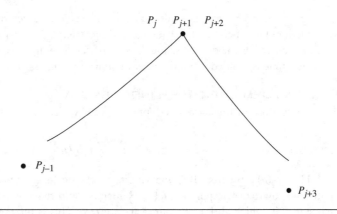

Figure 6.10   Three coinciding control points

SPECIFYING TRIPLE TERMINAL POINTS

Let us now adopt the usual terminology and talk simply of "repeating" a control point. An example will clarify this. If we have the control point sequence

$$P_0 \qquad P_1 \qquad P_2 \qquad P_3 \qquad P_4 \qquad P_5 \qquad P_6$$

in which $P_2 = P_3 = P_4$, we can use a notation in which we repeat the point P_2 in the control point sequence. The number of different subscripts is then identical to the number of "different" control points:

$$P_0 \qquad P_1 \qquad P_2 \qquad P_2 \qquad P_2 \qquad P_3 \qquad P_4$$

This notation is easy to read without being ambiguous. However, keep in mind that formally there are seven points, although only five have distinct coordinates.

Specifying a control point three times is useful if we do it with a terminal point P_0 or P_{n-1} because it causes the curve to attach to the triple point. In addition to being attached, near P_0 and P_3, the curve will partially coincide with the straight line from P_0 to P_1. Figure 6.11 shows such a curve.

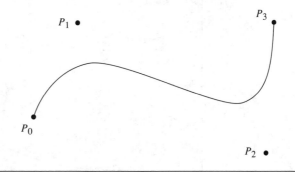

Figure 6.11   Triple specification of terminal points

In interactive design, it is quite valuable to be able to attach the curve to two end points and still mold it in between by changing, adding, deleting, and repeating other control points until the curve has the desired shape. In a user-friendly graphic system, the display will show how the curve is molded when the interior control points move.

THE UNIFORM CUBIC B-SPLINE FORMULA

We first review the above development. We have defined the B-spline curve as

$$C(u) = \sum_{i=0}^{n-1} p_i b_i(u)$$

Here, $b_i(u)$ is the basic B-spline with its peak at the location $u = i$. Each control point P_i is multiplied by the corresponding $b_i(u)$. Remember also that we draw the curve only for that range of u in which all four B-splines are nonzero. This is the range from $u = 1$ to $u = n-2$ (recall Figure 6.7). In each subinterval between 1 and $n-2$, the curve is determined by precisely four B-splines and the corresponding control points. In [1 2] these are the B-splines and control points with the subscripts 0, 1, 2, 3. That is:

$$C(u) = \sum_{i=0}^{3} p_i b_i(u) \quad \text{for } u \in \begin{bmatrix} 1 & 2 \end{bmatrix}$$

In [2 3] the subscripts are 1, 2, 3, 4:

$$C(u) = \sum_{i=1}^{4} p_i b_i(u) \quad \text{for } u \in \begin{bmatrix} 2 & 3 \end{bmatrix}$$

and so on. The reason for this is that all other B-splines are equal to zero outside these ranges.

Therefore, a drawing formula needs to use only four B-splines and corresponding control points. Of course, the four control points are not always the same when the parameter moves through its entire range. Studying the above two expressions for $C(u)$ will make it clear that the control points advance by one when u advances into the next subinterval. On the other hand, the B-splines weighted with the P_i are *identical*, in any subinterval! Figure 6.12 shows this.

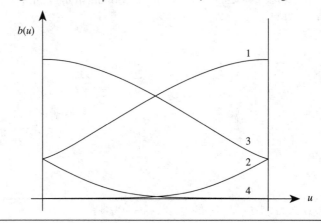

Figure 6.12   Parts of four different B-splines in a subinterval

We see two adjacent knots of a parameter subinterval. The knots correspond to P_{j+1} and P_{j+2}. The figure also shows the parts of the four basic B-splines that form C in this subinterval. We assume that the parameter's value is 0 at the left and 1 at the right, rather than i and $i+1$.

The polynomials multiplied by their weights produce the following equations:

$$1:\ \left(\tfrac{1}{6}(1+u)^3 - \tfrac{2}{3}u^3\right)x_{i+1}$$

$$2:\ \left(\tfrac{1}{6}u^3\right)x_{i+2}$$

$$3:\ \left(-\tfrac{2}{3}(1-u)^3 + \tfrac{1}{6}(2-u)^3\right)x_i$$

$$4:\ \left(\tfrac{1}{6}(1-u)^3\right)x_{i-1}$$

These equations are the same in any subinterval. We can therefore use one formula for evaluating $C(u)$ in all subintervals. In this formula, the parameter u will go from 0 to 1. The only varying factors from one subinterval to the next are the four control points that we plug into the formula. This formula is the most convenient way to compute or draw the B-spline curve. We can develop it by expressing the parts of the four different B-splines that participate in a subinterval as polynomials in u from 0 to 1 and by weighting them with $p_{i-1}, p_i, p_{i+1}, p_{i+2}$. These parts look identical to those in Figure 6.10, as they look in every subinterval.

$$C(u) = \left(\tfrac{1}{6}(1-u)^3\right)p_{i-1}$$
$$+ \left(-\tfrac{2}{3}(1-u)^3 + \tfrac{1}{6}(2-u)^3\right)p_i$$
$$+ \left(\tfrac{1}{6}(1+u)^3 - \tfrac{2}{3}u^3\right)p_{i+1}$$
$$+ \left(\tfrac{1}{6}u^3\right)p_{i+2}$$

Ordering on powers of u gives:

$$C(u) = u^3\left(-\tfrac{1}{6}p_{i-1} + \tfrac{1}{2}p_i - \tfrac{1}{2}p_{i+1} + \tfrac{1}{6}p_{i+2}\right)$$
$$+ u^2\left(\tfrac{1}{2}p_{i-1} - 1p_i + \tfrac{1}{2}p_{i+1}\right)$$
$$+ u^1\left(-\tfrac{1}{2}p_{i-1} + \tfrac{1}{2}p_{i+1}\right)$$
$$+ \left(\tfrac{1}{6}p_{i-1} + \tfrac{2}{3}p_i + \tfrac{1}{6}p_{i+1}\right)$$

We can write this conveniently as a matrix expression:

$$C(u) = \tfrac{1}{6}\begin{pmatrix} u^3 & u^2 & u & 1 \end{pmatrix} * \begin{pmatrix} -1 & 3 & -3 & 1 \\ 3 & -6 & 3 & 0 \\ -3 & 0 & 3 & 0 \\ 1 & 4 & 1 & 0 \end{pmatrix} * \begin{pmatrix} p_{i-1} \\ p_i \\ p_{i+1} \\ p_{i+2} \end{pmatrix}$$

We call this the *uniform cubic B-spline formula*. It expresses the value of C in any subinterval $[u \ u+1]$ with $u = 1, 2, \ldots, n-3$. Each subinterval determines one piece of the curve.

As the parameter u varies from 0 to 1, the formula gives the values of the curve from near P_i to near P_{i+1}. We say near because the curve does not go through the P_i. We call this a piece of the curve and the vector on the right the geometry vector. After advancing the control points in the geometry vector by 1, the parameter in the formula starts again with 0 and goes to 1. Although we originally had a parameter interval $[1 \ n-2]$ for the whole curve, now the parameter goes from 0 to 1 for each subinterval individually. We obtained this simplification by expressing all four B-splines in a common subinterval $[0 \ 1]$ and moving from one control point to the next, instead of from one subinterval to the next.

One can see that the curve is joined together from several pieces. Each piece is obtained by inserting the proper geometry vector into the formula. A smooth curve on the computer screen is drawn by stepping the parameter u in little increments from 0 to 1 for each geometry vector and connecting all curve values with straight lines. A curve unattached to the terminal control points is obtained by evaluating the formula for the following geometry vectors:

$$\begin{pmatrix} p_0 \\ p_1 \\ p_2 \\ p_3 \end{pmatrix} \quad \begin{pmatrix} p_1 \\ p_2 \\ p_3 \\ p_4 \end{pmatrix} \quad \cdots \quad \begin{pmatrix} p_{n-4} \\ p_{n-3} \\ p_{n-2} \\ p_{n-1} \end{pmatrix}$$

The graph of this curve will end near P_1 and P_{n-2} because this formula cannot evaluate curve values in the subintervals $[0 \ 1]$ and $[n-2 \ n-1]$. The reason is that for each subinterval, the formula needs to "reach out" to the adjacent control points on the left and right to obtain four points. The parameter subinterval $[0 \ 1]$ has no control point available to its left; similarly, $[n-2 \ n-1]$ has none on the right. Figure 6.7 shows that only three B-splines are nonzero there and that only three points control the curve.

We remind the reader to distinguish between control point vectors and geometry vectors. A control point vector is an array or list of all control points; a geometry vector is an array of only four numbers (the x-, y-, or z-coordinates of four successive control points). The geometry vectors that first enter the uniform formula are, for triple specification, $(p_0 \ p_0 \ p_0 \ p_1)^T$; for double specification, $(p_0 \ p_0 \ p_1 \ p_2)^T$, and for single specification, $(p_0 \ p_1 \ p_2 \ p_3)^T$.

HAND-DRAWING RULE

When working with B-splines, one should know the following rule for drawing B-splines by hand (see Figure 6.13). To obtain the curve point corresponding to any P_i, we connect the left and right neighbors of P_i with a straight line. Then we connect the midpoint, M, of this line to P_i. We find the point on this connector that lies $\frac{1}{3}$ of the line away from P_i. The B-spline curve goes through this point. The slope of the curve at this point is parallel to the line that connects the two neighbors. We can also use this drawing rule for doubled or tripled control points. We just assume that the two or three points are on top of each other.

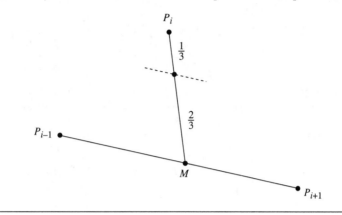

Figure 6.13   Hand-drawing a cubic B-spline curve

6.2.2   UNIFORM QUADRATIC B-SPLINES

We can approximate a set of control points with *uniform quadratic B-splines*, also called *parabolic B-splines*. The uniform quadratic B-spline curve stays closer to the points than the one we obtained from cubic B-splines. We do not go into the mathematical details of these B-splines as we did with the cubic ones, but just present the uniform quadratic B-spline formula. The analogies to the cubic case are quite obvious.

$$C(u) = \tfrac{1}{2}*\begin{pmatrix} u^2 & u & 1 \end{pmatrix}*\begin{pmatrix} 1 & -2 & 1 \\ -2 & 2 & 0 \\ 1 & 1 & 0 \end{pmatrix}*\begin{pmatrix} p_{i-1} \\ p_i \\ p_{i+1} \end{pmatrix}$$

In using this formula, we step the parameter u in small increments from 0 to 1 for each geometry vector of three adjacent control points. We force the curve through a control point or attach it to a terminal point by specifying the point twice. The curve will have a sharp corner at such a point.

Figure 6.14 shows cubic and parabolic B-spline curves to the same four control points; both are attached to the terminal points. The cubic B-spline curve is smoother than the quadratic one and stays farther away from intermediate control points.

HAND-DRAWING RULE

This rule is very simple for quadratic B-splines. We obtain the part of the curve near control point P_i by drawing one line segment between P_{i-1} and P_i and a second line segment between P_i and P_{i+1}. We mark the midpoints of the two segments. The piece of the curve starts at the first midpoint with the slope of the first segment and ends at the second midpoint with the slope of the second segment.

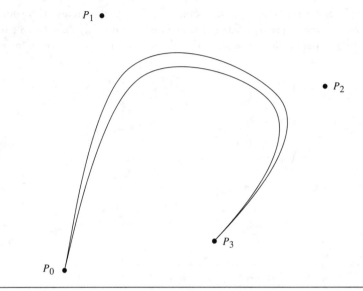

P_1 •

• P_2

• P_3

P_0 •

Figure 6.14   Comparison of quadratic and cubic B-spline curves

OO DESIGN AND CLASS SPECIFICATIONS

We have based our explanations of uniform B-splines on the cubic case because this one is more commonly used. We followed it with the quadratic case. Because we now see the similarities in both, we will base our design on the quadratic case and derive from it the cubic one. The other way is also possible, but seems unnatural to us.

Because a B-spline curve has an arbitrary number of points, we can represent it in the same manner as a polygon with all its points in a linked list of vertices. Deriving the class for a B-spline from convex_t has the following advantage: the data members that point to the vertex list, the counter of the vertices, the functions that deal with these, such as the operator += for adding new control points, and the constructor for constructing the class with the mouse are simply reused. Other member functions, such as filling, might or might not make sense for a curve—one can easily disable them if one so wishes. We must certainly respecify the functions draw() and copy().

With this design in mind, we derive the class ub3curve_t from convex_t and the class ub4curve_t from ub3curve_t.

```
//*********************** File ub3curve.h ***********************

#ifndef UB3CURVE_T
#define UB3CURVE_T

#include "../Shape2d/mouse.h"
#include "../Shape2d/scene.h"
#include "../Shape2d/convex.h"
```

```
class ub3curve_t : public convex_t //uniform B-spline curve of order 3
{
public:
   ub3curve_t() ;
   ub3curve_t(mouse_t&) ;
   ub3curve_t(const ub3curve_t&) ;
   ~ub3curve_t() ;

   void draw(const scene_t*) const ;
   prim_t* copy() const ;
} ;

#endif

//*****************************************************************
```

Drawing the B-spline curve is very convenient if one first puts all its vertices into a dynamically allocated array of points, where one can easily access them. Then, we draw the curve by drawing its consecutive pieces. The copy constructor for the curve simply calls the copy constructor of its base class convex_t.

The cubic B-spline curve is derived from the quadratic one and all that we have said for the class ub3curve_t applies here as well. In particular, we must redefine the functions draw() and copy().

```
//*********************** File ub4curve.h ***********************

#ifndef UB4CURVE_T
#define UB4CURVE_T

#include "../Curve/ub3curve.h"


class ub4curve_t : public ub3curve_t // uniform B-spline curve, order 4
{
public:
   ub4curve_t() ;
   ub4curve_t(mouse_t&) ;
   ub4curve_t(const ub4curve_t&) ;
   ~ub4curve_t() ;

   prim_t* copy() const ;
   void draw(const scene_t*) const ;
} ;

#endif

//*****************************************************************
```

The interested reader should study the implementation details in the codes `Curve/ub3curve.c` and `Curve/ub4curve.c`.

CLOSED B-SPLINE CURVES

To this point we have approximated only open curves. If we want to approximate a closed curve (one that connects to itself), we can most easily construct them with uniform B-splines of any order using the uniform B-spline formula. The only difference from what we did before is the way the control points enter the formula. We must also extend the control point sequence on one or both ends in a cyclic way.

QUADRATIC CURVES

If we have four control points (P_0, P_1, P_2, P_3), they could enter the formula in the following sequence:

$$P_3 \quad P_0 \quad P_1 \quad P_2 \quad P_3 \quad P_0$$

Therefore, we evaluate the parabolic B-spline formula with the following sequence of geometry vectors:

$$\begin{pmatrix} p_3 \\ p_0 \\ p_1 \end{pmatrix} \quad \begin{pmatrix} p_0 \\ p_1 \\ p_2 \end{pmatrix} \quad \begin{pmatrix} p_1 \\ p_2 \\ p_3 \end{pmatrix} \quad \begin{pmatrix} p_2 \\ p_3 \\ p_0 \end{pmatrix}$$

The first evaluation draws the curve from in between P_3 and P_0 to in between P_0 and P_1, and so on; the last one will close it.

Figure 6.15 shows a cubic and a quadratic closed curve with the same four control points. The quadratic curve is the one that goes closer to the control points.

CUBIC CURVES

If we have four control points P_0, P_1, P_2, P_3, they could enter the formula in the following order:

$$P_3 \quad P_0 \quad P_1 \quad P_2 \quad P_3 \quad P_0 \quad P_1$$

This results in an evaluation of the uniform cubic B-spline formula with the following sequence of geometry vectors:

$$\begin{pmatrix} p_3 \\ p_0 \\ p_1 \\ p_2 \end{pmatrix} \quad \begin{pmatrix} p_0 \\ p_1 \\ p_2 \\ p_3 \end{pmatrix} \quad \begin{pmatrix} p_1 \\ p_2 \\ p_3 \\ p_0 \end{pmatrix} \quad \begin{pmatrix} p_2 \\ p_3 \\ p_0 \\ p_1 \end{pmatrix}$$

The first evaluation draws the curve from near P_0 to near P_1 (the two middle control points in the geometry vector), the next from near P_1 to near P_2, and so on. The last evaluation closes the curve back to P_0. A cyclic permutation of the control point sequence will do the same.

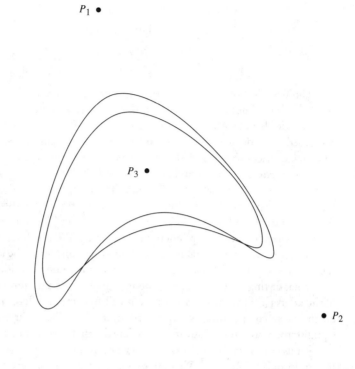

$P_1 \bullet$

$P_3 \bullet$

$\bullet \; P_2$

$P_0 \bullet$

Figure 6.15   Closed quadratic and cubic B-spline curves

6.3   NON-UNIFORM B-SPLINE CURVES

So far, we have restricted ourselves to uniform B-splines. These constitute a subset of the general B-splines, as Curry and Schoenberg originally introduced (CUSC47). In many computer graphics applications, it is sufficient to work with only uniform B-splines. The reason, as we mentioned, is that we are more concerned with the curve's visual appearance and less with its mathematical properties. The appearance of an approximating curve constructed with nonuniform B-splines differs little from one obtained with uniform B-splines (except in special cases).

Nonuniform B-splines are almost as easy to use as the uniform B-spline formula. However, their theoretical development is quite difficult and is well beyond the scope of this book. Therefore, we will not analyze them, only give the formulas. From now on, the term "B-spline" will refer to nonuniform B-splines, if not otherwise stated.

The B-splines of any degree and to any knot values u_i can be defined by the Cox-de Boor recursion formula (DEBO78):

$$b_{i1}(u) = 1 \text{ if } u_i \leq u < u_{i+1}$$

$$0 \text{ elsewhere}$$

$$b_{ik}(u) = \frac{(u - u_i)b_{i,k-1}(u)}{u_{i+k-1} - u_i} + \frac{(u_{i+k} - u)b_{i+1,k-1}(u)}{u_{i+k} - u_{i+1}}$$

The Cox-de Boor formula is elegant, but not intuitive. The two subscripts of b are i and k; i tells the knot range over which this B-spline stretches; b_{ik} goes from u_i until u_{i+k} (it is zero outside this range), and k is the order of the B-spline (the polynomials of which it is composed are of degree $k-1$). One can choose the knot values at will. They can even coincide. The only restriction is that the knot sequence must be nondecreasing. If two knots coincide, the denominators in the formula can become 0. In this case, the numerators are also 0; we adopt the convention that 0/0 = 0. Note that the second line gives a recursive relation for the b's; the B-splines of degree four are defined in terms of the B-splines of degree three, and these in terms of the B-splines of degree two, and so on. The first relation defines B-splines of degree 0; they are simple step functions. The sum of the B-splines of the same degree is identical to 1 everywhere in the range of the knot values, including the leftmost, but excluding the rightmost knot value. This last fact is important for coding considerations.

What distinguishes the curve we defined above from a uniform B-spline is the positioning of the knots u_i. If the knots are equidistant, all B-splines will look alike (uniform) and we can do the curve computation with a matrix formula, as shown in Section 6.2. If they are not equidistant, matrix formulas can be developed only for very special cases (Bezier curves).

Let us construct a special example of a nonuniform B-spline curve that looks very similar to a uniform B-spline curve. We want to obtain an approximating curve of order k to n control points, attached to the first and last point. For this, we choose the following $n+k$ knot values:

$$u_i = 0 \qquad \text{if } 0 \leq i < k$$
$$u_i = i - k + 1 \qquad \text{if } k \leq i < n$$
$$u_1 = n - k + 1 \qquad \text{if } n \leq i < n+k$$

This says that k knot values coincide at the ends of the parameter interval, which attaches the curve to the end points. The knots in between are equispaced. This arrangement produces a curve identical to a uniform B-spline curve in its center part if there are enough control points. We construct the curve C in the following way:

$$C(u) = \sum_{i=0}^{n-1} b_i k(u) * p_i$$

It would lead us too far astray to discuss all the aspects of nonuniform B-splines. We merely give an example for cubic B-splines, for which $k = 4$.

A SPECIAL KNOT ARRANGEMENT

According to the above discussion, if we have n control points P_0 to P_{n-1}, we choose $n+4$ knot values u_0 to u_{n+3}, for which:

$$u_i = 0 \qquad \text{if } 0 \le i < 4$$
$$u_i = i - 3 \qquad \text{if } 4 \le i < n$$
$$u_i = n - 3 \qquad \text{if } n \le i < n + 4$$

This defines a range of $n-2$ different knots. At each end of the range, the four terminal knots coincide, giving three knot intervals of length 0 at each end. The other knots are equally spaced over the range, thereby yielding $n-3$ knot intervals of length 1. (Observe that the knots are not equispaced throughout the entire range, so some of the B-splines are not uniform.) Now we can apply the above recursive formula to compute the B-splines.

The B-splines of degree 3 to this particular set of knots will consist of uniform B-splines in the middle of the range where the knots are equispaced. In the subintervals closer to the terminal knots, the B-splines will not be uniform because they include knot intervals of different length (length zero). These have different properties and shapes from the others. We demonstrate this with an example of nine control points, P_0 to P_8. Below, we will leave the subscript k of the B-spline out, as it is always 4.

$$u_0 = u_1 = u_2 = u_3 = 0$$
$$u_4 = 1,\ u_5 = 2,\ ...,\ u_8 = 5$$
$$u_9 = u_{10} = u_{11} = u_{12} = 6$$

Figure 6.16 shows the nonuniform cubic B-splines to these knots.

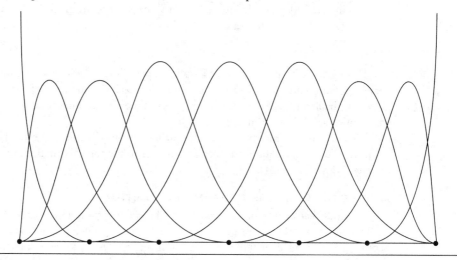

Figure 6.16   Nonuniform cubic B-splines

There are nine B-splines. All are composed of polynomials of degree 3 inside the interval, but are identical to 0 on the rest of the real number axis outside the interval and at the point $u = 6$. The three middle ones are uniform. The first three from the left are not uniform. They have discontinuities at the knot 0, either in the function value (the first or leftmost B-spline), the first derivative (the second one), or the second derivative (the third one). At the other end, similar things are true. There are only six nonzero knot intervals. If we define C as:

$$C(u) = \sum_{i=0}^{8} b_i(u) * p_i$$

then C is an approximating curve to the control points. We see that the B-spline curve to the given nine control points is again a weighted sum of the B-splines. At the left end of the interval, at $u = 0$ in the figure, only one B-spline is nonzero and has the value 1. At the right end, at $u = 6$, all B-splines are zero, although the last B-spline comes arbitrarily close to the value 1. From this we conclude that, at the end points of the interval, the function values $C(u)$ depend only on the corresponding control points (P_0 and P_8 in our example). This implies that $C(u)$ goes through the terminal points. At all other points in the interval, the value of $C(u)$ is a weighted sum of four B-splines between knots and a weighted sum of three B-splines at the knots.

As we described in the last section, we can attach a uniform B-spline curve to the terminal control points by tripling them. However, this curve would still differ from the above nonuniform B-spline curve in the following ways:

1. The uniform B-spline curve, attached to the terminal control points, depends on only two control points inside the terminal knot intervals and on three control points inside the next-to-terminal knot intervals. Inside the other knot intervals, it depends on four control points. At precisely an inner knot value, it depends on three.
2. Our nonuniform B-spline curve depends on four control points inside every subinterval. At precisely an inner knot value, it depends on three. In other words, the curve depends on four control points, even if only a small distance from a terminal point!

In the middle knot intervals the B-splines are uniform. Both types, the uniform B-spline curve and our nonuniform B-spline curve, are identical. Furthermore, the slopes of the curve at the terminal points are the same as the slopes of the straight lines from the respective terminal point to its adjacent control point.

There is no easy matrix formula for all nonuniform B-spline curves. The best way to calculate values of a nonuniform B-spline curve is to use the Cox-de Boor recursion formula directly (NESP79, p. 321).

A GENERAL B-SPLINE DRAWING ALGORITHM

The code that we now present generates a general B-spline curve of order 4 using the Cox-de Boor recursion. (Here, we purposely use the word "general" rather than "nonuniform," because this drawing algorithm draws the most general kind of B-spline curve. Depending on the setting of the knots, the curve could be nonuniform as well as uniform.)

Uniform and nonuniform B-spline curves are both composed of several curve pieces. In a curve of order k, each piece depends on only k consecutive control points and is computed as a weighted sum of these with the basic B-splines. So far, there is no difference between the two kinds. The difference is in how the basic B-splines are computed. In the uniform case, they are all identical, so they are computed once for all and condensed in the matrix formula.

In the nonuniform case, this is not possible. They depend on the knot values and must be computed on the fly for each point on the curve. When n control points are given, n basic B-splines must be computed, and these in turn need $n+k$ knot values. To draw the whole curve, the parameter u must go from the first knot to the last—not repeatedly through the interval [0 1], as it does in the case of a matrix formula.

Any given parameter value u will be in some knot interval. In this interval, there are precisely k basic B-splines with $b(u) > 0$. These depend on $2k$ knot values: the k to the left of u and the k to the right of u. The k control points associated with the nonzero B-splines and the $2k$ knot values on which the B-splines depend uniquely determine the value of the curve at u. Obviously, these stay the same inside the given knot interval. The part of the curve corresponding to a knot interval is again called a curve piece. The whole curve joins these separate pieces.

We specify the class `gb4curve_t` that represents a general B-spline curve of order 4. It has a linked list of vertices and an array of knot values. Since the order is 4, there must be four more knots than control points. The B-spline curve can be constructed with the mouse and the keyboard. After the user enters an arbitrary number of vertices with the mouse, the program will ask the user to enter a sequence of nondecreasing knot values from the keyboard—four more than the vertices. Alternatively, the user can choose not to enter knot values, in which case the knots will default to equispaced knots and the B-spline will become uniform.

We can conveniently derive this class from `convex_t`. We have to add only the pointer to the array of knots and write the proper constructor for entering the vertices with the mouse and the knots with the keyboard. We show the class specification below. The implementation is in `Curve/gb4curve.c`.

```
//*********************** File gb4curve.h ***********************

#ifndef GB4CURVE_T
#define GB4CURVE_T

#include "../Shape2d/convex.h"


class gb4curve_t : public convex_t // general B-spline curve, order 4
{
public:
   gb4curve_t(mouse_t&) ;
   gb4curve_t(const gb4curve_t&) ;
  ~gb4curve_t() ;

   void draw(const scene_t*) const ;
   prim_t* copy() const ;

private:
   double* knot ;
} ;

#endif

//****************************************************************************
```

A few comments about the implementation. We draw the curve by drawing its consecutive pieces. For piece 0, the parameter must go in little steps from knot[3] to knot[4], for piece 1 from knot[4] to knot[5], and so on. Straight lines connect the resulting curve values.

The function `bspline()` is the recursive Cox-de Boor formula. The call `bspline(i,k,u)` returns the value $b_{ik}(u)$ using the knots in the array.

The function `genbspl()` obtains the values of the four nonzero B-splines for a given u, weights them with the control points, and accumulates them. The result is the value of the curve at u.

An important remark: the function `piece()` that calls `genbspl()` with increasing u-values must avoid calling with u equal to or greater than the rightmost knot value knot[$n+3$] (n is the number of vertices). The curve can be attached to the terminal control points by repeating four knots at the ends of the knot range. The sum of the basic B-splines is 1 everywhere inside the knot range, excluding knot[$n+3$], where it is 0 (see DEBO78). If the last four knots coincide, a call with knot[$n+3$] would attach the curve to the origin. A mathematically clean solution is to call `genbspl()` only with u-values ranging from knot[$n+2$] to knot[$n+3$]–*eps* with a very small *eps*. This will make no visual difference in the curve pieces and will avoid attaching the curve to the origin in the case of terminal knot repetition.

By specifying nonequispaced knots or knots that coincide anywhere in the parameter range, we can give the B-spline curve a variety of shapes. Readers interested in B-splines should experiment with this code.

One can derive matrix formulas for computing or drawing nonuniform B-splines, but these must be different for every knot arrangement and even for different knot intervals within the same knot arrangement. Except for very special cases (Bezier curves are one special case of nonuniform B-splines), deriving those formulas is pointless. There is no simple rule for drawing nonuniform B-splines by hand.

CLOSED NONUNIFORM B-SPLINE CURVES

Closed nonuniform B-spline curves are a little harder to produce than closed uniform ones. We must specify the knots such that they form cyclicly repeating knot intervals.

When constructing a closed curve of order k to n control points, we first specify $n+1$ knot values u_0 to u_n. There are no restrictions, except that they must be in nondecreasing order. We then add $2k-2$ more knots, u_{n+1} to u_{n+2k-2}, at the right of the knot range, such that the added knot intervals are identical to those at the beginning of the knot range:

$$u_{n+1} - u_n = u_1 - u_0$$

$$u_{n+2} - u_{n+1} = u_2 - u_1$$

and so on. We augment the control point vector by appending the first $k-1$ control points to the end of the control point vector:

$$P_n = P_0$$

$$P_{n+1} = P_1$$

$$\ldots$$

$$P_{n+k-2} = P_{k-2}$$

THE CONVEX HULL PROPERTY

B-splines have the *convex hull property*, meaning that no individual piece of a B-spline curve will cross the convex hull of its four defining control points. Intuitively, the convex hull of points in a plane is the area defined by a rubber band stretched around all the points. Convex hulls are important in clipping a curve or in interactive B-spline drawing when speed is important. It is easiest if we first test the convex hull of the points that define the curve. If the convex hull does not intersect the clipping area, then neither does the B-spline curve. When redrawing part of a curve after changing a control point, we need only redraw that part within the convex hull of the changed control point and $k-1$ neighbors to the left and the right (k being the order of the B-splines).

6.4   CATMULL-ROM CURVES

As you have seen, a major difference between natural splines and B-spline curves is that the former interpolate while the latter approximate to the control points. The natural splines also lack local control. Can we somehow combine the advantage of local control and the ability to interpolate?

The answer to this question is yes, but it means sacrificing continuity of derivatives. With *Catmull-Rom curves*, we can define a locally controlled interpolating curve.

Catmull-Rom curves interpolate through given points. While we can construct them for any degree, only third-degree curves are popular in computer graphics. These we discuss below. Generalizing the Catmull-Rom curves leads to what is sometimes called *splines under tension*. They also interpolate through the control points.

Like a uniform B-spline curve, a Catmull-Rom curve is built from basic functions. It lacks continuity of the second derivatives at the knots. We obtain the basic functions in a fashion similar to that we described when discussing local control in Section 6.1, except that we remove the requirement of second-order continuity. We procure the 16 conditions needed to determine 16 constants in four cubic equations by adding three other requirements. These new requirements are specified values for the slopes at the three middle knots, which gives a fully determined system. The choice of these specified values exerts a strong influence on the resulting curve's appearance. If we select ½ in the left knot, 0 in the middle knot, and –½ in the right knot, we obtain the basis of a "proper" Catmull-Rom curve. Figure 6.17 shows the result of doing this. Compare it to Figure 6.6.

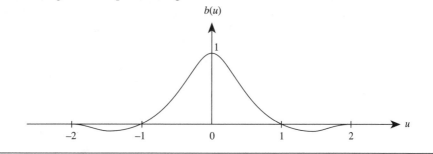

Figure 6.17   Catmull-Rom basis

We call this curve the *Catmull-Rom basis b*. To interpolate n control points $P_0, \ldots, P_{n-1}$, we use n bases, $b_0, \ldots, b_{n-1}$, which we obtain by shifting b by integer amounts in exactly the same way as for uniform B-splines:

$$b_i(u) = b(u - i)$$

The sum of these Catmull-Rom bases is equal to 1 throughout the interval [1 $n-2$]. We can therefore define the interpolating curve as:

$$C(u) = \sum_{i=0}^{n-1} b_i(u) * p_i$$

The curve goes through all control points. At each control point, the slope is parallel to the straight line that connects the two neighboring control points. The curve resembles a uniform cubic B-spline curve in this respect. The parts of the curve that correspond to terminal parameter intervals are again influenced by the origin. The drawing algorithm below will ignore these parts. Before we present the algorithm, we want to generalize.

To generalize the Catmull-Rom curve, we can set parameters for the values of the derivatives of the basis curve at the middle three knots. At the left knot we use c, at the middle knot 0, and at the right knot $-c$. When people obtain curves with bases defined in this way, they sometimes incorrectly call them splines under tension; we call them generalized Catmull-Rom curves. (Mathematically, these are really not splines, but the name "splines under tension" is suggestive and popular, as we explain below.)

The appearance of the resulting combined curve from a generalized Catmull-Rom basis fits the incorrect name "splines under tension" well. When c is small (less than 0.5), the resulting curve looks as if it has been pulled from its terminal points so as to be stretched out. The smaller c is, the more the curve is stretched, while still going through the control points. This makes the curve shorter with sharper bends. (This behavior is not apparent in the graphs of the single parameter curves.) Regardless of the value c, the tangent to the curve at the control points is always parallel to the line connecting its two adjacent neighbors.

Figure 6.18 shows three Catmull-Rom curves, all with the same control points, but with different values of c. The tightest one has $c = 0.3$, the next has $c = 0.5$ (which makes it a Catmull-Rom curve), and the loosest one has $c = 1$.

For $c = 0$, the combined curve degenerates to a polygon connecting the control points. Choosing $c = 0.5$ gives a Catmull-Rom curve. This curve is visually similar to a cubic B-spline curve, except that it interpolates through the control points rather than approximating to them. Since it has no second-order continuity, it lacks the grace of the B-spline curve. Values of c above 1 lead to a "slack" in the curve, which becomes so strong as c increases that the curve will make loops between the control points. For c values smaller than 0, the curve makes loops at the control points. Useful c values are therefore limited to the interval [0 1].

Catmull-Rom curves do not have the convex hull property and mathematically are not spline curves.

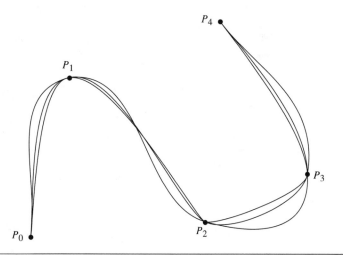

Figure 6.18   Generalized Catmull-Rom curves

A DRAWING ALGORITHM

Using the above conditions, we develop the equations for the four different polynomials that constitute the basis of the Catmull-Rom curves. If we transfer them all to the parameter interval [0 1], collect terms, and express $C(u)$ as a matrix formula, we obtain:

$$C(u) = \begin{pmatrix} u^3 & u^2 & u & 1 \end{pmatrix} * \begin{pmatrix} -c & 2-c & c-2 & c \\ 2c & c-3 & 3-2c & -c \\ -c & 0 & c & 0 \\ 0 & 1 & 0 & 0 \end{pmatrix} * \begin{pmatrix} p_{i-1} \\ p_i \\ p_{i+1} \\ p_{i+2} \end{pmatrix}$$

This formula generates the part of the Catmull-Rom curve between the middle two points in the geometry vector. If we repeatedly specify control points, this curve will behave quite differently from a B-spline curve. The curve will be attached to the terminal points if we specify them twice. When the curve enters a terminal point, the tangent to the curve will be parallel to the line connecting the terminal point to its neighbor. A triply specified terminal point produces one *overshoot* that sticks out beyond that point. If we specify a middle point twice, the curve makes a loop there, while a triple specification produces two overshoots. In that case, the curve will look as if two disconnected pieces cross each other at the point.

We can easily make generalized Catmull-Rom curves form closed curves if we specify the control points in a cyclic manner. Figure 6.19 shows a closed Catmull-Rom curve with four control points.

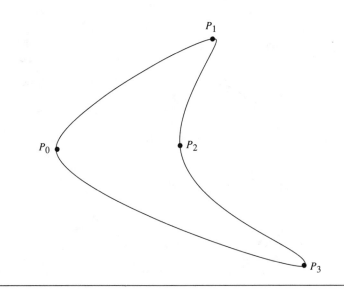

Figure 6.19   Closed Catmull-Rom curve

HAND-DRAWING RULE

The hand-drawing rule for Catmull-Rom curves is very simple. We know that the curve goes through the control points. The slope of the curve at point P_i is parallel to the line connecting P_{i-1} with P_{i+1}. This is enough information to draw an approximate outline of the curve.

6.5   BEZIER CURVES

We can use Bezier methods in a variety of ways to interpolate or approximate to a set of control points with curves of any degree. These methods stem from the *Bernstein polynomials*. There are $n+1$ Bernstein polynomials of degree n, defined on the interval [0 1] by:

$$b_i(u) = C(n,i) * u^i (1-u)^{n-i} \qquad i = 0, \dots, n$$

$C(n,i)$ is the binomial coefficient:

$$C(n,i) = \frac{n!}{i!(n-i)!}$$

For example, the four Bernstein polynomials of degree 3 are:

$$(1-u)^3, \ 3u^1(1-u)^2, \ 3u^2(1-u)^1, \ u^3$$

These polynomials are always nonnegative within [0 1]. Below, we discuss only cubic piecewise Bezier curves, as these are by far the most popular.

From the four cubic Bernstein polynomials, we can construct one cubic Bezier polynomial. Each of these is determined by four consecutive control points. Let us look at one. Given four consecutive control points $P_0, \dots, P_3$, we form the cubic Bezier polynomial as the sum of the Bernstein polynomials weighted with the control points:

$$\sum_{i=0}^{3} p_i * b_i(u) \quad \text{for } 0 \le u \le 1$$

According to our convention, the formula expresses a component curve for either the x-, y-, or z-coordinate, depending on which coordinates of the control points we insert. The combined curve is the cubic Bezier piece. It is attached to P_0 and P_3 and approximates P_1 and P_2, as Figure 6.20 shows. The slope of the curve at P_0 is identical to that of the straight line connecting P_0 and P_1. (The same is true at P_3.)

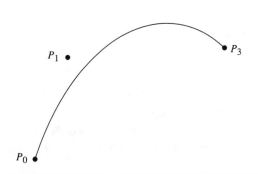

Figure 6.20   Cubic Bezier piece to four control points

Let us call an individual Bezier piece a *curve piece*. We can easily do the computation with a matrix formula:

$$C(u) = \begin{pmatrix} u^3 & u^2 & u & 1 \end{pmatrix} * \begin{pmatrix} -1 & 3 & -3 & 1 \\ 3 & -6 & 3 & 0 \\ -3 & 3 & 0 & 0 \\ 1 & 0 & 0 & 0 \end{pmatrix} * \begin{pmatrix} p_0 \\ p_1 \\ p_2 \\ p_3 \end{pmatrix}$$

If we have seven control points, as in Figure 6.21, we compute the second piece with the same formula using the geometry vector $(p_3 \ p_4 \ p_5 \ p_6)^T$. It is essential to observe that only control point P_3 appears in both geometry vectors. The pieces join at the point P_3, where in our example they form a sharp corner.

The control points P_2 and P_4 determine the slopes with which the pieces enter P_3. If we choose them to be collinear with P_3, there will be no corner at P_3 and the entire curve will be continuous in the first derivative.

If we have even more control points, we can continue in this manner. The number of control points must be any multiple of 3, plus 4. An individual curve piece will pass through the points P_{3i} and P_{3i+3}, but only approximate to the two control points in between. These points in the middle will define the slopes with which the curve enters the points P_{3i} and P_{3i+3}. The entire curve is usually called a *cubic Bezier curve*.

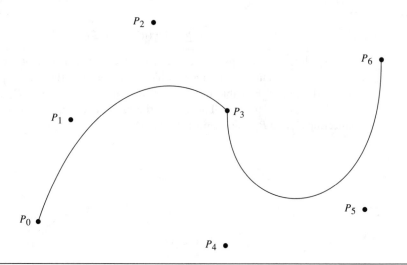

Figure 6.21   Two cubic Bezier pieces to seven control points

Figure 6.22 shows the curve to the same control points, except that P_4 has become collinear with P_2 and P_3. This makes the slopes of the two pieces identical where they meet at P_3; now the whole curve has a continuous first derivative.

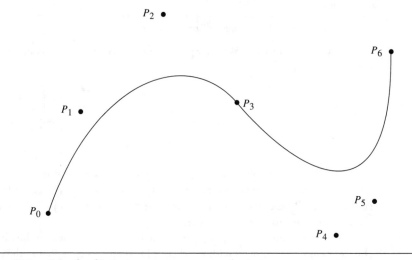

Figure 6.22   Smooth cubic Bezier curve to seven control points

We can continue this process to produce long, complicated curves with continuous first derivatives. The curve goes through every third point and through the terminal points. Setting the in-between points properly to achieve continuity is the user's responsibility. Because two inner points control the slopes for every piece, there is considerable flexibility in shaping the curve.

When drawing the pieces, one has to advance the geometry vectors in the following way:

$$\begin{pmatrix} p_0 \\ p_1 \\ p_2 \\ p_3 \end{pmatrix} \quad \begin{pmatrix} p_3 \\ p_4 \\ p_5 \\ p_6 \end{pmatrix} \quad \begin{pmatrix} p_6 \\ p_7 \\ p_8 \\ p_9 \end{pmatrix}$$

In an interactive drawing environment, one can fix the points P_0, P_3, P_6, and so on through which the curve will interpolate. Let us simply call these the control points. In other words, we specify a sequence of control points through which the curve should pass. We then specify auxiliary points (note that we do not call them control points). These are the points P_1, P_2, P_4, P_5, and so forth, which control the curve's slopes in the control points.

The piecewise Bezier curve with this set of points interpolates through all the control points and is still locally controlled. In a user-friendly drawing environment, the system helps the user set the auxiliary points to be collinear with "their" in-between control point. The resulting curve will look almost as smooth as a B-spline curve, will be attached to the terminal points, and will interpolate through all control points. These properties are more advantageous than the B-spline curve in many applications.

Some of the drawing programs for personal computers, such as Adobe Illustrator and Aldus FreeHand, allow the user to manipulate Bezier curves directly by "dragging" points with the mouse. The shape is controlled, while the changes appear on the screen in real-time.

We can easily make Bezier curves form closed curves by specifying the control points cyclicly much as we did before with closed curves. Bezier curves are a special case of a nonuniform B-spline curve, so they possess the convex hull property.

HAND-DRAWING RULE

The rule for sketching a cubic Bezier curve by hand is a little more complicated than for uniform B-splines. (We present it without mathematical proof.) One can geometrically find the point that the curve assumes for $u = \frac{1}{2}$ by finding the midpoint M_1 of the line from P_{i-1} to P_i, the midpoint M_2 of the line from P_i to P_{i+1}, and the midpoint M_3 of the line from P_{i+1} to P_{i+2}. Then, we find the midpoint M_4 of the line M_1–M_2, and the midpoint M_5 of the line M_2–M_3. Finally, we take the midpoint M of M_4–M_5. Point M will have the coordinates $C_x(\frac{1}{2})$ and $C_y(\frac{1}{2})$. The curve goes through M with the slope of this line. Figure 6.23 shows the process of finding M. The slope of the curve at a terminal point (P_{i-1} or P_{i+2}) coincides with the straight line from this point to its neighbor.

SUGGESTED READINGS

To the reader interested in parameterization and curves beyond the level presented here, I strongly recommend MORT85. Other good sources on these subjects are BARS88 and especially ROAD90.

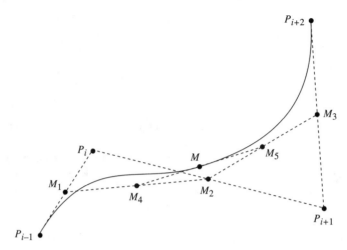

Figure 6.23   Hand drawing rule for cubic Bezier piece

EXERCISES

SECTION 6.0

Here are some curves for practice to make you familiar with parametric curve representations. They are called *hypocycloids*. You should write code that draws these curves either on the screen or on a plotter. The only graphics primitive you need is the straight line. Draw the curves by computing points along them that are connected by straight lines.

A hypocycloid is produced when a small circle with radius r rolls inside a larger circle with radius R. Any point a on the perimeter of the small circle describes a hypocycloid. The form of the curve depends on the ratio of R to r. We have a generalization if the point a does not lie on the perimeter of the small circle, but above or below. The point's distance from the center of the small circle is expressed by r_0 (see Figure 6.24).

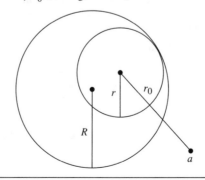

Figure 6.24   Constructing a hypocycloid

These curves demonstrate parametric representations' usefulness because we can easily express them in this way, while writing implicit formulas for them of the type $y = f(x)$ is extremely complicated. The parameterized form of a hypocycloid with u as the parameter is:

$$x = (R-r)*\cos(u) + r_0 \cos(u(R-r)/u)$$
$$y = (R-r)*\sin(u) - r_0 \sin(u(R-r)/u)$$

Below are some examples.

In Figure 6.25, $r_0 = r$. That is, point a lies on the perimeter of the small circle and $R/r = 2.5$. As this is not an integer ratio, the parameter u needs to go from 0 to 4π.

In Figure 6.26, we have $R/r = 8$ and $r_0 = 3*r$.

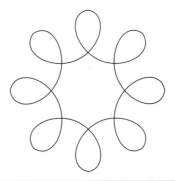

Figure 6.25   Example of hypocycloid   Figure 6.26   Another hypocycloid

In Figure 6.27, we again have an integer ratio: $R/r = 7$. r_0 is much greater than r: $r_0 = 5*r$.

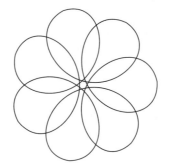

Figure 6.27   Another hypocycloid

1. Produce curves with different ratios of R/r and $r = r_0$.
2. Produce curves with different values for r_0. What is the characteristic feature of a curve with $r_0 > r$?
3. Find out how the curves look when r comes close to R and r_0 is much greater than r. What happens when $r > R$? This is not physically possible because the larger circle cannot roll inside the smaller one, but mathematically should still work and might produce an interesting curve.

4. What is the characteristic feature of the hypocycloids when r_0 is smaller than r? What happens for $r_0 = 0$? Find out by producing several such curves.

5. Draw by hand two smooth parameter curves whose combined curve has a sharp corner.

6. Draw by hand two parameter curves that both have a sharp corner, but whose combined curve is smooth.

SECTION 6.2

7. Write a function `void ub4piece(point3_t pv[4])` that draws one piece of a uniform cubic B-spline curve in the plane to four consecutive control points, using forward differences. Their coordinates are specified in the array `pv`. Use the type `point3_t` that we introduced in Chapter 5.

8. Extend the function `ub4piece()` to three dimensions by adding the computation of the z-coordinate.

9. Define more than four points in 3D space and use the three-dimensional function of Exercise 8 to draw a B-spline curve in space.
    a. Draw the curve on the screen with orthographic projection by ignoring the computation of the z-values.
    b. Draw the curve on the screen with perspective projection by using a `win_view3_t` system and the `line3_t::draw()` of Exercise 11 in Chapter 5.

10. Implement the class `ub3piece_t`, which specifies and draws a uniform quadratic B-spline curve piece analogous to `ub4piece_t`.

11. Show that one can draw a basic uniform cubic B-spline with the uniform B-spline formula by choosing the seven control points:

    (–3 0)   (–2 0)   (–1 0)   (0 1)   (1 0)   (2 0)   (3 0)

    (Observe that the y-coordinates are all equal, except for the middle one, and that the x-coordinates are equidistant.) Use the points in the listed order. What is the necessary sequence of geometry vectors? Draw this curve on the screen.

12. This exercise is analogous to Exercise 11, except for the order of the B-spline curve. What control points and what control point vector must you choose to draw a basic uniform quadratic B-spline? Draw this curve on the screen.

To become familiar with B-splines, you should practice drawing them by hand using the hand-drawing rule we presented in the text. The exercises below give you an opportunity to do this.

13. Draw by hand the open cubic B-spline curve to the control points (0 1), (1 2), (2 0), and (0.5 0.5).

14. Draw by hand the open uniform cubic B-spline curve to the five control points given in Figure 6.28.

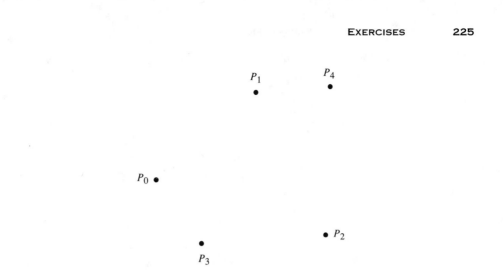

Figure 6.28   *Control points for practicing hand drawing*

15. Draw by hand the open uniform quadratic B-spline curve to the five control points of Exercise 14.

16. If we specify a control point twice, we can still use the hand-drawing rule to make the curve. The twice-specified point is considered to be two distinct points that are very close together, and so it almost plays a double role. Do this until you are proficient.

Hint: when advancing with the points, we consider the twice-specified point to be two points (see Figure 6.29). This figure shows only the part of the curve that is very close to P_3. The shape of the curve outside this part depends on other control points and is therefore not shown. With a little practice, you will be able to apply the drawing rule, while completely collapsing the two distinct images of P_3.

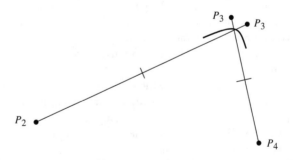

Figure 6.29   *Taking a double point as two distinct points*

17. Draw by hand the uniform cubic B-spline curve to the points in Figure 6.30, where P_1 and P_2 are specified twice.

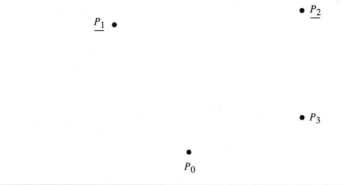

Figure 6.30   Control points for practicing hand drawing

18. If we specify a control point three times, using the hand-drawing rule is easy. We draw straight lines from this point in the direction of the adjacent control points to precisely $\frac{1}{6}$ the distance to these points. From then on, we use the hand-drawing rule with no change. Do this with the points of Figure 6.28, considering P_1 and P_2 to be triply specified.

SECTION 6.3

19. Use gb4curve_t and the knot sequence {0 0 0 0 1 2 3 3 3 3} to draw a general B-spline curve of order 4 to six control points. What is characteristic about this curve?

20. Use gb4curve_t and the knot sequence {0 0 0 0 1 1 2 2 3 3 3 3} to draw a general B-spline curve of order 4 to eight control points. What is characteristic about this curve?

21. Experiment with other knot sequences.

22. Define a class gbcurve_t that represents a general B-spline curve of any order. Derive it from gb4curve_t. Design the curve in analogy to class gb4curve_t. It holds the control points in a linked list and the knots in a dynamically allocated array. It is given control points and knots like the class gb4curve_t. It must have a member *k* for the order and its draw() function must check for sufficient number of control points and knots.

23. Use gbcurve_t to draw the same curves as in Exercises 19 and 20.

24. Define a class cgbcurve_t that represents a closed, general B-spline curve, as we explained in the text. The class is mostly identical to gbcurve_t, except that upon construction it initializes an augmented control point array and an augmented knot array. Then it draws an augmented number of pieces.

25. Use cgbcurve_t to draw a closed curve of order 4 to the control points (–2 –1), (–2.5 0.5), (0 0), (1.5 1.5), and (1.5 1). Use evenly spaced knot values.

26. Use cgbcurve_t to draw a closed general B-spline curve to the same control points, as in Exercise 23, but with nonequidistant or collapsing knot values.

27. Use gbcurve_t to draw a basic uniform B-spline of order 5. Simply use the default knot setting and the proper setting of control points.

28. Use `gbcurve_t` to draw basic general B-splines of various orders and to various knot settings. Example: specify ten knots $k[0]$ to $k[9]$ in nondecreasing sequence, then draw the six B-splines b_0 to b_5 of order 4. (Figure out the proper setting of the control points so that the resulting curves are B-splines.)

29. Draw by hand the closed cubic B-spline curve to the control points (0 1), (1 2), (2 0), and (0.5 0.5).

30. Choose four control points that form the vertices of a square, for example, (–1 –1), (1 –1), (1 1), and (–1 1). Draw the closed cubic B-spline curve to these points. It looks like a perfect circle. Is the curve in this particular case mathematically identical to a circle?

31. Draw the closed quadratic B-spline curve to the control points (0 1), (1 2), (2 0), and (0.5 0.5).

32. Draw by hand the closed cubic B-spline curve to the control points in Figure 6.31. Observe the sequence of the points!

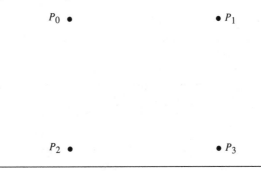

P_0 •   • P_1

P_2 •   • P_3

Figure 6.31   Control points for practicing hand drawing

SECTION 6.4

33. Write a class `crcurve_t` that specifies a generalized Catmull-Rom curve of degree 3 to a given sequence of control points. The control points are kept in a linked list of `vertex_t`. One class member is a pointer to the beginning of the list, another is the number of control points, and a third is the tension parameter.

    A `crcurve_t` object draws itself by drawing all its pieces and by using the nonmember function `void piece(point_t*, const win_view_t&)`. You can develop everything in analogy to the class `ub4curve_t` in the text.

34. Use `crcurve_t` to draw an open Catmull-Rom curve with tension parameter 0.5 to the five points in the given order: (0 0)   (0.5 2)   (2.5 –0.5)   (4 1)   (6.5 0.5)

35. Draw the same curve as above, but one that is attached to the terminal points. By which simple means can you achieve this?

36. Draw a generalized Catmull-Rom curve to the control points in Exercise 34 with varying parameter c. What do you observe when c nears and becomes 0? What if c becomes negative? What if c becomes bigger than 3?

37. Write the class `ccrcurve_t` that specifies a closed generalized Catmull-Rom curve of degree 3 to arbitrary control points. Draw closed Catmull-Rom curves to the control points in Exercise 34 with varying parameters c.

38. Write the class `crcurve3_t` that specifies a generalized Catmull-Rom curve of degree 3 in space. The control points are kept in a linked list of `vertex3_t`. Otherwise, everything else is analogous to `crcurve_t` of Exercise 33. Use `win_view3_t` and `line3_t`. If you have not implemented the 3D straight line clipper for `line3_t`, use a dummy clipper and see that the curve stays inside the frustum.

39. Use the hand-drawing rule to draw an open Catmull-Rom curve to the five control points:

    (–1 0)   (0.5 2)   (2.5 –0.5)   (4 1)   (3 0.5)

SECTION 6.5

40. Write a class `bezcurve_t` that specifies a piecewise Bezier curve of degree 3 to an arbitrary number of control points (the restriction $n = 3*i+1$ is valid). The class checks for the proper number of control points and exits with an error message if not fulfilled. A `bezcurve_t` object draws itself by drawing all its pieces using the nonmember function `void piece(point_t* p,const win_view_t& w)`. You can develop everything in analogy to the class `ub4curve_t` in the text. Pay attention to how geometry vectors advance in the control point vector.

41. Implement an additional feature of the class `bezcurve_t`. It checks for collinearity of those groups of three consecutive points that straddle over consecutive pieces. If not fulfilled, it exits with an error message. Use `bezcurve_t` to draw the Bezier curve to the ten control points in the given order:

    (–2 2) (–1 2) (–1 1) (0 0) (0.5 –0.5) (2 0) (2 1) (2 3) (3.5 1.5) (4.5 1.5)

42. Write a class `cbezcurve_t` that draws a closed Bezier curve to an arbitrary number of control points (the restriction is $n = 3*i$). Use it to draw a closed Bezier curve to the nine control points below in the given order:

    (0 0)   (–1.5 0)   (–2 –1)   (0 –2)   (1 –2.5)   (3 –1)   (2 0)   (1 1)   (1 0)

    Only three of these points can serve as knots. Which are they? *Hint:* watch for collinearity.

43. Write the class `bezcurve3_t` that extends the concept of `bezcurve_t` to three dimensions. Use `vertex3_t`, `win_view3_t`, and `line3_t` and develop the curve in analogy to Exercise 38.

44. Use the hand-drawing rule to draw a Bezier curve to the four control points:

    (–1 1)   (0 0)   (2 1.5)   (3.5 1)

7

Parametric Surfaces and the Oslo Algorithm

Chapter 7 discusses applying curves to generating surfaces and the Oslo algorithm.

7.0   INTRODUCTION

The objects in the real world that we wish to display on the screen are three-dimensional. We must be able to define their surfaces before we can project them onto a two-dimensional viewing surface. While some objects have planar surfaces that we can represent as joined polygons, this is too limiting. We need ways to represent curved surfaces. The two-dimensional curves of the last chapter form a basis for this important task.

The most important topic of this chapter is generating surfaces by extending the equations for 2D curves into three dimensions. While this idea is straightforward, it is difficult to visualize.

7.1   PARAMETRIC SURFACES

We move from curves to surfaces. A plane cannot contain a surface, so we must think in 3D space. A *surface* is a single function that establishes a relation between three variables x, y, and z:

$$z = f(x, y)$$

where both x and y are independent variables. For the same reason as in the plane, we prefer to use parametric representation. To describe a parametric surface in 3D space, we use three functions, but each function has two independent variables u and v as its parameters:

$$x = x(u, v)$$
$$y = y(u, v)$$
$$z = z(v, v)$$

If only one parameter varies and the other remains at a constant value, say $v = c$ with u allowed to vary, then the coordinates $x(u,c)$, $y(u,c)$, $z(u,c)$ describe a curve that runs within the surface. The slope of this curve's projection on the $(x\ y)$-plane is:

$$\frac{dy}{dx} = \left(\frac{dy}{du}\right) \div \left(\frac{dx}{du}\right)$$

The derivatives with respect to u are all partial. We can similarly derive the slopes of the projections on the other planes and the symmetric cases for fixed u with v varying. Note carefully that such curves' projections on any of the coordinate system's planes are not identical to the surface's intersections with any of these planes. For example, to obtain the intersection of the surface with the $(x\ y)$-plane, we observe that all such points in the surface will have $z = 0$. We then set $z(u,v) = 0$. This is a relation between u and v. We should transform this into a parameterized relation with a single parameter of the form:

$$u = U(w)$$
$$v = V(w)$$

The intersection is then described as a curve in the $(x\ y)$-plane with a single parameter, w:

$$x = x(U(w), V(w))$$
$$y = y(U(w), V(w))$$

We will not go into more detail here.

As with parameterized curves in 2D space, we can easily limit a surface to a certain region by restricting the parameters' range to a finite two-dimensional interval, for example, the rectangular area $[0\ n] \times [0\ m]$.

We obtain a surface that interpolates or approximates a set of control points in much the same way as we did for curves in the plane. We construct three parametric surfaces, one of which interpolates or approximates the control points' x-coordinates, one the y-coordinates, and one the z-coordinates. Each of these specific surfaces is defined on a rectangular area of the two arguments u and v, which can also be called a two-dimensional interval. Let this range be the rectangle $[0\ n] \times [0\ m]$. The particular parameter values (u,v) that determine the approximation or interpolation will be the same in all three surfaces.

An example will make this clearer. We want to construct a surface that contains a control point $P = (p_x\ p_y\ p_z)$. If we construct three surfaces with a given parameter range so that by choosing $(u_0\ v_0)$ within this range we obtain $x(u_0,v_0) = p_x$, $y(u_0,v_0) = p_y$, and $z(u_0,v_0) = p_z$, then it is evident that the surface goes through the point $(p_x\ p_y\ p_z)$.

The same idea applies to surfaces that approximate the point. We define basic surfaces $b(u,v)$, which we combine, as a weighted sum using the control points' coordinates as the weights. This is analogous to what we have done before in two dimensions.

7.2   UNIFORM CUBIC B-SPLINE SURFACES

We can define a uniform cubic basic B-spline surface $b(u,v)$ by multiplying the uniform cubic basic B-spline $b(u)$ (from Section 7.2.1) by itself, but with two different independent parameters u and v:

$$b(u,v) = b(u) * b(v)$$

The parameters u and v both range over the interval $[-2\ 2]$, so the parameter pair ranges over the area $[-2\ 2] \times [-2\ 2]$. We use the letter b for both the curves $b(u)$ and $b(v)$ and the basic B-spline surface $b(u,v)$. This should not cause confusion, as the context will differentiate; the surface b will have two arguments instead of one. Figure 7.1 shows a 3D view of this surface.

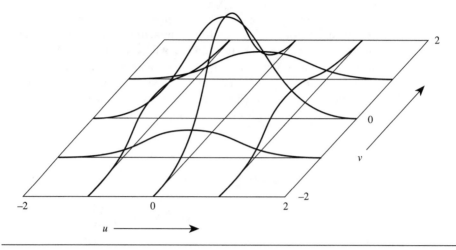

Figure 7.1   Basic uniform B-spline surface

Outside the range of definition, the surface $b(u,v)$ is identical to 0. Within its range, the surface b is pieced together from 16 different surface equations because the above definition involves multiplying each of the four curve pieces that comprise $b(u)$ by each of the four pieces of the curve $b(v)$. This surface is continuous up to its second partial derivative, as is true for each of the curves $b(u)$ and $b(v)$.

From the previously known values for $b(u)$ and $b(v)$, we have:

$$b(0,-1) = b(0,1) = b(-1,0) = b(1,0) = 1/9$$
$$b(-1,-1) = b(-1,1) = b(1,-1) = b(1,1) = 1/36$$
$$b(0,0) = 4/9$$
etc.

Here, the knots are the intersection points of the 10 grid lines shown in the drawing. These lines delimit 16 *subareas* (areas between adjacent gridlines) in which the 16 different surfaces that comprise $b(u,v)$ are defined. These specific surfaces are connected at the boundaries of the rectangular subregions.

In using this approach, be sure to observe the following. If we want to interpolate or approximate a set of points in space with a surface, we list the control points in a rectangular array. For this array, we use a *control point matrix*, just as we used a control point vector for curves. This does not mean that the surface will be rectangular or confined somehow to a rectangular area in any of the coordinates. The control points' spatial coordinates are independent of their position in the control point matrix. Two neighbors in the matrix can be far apart in space and vice versa. Points in different positions in the matrix can be very close or even coincident in space. This means that the number of different control points in space is not necessarily a product of two integers, as the matrix suggests.

What the matrix determines is the surface's course through (or near) the control points. Think of a B-spline curve in the plane, where the control points were arranged in a control point vector. The curve went from near P_i to near its two neighbors, P_{i-1} and P_{i+1}, no matter where these points were situated in the plane. In case of a surface, the surface will go from near the point P_{ij} to near its eight neighbors in the matrix, no matter where they lie in space. (If a control point has no neighbors, the curve or surface will end there.)

Once the control points are arranged in the matrix, we associate a basic surface with each of them; we need as many basic surfaces as there are points in the matrix. We obtain the surfaces by simply shifting the surface $b(u,v)$ by integer increments for u or v within the parameter range. Formally, we perform this with:

$$b_{ij}(u,v) = b(u-i, v-j) \quad \text{for} \quad i = 0, ..., n-1$$

$$\text{and} \quad j = 0, ..., m-1$$

This produces $m \times n$ basic surfaces, each of which spreads over a rectangular area of 25 knots (remember that the basic cubic B-spline stretched over 5 knots). Adjacent basic surfaces share either 16 or 20 of their knots, depending on whether they are diagonally or sidewise adjacent. For a matrix of size $m \times n$, the parameter range that contains the $m \times n$ basic surfaces will consist of $(m+4) \times (n+4)$ grid lines. The peaks of the basic surfaces are located at the inner knots (those that are at least two gridlines away from the range's boundaries). The sum of the basic surfaces is constant, equal to 1 over the whole inner parameter range, that is, up to two gridlines away from the boundaries. Between the inner range and the boundaries, it decreases smoothly and is 0 at the boundaries.

The shifting process we explained above also arranges the basic surfaces in a $m \times n$ rectangle over the parameter range. This gives the association between control points and basic surfaces. We obtain a uniform B-spline surface by multiplying the basic surfaces by the corresponding control points in the matrix and summing them.

$$S(u,v) = \sum_{i=0}^{m-1} \sum_{j=0}^{n-1} P_{ij} b_{ij}(u,v)$$

Of course, we must convert this to actual coordinates by inserting the x-, y-, or z-coordinates that define P. We get three expressions:

$$S_x(u,v) = \sum_{i=0}^{m-1} \sum_{j=0}^{n-1} x_{ij} b_{ij}(u,v)$$

for x, and likewise for y and for z.

Figure 7.1 showed how a basic B-spline surface is composed of 16 different surfaces. It follows that in an inner subarea there are 16 different surfaces—the parts of the 16 basic B-spline surfaces that are nonzero in this subarea. These are called the *blending surfaces* in this subarea. The part of the B-spline surface that corresponds to an inner subarea is called a *patch*. We construct a patch by multiplying that subarea's blending surfaces by the control points corresponding to the basic B-spline surfaces to which the blending functions belong. The parameters u and v range only over a distance of 1.

The blending surfaces are the same in all inner subareas where u and v range only over a distance of 1. Below, we will derive a formula for expressing any patch of the B-spline surface. Only the 16 control points used for weighting the basic splines will change; u and v will both range from 0 to 1.

A DRAWING ALGORITHM

We can derive a matrix formula for calculating the surface in an inner subarea that resembles the uniform B-spline formula for curves. We need to multiply all 16 blending surfaces by the proper control points and add them together.

The proper control points are the four associated with the corner points of the inner subarea, plus the 12 control points surrounding the subarea. Figure 7.2 shows a double-shaded inner subarea and its 16 associated control points.

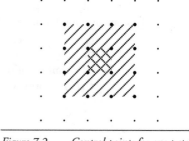

Figure 7.2   Control points for one patch

The next step is to group the powers of u and use the row vector $(u^3 \ u^2 \ u \ 1)$ on the left of the expression. Then we group the powers of v and use the column vector $(v^3 \ v^2 \ v \ 1)^T$ on the right. This gives an expression of the form:

$$S(u,v) = \mathbf{U} * \mathbf{Q} * \mathbf{V}^T$$

in which $S(u,v)$ is the surface, $\mathbf{U}$ and $\mathbf{V}$ are the two vectors above, and $\mathbf{Q}$ is a 4×4 matrix in which every element is a combination of all 16 control points with certain multipliers. We further decompose $\mathbf{Q}$ into three matrices. This calculation is lengthy, so we leave out the details.

The result is:

$$S(u,v) = \tfrac{1}{36} * \mathbf{U} * \mathbf{M} * \mathbf{P} * \mathbf{M}^T * \mathbf{V}^T$$

In this formula we have:

$$\mathbf{U} = \left(u^3 \ u^2 \ u \ 1 \right)$$

$$\mathbf{P} = \begin{pmatrix} p_{i-1,j-1} & p_{i-1,j} & p_{i-1,j+1} & p_{i-1,j+2} \\ p_{i,j-1} & p_{i,j} & p_{i,j+1} & p_{i,j+2} \\ p_{i+1,j-1} & p_{i+1,j} & p_{i+1,j+1} & p_{i+1,j+2} \\ p_{i+2,j-1} & p_{i+2,j} & p_{i+2,j+1} & p_{i+2,j+2} \end{pmatrix}$$

$$\mathbf{V} = \left(v^3 \ v^2 \ v \ 1 \right)$$

$\mathbf{M}$ is the matrix of the uniform cubic B-spline formula:

$$\mathbf{M} = \begin{pmatrix} -1 & 3 & -3 & 1 \\ 3 & -6 & 3 & 0 \\ -3 & 0 & 3 & 0 \\ 1 & 4 & 1 & 0 \end{pmatrix}$$

We call this the *uniform bicubic B-spline formula*. It expresses the part of S that is closest to the middle four control points in the matrix **P**. This is analogous to the uniform cubic B-spline formula for curves, which expresses the curve piece closest to the two middle points in the geometry vector. When we calculate the value of S in a subarea, we use the 16 control points surrounding this subarea. To display this part of S, we must evaluate the expression for both u and v, stepping in small increments from 0 to 1. This must be done three times, once for **P** filled with the x-coordinates, once with the y-coordinates, and once with the z-coordinates. The surface part obtained in this way is called a *bicubic B-spline patch*. The 16 control points that determine this patch form the *patch matrix*, (another name is *geometry matrix*, in analogy to the curves).

To move from patch to patch, we move the 4×4 patch matrix in some systematic way over the whole control point matrix and start u and v at 0 for every patch. The patches will join together with second-order continuity and form a smooth surface. The control point matrix can be of any size (though it must have a rectangular arrangement), but the patch matrix is always 4×4.

Figure 7.3 shows a surface consisting of two bicubic patches and the 20 control points for the two patches.

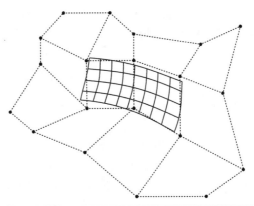

Figure 7.3   Two joined B-spline patches

We assume that the 20 control points are arranged in a 5×4 control point matrix:

$$\begin{pmatrix} P_{00} & P_{01} & P_{02} & P_{03} \\ P_{10} & P_{11} & P_{12} & P_{13} \\ P_{20} & P_{21} & P_{22} & P_{23} \\ P_{30} & P_{31} & P_{32} & P_{33} \\ P_{40} & P_{41} & P_{42} & P_{43} \end{pmatrix}$$

The patch matrices are submatrices of the control point matrix. Two patch matrices are possible in this case, as the shaded areas indicate:

$$\begin{pmatrix} P_{00} & P_{01} & P_{02} & P_{03} \\ P_{10} & P_{11} & P_{12} & P_{13} \\ P_{20} & P_{21} & P_{22} & P_{23} \\ P_{30} & P_{31} & P_{32} & P_{33} \\ P_{40} & P_{41} & P_{42} & P_{43} \end{pmatrix} \quad \begin{pmatrix} P_{00} & P_{01} & P_{02} & P_{03} \\ P_{10} & P_{11} & P_{12} & P_{13} \\ P_{20} & P_{21} & P_{22} & P_{23} \\ P_{30} & P_{31} & P_{32} & P_{33} \\ P_{40} & P_{41} & P_{42} & P_{43} \end{pmatrix}$$

We can see that the patch matrices must "overlap" within the control point matrix. The above two patch matrices yield the two joining bicubic B-spline patches of Figure 7.3.

REPEATING BOUNDARY CONTROL POINTS

This formula cannot calculate the surface in the outer subareas because there are not 16 surrounding control points in that location. We can attach the surface to the four corner points of the control point matrix by specifying the corner control points nine times and the other boundary control points three times. Then, the B-spline surface is attached to the four corner control points, and to the B-spline curves that approximate the boundary. It is not attached to the other control points on the boundaries.

Figure 7.4 shows how this works for control points on the lower left boundary. The subscripts show which control points are repeated.

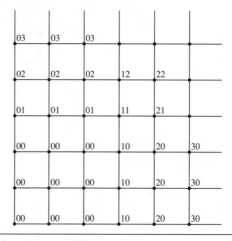

Figure 7.4   Repeating boundary control points

REPEATING INNER CONTROL POINTS

In this approach to constructing surfaces, we cannot pull the curve closer to or through a single, inner control point in the matrix by specifying this point two or three times. We force a cubic B-spline surface through a given point if we specify this point nine times in a 3 × 3 area. Similarly, we pull the surface more strongly in the direction of a control point if we specify the point four times in a 2 × 2 area of the grid. We are more restricted here because of the rectangular arrangement in which we must specify the control points. We cannot arbitrarily respecify one point without rearranging all the other points. Repeating a point along a row in the matrix's interior introduces an additional column of points in order to keep the matrix rectangular. We obtain similar results by repeating a point along a column in the matrix's interior. We will not go into more detail.

MOVEMENT OF A SURFACE POINT

The rules for matrix multiplication help us remember the direction in which a point moves in the parameterized surface with varying parameters u and v. Envision the schematic below:

$$\begin{pmatrix} u^3 & u^2 & u & 1 \end{pmatrix} * \begin{pmatrix} x & x & x & x \\ x & x & x & x \\ x & x & x & x \\ x & x & x & x \end{pmatrix} * \begin{pmatrix} v^3 \\ v^2 \\ v \\ 1 \end{pmatrix}$$

The matrix indicated by the x's is $\mathbf{M}*\mathbf{P}*\mathbf{M}^T$. For now, we call this matrix $\mathbf{P}'$. If u is a row vector at the left of $\mathbf{P}'$ and v is a column vector at the right of $\mathbf{P}'$, then u is multiplied by columns of $\mathbf{P}'$ and v is multiplied by rows of $\mathbf{P}'$.

This helps us remember: increasing u moves down in the patch matrix, while increasing v moves right in the patch matrix:

$$\begin{array}{c} \qquad \xrightarrow{\ v\ } \\ u \downarrow \begin{array}{cccc} x & x & x & x \\ x & x & x & x \\ x & x & x & x \\ x & x & x & x \end{array} \end{array}$$

If the patch matrix is:

$$\begin{matrix} 11 & 12 & 13 & 14 \\ 21 & 22 & 23 & 24 \\ 31 & 32 & 33 & 34 \\ 41 & 42 & 43 & 44 \end{matrix}$$

then varying u from 0 to 1 while keeping v fixed moves a surface point from near control point 22 in the direction of 32 or from 23 to 33, depending on where v is. (These are only approximate locations, but the schematic helps us to understand the parametric patches.)

OO DESIGN AND CLASS SPECIFICATIONS

Since a B-spline surface consists of several B-spline patches, we specify two classes: ub4surf_t (uniform 4th order B-spline surface) and ub4patch_t (uniform 4th order B-spline patch). The class ub4surf_t uses ub4patch_t; when it has to draw itself, it creates all the patches which comprise it and draws those, assuming a closed surface. (For an open surface, draw fewer patches.) The class `ub4surf_t` is derived from `prim_t`, so it can be treated like all the other graphics primitives we have introduced so far. We construct a `ub4surf_t` object by reading a file that contains first the two numbers specifying its size (rows and columns of the control point matrix) and then the control point coordinates in row major form. The class `ub4surf_t` specifies a copy constructor, a copy function, and a draw function, disabling the other virtual functions of the base class `prim_t`.

```
//*********************** File ub4curve.h *************************

#ifndef UB4SURF_T
#define UB4SURF_T

#include "../Shape3d/point3.h"
#include "../Shape2d/scene.h"
#include "../Surf/ub4patch.h"


class ub4surf_t : public prim_t  // uniform B-spline surface, order 4
{
public:
   ub4surf_t() ;
   ub4surf_t(char*) ;
   ub4surf_t(const ub4surf_t&) ;
  ~ub4surf_t() ;

   prim_t& rotx(double) ;
   prim_t& roty(double) ;
   prim_t& rotz(double) ;
   prim_t& translate(const point_t&) ;
   prim_t* copy() const ;
   void draw(const scene_t*) const ;

private:
   pmat_t givpatch(int,int) const ;

   point3_t cen ;                              // 3D centroid
   int rows ;
   int cols ;
   point3_t* cpt ;                             // control point matrix
} ;

#endif

//****************************************************************
```

The class `ub4patch_t` specifies one patch of the surface determined by 4×4 adjacent control points in the control point matrix. It declares a structure to hold just that matrix of 16 `point3_t`. It is not derived from anything, but serves only as a supplier module for `ub4surf_t`. Given a patch matrix, it draws that patch. For that purpose, it declares a variety of structures that are hidden in its implementation: a vector consisting of four `point3_t`, a `point4_t` consisting of four doubles, and so on. This allows it to take advantage of the operator overloading capabilities of C++. The drawing is a straightforward implementation of the uniform bicubic B-spline formula. The patch is drawn with a fixed number of constant *u*-curves and a fixed number of constant *v*-curves, which crosshatches the surface. You can look up the details in `Surf/ub4patch.c`.

```c
//************************* File ub4patch.h ************************

#ifndef UB4PATCH_T
#define UB4PATCH_T

#include "../Shape3d/point3.h"
#include "../Shape2d/scene.h"


struct pmat_t                      // patchmatrix: matrix of 16 point3-t
{
    point3_t m[16] ;
    pmat_t() ;                                      // default constructor
    pmat_t(const pmat_t&) ;                         // copy constructor
} ;


class ub4patch_t                   // uniform B-spline patch of order 4
{
public:
    ub4patch_t(const pmat_t&) ;
    void draw(const scene_t*) const ;

private:
    pmat_t pmat ;
} ;

#endif

//***************************************************************
```

The data file provided with the code specifies 16 control points that, when used to draw a closed surface, create a *torus*. In the main function, the reader can see the syntax of constructing a surface, rotating it, and adding it to the scene. We add the surface to a 2D scene because we do not need illumination and therefore do not need a light source. We will introduce 3D scenes, light sources, and other 3D objects in Chapter 10. Figure 7.5 shows the resulting torus.

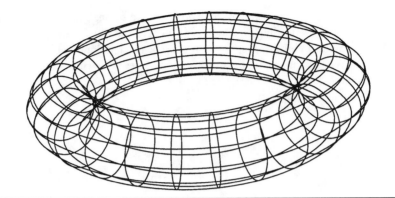

Figure 7.5   Torus formed by a bicubic B-spline surface

7.3   GENERAL B-SPLINE SURFACES

We derive general B-spline surfaces from general B-spline curves. We use the word "general" rather than "nonuniform" because the theory we explain below covers uniform as well as non-uniform surfaces, depending on the spacing of the knot-grid. If we specify the individual general B-spline curves for u and for v, as we did in Section 6.3, then we do not need to specify corner points and edge points repeatedly in order to attach the surface to the corners. This will automatically occur with this type of general B-spline surface. The basic surfaces from which the approximating surface is constructed are formed as a product of two general B-splines with two independent arguments u and v:

$$b_{ij}(u,v) = b_i(u) * b_j(v)$$

We assume below that both of the general B-splines are of degree three (that is, $k = 4$). (The above formulation is valid for all general B-spline surfaces and allows any degree and combination of different degrees.) The control point coordinates must be associated with a rectangular parameter range.

If we have $n \times m$ control points $P_{i,j}$, then we define a rectangular parameter range with $(n+k) \times (m+k)$ knots. The knots $(u_i \; v_j)$ must fulfill:

$$u_i = 0 \qquad \text{if } 0 \leq 1 < k$$
$$u_i = 1 - k + 1 \quad \text{if } k \leq i < n$$
$$u_i = n - k + 1 \quad \text{if } n \leq i < n + k$$

and

$$v_j = 0 \qquad \text{if } 0 \leq j < k$$
$$v_j = j - k + 1 \quad \text{if } k \leq j < m$$
$$v_j = m - k + 1 \quad \text{if } m \leq j < m + k$$

Usually entire rows and columns of knots will coincide at the edges of the parameter range. This will indeed give us "nonuniform" surfaces. (Remember, knots are not control points and coinciding knots do not mean coinciding control points!) Corresponding to this range, we define the basic surfaces as the above product and define both $b(u)$ and $b(v)$ as one-dimensional curves with the Cox-de Boor recursion formula (see Section 6.3 on general B-splines):

$$b_{i1}(u) = \begin{array}{l} 1 \text{ if } u_i <= u < u_{i+1} \\ 0 \text{ elsewhere} \end{array}$$

$$b_{ik}(u) = \frac{(u - u_i)b_{i,k-1}(u)}{u_{i+k-1} - u_i} + \frac{(u_{i+k} - u)b_{i+1,k-1}(u)}{u_{i+k} - u_{i+1}}$$

and correspondingly for $b(v)$.

For bicubic surfaces, we set $b_{ij}(u,v) = b_{i4}(u)*b_{j4}(v)$. The general B-spline surface for $n \times m$ control points is then:

$$S(u,v) = \sum_{i=0}^{n-1} \sum_{j=0}^{m-1} p_{ij}b_{ij}(u,v)$$

When u goes in small steps from 0 to $n-k+1$ and v from 0 to $m-k+1$, this produces the whole surface to all control points.

The above surface is a special type of nonuniform B-spline surface characterized by the choice of knots in the parameter range. We see that the knots are equispaced in the middle of the range. We therefore obtain a very similar surface to one constructed from uniform B-splines. Due to the choice of knots, it is attached to the corner points.

7.4 CATMULL-ROM PATCHES

What we have done with B-spline curves we can also do with Catmull-Rom curves. The Cartesian product of two Catmull-Rom curves defines a Catmull-Rom surface. This surface goes through the control points and is continuous up to its first partial derivative. We will not give a general formula, but will instead present the formula for calculating one Catmull-Rom patch below. A *Catmull-Rom patch* is the part of the whole surface that is stretched between four neighboring control points. The whole Catmull-Rom surface is calculated by calculating all of its patches:

$$S(u,v) = \tfrac{1}{4}*\begin{pmatrix} u^3 & u^2 & u & 1 \end{pmatrix}*\mathbf{M}*\mathbf{P}*\mathbf{M}^T*\begin{pmatrix} v^3 & v^2 & v & 1 \end{pmatrix}^T$$

$\mathbf{M}$ is the matrix:

$$\begin{pmatrix} -1 & 3 & -3 & 1 \\ 2 & -5 & 4 & -1 \\ -1 & 0 & 1 & 0 \\ 0 & 2 & 0 & 0 \end{pmatrix}$$

$\mathbf{P}$ is the patch matrix of the 16 control points surrounding this patch:

$$\begin{pmatrix} p_{i-1,j-1} & p_{i-1,j} & p_{i-1,j+1} & p_{i-1,j+2} \\ p_{i,j-1} & p_{i,j} & p_{i,j+1} & p_{i,j+2} \\ p_{i+1,j-1} & p_{i+1,j} & p_{i+1,j+1} & p_{i+1,j+2} \\ p_{i+2,j-1} & p_{i+2,j} & p_{i+2,j+1} & p_{i+2,j+2} \end{pmatrix}$$

The parameters u and v step in small increments from 0 to 1 for every patch. The Catmull-Rom patch is attached to the four inner control points of the patch matrix. We must take "overlapping" patches from the control point matrix. The surface can be attached to the corner points of the matrix and to the Catmull-Rom curves at the boundaries by specifying the boundary points twice. Thus, the corner points will be specified four times.

We can do the same with generalized Catmull-Rom curves. We need only to put the proper matrix into the surface formula.

7.5   BEZIER SURFACES

One defines a Bezier surface as the Cartesian product of two Bezier curves, much as one defines general B-spline surfaces as the Cartesian product of two general B-spline curves. The degree of the particular Bezier curve depends on the number of control points with which a surface is constructed. Again, the number of points in the matrix must be $m \times n$ for two integers m and n. These control points are associated with a rectangular parameter range. With a large number of control points, we will obtain a Bezier surface of high degree. Such a surface does not stay very close to the control points, so we use the piecewise Bezier surfaces more often. We describe both kinds of surfaces below.

7.5.1   GENERAL BEZIER SURFACES

To define this surface, we first define the basic elements from which it is composed. Just as a general Bezier curve is formed as a linear combination of Bernstein polynomials, the surface is formed from a linear combination of basic surfaces, which, by analogy to the polynomials, we can call *Bernstein surfaces*. These basic surfaces are all defined on the area $[0,1] \times [0,1]$ and are the Cartesian products of all Bernstein polynomials of some degree in these intervals. If we use $n \times m$ control points, then n polynomials $b_i(u)$ of order n and m polynomials $b_j(v)$ of order m result, as we showed in Section 7.3.1. The Cartesian products of all b_i with all b_j yields $n \times m$ surfaces:

$$b_{ij}(u,v) = b_i(u) * b_j(v)$$

We then define the surface from the given control points as:

$$S(u,v) = \sum_{i=0}^{n-1} \sum_{j=0}^{m-1} p_{ij} b_{ij}(u,v)$$

As the parameters u and v cover the area $[0,1] \times [0,1]$, the point $S(u,v)$ covers the surface.

This definition characterizes the general Bezier surface. This surface is attached to the four corner control points $P_{0,0}$, $P_{n-1,0}$, $P_{0,m-1}$, and $P_{n-1,m-1}$ in the control point matrix. The surface's edges consist of Bezier curves for the control points along the boundary.

A disadvantage similar to that of the Bezier curve is that this surface does not stay close to the control points, especially for larger quantities of points where the degree of the surface is accordingly higher. Together with the lack of local control over the surface, this inflexibility is a problem in interactive design. A solution is to use Bezier surfaces of lower degrees, accommodating larger numbers of control points by patching these surfaces together. We describe this below.

7.5.2 BEZIER PATCHES

As indicated above, the entire surface is not always best constructed as a single general Bezier surface. As with curves, we can piece together several patches of lower degree, usually of degree 2 or 3. Nine control points arranged in a matrix of 3×3 can be covered with a patch with degrees 2×2; 16 control points in a matrix of 4×4 will be covered by a patch with degrees 3×3. Figure 7.6 shows a patch for 4×3 control points.

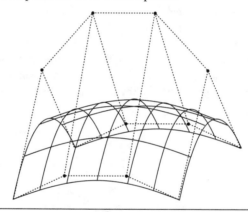

Figure 7.6   Bezier patch

We calculate surface points in this patch with a matrix formula. The matrices involved are for the appropriate lower degrees (3 and 2).

The formula for a Bezier patch with degrees 3×2 is

$$S(u,v) = \begin{pmatrix} u^3 & u^2 & u & 1 \end{pmatrix} * M_3 * (p_{ij}) * M_2^{\ T} * \begin{pmatrix} v^2 & v & 1 \end{pmatrix}^T$$

(p_{ij}) is the matrix of 4×3 control points:

$$\begin{pmatrix} p_{00} & p_{01} & p_{02} \\ p_{10} & p_{11} & p_{12} \\ p_{20} & p_{21} & p_{22} \\ p_{30} & p_{31} & p_{32} \end{pmatrix}$$

M_3 is the matrix:

$$\begin{pmatrix} -1 & 3 & -3 & 1 \\ 3 & -6 & 3 & 0 \\ -3 & 3 & 0 & 0 \\ 1 & 0 & 0 & 0 \end{pmatrix}$$

M_2 is the matrix:

$$\begin{pmatrix} 1 & -2 & 1 \\ -2 & 2 & 0 \\ 1 & 0 & 0 \end{pmatrix}$$

u and v step in small increments from 0 to 1.

We cover larger arrays of control points by joining patches computed from subsets of the points. Figure 7.7 shows two patches joined together at the boundary indicated by the arrows. Each patch is biquadratic and determined by nine control points. The two patch matrices of nine control points each share three points at the boundary. Altogether, there are 15 control points; they are the vertices of the underlying mesh in space.

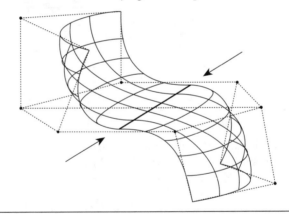

Figure 7.7   Two joined Bezier patches

The individual patch matrices overlap only by one row or column of points. Therefore, from a 7×7 control point matrix we can produce only four bicubic patches. We show the choice of control points for each patch to the right:

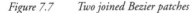

Bezier patches are automatically attached to the four control points at the corners of the patch matrix. It is not easy to get first-order continuity across the boundary between two patches when we enter the control points by hand or interactively. First, each boundary point must be collinear with the two nonboundary points adjacent to it, but this is not enough. Let us call these three collinear points a *collinear boundary triple*. If two adjacent collinear boundary triples are parallel, then the two polygons they span are planar and there is no problem. However, if they are not parallel, then the two polygons they span are not planar; in this case, the ratio of the collinear boundary triples' lengths must be constant. If this is not true, then the two patches will meet with a sharp ridge along the boundary.

In an interactive environment, even with three-dimensional visual feedback, it will not be easy to set the control points so as to satisfy these requirements. We must use a program to calculate the control points' three-dimensional coordinates properly in order to guarantee first order-continuity.

Figure 7.8 shows a mesh of 20 control points forming two patch matrices of 3 × 4 control points each, sharing four points along the boundary. Each patch matrix determines a degree 2 × 3 Bezier patch, which we do not show. We represent the boundary and the four collinear boundary triples with solid lines. The three closest collinear boundary triples are parallel, while the farthest is not, so those two quadrilaterals are not planar.

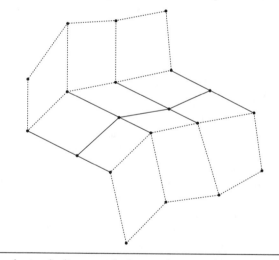

Figure 7.8   *Control points leading to a ridge between Bezier patches*

The length ratios of the last two boundary triples are obviously not equal. Therefore, the Bezier patches form a sharp ridge where they meet along the edge between the farthest two boundary points.

7.6   THE OSLO ALGORITHM

We use general quadratic B-splines in the plane to express the principle behind the Oslo algorithm.

For a given sequence of knot values, the general basic B-splines are defined by the Cox-de Boor recursion formula. In Figure 7.9, we show a sequence of arbitrarily spaced knots and the B-splines that result from those. Think of this figure as only a partial view of a knot and B-spline sequence that extends to the left and right. The B-splines on the left and right are only partially shown. We identify the B-splines as shown: b_0 to b_6. Identifying the knots is not necessary.

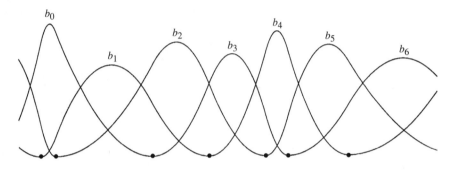

Figure 7.9   Quadratic B-splines for a given knot sequence

Let us take a closer look at the B-splines. Because they are quadratic, each B-spline extends over precisely three knot intervals (or four knot values). They vary in shape (they are not uniform) because the knots are not equispaced.

Now let us insert two additional knot values at arbitrary locations, as the arrows in Figure 7.10 indicate, and compute new B-splines, n_i, to the refined knot values (old plus new knots). We call these "refined" because they are more closely spaced. As Figure 7.10 shows, the new B-splines are named n_0 to n_8. A closer look will reveal that some of the n's are identical to the b's and some are not. More precisely, *every b that did not straddle a newly inserted knot will be identical to some n*, but those b's that straddled a new knot have disappeared. This means that four b's have disappeared, because three quadratic B-splines straddle a knot interval and two consecutive intervals have received a new knot. Six new B-splines, n_1 to n_6, have appeared in their place, and are represented by dashed lines.

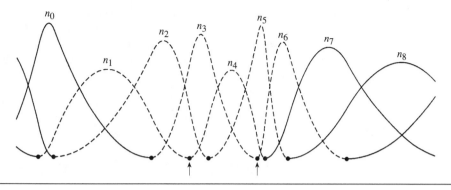

Figure 7.10   B-splines for the refined knot sequence

In particular, we have:

$$b_0 = n_0 \qquad b_5 = n_7 \qquad b_6 = n_8$$

We see that b_1 to b_4 have disappeared and that n_1 to n_6 have appeared in their place.

The Oslo algorithm states: Every old B-spline can be expressed as a weighted sum of those new B-splines that are contained in the knot range over which the old B-spline stretches.

In the case of an old B-spline being identical to a new one, this is obvious. We simply have $b_i = n_j$ for some i and j. For those old ones that have disappeared, the validity of the statement is not obvious. The Olso algorithm is essentially a method to compute the weights α for the weighted sums. Using these, one can write:

$$b_1 = \alpha_{11} n_1 + \alpha_{12} n_2$$
$$b_2 = \alpha_{22} n_2 + \alpha_{23} n_3 + \alpha_{24} n_4$$
$$b_3 = \alpha_{33} n_3 + \alpha_{34} n_4 + \alpha_{35} n_5$$
$$b_4 = \alpha_{45} n_5 + \alpha_{46} n_6$$

The first subscript of α is the subscript of the old B-spline, b, that is being expressed and the second one is the subscript of the new B-spline, n, with which this α is multiplied. Below, when we present the algorithm more formally, the α's will have one additional subscript.

7.6.1   A MORE FORMAL PRESENTATION

Now that you have a general idea of the Oslo algorithm, we will present it formally.

A general B-spline curve of order k is a weighted sum of general B-splines of order k. If we have n control points $P_0 \ldots P_{n-1}$, we can define an approximating curve as:

$$C(u) = \sum_{i=0}^{n-1} P_i b_{ik}(u) \ldots \qquad (1)$$

using n B-splines b_0 to b_{n-1}, where u is the parameter and P_i are the control points. The above sum represents any one of the individual parameter curves in x, y, or z.

The basic B-splines of order k are defined over a sequence of $n+k$ knots in the parameter interval:

$$\{u_0 \ u_1 \ \ldots \ u_{n+k-1}\}$$

We can space these knots at will. A convenient choice for spacing the knots is to set the first k knots equal to zero, the next $n–k$ knots to 1, 2, ... $n–k$, and the last k knots to $n–k+1$. We have described this type of general B-spline curve in Section 6.3. The resulting B-spline curve is attached to the terminal control points. Its values can be computed with the recursive Cox-de Boor B-spline formula. Another convenient choice is to space all $n+k$ knots equidistantly:

$$u_i = i \quad \text{for } i = 0, \ldots n+k-1$$

The resulting B-splines are uniform. We can compute the B-spline curve either with the Cox-de Boor formula or with uniform matrix formulas. These are easy to handle and compute quickly.

Now we insert additional m knots at arbitrary locations into the given sequence of u-values and obtain a refined sequence of $n+m+k$ knots; all knots (old and new ones) are named w_i:

$$\{w_0 \; w_1 \; \ldots \; w_{n+m+k-1}\}$$

The B-splines of order k over the refined knot sequence are $n_0, \ldots, n_{n+m-1}$. We can express each b_i as a weighted sum of the n_j.

$$b_{ik} = \sum_{i=0}^{n+m-1} \alpha_{ikj} n_{jk} \quad \ldots \quad (2)$$

using proper weights α_{ikj}. The index i refers to the B-spline b_{ik} that is expressed using this α, k is the order of the B-splines, and j refers to the B-spline n_{jk} for which this α is a weight.

The Oslo algorithm determines these α's. The formula is recursive and very similar to the definition of the general B-splines. Any ratio is considered zero if its numerator and denominator are both zero. (We leave commas between subscripts out whenever possible.)

$$\alpha_{i1j} = \begin{array}{l} 1 \text{ if } u_i \leq w_j < u_{i+1} \\ 0 \text{ otherwise} \end{array}$$

$$\alpha_{ikj} = \frac{u_{i+k} - w_{j+k-1}}{u_{i+k} - u_{i+1}} * \alpha_{i+1,k-1,j} + \frac{w_{j+k-1} - u_i}{u_{i+k-1} - u_i} * \alpha_{i,k-1,j}$$

It turns out that:

$$0 \leq \alpha_{ikj} \leq 1 \text{ for all } i, k, j \text{ and } \sum_{i=0}^{n-1} \alpha_{ikj} = 1$$

Inserting equation (2) into equation (1) gives:

$$C(u) = \sum_{i=0}^{n-1} P_i b_{ik}(u) = \sum_{i=0}^{n-1} P_i \sum_{j=0}^{n+m-1} \alpha_{ikj} n_{jk}(u)$$

Rearranging the sum on the right yields:

$$C(u) = \sum_{j=0}^{n+m-1} n_{jk} \sum_{i=0}^{n-1} P_i \alpha_{ikj} = \sum_{j=0}^{n+m-1} n_{jk} W_j$$

$$\text{with} \quad W_j = \sum_{i=0}^{n-1} P_i \alpha_{ikj}$$

The W_j are weighted sums of the original control points (P_i). We see from this that the curve $C(u)$ can be expressed as a sum of the new B-splines (n_j) weighted with the control points (W_j), summed over $n+m$ terms. We are not interested in the new B-splines (n), only in the new control points (W). (Observe that the w_i designate inserted knot values, while the W_j, with capital W, designate new control points.)

Knowing the weights (α) for a certain knot refinement, we compute from the original control points (P) the set of new control points (W). These are more numerous and lie closer to the B-spline curve. Computing the new B-splines (n) that correspond to the refined knot sequence is superfluous. Their weighted sum with the new control points would lead to the same B-spline curve.

7.6.2   CONTROL POINT DOUBLING FOR UNIFORM B-SPLINES

Let us now concentrate on a special case of the Oslo algorithm that is useful in certain areas of computer graphics. It allows us to refine the control point grid to such a degree that the surface can be approximated by the control points themselves.

The α's depend on the original knots and on the locations and number of the additional knots. If the original knots are equispaced and new knots are inserted strictly in the middle of consecutive knot intervals, then the α's repeat in a simple fashion. These α's are computed with the Oslo algorithm and given below for several orders. We call these *refinement tables*.

The new control points (W_j) are weighted sums of the old control points (P_i) with weights from the refinement tables. We produce these tables by assuming an original sequence of enough equispaced knots and inserting one or more additional knots in the middle of one or more consecutive knot intervals.

If we insert only one new knot in the middle of a knot interval and the B-splines are of order k, then precisely k old B-splines (b) disappear and are replaced by $k+1$ new ones (n). The part of a uniform B-spline curve that was built from the removed b's and corresponding k control points (P) can now be expressed with the new B-splines (n) and the corresponding $k+1$ new control points (W). Let us number the k control points that correspond to the removed B-splines P_0 to P_{k-1}. The new control points that replace them are named W_0 to W_k. It always turns out that $W_0 = P_0$ and $W_k = P_{k-1}$. We derive the W_j in between by weighting the proper P_i with the proper weights α. All other control points P remain unchanged.

The refinement tables are arranged so that the closest unchanged control point on the left has subscript 0: $P_0 = W_0$. The subscript of the closest unchanged control point on the right is then $k-1$: $P_{k-1} = W_k$. Let us demonstrate this with the table for $k = 4$ with just one inserted knot value. Blank spaces in the table indicate α's that are equal to zero.

$k = 4$	P_0	P_1	P_2	P_3
W_0	1			
W_1	$\frac{1}{6}$	$\frac{5}{6}$		
W_2		$\frac{1}{2}$	$\frac{1}{2}$	
W_3			$\frac{5}{6}$	$\frac{1}{6}$
W_4				1

This says that

$$W_0 = P_0$$
$$W_1 = \tfrac{1}{6}P_0 + \tfrac{5}{6}P_1$$
$$W_2 = \tfrac{1}{2}P_1 + \tfrac{1}{2}P_2$$
$$W_3 = \tfrac{5}{6}P_2 + \tfrac{1}{6}P_3$$
$$W_4 = P_3$$

Now, suppose we halve two consecutive knot intervals by inserting knots in the middle. Then, $k+1$ P's will be replaced by $k+3$ W's. Again, we number the points so that the closest unchanged control point on the left is $P_0 = W_0$. The closest unchanged control point on the right is $P_k = W_{k+2}$. The table looks like this:

$k = 4$	P_0	P_1	P_2	P_3	P_4
W_0	1				
W_1	$\frac{1}{6}$	$\frac{5}{6}$			
$\rightarrow$ W_2		$\frac{1}{2}$	$\frac{1}{2}$		
$\rightarrow$ W_3		$\frac{1}{8}$	$\frac{6}{8}$	$\frac{1}{8}$	
W_4			$\frac{1}{2}$	$\frac{1}{2}$	
W_5				$\frac{5}{6}$	$\frac{1}{6}$
W_6					1

Observe that the table has two new rows inserted. In general, we can say that the more intervals we divide by inserting knots, the more new rows will be inserted.

However, if we halve $k-1$ or more consecutive intervals, the Oslo algorithm produces no different weights. Instead, because of the regular repetition of the half-sized knot intervals, the new B-splines (n) become uniform and therefore the pattern of α's keeps repeating. Thus, the weights are uniform. In the above table, we have indicated these with arrows. If we compute the weights for $k = 4$ and three halved intervals, two additional rows that are identical to those with the arrows, though they are shifted to the right, will appear in the table. Repeating the table for three inserted knots and for $k = 4$ will produce:

$k = 4$	P_0	P_1	P_2	P_3	P_4	P_5
W_0	1					
W_1	$\frac{1}{6}$	$\frac{5}{6}$				
→ W_2		$\frac{1}{2}$	$\frac{1}{2}$			
→ W_3		$\frac{1}{8}$	$\frac{6}{8}$	$\frac{1}{8}$		
→ W_4			$\frac{1}{2}$	$\frac{1}{2}$		
→ W_5			$\frac{1}{8}$	$\frac{6}{8}$	$\frac{1}{8}$	
W_6				$\frac{1}{2}$	$\frac{1}{2}$	
W_7					$\frac{5}{6}$	$\frac{1}{6}$
W_8						1

What this means is that we need refinement tables for each order of the B-splines with only $k-2$ knots inserted. This gives all possible weights. Here are the tables for $k = 3$, 4, and 5 with arrows.

$k = 3$	P_0	P_1	P_2
W_0	1		
→ W_1	$\frac{1}{4}$	$\frac{3}{4}$	
→ W_2		$\frac{3}{4}$	$\frac{1}{4}$
W_3			1

$k = 4$	P_0	P_1	P_2	P_3	P_4
W_0	1				
W_1	$\frac{1}{6}$	$\frac{5}{6}$			
→ W_2		$\frac{1}{2}$	$\frac{1}{2}$		
→ W_3		$\frac{1}{8}$	$\frac{6}{8}$	$\frac{1}{8}$	
W_4			$\frac{1}{2}$	$\frac{1}{2}$	
W_5				$\frac{5}{6}$	$\frac{1}{6}$
W_6					1

$k=5$	P_0	P_1	P_2	P_3	P_4	P_5
W_0	1					
W_1	$\frac{1}{8}$	$\frac{7}{8}$				
W_2		$\frac{6}{16}$	$\frac{10}{16}$			
$\rightarrow$ W_3		$\frac{1}{16}$	$\frac{10}{16}$	$\frac{5}{16}$		
$\rightarrow$ W_4			$\frac{5}{16}$	$\frac{10}{16}$	$\frac{1}{16}$	
W_5				$\frac{10}{16}$	$\frac{6}{16}$	
W_6					$\frac{7}{8}$	$\frac{1}{8}$
W_7						1

It is important to realize the following: although the new control points determine the same B-spline curve, one cannot use the uniform B-spline formula (of order k) with the new control points to draw this curve. The B-splines that cross over from intervals with inserted knots to intervals without inserted knots are not uniform! Only if we insert new knots in all knot intervals will the curve be a uniform B-spline curve to the new control points.

The main use of the Oslo algorithm in computer graphics is for control point doubling. One achieves this by inserting a new knot in the middle of every knot interval, even those intervals outside the region over which the curve is drawn. Halving all knot intervals guarantees that the new B-splines (n) will be uniform. As a consequence, we use only uniform weights when computing the new control points and we compute new control points from all old control points. This creates simple algorithms for control point doubling. (Actually we do not really insert the new knots; that is only the theoretical basis for control point refinement.)

We now present the simple control point doubling algorithm for uniform B-spline curves of the orders $k = 3$, 4, and 5. (This repeats the above tables in a different format.) We perform this with so-called *weight vectors*. We lay these vectors over consecutive points in the old control point vector and then multiply each control point by its associated weight. Observe that the sum of the weights is always equal to 1 and that, with increasing order, the number of old control points involved in forming a new one also increases. Remember that we must entirely discard the old control points (P). For open curves, we have a simple relation of the subscripts of old and new control points. For closed curves, we must consider P_0 as identical to P_n, and so forth, to apply this subscript relation.

Quadratic B-splines—weight vectors:
    (3 1)/4
    (1 3)/4

Interpret this as:
    $W_{2i-2} = (3P_{i-1} + 1P_i)/4$
    $W_{2i-1} = (1P_{i-1} + 3P_i)/4$

Cubic B-splines—weight vectors:
    (4 4)/8
    (1 6 1)/8

Interpret this as:
    $W_{2i-2} = (4P_{i-1} + 4P_i)/8$
    $W_{2i-1} = (1P_{i-1} + 6P_i + 1P_{i+1})/8$

Quartic B-splines—weight vectors: Interpret this as:

$(1 \quad 10 \quad 5)/16$ $W_{2i-2} = (5P_{i-1} + 10P_i + 1P_{i+1})/16$

$(5 \quad 10 \quad 1)/16$ $W_{2i-1} = (1P_{i-1} + 10P_i + 5P_{i+1})/16$

We now provide a few examples. Figure 7.11 shows five control points (black squares) for a uniform cubic B-spline curve, which we have not drawn. The circles and crosses are the new control points obtained through doubling. We obtain them by taking all sequences of two consecutive old points and producing a new one at the midpoint, according to $W_{2i-2} = \frac{1}{2}P_{i-1} + \frac{1}{2}P_i$; these are the circles. We obtain the crosses by taking all sequences of three consecutive points and producing a new one, according to $W_{2i-1} = \frac{1}{8}P_{i-1} + \frac{6}{8}P_i + \frac{1}{8}P_{i+1}$. We can do the latter geometrically by taking the middle of the line connecting P_{i-1} and P_{i+1}, connecting this middle to P_i, and marking $\frac{3}{4}$ of the distance to P_i.

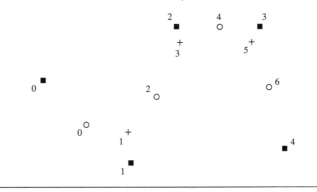

Figure 7.11   Doubling of open control point sequence

In this example, we produce only seven new control points from five old ones, which is hardly a doubling. However, this happens only with open curves. The lack of additional points outside the range does not allow us to draw more of the refined points. The more original points we have, the closer we come to doubling. With 10 old points, for example, we obtain 17 new ones.

In the case of closed curves, there is no such problem, because we can cyclicly repeat. The old control points are the black squares, while the new ones are the crosses and circles. The control points indeed double; see Figure 7.12.

If a B-spline curve of order k is attached to the terminal control points with $k-1$-fold repetitions, control point doubling maintains this feature in the refined control point sequence. This easily follows from the formulas. For example, for a triple terminal point $P_0 = P_1 = P_2$, the formula for $k = 4$ gives us:

$$W_0 = (P_0 + P_1)/2 = P_1$$
$$W_1 = (P_0 + 6P_1 + P_2)/8 = 8P_1/8 = P_1$$
$$W_2 = (P_1 + P_2)/2 = P_1$$

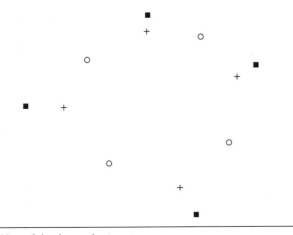

Figure 7.12   Doubling of closed control point sequence

Keep in mind that control point doubling is a very specialized application of the Oslo algorithm, where the original knot sequence is equispaced with one new knot per interval precisely in the middle. If, for example, we insert two new knots in every interval, one at $\frac{1}{3}$ and one at $\frac{2}{3}$ of its length, we would again produce uniform α-values. These could be used for control point tripling. This, however, seems less popular than repeated control point doubling.

Any B-spline curve can be approximated through repeated doubling of its control points. The arithmetic involved is not expensive, as divisions occur only by powers of 2. When the control points are sufficiently dense, they can be connected with straight lines, which gives a very good approximation of the B-spline curve. This is a major application of the Oslo algorithm.

One can use the Oslo algorithm to refine the control points or to compute new control points for Bezier curves. (Remember that Bezier curves are a certain type of general B-spline curves.) The exercises will present such a case.

7.6.3   CONTROL POINT REFINEMENT IN SPACE

Another important application is control point refinement for uniform B-spline surfaces in space. We will present this without going into much mathematical detail. Everything is analogous to the curves.

Theoretically, a basic (uniform) B-spline surface is defined as a tensor product of two basic (uniform) B-splines in independent parameters. If we halve the knot intervals of both parameters, the basic B-spline surfaces will be defined over a finer knot-grid and will again be uniform. The old B-spline surfaces are expressible as weighted sums of the new ones. The weights are now tensor products of the weights that we had for curves. We will again restrict ourselves to the uniform weights. These same weights can be used to express the new control points as weighted sums of the old ones.

Using tensor products is certainly easiest, because one can derive the weights from the weights for curves. The tensor product of two vectors is a matrix (see the appendix for tensor products). When doubling the control points for curves, we applied a vector of weights to consecutive points in the control point vector. Here, we apply a matrix of weights to adjacent points in the control point matrix.

For the order $k = 3$, the weight vectors are $(3\ \ 1)/4$ and $(1\ \ 3)/4$. This allows four different tensor products. They are just simple variations on the same theme.

$$\frac{1}{4}\begin{pmatrix} 3 \\ 1 \end{pmatrix} * \frac{1}{4}\begin{pmatrix} 3 & 1 \end{pmatrix} = \frac{1}{16}\begin{pmatrix} 9 & 3 \\ 3 & 1 \end{pmatrix} \qquad \frac{1}{4}\begin{pmatrix} 3 \\ 1 \end{pmatrix} * \frac{1}{4}\begin{pmatrix} 1 & 3 \end{pmatrix} = \frac{1}{16}\begin{pmatrix} 3 & 9 \\ 1 & 3 \end{pmatrix}$$

$$\frac{1}{4}\begin{pmatrix} 1 \\ 3 \end{pmatrix} * \frac{1}{4}\begin{pmatrix} 3 & 1 \end{pmatrix} = \frac{1}{16}\begin{pmatrix} 3 & 1 \\ 9 & 3 \end{pmatrix} \qquad \frac{1}{4}\begin{pmatrix} 1 \\ 3 \end{pmatrix} * \frac{1}{4}\begin{pmatrix} 1 & 3 \end{pmatrix} = \frac{1}{16}\begin{pmatrix} 1 & 3 \\ 3 & 9 \end{pmatrix}$$

For the order $k = 4$, the weight vectors are $(4\ \ 4)/8$ and $(1\ \ 6\ \ 1)/8$. We again have four different tensor products:

$$\frac{1}{8}\begin{pmatrix} 4 \\ 4 \end{pmatrix} * \frac{1}{8}\begin{pmatrix} 4 & 4 \end{pmatrix} = \frac{1}{64}\begin{pmatrix} 16 & 16 \\ 16 & 16 \end{pmatrix} \qquad \frac{1}{8}\begin{pmatrix} 4 \\ 4 \end{pmatrix} * \frac{1}{8}\begin{pmatrix} 1 & 6 & 1 \end{pmatrix} = \frac{1}{64}\begin{pmatrix} 4 & 24 & 4 \\ 4 & 24 & 4 \end{pmatrix}$$

$$\frac{1}{8}\begin{pmatrix} 1 \\ 6 \\ 1 \end{pmatrix} * \frac{1}{8}\begin{pmatrix} 4 & 4 \end{pmatrix} = \frac{1}{64}\begin{pmatrix} 4 & 4 \\ 24 & 24 \\ 4 & 4 \end{pmatrix} \qquad \frac{1}{8}\begin{pmatrix} 1 \\ 6 \\ 1 \end{pmatrix} * \frac{1}{8}\begin{pmatrix} 1 & 6 & 1 \end{pmatrix} = \frac{1}{64}\begin{pmatrix} 1 & 6 & 1 \\ 6 & 36 & 6 \\ 1 & 6 & 1 \end{pmatrix}$$

The reader should try to derive the four different weight matrices for the order $k = 5$. Observe that the sum of all weights in every matrix is equal to one.

When we lay all four weight matrices over all possible positions in the control point matrix and compute new control points, we achieve control point quadrupling. With open surfaces, we will end up with fewer than four times the number of old control points. With closed surfaces, when we can cyclically repeat in all directions, we will achieve proper quadrupling in every refinement step.

With each refinement step, the control points are more numerous and therefore lie closer to the surface. Through repeated refinement, we can approximate the surface until the control points are arbitrarily close. This technique is used in ray tracing of B-spline and other bicubic surfaces.

CODED ALGORITHM

There is no graphics primitive associated with the Oslo algorithm. Therefore, we do not specify a class, such as `oslo_t`. We show only the algorithm as a so-called "free" function. The code is short, so we can include it in the text. It produces textual output, but no graphics, and computes the α-values for any general original and refined knot sequence. A given sequence of knots $u_0, u_1, u_2 \dots$ is augmented by additional knots leading to a refined sequence of knots $w_0, w_1, w_2 \dots$. The B-splines for the original sequence are $b_0, b_1, \dots$. The refined knot sequence implies new B-splines $n_0, n_1, \dots$. We can express the b's as weighted sums of the n's, using the weights $alpha(i,k,j)$. Index i refers to the B-spline, which we express as a weighted sum of the n's, while k is the order of the b's and n's, and j is the index of the n for which this alpha is a weight. For example:

$b_3 = alpha(3,4,5)*n_5 + alpha(3,4,6)*n_6$; order is 4.

The other interpretation of the weights is used for control point refinement. For example:

$W_3 = alpha(5,4,3)*P_5 + alpha(6,4,3)*P_6$; order is 4.

The printout reads as follows: the numbers under a B_i are the coefficients of the **N**'s on the left to form this B_i. Another reading is: the numbers in row j are the coefficients that express the new control point j as a linear combination of the old control points with the subscripts i above these numbers.

```c
//*********************** File oslo.c ***************************
//                    The Oslo algorithm

#include <stdio.h>

double u[30] , w[30] , adknot[30];

double alpha(int i, int k, int j)              // recursive Cox-de Boor
{
    if (k == 1)
        return (u[i] <= w[j] && w[j] < u[i+1]) ? 1 : 0 ;
    else
    {
        double nom , sum = 0 ;

        if (nom = u[i+k-1]-u[i])
            sum  = (w[j+k-1]-u[i])/nom*alpha(i,k-1,j);
        if (nom = u[i+k] - u[i+1])
            sum += (u[i+k]-w[j+k-1])/nom*alpha(i+1,k-1,j);
        return sum;
    }
}

void main()
{
    int m , n , i , j , k ;
    int order ;

    printf("input number of knots: ");
    scanf("%d",&m);
    printf("\ninput %2d knot values\n",m);
    for (i = 0; i < m; i++)
        scanf("%lf",&u[i]);
    u[m] = 100000;

    printf("input number of additional knots: ");
    scanf("%d",&n);
    printf("\ninput %2d additional knot values\n",n);
    for (i = 0; i < n; i++)
        scanf("%lf",&adknot[i]);
    adknot[n] = 100000;
```

```
      printf("input order of alpha: ");
      scanf("%d",&order);

      i = 0; j = 0;
      for (k = 0; k < m+n; k++)                    // refined knot sequence
         if (u[i] <= adknot[j])
            w[k] = u[i++];
         else
            w[k] = adknot[j++];

      printf("\n\nk=%d | i   ",order);             // print table
      for (i = 0; i < m-order; i++)
         printf("B%d      ",i);
      printf("\n—+-");
      for (i = 0; i < m-order; i++)
         printf("——");
      printf("\n j  |\n");

      for (j = 0; j < m+n-order; j++)
      {
         printf("N%2d |",j);
         for (i = 0; i < m-order; i++)
         {
            double a = alpha(i,order,j);

            if (a == 0)
               printf("        ");
            else
               printf("%7.5f",a);
         }
         printf("\n");
      }

      getchar();
}

//********************************************************************
```

To obtain the uniform *alphas*, we must provide an original equispaced knot sequence with enough knots and insert at least $k-2$ new knots in the intervals in the center of the sequence. For a cubic B-spline, we choose the original sequence {1 2 3 4 5 6 7} and add the two knots {3.5 4.5}. We obtain the refined sequence {1 2 3 3.5 4 4.5 5 6 7}. We can, of course, choose a longer original sequence.

We supply these two knot sequences as globals to the function alpha(). Then

> *alpha*(0,4,1)   *alpha*(1,4,1)

and

> *alpha*(0,4,2)   *alpha*(1,4,2)   *alpha*(2,4,2)

will be the uniform weights.

The clearest way to present the weights is to display them in tables, such as the ones in the text. Then, we can easily recognize the uniform weights.

An algorithm for control point doubling would not compute the weights, but would simply hard-code them in the program.

SUGGESTED READINGS

You can find excellent and elaborate (althought mathematically demanding) explanations of Bezier and B-spline surfaces in ROAD90. For further readings on the OSLO algorithm, I also recommend ROAD90, which contains meticulously worked out examples for B-spline subdivision and for computing the alphas. The original work on curve subdivision is CLRI80. For an application of the OSLO algorithm in space, consult SWBA86.

EXERCISES

SECTION 7.2

1. Consider the following control point matrix (the letter P is omitted; only the two subscripts are shown):

    $$\begin{matrix} 00 & 01 & 02 & 03 & 04 \\ 10 & 11 & 12 & 13 & 14 \\ 20 & 21 & 22 & 23 & 24 \\ 30 & 31 & 32 & 33 & 34 \\ 40 & 41 & 42 & 43 & 44 \end{matrix}$$

    How many different cubic B-spline patches are used to produce the open uniform cubic B-spline surface to the above control point matrix? Indicate the corresponding patch matrices in the control point matrix.

2. Use the control point matrix of Exercise 1. How many different quadratic B-spline patches are used to produce the open uniform quadratic B-spline surface to the above matrix? Indicate the corresponding patch matrices in the control point matrix.

    A B-spline patch is not attached to any control points, but is near the patch matrix's four inner control points (see Figure 7.13). The patch is near the four center control points and hovers above them in space as the patch's 16 control points form a trough.

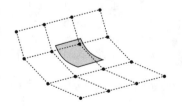

Figure 7.13   B-spline patch for 16 control points

Figure 7.14 shows an arrangement of the 25 control points of Exercise 1 in space.

3. Sketch by hand the patches resulting from the four possible patch matrices for this control point arrangement.

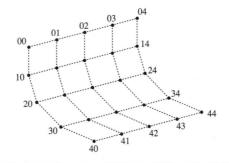

Figure 7.14   25 control points in space

4. Show the curves of constant u and of constant v in the four patches sketched in Exercise 1.
5. Show analytically that the last row of the patch matrix is not involved in forming the patch when $u = 0$ and that the first row is not involved when $u = 1$. What follows from this for the curves of constant u in the patch when $u = 0$ and when $u = 1$?
6. Show analytically that the last column of the patch matrix is not involved in forming the patch when $v = 0$ and that the first column is not involved when $v = 1$. What follows from this for the curves of constant v in the patch when $v = 0$ and when $v = 1$?
7. Write a class `ub3patch_t` that represents a uniform quadratic B-spline patch. It is constructed with a patch matrix of size 3×3 and has a member function to draw itself with crosshatch lines. One set of lines is the constant u-curves, the other set the constant v-curves. Project and draw the lines either orthographically, by not computing the z-coordinate, or perspectively, by using a `win-view3_t`.
8. Write a class `ub4surf_t` that represents an entire uniform cubic B-spline surface. It has a member that points to a control point matrix and two members that specify the matrix size. The surface is initialized with a control point matrix and its size. It takes the patches without cyclic wraparound across the boundaries.
9. Specify the control point matrix needed to draw the basic uniform cubic B-spline surface shown in the text in Figure 7.1. *Hint*: you need 49 control points. Use `ub4surf_t::draw()` of Exercise 8 to draw this surface.
10. Define a 5×5 control point matrix so that the control points have approximately the positions shown in Figure 7.14. Use `ub4surf_t()::draw()` to draw the surface to these control points.
11. The following 20 control points are specified to form a pipelike construct. The control point matrix is:

$$
\begin{pmatrix} 00 & 01 & 02 & 03 & 04 \\ 10 & 11 & 12 & 13 & 14 \\ 20 & 21 & 22 & 23 & 24 \\ 30 & 31 & 32 & 33 & 34 \end{pmatrix} = \begin{pmatrix} (1\ 0\ {-2}) & (1\ 0\ {-1}) & (1\ 0\ 0) & (1\ 0\ 1) & (1\ 0\ 2) \\ (0\ 1\ {-2}) & (0\ 1\ {-1}) & (0\ 1\ 0) & (0\ 1\ 1) & (0\ 1\ 2) \\ ({-1}\ 0\ {-2}) & ({-1}\ 0\ {-1}) & ({-1}\ 0\ 0) & ({-1}\ 0\ 1) & ({-1}\ 0\ 2) \\ (0\ {-1}\ {-2}) & (0\ {-1}\ {-1}) & (0\ {-1}\ 0) & (0\ {-1}\ 1) & (0\ {-1}\ 2) \end{pmatrix}
$$

Define a control point matrix of these points. Rotate all points slightly about the x-axis and about the y-axis before you draw patches; this gives a more interesting display. The pipe has four points around its perimeter and five points lengthwise. With the above arrangement u goes around the pipe and v goes lengthwise. Without cyclic wraparound you can draw two patches.

12. You can draw two patches lengthwise and four patches around the pipe if you take the patch matrices in a cyclic manner. This gives us a pipelike-shaped B-spline surface that is closed around the pipe, but open at the ends. *Hint:* wrap around cyclicly in one direction but not in the other. Use `ub4patch_t::draw()` to draw these eight patches.

13. You can make the pipe longer, that is, continue it in both directions so that it ends flush with the first and last column of control points by specifying the first and the last column in the control point matrix three times (no cyclic wraparound in this direction!). This gives you 20 patch matrices. Use function `ub4patch_t::draw()` to draw the resulting surface.

14. The following 16 control points lie on a torus. To draw the whole torus surface, you need to draw 16 patches. You can obtain the 16 patch matrices through cyclic wraparound across all boundaries of the control point matrix.

$$
\begin{pmatrix} 00 & 01 & 02 & 03 \\ 10 & 11 & 12 & 13 \\ 20 & 21 & 22 & 23 \\ 30 & 31 & 32 & 33 \end{pmatrix} = \begin{pmatrix} (3\ 0\ 0) & (0\ 0\ 3) & ({-3}\ 0\ 0) & (0\ 0\ {-3}) \\ (2\ 1\ 0) & (0\ 1\ 2) & ({-2}\ 1\ 0) & (0\ 1\ {-2}) \\ (1\ 0\ 0) & (0\ 0\ 1) & ({-1}\ 0\ 0) & (0\ 0\ {-1}) \\ (2\ {-1}\ 0) & (0\ {-1}\ 2) & ({-2}\ {-1}\ 0) & (0\ {-1}\ {-2}) \end{pmatrix}
$$

Make a hand sketch of this torus and show how the constant u-curves and the constant v-curves run on the torus surface.

15. Make a hand sketch of the torus of Exercise 14 and show the patch corresponding to the control point matrix.

APPROXIMATING SPHERES WITH CUBIC B-SPLINE PATCHES

This is a little more tricky than for a torus, because the parametric description of a sphere surface always leads to poles. However, we can overcome this problem.

16. Consider the following 10 control points in space (we now use a different notation to enhance the geometric meaning of the points):

$$N = (0 \ 2 \ 0)$$

$$
\begin{array}{llll}
N_0 = (2 \ 1 \ -2) & N_1 = (2 \ 1 \ 2) & N_2 = (-2 \ 1 \ 2) & N_3 = (-2 \ 1 \ -2) \\
S_0 = (2 \ -1 \ -2) & S_1 = (2 \ -1 \ 2) & S_2 = (-2 \ -1 \ 2) & S_3 = (-2 \ -1 \ -2)
\end{array}
$$

$$S = (0 \ -2 \ 0)$$

(N stands for north, S for south.)

These points form a closed polyhedron in space with 12 facets, as Figure 7.15 shows. We can approximate it with a completely closed B-spline surface. The four side patches will be of normal "rectangular" form, but the top and bottom patches degenerate to triangular form because they must be "pulled" over the poles. An example of a corresponding patch matrix is:

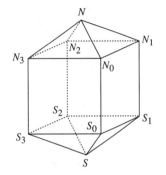

$$
\begin{array}{cccc}
N_2 & N_3 & N_0 & N_1 \\
N & N & N & N \\
N_0 & N_1 & N_2 & N_3 \\
S_0 & S_1 & S_2 & S_3
\end{array}
$$

Figure 7.15   *Control points for a spherical surface, arrangement 1*

It corresponds to the patch near the triangle $N \ N_1 \ N_2$. Follow the four paths of varying u when moving down the columns of this matrix to see how they cross over at the north pole. The same happens at the south pole. The following control point matrix allows the definition of the 12 patch matrices to produce the closed surface by repeating it cyclicly from left to right:

$$
\begin{array}{cccc}
N_2 & N_3 & N_0 & N_1 \\
N & N & N & N \\
N_0 & N_1 & N_2 & N_3 \\
S_0 & S_1 & S_2 & S_3 \\
S & S & S & S \\
S_2 & S_3 & S_0 & S_1
\end{array}
$$

Use `ub4patch_t::draw()` to draw this surface.

17. We can approximate the control point polyhedron in Figure 7.16 with a completely closed B-spline surface. Define the control point matrix that can be repeated cyclicly from left to right and from top to bottom to yield the minimum required number of patch matrices.

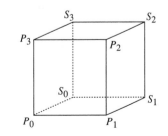

Figure 7.16   *Control points for a spherical surface, arrangement 2*

SECTION 7.3

18. Write a class gb4patch_t that uses the Cox-de Boor formula to draw one patch of a general cubic B-spline surface to 4×4 control points and 8×8 knots. Use the analogy to gb4piece_t. Do not worry about computation efficiency or speed.

19. Define 25 control points in space, similar to the arrangement of Exercise 20, and use gb4patch_t::draw() to draw a general cubic B-spline surface to these points.

SECTION 7.4

The exercises for this section consist of doing the exercises for Section 7.2 with Catmull-Rom patches, instead of B-spline patches. The only exception is the repetition of control points.

20. Write a class crpatch_t that specifies a Catmull-Rom patch. It is initialized with a patch matrix and a tension parameter and has a member function to draw itself. Comparing this class to ub4patch_t, you will find many similarities and will need to change very little.

SECTION 7.5

General higher order Bezier curves and surfaces are not useful in computer graphics, but piecewise cubic curves and patches are very popular. To draw a piecewise Bezier surface, we must define the control points properly, meeting all the requirements specified in the text to avoid ridges. We do not have as much freedom as with uniform B-spline surfaces. Obtaining a smooth surface depends on how we define the control points.

21. Write a class bezpatch_t that specifies a bicubic Bezier patch. It is initialized with a 4×4 patch matrix and has a member function to draw itself. Here, too, you will find that there is much similarity to ubpatch_t and that you have to change very little.

22. Consider the following control point matrix of 48 points:

(0 4 –2)	(0 2 –4)	(0 –2 –4)	(0 –4 –2)
(1 4 –2)	(2 2 –4)	(2 –2 –4)	(1 –4 –2)
(2 4 –1)	(4 2 –2)	(4 –2 –2)	(2 –4 –1)
(2 4 0)	(4 2 0)	(4 –2 0)	(2 –4 0)
(2 4 1)	(4 2 2)	(4 –2 2)	(2 –4 1)
(1 4 2)	(2 2 4)	(2 –2 4)	(1 –4 2)
(0 4 2)	(0 2 4)	(0 –2 4)	(0 –4 2)
(–1 4 2)	(–2 2 4)	(–2 –2 4)	(–1 –4 2)
(–2 4 1)	(–4 2 2)	(–4 –2 2)	(–2 –4 1)
(–2 4 0)	(–4 2 0)	(–4 –2 0)	(–2 –4 0)
(–2 4 –1)	(–4 2 –2)	(–4 –2 –2)	(–2 –4 –1)
(–1 4 –2)	(–2 2 –4)	(–2 –2 –4)	(–1 –4 –2)

You can use this matrix to define four bicubic Bezier patches. Knot points are the points in rows 1, 4, 7, and 10. If the first row is repeated as row 13 to close the fourth patch back to the first one, these four patches form a partly closed piecewise Bezier surface. Rotate these points in space slightly around the *x*-axis, then use `bezpatch_t::draw()` repeatedly to draw the surface. (This surface is similar to the one Martin Newell used for his teapot, described in CROW87.)

SECTION 7.6

23. Given are four control points P_0, P_1, P_2, and P_3 for an open cubic B-spline curve. Applying the "control point doubling" algorithm, discard P_0 through P_3 and obtain five new control points, W_0 through W_4. The curve obtained with the uniform cubic B-spline formula with the points P_0 through P_3 consists of one curve piece. The curve obtained with W_0 through W_4 consists of two pieces. Show that the two curves are mathematically identical except for a parameter substitution, $u' = u/2$.

24. Determine the three weight vectors for control point tripling of uniform B-splines of order 3.

25. Determine the three weight vectors for control point tripling of uniform B-splines of order 4.

26. Determine the four weight vectors for control point quadrupling of uniform B-splines of order 4.

SPLITTING OF A BEZIER CURVE

Given one piece of a Bezier curve determined by the main points, P_0 and P_3, and the auxiliary points, P_1 and P_2. We now choose an arbitrary point, M, on the curve (see Figure 7.17) and discard the two auxiliary points. Then we try to determine four new auxiliary points, N_1, N_2, N_3, and N_4, so that the four points P_0, N_1, N_2, M determine the curve piece from P_0 to M, and the four points M, N_3, N_4, P_3 determine the piece from M to P_3. We actually split the original curve piece into two at the point M. We can find N_1 through N_4 with the Oslo algorithm.

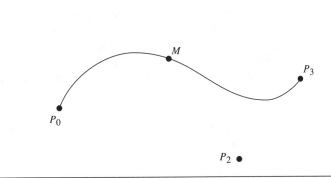

Figure 7.17   Splitting a Bezier curve at M

A piecewise cubic Bezier curve is a general B-spline curve in which the knots coincide in triples, while the distance between noncoinciding knots is arbitrary. For example:

$$u_0 = u_1 = u_2 = 0$$
$$u_3 = u_4 = u_5 = 1.5$$
$$u_6 = u_7 = u_8 = 2.1$$
etc.

There is one knot-triple for every main point. With four control points (two main and two auxiliary), the curve is drawn over one interval and six knots. Figure 7.18 shows the four basic B-splines in this interval.

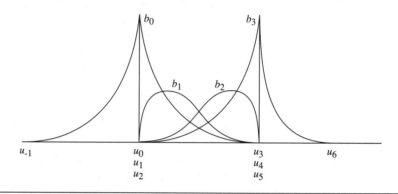

Figure 7.18   Basic splines for a Bezier curve piece

The knot range for b_i is from u_{i-1} to u_{i+3}. The drawing range is from u_2 to u_3. With seven control points (three main and four auxiliary), the curve is drawn over two intervals containing nine knots and seven different B-splines. No matter how long an interval, the four basic splines in it are symmetric to each other with respect to its center. Therefore, the length of an interval is insignificant.

We arbitrarily set $u_0 = u_1 = u_2 = 0$ and $u_3 = u_4 = u_5 = 1$. Inserting a triple knot at location w in the interval and refining the control points with the Oslo algorithm replaces the control points P_1 and P_2 with five new ones: $N_0, N_1, M, N_3,$ and N_4. P_0 and P_3 will not change. M will be the point on the curve piece corresponding to the parameter value w, where the triple knot was inserted. The new points will be weighted sums of P_0 through P_3, with the weights given by the Oslo algorithm.

To use the algorithm, we must specify the old knot sequence and the refined knot sequence. We must specify enough knots to contain all B-splines affected by inserting the new knots. In Figure 7.18, we see that the affected B-splines are b_0 through b_3. We see, too, that b_1 and b_2 are contained within the knot range u_0 to u_5, but that b_0 stretches to one more knot to the left, u_{-1}, and b_3 to one more knot to the right, u_6. We can choose arbitrary values for these, so that $u_{-1} < u_0$ and $u_5 < u_6$. We choose the old knot sequence:

{–1 0 0 0 1 1 1 2}

The refined sequence will then be:

{–1 0 0 0 w w w 1 1 1 2}

With these two sequences, the order 4 and $w = 0.5$ we obtain the weights:

α_{ij}	$j = 0$	1	2	3	4	5	6
$i = 0$	1	0.5	0.25	0.125			
1		0.5	0.5	0.375	0.25		
2			0.25	0.375	0.5	0.5	
3				0.125	0.25	0.5	1

(The order is not indicated in the subscripts.) We interpret this table as we explained in the text. There will be seven new control points, W_0 through W_6, expressed as follows:

$$W_j = P_0 \alpha_{0j} + P_1 \alpha_{1j} + P_2 \alpha_{2j} + P_3 \alpha_{3j}$$

We see that $W_0 = P_0$ and $W_6 = P_3$, but in between there appear five new ones. One of these, W_3, will lie on the curve (see the explanation of the hand-drawing rule for Bezier curves and compare the coefficients of W_3 to those derived there).

If we want to split at a different w value, we have to run the above algorithm with the changed w. However, we can express the weights as functions of w, enabling us to hardcode the computation of the new control points in the splitting program. Below, we show these functions.

α_{ij}	$j = 0$	1	2	3	4	5	6
$i = 0$	1	$1-w$	$(1-w)^2$	$(1-w)^3$			
1		w	$2w(1-w)$	$3w(1-w)^2$	$(1-w)^2$		
2			w^2	$3w^2(1-w)$	$2w(1-w)$	$1-w$	
3				w^3	w^2	w	1

If you study this table, you will see that these functions are Bernstein polynomials in w.

27. Write a program that computes and draws the refined control points for a Bezier curve split at an arbitrary location using the hardcoded functions for finding the weights.

28. Derive the values of the a_{ij} as functions of w. You can do this by symbolically computing the weights, using the Oslo algorithm for the given knot sequences (w) and the order 4. Another way is to express the refined B-splines n_0 to n_6 explicitly as Bernstein polynomials (see Section 6.6) and as linear combinations of the b_i with unknown weights. Then you would compare the coefficients. You can use the fact that the sum over each column is equal to 1.

8

LIGHT AND COLOR

This chapter has five sections that explain how we perceive light and colors, how we can describe a color precisely, and how we compute colors.

8.0   **Introduction** points out how the use of color is important in computer graphics.

8.1   **Light** summarizes the physics of light.

8.2   **Colors** explains how we perceive colors and how color primaries or their complements can be mixed to produce other colors.

8.3   **Color Descriptions** explains four systems for describing colors quantitatively, how these relate to color displays, and how they are interrelated.

8.4   **Illumination Models** considers both the sources of light and light's interaction with the surfaces of the objects that we display on the screen.

8.0   INTRODUCTION

Until now, when we spoke of light, the major variable was its intensity. We imagined a monochrome display. If pixels can be just black or white, the only way to vary light's intensity is to vary the ratio of black and white pixels in a given area. However, we cannot continue to overlook color, an extremely important property of light. This brings us to a new aspect of computer graphics.

Observe how thoroughly we ignored color. In scan conversion, we just computed locations in a raster; in windowing and clipping, we transformed numbers from one coordinate system to another and computed the intersection of lines. Transformations in the plane and in space redefined objects' coordinates. Curves and surfaces allowed us to define the smooth outlines of an object independently of how they were to be displayed. However, all these things can very well be done in a black-and-white environment.

Now we are about to enter the exciting area of colors—colors that are taken from the real world around us, colors that we try to analyze and understand as a topic in themselves, colors that are governed by the laws of physics and that add another dimension to our pictures.

8.1   LIGHT

From physics, we learn that light is a narrow band of electromagnetic frequencies with wavelengths that range from approximately 400 to 700 nanometers. When electromagnetic energy at these wavelengths hits the eye's retina, we experience the sensation of light. The measurement of light is therefore inseparable from the physiological aspects of human sight. A wavelength of 400 nanometers (nm) is perceived as violet; increasing wavelengths are blue, cyan, green, yellow, and finally red, at 700 nm.

Three terms are used to specify the quality of a light source, beyond its purely physical description as a spectrum of different wavelengths and intensities. These terms are *radiance*, *luminance*, and *brightness*. They are not independent from one another, but their interrelationship is very complex. We will look at them individually.

Radiance is the total amount of energy that flows from the electromagnetic (light) source. One can measure the amount with instruments and usually express it in watts, a standard measure of any kind of energy.

Not all energy from light sources excites the sensors in the human eye equally. Subjectively speaking, some wavelengths seem brighter to us than others, although their sources radiate the same energy measured in watts. We need a different measure for the amount of energy we perceive from a given light source. This perceived energy is called *luminance*; its measuring unit is the *lumen*. It tells how much a certain quality of light excites the sensors in the human eye. For example, a light with a wavelength of 380 nm can have considerable energy (radiance) and yet will hardly be perceived because this light is at the higher frequency end of the band for which we have a sensation. The luminance of such a light source is almost zero.

Brightness is very subjective and is practically impossible to measure. A source's brightness tells how "bright" the light looks to the viewer. We know that when we turn on a light in a dark room, it first seems very bright to us. As soon as our eyes have adapted to it, it will look "normal," no matter how many watts the light emits. This is because the eye-brain system adjusts to the given light environment. Now, brightness does not mean this immediate sensation before we adapt; rather, it means our subjective feeling of a given light source's brightness after we have adapted to it. For example, the light of a burning candle in a dark room will look bright, even after we have fully adapted; this is probably because it is much brighter than everything else in this room. The same candle will not look bright to us if we see it in the sunlight.

The relation between luminance and wavelength can be established experimentally. Figure 8.1, which plots wavelength against relative sensitivity, shows this relationship. The light in this graph has a constant radiance of 1 watt for all wavelengths. If this watt of energy is emitted at a wavelength of 560 nm (green), the luminance is highest (680 lumens) and we take this as 100 percent sensitivity. The luminance decreases rapidly as the wavelength changes slightly, and is practically zero at 380 and 740 nm. This does not mean that a lumen of red light is less than a lumen of green light; these two lumens of light produce the same sensory response. However, we need many more watts of red light energy to produce one lumen of sensation than we need to produce one lumen of sensation from green light.

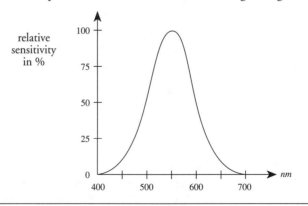

Figure 8.1   *Light sensitivity against wavelength*

MEASURING POINT LIGHT

To discuss the measurement of light, we must make some abstractions. One concept that is not very close to reality but is still very helpful is that of a *point light source*. This abstraction assumes that an infinitely small light source (a point) can emit light. In Section 4, we will work with these point light sources, because distributed sources, which are more realistic, are mathematically difficult to handle.

The light emitted by a point source radiates in all directions. We can conceptualize the point source as surrounded by a sphere that catches all the source's light. If the sphere is large, the light will have a low intensity per unit area when it reaches the surrounding surface. If the sphere is small, the unit intensity will be high. However, the total amount of light reaching the sphere will be constant. The intensity of a point source therefore must be measured as the amount of light it produces in relation to a certain spatial angle.

A *radian* is the unit of an angle that intercepts an arc of length r when the angle's vertex is at the center of a circle of radius r. In three dimensions, the analogous angle has a vertex centered in a sphere of radius r that subtends an area of r^2. This unit of spatial angles is called a *steradian*. In Figure 8.2, we see a sphere of radius r surrounding a point light source with an area of r^2 on its surface. The spatial angle subtended by this area is one steradian, no matter what the area's shape is.

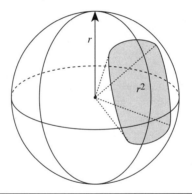

Figure 8.2   Concept of a steradian

The amount of light, measured in lumens, that falls on one steradian of a sphere containing the point light source is constant, regardless of the sphere's size. It makes sense to measure the strength of a point light in lumens per steradian. It follows from this that the amount of light hitting an area of constant size decreases with the square of the distance to the light source.

MEASURING DISTRIBUTED LIGHT

The alternative to point light is light coming from a surface. All light sources in the real world (except possibly stars) are distributed sources. When we "see" a surface, what we see is light coming from every point on that surface. We can think of this as infinitely many point sources, each of which has practically zero light intensity. To compute the total amount of light from a surface, we must evaluate an integral, but we will not pursue this.

Luminance is defined as the amount of light coming from a luminous surface, measured as light intensity per unit of surface. With a real surface, these infinite, very weak point light sources do not emit their light with equal strength in all directions. That is, they do not *diffuse* perfectly, so in reality the light coming from a surface depends on the angle from which we look at it. Here, we make a second useful abstraction. We assume that surfaces diffuse perfectly, a property called *lambertian*. This means that the light coming from them has the same strength, regardless of the viewer's angle. In Section 8.4, we will add some more abstractions to arrive at a workable illumination model.

8.2   COLORS

COLOR SENSATION

Humans have known about colors since long before they could describe them physically as certain wavelengths in the spectrum of electromagnetic waves. Still, the knowledge of color's physical nature really only tells us that we create the entire sensation of color. There are no colors in the physical universe; electromagnetic radiation has nothing that resembles color. Only our perception creates color. Figure 8.3 shows which wavelengths we perceive as which colors. The horizontal scale is in nanometers.

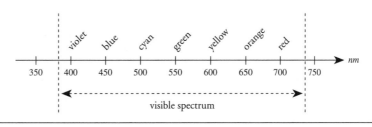

Figure 8.3   Color spectrum

Color sensation is an important element in our visual recognition process. It influences what we see and helps us recognize complicated visual information. It even influences our mood; for example, we usually view red and orange as "warm" colors and blue and cyan as "cold."

Two facts concerning our visual recognition system have been experimentally established and widely accepted:

1. We see color through *cones*, special sensors in the eye's retina. These sensors are concentrated in a small area called the *fovea*, which is only 0.25 millimeter in diameter. Outside the fovea, we have very few cones and therefore have reduced color sensation, mainly perceiving grayscale intensities.
2. We can obtain all the colors we perceive by mixing red, green, and blue. This leads to the assumption that there are three types of cones, each responding to red, green, or blue light. An object's color is perceived by the degree to which each of these types of cones is excited.

This is the background underlying the concept of a color monitor, which produces all colors with a mixture of red, green, and blue. The process corresponds directly to the way our visual system perceives colors.

Color CRT Techniques

Almost every color CRT displays a color image with the *shadow mask technique* (defined below). All the varied colors that we see are produced by mixing the three primaries: red, green, and blue. These three colors are produced on the CRT surface by exciting three types of phosphors. These emit either red, green, or blue light when hit by an electron beam. The phosphors are laid down carefully in various patterns on the CRT's inner front surface.

We now present three common techniques. In one, the *delta construction*, these phosphors are laid down as dots of about 0.35 mm size. The pattern is such that one red, one green, and one blue dot form a delta-shaped (equilateral) triangle called a *triad*.

Figure 8.A shows part of such a layout, in which two triads are highlighted. These triads repeat in an interlaced pattern over the whole inner surface of the tube. To produce a red dot, we just aim an electron beam precisely enough so that it will hit only the red phosphor, never a green or blue phosphor. While the principle is simple, accomplishing it is very difficult.

Figure 8.A   Phosphor dot pattern

There is a good reason for laying down the phosphor dots in such a pattern. This pattern, together with a shadow mask, allows a subset of the electrons to strike only phosphors of the correct color without hitting phosphors of another color. The *shadow mask* is a thin metal plate with tiny apertures, such that there is precisely one aperture per triad. The center-to-center spacing of the apertures is about 0.3 mm (this is called the shadow mask's *pitch*). The mask is mounted inside the tube, about 13 mm from the front surface. Three separate electron guns are also mounted in a delta-shaped cluster. The beams of these three guns are deflected together in such a way that they converge and cross over at the plane of the shadow mask. The arrangement of guns, shadow mask, and triads ensures that the beam from one gun can impinge on only one of the three phosphor types and is "shadowed" from the other two. Because the beams originate at different points, they pass through the apertures at different angles; this permits electrons from only one gun to strike the corresponding phosphor dot.

Figure 8.B shows how apertures and triads correspond. The apertures, shown in black, sit in the centers of their triads. This is the view we might have when looking at the shadow mask and the triads from a point in the center between the three guns (except that we would see only those parts of the triads that are now covered by the black apertures). Moving to the red gun, we would see only the red phosphor dots. The same holds for green and blue.

Figure 8.B   *One shadow mask hole per triad*

The arrangement of triads and apertures as shown in Figure 8.B represents only the center portion of the screen. It is not as regular in the outer portions, in order to compensate for the slant of the electron beams. The overall arrangement is shown in Figure 8.C.

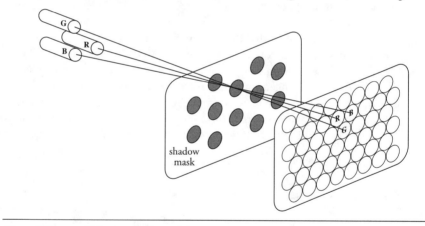

Figure 8.C   *Delta arrangement of electron guns*

You can see in the figure how the beams cross over in the plane of the shadow mask when they penetrate through an aperture. The green gun is at the top of the triangular gun arrangement, so its beam can strike only the green phosphor dot at the bottom of its triad. Red and blue work similarly.

The pixel data in the frame buffer contain information about the intensities of the three primaries R, G, and B. We describe later in this chapter precisely how the pixel data, which are just numbers, are transformed into the three primary intensities.

It is essential that although the three guns' beams always move together, their intensities change individually. For example, if only the red gun is at full intensity, with green

(continued)

and blue at zero, then that location will look red on the screen, because an electron beam will hit only the red phosphor dot.

It is important to recognize that the thickness of the three guns' combined beams is much wider than one aperture in the shadow mask. If it were exactly the same size, it would be almost impossible to attain the precision required for sending the correct color information at exactly the right instant. The ratio between holes to metal in the shadow mask is only about 1:4. If the combined beam were just a little off, the screen could look much darker or completely dark, even if all three intensities were full for each pixel. This would happen if the beam were turned on when it was between two apertures on its horizontal path. The vertical adjustment would be very difficult as well; for certain scan lines, the beam's horizontal path might never hit an aperture in the mask. If the positions where the beam sends pixel information "beats" with the aperture positions, then strong *moiré* patterns develop on the display. In short, a precise adjustment would not be possible.

One can overcome the above difficulties by making the combined beam thick enough to always cover at least two apertures in the mask. Therefore a single pixel extends over two to three apertures. If a single green pixel is displayed, it can very well have been formed by two green phosphor dots or even two and a half, depending on its position on the screen. If you examine a color monitor or a TV display with a magnifying glass, you can confirm this.

The net result is that there is no fixed relation between the size of the frame buffer and the shadow mask pitch. This makes the resolution of a color CRT display independent of the shadow mask pitch; it is merely a function of the frame buffer size.

Another arrangement is the *inline tube*, which has its three electron guns in one horizontal line rather than in a triangle. This allows somewhat higher precision. The phosphor dots on the screen form groups of three, just as in the delta system, but the individual triad consists of three dots in one horizontal line (see Figure 8.D).

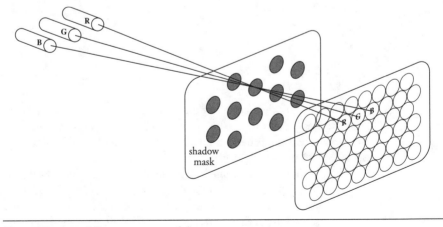

Figure 8.D   *Inline arrangement of electron guns*

Sometimes the phosphor dots on the screen are not round, but elongated rectangles (maybe this is so on your TV monitor). In such a case, the apertures in the shadow mask are also rectangles. This is carried to the extreme in another arrangement. The phosphors are not in triads, but in narrow, vertical stripes. The shadow mask looks like a very fine grill consisting of vertical bands. The electron guns in this case are arranged as in the inline tube. Consult RAST85 for more information on this.

THE PRIMARIES

In Figure 8.3, we saw that colors correspond to wavelengths. The color range in the spectrum of visible light represents the *rainbow colors*, because a rainbow consists of these colors. However, many colors do not appear in the rainbow, for example, pink, brown, black, white, ochre, and magenta. How are these generated?

The rainbow colors are those with a single pure wavelength. In the real world, however, light will usually be a mixture of colors of different wavelengths. A true white light consists of equal radiance levels across the entire rainbow spectrum; it is a combination of wavelengths, each radiating with the same radiance. It has been experimentally established that a proper mixture of only three colors in the spectrum can produce the same sensation of white light. We cannot take just any three colors; they must be chosen so that no two of them can produce the sensation of the third. Whenever we have a combination of three colors that achieves this, we call them *primaries*.

The most widely used primaries are red, green, and blue. (Other primaries are possible, but have not become popular, maybe because the human eye-brain system works with something close to red, green, and blue.) When mixed properly, these primaries can produce not only white, but almost every other color that we can perceive, because the primaries are widely separated on the spectrum. Thus, we can sense the color yellow in two different ways: as light with a wavelength of about 600 nm, or as a mixture of green and red light. In the first case, the cones for green and red are excited by the yellow wavelength, because it is about halfway between these two. In the second case, these two groups of cones are each excited precisely by the light for which they have their peak response. Physiologically, almost the same process is involved—impulses from the red and green cones combine in the brain to give the sensation of yellow (there are no cones for yellow). (Note carefully that we are mixing light. Mixing paint colors is entirely different.)

The color cyan can be produced in two similar ways. However, the color magenta is really an artifact of the brain; it does not occur in the spectrum. The only way to produce it is by properly mixing red and blue. We perceive this color by internally calculating the ratio between the radiances of red and blue light.

After the colors yellow, cyan, and magenta (and their shades), we have exhausted the colors that can be produced with a mixture of only two of the primaries red, green, and blue (abbreviated RGB). However, mixing three of the primaries can produce a huge range of color sensations, all artifacts of the brain. The most important and easiest to remember is white. A color such as pink would be similar to white, but with a stronger contribution from red than green and blue.

Gray is a white with all primaries equally strong, but with each weaker than in full white.

We can go continuously down the gray scale by diminishing all radiances equally until they are at zero; then we have black.

A color such as brown is a mixture of red, green, and blue, in which the red has a radiance approximately two times as strong as the green and about four times as strong as the blue. In addition, all primaries are at a low luminance. Figure 8.4 shows the additive color-mixing scheme. As a two-dimensional layout, it cannot show all possible combinations.

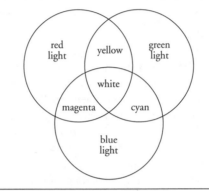

Figure 8.4   *Additive color mixing*

Because colors are produced by adding light of the primaries in the proper radiances, we call such a system *additive*. Color monitors follow an additive principle. The lights emitted by the different phosphors combine to produce the desired color sensation. The amount of light emitted by a given phosphor depends on the intensity of the electron beam hitting it. Therefore, the radiance of a certain primary is often called its *intensity*.

COMPLEMENTARY COLORS

When we take white light and subtract one of the RGB primaries, we obtain a mixture of the remaining two primaries. This mixture will be either yellow, cyan, or magenta. We call those the three *complementary colors*. Can we produce all the other colors by adding combinations of these on a monitor? No, because whichever two we add, we will always have a mixture of all three primaries and hence a color close to white. For example, adding yellow and cyan gives R+G plus G+B, which is white with a strong green component, or a greenish white. Actually, we will always end up with a tint of white when the luminances are high and with a tint of gray when they are low. There is no way we could create a pure blue, for example.

Still, these complementary colors are extremely important, perhaps even more so than the RGB primaries. We can view them as primaries when we consider paints and dyes, which are quite different from light-emitting sources. They never produce their own light; instead, they reflect light that falls onto them or filter light that passes through them, absorbing more or less light in the process.

Consider a cyan dye painted onto white paper. Without the dye, the paper would reflect the whole of the white light falling onto it from the environment, so it would look white. With the cyan dye painted on it, the light passing through and coming back from the paper surface consists only of green and blue (and cyan) wavelengths. The red wavelengths are missing—

they were absorbed while passing through the cyan dye. We can think of the cyan dye as a mass of fine particles that is able to reflect and scatter all wavelengths, except for red ones. Thus, the light that passes through this mass is reflected and scattered from one particle to the other. When it finally manages to escape, it has lost its red wavelength; this has been subtracted.

As another example, consider what yellow dye does. Obviously, it consists of particles that can reflect and scatter everything except the blue wavelengths, so light that passes through will contain only the wavelengths red and green (and yellow), and will therefore appear yellow to us. The blue wavelength has been subtracted.

If we mix cyan and yellow dye, what color results? White light that falls on this mixture will lose the red wavelength through the cyan particles and the blue wavelength through the yellow particles. All that is left will be green light. This is something we can easily verify; every painter can confirm that green will be the result of such a mixture.

SUBTRACTIVE SYSTEMS

We call a color system that behaves this way *subtractive*. This subtractive system is more familiar to us than the additive system. However, the additive system seems unnatural, only because we are not used to it. It is physically as "real" as our practical experience with mixing paints and dyes.

Figure 8.5 shows the subtractive color-mixing scheme. Whenever two colors are mixed, they produce the color shown in the intersection. White does not show in this scheme, because white is obtained by "not mixing" any colors, in other words, not painting anything onto the originally white paper.

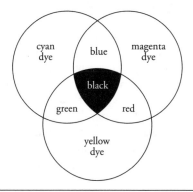

Figure 8.5   Subtractive color mixture

A very light pink can be obtained by painting only a tiny portion of magenta and yellow onto the white surface so that much of its white will still shine through. In other words, only a little of the green light and a little of the blue light will be subtracted by magenta and yellow. The result can be compared to a mixture of RGB, in which all three primaries are about equally strong, but the red primary is somewhat stronger than the other two. In this situation, we eventually obtain the same mixture of red, green, and blue as the one we used above to produce pink.

If we paint onto a nonwhite background, we cannot obtain white or any light color that has white in it, such as pink. Because the system is subtractive, the more dye we put onto the background, the more we subtract from it, so nothing can get lighter. Here, we seem to run into difficulties. Can we paint a black background so that it becomes the color of the paint? Yes, but in such a case, the layer of paint is so thick that the light never penetrates through to the background. The light is reflected (maybe minus some wavelengths) before it can ever reach the background. In this case, we are actually creating a new background or replacing the given one with a background of a different color. The dyes we are using to explain the subtractive system are transparent. The paints that most closely demonstrate the subtracting effect are watercolors. These must be used on a white background.

There is another seeming contradiction. If we paint all three subtractive primaries with watercolors onto a white paper, we do not produce black, but a grayish brown. This happens because although the yellow watercolor subtracts the blue wavelengths, it does not do so completely. Some blue light will always escape. The same is true for the other two primaries. What sounds so easy in theory is only imperfectly realized in practice. The combination lets a variety of wavelengths pass whose composition depends on a number of factors beyond our control.

Practically all the light that we see in the world has gone through a subtractive colorforming process. The only exceptions are the light of the sun, stars, lamps, and the light coming from a TV screen or some color CRT display. The surfaces of objects, such as cars, plants, houses, and practically everything else do not produce their own light, but subtract more or less of the light that falls on them. *Nonemitter displays*, such as photographs, printed matter, and paintings belong in this group.

8.3   COLOR DESCRIPTIONS

We have seen that we can choose three primaries and express practically all other colors as a combination of those. Which primaries we choose and how they interact depends on whether we use an emitter or nonemitter display. In the following discussion, we will use the word *color* in a broader sense. Color means not only a primary or a color of the rainbow spectrum, but everything we can perceive as a visual color sensation from the world around us: white, black, and the numerous other mixtures that we can see.

We need some way to define the colors we see precisely. It would be convenient if we could do this by specifying the color's wavelength; then, we could describe the color with a single number. However, several facts make this impossible. One is that only the rainbow colors can be specified by wavelength. Most colors, including sunlight, are conglomerates of several rainbow colors. Another is that even a rainbow color cannot be sufficiently described by its wavelength. Two objects of the same color can still appear different because of the amount of color that comes from them. One object could be a bright blue and the other a darker blue, though they are the same blue in both cases. One possibility is to use the primaries themselves to describe a given color. What we must specify is the amount of each primary in a mixture.

8.3.1   THE RGB SYSTEM

When working in an environment that uses a color CRT as a display, we can use the RGB color system for specifying colors. RGB stands for the red, green, and blue primaries of an additive display, such as a CRT. The colors that can be produced by a color monitor can easily be described by three numbers: the three *luminances* (adjusted by the amount of white, see below), also called the *intensities*, of these primaries. The number of different intensities possible for each primary depends on the size of one entry in the color lookup table (see sidebar). These sizes presently range from about three bits, corresponding to eight intensities in small desktop computers, to eight, corresponding to 256 intensities in better graphics boards. As each intensity can combine with others to yield a different color, this gives in the first case $8^3 = 512$, and in the second $256^3 = 16$ million different colors. The monitor itself (except for its quality) has nothing to do with the number of colors that can be displayed on it.

The Lookup Table Technique

The most widely used technique to display frame buffers on color monitors is with a *lookup table*. A lookup table is a convenient way to increase the number of colors displayable on the monitor without increasing the depth of the frame buffer. There are several variations of this technique; we will explain just the most straightforward one.

A frame buffer contains only numbers. These numbers specify the pixels' color. The color actually produced depends on the entry in the lookup table that corresponds to the frame buffer number, which we can conveniently change. In effect, the lookup table translates frame buffer values to RGB intensities.

We explain this technique with an example. Figure 8.E shows the circuitry schematic of a frame buffer and a lookup table. We assume a frame buffer of depth four, which is shown in the drawing as four layers. Four bits correspond to each pixel. These bits are at the same location in the frame buffer, but in different layers. (These layers are often called *bit planes.*) The four-bit group corresponds to a specific address in the frame buffer. Its content is a number between 0 and 15. The association between the number at a frame buffer address and the color of the corresponding pixel is established through the color lookup table, which, like a frame buffer, is a RAM area addressable by the main processor. We see the lookup table on the right in the figure.

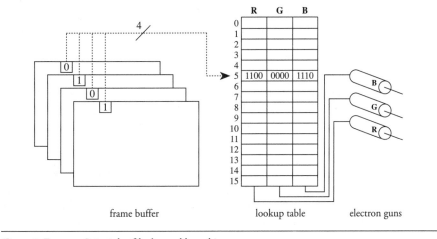

frame buffer   lookup table   electron guns

Figure 8.E　　*Principle of lookup table architecture*

(continued)

When the CRT controller produces a certain frame buffer address, the content of this address is put on the four-bit-wide data bus (in our example). This value is then used for addressing the lookup table. If the value in the frame buffer location is 5, then location 5 in the lookup table is addressed. The table contains intensities for the three primaries. In our example, the table has an overall width of 12 bits, four bits for each primary. The intensity for each primary can therefore be a number between 0 and 15. The contents of the three addressed entries in the table are read out, transformed into analog intensities, and fed to the electron guns for the respective primaries. Our example gives an intensity of 12 for red, 0 for green, and 14 for blue. The given pixel would therefore look magenta on the display.

The table of our example allows 16 intensities each for red, green, and blue. By writing any of these values into a table location we can produce any combination of the primaries with these intensities. This amounts to $16^3 = 4096$ different colors. Unfortunately these combinations cannot all be present at the same time in the table, because its size is only 16. Therefore, only 16 different colors can be present simultaneously on the screen, even with the lookup table. However, we can choose these 16 colors from an overall palette of 4096.

A frame buffer with one byte per pixel would require a lookup table of length $2^8 = 256$. The width is independent of the length. One byte per primary would result in an overall width of 24 bits, which is not farfetched for a good-quality graphics board. This corresponds to a palette of $2^{24} = 16$ million colors. Only 256 colors of this huge palette could be present simultaneously on the screen.

The hardware must address a pixel, read its content, use it to address the lookup table, read out the three intensities, transform those to analog, and feed them to the display circuitry for each pixel on the screen. Imagine a screen with one million pixels, a noninterlaced display, and a refresh rate of 60 frames per second. The hardware does this 60 million times per second, which leaves about 14 to 15 nsec for each pixel (horizontal and vertical sync pauses must be included). No wonder only the fastest RAMs can be used for lookup tables!

If a frame buffer has 24 bits per pixel, 16 million colors can be produced without a lookup table.

To represent the RGB color system, we need a three-dimensional model, because three independent parameters describe a color. These parameters are the luminances of the primaries. In nature, these values have a lower limit of zero, but an upper limit physically does not exist. On a color monitor, the upper limit is the strongest luminance the monitor can produce for any of the primaries. Therefore, we set the lowest luminance to 0 and the highest to 1, in effect normalizing the values.

With these conventions, we can use a Cartesian coordinate system and associate the primaries with the spatial coordinate axes, which we call R, G, and B. The origin will be luminance 0, which gradually increases to 1 along any of the axes. The set of all possible combinations is then contained in a cube whose side is equal to 1. This is called the *RGB color cube*, shown in Figure 8.6.

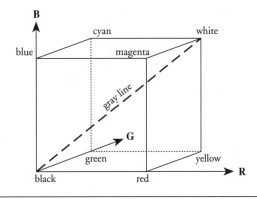

Figure 8.6   The RGB color cube

The gray levels lie along the diagonal (shown here as a heavy-dashed line) from black (0 0 0) to white (1 1 1). Points on this diagonal have equal amounts of all primaries. There are other ways to represent color systems, and we shall explore several.

The RGB-system is the most useful for specifying the colors of objects and we will use it in all programs that produce colored CRT output. We define the class rgb_t with one double for each of the primaries red, green and blue. RGB-values can be added and multiplied component-wise and can be multiplied with a scalar. Also, we define an overloaded operator for reading an RGB-value from a file.

```cpp
//*************************** File rgb.h ****************************

#ifndef RGB_T
#define RGB_T
#include <fstream.h>


class rgb_t
{
public:
    rgb_t() : r(0) , g(0) , b(0) {}
    rgb_t(double r,double g,double b): r(r) , g(g) , b(b) {}
    rgb_t(const rgb_t& rgb) : r(rgb.r) , g(rgb.g) , b(rgb.b) {}

    double givr() const { return r; }
    double givg() const { return g; }
    double givb() const { return b; }
    void setr(double r) { rgb_t::r = r; }
    void setg(double g) { rgb_t::g = g; }
    void setb(double b) { rgb_t::b = b; }
    rgb_t operator + (const rgb_t&) const ;
    rgb_t operator * (const rgb_t&) const ;
    rgb_t operator * (double) const ;
    int   operator == (const rgb_t&) const ;
    rgb_t trim_to_1() ;
```

```
protected:
   double r , g , b;
} ;

rgb_t operator * (double,const rgb_t&) ;
ifstream& operator >> (ifstream&,rgb_t&) ;

#endif


//******************************************************************
```

Here is a good place to introduce the class light_t that describes a point light source. It consists simply of an rgb_t member giving its intensity and a point3_t member giving its location in space. For reasons of implementation, such as linking several point light sources in a list, we provide the structure with a link. A destructor must be present to free allocated memory. We will also use this class to specify ambient light. In this case, the direction component is simply ignored. We will speak more about computing intensities and using these structures in Section 8.4.

```
//*********************** File light.h ***************************

#ifndef LIGHT_T
#define LIGHT_T

#include "../Shape3d/rgb.h"
#include "../Shape3d/point3.h"


class light_t
{
public:
   light_t() : pos(0,0,0), rgb(0,0,0) , next(0) {}
   light_t(point3_t pos,rgb_t rgb,light_t* next) :
      pos(pos) , rgb(rgb) , next(next) {}

   point3_t givpos() const { return pos; }
   void setpos(const point3_t& p) { pos = p; }
   rgb_t    givrgb() const { return rgb; }
   light_t* givnext() const { return next; }

private:
   point3_t pos ;                      // position in space (or direction)
   rgb_t    rgb ;                                            // intensity
   light_t* next ;
} ;

#endif


//******************************************************************
```

8.3.2 THE HSV SYSTEM

The letters HSV stand for *hue, saturation,* and *value*. This system offers a more intuitive and user-friendly definition of colors. We can easily derive it from the RGB color cube. If we look at the cube from a point on the black-white diagonal at some distance from the white corner, the corners will surround us and the cube will look like a regular hexagon. In the middle of the hexagon we will have white and on the six corners the colors red, yellow, green, cyan, blue, and magenta (see Figure 8.7).

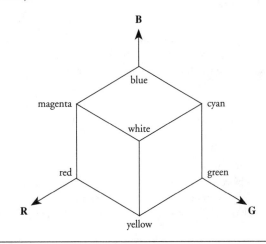

Figure 8.7   RGB color cube viewed from the black-white diagonal

Figure 8.8 shows only the hexagon without any cube edges. The hexagon is also rotated so that we have green at the top. This hexagon shows us all colors. There are gradual transitions along the edges and the colors become more white as we move toward the center. Only black is missing.

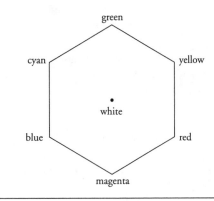

Figure 8.8   The RGB-hexagon

This problem is solved by adding a third dimension to the hexagon. The hexagon will become the base of a six-sided pyramid, with the apex below the center (see Figure 8.9). The height of the hexpyramid is 1. The point at the apex represents the color black. The vector from the apex upward is called the value vector **V**. The hexagon corresponds to **V**-values of 1. Any color now corresponds to a point within this hexpyramid. Full-intensity colors are located in the hexagon; their **V**-values are 1. The further down we go, the lower the intensity and the darker the color. At **V** = 0 we have black, so **V** expresses the value (intensity) of a color.

Hue, H, is relatively easy to describe. In a sense it means color, which we describe with the words red, green, and so on, even if the given color in the broad sense is only a reddish or greenish white or gray. The hue will be described by a number between 0 and 360, which is the angle in a ccw sense starting at red = 0°. A certain hue angle comprises all points on the radial that emanates from the center with this angle and all points on a vertical half-plane intersecting the hexpyramid along this radial. A point below the hexagon represents a color that is darker, but still has the same hue as the point vertically above it. A point further from the

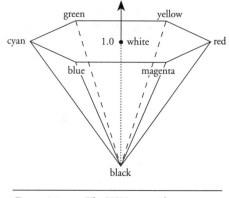

Figure 8.9   The HSV pyramid

boundary represents a color that is less saturated (see below) than a color of a point on the same radial and closer to the boundary. Complementary colors are opposites, 180° from each other.

Saturation, S, also called *purity*, is the most difficult to visualize. Look at Figure 8.10, which shows a certain color's spectral energy distribution. Most wavelengths in the spectrum radiate with an almost equal energy, but one wavelength is much stronger. This *dominant wavelength* determines the given color's hue. The other wavelengths that radiate about equally strongly, but less than the dominant one, produce a lighter or darker white, which is added to the hue and thereby dilutes, or *desaturates*, it. The ratio between r_1 and r_2 represents the color's saturation. An absolutely pure light has no white (gray) tones, so $r_1 = 0$. When $r_1 = r_2$, we have just white and the saturation is 0.

The saturation's value is a ratio ranging from 0 on the center line (**V**-axis) to 1 on the hexagon's boundary. Saturation is a color's distance from the center line. Fully saturated colors lie on the hexagon's boundary. The center line represents all colors with a saturation of 0. Moving along this line from the white point down to the apex gives white through gray until black is reached. These colors have no hue in them, because this line is equally far from all perimeter points.

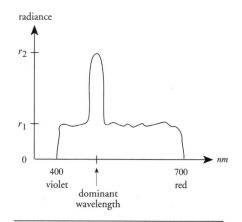

Figure 8.10   Desaturated color mixture

8.3.3 THE HLS SYSTEM

Similar to the HSV system, the HLS system is frequently used in color CRT displays, especially in Tektronix hardware. The letters HLS stand for *hue, lightness,* and *saturation.* In a broader sense, a color's physiological characteristics are its hue (in the sense of rainbow color), its lightness (its brightness or luminance), and its saturation (the degree to which it is undiluted by white), as we have seen above. The HLS system is based on the Ostwald color system, proposed in 1931. Similar to the HSV system, it needs a three-dimensional representation, called the *color double cone* (see Figure 8.11).

On a disk's perimeter are located the colors blue, magenta, red, yellow, green, and cyan, spaced 60° apart from each other. The cone's upper apex is white and the lower apex is black. The colors on the perimeter blend gradually into each other. Each point on the disk's perimeter describes a color that is a blend of the two adjacent colors. The ratio of the blend depends on the ratio of the color's distances from the adjacent two colors. Here, a blue hue is at angle 0.

A point not on the perimeter contains a blend of all colors. The greater the point's distance from any of the perimeter colors, the less that color appears in the blend. Therefore, these points describe pastel colors that contain a certain amount of white. Hue and saturation mean the same as in the HSV system, but here angle 0 corresponds to blue.

The lightness depends on the height in the double cone. It is specified as a number between 0, corresponding to the lower apex, and 1, corresponding to the upper apex. The lightness is the color's intensity. At the highest intensity all colors merge into white, and at the lowest they merge into black.

The middle of the central disk describes white of medium intensity, not full intensity as in the hexpyramid diagram. We can understand it as a mixture of all colors with equal intensity. The higher we move up in the cone, the more we move toward

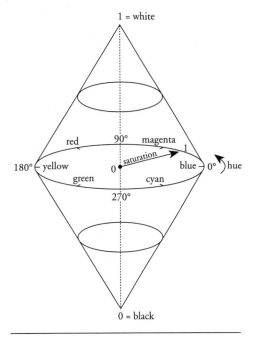

Figure 8.11   The HLS color cone

white; the more we move down, the more we move toward black. If we start at the perimeter at the angle 0 (color blue) and move in a straight line toward the top, we add more and more white, so we will go through light blue to an almost white pastel blue until we finally have the brightest white. This will happen with any color with which we start. The shrinking of the cone's diameter toward the top and bottom expresses the idea that all colors converge to white as we move up or to black as we move down. Moving along the straight line between top and bottom gives all the gray levels from white to black.

8.3.4   THE CIE SYSTEM

CIE stands for Commission Internationale de l'Eclairage. In 1931, this commission worked out a color system that is very adaptable to color programming. To explain it, we first discuss color triangles.

COLOR TRIANGLES

When we have a color system consisting of three primaries, we can represent it graphically with an equilateral triangle. As mentioned before, we can use any three colors as primaries, as long as no one of them can be created by a combination of the other two.

In Figure 8.12, the primaries are at the corners of the triangle, called X, Y, and Z. Any color is a point within this triangle, such as C. The point's position with respect to the corners expresses the primaries' relative contribution to the color.

More precisely, the contribution of X is proportional to the area of the triangle CYZ opposite to X. The same is true for the primaries Y and Z. A primary's contribution to a point C is "full" if C is at the corner and zero if C is on the opposite edge. The areas have certain absolute sizes that depend on the original triangle's size. The sizes can be considered as the luminances that the primaries contribute to the color.

A color can then be expressed with three numbers, the areas of the subtriangles, which constitute its *chromaticity values*. The sum of the chromaticity values will always be the same, no matter where C is located.

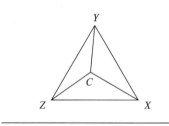

Figure 8.12   Color triangle

The size of the original whole triangle still varies. If we work with primaries of high luminances, we will have large triangles; otherwise, we will have small ones. We can represent this system of expressing colors with a three-dimensional geometric model with the Cartesian coordinates X, Y, and Z. The primaries are points on the axes whose distances from the origin depend on their luminance. With all three primary luminances equal, these three points define an equilateral triangle—the triangle we had above. The vector from the origin to the point C in this triangle expresses C's hue. The vector's length expresses C's luminance. Colors that differ only in luminance but not in hue lie on the same vector.

If we want a system that describes just a color's hue and not its luminance, we must ignore the vector's length. The purpose of the color triangle is to develop such a system. Intuitively, we could later multiply in luminance as a common factor. We can achieve this by dividing C's chromaticity values by their sum:

$$x_c = \frac{X_c}{X_c + Y_c + Z_c} \qquad y_c = \frac{Y_c}{X_c + Y_c + Z_c} \qquad z_c = \frac{Z_c}{X_c + Y_c + Z_c}$$

We call these normalized chromaticity values chromaticity coefficients. Their sum is always equal to 1:

$$x_c + y_c + z_c = 1$$

Geometrically, this corresponds to using only the triangle spanned by the points at a distance of 1 from the origin, as Figure 8.13 shows. (The view is from below that triangle.)

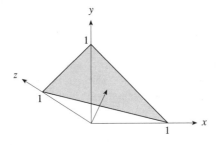

Figure 8.13   Normalized color triangle

Because the sum of the three values equals 1, it suffices to specify only two of them, say x_c and y_c. Then, z_c equals $1 - x_c - y_c$. We can express this geometrically by projecting the equilateral triangle onto the $(x\ y)$-plane. A color is now expressed by only two parameters, x and y, in a Cartesian coordinate system, shown in Figure 8.14. The primaries we choose sit on the corners of a right triangle. We have now made a step toward understanding the CIE color system.

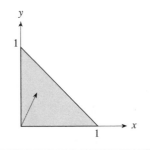

Figure 8.14   Two-dimensional color triangle

ALIGNMENT TO WHITE

We have assumed that the luminances of the three primaries at the corners are equal. Consequently, the point within the triangle where the primaries combine to produce white will not lie in the center. White light consists of light of all visible wavelengths, each radiating with the same energy. The luminance values of these component lights will be far from equal, as we saw in the luminance curve in Figure 8.1.

In addition, when we compose white light from three primaries, they must radiate with about equal energy. This implies that their luminance values will not be equal. If the primaries are, for example, red, green, and blue, only small luminances of blue and red compared to a large luminance of green are required to form white. Equal luminances on the corners mean that the white point will be far from blue and red and close to green. If we mix equal luminances of red and green and blue, we will not produce white.

Still, we prefer to have the white point in the middle of the triangle. We can achieve this by lowering the luminances of the primaries that have too much "weight" in the mix. The factors that accomplish this are called the primaries' *luminosity coefficients*. They depend on which primaries are used and to which white they are aligned.

The problem of aligning to white is not theoretical; it occurs with every color monitor. To align a color monitor, one adjusts the amplifier circuits for the three primaries (whatever these are), so that equal intensity specifications for the primaries (in the lookup table) will result in the desired white and from there through the whole gray scale down to black. The luminance of full-scale blue or full-scale red will always be much lower than that of full-scale green.

THE CIE DIAGRAM

Let us choose any three primaries, say red, green, and blue, and try to match all possible colors with combinations of these. We will always find some colors that we cannot make, no matter how pure and how saturated the primaries. This will not change if we use a different set of three primaries. Some colors not achievable with the former set of primaries might now be possible, but there will be other colors that we can no longer match.

Assume we have a color, for example, some full-saturated cyan, that we cannot match with our given set of three primaries, red, green, and blue. We will now apply a scheme that allows us to express which combination of our primaries could theoretically define that color. If we add a little red (r) to the cyan we will be able to match it in terms of green (g) and blue (b). In our example, let the amount of red added to cyan be 0.05, and let this desaturated cyan be matchable by $0.4*g + 0.4*b$. Now we have:

$$cyan + 0.05*r = 0.4*g + 0.4*b$$

From this, we deduce:

$$cyan = -0.05*r + 0.4*g + 0.4*b$$

We have a negative weight in the combination. This theoretical match does not help us, because we cannot apply negative weights. This scheme is demonstrated in Figure 8.15, which shows what weights of red, green, and blue are necessary to match any colors in the rainbow spectrum. For many colors, we need negative weights.

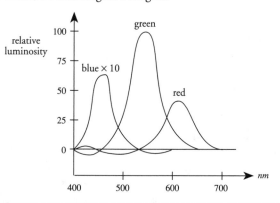

Figure 8.15   Response characteristic for red, green, and blue

The fact of negative weights suggests that our primaries were not pure enough or saturated enough. We had to desaturate the cyan, that is, pull it more toward white by adding some of the third primary in order to match it with the first two primaries. If our blue and green were more saturated (farther away from white), we should be able to match the given cyan without pulling it closer to white. We should have a "bluer" blue and a "greener" green. The same applies to the third primary, red.

This thought led the CIE to introduce three supersaturated colors as primaries which do not exist in reality: X, Y, and Z. These primaries will never be used to generate colors on any real device. They will be used only to describe colors in terms of a two-dimensional Cartesian coordinate system and permit us to read some important true color relationships directly from the diagram. The system will be two-dimensional, because the sum of the primary weights (the chromaticity coefficients) will always be 1 (see the color triangles above) and the weights can now always be positive. It is of course possible to describe colors that do not exist, but this is insignificant. What counts is the fact that we can describe all visible colors with positive chromaticity coefficients.

Note that here we observe the same distinction between chromaticity values and chromaticity coefficients (that add up to 1). The coefficients do not describe a color's luminance, however; that must be provided by a luminance value Y. In the CIE system, then, a color can be fully described with the two coefficients $(x\ y)$ and a luminance value Y. This is again essentially a three-dimensional description, but if we do not need a color's luminance, we have a two-dimensional color definition.

We can transform from chromaticity coefficients $(x\ y\ z)$ to chromaticity values $(X\ Y\ Z)$, not by multiplying by the luminance value Y, but by scaling the coefficients with the proper factor so that y transforms into Y. The convention is that the Y chromaticity value directly expresses the color's luminance. The factor to use is Y/y.

Figure 8.16 on the next page shows the CIE diagram. The whites lie in the center of the area. Blue in the lower left corner and red in the lower right corner are connected by a straight line, called the *purple boundary*.

All visible colors are now expressed as points on this two-dimensional diagram. The fully saturated rainbow colors lie on a horseshoe-shaped curve. The diagram is arranged so that the y chromaticity coefficient has a dual function; it not only expresses a color's position in the chart, but also can be interpreted as a color's relative (as opposed to absolute) luminance. What does this mean?

Assume we have the CIE descriptions of two colors, $A = (x_A\ y_A)$ and $B = (x_B\ y_B)$. If these two are radiating with the same energy, then y_A/y_B is not only the ratio of their relative luminances, but also the ratio of their absolute luminances (because it is only a ratio). If we want these colors to shine with the same absolute luminances Y, we have to scale the first one with the factor Y/y_A and the second with Y/y_B. In doing so, we obtain their chromaticity values: $(X_A\ Y\ Z_A)$ and $(X_B\ Y\ Z_B)$. (Remember that $z_A = 1 - x_A - y_A$, and $z_B = 1 - x_B - y_B$.) These three values are the contributions of the hypothetical supersaturated primaries assumed in the CIE diagram and therefore are of no help in producing these colors. However, they do help us in analyzing them. We can use them to compute the colors' total chromaticities: $T_A = X_A + Y + Z_A$ and $T_B = X_B + Y + Z_B$. A color's total chromaticity is not the same as its luminance, but is in effect the weight that this color has in mixtures.

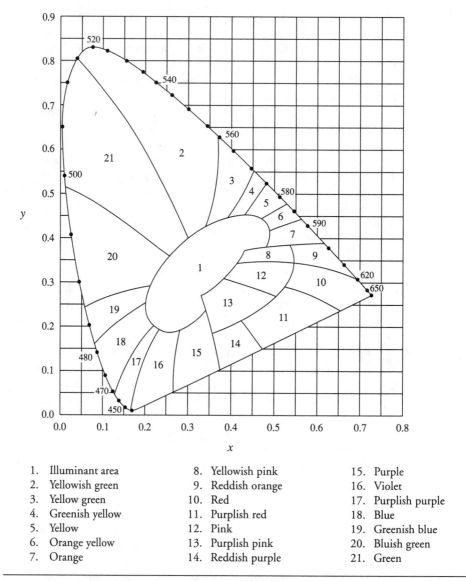

1. Illuminant area
2. Yellowish green
3. Yellow green
4. Greenish yellow
5. Yellow
6. Orange yellow
7. Orange
8. Yellowish pink
9. Reddish orange
10. Red
11. Purplish red
12. Pink
13. Purplish pink
14. Reddish purple
15. Purple
16. Violet
17. Purplish purple
18. Blue
19. Greenish blue
20. Bluish green
21. Green

Figure 8.16   The CIE diagram

What this tells us is that colors very low down in the CIE diagram (blue, etc.) have very weak luminances compared to colors high up (green, etc.). If we crank up the radiance of a blue color to achieve the same luminance as a green one, then these two will look equally bright to us. If we then mix them together, the result will appear blue because the weight (total chromaticity) of this cranked-up blue in mixtures is overwhelming. The CIE diagram has other uses, too, some of which we explain below.

Color gamuts

If we ignore luminance, we can describe a color in an RGB system with color triangles. It then becomes essentially the same as a CIE description. Both use triangular coordinates; the only difference is that the primaries in CIE are hypothetical, while the primaries in RGB are real. Transformations between RGB and CIE descriptions are expressed with simple linear equations and can be done geometrically. The CIE chart spans an area so wide that it contains all visible colors. If we choose any three real primaries, they will lie somewhere in the CIE chart. All colors that we can obtain with these three primaries are contained in the triangle they span. We can see that no triangle entirely inside the outward bent horseshoe curve can cover the whole area within the curve. Choosing more than three primaries would allow us to draw a quadrilateral, pentagon, or other figure, but such polygons still cannot cover the whole area.

Using the CIE diagram, we can choose primaries and see immediately which colors we can obtain from them. The triangle spanned by the primaries within the diagram shows that range. We call such a color range a *color gamut*. Figure 8.17 uses dotted lines to show the triangle of primaries that the National Television Standards Committee (NTSC) chose in 1953. Solid lines form the triangle of a good-quality graphics color monitor. The diagram is very useful for comparing the color gamuts of different monitors.

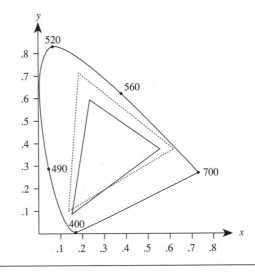

Figure 8.17   Color gamuts

The table below shows the chromaticity coefficients $(x \ y)$ for the color monitor in Figure 8.17. The z coefficient is $1 - x - y$.

R: 0.628   0.346
G: 0.268   0.588
B: 0.150   0.070

We can also show the color gamuts for color printers and hard-copy devices with the CIE diagram. Mixing colors on a white background as done by a printer is basically a subtractive process. The difference between an additive and subtractive process is not that different hues are produced when mixing given colors, but that additive mixing produces increased luminance and subtractive mixing produces decreased luminance. As the CIE diagram is luminance-independent, it is also independent of the type of color mixing. It is hard, however, to visualize the resulting color in a subtractive case. Mixing red and green gives orange-yellow on a screen and in the diagram. Mixing it on paper gives brown, which is actually orange-yellow with a very low luminance and is therefore not shown in the diagram. To add to the problem, printers work with a fourth color, black, which has no corresponding point in the diagram.

DOMINANT WAVELENGTH

The diagram allows us to obtain the *dominant wavelength* (the hue) of any given color, such as that given by point A. We draw the dominant wavelength vector, which is a line connecting the point A and the white point, W. Moving away from W along this vector, we will intersect the boundary of the area, say at point B. The wavelength corresponding to B is the color's dominant wavelength (see Figure 8.18).

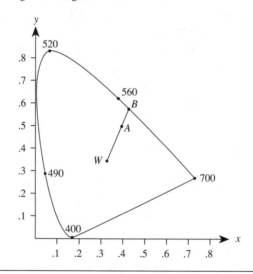

Figure 8.18   Dominant wavelength of color A

If we hit the purple boundary, as at point B in Figure 8.19, we have a *nonspectral color*, because purple hues do not occur in the rainbow spectrum. Consequently, there is no dominant wavelength. In such a case, we elongate the connecting line in the opposite direction and hit the boundary there, say at point D. That color, approximately 500 nm, is said to be the *complementary dominant wavelength* of color A.

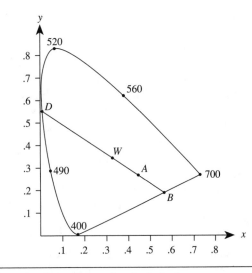

Figure 8.19   Complementary dominant wavelength of color A

The color's purity is expressed by the ratio of the length A_W to the length of the whole line. We see immediately that white has a purity of 0 and that colors on the boundary have a purity of 1.

MIXING COLORS

When we mix two colors A and B, we plot the corresponding points in the diagram and connect them with a straight line. All colors along this line can be produced by mixing A with B in varying luminances. This is called *interpolation in color space* or *color programming* (see Figure 8.20).

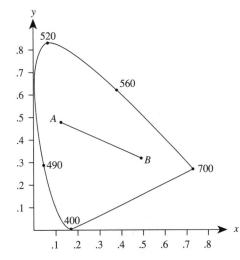

Figure 8.20   Mixing colors A and B

There is more to it than just drawing a line. We have merely stated that we can obtain all colors on the line from A to B. However, the color that results from a given mixture depends on a nontrivial relation. If we do not need precise results, we can say that, for example, mixing A with B at equal luminances will produce a color at the center of the line. This rough estimate is often inadequate because colors have different weights. We know that to achieve white, we require only a very small luminance of blue compared to somewhat more of red and a very great luminance of green. If we mix A and B with equal luminances, the resulting color will not usually lie at the center of the line. The CIE chromaticity diagram is helpful in determining the result. As we explained above, a color's y-coordinate in the diagram also expresses this color's luminance in relation to the luminances of all other colors in the diagram; the y-coordinate is the color's *relative luminance*.

Take the line of Figure 8.20 as an example. A has the chromaticity coefficients $(x\ y\ z) = (0.08\ 0.5\ 0.42)$ and B has $(x\ y\ z) = (0.5\ 0.3\ 0.2)$. This means that the luminances of A and B are in a ratio of $\frac{5}{3}$ if we make no other adjustments. In order for B to radiate with the same luminance as A, B has to radiate with 5/3 as much power as A. In this analysis, we do not need any absolute luminance values, because we just want to express our result on the CIE diagram. (The relative values may fall outside the diagram; that is not important.)

After we apply the factor $\frac{5}{3}$, B has the coefficients $(0.83\ 0.5\ 0.33)$ compared to A, which has $(0.08\ 0.5\ 0.42)$. Observe that we have made the y-coefficients equal, which means that A and B have equal luminance. Adding the coefficients of A and B together, we obtain $(0.91\ 1.0\ 0.75)$, which is not in the diagram. We normalize this point to 1 so that we can associate a point in the CIE diagram with it and obtain $(0.342\ 0.37\ 0.28)$. This point lies on the line from A to B, because it is a linear combination of the A and B coordinates, but it is much closer to B than to A. In this example, we have assumed only that the absolute luminances of A and B are equal; their relative values do not matter. (If we were to mix the colors without equalizing their absolute luminances, the resulting color would be at the midpoint between A and B.)

To program such color computations is not difficult. We need to do this when, for example, we want to see what colors we produce when we merge two separate color images on the screen. In a practical application, the colors A, B, and so on will be described with the triples $(x_A\ y_A\ Y_A)$, $(x_B\ y_B\ Y_B)$, and so on, where Y is the luminance. In such a case, the color weights are computed as:

$$T_A = \frac{Y_A}{y_A} \qquad T_B = \frac{Y_B}{y_B}$$

The chromaticities of the mixture are then computed as:

$$x_M = \frac{x_A T_A + x_B T_B}{T_A + T_B} \qquad y_M = \frac{y_A T_A + y_B T_B}{T_A + T_B} \qquad Y_M = Y_A + Y_B$$

The main value of the CIE diagram is that it helps us visualize the color we should obtain when we merge colors on the screen. If the screen is badly gamma-corrected or badly white-aligned, the CIE diagram will be the only reliable source for visualizing the result. With a perfectly gamma-corrected and white-aligned monitor, we obtain correct results just by linearly interpolating color data, as for example that represented in the lookup tables. (A white-aligned monitor produces a white color from equal intensity values for the primaries in the lookup table. Adjustable potentiometers can be set to compensate for the difference in phosphor reactions to the electron beam. We described gamma correction in Chapter 2.)

8.3.5 THE CMYK SYSTEM

We described the complementary colors to RGB in Section 8.2. These are: cyan (white minus red), magenta (white minus green), and yellow (white minus blue). If we use these in a subtractive environment, that is, by putting transparent inks or dyes onto white paper, we can produce every color except black. Therefore, we add black as a fourth color for the reasons we mentioned in Section 8.2: when cyan, magenta, and yellow inks print on top of each other, they should theoretically produce black, but this does not actually happen because of imperfections in the inks. The abbreviations for the colors are C, M, Y, and K for black (to avoid confusion with B for blue).

When printing on white paper, transparent inks of the above four colors are used. Every color can be described by its CMYK components given a certain set of the colored inks.

The system is easy to understand if one assumes perfect inks. A perfect ink would subtract all the red, green, or blue wavelengths respectively from the white light, but nothing more! Black would not be needed. The result of mixing inks of different intensities could be explained mathematically by subtracting the corresponding amount of wavelengths from white.

For example, a full intensity cyan plus a full intensity magenta would theoretically result in a full intensity blue. In practice, however, some red and green wavelengths are still present, making the blue a little grayish. This might be imperceptible, depending on the quality of the inks, but it may have to be counteracted by adding a little black. The CMYK color description is of paramount importance in the printing industry.

8.3.6 TRANSFORMATIONS

Obviously the same color can be expressed in various ways, five of which we have covered: RGB, HSV, HLS, CIE, and the CMYK subtractive system. It is possible to transform from one description into another. We will describe some of the more common transformations.

RGB AND CMYK

We need this transformation when we have to make a hard copy of a CRT display on a color hard-copy device (dot matrix, ink jet, laser printer, or printing plates). Whenever a picture has been created for a CRT display using RGB color descriptions, producing a hard copy of the screen picture involves transforming between these two different descriptions.

If we directly produce the same colors on the paper as we have on the screen, namely red, green, and blue, in the same intensities, we obtain completely wrong results. Red + green is yellow on the screen, but brown on the paper. Red + green + blue is white on the screen, but a very dark brown on the paper. No colors at all produce black on the screen, but white on the paper, and so on. Mixing more and more colors together gives us an ever brighter result on a CRT display, while it gives us an ever darker result on the paper.

When producing hard copies, it is not possible or desirable to avoid overlapping different colors on the paper. We actually need this overlap to blend the subtractions. It is best to work on the paper with primaries that each extinguish only one of the wavelengths. These primaries are cyan, magenta, and yellow (CMY). While a certain color on the screen is produced by adding the necessary wavelengths to the original black, this color is produced on the paper by subtracting the unnecessary wavelengths from the original white. This explains the transformation formulas below.

Two different formulas are often encountered. A formula for deriving the CMY intensities for any given RGB intensities is:

$$C = 1 - R$$
$$M = 1 - G$$
$$Y = 1 - B$$

The intensities in both systems are given in fractions, with 1 as the highest intensity. This formula is purely theoretical, as it assumes that full intensities of CMY together produce black, which is not the case.

For real hard-copy output, we must use the CMYK system, so the formulas become:

$$C = \max(RGB) - R$$
$$M = \max(RGB) - G$$
$$Y = \max(RGB) - B$$
$$K = 1 - \max(RGB)$$

Again, the intensities are given as fractions, with 1 as the maximum. The term $\max(RGB)$ is the maximum of any primary intensity of the RGB combination.

We do not need an inverse transformation, because there are no applications in which a color hard copy must be transformed to RGB. When we scan a color hard copy, the hardware (the video digitizer or the scanner) automatically gives RGB values.

For example, transform a dark greenish yellow on the screen to the proper CMYK values. Our dark greenish yellow is given as $(RGB) = (0.4 \ 0.5 \ 0)$, which stands for low red, not so low green, no blue. In this case, $\max(RGB) = 0.5$, so we have:

$$C = 0.5 - 0.4 = 0.1$$
$$M = 0.5 - 0.5 = 0.0$$
$$Y = 0.5 - 0.0 = 0.5$$
$$K = 1.0 - 0.5 = 0.5$$

We obtain mainly a mixture of yellow and black dots on the paper, resulting in dark yellow. A little bit of cyan (a few cyan dots) will be strewn in to give the dark yellow a greenish tint. There are more examples in the exercises.

In the printing industry, this transformation from RGB to CMYK involves more complicated conversion formulas for several reasons. One is that the available cyan printing ink is probably not equal to white minus the actual red on the CRT, nor is the available magenta equal to white minus the actual green on the CRT, and so on. Also, the transparencies of the inks usually leave much to be desired. To produce a printed picture that is very much like the CRT display in its color values is largely a matter of the personal experience and intuition of those running the printing press.

RGB AND HLS

These transformations are more awkward. Both systems are used to define colors for CRT displays. In these transformation formulas, we assume that the RGB values are defined in a range from 0 to 1, H is defined in a range from 0 to 360, and L and S are defined in a range from 0 to 1.

In a transformation from RGB to HLS, we first set $M = \max(RGB)$ and $m = \min(RGB)$ and compute $(r\ g\ b)$:

$$r = \frac{M - R}{M - m} \qquad g = \frac{M - G}{M - m} \qquad b = \frac{M - B}{M - m}$$

At least one of the $(r\ g\ b)$ values will be 0, depending on which of the RGB intensities equals the maximum, and at least one of them will be 1, depending on which of the RGB intensities equals the minimum.

Then we compute the intensity L: $L = (M + m)/2$.

We compute the saturation S with one of two formulas, depending on whether L is smaller or greater than 0.5:

$$\text{if } L \le 0.5, \ \ S = \frac{M - m}{M + m} \qquad \text{if } L > 0.5, \ \ S = \frac{M - m}{2 - M - m}$$

To compute H, we use one of three different formulas, depending on which of the $(r\ g\ b)$ is 0:

$$\text{if } r = 0, \quad H = 60*(2 + b - g)$$
$$\text{if } g = 0, \quad H = 60*(4 + r - b)$$
$$\text{if } b = 0, \quad H = 60*(6 + g - r)$$

If the saturation S is 0, we can assign an arbitrary value to H. In a transformation from HLS to RGB, we first compute M and m:

$$\text{if } L \le 0.5, \ \ M = L(1 + S) \qquad \text{if } L > 0.5, \ \ M = L + s - LS$$
$$m = 2L - M$$

Then we compute R:

$$\text{if } H < 60, \quad R = m + (M - m)\frac{H}{60} \qquad \text{if } H < 180, \ \ R = M$$
$$\text{if } H < 240, \quad R = m + (M - m)\frac{240 - H}{60} \qquad \text{if } H < 360, \ \ R = m$$

Then G:

$$\text{if } H < 120, \ \ G = m \qquad \text{if } H < 180, \ \ G = m + (M - m)\frac{H - 120}{60}$$
$$\text{if } H < 300, \ \ G = M \qquad \text{if } H < 360, \ \ G = m + (M - m)\frac{360 - H}{60}$$

Then B:

$$\text{if } H < 60, \quad B = M \qquad \text{if } H < 120, \ \ B = m + (M - m)\frac{120 - H}{60}$$
$$\text{if } H < 240, \ \ B = m \qquad \text{if } H < 300, \ \ B = m + (M - m)\frac{H - 240}{60}$$

A system that allows the user to specify colors in HLS must be able to do a transformation to RGB, because technically, at the lowest hardware level, every CRT monitor is driven with RGB primaries. The transformation from HLS to RGB is often built into the system.

RGB AND CIE

To establish a relation between these two systems, we must know the CIE chromaticity coefficients of the RGB primaries for the given CRT monitor and for the white to which the monitor is aligned (or not so well aligned!):

$$R: x_R, y_R, z_R \qquad G: x_G, y_G, z_G \qquad B: x_B, y_B, z_B \qquad W: X_W, Y_W, Z_W$$

The z-coordinates are really redundant, as they can be derived from x and y. Notice that the white alignment is given in absolute chromaticity values. On a monitor the white alignment is produced by combining the primaries with unequal luminances. Primaries with a low relative luminance, such as blue, must be brought into the combination with a reduced absolute luminance, which implies a reduced total chromaticity, in order not to exert too much weight. The sum of the total chromaticities (the adjusted weights) of the three primaries gives the desired white. We can express this with the linear system:

$$\begin{pmatrix} x_R & x_G & x_B \\ y_R & y_G & y_B \\ z_R & z_G & z_B \end{pmatrix} * \begin{pmatrix} T_R \\ T_G \\ T_B \end{pmatrix} = \begin{pmatrix} X_W \\ Y_W \\ Z_W \end{pmatrix}$$

Expressing a color given in one system in terms of the other is basically simple, but requires several computations. What we show now is nothing but the application of Cramer's rule to that system. We first compute the transformation determinant k_D:

$$k_D = \begin{vmatrix} x_R & x_G & x_B \\ y_R & y_G & y_B \\ z_R & z_G & z_B \end{vmatrix}$$

Then we compute nine conversion factors k_1 through k_9:

$$k_1 = \frac{y_G z_B - y_B z_G}{k_D} \qquad k_2 = \frac{x_B z_G - x_G z_B}{k_D} \qquad k_3 = \frac{x_G y_B - x_B y_G}{k_D}$$

$$k_4 = \frac{y_B z_R - y_R z_B}{k_D} \qquad k_5 = \frac{x_R z_B - x_B z_R}{k_D} \qquad k_6 = \frac{x_B y_R - x_R y_B}{k_D}$$

$$k_7 = \frac{y_R z_G - y_G z_R}{k_D} \qquad k_8 = \frac{x_G z_R - x_R z_G}{k_D} \qquad k_9 = \frac{x_R y_G - x_G y_R}{k_D}$$

With these we compute the total chromaticity values T_R, T_G, and T_B for the primaries:

$$T_R = k_1 X_W + k_2 Y_W + k_3 Z_W$$

$$T_G = k_4 X_W + k_5 Y_W + k_6 Z_W$$

$$T_B = k_7 X_W + k_8 Y_W + k_9 Z_W$$

The k and T values are constant for white and a given set of primaries, so we can keep them as fixed constants for a given monitor and use them for the conversions in both directions.

In order for the following transformations to be correct, we assume that the monitor is gamma-corrected. This means that the data-to-luminance relation is linear on this monitor.

CIE TO RGB

If a color C is given as $(x_C \ y_C \ Y_C)$, we first compute its chromaticity values:

$$X_C = \frac{x_C}{y_C}Y_C \qquad Y_C = Y_C \qquad Z_C = \frac{z_C}{y_C}Y_C$$

Then we compute the RGB components of the color C:

$$R_C = \frac{k_1}{T_R}X_C + \frac{k_2}{T_R}Y_C + \frac{k_3}{T_R}Z_C$$

$$G_C = \frac{k_4}{T_G}X_C + \frac{k_5}{T_G}Y_C + \frac{k_6}{T_G}Z_C$$

$$B_C = \frac{k_7}{T_B}X_C + \frac{k_8}{T_B}Y_C + \frac{k_9}{T_B}Z_C$$

RGB TO CIE

If a color is given by its RGB values as $(R_C \ G_C \ B_C)$, we first compute its chromaticity values:

$$X_C = x_R T_R R_C + x_G T_G G_C + x_B T_B B_C$$
$$Y_C = y_R T_R R_C + y_G T_G G_C + y_B T_B B_C$$
$$Z_C = z_R T_R R_C + z_G T_G G_C + z_B T_B B_C$$

These are transformed into the chromaticity coefficients:

$$T_C = X_C + Y_C + Z_C$$

$$x_C = \frac{X_C}{T_C} \qquad y_C = \frac{Y_C}{T_C} \qquad z_C = \frac{Z_C}{T_C}$$

The exercises give you opportunities to practice all of these transformations.

8.4   ILLUMINATION MODELS

We have investigated the properties of light and its colors; now we focus on the interaction of light with surfaces. This interaction modifies the light in several ways. One interaction modifies the light's qualities, (such as wavelength, composition, and intensity) while another changes the direction of the light rays.

For a realistic scene, we must render the objects of the scene in colors that closely resemble their real colors. This is not a trivial matter. What happens when we look at a object? We see it because of the light that comes from the object's surfaces to our eyes. Visual perception is a complicated process that has been studied extensively; we will not go into detail here.

In this section, we concentrate on the location and qualities of the light that falls on our objects and how the object interacts with it. A model for the interaction of light with a surface is called an *illumination model*. This section describes one such model, a simplified explanation of what occurs in the real world. Our model gives good results in our quest for visual realism.

8.4.1   LIGHT SOURCES

Every object that we see in the real world emits light. This light has different origins. The object itself may produce and emit light, for example, a lamp, the sun, or the stars (see Figure 8.21). We call such an object a *light-emitting source*.

Figure 8.21   Light-emitting source

More commonly, the light comes from somewhere else and the object reflects it. In Figure 8.22, the sun's light is reflected by the gray sphere. We call such an object a *light-reflecting source*.

Light-emitting sources can be either *point sources* or *distributed sources*. If the light-emitting surface is small compared to the surface onto which it shines, we have a point source. Otherwise, we have a distributed source. The distinction is not very sharp, but that is unimportant, because the mathematical models we use are inaccurate anyway. We will call the light from the first source *point light* and light from the other *distributed light* (see Figures 8.23 and 8.24).

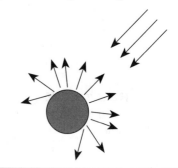

Figure 8.22   Light-reflecting source

All nonemitting objects in a scene are light-reflecting sources. This includes objects that are not shown in the scene—in other words, the whole environment. When we try to produce realistic displays, we must recognize that reflected light is coming from practically all directions: the walls of the room, all illuminated objects, the sky, and the landscape. It follows that a surface that is not exposed directly to a light-emitting source will still be visible, because of the multitude of reflecting light sources around it. For example, something that is out-

Figure 8.23   The sun as a point light source

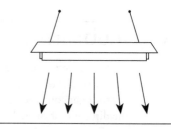

Figure 8.24   A fluorescent lamp as a distributed light source

side but shaded from the sun is still visible because the sky and many other things are light-reflecting sources. Light coming from such sources is called *ambient light* or *background light*.

We need to consider these two types of sources in order to compute how much light is reflected from an object's surface. Each type of source contributes to the illumination of the particular surface. Figure 8.25 shows an example. The viewed object is a cube. Its front surface is illuminated by point light coming from the light bulb and by ambient light coming from the wall.

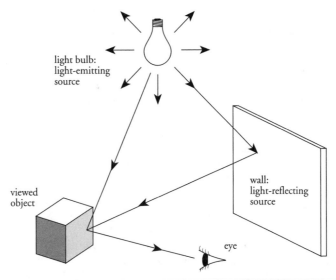

Figure 8.25   Object simultaneously illuminated by two types of light sources

8.4.2 REFLECTIONS

When light falls on a surface, it can be reflected, absorbed, or transmitted by the surface. These three effects are not mutually exclusive; all of them usually take place. At this point, however, we are concerned only with reflection, because reflected light makes an object visible. The precise physical process of reflection is very complicated, well beyond the scope of this book, but a precise simulation of the physical process is unnecessary. We can obtain good results from simple models.

Because there are two types of light sources, we have two different types of light. There are also two types of reflection: *diffuse reflection* and *specular reflection*. The reflection model we use works with both sources. We now investigate how the two types of light sources interact with the two types of reflection.

DIFFUSE REFLECTION

In diffuse reflection, incoming light is not reflected in a single direction but is scattered almost randomly in all possible directions. In addition, the incoming light is influenced by the surface.

A surface will hardly reflect all the incoming light; part will be absorbed. The part that is not absorbed will be reflected randomly in all directions. Therefore, the direction from which the incoming light comes is unimportant (see Figure 8.26).

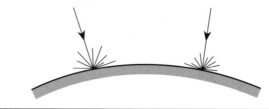

Figure 8.26   Diffuse reflection

How much of the light is absorbed varies for different wavelengths of the incoming light. If a surface completely absorbs the red and blue wavelengths and partially absorbs the green, it then reflects no red or blue light and only part of the green light. The surface will appear dark green.

Because we are working in the RGB color system, we describe the diffuse reflectivity of a surface with three parameters:

k_{dr} = diffuse reflectivity for red
k_{dg} = diffuse reflectivity for green
k_{db} = diffuse reflectivity for blue

These parameters are specified as values in the range [0 1]. The above example of a dark green surface might have a diffuse reflectivity of $(k_{dr}\ \ k_{dg}\ \ k_{db})$ = (0.0 0.5 0.0).

The incoming light, whether ambient, point light, or diffuse light, will also consist of three components that describe its intensity in terms of red, green, and blue: I_r, I_g, I_b. In the real world, there is no upper limit to the intensity of light, but in computer graphics we have a maximum intensity for any of the three colors. These intensities are usually numbers assigned to the primaries of a particular color in the lookup table. The greatest value number depends on the hardware; the lowest intensity is always 0. We assign 1 to the highest intensity and 0 to the lowest in order to be machine independent.

Let us consider diffuse reflection of the different types of light sources. First, we consider the diffuse reflection of ambient light. Ambient light comes randomly from all possible directions and is also reflected randomly in all possible directions. There is no single angle from which the light comes and no single angle to which it goes. We can think of it as being reflected equally in all directions. This means that the angle at which the reflecting surface is tilted in space is insignificant. The light coming from it will always be the same. This results in a uniform illumination of the surface at any viewing position, no matter whether the surface is curved or not.

The ambient light that hits the surface is described by the three components $(I_{ar}\ \ I_{ag}\ \ I_{ab})$. Let us describe the reflected light by the three components $(I_r\ \ I_g\ \ I_b)$. We can compute the intensity of each component of the reflected light separately:

$$I_r = k_{dr} * I_{ar} \qquad I_g = k_{dg} * I_{ag} \qquad I_b = k_{db} * I_{ab}$$

These values for I_r, I_g, and I_b describe the contribution from ambient light to the total illumination of a surface. Other light sources and other reflection mechanisms will add their share to the overall illumination.

Next, we consider the diffuse reflection of point light. Point light differs from ambient light in that we must consider the angle from which it comes in our reflection model. Light from a distributed light source also comes in at an angle. We will not further distinguish between these two types of light and will treat them equally. They both constitute light that comes in at some incident angle. The *incident angle* is the angle ϕ between the vector that points to the light source **L** and the surface normal **N** at this point (see Figure 8.27).

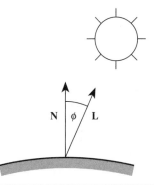

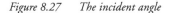

Figure 8.27   The incident angle

A surface that reflects diffusely randomly scatters a part of any incoming light ray, no matter from what angle the light ray comes. The rest is absorbed. However, a light ray that hits a surface directly brings more light per unit area of the surface than an equally intense light ray that hits the surface obliquely. To clarify this concept, we make a slight simplification.

We consider the incoming light rays to be parallel. This comes very close to reality for two reasons. First, the light sources are either very, very far away (like the sun) or very far compared to the size of the illuminated object. The light rays are so nearly parallel that the slight variations of the incident angles for a light source at a finite distance do not create perceptible differences in intensity. Second, real "point" light sources are not really points, but areas. Strictly speaking, the light rays hitting a certain area are never completely parallel, but hit at different angles. A model in which the rays were not parallel would become tremendously complicated and would contribute little.

We account for the intensity of impinging light by assessing the density of the light rays that come from the source. Figure 8.28 shows this. A certain number of light rays come from the left, hitting a flat surface perpendicular to the light rays. When the surface is tilted, it is hit by fewer light rays. When it is parallel to the light rays, no light at all will hit the surface. This shows that the intensity of the impinging light decreases when the surface is tilted. The intensity of the impinging light is proportional to the number of light rays that hit an area of constant size. This proportion is the cosine of the incident angle ϕ, $0 \leq \phi \leq \pi/2$. We call this *Lambert's cosine law.*

The lines in Figure 8.28 represent the density of the incoming light. In case a, the incident angle is 0; five light rays hit the surface. In case b, the incident angle is 45°; only about 3.5 rays hit the surface, although the rays are equally dense. In case c, the incident angle is 90°; no light rays hit the surface.

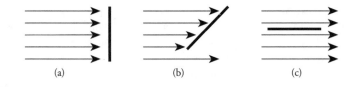

Figure 8.28   Light striking surfaces at different incident angles

This means that we must multiply all intensities of the incoming light by $\cos\phi$ to obtain the actual intensity with which light hits the surface. It is the actual intensity at the surface that is reflected diffusely.

Another factor that influences a point light's density is the point light source's distance from the surface. Often, the distances involved are so large compared to the size of the illuminated surface that the discrepancies due to distance for various points on an object's surfaces are negligible. In many applications, then, we can ignore the distance from the point source, but in a minority of scenes, it is important to allow for this, so the formula will include a distance parameter d.

Suppose that the intensity of light coming from a point source (or distributed source) is $(I_{pr}\ I_{pg}\ I_{pb})$. The contribution of the point light to the overall illumination is:

$$I_r = I_{pr} * \cos\phi * \frac{k_{dr}}{d} \qquad I_g = I_{pg} * \cos\phi * \frac{k_{dg}}{d} \qquad I_b = I_{pb} * \cos\phi * \frac{k_{db}}{d}$$

The cosine of the incident angle ϕ can be computed as the dot product of the vector $\mathbf{L}$ pointing to the light source and the vector $\mathbf{N}$ normal to the surface: $\cos\phi = \mathbf{N} \cdot \mathbf{L}$. Both vectors must be normalized for this computation. For scenes that are illuminated by the sun or by a far light source, we ignore the division by d. (Actually, the intensity of light coming from a point source decreases as $1/d^2$, but this is only for true point light sources, which never really exist. When a light source is an area, the decrease is less rapid. The above formula is a realistic model.)

We have then, for diffuse reflection of both ambient light and point light,

$$I_r = I_{ar} * k_{dr} + I_{pr} * k_{dr} * \frac{\cos\phi}{d}$$

$$I_g = I_{ag} * k_{dg} + I_{pg} * k_{dg} * \frac{\cos\phi}{d}$$

$$I_b = I_{ab} * k_{db} + I_{pb} * k_{db} * \frac{\cos\phi}{d}$$

SPECULAR REFLECTION

Specular reflectivity occurs when a surface reflects incoming light in a nearly fixed direction without affecting its quality. This reflection produces highlights on shiny objects. We will use Bui-Truong Phong's empirical model (PHON75) to simplify the very complex physical characteristics of specularly reflected light. In this model, the specular reflection has no influence on the wavelength of the incoming light. All wavelengths (or RGB components) of the incoming light are reflected equally.

Figure 8.29 illustrates specular reflection. The vector **L** points in the direction of the light source. **N** is the surface normal at the point where the light hits. The vector **R** points in the direction of the reflected light. **L**, **N**, and **R** always lie in the same plane. The spatial angle between **L** and **N** is identical to the angle between **N** and **R**.

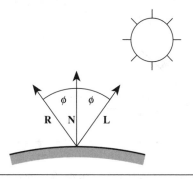

Figure 8.29   *Geometric reflection model*

If we continue the systematic approach, we should now consider specular reflection of ambient light. In our model, there simply is no such thing. This is sensible, because ambient light comes from all possible angles, so specular reflection must have the same effect on ambient light as diffuse reflection has—both reflect in all possible directions. The only difference is that the ambient light is reflected without any change in quality. This amounts to giving the object some of the ambient light's color in addition to its own color. The practical effects are subtle and are usually ignored.

This leaves only the specular reflection of point light to be considered. The essential characteristic of specular reflection is that it depends on the angle of the incoming light. Only point light comes in at a prescribed angle.

We use one parameter to describe the quality of a specular reflection. This parameter tells how the reflected light is concentrated around the reflection vector. The parameter describes the *shiniess* of the surface. A very shiny surface will reflect almost all the incoming light precisely in the direction of the reflection vector. A less shiny surface will reflect much of the incoming light along this vector, but will scatter another part a little around the reflection vector. In Phong's model, the shiniess of a surface is characterized by an integer n. The intensity of the reflected light is computed by multiplying the intensity of the incoming light by $\cos^n\theta$. The angle θ is the spatial angle by which the direction of reflected light deviates from the precise direction of reflection. Figure 8.30 shows a plot of $\cos^n\theta$ for several values of n.

Assume that light with intensity I is coming from direction **L**. The reflection vector is **R**. Light that is reflected precisely in the direction of **R** has a deviation angle 0. The light will therefore be reflected with intensity $I*\cos^n 0 = I$. Light reflected almost in the direction of **R** is at an angle $\theta > 0$ to **R**. It is reflected with intensity $I*\cos^n\theta$, which is small when n is large. In other words, for a large n, little of the light is reflected in directions that deviate from **R** and will be practically 0 even for small values of θ.

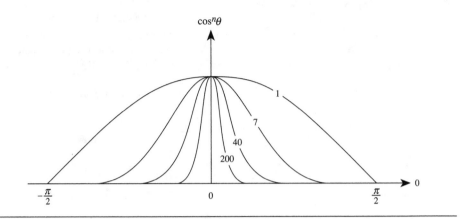

Figure 8.30   *Spatial distribution function for specular reflection*

Figure 8.31 shows how the angle θ is involved in the intensity of the light ray coming from the incident point to the eye (the dotted line). We call this line the *line of vision*. Its direction is described by the vector $\mathbf{V}$, also called the *viewing direction*. This line is not necessarily in the same plane with $\mathbf{L}$, $\mathbf{N}$, and $\mathbf{R}$. If $\mathbf{R}$ and $\mathbf{V}$ are normalized, $\cos\theta = \mathbf{R} \cdot \mathbf{V}$.

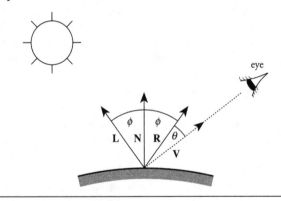

Figure 8.31   *The line of vision's deviation from* $\mathbf{R}$

Very shiny surfaces, for example polished silver, will have a large value of n (150 or more); less shiny surfaces have values of n as small as 1, for example, cardboard or paper.

Our model simplifies the true case. Specular reflection actually depends on the angle of incidence and on the wavelength (see below). In general, the amount of reflected light increases as the angle of incidence grows. Light that strikes a surface at the grazing angle will be completely reflected, while light that strikes at a small incident angle may be only partially reflected. The rest is either absorbed, reflected diffusely, or transmitted.

You are familiar with this effect in glass. When we look at a sheet of glass at a low incident angle (almost face-on), we see "through" the glass because the light rays emanating from the objects behind the sheet pass through and reach our eyes. Very little is absorbed and very little reflected. It is hard, however, to see objects through the glass when the glass surface is almost in line with the line of vision. The light coming from those objects strikes the surface opposite to us at a high incident angle and is therefore reflected from the surface. Only a small part of these light rays reach our eyes, making these objects almost invisible to us. To further impair our view of the objects, there will be mirror images of objects on our side of the sheet because the light emitted from them will be reflected toward us. Figure 8.32 shows such a situation. Object 1 will be clearly visible; object 2 is almost invisible. What reaches our eyes are reflected light rays from other objects on our side of the sheet.

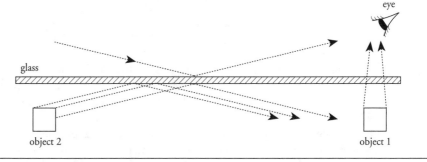

Figure 8.32   Dependence of reflection on the incident angle

How much is reflected depends not only on the incident angle ϕ, but also on the wavelength l of the incoming light. It is expressed by $w(\phi,l)$, which is the ratio of specularly reflected light to the incident light. This $w(\phi,l)$ is called the specular reflection coefficient (NESP79) or specular reflectance (COTO82). Figure 8.33 shows the curves of $w(\phi,l)$ for glass, gold, and silver as a function of only the incident angle. A complete description of $w(\phi,l)$ requires a surface function or a table. The surface description of $w(\phi,l)$ for copper appears in COTO82.

Figure 8.33 shows the specular reflection as a function of the incident angle ϕ.

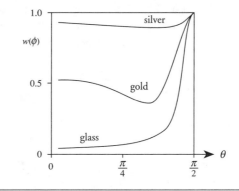

Figure 8.33   Specular reflectance for some materials

As $w(\phi,l)$ is very complex, it is usually replaced by a constant k_s. This constant plays the same role as the constants k_{dr}, k_{dg}, and k_{db} in the diffuse reflection model, except that there is no distinction between red, green, and blue. The formula for Phong's reflectance model is:

$$I_r = I_{pr} * k_s * \cos^n \theta \qquad I_g = I_{pg} * k_s * \cos^n \theta \qquad I_b = I_{pb} * k_s * \cos^n \theta$$

Combining the results for diffuse ambient light, diffuse reflected light, and specularly reflected point light yields the model:

$$I_r = I_{ar} * k_{dr} + I_{pr} * \left(k_{dr} * \frac{\cos\phi}{d} + k_s * \cos^n\theta \right)$$

$$I_g = I_{ag} * k_{dg} + I_{pg} * \left(k_{dg} * \frac{\cos\phi}{d} + k_s * \cos^n\theta \right) \quad \dots \ (1)$$

$$I_b = I_{ab} * k_{db} + I_{pb} * \left(k_{db} * \frac{\cos\phi}{d} + k_s * \cos^n\theta \right)$$

If there are several point light sources, their contributions are added.

The above formula is not precise enough for physical reflection effects, but is usually adequate for producing realistic highlights similar to real specular reflections. We call these *soft highlights* because they do not have a sharp boundary. This model is not adequate for materials whose reflectance changes significantly with the incident angle, such as glass. For such a material, we should not use a constant k_s, but should at least approximate the curve for $w(I)$. The model is fine for silver, acceptable for gold, and good for all materials with low reflectivity.

Figure 8.34 shows how a soft highlight is produced on a spherical shiny surface if one distant light source is present. In the figure, the light source is outside the picture. The surface is of medium specular reflectivity, with $n = 12$. At the surface points a, b, and c, the light is reflected for the most part in the directions $\mathbf{R}_a$, $\mathbf{R}_b$, and $\mathbf{R}_c$. At point b, almost all the incoming light is reflected toward the eye, but much less light will reach the eye from points a and c, because the ray from those points to the eye deviates considerably from $\mathbf{R}_a$ and $\mathbf{R}_c$.

These deviation angles are about 35°, so the intensity of the light coming from a and c to the eye is $(\cos 35°)^{12} = 0.09$ times the intensity of the incoming light; only $\frac{1}{11}$ of the incoming light goes to the eye from those points. From points still farther from point b, practically no light will reach the eye. We will therefore see a bright spot around point b whose brightness at a and c (and all other points at that distance from b) is only $\frac{1}{11}$ of its central brightness.

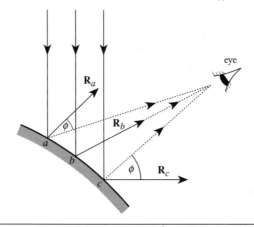

Figure 8.34   Geometry of a soft highlight

8.4.3   COMPUTING THE ILLUMINATION

When we render an object on a CRT in the most general case, we have to compute the illumination pixelwise. Pixels are the smallest indivisible units that we can display, so we compute the illumination for each point on the object's surface that corresponds to a pixel on the display. Then we set the pixel to that value. If the scene has more than one light source, we must compute and add their contributions to the overall illumination of that pixel. In many cases, (for example, displaying objects bounded by flat surfaces) larger areas will have one constant illumination; then we need only one computation for the whole area.

Below, we list the computations needed to find the illumination of one pixel. We assume that we know the coordinates of the point being displayed in that pixel.

1. The direction vector, $\mathbf{L}$, to the light source (for more than one light source, we must find $\mathbf{L}_1$, $\mathbf{L}_2$, etc.).
2. The viewing direction $\mathbf{V}$.
3. The normal vector $\mathbf{N}$.
4. The reflection vector $\mathbf{R}$ of the viewing direction.

We often assume that point light sources are distant enough that the rays coming from them are parallel; when this is the case, the vectors $\mathbf{L}_1$, $\mathbf{L}_2$, etc. are the same for all pixels. If the light sources are at a finite distance, we compute the $\mathbf{L}_s$ anew for each pixel. Instead of computing the reflection of $\mathbf{L}$ about $\mathbf{N}$ and finding its angle with $\mathbf{V}$, we can also compute the reflection of $\mathbf{V}$ about $\mathbf{N}$ and find its angle with $\mathbf{L}$. These angles are identical. The first model directly follows the movement of the light beams. Because we need only the angles, however, we usually use the second one in computations (see Chapter 15, Ray Tracing).

Here is an example. We consider three points: $(x \; y \; z)$ is the point on an object's surface that corresponds to the pixel being illuminated, $(S_x \; S_y \; S_z)$ is the location of a point light source, and $(E_x \; E_y \; E_z)$ is the position of the eye. This point normally coincides with the center of perspective projection and then has the coordinates $(0 \; 0 \; -d)$ with some positive value d in a left-handed coordinate system.

1. We compute $\mathbf{L}$: $\mathbf{L}_x = S_x - x$, $\mathbf{L}_y = S_y - y$, $\mathbf{L}_z = S_z - z$ and normalize it.
2. We compute $\mathbf{V}$: $\mathbf{V}_x = E_x - x$, $\mathbf{V}_y = E_y - y$, $\mathbf{V}_z = E_z - z$ and normalize it.
3. We compute $\mathbf{N}$: This is usually more complicated. It depends on the type of surface we have. If we have an analytical description of the surface, computing the surface's normal at a given point is straightforward, but not always easy. For example, on a bicubic B-spline or Bezier patch, we must evaluate a biquintic expression. If the object is described by a polygon mesh or similar structure, its surfaces are planar polygons. If such an object is rendered with faceted shading, there is just one surface normal for each polygon. We can easily derive this surface normal from the plane equation (see Section 10.1). If the object is rendered with smooth shading, we need the surface normals at each vertex. We cover smooth shading and vertex normals in Chapter 13.
4. We compute $\mathbf{R}$: the reflection of $\mathbf{E}$ about $\mathbf{N}$.

COMPUTING THE REFLECTION VECTOR

We present a simple method for computing the reflection vector, using geometry and vector algebra. There are some other methods (see ROGE85) that we do not discuss.

In Figure 8.35, the vector that impinges on the surface is $\mathbf{H}$, the normal is $\mathbf{N}$, and the reflection vector is $\mathbf{R}$. They all lie in one plane. Each is a unit vector of length 1 and each points away from point P. A line parallel to $\mathbf{R}$ through the end point of $\mathbf{H}$ meets $\mathbf{N}$ at the point Q. P, Q, and the end point of $\mathbf{H}$ form an isosceles triangle. The length from P to the middle of this triangle's base is the length of the projection of $\mathbf{H}$ onto $\mathbf{N}$: $\mathbf{N}\cdot\mathbf{H}$. Hence, the vector from P to Q is $2(\mathbf{N}\cdot\mathbf{H})\mathbf{N}$. P, Q, and the end point of $\mathbf{R}$ form another isosceles triangle—the mirror image of the first triangle. The vector from Q to the end point of $\mathbf{R}$ is parallel to $\mathbf{H}$ and is of length 1; in fact, the vector is $-\mathbf{H}$. We can therefore express the vector $\mathbf{R}$ with vector addition:

$$\mathbf{R} = 2(\mathbf{N}\cdot\mathbf{H})\mathbf{N} - \mathbf{H}$$

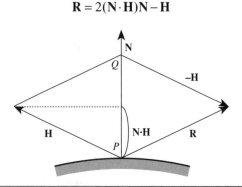

Figure 8.35   Reflection model

The computation of the reflection vector assumes normalized vectors $\mathbf{H}$ and $\mathbf{N}$. It is done by a member function of `point3_t`. The `point3_t` object assumes to be the outwardly directed surface normal. Only one argument is needed: the impinging hit-vector, assumed to be facing in.

```
//******************************************************************
point3_t point3_t::reflec(const point3_t& hit)
{                                    // reflection vector facing out
    return h - *this * 2*(*this*hit);
}
//******************************************************************
```

As soon as we have $\mathbf{L}$, $\mathbf{V}$, $\mathbf{N}$, and $\mathbf{R}$, we can compute $\cos\phi = \mathbf{L}\cdot\mathbf{N}$ and $\cos\theta = \mathbf{L}\cdot\mathbf{R}$. We must normalize all vectors involved in the cosine computations. Then we compute the illumination with formula (1).

SETTING THE COLOR MAP

As you have seen, there are three contributors to the illumination of any point on a surface: ambient light, diffusely reflected point light, and specularly reflected point light. These contributions will usually vary over the surface of the object. The problem now is to adjust the contributions so that their sum will not exceed the maximum intensity settings of a particular display. If formula (1) yields a value larger than the maximum intensity for any of the primary colors, we could just reduce that value to the maximum. While this is safe to do, trimming too many of the computed illuminations will decrease the variety of colors and intensities. On the other hand, we could scale down all the contributions by a certain factor, say 0.9. This avoids illuminations that are too high for extended areas of the object, but may make some areas on the object so dark that they will appear black without exhibiting any hue. We usually find the proper weighting of the three different types of light through experimentation.

Another problem is that the CRT can display only a limited number of different colors. This limit is determined by the depth of the frame buffer. When computing a pixel's illumination, we could make an entry in the color map for that *rgb*-value and use its location number for that pixel. Even if the hardware allows the simultaneous display of 256 different colors, we will soon exceed this limit.

A way to solve this problem is to prepare a certain set of color entries beforehand. Depending on the color we want to give the object, we prepare a lowest and a highest intensity for that color. Suppose that for our hardware the intensities of all three primaries go from 0 to 255. We want the object to be brown. We will set the darkest brown to $(r\ g\ b) = (150\ 100\ 50)$ and the lightest to (255 220 200) to allow for specular highlights (this is a yellowish white). If we want 50 different intensities of brown, we will distribute the intensities from the lowest to the highest over 50 places and enter them in the color map. Let us put the darkest brown in position 1 and the brightest in position 50. The positions from 2 to 49 are filled with the in-between values. Interpolating linearly for the in-between values gives a distribution that is sufficient for practical purposes. For a given *rgb*-value, we can quickly compute the location of the closest color in the color map. We use this technique in Phong shading, Chapter 13.

If an *rgb*-value results from the color computation and there is no simple relation between the *rgb*-value and the color map position, we have to search through the color map for the closest matching color. This is very time-consuming, but sometimes unavoidable.

Consider also that the same intensities will produce different colors on different monitors. Familiarity with your monitor and experimentation are necessary for good results.

SUGGESTED READINGS

Raster scan technology is explained in RAST85. You can find an introduction to the subject of light in BUGI89 pp. 320–338. Lookup table (colormap) technology is not covered very thoroughly in most other textbooks, but you can find the basic concepts in NYEX92 p. 187 and in HILL90.

EXERCISES

SECTION 8.3.1

1. Assume a frame buffer with one byte per pixel. How many different colors can be displayed simultaneously on the screen?

2. Assume a frame buffer with one byte per pixel and a lookup table with length 256 and width 24 bits (eight for red, eight for green, and eight for blue). How many different colors can be displayed overall?

3. Assume a frame buffer of depth four (four bits per pixel). Specify the size of the lookup table needed to display 16 colors simultaneously from a palette of 512.

4. Approximately where in the RGB color cube (Figure 8.6) is the color brown? Remember that brown is just a dark yellow. Approximately where is it in the HSV hexpyramid (Figure 8.9)? Approximately where is it in the HLS double cone (Figure 8.11)?

5. For this exercise you need a colored CIE diagram. (See Color Plate 1.) Locate the two colors A = (0.2 0.1 0.7) and B = (0.5 0.4 0.1) in the diagram and find what color results from mixing them with equal luminances. The resulting color lies on the straight line connecting A and B. Compute the location of this point and indicate it in the diagram.

SECTION 8.3.6

6. Transform the RGB color (0.8 0.3 0.4) into the equivalent CMYK expression.

7. Write a function for transforming RGB into CMYK.

8. Transform the RGB color (0.5 0.1 0) into the equivalent HLS expression.

9. Write a function for transforming RGB into HLS.

10. Write a function for transforming HLS into RGB.

SECTION 8.4

For the functions d_reflec() and ds_reflec() below, use the structures point3_t from Chapter 5 and rgb_t as specified in this chapter.

11. (Diffuse reflection) Write a function d_reflec that computes the intensity of a surface using the diffuse reflection model portion of equation (1). Given are the normalized surface normal $(n_x\ n_y\ n_z)$ pointing out of the object, the ambient light intensity $(I_{ar}\ I_{ag}\ I_{ab})$, the point light intensity $(I_{pr}\ I_{pg}\ I_{pb})$, the diffuse reflectivity factors of the surface $(k_{dr}\ k_{dg}\ k_{db})$, and the normalized vector pointing to the point light source $(l_x\ l_y\ l_z)$. The parameters norm and lvect are of type point3_t; alight, plight, and diff are of type rgb_t.

   The cosine of the incident angle can be negative if the light comes from the side opposite to where the surface normal points. In that case, set the cosine to 0.

12. (Specular reflection) Write a function ds_reflec() that computes the intensity of a surface using the specular reflection model of equation (1). Given are the normalized surface normal $(n_x\ n_y\ n_z)$, the ambient light intensity $(I_{ar}\ I_{ag}\ I_{ab})$, the point light intensity $(I_{pr}\ I_{pg}\ I_{pb})$, the diffuse reflectivity factors of the surface $(k_{dr}\ k_{dg}\ k_{db})$, the specular reflectivity factors $(k_{sr}\ k_{sg}\ k_{sb})$, the normalized vector pointing to the point light source $(l_x\ l_y\ l_z)$, and the normalized vector pointing to the viewer's eye (the center of projection).

FRACTALS

Fractals are an interesting way to produce computer-generated pictures that simulate the irregularities of natural scenes.

9.0   INTRODUCTION

Until now, we have displayed objects comprised of planar polygons or described by smooth curves. Suppose we want to show a natural scene, one with mountains, trees, clouds, and so on. It is hardly feasible to define the many points that would be required to project that scene, especially if we want to reproduce the colors, shapes, and textures. It is impractical to try to replace a camera with the computer screen. Often, though, it is not some existing natural scene that we desire, but one that we see in our imagination, one that an artist might paint. If we do this with only the methods so far described, the result will look "unnatural." A picture made up of drawn curves or polygons differs from nature in being too precise, too regular, too contrived.

A mathematical entity called a *fractal* presents a solution to this problem. A fractal is a set of points with a fractional dimension.

Fractals are highly irregular shapes that have countless counterparts in the real world. Some examples are coastlines, island clusters, turbulences, river networks, clouds, snowflakes, and galaxies. No natural surface, when examined closely enough, is smooth and regular; it actually contains tiny pits and irregularities. One can say that nature is always irregular. If we create fractals on a computer, we can mimic nature. Because a fractal is a mathematical entity, this should be possible.

The term *fractional dimension* explains the origin of the word "fractal." Consider an infinite line or finite line segment. It is always possible to specify every point on it with a single number, which can be interpreted as the distance from some reference point. This fact tells us that this line is of dimension one. This seems so trivial that we pay it no attention. This concept is identical to the fact that we measure a line with a one-dimensional measure, such as length. No one would try to measure a line in terms of area. Such a measurement can never yield a useful result, because that would apply a two-dimensional measuring unit to a one-dimensional set. Intuitively, we know that the area of a line is 0, no matter how long the line is.

When we measure an area, we use a two-dimensional unit (square feet, square meters, etc.). We certainly would not try to use length to measure an area, because the result would be infinity; no matter how small the area, an infinitely long line can be fitted into it. Areas, then are two-dimensional.

The volume of any line or any area is always 0, because volume is a three-dimensional unit. We can fit an infinitely long line or infinitely big area into any volume, no matter how small. An intuitive explanation of this situation might be that a one-dimensional unit is too weak for measuring a two-dimensional or three-dimensional entity. It will always produce an infinite number, no matter what the real extent of the measured object. A two-dimensional unit is too strong for measuring a line and too weak for measuring a volume. In the first case, the result will always be 0; in the latter case, it will always be infinite. Measuring units must be of the same dimension as the measured object!

We can reason the other way around. If we have a measuring unit that yields a proper result when applied to some object, then the object must have the same dimension as the unit. This will help us to find the dimension of fractals.

Let us now look at some fractals. The first one is the coastline of England. (This topic is part of the fascinating history of fractals.) Looking at a map, we see that this is a very rugged line. How long is England's coastline? The answer to this question reveals one of the strange properties of fractals. To obtain an answer, we will use a method for measuring the length of a curve.

MEASURING THE LENGTH OF A CURVE

The method we will use consists of repeatedly aligning a yardstick with the curve, continuing where the end of the yardstick touches the curve, and counting how often this occurs. This method works well for many sorts of curves. We will demonstrate it for a semicircle.

We take the radius as our first measuring unit and align it against the curve. It will fit three times; 3 is therefore our first approximation for the length of the semicircle (see Figure 9.1). Because there was a piece left over, we may obtain a better result by applying a shorter measuring unit, so we take 0.1*radius for our unit. This unit will fit 31 times into the curve; our new approximation is 3.1. This result is larger than the one before, but we expected that. To obtain an even better result, we measure the curve once more with an even shorter unit, this time 0.01*radius, and we see that this one fits into the curve 314 times. Again this result, 3.14, is larger than the one before, but we see that the amount of growth is very small.

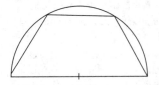

Figure 9.1   Semicircle measured with the radius as unit

Indeed, if we perform more measurements, say, with 0.001*radius as the unit, then 0.0001*radius, the results will be 3.141 and 3.1415. The numbers grow, but the amount of increase becomes smaller, showing that the results do not grow without limit. Of course, we need mathematical proof, but we can clearly grasp the concept of measuring the length of a curve this way from the example. In the case of a semicircle, the measured lengths for ever-smaller measuring units approach a limit that we consider to be the semicircle's true length.

Suppose we use this method to measure the length of the seacoast or, more practically, some part of it. We start out with a measuring stick one sea mile long and we end up with a result of perhaps 1000 sea miles in length. We know that this is certainly a very rough approximation, so we try a second measuring process with a 100-meter measuring stick. The result we obtain might be 3000 sea miles.

We certainly expected the larger result, but it is astonishing that it grew by such a great amount. We hope the approximate lengths will settle down to a smaller growth, so we try another measurement process, this time with a 10-meter measuring stick. The result we get now really discourages us, as it will be much larger than before—it might be about 8000 sea miles.

In the case of measuring a seacoast, we find no improvement when we use smaller measuring units. A man could walk right along the coast in steps one meter long. When we add together the number of steps, we see no tendency for the results to slow down in their growth. Whenever we decrease the length of the measuring stick, the measured length will grow considerably. If we let a mouse run along the coast and make it follow the boundary between water and land exactly, the resulting length will again be several factors larger than before. The measured length apparently grows without bound (see MAND77, RICH61). In short, it is not possible to measure the length of the coastline exactly and precisely. The reason is the coastline's "ruggedness." Figures 9.2 through 9.4 show what the coastline might look like when seen from very high above.

If we focus on a small part of the line, we see that the details of the line are as rugged as the whole line. The next step of focus does not change the overall impression. This will continue, no matter how close we go. We must characterize a coastline as infinitely rugged.

We certainly approach a limit as we come closer to the molecular or atomic structure of matter. We also meet a limit in the macro scale in the structure of the planet and solar system. The existence of

Figure 9.2   Rugged coastline

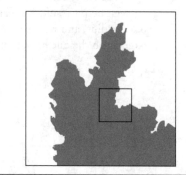

Figure 9.3   Magnified detail

these limits, however, will not enable us to measure the length of the coastline exactly.

The coastline is an example of a line in which the details, no matter how small, bear a strong resemblance to the whole line. Here, the attribute "rugged" seems to stick to the line endlessly, always showing up, no matter how closely we look. This attribute is repeated continuously in forever smaller details of the whole.

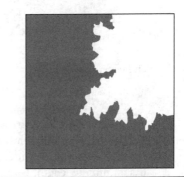

Figure 9.4   Further magnified detail

9.1   AN ARTIFICIAL FRACTAL

We began this chapter with the notion that fractals might help us draw curves that mimic nature. Now we know a little about what must be done to accomplish this. Can we produce a fractal in the computer? The answer is yes, so we will look at an example. Our first artificially created fractal is the *triadic von Koch curve*, which we simply call the *von Koch curve*. This curve is easy to create. We start with a straight line of length 1. We call this line the curve of order zero.

We create the von Koch curve of order 1 by taking out the middle third of the straight line and replacing it with two lines of equal length, meeting at a 60° angle, as in Figure 9.5.

Figure 9.5   von Koch curve of order 1

We obtain the curve of order 2 by repeating the replacement process with each of the four line segments. The resulting curve of order 2 is a little more rugged, as in Figure 9.6.

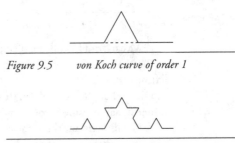

Figure 9.6   von Koch curve of order 2

We do the same thing with each of the 16 segments in the order 2 curve to obtain the von Koch curve of order 3. Assume that we continue this process ad infinitum; this gives a mathematically precise definition of a von Koch curve. How long is it, we ask?

It turns out that this is impossible to measure. When we attempt to measure the length of this line, we will get the same surprise as with the coastline. We will first apply a measuring stick of length $\frac{1}{3}$ to the line. Due to the completely regular rule of the curve's construction, we can definitely say that this unit will fit exactly four times into the curve, and the measuring result will be $\frac{4}{3}$. Therefore, the approximate length of the curve measured with this unit will be $\frac{4}{3}$ (ignoring all the rugged detail in the curve). Let $L(m)$ be the length obtained with a measuring unit m. Then we have:

$$L\left(\tfrac{1}{3}\right) = \tfrac{4}{3}$$

The measuring unit $\frac{1}{9}$ will fit exactly 16 times into the curve, so we have:

$$L\left(\tfrac{1}{9}\right) = \tfrac{16}{9}$$

and generally,

$$L\left(\tfrac{1}{3^k}\right) = \left(\tfrac{4}{3}\right)^k$$

This shows that shortening the measuring unit will make the results approach infinity, so the true length of the von Koch curve is infinite. A line of infinite length is crammed into a finite area of the plane without intersecting itself! Every small part of the von Koch curve also has an infinite length, because it consists of reduced instances of the von Koch curve. We cannot measure this curve in terms of length. In what terms can it be measured? This is actually a question about this curve's dimension. Let us look at the von Koch curve as simply a set of points in the plane and ask what dimension it has.

The problem with the von Koch curve is not that it is infinitely long. Even if a line has infinite length, we can define every point on the line with a single number. This shows that an infinitely long line can be one-dimensional. Figure 9.7 shows the real number axis that stretches from -∞ to +∞. Every point on this line is described by one single number that specifies its distance from the origin.

Figure 9.7   Real number axis

We can readily indicate specific points on the von Koch curve, but we cannot describe any of them with a single number specifying, for example, its distance along the curve from the leftmost point. All these distances and all distances between single points on that line are infinite. That shows that length or distance is not a proper measure for this curve. A one-dimensional measure is too weak for the von Koch curve.

The dimension, then, must be more than one. Could we measure the curve in terms of area with a dimension of two? No, we cannot find any part of the curve that has a positive area. If we try to find the area of the von Koch curve, we end up with an area of 0, which shows that a two-dimensional measure is too strong for the von Koch curve. The solution to this dilemma lies in between. The von Koch curve is a set of points with a dimension greater than one and smaller than two. It has a fractional dimension, and is therefore a fractal.

There are actually different notions of dimension. Here, we mention only two: the Hausdorff-Besicovitch dimension and the topological dimension. These can differ for the same set of points. The von Koch curve has a topological dimension of one, because topologically, this set of points is a line. If a single point is taken out anywhere in the curve, then it is severed, giving two distinct and noncoherent parts. However, the topological dimension does not measure the curve's length, area, or anything else. To obtain those, we must use the Hausdorff-Besicovitch dimension. Unfortunately, this theory is too complicated to be presented in this book and is of limited use in computer graphics, but it does help us define a real number as the dimension of this type of object. The interested reader can find the precise definition of the Hausdorff-Besicovitch dimension in BEUR37.

There is a relatively simple method to determine this curve's dimension. Using it will let us find out a little more about fractals. This method uses a similarity relation, which is helpful in determining the dimension of many different fractals.

9.2   THE SIMILARITY RELATION

The first steps we take here are mostly of a suggestive nature and are so trivial that it may be difficult to see the essential point. Assume we have a set of points whose dimension we do not know; let this set be a segment of a straight line. We define the length of the whole line segment as 1 and divide it into equal parts, say into thirds (see Figure 9.8).

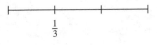

$$\frac{1}{3}$$

Figure 9.8   Line segment consisting of three thirds

Obviously, we can compose the whole line from the three parts, all of which are similar to the whole, but scaled down to one-third the size. This scaling relation is r, so that $r = \frac{1}{3}$. We express the whole as 3 times the *similarity relation*:

$$1 = 3 * r$$

What is inconspicuous but important in this equation is that r is raised to the power 1. As the exponent 1 satisfies this equation, it follows that the dimension of our original set is one.

Figure 9.9 will illuminate this reasoning. Here, we have a rectangular-shaped area, which constitutes the whole and is equal to 1. We will divide all its sides into three equal parts.

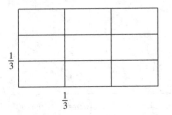

$$\frac{1}{3}$$

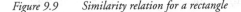

$$\frac{1}{3}$$

Figure 9.9   Similarity relation for a rectangle

We obviously obtain nine parts, which relate to the whole with a similarity relation of $r = \frac{1}{3}$. (Note that it is not $r = \frac{1}{9}$. Every part is obtained from the whole by scaling it down by $\frac{1}{3}$.) We express the whole as the sum of nine of its parts times the similarity relation r, which we must now raise to the power 2 in order to satisfy the equation:

$$1 = 9 * r^2$$

We can use the similarity relation r to write the equation that expresses the whole as the sum of its parts:

$$1 = 9 * r^D$$

The value of D to satisfy this equation is 2. It follows that our set of points is two-dimensional.

If we repeat this for any parallelepiped and choose a similarity relation of $r = \frac{1}{3}$, then the whole is composed of 27 similar parts (Figure 9.10) and we get the equation $1 = 27*r^D$, which requires $D = 3$, so this is the dimension of the parallelepiped. All this is very simple but important.

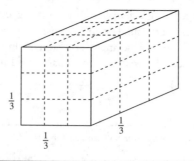

Figure 9.10   Similarity relation for a parallelepiped

A similar object is obtained by enlarging or shrinking the original object. To do this, we multiply each of its dimensions in one-, two-, or three-dimensional space by the same number. The similarity relation is precisely this number. In the case of a one-dimensional object, one multiplication is necessary to scale it to a similar object. In the case of a two-dimensional object, two multiplications are necessary, and so on. This operation is not trivial when we apply it to the von Koch curve. The whole curve can be composed of exactly four similar parts (see Figure 9.11).

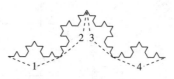

Figure 9.11   von Koch curve consisting of four similar parts

Do not forget that the parts are as "rugged" as the whole curve, because the ruggedness is infinite. Thus, these four parts are really identical to the whole, except for their size. Furthermore, we can see that the size (perhaps as indicated by the straight line distance from one end to the other) of each of these four parts is just $\frac{1}{3}$ of the whole, so the similarity relation is $r = \frac{1}{3}$. Therefore, we have the equation $1 = 4*(\frac{1}{3})^D$. D must be log4/log3, which is 1.2857; the Hausdorff-Besicovitch dimension of the von Koch curve is 1.2857. A von Koch curve can be measured only in terms of unit von Koch curves or any other unit curves with exactly the same dimension.

Because the dimension is fractional for most sets of this type, Mandelbrot coined the term "fractal" for them (MAND82). The exact definition of a fractal, as given in MAND82, still looks pretty complicated and may not make much sense to some readers, but you should at least see it:

A fractal is a set of points whose fractional dimension
is strictly bigger than its topological dimension.

According to this, the von Koch curve is a fractal. As its dimension is greater than one, it fills more of 2D space than a simple line, which has the dimension $D = 1$, but it fills less than an area, which has the dimension $D = 2$. We will look at other fractals of higher dimension than the von Koch curve and these will fill more of 2D space than the von Koch curve. The dimension can be as great as two with the Dragon curve, which is an area-filling curve, but which is still a fractal and not an area; its topological dimension is still one and is therefore smaller than the fractional dimension.

9.3   FRACTAL-GENERATING ALGORITHMS

Now that we have seen an example of a fractal and how to construct it, we will see how a computer can generate a fractal using *production rules*. We will demonstrate this geometrically. For the triadic von Koch curve, the production rule appears in Figure 9.12.

Figure 9.12   von Koch curve production rule

This rule says that the straight line on the left must be replaced by the shape on the right. Here, as in all production rules, the element to start with is a straight line. Therefore the line and the arrow can be omitted; it is enough to show just the replacement part. This is the same as in MAND82, with the exception that Mandlebrot sometimes starts with a square or other shape. In such a case, the production rule must be applied to all four sides of the square. Figure 9.13 shows the von Koch curve after five generating steps.

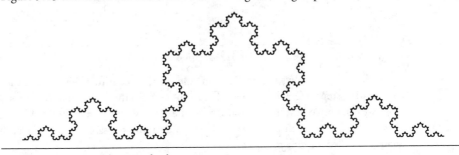

Figure 9.13   von Koch curve of order 5

We will now look at some more regular fractals that show the infinite variety and beauty of these objects. Figure 9.14 shows the production rule for a von Koch curve variation, which produces a fractal line of higher dimension than the previous one.

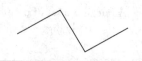

Figure 9.14   von Koch curve variation—production rule

The three lines meet at right angles and are of the same length. From this, and with some geometric analysis, we find that the similarity relation is $r = 1/\sqrt{5}$ and that three such pieces form the whole curve. Thus, we have $1 = 3*(1/\sqrt{5})^D$, which yields $D = 1.365$. Figure 9.15 shows the curve that develops from this production rule after three steps.

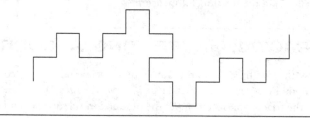

Figure 9.15   Curve from the previous rule

Another von Koch curve production rule and the resulting curve after two generating steps is shown in Figure 9.16. The similarity relation is $r = \frac{1}{4}$; eight parts constitute the whole, so we get $D = 1.5$.

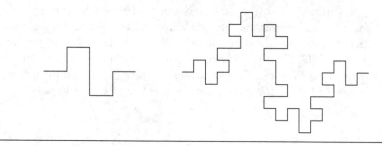

Figure 9.16   Another von Koch curve variation

Figure 9.17 shows the production rule for the beautiful C-curve and the curve after 12 generating steps. Here, it is more difficult to see from the curve what the similarity relation is, but we can derive it from the production rule: $r = \frac{1}{2}*\sqrt{2}$; two parts form the whole, so we have $1 = 2*(\frac{1}{2}*\sqrt{2})^D$, which yields $D = 2$. This dimension is the same as for an area, therefore the C-curve is called an *area-filling curve*.

We mention one more curve, one that is often produced because it is eye-catching: the dragon curve. Its production rule, shown in Figure 9.18, does not start from a straight line, but from two sides of a rectangular isosceles triangle. Each side is then replaced with the two sides of a rectangular isosceles triangle, but the replacement must alternate between left and right and the alternation sequence must be strictly the same in all generation steps. In Figure 9.18 we use first left and then right.

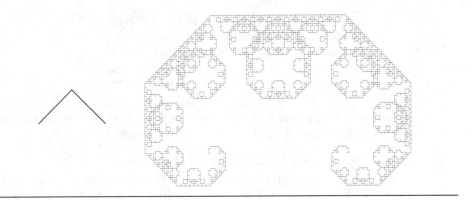

Figure 9.17   C-curve of order 12

Figure 9.18   Production rule of the Dragon curve

It is somewhat difficult to see from the curve itself what the similarity relation is, but we can derive it from the production rule: $r = \frac{1}{2} * \sqrt{2}$. Two dragons scaled by this ratio form a whole dragon. We have $1 = 2 * (\frac{1}{2} * \sqrt{2})^D$, which yields $D = 2$. The dragon curve, too, is an area-filling curve. It appears in Figure 9.19.

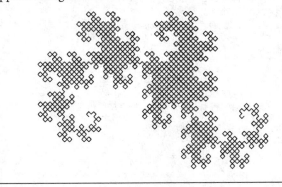

Figure 9.19   Dragon curve

All the fractal curves listed above can be drawn on a line plotter and are easy to program with recursion. Changing the line color in some systematic way produces amazing effects.

Here is an example that draws a von Koch curve. When following the course of a horizontal von Koch curve from left to right, we first pass through a von Koch curve of $\frac{1}{3}$ the length, which is also horizontal (direction 0°). Then we pass through a von Koch curve of the same length that goes upward in a direction of 60°. Then we pass through one that goes downward by −60°. The last one is like the first. The code directly implements this rule by recursion.

Drawing a vkcurve of length 1 in direction 0° consists of:

1. drawing a vkcurve of length $\frac{1}{3}$ in direction 0°
2. drawing a vkcurve of length $\frac{1}{3}$ in direction 60°
3. drawing a vkcurve of length $\frac{1}{3}$ in direction –60°
4. drawing a vkcurve of length $\frac{1}{3}$ in direction 0°

The directions in the tilted von Koch curves are multiples of 60°. Altogether, only six different directions occur, so we compute these angles' sin and cos values in advance. This last device only improves speed and has nothing to do with the algorithm.

OO DESIGN AND CLASS SPECIFICATIONS

We can consider the von Koch curve to be a certain type of line and, as such, a drawable object. We derive it from `prim_t` in order to add it to a 2D scene. Below is the class `vkcurve_t`. It is initialized with starting point and length in world coordinates, and an integer "depth" that specifies the order of the curve. We draw the curve by issuing a draw command to the scene that contains the curve.

```
//******************* File Frac/vkcurve.h *************************

#ifndef VKCURVE_T
#define VKCURVE_T

#include "../Shape2d/scene.h"
#include "../Shape2d/point.h"
#include "../Shape2d/prim.h"

class vkcurve_t : public prim_t
{
public:
   vkcurve_t(point_t,double,int) ;
   vkcurve_t(const vkcurve_t&) ;
   prim_t* copy() const ;
   void draw(const scene_t*) const ;

private:
   point_t start ;
   double length ;
   int depth ;
} ;

#endif
//*****************************************************************
```

The implementation of this class serves as an example for the recursive drawing technique used for this type of fractal. Two global `point_t` serve as the end points of the individual line pieces and are updated during the recursion. The six possible drawing directions are kept in two global arrays. We must perform modulo six arithmetic explicitly, because the % operator in the C++ language does not give the desired result for a negative operand. The code below draws a horizontal von Koch curve (direction = 0) of the order "depth." We must pass the length and direction as parameters because they are modified and passed to the recursive calls.

```
//******************** File Frac/vkcurve.c ********************

#include <math.h>

#include "../Shape2d/scene.h"
#include "../Frac/vkcurve.h"
#include "../Shape2d/line.h"


vkcurve_t::vkcurve_t(point_t start,double length,int depth) :
      start(start) , length(length) , depth(depth) {}

vkcurve_t::vkcurve_t(const vkcurve_t& v) :
      start(v.start) , length(v.length) , depth(v.depth) {}

prim_t* vkcurve_t::copy() const
{
   return new vkcurve_t(*this);
}

static point_t a , b ;
static int depth ;
static scene_t* scene ;
static double c[6] , s[6] ;               // to hold sin and cos values

static void vonkoch(int dir,double len)    // recursive generation
{
   static dep = 0 ;

   dep++;
   int dup = dir == 5 ? 0 : dir + 1 ,      // modulo 6 arithmetic
       ddn = dir == 0 ? 5 : dir - 1 ;      // in both directions

   if (dep <= depth)
      vonkoch(dir,len/3),                             // same direction
      vonkoch(dup,len/3),                             // direction up
      vonkoch(ddn,len/3),                             // direction down
      vonkoch(dir,len/3);                             // same direction
   else
      b += point_t(len*c[dir],len*s[dir]),
      line_t(a,b).draw((const scene_t*)scene),
      a = b;
   dep—;
}

void vkcurve_t::draw(const scene_t* scene) const
{
   a = b = start;
   ::depth = depth;
   ::scene = (scene_t*)scene ;

   for (int i ˜= 0; i < 6; i++)
   {
      c[i] = cos(1.04719*i);                       // pi/3 = 1.04719
```

```
        s[i] = sin(1.04719*i);
    }


    vonkoch(0,length);
}
//******************************************************************
```

9.4   RANDOM FRACTAL SURFACES

Objects in nature rarely exhibit *self-similarity* (the parts mimic the whole) as do the von Koch curve, C-curve, dragon curve, and so on, but they possess a related property, called *statistical self-similarity*. Nature is full of such fractals. The coastline at the beginning of the chapter is a good example. The more closely we look at the line, the more detail we see. A set is statistically self-similar with a ratio r if it is composed of several distinct subsets, each of which is identical in all statistical respects to the set S, scaled down by r. A subset will never be congruent or identical to the scaled-down whole set S, as the von Koch curve was. Therefore, the definition of self-similarity is more difficult to handle and verify.

In statistics, two distributions are said to be similar if all *moments* are equal. In practice, it is impossible to verify that all moments of the statistical distribution are identical. Claims of statistical self-similarity are usually based on the identity of only a few moments. However, if a statistical self-similarity can be found for a certain scaling ratio r with sufficient certainty, and if the whole set S consists of N such distinct parts, then by analogy to the artificially created regular fractals, the dimension of this fractal can be calculated as:

$$D = \frac{\log N}{\log\left(\frac{1}{r}\right)}$$

This r will often be difficult to find for fractals in nature because part of a random fractal, such as a coastline, is often statistically self-similar to the whole scaled down by any ratio r. In other words, if we take some part of the coastline, then we can scale the whole coastline, say by three, four, or five, and always find statistical self-similarity with the part. In such cases, we must compute the fractal dimension by using a different concept, the so-called *box dimension*. We will not go into this here, but the interested reader can find an explanation in VOSS85.

Fractals that resemble such natural phenomena are generated in computer graphics. You may have seen these in television commercials. The generating algorithms differ from the production rules of Section 9.3, in that they include random numbers. The fractals that are so created are different every time. We use them to forge landscapes, mountains, surfaces, island clusters, waves, and clouds. All are of higher dimension than the ones we have looked at until now; all are higher than two. Not all random fractals are of such high dimensions, but the ones that are useful for fractal forgeries in computer graphics are. This section deals with random fractals, but is limited to fractal surfaces.

Fractal surfaces are sets of points whose fractional dimension is between two and three. What a von Koch curve, coastline, or some other fractal line is in the plane, this fractal surface is in space. Usually, these are very complex surfaces with infinitely great detail. As the fractal dimension of such a surface is greater than two, it somehow fills more of the 3D space than a mathematically exact 2D surface, but it does not fill the whole space. Generally, one can say that the greater the dimension, the more rugged the appearance. Natural landscapes normally have a fractional dimension of about 2.15; very rugged landscapes, some areas in the French Alps, for example, can have a dimension of up to 2.5, but this is about the limit. An artificially created fractal landscape, such as the landscape in Color Plate 6 has a statistical self-similarity range that extends from arbitrarily large to arbitrarily small scales, because of the properties of the statistical factors.

Natural landscapes never have such a tremendous range for the ratio. The similarity ratio can vary and can extend over a range of values as we mentioned above for the coastline, but the scale over which we can observe self-similarity must be finite. The lower limit is set by the regular, nonfractal, crystalline structure of sand, clay, and so forth, and the upper limit by the finite strength of matter, which gravity ultimately forms into spheres of various sizes. A fractal is a mathematical ideal and serves only to approximate the real world. Fractal geometry, though, is the best known approximation and is superior to other geometries (Euclidian, etc.) when it comes to describing the real world.

GENERATING RANDOM FRACTALS

A truly random fractal cannot be generated on a computer because it has an infinitely complex shape. We are limited to generating and rendering only a finite approximation of the fractal. There are several methods for generating fractal curves and surfaces. A few of these are shear displacement, modified Markhov processes, and random displacement.

SHEAR DISPLACEMENT AND MARKHOV PROCESSES

We briefly describe and outline these two older methods because of the considerable literature about them. We can apply them in some situations, but they are not as good as newer methods.

In a *shear displacement process* (MAND75), a line is cut at a point chosen from a set with a uniform random distribution. Then the left and right parts are displaced vertically in opposite directions for a distance chosen from a set with a Gaussian random distribution. This is repeated on the parts, producing finer and finer detail and stops when the detail is fine enough. An analogous process can be performed for a plane. A random point in the plane is determined from a uniform distribution and then a random angle is determined from a uniform distribution. A line through this point at this angle constitutes a shear line of the plane. The two parts are then displaced in opposite directions by random distances with a Gaussian distribution. The shear displacement method is computationally very expensive; newer methods are an improvement.

Mandelbrot also developed the *Markhov process method* (MAND69, MAND71). It can create fractals of dimensions between one and two, that is, fractal lines. It does not create fractal surfaces. We move in the x-direction with constant steps; y-values are created as random points at each x-value. First, n random values from a Gaussian distribution are selected. Each y-value is computed as a weighted sum of the last n values and multiplied by a random variable. The sequence of $(x\ y)$-pairs constitutes the points on a fractal curve. In such a curve, current values are affected by values in the recent past. Although the points are random, they are still related to each other and not completely independent. This method has certain shortcomings for graphics applications. One is that the step size is constant and that it is difficult to produce a local scale magnification of the line afterward. Another is that the line cannot be made to pass through specified points; it tends to run away in either the positive or negative direction as it is created.

RANDOM MIDPOINT DISPLACEMENT

This is a generalization of conventional subdivision methods (LCWB80). We explain it first for a line and then for a surface.

GENERATING A FRACTAL LINE

We start with the two end points of a straight line segment, say A and B. We then displace the midpoint of the line vertically by a random amount h. Call this displaced midpoint Md. We then connect the displaced midpoint to A and B and repeat the process with the lines A to Md and Md to B. We repeat this with all subdivisions until there is sufficient detail. The mean of the distribution of the random number h must be 0 and the mean of the displacement amount abs(h) must be proportional to the distance between the end points of the segment.

It is essential that the mean of the displacement amount be proportional to the length of the line whose midpoint is being displaced. This ensures that the fractal's roughness is at all times independent of the scale. If we did not make the mean of the displacement proportional to the current length, we would have increased roughness as we proceeded and we would lose the required statistical self-similarity. If we carry this process out to the limit, we create a fractal.

If the initial line starts with a height of $h(a)$, ending at b with a height of $h(b)$, then the height at the midpoint is $(h(a)+h(b))/2$. This value is displaced by a random amount proportional to b minus a. Figure 9.20 shows one displacement step.

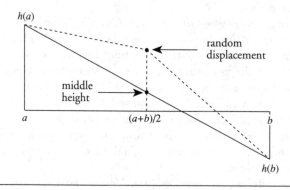

Figure 9.20   Random midpoint displacement

OO DESIGN AND CLASS SPECIFICATIONS

Like the von Koch curve, the fractal line is a certain line type and is derived from prim_t. Below, we show the class fline_t that represents the fractal line. It is constructed with the starting point and length in world coordinates, the number of fracture points or "knots," and the ruggedness parameter.

The constructor allocates an array of *num* doubles. The data member "knot" points to the beginning of this array. The element *knot*[*i*] stores the displacement (up or down) of "fracture point" *i* on the line. The line can be displaced only on the locations *knot*[1] through *knot*[*num*−2]. The locations *knot*[0] and *knot*[*num*−1] are the end points and are set to zero.

```
//********************** File Frac/fline.h **********************

#ifndef FLINE_T
#define FLINE_T

#include "../Shape2d/scene.h"
#include "../Shape2d/prim.h"

class fline_t : public prim_t
{
public:
   fline_t(point_t start,double len,int num,double rug) ;
   fline_t(const fline_t&) ;
   ~fline_t() ;

   prim_t* copy() const ;
   void draw(const scene_t*) const ;

private:
   point_t start ;                              // start point
   double  len   ;                              //     length
   int     num   ;                      // number of knots
   double  rug   ;                          // ruggedness
   double* knot  ;                  // pointer to array of knots
   void frac(int,int) ;
} ;

#endif
//*************************************************************
```

The line is fractured immediately upon construction (unlike the von Koch curve, which is fractured during the time of drawing). The fracturing function first displaces the line's midpoint with a random value scaled by (*b*–*a*)/(*num*−1), which is used instead of the current segment's true length (the true length is somewhat longer, since individual line pieces might be slanted). The displacement is also multiplied by the ruggedness factor, *rug*. A factor near 0 keeps the displacement small, giving a nearly straight line. Then it fractures the left and right half with two recursive calls. The recursion ends when the difference between the terminal subscripts of the piece to be fractured is less than two. When drawing the line, one must find a good value for *rug* through experimentation.

The above recursive algorithm that creates a random fractal line uses the same principle as the algorithm for fractal surface generation. Understanding it will help you understand that more complicated process.

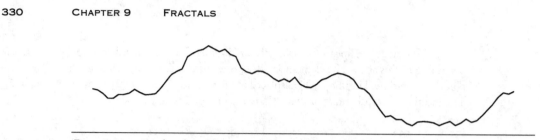

Figure 9.21   Random fractal line

GENERATING A FRACTAL SURFACE

We now extend the above to three dimensions to generate a random fractal surface. We start with a rectangular surface with the corner points a, b, c, and d. The initial heights at the corner points are $h(a)$, $h(b)$, $h(c)$, and $h(d)$. We displace the midpoint of each side just as above. At the point $(a + b)/2$, we obtain $(h(a) + h(b))/2$ plus a random displacement proportional to the length from a to b; we do the same for all four sides. We must also displace the height at the rectangle's center point: $(a + b + c + d)/4$. We take the mean of the height values at the corners: $(h(a) + h(b) + h(c) + h(d))/4$, plus a random displacement proportional to the sum of the lengths of all sides. At the left in Figure 9.22 is a surface at the start and the five displacement points; at the right is the resulting surface after this one step.

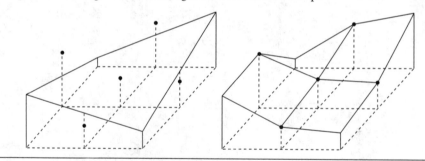

Figure 9.22   One step of surface displacement

In the next step, each of the four new rectangles will have its five midpoints displaced. (The resulting facets are not planar.) This leads to a fractal grid surface. Such a surface is easy to display with hidden lines removed, as we will explain in Chapter 12.

OO DESIGN AND CLASS SPECIFICATIONS

The above fractal surface is essentially an array of points in 3D space. The x- and z-coordinates of these points lie in a rectangular arrangement. The x-coordinates of all leftmost points in the array are equal and so are the x-coordinates in all columns; similarly, the z-coordinates of all points in the first row are equal and so are the z-coordinates in all rows. Furthermore, in our case the x- and z-coordinates are equidistant.

One might at first assume that it is sufficient to store only the number of rows, the number of columns, and the two-dimensional array of distorted y-values. However, once the surface is rotated in space, this simple pattern does not hold true anymore. It is therefore better to store the surface as a two-dimensional array of 3D points. We then rotate and translate all of the surface's points. We still keep the number of rows and columns as data members; they are needed to initially compute the *x*- and *z*-coordinates of the surface points and to do correct subscript computation in the 2D array.

The class `frect_t` below represents a fractal surface. It is a 3D drawable primitive derived from `prim_t` and can be added to a `scene_t` or `scene3_t`. It has two `point3_t` members that signify its corners in the *x-z* plane in world coordinates (the *y*-coordinates are ignored). It has the number of rows and of columns, so the total number of knots is `rows*cols`. It has a centroid to be rotated about, a ruggedness parameter, and a pointer to the array of knots. Each knot is a `fpoint_t`, rather than a `point3_t`, to reduce the memory requirement.

```
//********************** File Frac/frect.h **********************

#ifndef FRECT_T
#define FRECT_T

#include "../Shape3d/scene3.h"
#include "../Frac/fpoint.h"
#include "../Shape2d/prim.h"

class frect_t : public prim_t
{
public:
   frect_t(point3_t,point3_t,int,int,double) ;
   frect_t(const frect_t&) ;
  ~frect_t() ;
   prim_t* copy() const ;
   void draw(const scene_t*) const ;
   prim_t& rotx(double) ;
   prim_t& roty(double) ;
   prim_t& rotz(double) ;
   prim_t& translate(const point_t&) ;
   fpoint_t* operator [] (int row) { return knot + row*rows; }

private:
   point3_t a , b ;                         // corner points
   point3_t cen ;                           // centroid
   int rows , cols ;                        // rows*cols knots
   double rug ;
   fpoint_t* knot ;                         // pointer to array of knots
   void frac(int,int,int,int) ;
} ;

#endif

//****************************************************************
```

The class `fpoint_t` differs from `point3_t` in that its coordinates are floats, rather than doubles. All class members are private. Derivation from `point3_t` would not make sense. However, rotation and translation can reuse the code in `point3_t`.

```
//************************** File fpoint.h **************************

#ifndef FPOINT_T
#define FPOINT_T

#include "../Shape3d/point3.h"


class fpoint_t
{
friend class frect_t ;
public:
    fpoint_t(float x,float y,float z) :
        x(x) , y(y) , z(z) {}
    fpoint_t () : x(0) , y(0) , z(0) {}
    float    givx() const { return x; }
    float    givy() const { return y; }
    float    givz() const { return z; }
    point3_t giv()  const { return point3_t(x,y,z); }
    fpoint_t& rotx(double) ;
    fpoint_t& roty(double) ;
    fpoint_t& rotz(double) ;
    fpoint_t& translate(const point_t&) ;
    double operator * (const fpoint_t&) ;                // dot product
    double operator * (const point3_t&) ;                // dot product

private:
    float x , y , z ;
} ;

#endif

//**********************************************************************
```

An `frect_t` object is constructed with two corner points in the *x-z* plane, the number of rows, the number of columns, and the ruggedness parameter. Upon construction, the array of knots is allocated, the fractal surface computed and stored in the array. Operations applied to the scene such as rotations and translations are runtime bound to `frect_t` and explicitly transform all points.

Drawing the surface is easy. For each pair of adjacent surface points, a `line3_t` is constructed and its `draw()` function is called with the containing scene as a parameter. This gives access to the 3D window specified for the scene. The drawing will automatically do a perspective projection and clipping to the view volume.

"Fracturing" the surface is done by the member function `frac()`, called with the subscripts *l*, *r*, *n*, *f*, meaning left, right, near, far. They determine a rectangle as follows: the left, near corner of the rectangle has the subscripts *l* and *n*; the right, near corner has *r* and *n*, and so on. Before the computation starts, all boundary values of the surface are set to zero. The function `frac()` computes heights at the midpoints and then calls itself recursively for the four new rectangles.

The first recursive call is for the near left rectangle; it will compute five new height values. The second recursive call is for the near right rectangle; it must not compute a new height value on the left side of this rectangle. This value has already been computed by the first call and will consequently be used in computing all smaller rectangles adjacent to the point by the subcalls of the first call! Changing the value would destroy the fractal property of the resulting surface, turning it into an almost random surface. The same is true for the value at the bottom of the far left rectangle, and for the left side, and the bottom of the far right rectangle. In other words, once any value in the array has been set, it must not be reset. We can readily solve this problem by checking whether a value in the array has been set or not. One can tell this by initializing all values to a number that will never occur in the process.

The `main()` function, supplied in `Frac/main.c`, is an example of the flexibility and suppleness of C++. It declares a `scene_t` and initializes it with a 3D window-viewport system. Then it adds a von Koch curve, a fractal line, and a fractal surface to the scene. The command `draw()` issued for the scene will draw all three objects correctly, although the first two objects need a 2D window-viewport system to be drawn. Their draw functions, evoked through runtime binding, will cast the `win_vie3_t` to the base class `win_view_t` and use only the 2D portion.

Figures 9.23 and 9.24 show two fractal surfaces with 20×20 knots produced with different values of *rug*. They are drawn without hidden line removal.

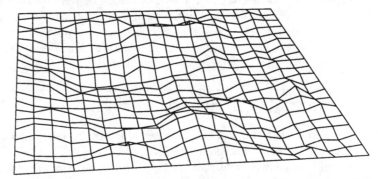

Figure 9.23   Fractal grid surface

Fractal grid surfaces are useful for producing fractal forgeries of landscapes, especially of mountains. The grid is ordinarily much finer, 150×150, for example. It is not the production of the grid heights, but doing the display, that is time-consuming. Obviously, the factor *rug* has some relationship to the fractional dimension of the surface.

We should be aware that we do not fulfill the precise requirements of self-similarity when we create a line or a surface in this way. One reason is that the displacement amount is not proportional to the length of the line or to the length of the facet's side, but it would be more costly to compute the length through a square root in every step. Another reason is that the direction of displacement is not perpendicular to the line piece or surface piece for which it is performed. This, too, is a deviation from the precise requirement. The approximations we use are good enough for practical purposes. A mountain landscape produced with this method is shown in Color Plate 6.

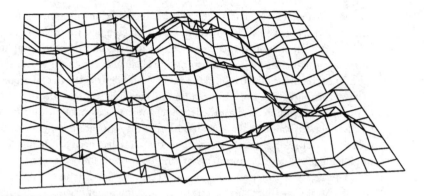

Figure 9.24   Fractal grid surface

We can preshape the surface by properly presetting height values in the grid. When presetting height values, one sets a value only if its immediate predecessors in the generation process are set. Otherwise, one produces abrupt and too-regular-looking height changes. The height at the center is the predecessor of all other values, so one can always set it. One can also set any of the centers and side midpoints of the four subsquares. One can continue in this way to predefine a certain "skeleton," the "in-betweens" of which the algorithm would then fill in. If, for example, the center point is set to a higher value before fracturing, the result will have a peak in the middle. It is as if this point had assumed this value by chance. After the first subdivision, this point is used in computing the heights of all subrectangles and consequently in computing the whole surface.

9.5   FRACTAL CLOUDS

As stated in MAND82 and LOMA85 and supported by observation and research, clouds are fractals. They have a fractal dimension between 3 and 4. They do not completely fill a four-dimensional space. It is difficult to imagine the fractal shape of a cloud for two reasons. One reason is that all fractals, even of lower dimension, are hard to imagine. The other is that a four-dimensional space is hard to imagine. The following concept might help: if all points of three-dimensional space are allowed to vary in density, then we can consider the density to be the fourth dimension. Density can be directly translated into mist or fog and can be represented by a certain gray level on a computer screen.

Displaying a cloud on a computer screen involves displaying a two-dimensional projection of the cloud onto a plane. An orthographic projection of a cloud would mean accumulating the densities in the cloud along all lines perpendicular to the projection plane and assigning the accumulated densities to the points in the plane where the perpendicular lines emanate.

What is thus created is a fractal set of points with dimension between 2 and 3. The fact that the set is at least two-dimensional is trivial, because it consists of all points on a two-dimensional plane. Also, the points' densities vary from one point to the next in a noncontinuous way, which gives the set a dimension greater than two. However, the set cannot be three-dimensional, because every point has precisely one density and not infinitely many, as would be required to make it three-dimensional.

We will not attempt to produce such projections. First, it is practically impossible to generate the cloud-fractal with its precise dimension, because that would require an enormously big memory. Every point in space would have to be represented by a memory cell containing a density. Second, all densities would have to be accumulated along one coordinate axis, certainly a time-consuming process.

Consider the following: the intersection of a fractal of dimension between 3 and 4 with a plane yields a fractal of dimension between 2 and 3, because exactly one spatial dimension is lost. In other words, the intersection of a cloud with a plane yields a fractal with dimension between 2 and 3. There is reason to believe that this intersection looks essentially the same as the projection of a cloud onto a plane and therefore appears as a cloud. To produce this cloud-picture with a computer, one would have to start out with a plane and assign intensities to all its points in a "fractal" manner. We will do this using a similar algorithm to that we used in constructing landscapes and mountains—the midpoint-displacement algorithm.

Clouds are not fractals on all scales of magnification. This becomes clear when we look at cumulonimbus clouds. These have a definite characteristic shape. The fractal property of clouds certainly exists on a small scale and sometimes, depending on the type of cloud, in bigger scales. The cirrus cloud is fractal on almost all scales. Fractal techniques can indeed produce these clouds; we will consider cirrus clouds here. Below, we refer to only this type of cloud if not otherwise stated.

A digitized elevation map of a natural landscape can be displayed as one or more clouds by replacing "height" with "gray value." The clouds thus obtained are indistinguishable from natural ones. PIXAR company of San Rafael, California, which produces image processing hardware and software, has done this with excellent results for several of their presentation portfolios.

To create a single cloud, it seems sufficient to produce a single peak surface of type `frect_t` and interpret the heights as gray values. One presets the center point to a positive value and all boundary points to zero, because a cloud is supposed to disappear smoothly into the sky. The construction of `frect_t` will not change preset values. The fractal surface will be built around them. If the proper points are preset, they become the skeleton of the surface. One exercise produces a cloud with this technique.

Strangely though, when we display the surface thus obtained as a cloud, regularities appear in the form of various sized "crosses." The reason is that the surface of type `frect_t` has cross-shaped ridges. If we suppress fractal distortions by setting *rug* = 0, the surface will consist of one cross-shaped ridge centered at the peak. Using a positive value for *rug* will overlay the main ridge with distortions and somewhat blur it. However, subpeaks will be created at arbitrary locations and local subshapes of the same kind will appear imposing their own cross-shaped ridges.

The problem is that the human eye detects density regularities very readily, making such clouds unacceptable; natural clouds do not have these regularities. On the other hand, when this surface is displayed as a landscape, the regularities look like natural ridges and are not disturbing to the human observer; they usually even defy detection.

We have to vary the `frect_t` construction algorithm to remove regularities. Below, we present a method that produces very good results. To explain it, we again consider the construction of a fractal line.

The construction of an `fline_t` object involves distorting the midpoints of connecting straight lines by random amounts. Presetting one height value at the center and using a zero distortion factor gives us what we call the basic shape. Clearly, it will consist of two straight lines connecting the line end points to the peak in the center. The basic shape indicates the character of the fractally distorted line, because that line is an accumulation of many basic shapes of different sizes. The shape tells us that the line will consist of many small peaks. It is analogous to `frect_t`, because the interpolations are linear. The lines and surfaces of types `fline_t` and `frect_t` support this fact.

THE "SMOOCLOU" ALGORITHM

The essential change to the construction of a `frect_t` consists of distorting the midpoints of connecting curves instead of connecting straight lines. If we distort connecting curves, we will not create any sharp peaks. The curve that comes to mind is the cubic Catmull-Rom curve, because it interpolates through the points.

If P_0 and P_1 are points to be connected by a Catmull-Rom curve, we must use one more point on the left, P_{-1}, and one more on the right, P_2. These four points determine the curve piece connecting P_0 and P_1. The curve value at the center point, P_c, is easily computed and then distorted by a random amount, as in `frect_t::frac()` (see Figure 9.25).

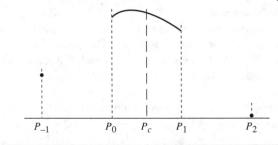

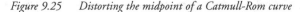

P_{-1} P_0 P_c P_1 P_2

Figure 9.25   Distorting the midpoint of a Catmull-Rom curve

Recursive programming is not possible because the algorithm must access height values outside the currently computed fractal line piece. If you understand the principle of distorting one line piece, which we explain next, you will understand the cloud algorithm better.

Consider a line with two end points at height 0 and the midpoint at height 1. We interpret these as three control points in the $(x \ y)$ plane with $(x \ y)$-values of: $(-1 \ 0)$, $(0 \ 1)$, and $(1 \ 0)$. (The x-values are actually insignificant; we simply assume them to be equidistant.)

To find the undistorted height at the midpoint of the left half, we compute the y-value of the curve at $x = -0.5$ through the four points $(-2 \ 0)$, $(-1 \ 0)$, $(0 \ 1)$, and $(1 \ 0)$. Observe that we have simply assumed one more control point to the left of $(-1 \ 0)$ to give us a total of four points. The point $(-2 \ 0)$ is equispaced in x with the others and its y-value is the same as that of $(-1 \ 0)$; we are just doing control point repetition. We will always do this when we compute the midpoint in a terminal interval. First, let us develop the midpoint computation as a general formula. The four y-values for the interpolation are $(y_{-1} \ y_0 \ y_1 \ y_2)$. The Catmull-Rom matrix formula with $c = \frac{1}{2}$ and this geometry vector at $u = \frac{1}{2}$ is:

$$C_y\left(\tfrac{1}{2}\right) = \tfrac{1}{2}\begin{pmatrix} \tfrac{1}{8} & \tfrac{1}{4} & \tfrac{1}{2} & 1 \end{pmatrix} \begin{pmatrix} -1 & 3 & -3 & 1 \\ 2 & -5 & 4 & -1 \\ -1 & 0 & 1 & 0 \\ 0 & 2 & 0 & 0 \end{pmatrix} \begin{pmatrix} y_{-1} \\ y_0 \\ y_1 \\ y_2 \end{pmatrix}$$

This becomes: $C_y\left(\tfrac{1}{2}\right) = (-y_{-1} + 9y_0 + 9y_1 - y_2)/16$.

For our particular first midpoint computation, we insert the four y-values (0 0 1 0) and obtain $C_y\left(\tfrac{1}{2}\right) = \tfrac{9}{16}$ as the height value. The x-coordinate interpolation is unnecessary, as it automatically gives the midpoint with equispaced x-values. In the right half at +0.5, we obtain the same value. We see immediately that this value is higher than the midpoint of a connecting straight line.

In the next pass, we compute four new height values in the middle of the four intervals. We never use midpoints and height values computed within the same pass, but restrict ourselves to the previous points and height values. We continue with passes until everything is refined enough.

Running this with zero distortion gives us the basic shape—a smooth curve. If we want the line to become fractal, we will distort each y-value by a random amount proportional to the length of the interval and will obtain a smooth fractal line! What we have to do now is to extend this algorithmic concept from the line to the surface.

In the case of a surface, we start with a square where the heights at the boundary points and corner points are preset to 0 and the height at the center point is preset to 1. This gives us four subsquares, each with four preset corner points. We now interpolate at the center of each subsquare and at the four midpoints of its sides. (Usually, two of those midpoints are already computed, so we have to compute only two side-midpoints.) For the Catmull-Rom patch evaluation, we take the four corner points and "reach out" to the 12 surrounding neighbors, giving us a total of 16 control points. (If we are at the boundary of the area, we achieve this again through control point repetition.)

Figure 9.26 shows the layout for these interpolations. The control points are simply named P_0 through P_{15}. We obtain the values of the bicubic Catmull-Rom patch at P_a, P_b, and P_c by evaluating the bicubic Catmull-Rom matrix formula for the $(u\ v)$ pairs $(\tfrac{1}{2}\ 0)$, $(0\ \tfrac{1}{2})$, and $(\tfrac{1}{2}\ \tfrac{1}{2})$.

$$
\begin{array}{cccc}
P_{12} & P_{13} & P_{14} & P_{15} \\
\\
P_8 & P_9 & P_{10} & P_{11} \\
& P_a\ \ P_c & \\
P_4 & P_5\ \ P_b\ \ P_6 & & P_7 \\
\\
P_0 & P_1 & P_2 & P_3
\end{array}
$$

Figure 9.26 Gridpoint layout for Catmull-Rom interpolation

$$y(P_a) = S_y\left(\tfrac{1}{2} \ 0\right) = (-P_1 + 9P_5 + 9P_9 - P_{13})/16$$

$$y(P_b) = S_y\left(0 \ \tfrac{1}{2}\right) = (-P_4 + 9P_5 + 9P_6 - P_7)/16$$

$$\begin{aligned}
y(P_c) = S_y\left(\tfrac{1}{2} \ \tfrac{1}{2}\right) = (&+P_0 \ -9P_1 \ -9P_2 \ +P_3 \\
&-9P_4 + 81P_5 + 81P_6 \ -9P_7 \\
&-9P_8 + 81P_9 + 81P_{10} - 9P_{11} \\
&+P_{12} - 9P_{13} - 9P_{14} + P_{15})/256
\end{aligned}$$

The formulas for the other two side midpoints are analogous. If the sequence of computations proceeds from left to right and bottom to top, we must compute only the midpoints in the center and at the sides. Running this with zero distortion produces a smooth bump as the basic shape. If we distort with a certain ruggedness, we obtain a smooth bumpy surface.

OO DESIGN AND CLASS SPECIFICATIONS

An object of type "smooth cloud" is described by the class smoocloud_t. Its members are two point_t that use device coordinates to specify the upper left and the lower right corner point of the cloud-area on the screen. Another member is the cloud's ruggedness. The class has a draw function that creates the cloud on the screen.

The cloud is positioned in absolute device coordinates. Using world coordinates would increase the memory requirements and the algorithm's complexity—it is not advisable. The type smoocloud_t has no relation to any of the 2D or 3D drawable primitives introduced so far. This class is therefore not derived from prim_t, but stands alone.

```
//******************* File Cloud/smooclou.h *******************

#ifndef SMOOCLOUD_T
#define SMOOCLOUD_T

#include "../Shape2d/point.h"

class smoocloud_t
{
public:
   smoocloud_t(point_t,point_t,double) ;
  ~smoocloud_t();
   void draw() ;
   void setvalue(int,int,unsigned char);

private:
   point_t a ;                              // upper left corner
   point_t b ;                              // lower right corner
   double rug ;
   void cr_int(int,int,int,int,int,int,int,int,int*,int*) ;
} ;

#endif

//*************************************************************
```

Some comments about the implementation: the constructor of `smoocloud_t` initializes the data members and sets the "skeleton" for a default cloud with one peak in the center. The cloud itself is produced during `draw()`. Instead of using an array, the code works in the frame buffer memory, so the cloud is created directly on the display. For this it requires the two functions `setpix()` and `readpix()` (in X Windows) or `put_pixel()` and `get_pixel()` (in Tiga).

The `draw()` function initializes the array of subscripts in the *j*-direction (left to right), `jpos`, and the array of subscripts in the *i*-direction (top to bottom), `ipos`. These arrays contain the subscripts of those pixels that have already been computed. We can consider each array as a set of parallel lines laid over the cloud rectangle. The two sets of lines cross at right angles. Wherever two lines cross, there is a pixel that has already been computed.

The function `cr_int()` (Catmull-Rom interpolation) reads the values of 4×4 adjacent computed pixels and interpolates one new pixel value from those. Then it sets that pixel. The pixel's subscripts are merged into `ipos` and `jpos`. `Cr_int()` is called for all adjacent 4×4 pixel groups. Thus, the sets of subscripts are refined when new subscripts are added in between the old ones.

Successive sweeps over the cloud rectangle interpolate smaller and smaller 4×4 groups. The sweeps continue until both sets of lines are "dense," that is, no uncomputed pixels remain. All computed values must be trimmed to the range from 0 to 255, as this is the intensity range for each *rgb*-component.

The cloud is produced in white on a blue background. The lowest color value is pure blue, the highest is pure white. This means that the blue component is 255 (full intensity) in all cases, while the green and red intensities vary together from 0 to 255.

In an environment with a lookup table (Xwin8), we have to set lookup table entries that vary smoothly from (0 0 255), pure blue, to (255 255 255), pure white, over a considerable range to achieve a smooth variation. If we need other colors in the picture, the range must be reduced.

The implementations for the X Window environment (Xwin8 and Xwin24) allocate a matrix of unsigned characters corresponding to the size of the cloud. Each entry in the matrix stores the red and green intensity written into the corresponding pixel. When computing new pixels, the program reads the entries in the matrix rather than the stored pixel values in the frame buffer. The latter would be extremely slow because program and display are not necessarily running on the same machine—the request may have to travel through the network. The constructor of the cloud object allocates the memory and the destructor deallocates it.

In an MS-DOS environment, such amounts of memory cannot be allocated. The frame buffer of the graphics board itself serves as that memory. The implementation for the #9GXi graphics board (Tiga) uses the fourth (rightmost) byte per pixel, which is not displayed, to store the pixel value. The repeated accesses to the graphics board, however, slow the computation down considerably.

One can give the cloud a horizontal shape by specifying an area that has a greater width than height. Also, by properly presetting density values in the cloud area with `setvalue()`, one can even produce clouds with several density centers. When presetting density values, one sets a value only if its immediate predecessors in the generation process are set. Otherwise, one produces abrupt and too-regular-looking density changes. The center value precedes all other values, so it can always be set. However, one can also set any of the centers and side-midpoints of the four subsquares. One can continue in this way to produce a cloud of a certain shape. Color Plate 8 shows an example of a horizontal cirrus cloud.

THE "SIMPCLOU" ALGORITHM

Another algorithm for creating fractal surfaces that is also used for creating clouds can be found in the literature. It computes densities only at the centers of subsquares using the four corner values, but never those at side-midpoints. The algorithm computes densities by considering the corners and centers of all subsquares during a given pass as the corners of another set of subsquares that are tilted by 45 degrees and reduced in size. After the densities in those centers are computed, the algorithm then considers them as corners of another set of nontilted squares of reduced size. These two types of passes alternate until all pixels are set. In Figure 9.27, we see on the left how the points "1" are computed as centers of squares with corners "0." On the right each "0" and "1" forms a corner in a set of tilted squares whose centers, "2," are computed. The subsquares decrease from one pass to the next is by a factor of $\frac{1}{2}\sqrt{2}$.

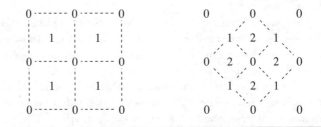

Figure 9.27   Sequence of pixel computation

The basic shape of this surface (taking heights instead of densities) does not have ridges, but has a very sharp peak in the center. The clouds produced with this algorithm tend to have small sharp density concentrations. The algorithm is simple, but needs to use a square array in which the row and column numbers are a power of two plus one. It is impossible to write this algorithm for a different array size without making drastic changes. It is possible to preset density values other than just the boundary and center, but one needs to be more careful than in smooclou().

We present a class specification for this type of cloud: simpcloud_t. The area in which the cloud is computed is always square and consists of size * size pixels; size is a data member of the class. Another data member is the ruggedness. An object of this type is constructed with these two parameters. The upper left corner of the cloud square is at absolute screen position (0 0). One can generalize the algorithm to put the cloud at any position on the screen. We have left this as an exercise.

What we said about the simpcloud_t implementation is also true here. The cloud has no relation to 2D or 3D objects introduced so far. This class is not derived from prim_t, but stands alone. The implementation is in Cloud/simpclou.c.

```
//******************** File Cloud/simpclou.h ********************

#ifndef SIMPCLOUD_T
#define SIMPCLOUD_T

class simpcloud_t
{
public:
  ~simpcloud_t();
  simpcloud_t(int size,float rug) : size(size) , rug(rug) {}
  void draw() ;

private:
  int size ;                    // cloud size is size*size pixels
  double rug ;                          // ruggedness factor
} ;

#endif
//***************************************************************
```

9.6 THE MANDELBROT SET, JULIA SETS, AND FATOU DUSTS

We will now discuss three very popular fractals: the Mandelbrot set, Julia sets, and Fatou dusts. The computational method for these prevents them from being drawn on a line plotter, although some of these fractals are indeed lines. Instead, they must be produced on a raster display. These fractals are all defined in the complex plane, so we must use complex arithmetic in the complex plane to produce them.

The complex number plane is practically identical to the two-dimensional Cartesian drawing plane. The horizontal axis is the real axis, while the vertical axis is the imaginary axis. Complex numbers can be plotted on this plane as number pairs, almost exactly as with Cartesian coordinate pairs. We refer to the complex numbers as $(a_1\ b_1)$, $(a_2\ b_2)$, and so on; the real part is given first, the imaginary part second. Therefore, $(a\ b)$ and $a+bi$ mean the same thing. The whole complex plane, together with ∞, is designated by C. The rules for adding and subtracting complex numbers and for multiplying a complex number by a real factor are identical to those for vector addition, subtraction, and scalar multiplication in Cartesian coordinates. The rules for multiplying and dividing complex numbers by each other are different and are presented in the appendix.

THE MANDELBROT SET

The *Mandelbrot set* is named after Benoit Mandelbrot, who first studied it in the 1970s (MAND77). It is easy to create. Strictly speaking, the Mandelbrot set is not a fractal; it is a subset of the complex plane, but its boundary is a fractal. It is this boundary which reveals infinite detail of amazing variety when examined under high magnification.

To create the Mandelbrot set, we perform a simple iteration in the complex plane. We will indicate a complex number by just one letter: $z = (z_r\ z_i)$, $c = (c_r\ c_i)$, and so on. If z_i is a complex number in the iteration process, the next number is z_{i+1}. We obtain this number with $z_{i+1} = z_i^2 + c$, in which c is a fixed complex number not farther than 2 away from the origin.

We choose some such number c and a starting value $z_0 = (0 \; 0)$, then iterate $z_1, z_2, z_3, \ldots$. After every step, we check the distance of z_i from the origin. As soon as it exceeds 2, we stop the iteration because this sequence will go to ∞. If so, then the number c is not in the Mandelbrot set. If the distance of z_i from the origin never becomes greater than 2, then c belongs to the Mandelbrot set because the Mandelbrot set is defined as:

$$\left\{ c \in C: \lim z_i \neq \infty \text{ under } z_{i+1} = z_i^2 + c, \; z_0 = (0 \; 0) \right\}$$

We cannot know with certainty that an iteration will never go to ∞, because we cannot run the iteration forever to see if this will eventually occur. But we can set a limit, say 50 iteration steps, and if after so many steps z_i is still not farther than 2 from the origin, we assume that c is in the Mandelbrot set.

We can create the figure by trying all c-values from some rectangular area of the complex plane. We make the rectangular area correspond to pixel locations on the screen. If c belongs to the set, we make this pixel black; if c does not belong to the set, we set the pixel to white. Figure 9.28 shows the Mandelbrot set. There seem to be parts isolated from the main set, but this is only a deficiency of the display. The Mandelbrot set is really connected (DOHU82).

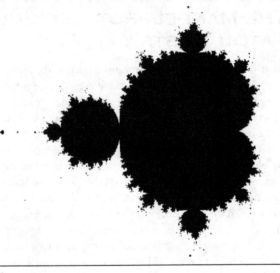

Figure 9.28   Mandelbrot set

Close-ups of the Mandelbrot set can be shown in a beautiful color display. To obtain such beautiful Mandelbrot pictures, we see whether a c-value belongs to the set. If it does not belong, we do not set the corresponding pixel to white, but we remember how many iteration steps it took to make z_i jump over the boundary. We set the pixel to a color according to this number of iterations. That is really all! Color Plate 15 shows a Mandelbrot close-up.

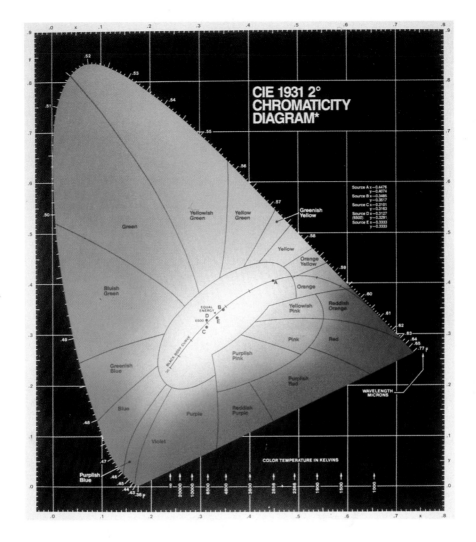

Color Plate 1

The C. I. E. Chromaticity Diagram is an industry standard for describing the color reproduction capability of a color monitor. Shown here are all perceivable colors in a two-dimensional arrangement. The pure colors are located on the upper boundary of the curve. In nature most colors are mixtures of pure colors and correspond to the ones found within the boundaries of the curve. Color intensity is ignored in this diagram—that is why colors such as brown and gray are not visible. (Courtesy Photo Research)

Color Plate 2
"Everything"
by Cornel Pokorny

Shows all solid primitives covered in this book. Ray tracing in 24-bit color; transparency, refraction, reflection (glass objects); shadows; solid texturing (marble and granite); flat texturing (plumber's tee).

Color Plate 3
"Free Composition"
by Cornel Pokorny

Ray tracing in 24-bit color; glass torus and marble dodecahedron over checkerboard; shows reflection, refraction, and solid texturing.

Color Plate 4 "Someone's Thinking of You"

by Cornel Pokorny

Ray tracing with constructive solid geometry (glass, pencil, table top); framed picture is flat texturing of a scanned photograph of the author's daughter. Solid texturing, reflection, refraction; tinted shadows.

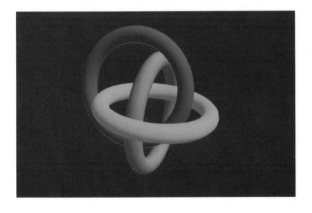

Color Plate 5 "Tri-torus"

by Cornel Pokorny

Each torus is a quadrangle mesh produced by Phong\surfrev.c as a surface of revolution; rotated and translated into position; rendered in 24-bit color with painter's algorithm and Phong shading.

Color Plate 6
"Fractal Mountains"
by Cornel Pokorny

The mountains are fractally distorted surfaces. Displayed with faceted shading in 8-bit color, drawing the farthest ones first and the closest ones last; one light source in upper right corner.

Color Plate 7
"Chesspiece and Saucer"
by Cornel Pokorny

Objects are quadrangle meshes, produced by Phong\surfrev.c as surfaces of revolution. Rendered in 24-bit color with painter's algorithm and Phong shading.

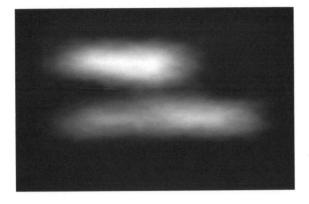

Color Plate 8
"Cirrus Clouds"

by Cornel Pokorny

Produced with the "smoocloud" algorithm in 24-bit color. A "skeleton" of predefined height values outlines the shape of two cirrus clouds. Technique similar to fractal surface distortion.

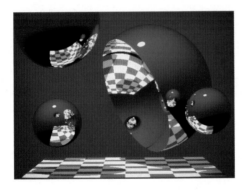

Color Plate 9
"Spheres"

by Adrian Brandt

Ray tracing in 8-bit color, difference of spheres, total reflectivity, multiple reflections.

Color Plate 10
"Phong Shading"
by Cornel Pokorny

Simple quadrangle meshes representing two cylinders and a cone; rendered in 24-bit color with painter's algorithm and Phong shading.

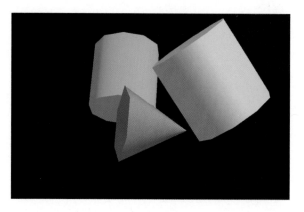

Color Plate 11
"Warnock Algorithm"
by Cornel Pokorny

Warnock screen subdivision method with acceleration through list management. Arbitrary polyhedra penetrating each other.

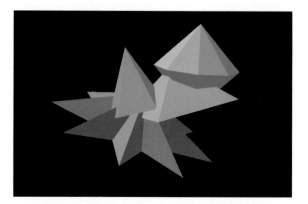

Color Plate 12
"Painter's Algorithm"
by Cornel Pokorny

Depth sorting and painter's algorithm; arbitrary polyhedra, no mutual penetration of objects is allowed.

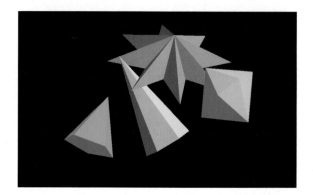

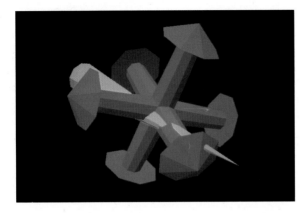

Color Plate 13
"Hexarrow"
by Cornel Pokorny

A 3D arrow construct and a many-sided, narrow cone defined with triangle meshes penetrating each other; rendered with Warnock screen subdivision method in 8-bit color.

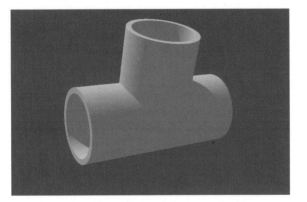

Color Plate 14
"Plumber's Tee"
by Cornel Pokorny

Ray tracing in 24-bit color; constructive solid geometry; two cylinder tees are defined, the thinner (inner) one is subtracted from the thicker (outer) one.

Color Plate 15
"Mandlebrot Set"
by Cornel Pokorny

A close-up of a Mandlebrot set (see Section 9.6). The Mandlebrot set has an enormous variety of differently shaped details.

Color Plate 16

by Cornel Pokorny

Julia set of the function $z^2 + (0.421\ 0.30795)$ and its immediate vicinity. The display was created by testing only for the attractor ∞. The color of a point is determined by its distance from the point of origin.

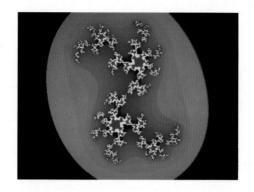

Color Plate 17

by Cornel Pokorny

Julia set of the function $1/(z^2 + (0.5\ 0.1))$ and its immediate vicinity. The display was created by testing only for the attractor ∞. The Julia set is inside the grapevine-shaped garland.

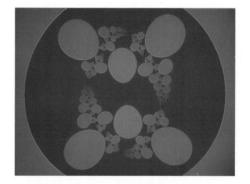

Color Plate 18
"Rabbit"

by Cornel Pokorny

Attractor method for Julia sets; four attractors; iteration is $z \to z^2 + (-0.12\ 0.74)$; the boundary of the colored area is the Julia set.

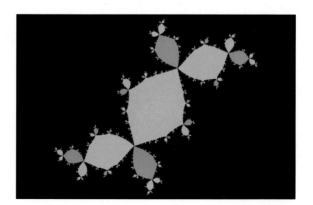

Color Plate 19
"Art Gallery"
by Eric Anderson

Ray tracing in 24-bit color, solid texturing on table tops, flat mapping on paintings, constructive solid geometry, tinted transparent bowls with shadows, light sources inside and outside room.

Color Plate 20
"Free Composition"
by Victor Solanoy

Ray tracing in 24-bit color, multicolored light sources, flat mapping on background, solid texturing on vase and granite objects, refractive glass sphere and glass beams.

Color Plate 21
"Toys"
by Dave Meny

Ray tracing in 24-bit color; texture mapping (floor and star); procedural texturing on ball; reflections (floor); shadows; functional modeling (blocks); antialiased through supersampling.

Color Plate 22
"Cola Cans"
by Allen Do

Ray tracing in 24-bit color; cylinders with flat texturing on mantle and cut-off planes; reflective checkerboard. The texture maps were scanned from real cans.

Color Plate 23
"Free Composition"
by Tuyet-Nhi Luu

Ray tracing in 24-bit color; glass and marble torus mutually penetrating; elliptical spiral; flat texturing on board.

Color Plate 24
"Table Setting"
by Jennifer Courter

Ray tracing in 24-bit color; all objects with constructive solid geometry; solid texturing on table top; transparent wine glass.

Color Plate 25
"Solid Textures"
by David Fletcher

Ray tracing in 24-bit color; solid texturing (spheres and table top); textures composed with David Fletcher's texture specification tool.

Color Plate 26
"Mountain Bike"
by John Gieske

Ray tracing in 24-bit color; constructive solid geometry with high detail; reflections; multiple light sources; solid texturing on saddle.

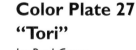

Color Plate 27
"Tori"
by Paul Cerra

Ray tracing in 24-bit color, green glass dodecahedron, chains of reflective and transparent tori, full and tinted shadows; reflections, refractions.

Color Plate 28
"Magician's Sphere"
by Daniel Gong

Ray tracing in 24-bit color; constructive solid geometry; solid texturing on table top; transparent sphere; hands composed of ellipsoids; shadows; refractions.

Color Plate 29
"Planets"
by Brendan Miller

Ray tracing in 24-bit color; solid texturing on spheres, flat texturing on ground.

Color Plate 30

© 1993 Photo Provided Courtesy of Industrial Light & Magic

Color Plate 31

© 1993 Photo Provided Courtesy of Industrial Light & Magic

Color Plate 32

© 1993 Photo Provided Courtesy of Industrial Light & Magic

Many people's first exposure to computer graphics was in a movie theater. The number of films incorporating computer-generated images into their special effects has increased over the last several years.

These three scenes are from *Terminator 2: Judgment Day*. Industrial Light & Magic won the Academy Award for Visual Effects in 1991 for their groundbreaking contribution to this film.

Color Plate 33

Artists use computer graphics to simulate fantasy worlds. Superimposed photographs are sometimes used to make a graphic look more realistic. (Courtesy Evans & Sutherland)

Color Plate 34

Engineers and architects use computer graphics to simulate the completion of a project, as in this example of a train station. (Courtesy Evans & Sutherland)

Color Plate 35

City planners use computer graphics to simulate how a proposed project might look. (Courtesy Evans & Sutherland)

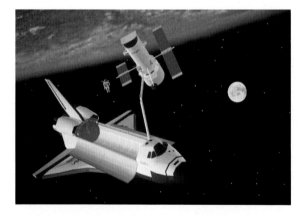

Color Plate 36

Computer graphics are often used by NASA to simulate space shuttle missions. (Courtesy Evans & Sutherland)

Color Plate 37

Military simulations were a very early use of computer graphics. (Courtesy Evans & Sutherland)

Color Plate 38

Color Plate 39

Color Plate 40

Color Plate 41

This is an example of *morphing*, the blending of one image into another via computer software. Once the beginning and end images are chosen, the morphing software determines how many in-between images should be generated for an optimally smooth blend. Note how the before and after scenes are set up to be nearly identical—the position of the two men, their hairstyles, the background. Limiting the blend to the face accentuates the blend's effectiveness.

Photos courtesy of Warner-Lambert Shaving Products Group/Schick Division © 1993

Figure 9.29 shows a close-up of the set, namely the area from −0.734792 to −0.732708 on the real axis and from 0.194988 to 0.197072 on the imaginary axis. This area is displayed with 200 × 200 pixels. The limit for the iterations is 90.

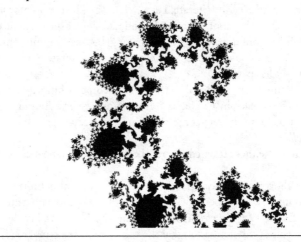

Figure 9.29   Mandelbrot set closeup

Experience is needed to choose good colors for pixels and good boundary regions for the Mandelbrot subset. If we are too far away from the set, we obtain just one or two plain colors; if we are too close—inside the set—we obtain plain black. To have good, interesting close-ups, we might need to scan a very small area; double precision arithmetic is necessary. In addition, the limit we set for the iterations must be high, even 700 is not too high. Mandelbrot close-ups are extremely computation intensive. A very fast processor or a math chip can save days and even weeks of processor time.

JULIA SETS

(This section can be omitted without loss of continuity.) Julia sets are one of the most widely studied fractals, but many questions about them remain. For example, we know almost nothing about their fractional dimension. A Julia set is not necessarily a fractal, but most Julia sets are. Work on these sets was begun by Gaston Julia and Pierre Fatou around the time of World War I (JULI18, FATO19).

As with the Mandelbrot set, Julia sets are defined in the complex plane C. Let $P(z)$ and $Q(z)$ be two polynomials with complex arguments and without common divisors; then $R(z) = P(z)/Q(z)$ is a rational function in C. For each rational function, a Julia set can be defined as explained below.

The rational function $R(z)$ is used to iterate any given point of C: $z_{i+1} = R(z_i)$. Depending on the starting point, such an iteration sequence can behave in several ways. Consider only those starting values that repeat themselves cyclically when iterated. For example, take $P(z) = z^2$ and $Q(z) = 1$; then $R(z) = z^2$. The point $e^{2i\pi/7} = (.6234\ \ .7818)$ iterates to $(-.2225\ \ .9749)$, then to $(-.9009\ \ -.4338)$, then back to $(.6234\ \ .7818)$, and repeats this cycle forever. Denote such a periodic cycle with Γ. The above three points are called periodic; their periods are of length 3. Points with a period of 1 are also considered periodic.

We will characterize the periodic cycles further. If z_0 is a periodic point with period n for the function R, then it is a periodic point with period 1 for the function R^n ($R^n = R*R* \ldots R$, applied to itself n times). Iterating a point in R^n is the same as iterating it in R and paying attention only to every nth iterate. Let $z_0, z_1, \ldots, z_{n-1}$ be the points of the cycle Γ with period n. Now consider the iteration function R^n and take any of the periodic points z_i from Γ. Iterating with a point z_i from the cycle is not interesting, because it jumps onto itself forever (the period is 1 for R^n!). If we take a point very close to z_i and iterate with it, however, several different things might happen:

1. The point can be attracted by z_i, that is, it comes arbitrarily close to z_i; we call z_i *attractive*.
2. It can be repelled by z_i. That is, it is not attracted by z_i, but may be attracted by some other point or by ∞. It may come closer and withdraw again in a chaotic manner; we call z_i *repelling*.
3. It can be neither attracted nor repelled, but circles z_i on a curve forever; we call z_i *indifferent*.

The above explanations have precise mathematical definitions. To find in which of the three groups an n-cycle periodic point z_i of R belongs, we compute the derivative of R^n at the point z_i: $L = (R^n)'(z_i)$. In case a, $|L| < 1$; in case b, $|L| > 1$; and in case c, $|L| = 1$. It follows from the chain rule of differentiation that the value of L is the same for all z_i in a cycle; therefore the whole cycle Γ belongs to one of these groups. This allows us to categorize all periodic cycles of a function R into one of the three classes.

We want to examine the repelling periodic cycles of R. Without going into mathematical detail, we state that for every rational function $R(z)$ there are infinitely many repelling periodic cycles and therefore infinitely many repelling periodic points. Let P be the set of all repelling periodic points of R. The Julia set of R, J_R, is defined as the closure of P. In other words, J_R is the set of all limit points of P. In this sense, P more or less outlines J_R.

In some cases, there is a more intuitive way to describe the Julia set of R. Attractive cycles do not always exist. However, if there is one (Γ) consisting of the points $z_0, \ldots, z_{n-1}$, we group into one set all points attracted to each z_i through iteration with R^n and call this set $A(z_i)$, the *basin of attraction* of z_i. J_R is the boundary of $A(z_i)$; that is, it is the set of all limit points of $A(z_i)$, no matter which z_i we take. The union of $A(z_0), A(z_1), \ldots, A(z_{n-1})$ is the basin of attraction for this cycle, $A(\Gamma)$. J_R is also the boundary of $A(\Gamma)$. This is an interesting property, because there are usually several basins of attraction with completely different shapes, but with identical boundaries. From this, it follows that in many cases, J_R must be fractal.

Another property of J_R is that J_R is identical to $J_R{}^n$. We can therefore display $J_R{}^n$ instead of J_R if this is easier. J_R is also invariant under R: $R(J_R) = J_R$.

As an example, take z^2+c as the rational function $R(z)$, where c is the complex constant $(-.12\ .74)$. This R has an attractive three-cycle consisting of the three points $a = (-.65306\ .56253)$, $b = (-.00995\ 0.00527)$, and $c = (-.11993\ .73990)$. If we iterate with R $*R*R$, then each of these points is attractive with period 1. The point ∞ is also attractive. Each of these four points has its basin of attraction; they are shown in black in Figures 9.30 through 9.33. As we can see, the basins are in the first three cases the union of countless many disjoint sets. Most of them are so small that they we cannot see them in the display. $A(a)$, $A(b)$, $A(c)$, and $A(\infty)$ are very different from each other, yet their boundaries are identical and equal to J_{R*R*R}. Therefore, they are identical to J_R.

In Figure 9.30, the union of the black areas is the basin of attraction of the point $a = (-.65306\ .56253)$. The boundary of this set is J_R. The point a lies in the large area at the upper left.

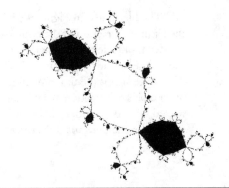

Figure 9.30   Basin of attraction of (–.65306 .56253)

In Figure 9.31, the union of the black areas is the basin of attraction of the point $b = (-.00995\ 0.00527)$. The boundary of this set is J_R. The point b lies in the large center area.

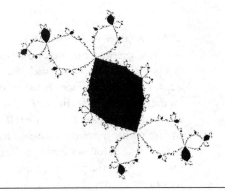

Figure 9.31   Basin of attraction of (–.00995 .00527)

In Figure 9.32, the union of the black areas is the basin of attraction of the point $c = (-.11993\ .73990)$. The boundary of this set is J_R. The point c lies in the upper of the two big parts.

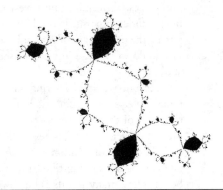

Figure 9.32   Basin of attraction of (–.11993 .73990)

The black area in Figure 9.33 is the basin of attraction of the point ∞; it extends outside the rectangle to infinity. The boundary of this set is J_R. The white area is the union of all the other basins of attraction. $A(\infty)$ is connected and its boundary is easier to see than in the previous three cases.

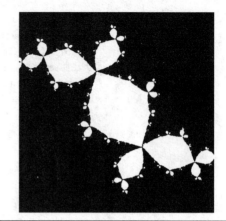

Figure 9.33   Basin of attraction of ∞

DISPLAYING A JULIA SET: PRE-IMAGE METHOD

Julia sets are harder to display than the Mandelbrot set. Here is one method. A *pre-image* of a point z_0 is any point z such that $R(z) = z_0$. Given R and a point z_0, then $I(z_0) = \{z \in :R^k(z) = z_0$ for $k = 1,2,...\}$ describes the set of all pre-images of z_0. A Julia set J_R has the property that, for every point $z_0 \in J_R$, the set $I(z_0)$ is dense in J_R. In other words, the set of all pre-images of z_0 pretty much outlines the Julia set. If R is not too complicated, we can express the pre-image of a point with a formula. For example, let $R(z) = z^2+c$. The pre-image z of z_0 satisfies $R(z) = z_0$, so $z^2+c = z_0$; it follows that there are two pre-images $z_1 = +\sqrt{z_0-c}$ and $z_2 = -\sqrt{z_0-c}$. We will further explain the pre-image method only for $R(z) = z^2+c$. For more complicated functions, we cannot express the inverse as a formula, and we must find the pre-images with a method such as Newton's.

Beginning with a starting point and repeating the formula, we can compute pre-images of pre-images, continuing until we reach a preset limit n. There are always two possible pre-images for each point. It would be most complicated and require tremendous buffer space to pursue the pre-images of each solution when they double with every step, but it is not necessary to do so. We use just one of the two pre-images randomly so that they are chosen with about equal probability.

How do we find a starting point in the Julia set? Luckily, we do not really need one. If we iterate inversely and choose any pre-image at random, then, for mathematical reasons beyond the scope of this book, every point from C will be pulled toward J_R. Once there, it will jump into J_R forever. We take, for example, (1 0) as the starting point, compute the two pre-images, and choose one at random. We can still set both pixels corresponding to both solutions. It takes only a few steps until the pre-images are in the Julia set. The more points we produce, the better. How many points should we produce? For cases in which the Julia set is not very ragged, we obtain a pretty good picture with about 2000 iterations (see Figures 9.34 and 9.35).

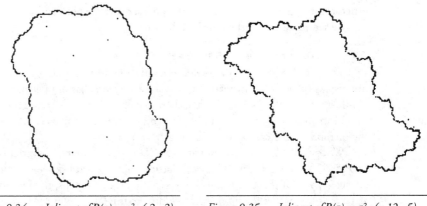

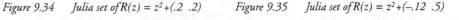

Figure 9.34   Julia set of $R(z) = z^2 + (.2 \ .2)$ Figure 9.35   Julia set of $R(z) = z^2 + (-.12 \ .5)$

The method's shortcoming quickly becomes obvious when we try to display more complicated sets. Figure 9.36 shows two such attempts for $R(z) = z^2 + (-.12 \ .74)$. Compare these to Figure 9.35. In Figure 9.36, the outline of J_R is recognizable, but there are still gaps in the line, although 10,000 (left) and 20,000 (right) iterations were performed. In the right display, J_R is outlined better. The gaps result from the fact that the pre-images seldom reach these areas. Increasing the number of iterated points does not help very much; gaps will be visible even after 40,000 iterations.

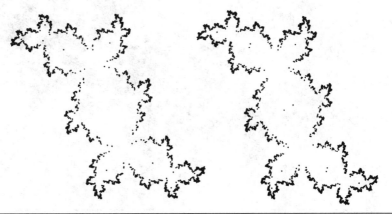

Figure 9.36   Julia set of $R(z) = z^2 + (-.12 \ .74)$ displayed with 10,000 points (L) and 20,000 points (R)

ATTRACTOR METHOD FOR THE JULIA SET

When the pre-image method does not yield good results, we can try the following. Essentially, we work with just one attractor. Call this point a (a can be ∞). We check whether a point x_0 that corresponds to a pixel is attracted to a. This test is $|x_i - a| < \varepsilon$ (except if $a = \infty$, it is $|x_i| > r$). If this terminating condition is not met after, say, fifty iterations, we assume that the starting point is not attracted to a. We do this testing for the pixel's four corner points. If all four corner points are attracted, or if none of the four corner points are attracted, we assume that the boundary is not within the pixel. However, if one, two, or three are attracted and the others are not, then the boundary of the Julia set is in the pixel and we set the pixel. The pixels that we set display an outline of the Julia set.

ATTRACTOR METHOD FOR BASINS

This method works under the same conditions as the attractor method above, but it does not display the Julia set. Instead it displays one or several basins of attraction. Such displays are as informative as the Julia set itself and are usually much prettier and more colorful. We need to find an attractive point (including ∞). To have the attractor ∞ is sufficient. We first explain the method for the case when ∞ is the attractor.

We cover the area of interest with a fine lattice, such that each lattice point corresponds to one pixel. Then we iterate with each lattice point x_0 until $|x_i| > r$, which means that x_0 is attracted by ∞. If this condition is not met after, say, 50 steps, then we assume that x_0 is not attracted by ∞; we set the pixel corresponding to this lattice point to black, otherwise to white. This method is the easiest to program and produces a filled-in Julia set if J_R is connected. Figure 9.37 shows the filled-in Julia set for $z^2+(-.544\ -.54)$ produced with this method. The lattice consists of 361×361 points, the area is $[-1.5\ 1.5] \times [-1.5\ 1.5]$, and the limit for iterations is 42. It would be almost impossible to display this J_R using the pre-image method.

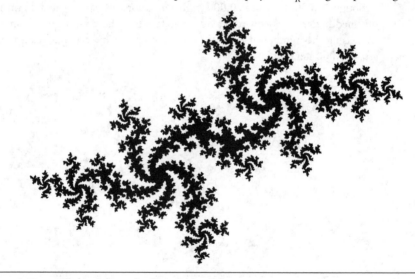

Figure 9.37   Filled-in Julia set for $z^2+(-.544\ -.54)$

The relation between lattice points and pixels will be apparent from this example. Suppose the rectangle of interest is from -1 to $+1$ on the real axis and from -0.625 to $+0.625$ on the imaginary axis. We want to display this using the entire screen, which has 640×400 pixels with a square pixel ratio. (Since the area of interest has the same proportions as the screen, no distortions are introduced.) This is the relation that associates a pixel $(x_s\ y_s)$ with a point $(a\ b)$ in the complex lattice plane:

$$a = \frac{(x_s - 320)}{320} \qquad b = \frac{(y_s - 320)}{320}$$

For Figure 9.37, we tested only ∞. Suppose we have several attractors $a_1, a_2, a_3, \ldots$ (one of them might be ∞). Then we again cover the area of interest with a fine lattice and iterate for each lattice point x_0, but we expand the stopping condition to include every possible attractor. The stopping condition must be: if $|x_i| > r$ or $|x_i-a_1| < \varepsilon$ or $|x_i-a_2| < \varepsilon$ or $|x_i-a_3| < \varepsilon$, and so on, with ε and r as above. The iteration will always stop and meet one of the conditions (if we test for all existing attractors). We keep track of which particular "or" clause was met and set the corresponding pixel to a certain color. This fills each of the basins with a different color. With more than two attractors, the boundaries between them are fractal, which makes such displays very interesting.

Figures 9.30 through 9.32 were produced with this method. The iteration function was $(R*R*R)(z)$ with $R(z) = z^2+(-.12 \;\; .74)$. The attractors are listed with the figures. Only one attractor was checked for each display because of the black/white restriction. With a color display all four attractors can be checked in the iteration and the four basins can be produced simultaneously.

The above shows that we always need some additional information about a Julia set and have to do some preparations before we can successfully compute and display it. The Mandelbrot set is much easier to display because there is only one, so one program will do all possible close-ups. However, there are infinitely many different Julia sets; the function z^2+c alone gives us an infinite and amazing variety of different pictures depending on c.

The same phenomenon occurs here as with the Mandelbrot set. We usually produce nicer pictures if we do not go for the Julia set itself (which is just a fractally distorted line or a dust), but instead count how many iteration steps it takes before making a decision. This number determines the color of the particular pixel. Julia sets are shown in Color Plates 16, 17, and 18. For further information on Julia sets, consult PERI86 and CUGS83.

FATOU DUSTS

Julia sets that are topologically not lines but are totally disconnected, are sometimes called *Fatou dusts*. They are hard to create because the only attractive point is ∞. If an iteration does not start very close to the Fatou dust, it will quickly drop into $A(\infty)$, so the dust points can easily escape the scanning process. We can catch the dust points more easily if the iteration limit is not set high and the scanning raster is dense. Theoretically, the chance that a grid point is in the Fatou dust is 0 and the chance that it is in $A(\infty)$ is 1, so if we iterate too long we will always go to ∞.

9.7 CREATING FRACTALS THROUGH ITERATED TRANSFORMATIONS

Any geometric shape (not necessarily a fractal) that exhibits self-similarity can be produced with a succession of linear transformations that fulfill certain conditions. These are called *contractive affine transformations* and they consist of rotations, translations, and scalings designed to produce an image smaller than the original one. An image that consists of several self-similar parts can be expressed as the union of several of its affine transformations. These parts may be scaled or rotated before being joined.

A simple but illustrative example is a rectangle. Figure 9.38 shows how the contractive affine transformation A_1 transforms a rectangle into a smaller one that covers $\frac{1}{4}$ of it.

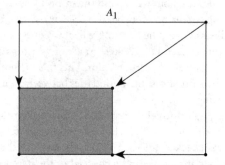

Figure 9.38   Affine transformation of a rectangle

Figure 9.39 shows how a rectangle can be covered with four scaled-down images of itself. The scaled-down images are marked with the affine transformations A_1 through A_4 that produce them. Rectangle A_1 is obtained by scaling the original rectangle by a factor of 0.5. Rectangles A_2, A_3, and A_4 are obtained through scaling by the same factor and subsequent translation.

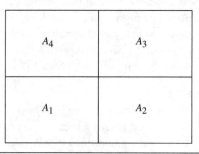

Figure 9.39   Covering a rectangle with four transformations

The matrices below express the four corresponding affine transformations A_1 through A_4. It is assumed that the original rectangle has its lower left corner at the origin:

$$A_1 = \begin{pmatrix} .5 & 0 & 0 \\ 0 & .5 & 0 \\ 0 & 0 & 1 \end{pmatrix} \quad A_2 = \begin{pmatrix} .5 & 0 & 0 \\ 0 & .5 & 0 \\ .5 & 0 & 1 \end{pmatrix} \quad A_3 = \begin{pmatrix} .5 & 0 & 0 \\ 0 & .5 & 0 \\ .5 & .5 & 1 \end{pmatrix} \quad A_4 = \begin{pmatrix} .5 & 0 & 0 \\ 0 & .5 & 0 \\ 0 & .5 & 1 \end{pmatrix}$$

If we take the point (0 0) and compute its four images with A_1 through A_4, we obtain the four points shown in Figure 9.40. As (0 0) is the left lower corner of the original rectangle, the four transformations of (0 0) are the left lower corners of the rectangle's four images.

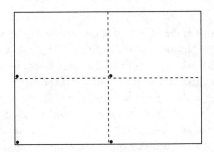

Figure 9.40   The four images of point (0 0)

If we compute the images of these four points with the four transformations, we obtain the 16 points shown in Figure 9.41. Each transformation produces four points in its corresponding image rectangle.

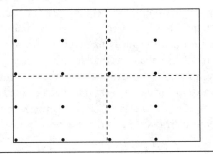

Figure 9.41   The 16 subsequent images

Computing the images of these 16 points with all four transformations gives us 64 points, as shown in Figure 9.42.

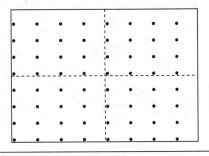

Figure 9.42   The 64 subsequent images

By repeating this over and over again, we fill up the whole rectangular area. The number of points increases by four with each step, and the rectangle is filled in a systematic and regular manner.

It is not necessary to proceed so systematically. If we apply not four transformations to the starting point, but one chosen at random with equal probability, there is equal probability that we will obtain any of the four successor points. Let us find out what happens if we iterate in this way. Again applying any of the transformations at random to the successor point, we obtain any one of the 16 points of the second step. After the third iteration, we obtain any one of the 64 possible points of the third step. The first, second, and third iterated points all lie on different grids that become finer and finer. Theoretically, we will never produce a point twice with this method. In practice, however, it is different.

Because of the limited accuracy of machine arithmetic, the machine can produce only a finite number of points within the rectangular area. Therefore, we will not continue to obtain points on finer and finer grids. After reaching the finest grid possible with the given machine arithmetic, we will produce points only on this grid, and will therefore eventually produce points identical to former points in the iteration. This opens the possibility that all successors of all points will eventually be produced. In other words, if we continue such an iteration long enough, we will finally cover the whole rectangle with points.

Because the above affine transformations can generate the rectangle, they serve as a definition of it. The rectangle is produced by applying the transformations with equal probability to an arbitrary starting point and iterating just long enough. This is certainly a clumsy way to define a rectangle, but it is a very good way to define a highly complex fractal image.

A fractal image can usually be covered with several transformed instances of itself. If we can specify the transformations that do this, we have a description of the fractal. Let us look at a way to find these transformations when they are not obvious, as in the case of the rectangle.

An affine transformation is uniquely determined by three different points and their transformations; we show this below. We use homogeneous coordinates to describe the points and "homogeneous matrices" to describe the transformations. Let the three points be:

$$P_1 = \begin{pmatrix} x_1 & y_1 & 1 \end{pmatrix} \qquad P_2 = \begin{pmatrix} x_2 & y_2 & 1 \end{pmatrix} \qquad P_3 = \begin{pmatrix} x_3 & y_3 & 1 \end{pmatrix}$$

Let their transformations be:

$$Pt_1 = \begin{pmatrix} xt_1 & yt_1 & 1 \end{pmatrix} \qquad Pt_2 = \begin{pmatrix} xt_2 & yt_2 & 1 \end{pmatrix} \qquad Pt_3 = \begin{pmatrix} xt_3 & yt_3 & 1 \end{pmatrix}$$

Let the affine transformation be expressed by the matrix:

$$\begin{pmatrix} a & b & 0 \\ c & d & 0 \\ e & f & 1 \end{pmatrix}$$

Then we have the equations:

$$\begin{pmatrix} xt_1 & yt_1 & 1 \end{pmatrix} = \begin{pmatrix} x_1 & y_1 & 1 \end{pmatrix} \begin{pmatrix} a & b & 0 \\ c & d & 0 \\ e & f & 1 \end{pmatrix}$$

$$\begin{pmatrix} xt_2 & yt_2 & 1 \end{pmatrix} = \begin{pmatrix} x_2 & y_2 & 1 \end{pmatrix} \begin{pmatrix} a & b & 0 \\ c & d & 0 \\ e & f & 1 \end{pmatrix}$$

$$\begin{pmatrix} xt_3 & yt_3 & 1 \end{pmatrix} = \begin{pmatrix} x_3 & y_3 & 1 \end{pmatrix} \begin{pmatrix} a & b & 0 \\ c & d & 0 \\ e & f & 1 \end{pmatrix}$$

The unknowns are a, b, c, d, e, and f. This leads to two linear systems:

$$\begin{pmatrix} x_1 & y_1 & 1 \\ x_2 & y_2 & 1 \\ x_3 & y_3 & 1 \end{pmatrix}\begin{pmatrix} a \\ c \\ e \end{pmatrix} = \begin{pmatrix} xt_1 \\ xt_2 \\ xt_3 \end{pmatrix} \quad \text{and} \quad \begin{pmatrix} x_1 & y_1 & 1 \\ x_2 & y_2 & 1 \\ x_3 & y_3 & 1 \end{pmatrix}\begin{pmatrix} b \\ d \\ f \end{pmatrix} = \begin{pmatrix} yt_1 \\ yt_2 \\ yt_3 \end{pmatrix}$$

The solutions are:

$$a = \frac{\begin{vmatrix} xt_1 & y_1 & 1 \\ xt_2 & y_2 & 1 \\ xt_3 & y_3 & 1 \end{vmatrix}}{\det} \qquad c = \frac{\begin{vmatrix} x_1 & xt_1 & 1 \\ x_2 & xt_2 & 1 \\ x_3 & xt_3 & 1 \end{vmatrix}}{\det} \qquad e = \frac{\begin{vmatrix} x_1 & y_1 & xt_1 \\ x_2 & y_2 & xt_2 \\ x_3 & y_3 & xt_3 \end{vmatrix}}{\det}$$

$$b = \frac{\begin{vmatrix} yt_1 & y_1 & 1 \\ yt_2 & y_2 & 1 \\ yt_3 & y_3 & 1 \end{vmatrix}}{\det} \qquad d = \frac{\begin{vmatrix} x_1 & yt_1 & 1 \\ x_2 & yt_2 & 1 \\ x_3 & yt_3 & 1 \end{vmatrix}}{\det} \qquad f = \frac{\begin{vmatrix} x_1 & y_1 & yt_1 \\ x_2 & y_2 & yt_2 \\ x_3 & y_3 & yt_3 \end{vmatrix}}{\det}$$

$$\text{with } \det = \begin{vmatrix} x_1 & y_1 & 1 \\ x_2 & y_2 & 1 \\ x_3 & y_3 & 1 \end{vmatrix}$$

Here is how we can find values for the parameters a, b, ..., f. As we mentioned above, we have to cover the original image with transformed instances of itself. To derive an individual affine transformation for this covering process, we first identify a self-similar part. Then, we specify three points on the original—P_1, P_2, P_3—and the three corresponding points on its self-similar part—Pt_1, Pt_2, Pt_3. From their coordinates, we determine the transformation matrix using the above formulas.

We must do this until the whole original is covered. After we determine all transformations in this manner, we use them with equal probabilities to iterate on an arbitrary starting point. (For better probability distributions, see BASL88.) The probabilities with which we use the different transformations should be proportional to the areas of their respective images. After a few iterations, any starting point will reach the original image and once there, the further iterates will randomly jump around within it, eventually reaching every point of it. This reproduces the original image more or less accurately. The better the original is covered by its transformed images and the more precise the individual transformations are, the better the approximation. A slight inaccuracy produces only a small deviation from the precise image because the underlying mathematical process is stable.

Let us look at the fractal in Figure 9.43. There are many ways to cover it with self-similar images. Of course, we are looking for the simplest way.

Figure 9.43   A fractal "scroll"

Figure 9.44 will help us identify self-similar parts. One of these parts is shaded. The unshaded part is also self-similar. We can therefore cover the whole image with just two transformations.

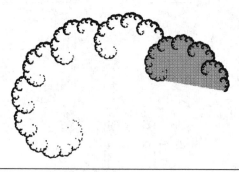

Figure 9.44   Finding self-similar parts in a fractal

We could just as well take the scroll to the left of the shaded one as another self-similar part. The remaining unshaded part would then be smaller by one scroll, but it would still be self-similar. Thus, we could cover the whole image with three transformations instead of two. Applying the three-point method to find the two transformations, we obtain:

$$A_1 = \begin{pmatrix} .693 & .400 & 0 \\ -.400 & .693 & 0 \\ .0 & .0 & 1 \end{pmatrix} \quad \text{and} \quad A_2 = \begin{pmatrix} .346 & -.200 & 0 \\ .200 & .346 & 0 \\ .693 & .400 & 1 \end{pmatrix}$$

All we need to store this fractal are the coefficients of A_1 and A_2. Indeed, this technique is used to "store" pictures that consist mostly of fractal parts. What is stored are only the affine transformations necessary to recreate the picture. This requires much less storage space than a bitmap; compression rates of 1 to 10,000 are commonly achieved. Finding the original fractal image, detecting self-similarities, and so forth are done automatically with image processing techniques.

To show that we can use this technique to create some of our well-known fractals, we will produce the C-curve and the dragon curve. We know from the generating rule that the C-curve consists of two instances of itself, both scaled down by $\frac{1}{2}\sqrt{2}$. If we imagine the whole curve as a horizontal line of length 1 starting at the origin, then its first self similar part is rotated by 45° cw and starts at the origin. Its second self similar part is rotated by 45° ccw and starts at the point (0.5 −0.5). (This describes a downward bent C-curve.) Here, we do not need to use the three-point method to find the transformations, as we already know what they are. Below, we see a code fragment that shows the two transformations and iterates an arbitrary starting point 100,000 times, subjecting it randomly to the first or second transformation. The function `random()` produces the numbers 0 and 1 with equal probability. Figure 9.45 shows the result.

```
for (i = 0; i < 100000; i++)
{
    switch (random())
    {
    case 0:
        x1 = ( x+y)*0.5,
        y  = (-x+y)*0.5,
        x  = x1;
        break;
    case 1:
        x1 = (x-y+1)*0.5,
        y  = (x+y-1)*0.5,
        x  = x1;
        break;
    }

    setpix((int)x,(int)y);
}
```

Figure 9.45   C-curve produced with affine transformations

The self-similarity in the dragon curve is somewhat harder to detect. This curve also consists of two instances of itself, both scaled down by $\frac{1}{2}\sqrt{2}$. If we imagine the whole curve as a horizontal line of length 1 starting at the origin, then its first self-similar part is rotated by 45° cw and starts at the origin. Its second self-similar part is rotated by 135° cw and starts at the point (1 0). Below, we see the code fragment for these two transformations. Figure 9.46 shows the result of 100,000 iterations of a point.

```
for (i = 0; i < 100000; i++)
{
    switch (random())
    {
    case 0:
        x1 = ( x+y)*0.5,
        y  = (-x+y)*0.5,
        x  = x1;
        break;
    case 1:
        x1 = (-x+y)*0.5 + 1,
        y  = (-x-y)*0.5,
        x  = x1;
        break;
    }

    setpix((int)x,(int)y);
}
```

Figure 9.46   Dragon curve produced with affine transformations

The iterated transformation method allows us to produce fractals with short and simple codes. However, the method is applicable only to raster displays. We can make the resulting fractals look more interesting and prettier by setting the pixels in different colors, depending on which transformation is used. See BASL88 for more information.

SUGGESTED READINGS

Presentations of fractal curves can be found in HILL90 and MIEL89; the latter with more detail about the Mandelbrot set. A thorough coverage of fractals in general is PERI86.

EXERCISES

SECTION 9.3

1. Generate a C-curve. In a C-curve, there are eight possible directions in which any line can be drawn. They are cyclic: 0, 1, 2, 3, 4, 5, 6, and 7 (see Figure 9.47). A C-curve in direction 0 consists of two C-curves, one in direction (0+1) mod 8 followed by one in direction (0−1) mod 8 (see Figure 9.48). Verify that this is true for all eight directions. The length of each of these two curves is $\frac{1}{2}\sqrt{2}$ of the original C-curve's length.

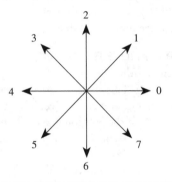

Figure 9.47   The eight possible line directions in a C-curve

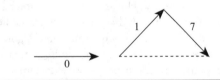

Figure 9.48   C-curve—generating rule

Using these simple rules, write a recursive function for drawing a C-curve. The function needs two arguments—the curve's direction and length. Keep track of the depth of recursion through a global depth counter, and stop further calls when a certain depth is reached, for example, eight. In such a case, just draw a straight line. You need a line-draw primitive that draws a straight line given one of the eight possible directions and the length.

2. In a von Koch curve, there are six possible drawing directions. Use reasoning similar to that in Exercise 1 to write a recursive function that draws a von Koch curve. Demonstrate that it works correctly on all hardware you have at your disposal.

3. Show in an informal way that the von Koch curve does not intersect itself.

4. Generate a dragon curve. Use reasoning similar to that in Exercise 1 to write a function for drawing a dragon curve. Use the generating rule given in the text.

For Exercises 5 through 7, investigate a variation to the von Koch curve, described by the following generating rule. Start with a straight line. Take out the middle and replace it with an isosceles triangle with an angle of 120° at the top so that the resulting four line pieces are equally long (Figure 9.49).

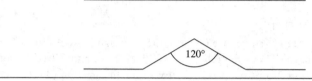

Figure 9.49   von Koch curve variation—generating rule

5. Determine the fractal dimension of the resulting curve with the similarity relation.
6. Show that this curve does not intersect itself.
7. Write a recursive function to draw this curve.

SECTIONS 9.4 AND 9.5

8. Write a member function `ldraw()` for `frect_t` that displays the fractal surface as a line display using "fake" hidden line removal. Take 2 × 2 adjacent points in the surface, make a polygon out of them, project it, and fill it solid with the background color. Then draw the outline of the polygon in a different color. Do not write any new code. Use the functions `solid()` and `draw()` of the class `polygon_t`. Do this for all 2 × 2 groups of points.

   It is essential that you draw the polygons in an occlusion-compatible order. Start with the polygons that are in the farthest row and end with those in the closest row. Hard code the drawing order—do not use algorithms to determine the occlusion-compatible order in a general way. (This is a topic of Chapter 12.)

9. Write a C++ program that draws a smooth fractal line using Catmull-Rom interpolation as explained in Section 9.5—the "smooclou" algorithm.

10. Add a member function `set()` to `frect_t` that allows you to preset points in the grid to influence the surface's shape. Observe the remark in the text about which points can be preset and in which order.

11. Draw a `frect_t` surface with all boundary points preset to 0 and the center preset to 1 and ruggedness 0. Rotate slightly about the x- and y-axis. Observe the resulting cross-shaped ridge in the "basic shape."

12. Generalize the class `simpclou_t` to specify and draw clouds at any location on the screen. You simply have to increase all x- and y-values in the computation by the coordinates of the left upper corner point.

SECTION 9.6

13. Specify a class `complex_t` that represents complex numbers. Overload the operators `*` and `+` to do complex arithmetic with objects of this type. Write a conversion operator that returns the modulus (distance from (0 0)) of a complex number as a double.

14. Using `complex_t`, write a program that computes and displays a Mandelbrot close-up.

15. Add operators – (minus) and / (divide) for complex numbers to the class `complex_t`. With these, we can program the Newton iteration step in Exercise 16.

16. Find three-cycles of $R(z) = z^2+c$ with $c = (-.39054 \ -0.58679)$. *Hint:* you have to find solutions of $(R*R*R)(z) = z$ or the zeros of $(R*R*R)(z) - z = 0$. You can do this using Newton's iteration method:

$$z_{i+1} = z_i - \frac{(R*R*R)(z_i) - z_i}{(R*R*R)'(z_i) - 1}$$

The chain rule of differentiation gives:

$$(R*R*R)'(z) = (R*R*R)(z)*(R'*R)(z)*R'(z) \ \text{ and } \ R'(z) = 2z$$

Use the class and operators written in Exercises 1 and 3 to program the Newton iteration.

SECTION 9.7

17. Reproduce the spiral of Figure 9.50 as closely as possible. You need four different transformations. One scales the whole image by 0.8 and rotates it ccw by 20°. The other three scale it by 0.2 and translate it to the ends of the arms of the first transformed image.

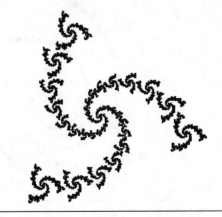

Figure 9.50   Fractal from affine transformations

18. Reproduce the image of Figure 9.51 as closely as possible. You need five different transformations that are analogous to the ones we explained in Exercise 17. Just the scaling factors and the rotation angle are different.

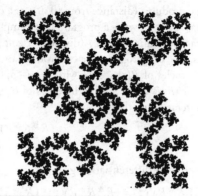

Figure 9.51   Fractal from affine transformations

19. This example uses an image in which the self-similar parts are vastly different in size (see Figure 9.52). Reproduce this image with four different transformations. It is essential that you use different probabilities here.

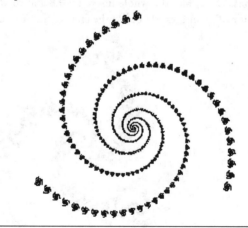

Figure 9.52   Fractal from affine transformations

10

HIDDEN LINES AND SURFACES

DEPTH SORTING METHODS

Chapter 10 is the first of three chapters that develop methods for recognizing the parts of a scene that are behind other objects. Because we cannot see these parts, we should not draw them. The methods of this chapter are practical only when the surfaces of objects are planar polygons.

10.0   **Introduction** shows why removing hidden lines and surfaces is important and how curved surfaces can be represented by planar polygons.

10.1   **Polygon Meshes** considers the data structures that can represent a set of polygons making up the surface of an object.

10.2   **Backface Removal** requires that we identify those faces of an object that point away from the viewer and are therefore not seen. We remove a backface simply by not drawing it. However, this does not handle faces that point to the viewer but are occluded by other faces in the scene.

10.3   **Depth Sorting Methods** are a more general class of methods for removing hidden surfaces. These methods depend on finding which faces lie behind other faces. It is practical to do this only for triangular or quadrangular faces.

10.0   INTRODUCTION

Many three-dimensional objects have surfaces that are planar polygons, for example, cubes, pyramids, prisms, and so on. More complex objects, such as houses, are often built from these. Many machine parts are formed from plates and have no curved surfaces. Even when an object has curved surfaces, it can often be well approximated by simple polyhedra joined together; these simulate the actual surface. For example, the surface of a cylinder can be represented by many long narrow rectangles. When such an approximation is inadequate, the description of the curved surface must be done with a mathematical definition in three variables. Often, though, properly rendering a surface composed of planar polygons can make the surface appear curved, as we will describe in Chapter 13. Rendering objects that are really defined by curved surfaces is much more complicated and is beyond the scope of this chapter.

Throughout this chapter, then, our spatial objects will have plane polygonal surfaces. When we display such an object by drawing only the edges, the result is a *wireframe model.* This is easy to do, hence wireframe models are often used, even when the real object is opaque. However, such a wireframe representation of a solid object may appear ambiguous, because it shows all edges of the object, including those that should not be visible. Figure 10.1 is an example. Most of these ambiguities disappear if the hidden lines are removed. This also makes the object appear to have depth.

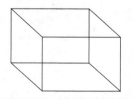

Figure 10.1   Ambiguous wireframe model

It is difficult and requires considerable computation to distinguish between an object's visible and invisible edges. It is easier to remove the hidden parts of surfaces than the hidden parts of lines. The first efforts in this area, however, focused on techniques for removing hidden lines rather than hidden surfaces. The reason for this is that, initially, all displays were vector scan devices that could not display a solidly filled area, something that is easy for today's raster scan displays. When solid objects are displayed using filled areas, the display problem reduces to the easier problem of eliminating hidden surfaces.

Even so, hidden line removal algorithms deserve special attention because the popular line plotters are physically vector devices and have difficulties displaying solid surfaces. Hidden surface algorithms will not work for them.

One of the goals in computer graphics is to generate the images of real-world objects as realistically as possible. Another is to produce images that exist only in our imagination (computer graphic art). A most important application is computer-aided design in which objects are fully specified. In all cases, the shapes that we are to display are usually complex. How shall we describe them?

At the one extreme, completely describing a random 3D shape can require an infinity of number triples to fully define its surface. At the other extreme, a sphere can be described with a single mathematical formula. The same is true for a torus (a shape like an inner tube) as well as for other ideal shapes. A cylinder is a bit more complicated to describe. However, all of these can be approximated with polyhedra to an arbitrarily fine precision. Such approximations are realistic and manageable as long as we see that the number of faces is not too great. Otherwise, they become very awkward.

A method that works well for rendering shapes bounded by curved surfaces is to approximate the shape with a modest number of planar surfaces and then to render it in a way that makes it appear smooth.

There are, then, two types of objects that we internally represent as polyhedra: those that are really bounded by planar polygons, such as pyramids, cubes, prisms, and so forth, and those that are bounded by curved surfaces that we internally approximate with a modest number of polygons and then smooth by rendering. In both cases, we have to know how to store polyhedra internally and how to distinguish between visible and hidden parts. We will also render these objects with simple methods: drawing straight lines and filling polygons with constant colors. This chapter concentrates on these techniques. Shaded and smooth rendering are the topics of another chapter.

This chapter is accompanied by complete C++ code for backface removal, depth sorting, and the painter's algorithm. Backface removal is not an algorithm in itself, but rather a principle to be included in more complicated algorithms. Neither depth sorting nor the painter's algorithm are difficult to program. Hidden line removal is more difficult to program, but is explained in detail.

We concentrate instead on presenting the data structures for the algorithms in this chapter and include pieces of C++ code in critical spots.

Before we discuss the removal of hidden lines and faces, we need to describe how polyhedra can be represented within the computer. A commonly used method to do this is with polygon meshes, which we will introduce here.

10.1   POLYGON MESHES

The *polygon mesh* method is well adapted for describing objects that contain many planar surfaces and straight edges. Buildings fall in this category, as do cubes and boxes. However, the polygon mesh method is not limited to objects with planar surfaces. An object with smooth curved surfaces can be described in this way, at least roughly. The rough polygon mesh can later be rendered in such a way that it looks smoothly curved, although it is actually only a grouping of polygons. (We will discuss this in Chapter 13 when we talk about shading.) For these reasons, polygon meshes play a most important role in the representation of all three-dimensional shapes.

A polygon mesh is not simply a set of unrelated polygons. The polygons that constitute a mesh have the property of *adjacency*. A polygon mesh must reflect this property and record the sequence of vertices or edges that compose the individual polygons (we discussed this in Chapter 2). There are several ways to represent a polygon mesh, each with advantages and disadvantages. Figure 10.2 shows an example of a mesh.

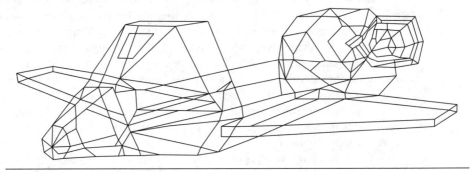

Figure 10.2   *Example of a polygon mesh*

A polygon mesh should permit us to do the following:
1. Identify a specific polygon in the mesh.
2. Identify all the edges belonging to a polygon.
3. Identify those polygons that share a given edge.
4. Identify the vertices (end points) of any edge.
5. Change the mesh.
6. Display the mesh.

Any acceptable mesh representation must provide for the above. However, the quality of the representation depends on the ease of obtaining that information. In addition, the speed and storage space required are important. We limit ourselves to describing one simple but useful type of polygon mesh.

In an *explicit polygons mesh*, each vertex is stored once as a number triple in a vertex table. We then define a polygon as a sequence of such vertices. We do this by defining the polygon as a linked list of pointers into the vertex list. Figure 10.3 illustrates this; Figure 10.4 shows the corresponding data structure.

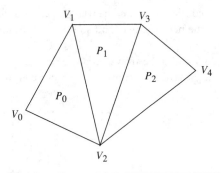

Figure 10.3   Polygon mesh

	V_0	V_1	V_2			X	Y	Z
$P_0 \rightarrow$			0		V_0	1.0	1.0	1.0
	V_1	V_3	V_2		V_1	3.0	3.5	0.5
$P_1 \rightarrow$			0		V_2	3.5	0.5	0.5
	V_2	V_3	V_4		V_3	4.2	3.0	1.5
$P_2 \rightarrow$			0		V_4	4.7	2.0	1.8

Figure 10.4   Data structure

This representation of a mesh takes up the least amount of storage. Changing the mesh is also very easy and efficient. To change one vertex, we change only this number triple in the vertex list. Deleting and adding polygons is also quite easy.

The problem with a vertex table, however, is that to find the polygons sharing a specified edge, we must check all polygons to see whether or not they incorporate this edge. The same is true of finding all polygons that share a given vertex. This is no real handicap for small meshes, but becomes increasingly time-consuming with larger ones. Furthermore, displaying the mesh requires traversing the entire list of polygons and connecting their vertices with straight lines. This displays the mesh correctly, but draws every edge twice. Again, this is not important for small meshes but, for large ones, the factor of two in speed of display can be important. This is particularly true in time critical applications, for example, in the real-time animated displays of flight simulation.

AN IMPLEMENTATION EXAMPLE

A realization of this mesh type is simple when all the polygons are triangles. In this case, one can use a structure of three pointers instead of a linked list to store the pointers. (Instead of pointers, one could also store the subscripts from the vertex table in the structure in the order in which they define the triangle.) More information can be included in the structure, depending on what is useful for the application. Examples are the triangle plane, the perspective-transformed triangle plane, the triangle's color or illumination, whether it is a backface or not, a link to the next triangle, and so forth. All triangles of the mesh are then stored in an array of triangles.

Figure 10.5 shows the array of triangle structures representing the triangle mesh of Figure 10.3. The triangle structure consists of subscripts into the vertex table

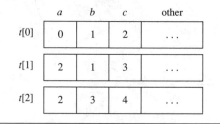

Figure 10.5   Data structure for the triangle mesh of Figure 10.3

The reader who so desires can easily develop structures for polygons with more than four vertices, although there is no advantage in having those. It is better to do a little more work when specifying the polygons of the scene, using only triangles or quadrangles. (Here we mention quadrangles because some special applications, for example Phong shading, perform better with quadrangles.) To see how a polygon can be composed of several triangles, see Figure 10.21 in Section 10.3.3.

10.2   BACKFACE REMOVAL

If a spatial object is composed of polygons, it is easy to identify those surfaces of the object that face away from the viewer. These surfaces are not seen and therefore will not be displayed. The technique to do this is called *backface removal.*

A short review of vectors is in order. (A fuller discussion is in Appendix A.) A vector has direction in space and length. Its starting point is not significant, so two parallel vectors of equal length are identical. This means that we can move a vector freely, as long as it stays parallel to its original direction. We use a number triple $(x\ y\ z)$ to define the vector, assuming that its start point is at the origin. When the vector's start point is the origin, its end point is the point $(x\ y\ z)$. In this sense, a point and a vector from the origin are identical. Distinguishing between these is not necessary for mathematical formalism, but the difference is important for clear understanding. In this book, we will use number triples to define both points and vectors and will call the triple a point or a vector, whichever is appropriate.

If two vectors $(A\ B\ C)$ and $(x\ y\ z)$ are normal to each other in space, then their dot product is 0:

$$(A\ B\ C) \cdot \begin{pmatrix} x \\ y \\ z \end{pmatrix} = 0$$

Therefore, all vectors (points) $(x\ y\ z)$ for which $Ax + By + Cz = 0$ lie on a plane that contains the origin; vector $(A\ B\ C)$ is normal to that plane. We also say that the plane is normal to that vector. This vector is called the *plane normal.* The plane has two sides. We will use the term *positive side* to designate the side that looks in the same direction as the plane normal points.

Let us go one step further. We know that $Ax + By + Cz = 0$ expresses a plane through the origin. Similarly, $Ax + By + Cz = D$, where D is any nonzero number, expresses a plane that does not go through the origin, but is still normal to the vector $(A\ B\ C)$. A, B, C, and D are called the plane coefficients. To know where this plane lies, we need to know only how far it is from the origin. D is indicative of this distance; as D increases, the distance increases. However, D is not this distance. We will find this distance below.

Figure 10.6 shows this concept. The board-like shape indicates the plane. The heavy line is the vector $(A\ B\ C)$, which is normal to the plane. The point where it penetrates the plane is marked by a cross and the dotted part of the vector is behind the plane.

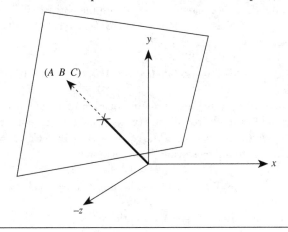

Figure 10.6   Plane in space

We adopt the expression $Ax + By + Cz - D = 0$ with any numbers A, B, C, and D, where $(A\ B\ C)$ do not equal $(0\ 0\ 0)$, as the representation of an arbitrary plane (also called the *plane equation*). If we multiply all plane coefficients by the same factor, the equation will still express the same plane because all points $(x\ y\ z)$ that fulfill the first also fulfull the second. This tells us that there are infinitely many ways to express the same plane. We single out one of those representations—the *normalized plane equation*—and use it most often. In that equation, the plane normal $(A\ B\ C)$ has the length one. We can normalize any plane equation by computing $L = \sqrt{A^2 + B^2 + C^2}$ and then dividing all four coefficients by L. From now on, we will use lowercase a, b, c, and d to indicate a normalized plane equation.

If $ax + by + cz - d = 0$ is the normalized equation of a plane, then its plane normal is $(a\ b\ c)$ and its distance from the origin is d. This is almost enough to locate that plane in space. First, we imagine the vector $(a\ b\ c)$ starting at the origin. Then, we go the distance d along this vector and at that point we imagine a plane normal to $(a\ b\ c)$.

However, there are two planes normal to $(a\ b\ c)$ and at distance $|d|$ from the origin.

Which of those is our plane? If we pay attention to the sign of d, we can find the plane expressed by the above equation; positive d means go along vector $(a\ b\ c)$ from the origin, negative d means go the other way. This is easy to remember, but we urge the reader to be careful with interpreting positive and negative d. Observe that in our plane representation, d carries a minus sign. Therefore, in the plane

$$.2672x + .5345y + .8018z + 1.069 = 0$$

the plane normal is $(.2672\ .5345\ .8018)$ and d is -1.069!

Any point in space $(x\ y\ z)$ inserted into the left-hand side gives one of three possible results:

> 0: the point lies on the positive side
= 0: the point fulfills the equation, it lies in the plane
< 0: the point lies on the negative side

Each plane divides space into two halves. We call the positive side the *positive halfspace* and the negative side the *negative halfspace*.

Given the above plane, is $(3\ 5\ -6)$ on the positive side?

$$.2672*3 + .5345*5 + .8018*(-6) + 1.069 = -0.2677$$

No.

What about $(0\ 0\ 0)$?

$$.2672*0 + .5345*0 + .8018*0 + 1.069 = 1.069$$

Yes.

We often want to determine the equation of a plane from three points in that plane. If $P_1, P_2,$ and P_3 with the coordinates $(x_1\ y_1\ z_1)$, $(x_2\ y_2\ z_2)$, and $(x_3\ y_3\ z_3)$ are three noncollinear points, then the coefficients of the equation $Ax + By + Cz - D = 0$ for the plane through these points can be found by solving the linear system:

$$Ax_i + By_i + Cz_i - D = 0 \quad \text{for } i = 1, 2, 3$$

for the unknowns A, B, C, and D. This linear system is always solvable if the three points are noncollinear.

These determinants give the solution:

$$A = \begin{vmatrix} 1 & y_1 & z_1 \\ 1 & y_2 & z_2 \\ 1 & y_3 & z_3 \end{vmatrix} \quad B = \begin{vmatrix} x_1 & 1 & z_1 \\ x_2 & 1 & z_2 \\ x_3 & 1 & z_3 \end{vmatrix} \quad C = \begin{vmatrix} x_1 & y_1 & 1 \\ x_2 & y_2 & 1 \\ x_3 & y_3 & 1 \end{vmatrix} \quad D = \begin{vmatrix} x_1 & y_1 & z_1 \\ x_2 & y_2 & z_2 \\ x_3 & y_3 & z_3 \end{vmatrix}$$

We can specify the three points as $P_1P_2P_3$, $P_2P_3P_1$, or $P_3P_1P_2$ (these are in the same cyclic order). However, if the points' cyclic order changes, the direction of the normal vector is reversed.

A plane has intercepts on the x, y, and z axes of D/A, D/B, and D/C. Remembering this will help us visualize or sketch the plane.

THE "CORKSCREW" RULE

It is worth remembering this rule when determining the plane equation. When we drive a corkscrew into a cork by turning our right hand clockwise, the screw moves away from us (into the cork). If we specify three points in space in a clockwise sense in a right-handed system and compute the plane equation with the above determinants, the plane normal will point away from us like the corkscrew. If we change rhs to lhs, the plane normal reverses its direction. The same happens if we change clockwise to counterclockwise.

Example: if, in a lhs, we specify three points in a ccw sense while looking onto them from a point Z in space and obtain the plane equation $Ax + By + Cz - D = 0$, then $(A\ B\ C)$ is pointing away from us. This is because we have negated the corkscrew rule twice: rhs to lhs and cw to ccw. Also, Z inserted into the plane equation gives a negative result.

Each surface of a solid object has an inside and an outside. The inside is certainly invisible because it is always occluded by the object's mass. Only the outside can be visible. We will agree to determine the equation of a plane in which a surface lies so that the surface's outside lies in the positive halfspace and the inside in the negative one. To accomplish this, we specify three points in the plane, usually three vertices of the polygon, and we agree that the points will be specified in a clockwise sense as viewed from a point Z in space from which the surface is visible.

This now lets us determine whether a surface is visible from any given point in space. Any point for which the plane equation of that surface yields a positive result lies on the same side of the plane as Z (the positive side), so the surface is visible from such a point. If a point produces a negative result, then it lies on the negative side of that plane, the side that contains the inside of the surface in question. The surface is, therefore, invisible from that point.

The net result of this is that the normal vector to the plane that contains the surface of the object points to the outside.

Figure 10.7 shows a solid prism together with a point Z, first in front view and then in top view. Z is behind and to the left of the prism. The top view is very informative for our purpose. The three side surfaces are indicated by the letters α, β, γ, and the planes in which they lie are shown as straight lines.

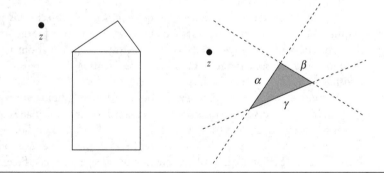

Figure 10.7   Prism in side view and top view

We assume a lhs and position ourselves at Z, from which α is visible (β and γ are invisible). We now specify three vertices on α in a cw sense and determine the plane equation from those. Z lies on the positive side of the plane containing α. From every point on the positive side, α will be visible. The essence of all this is that later on, we can readily find out whether an arbitrary point is on the positive side of this plane. We insert it into the plane equation. If it gives a positive result, then α is visible; otherwise, α is invisible.

To determine the equation for the plane containing β, we will position ourselves so that β is visible, then specify three vertices on β in a cw sense and determine the plane equation from those. We will do the same for γ. Surface γ, for example, is the one we see straight on in the side view of Figure 10.7. We do all this when we specify the object.

Once we have determined all plane equations, we can readily find out whether a surface is visible from any given point. If V is our own position in relation to the front view at the left in Figure 10.7, we would insert V into the plane equations for α, β, and γ, obtain the results <0, <0, and >0 respectively, and then display only surface γ. We ignored the prism's top and bottom surfaces in this example, but would handle them in exactly the same way.

REMOVING BACKFACES

Backface removal can be performed if all polygons describing an object have been entered so that the plane's orientation can be retrieved unambiguously from the polygon information. Polygons are sometimes defined by their vertices, sometimes by their edges. In both cases, we have to specify them in a cw sense when we view them from outside the object. In some data structures, the plane equation's coefficients for each polygon are calculated once and stored. In others, they are calculated upon demand. If the polygon has more than three vertices, we base the calculation on the first three and ignore the rest. (If the polygon is defined by edges, then the first two edges will determine the first three vertices.) When an object is transformed in space, the plane coefficients must be either recalculated from the transformed vertices or transformed themselves.

We must be careful when concave polygons are involved. Fortunately, they need not occur as bounding planes of solid objects, because we can always avoid them when specifying any solid object. When a concave polygon is traversed in a cw manner, not every sequence of three consecutive vertices is cw. In such a case, we should renumber the vertices so that the first three vertices determine a cw sense.

The backface test differs, depending on whether the projection is perspective or orthographic. We assume a left-handed system and a cw specification for the vertices. With perspective projection, the point we are checking against all plane equations is the center of projection; its coordinates are inserted into each plane equation. If the result is positive, the surface is visible; otherwise, it is invisible.

In contrast, when backface removal is done with orthographic projection, the test is much simpler. It is not necessary to insert the viewer's position into the plane equations. The normal vector of a plane equation is $(A \ B \ C)$. This vector will point toward the viewer if its z-component is negative, because in a lhs, the viewer looks in the direction of positive z-coordinates. Hence, a face is a frontface if its plane equation has a negative C coefficient. We need only look at the sign of C, but to allow for round-off, we should deem a face invisible if $C > \varepsilon$ with a small negative ε. In fact, it would be sufficient to compute only the C from the above four determinants. However, it is better to provide for computing all four coefficients in any program because one can then easily change to the perspective backface test.

Figure 10.8 shows an object for which we perform backface removal. A left-handed system is assumed, and the plane normals are shown. The results differ, depending on the projection. With orthographic projection, surfaces a, b, and c are visible because their plane normals have a negative z-component. With perspective projection, only surface b is visible because the center lies on the negative sides of a, c, and d.

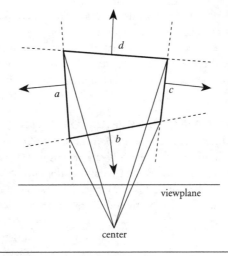

Figure 10.8 *Perspective and orthographic projection*

DISPLAYING A SINGLE CONVEX OBJECT

The backface test can be used to remove hidden surfaces or hidden lines when a single convex object is displayed, no matter whether the object is to be displayed by solid filled areas or just by its edges (wireframe with hidden lines removed). On such objects, no frontfaces can be hidden; they are all visible. Therefore, backface removal is all that needs to be done. If we are to remove hidden lines, the technique is simple. We define the object as a collection of polygons and determine the backfaces. We then draw only the edges of the frontfaces.

Figure 10.9 shows an octahedron with numbers indicating the vertices. Edges drawn twice appear as heavy lines, edges drawn once appear as normal lines, and edges drawn no times appear as dotted lines. From the viewer's standpoint, four surfaces are visible and four are not. This causes the edges 21, 23, 25, and 26 to be drawn twice. All other edges are drawn one or no times.

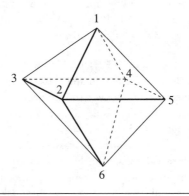

Figure 10.9 *Octahedron drawn by outlines*

The object's outlines are drawn exactly once because they are the edges of only one visible polygon. If the plane of a polygon is precisely edge-on (with orthogonal projection, coefficient C of the plane equation equals 0; with perspective projection, the plane equation yields 0 for the projection center), it is just a straight line and it is immaterial whether this line is drawn or not. There will always be another edge of a visible polygon that coincides with this line.

CONCAVE OBJECTS, SEVERAL OBJECTS

If an object is concave, some parts of the object can partly or completely hide the object's frontfaces. Similarly, if several objects are displayed, even if all are convex, one object can occlude parts of another. Backface removal does not solve the problem, because it displays all frontfaces regardless of occlusion. Figure 10.10 shows a concave object in which face *a*, which would normally show, is partly hidden by other faces.

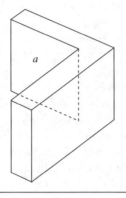

Figure 10.10   Concave object

Even though it does not solve this type of problem, backface removal is useful as a preprocessor for general hidden surface or hidden line removal techniques because it typically cuts in half the number of polygons that the more general and complex algorithms will consider. The backface test is performed in the implementation of the member functions `tmesh_t::draw()` and `tmesh_t::solid()`. If the tmesh describes a convex object, the functions `draw()` and `solid()` will display it correctly.

OO DESIGN AND CLASS SPECIFICATIONS

Below, we develop the design and class specifications for a triangle mesh. Using this design, we can specify every convex solid object bounded by planes. The object can be constructed from an input file, displayed as a wireframe or solid with hidden surfaces removed, and rotated or translated in space.

First, we introduce two supplier classes—the plane and the triangle. The first is `plane_t`, which describes a plane equation by its four coefficients. It can be constructed from four doubles or from three points in space using the type `point3_t` introduced in Chapter 5. This class has several member functions that make its use convenient, some of which are described in the next chapter. A plane can rotate, translate, or normalize itself.

```
//************************** File plane.h **************************

#ifndef PLANE_T
#define PLANE_T

#include "../Shape3d/point3.h"


class plane_t
{
public:
   plane_t() ;
   plane_t(const plane_t&) ;
   plane_t(double,double,double,double) ;
   plane_t(const point3_t&,double) ;
   plane_t(const point3_t&,const point3_t&,const point3_t&) ;

   double giva() const { return a; }
   double givb() const { return b; }
   double givc() const { return c; }
   double givd() const { return d; }
   point3_t givnorm() const { return point3_t(a,b,c); }
   int frontface(const point3_t& p) const ; //true if frontface for p
   void rotx(double) ;
   void roty(double) ;
   void rotz(double) ;
   void translate(const point3_t&) ;

protected:
   double a , b , c , d;          // coefficients of the plane equation
} ;

#endif

//************************************************************************
```

The next class is `triangle_t`. It has a pointer (`vertex`) to the beginning of the vertex table of the triangle mesh. This pointer is of type `vertex3_t**` because the vertex table is an array of pointers to `vertex3_t`. Another member is a pointer (`v`) to an array of three integers that point into the vertex table. This arrangement provides more flexibility than making the array itself a data member. It will be easy to derive a quadrangle and maybe other shapes from triangle. Another member is the plane (`p`) spanned by the three vertices. Two more members are an *rgb*-value (`rgb`), used in a true-color environment, and an integer (`lutloc`), used when a lookup table is necessary.

A triangle is not a polygon because it does not have vertices. If we used `convex_t` for a triangle, all vertices of the mesh would be stored multiple times and transformations would be very time-consuming. Member functions are the interface functions for obtaining the triangle's members and some virtual functions, explained after the class specification.

```
//********************** File triangle.h **************************

#ifndef TRIANGLE_T
#define TRIANGLE_T

#include "../Shape2d/scene.h"
#include "../Shape3d/plane.h"
#include "../Shape3d/vertex3.h"
#include "../Shape3d/rgb.h"
#include "../Shape3d/light.h"


class triangle_t
{
public:
  ~triangle_t() ;
   triangle_t() ;

   vertex3_t& giva() { return *vertex[v[0]]; }
   vertex3_t& givb() { return *vertex[v[1]]; }
   vertex3_t& givc() { return *vertex[v[2]]; }
   int*       givv() { return v; }
   plane_t&   givp() { return p; }
   rgb_t      givrgb() { return rgb; }
   int        givlutloc() { return lutloc; }
   void setvertex(vertex3_t** ver) { vertex = ver; }

   virtual void draw(const scene_t*) const ;
   virtual void solid(const scene_t*) const ;
   virtual void setcolor(light_t*,const rgb_t&,int&) ;
   virtual void read(ifstream&,vertex3_t**) ;
   virtual void operator = (const triangle_t&) ;

protected:
   int* v ;                     // subscripts into vertex table of mesh
   plane_t p ;
   rgb_t rgb ;                                   // triangle's rgb color
   int lutloc ;                      // used for lookup table reference
   vertex3_t** vertex ;
};

#endif

//****************************************************************
```

The function setcolor() computes the triangle's color from a light source and the tmesh's *rgb*-value, using the triangle's plane equation. It stores the computed color in the member rgb. In a lookup table environment, it enters the computed *rgb*-value into the lookup table at the location given by the third parameter. This parameter is increased by 1 before the entry is made and is then stored in the member lutloc. The scene whose tmeshes are to be drawn maintains this parameter globally. In a lookup table environment, a scene can be drawn correctly only if the number of all of its tmeshes' frontfaces does not exceed the size of the lookup table. If there are more frontfaces than possible lookup table entries, the program will exit with an error message.

The functions draw() and solid() simply construct a convex_t with the triangle's vertices and then call the draw() and solid() of the convex_t. In a true-color environment, the foreground color is set to the triangle's *rgb*-value before the triangle is filled solid. In a lookup table environment, the drawing color is set to the number stored in lutloc.

The member function read() reads three numbers from an input stream and stores them in the subscript array v. It also sets the pointer, vertex, to the vertex list. The overloaded operator = is necessary because triangle_t is a "deep" structure.

The next class describes a triangle mesh, tmesh_t, which is derived from prim_t. It contains the number of vertices (vernum), the number of triangles (facnum), a pointer (facet) to an array of triangles, and a pointer (vertex) to an array of vertex3_t pointers. This provides more flexibility than an array of vertices. Such flexibility is an advantage, as we explain below. It also has a member cen, which holds its centroid, and a member rgb, which holds its *rgb*-value.

The class tmesh_t needs a destructor to free allocated memory. It has a default constructor which initializes all its data to zero and a copy constructor which constructs a tmesh_t through a deep copy, during which the individual vertices are copied by calling the vertices' virtual copy function. Like all classes derived from prim_t, tmesh_t has a copy function (not to be confused with the copy constructor). It has interface functions to access its protected members. Other member functions are described below.

```
//************************** File tmesh.h **************************

#ifndef TMESH_T
#define TMESH_T

#include "../Shape3d/plane.h"
#include "../Shape3d/triangle.h"
#include "../Shape2d/prim.h"
#include "../Shape3d/win_vie3.h"
#include "../Shape3d/rgb.h"
#include "../Shape3d/scene3.h"


class tmesh_t : public prim_t                              // triangle mesh
{
public:
  ~tmesh_t() ;
  tmesh_t() ;
  tmesh_t(const tmesh_t&) ;

  prim_t& read(char*) ;
  virtual vertex3_t* alloc_vertex() const ;
  virtual triangle_t* alloc_facets() const ;
```

```
    prim_t* copy() const ;
    void setcolors(const scene_t*,int&) const ;
    void draw(const scene_t*) const ;
    void solid(const scene_t*) const ;
    prim_t& rotx(double) ;
    prim_t& roty(double) ;
    prim_t& rotz(double) ;
    prim_t& translate(const point_t&) ;
    prim_t& viewtrans(const point_t&,const point_t&,const point_t&) ;

    vertex3_t** givvertex() const { return vertex; }
    triangle_t* givfacet() const { return facet; }
    int givvernum() const { return vernum; }
    int givfacnum() const { return facnum; }
    rgb_t givrgb() const { return rgb; }

protected:
    vertex3_t** vertex ;                           // vertex table
    triangle_t* facet ;                            // triangle table
    int vernum ;                                   // # of vertices
    int facnum ;                                   // # of facets
    rgb_t rgb ;                                     // diffuse reflectivity
    point3_t cen ;                                 // centroid
} ;

#endif

//***********************************************************************
```

The member function read() reads the whole tmesh from a file. It reads from that file its *rgb*-value and number of vertices, and then allocates memory for the vertices through calls to the virtual member function alloc_vertex(). This function allocates a vertex3_t. Further reading from the file provides all coordinates for the vertices.

The next number read from the file is the number of facets (triangles in this case). A call to the virtual member function alloc_facets() allocates an array of triangle_t. The subscripts for the triangles are read by calling the facet's own virtual member function read(). Because this facet is a triangle_t, each call reads three numbers from the file and also sets the triangle's vertex pointer to the vertex pointer of the tmesh.

Why we do it this way? Using a vertex list and a list of facets makes it easier to derive other types of meshes from tmesh_t, whether with different vertices (such as zvertices for the Z-buffer algorithm, pvertices for Phong filling, etc.) or with different types of facets (such as dstriangles for depth sorting, quadrangles for Phong shading, etc.).[†]

[†] An elegant and straightforward solution is a template class mesh_t<class V, class F> where V is the type of vertex and F the type of facet, supplied during instantiation. Unfortunately, both platforms on which the author was working had linker problems with instantiations other than vertex3_t and triangle_t. The author has therefore decided to use a platform-independent solution that uses derived meshes and virtual functions. The simplification of the code to a template class is left for an exercise.

The function `tmesh_t::setcolors()` walks through all facets and tests them for frontface. If frontface is true, the facet's `setcolor()` is called. This call supplies a pointer to the scene to which the tmesh belongs, giving access to the list of light sources, its own *rgb*-value, and the global integer maintained by the scene for the entry location in the lookup table.

The functions `tmesh_t::draw()` and `solid()` are equally simple. They both walk through all facets, test them for frontface, and call this facet's `draw()` or `solid()` if frontface is true. The facet's `draw()` and `solid()` functions are given the pointer to the scene as a parameter. As explained above, they simply construct a `convex_t` from the vertices and call that object's `draw()` or `solid()`. For this call, they need the pointer to the scene.

Five transformations are provided: rotation about the *x*-, *y*-, and *z*-axes, translation, and view-transformation. The simplest is the translation, so we explain it first. Its parameter is of type `point_t&`, but refers in reality to a `point3_t`, and therefore must first be upgraded to a `point3_t`. The tmesh then translates all its vertices, the centroid, and all the facet's planes by this `point3_t`.

The tmesh rotates itself around its centroid by translating itself to (0 0 0), rotating all its vertices and planes, and then translating itself back to the position of the original centroid.

The view transformation computes the transformation matrix and then multiplies all its vertices, the centroid, and all planes with this matrix.

Below, we show an example of an input file for a `tmesh_t`. We have appended comments, although these are not part of the input file.

```
 0 1 0                          // rgb-value green
 5                              //  5 vertices
   0    1    0                  // vertex values
  -1    0   -1
   1    0   -1
   1    0    1
  -1    0    1
 6                              // 6 triangles
 0    2    1                    // pointers into vertex table
 0    3    2                    // these are subscripts here
 0    4    3
 0    1    4
 1    2    4
 3    4    2
```

Tmeshes are 3D objects. To display them correctly, not only with respect to the removal of hidden surfaces but also with proper illumination, we must consider the position of a given light source. For this purpose, we define a class `scene3_t` that specifies a three-dimensional scene. It is derived from `scene_t` (the 2D scene), from which it inherits the operator `+=` that adds an object to the scene, and the reference to a window-viewport system. An additional member is now a pointer to a linked list of `light_t` objects. The `win_view_t` reference member should now refer to a `win_vie3_t` (a 3D window-viewport system) and the `light_t` pointer should point to a list of at least two `light_t` objects. The first one is interpreted as ambient light, the second one as point light.

```
//************************* File scene3.h *************************

#ifndef SCENE3_T
#define SCENE3_T

#include "../Shape3d/light.h"
#include "../Shape2d/scene.h"
#include "../Shape3d/win_vie3.h"


class scene3_t : public scene_t
{
public:
    scene3_t(const win_view3_t& wv,light_t* l) :
        scene_t(wv) , light(l) {}

    light_t* givlight() { return light; }
    void solid() const ;
    scene3_t& rotx(double) ;
    scene3_t& roty(double) ;
    scene3_t& rotz(double) ;
    scene3_t& translate(const point3_t&) ;
    scene3_t& viewtrans(
        const point3_t&,const point3_t&,const point3_t&) ;

protected:
    light_t* light ;
} ;

#endif

//*****************************************************************
```

10.3 DEPTH SORTING METHODS

The methods described in this section are more powerful than those described before because they are not restricted to single convex objects. We still deal only with scenes whose objects are all defined by planar polygonal surfaces, but there may be multiple objects that can be concave as well as convex. This covers the majority of cases. We impose two restrictions, however. The scenes cannot have surfaces that mutually penetrate or mutually occlude each other or themselves.

The polygons that make up the scene are stored in some data structure. Without excluding generality, we make two assumptions:

1. The objects are given as one or more polygon meshes.
2. All polygons are triangles or convex quadrangles.

The second assumption is a necessity for the depth sorting algorithm below. In fact, we will present it only for triangles; the extension to convex quadrangles is easy. A general algorithm for convex or concave polygons would be much more complicated. On the other hand, this assumption is not a restriction because we can specify every polygon as several triangles, as in Figure 10.21. When these are filled with the same color, they merge into one polygon and the boundaries of the individual triangles become invisible. We still need to allow for quadrangles because certain algorithms work better with quadrangles.

When the scene is to be displayed as a line drawing with hidden lines removed, we initially define all faces as triangles and associate each triangle vertex with either a "move" or "draw" command. This will assure that the lines that subdivide the polygons will not be drawn. The "move" and "draw" commands are explained in Section 10.3.3.

To draw the scene with hidden surfaces or lines removed, we do a perspective transformation (not projection!) on all polygon vertices. This puts the objects to be displayed into the desired position for depth sorting.

With the polygons in position, we do a backface test on each polygon in turn. We can do the test with either the transformed polygons, using the condition for orthographic projection, or with the original vertices, using the condition for perspective projection. If the polygon is a backface, we do not consider it further.

The next step is to put the frontface polygons into order, based on their depth behind the view plane. After depth sorting, we can continue in two different ways. First, if we are to draw the scene as solid objects, we must remove occluded parts of the polygons. In this case, we can draw all polygons starting with the farthest first; when we draw another polygon on top, it is automatically hidden. This method is called the *painter's algorithm.*

Second, if we are to draw only the object's edges, creating a scene consisting entirely of lines, we must remove hidden lines. This is more complex because a line can be completely hidden by some polygon, cut so that only one portion remains, or cut so that two portions remain. On the other hand, in this case it is possible to define the whole scene initially with only triangles. We will say more about this later.

We will now explain algorithms for each of these steps in the order in which they are applied: depth sorting, painter's algorithm, and hidden line removal.

10.3.1 DEPTH SORTING

We explain this algorithm only for triangles and later extend it to quadrangles in a simple way. To find which triangles in the scene can occlude others we put them in an *occlusion-compatible order.* This term means to arrange items sequentially such that one member can hide the following members. Doing so is not a trivial matter. In the case of a mutual occlusion or penetration of triangles, as in Figures 10.11 and 10.12, such an order does not even exist. To handle such cases requires decomposing the triangles into still smaller ones. We have assumed, however, that this does not occur.

If we exclude these cases, we can derive the occlusion-compatible order by comparing the triangles in pairs. In this comparison, we want to find a point in one triangle and a point in the other whose x- and y-coordinates are equal, but whose z-coordinates differ. The depth order will then depend on the z-coordinates. Only when the two triangles overlap do we need to compare their z-coordinates, so we look at this topic now.

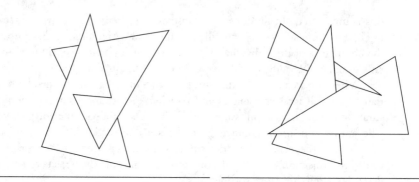

Figure 10.11 Two triangles penetrating each other *Figure 10.12 Three cyclic overlapping triangles*

TESTING FOR OVERLAPPING TRIANGLES

The triangles we use in depth sorting are those we obtained from the original ones by doing a perspective transformation with each vertex. We simply create perspective-transformed versions of the triangles and work with those. We call these *depth-sorting records* or simply *records*. We compute each record's plane equation. Only the *x*- and *y*-coordinates are used for overlap tests and the plane equations for depth comparisons. Each record represents a 2D triangle and the overlap tests thus work with 2D triangles. From now on, "triangle" refers to a 2D triangle.

The first test we perform is a minimax test for two triangles. This test can tell in some cases that two triangles do not overlap. For each triangle, we compute the smallest containing rectangles and check these for overlapping. (The overlapping check for rectangles is so obvious that we need not explain it.) If the rectangles do not overlap, neither do the triangles. If they do, we need to examine them more closely (see Figure 10.13).

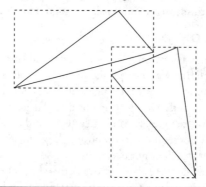

Figure 10.13 The smallest containing rectangles overlap

We apply increasingly more expensive tests to narrow down the cases that remain after minimax. To verify that two triangles (T_1 and T_2) do overlap, we check each edge of T_1 against each edge of T_2 for intersections. (Remember, we are working with projections now.) As soon as we find an intersection, we can stop testing; they overlap. We should keep in mind, however, that two triangles can overlap even if none of their edges intersect; this can occur when one triangle is completely contained in another, which will be our last test.

If we know the end points of two line segments, the first going from $(x_1 \ y_1)$ to $(x_2 \ y_2)$ and the second from $(x_3 \ y_3)$ to $(x_4 \ y_4)$, we can test them for intersection by first performing a minimax test:

$$\max(x_1,x_2) < \min(x_3,x_4)$$
$$\max(x_3,x_4) < \min(x_1,x_2)$$
$$\max(y_1,y_2) < \min(y_3,y_4)$$
$$\max(y_3,y_4) < \min(y_1,y_2)$$

If any of these conditions is true, the lines do not intersect. This minimax test is less expensive than the intersection test below.

If none of the above conditions is true, then we must continue as follows. First, we check to see if the lines are parallel. This is true if they have the same slopes. If the slopes are equal, then $D = 0$ in:

$$D = (x_3 - x_4)(y_1 - y_2) - (x_1 - x_2)(y_3 - y_4)$$

If $D = 0$, there is no intersection. (It is best to check $|D| < \varepsilon$, with ε depending on the machine arithmetic to allow for numerical imprecision.)

If $|D| > \varepsilon$, we proceed with a second test. Compute:

$$s = \left[(x_3 - x_4)(y_1 - y_3) - (x_1 - x_3)(y_3 - y_4)\right] / D$$
$$t = \left[(x_1 - x_2)(y_1 - y_3) - (x_1 - x_3)(y_1 - y_2)\right] / D$$

If $0 < (s,t) < 1$, then the lines intersect at point $(x \ y)$ between their end points. The coordinates of the intersection point $(x \ y)$ are:

$$x = x_1 + s(x_2 - x_1)$$
$$y = y_1 + s(y_2 - y_1)$$

(We do not usually need the coordinates of the intersection; it is enough to know that they do intersect.) When one line just touches the other at its end point, this test does not consider that to be an intersection. This means that a triangle touching another on its perimeter will not be treated as an overlap. We must test each edge of T_1 against each edge of T_2, a total of nine tests for nine pairs of edges.

If all nine tests of the two triangles' edge pairs do not show an intersection, then there are two possible cases—either one triangle is contained in the other or they do not overlap (see Figure 10.14).

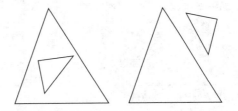

Figure 10.14   No intersection between triangle edges

After the above minimax and edge-intersection tests, our last test looks for one triangle's containment within another. Before we do a general triangle-inside test, we can use minimax again with the center of one of the triangles against the other's containing rectangle. Let $(x_1\ y_1)$, $(x_2\ y_2)$, and $(x_3\ y_3)$ be the vertices of a triangle (ignore the z-coordinates because we are working with projections). Its center is:

$$x_c = (x_1 + x_2 + x_3)/3$$
$$y_c = (y_1 + y_2 + y_3)/3$$

The minimax test is straightforward. The general containment test is described below. Based on these final tests, we have either "inside" or "outside" (see Figure 10.14).

THE TRIANGLE-INSIDE TEST

To develop the triangle-inside test, we first look at the formula for a line through two points. Remember, triangle here means a triangle's projection onto the plane $z = 0$. The expression:

$$f(x,y) = (x - x_1)(y_2 - y_1) - (x_2 - x_1)(y - y_1)$$

determines a straight line through the points $(x_1\ y_1)$ and $(x_2\ y_2)$ in the following way:
   $f(x,y) = 0$ for $(x\ y)$ on the line
   $f(x,y) < 0$ for $(x\ y)$ on one side of the line
   $f(x,y) > 0$ for $(x\ y)$ on the other side of the line

Two arbitrary points lie on the same side of the line if the expression yields the same sign for both.

We can use this property for the triangle-inside test. A point can be inside a triangle only if it lies on the same side as the vertex that is opposite the line. We must check against all three sides (see Figure 10.15).

The point p_1 lies on the same side as A with respect to the side BC and the analog is true for the other two sides. The point p_2 does not lie on the same side as C with respect to the side AB, so it is outside the triangle.

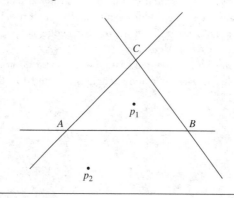

Figure 10.15   Points inside and outside a triangle

We first test whether the first triangle's center is inside the second. If this is not true, we still must test whether the second triangle's center is inside the first. If this also is not true, there is no overlap.

There are some rare cases of possible overlap that we can miss with the above tests, but we can ignore them because they hardly ever occur when working with floating point numbers. On the other hand, their inclusion would add an enormous amount of complicated code.

DEPTH COMPARISON

Because of all these tests, we now know if each pair of triangles overlaps. If they do not, their relative depths are insignificant. If they do overlap, we have to decide which triangle is in front. Again, there are simple tests that give us results in many cases and more complicated tests that we must apply if the simpler ones fail.

A simple testing method is the minimax test, this time applied to the z-coordinates. If all z-coordinates of one triangle are smaller than all z-coordinates of the other, we know which triangle is in front.

Figure 10.16 shows two triangles, A and B, with overlapping projections, viewed from a point high up on the y-axis. The positive z-axis extends upward and the $(x\ y)$-plane looks like a horizontal line. The user's actual view is through the $(x\ y)$-plane from a point below the figure. Keep in mind that the triangles shown in the figure are already perspective-transformed images so that we need only project them orthographically onto the $(x\ y)$-plane to put their projections onto the screen.

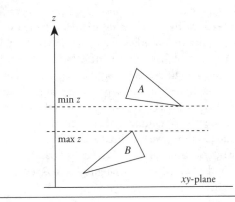

Figure 10.16   Example for the z-minimax test

In Figure 10.16, A's minimum z-coordinate is greater than B's maximum z-coordinate. Triangle B therefore partly or totally occludes triangle A. This z-minimax test is easy to perform. For overlapping triangles A and B, we test:

$$\min(z\text{-coord of } A) > \max(z\text{-coord of } B) \ \rightarrow \ A \text{ behind } B$$
$$\min(z\text{-coord of } B) > \max(z\text{-coord of } A) \ \rightarrow \ B \text{ behind } A$$

However, the depth question is not always so easily solved. Figure 10.17 shows a possible case. None of the z-minimax conditions is true. In this case, we must find a point within the projection of each triangle with the same $(x\ y)$-values and then compute the z-coordinates of the two points. The relation between these z-coordinates determines the depth relation between A and B. This depth relation may not apply between the entire triangles, but it is certainly true for their overlapping parts, which is all that concerns us.

The vertical line through q and p in Figure 10.17 indicates the points whose relationship concerns us. In this case, they lie on the intersection of two triangle edges in the $(x\ y)$-plane. Point p on triangle A corresponds to these $(x\ y)$-coordinates, as does point q on B. Because q has the smaller z-coordinate, we conclude that A is behind B. Finding points p and q is discussed later.

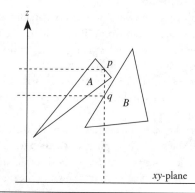

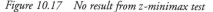

Figure 10.17   No result from z-minimax test

If the z-minimax test is inconclusive, we proceed to find points with the same $(x\ y)$-coordinates on each of the overlapping triangles. Remember that we already know that the triangles overlap. Since they overlap, there is always such a point and we already have information about it. Further, we have already determined that either one projected edge intersects another or that one triangle is completely contained in the other. If we have performed an edge intersection test, we know the values of s and t at an intersection point; if we have done a containment test, we know a center point. Each of these points lies in both of the participating triangles. When there is containment, we just check the two z-values at the center point. When we have edge intersections, we continue as follows.

When the intersection point is on an edge of triangles A and B, let $(P_1\ P_2)$ and $(P_3\ P_4)$ be the end points of the two edges for triangles A and B respectively. Using the known values of s and t, we compute:

$$z_A = z_1 + s(z_2 - z_1) \quad \text{and} \quad z_B = z_3 + t(z_4 - z_3)$$

z_A and z_B are the relative depths of the two triangles at the common point. If $z_A < z_B$, then A occludes B; if $z_A > z_B$, then B occludes A.

What if $z_A = z_B$? Then we cannot yet decide and must do further testing. We look for additional edge intersections. It is not necessary to find a second intersection on one of the current edges. It is enough to find just any other place where the edges of these two triangles intersect. Because the triangles are never coplanar (see below), we can always find a common point with differing z-coordinates.

The above equality $z_A = z_B$ must be interpreted with consideration for round-off errors. Exact equality will probably never occur, so we use the test $|z_A - z_B| < \varepsilon$, with a small value for ε. If we do not do this, two triangles might touch or be very close to each other at that one point in space, but otherwise be far apart in depth. Numerical imprecision in the computer arithmetic can give us $z_A < z_B$ when it actually should be $z_A \geq z_B$. If we base the decision on the first, we occlude one triangle by the other in the wrong way. The value we choose for ε depends on the hardware.

It is clear that two overlapping triangles are never exactly coplanar, but what if they test as coplanar for the given machine precision? In this case they would really be almost coplanar and the objects to which they belong would practically touch in space. Real-world objects are solid, so the objects' interiors are on opposite sides of the planes in question. Hence, one of the planes is a backface and has already been eliminated from consideration. In other words, two overlapping triangles can never test as coplanar!

It will help to summarize this rather involved set of tests. If the z-minimax test fails, we test triangle edges for intersections. If an intersection results in two numerically equal z-values, we look for a second intersection. If the difference in these z-values exceeds ε, we decide which triangle is in front. Otherwise, we look for a third intersection. Now, there are two possibilities.

First, a third edge intersection exists. Here, the z-values must be unequal by more than ε, and we can decide which triangle is in front. (We know from the above that the triangles are not coplanar.)

Second, a third intersection does not exist. This is the case when just the tip of one triangle reaches into the other.

In this case (see Figure 10.18), we must find which of the triangle's vertices lies inside the other. Sometimes there is only one solution, sometimes there are two. Therefore, we do a point-triangle minimax test, followed if necessary by a triangle-inside test for all combinations of vertices and triangles until we find this vertex. At that point, p, we compute the z-coordinate of the plane in which the other triangle lies. (Actually, there is a subcase for two edge intersections where we do not find a vertex inside the other triangle. This is when the vertex just touches a side of the other triangle. You will be asked to explore this situation in an exercise.)

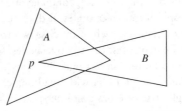

Figure 10.18   Only two edge intersections

Let A be the triangle whose projection contains the point $p = (p_x \ p_y)$ in Figure 10.18 and let $(x_1 \ y_1 \ z_1)$, $(x_2 \ y_2 \ z_2)$, and $(x_3 \ y_3 \ z_3)$ be its vertices. Let B be the other triangle. The depth of the point $(p_x \ p_y)$ in the plane of triangle A is:

$$z_A = -\frac{a}{c(p_x - x_1)} - \frac{b}{c(p_y - y_1)} + z_1$$

with

$$a = (y_2 - y_3)(z_1 - z_3) - (z_2 - z_3)(y_1 - y_3)$$
$$b = (z_2 - z_3)(x_1 - x_3) - (x_2 - x_3)(z_1 - z_3)$$
$$c = (x_2 - x_3)(y_1 - y_3) - (y_2 - y_3)(x_1 - x_3)$$

The point $(p_x \ p_y \ p_z)$ lies in the plane of triangle B, so we have $z_B = p_z$. If $z_A < z_B$, then A occludes B. If $z_A > z_B$, then B occludes A.

ESTABLISHING DEPTH ORDER

We are now able to determine whether each pair of triangles (records) overlaps and, if so, which is nearer to us. To express this *depth order*, we create a linked list for each triangle containing pointers to those triangles that are in front of it. All our triangles are stored in an array. Therefore, the list will essentially be a linked list of integers. We also create a counter for each triangle that records how many triangles are behind it. Figure 10.19 presents an example with the lists for the six triangles:

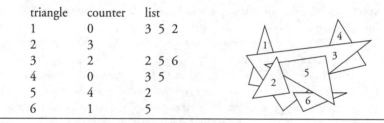

triangle	counter	list
1	0	3 5 2
2	3	
3	2	2 5 6
4	0	3 5
5	4	2
6	1	5

Figure 10.19   Depth-sorted triangles with counters and lists

ESTABLISHING DEPTH ORDER FOR QUADRANGLES

We will implement Phong shading with convex quadrangles. It is not too difficult to depth sort those or a mixture of quadrangles and triangles. Both quadrangles to be tested can each be easily split into two triangles. It does not matter where we put the splitting diagonal line. Then we overlap-test each of the first two triangles against each of the other two. If any overlap exists, we depth-test these two triangles, sort the quadrangles into order according to the result, and do no further testing.

We establish a depth order with quadrangles in precisely the same way as with triangles, each quadrangle structure has a pointer that points to the quadrangles in front of it and a counter counting how many are behind it.

10.3.2 HIDDEN SURFACE REMOVAL (PAINTER'S ALGORITHM)

Polygon in this section means either triangle or quadrangle. At this point, we have removed backfaces and sorted the remaining polygons into occlusion-compatible order. We have set up the data structure we just described and are ready to display the polygons as solid surfaces or as their boundary lines. For the former, we will use the painter's algorithm. Displaying just the boundary lines requires hidden line removal, as we explain in the next section.

In comparison to the work we have already done, the painter's algorithm is no big deal. We go through the array and draw all those polygons that have a behind-counter of 0. These are the ones with no other polygons under them. Whenever we draw such a polygon, we step through the polygons in its frontlist and decrease their behind-counters by 1. (The number of polygons behind them is reduced by the one we draw.) We mark the polygon drawn by setting its behind-counter to −1 in order not to draw it again. Through these operations, new 0's will appear. We continue this process until no polygons are left.

The sequence in Figure 10.20 shows the individual steps of the painter's algorithm using triangles. The original data is that of Figure 10.19. Changes occur in the counters and the picture. The frontlists are shown for reference; marked triangles are expressed by −1.

— Data before the step —			— after —	
triangle	frontlist	behind	picture	behind
1 draw	3 5 2	0		−1
2		3		2
3	2 5 6	2		1
4	3 5	0		0
5	2	4		3
6	5	1		1
1	3 5 2	−1		−1
2		2		2
3	2 5 6	1		0
4 draw	3 5	0		−1
5	2	3		2
6	5	1		1
1	3 5 2	−1		−1
2		2		1
3 draw	2 5 6	0		−1
4	3 5	−1		−1
5	2	2		1
6	5	1		0
1	3 5 2	−1		−1
2		1		1
3	2 5 6	−1		−1
4	3 5	−1		−1
5	2	1		0
6 draw	5	0		−1

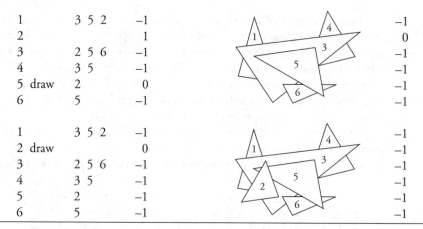

1		3 5 2	−1		−1
2			1		0
3		2 5 6	−1		−1
4		3 5	−1		−1
5	draw	2	0		−1
6		5	−1		−1

1		3 5 2	−1		−1
2	draw		0		−1
3		2 5 6	−1		−1
4		3 5	−1		−1
5		2	−1		−1
6		5	−1		−1

Figure 10.20   Process of painter's algorithm

The painter's algorithm works only on raster devices and then only if we draw solid objects with filling polygons. The essential principle that makes it work is that an area, set to a certain color, can be reset to a different color. (For monochrome, this is just white or black.) Every pixel's color can be changed repeatedly. What this means is that when a polygon is drawn, it superimposes itself onto whatever was there before.

OO DESIGN AND CLASS SPECIFICATION

What guides our design at this stage is the fact that no individual tmesh can be displayed by itself when using the painter's algorithm. It is essential to deal with all the scene's triangles together, no matter how many objects there are. All triangles must be thrown into a common pool, perspectively transformed, compared against each other, sorted, and finally drawn. The drawing sequence will have no relation to the objects to which the triangles belong. Therefore, there cannot be a member function `painters_draw()` or the like for a tmesh. Such a function makes sense only for the entire scene.

We define a class `dsscene_t` (depth sorting scene), which is a three-dimensional scene, in order to display its tmeshes with the painter's algorithm. This class is derived from `scene3_t` and is identical to it in that it has the same data members; no new members are defined. However, the function `solid()` of `dsscene_t` is redefined; it walks through the list of all its tmeshes and counts how many frontface triangles there are. Then it allocates memory to store enough information for each frontface triangle. This information is stored in an array of class `dsrec_t` (depth sorting record).

```
//*********************** File dsscene.h ************************

#ifndef DSSCENE_T
#define DSSCENE_T

#include "../Shape3d/scene3.h"
#include "../Shape3d/light.h"
```

```
class dsscene_t : public scene3_t
{
public:
    dsscene_t(const win_view3_t& wv,light_t* l) : scene3_t(wv,l) {}
    void solid() const ;
} ;

#endif

//*****************************************************************
```

The class `dsrec_t` represents one triangle that is to be depth sorted. It holds all information needed for this purpose: the triangle's three perspective-transformed vertices; the plane equation determined by these (for the depth test); a counter holding the number of triangles behind this one; a pointer to a linked list of subscripts indicating the dsrecs that are in front of this one; a pointer to the original, non-transformed triangle (for illumination computation and drawing); and a static member that holds a common point when two triangles have been found to overlap. All dsrecs share this member—it is needed only for the short period from the discovery of the overlap to the computation of the depth at the common point.

For the overlap test, we overload the operator ^ to return true or false; for the depth comparison, we overload the operator < to return true or false. The functions `edge_sec()` and `same_side()` perform the edge-intersection test and the same-side test. Edge_sec is a member function. The details of these operators and functions are hidden away in the implementation of `dsrec_t`.

The class `infront_t` is a supplier class used for implementing the list of triangles in front.

```
//*********************** File dsrec.h **********************

#ifndef DSREC_T
#define DSREC_T

#include "../Shape3d/point3.h"
#include "../Shape3d/plane.h"
#include "../Shape3d/rgb.h"
#include "../Dsort/dstriang.h"

class scene_t ;
class tmesh_t ;


class infront_t
{
public:
    infront_t(int tri,infront_t* n) : tri(tri), next(n) {}
    ~infront_t() { delete next; }
```

```
      int tri ;
      infront_t* next ;
   } ;


   class dsrec_t                    // triangle record for depth sorting
   {
   public:
      virtual ~dsrec_t() ;
      dsrec_t() ;
      dsrec_t(const dsrec_t&) ;
      dsrec_t(const point3_t&,const point3_t&,const point3_t&) ;
      dsrec_t(const scene_t*,triangle_t*) ;

      point_t giva() const { return trans[0]; }
      point_t givb() const { return trans[1]; }
      point_t givc() const { return trans[2]; }

      plane_t plane ;                 // plane eq of transformed vertices
      triangle_t* orig ;              // pointer to original triangle
      int num_behind ;                // number of faces behind
      infront_t* infront ;            // list of faces in front
      static point_t common ;         // common point for depth computation

      void operator = (const dsrec_t&) ;
      virtual int operator ^ (const dsrec_t&) const;    // overlap test
      virtual int operator < (const dsrec_t&) ;         // depth test

   protected:
      point3_t* trans ;               // pointer to transformed vertices
      point_t min() const ;
      point_t max() const ;
      point_t cen() const;                          // center of triangle
      int in(const point_t&) const;         // true if point_t in triangle
      int edge_sec(point_t,point_t,point_t,point_t) const ;
   } ;

   #endif

   //**********************************************************************
```

With these syntactic conveniences, the code for establishing the depth order reads almost like a description of the algorithm. The same is true for using the sorted dsrecs to draw the triangles. The code is implemented in the function `dsscene_t::draw()` in the file `Dsort/dssene.c`.

We need two more classes: `dsmesh_t` (depth sorting mesh) and `dstriang_t` (depth sorting triangle). A `dsmesh_t` differs from a `tmesh_t` only in that its triangles are of type `dstriang_t`. It is derived from `tmesh_t` with no additional data members, has a destructor, a default constructor, a copy constructor, and a copy function. The constructors simply call the base class constructors. All other data and functions are inherited. The only reason for introducing it is to redefine the function `alloc_facets()` to allocate and return an array of `dstraing_t` instead of `triangle_t`. In a `dsmesh_t`, therefore, the pointer facet will at runtime point to dstriangles.

```
//************************* File dsmesh.h *************************

#ifndef DSMESH_T
#define DSMESH_T
#include "../Shape3d/tmesh.h"


class dsmesh_t : public tmesh_t              // tmesh with dstriangles
{
public:
  ~dsmesh_t() ;
  dsmesh_t() ;
  dsmesh_t(const dsmesh_t&) ;

  prim_t* copy() const ;
  triangle_t* alloc_facets() const ;
} ;

#endif

//**********************************************************************
```

The class `dstriang_t` is derived from `triangle_t` with only one additional member function: `virtual dsrec_t* make_dsrec()`. This function creates a depth sorting record from the triangle as described in the text by projecting the vertices, etc. It is used in `dsscene_t::solid()` to create an array of `dsrec_t` of all frontface triangles in the scene.

We introduce this class only to demonstrate the OOP principle of adding functionality to a class without changing its code. Our alternative would have been to add the member function `make_dsrec()` simply to `triangle_t` when necessary. In the development of large software projects, late changes to finished and approved classes are usually not possible.

Thus, a dsscene must contain dsmeshes, which have `dstriang_t` as faces. There is no difference in data, only in type. The dstriangles create their own depth sorting records. This design makes it possible to add other types of meshes to a depth sorting scene as we will see in Chapter 13 (Phong shading).

```
//************************* File dstriang.h *********************

#ifndef DSTRIANG_T
#define DSTRIANG_T

#include "../Shape3d/triangle.h"
#include "../Shape3d/tmesh.h"
class dsrec_t ;
```

```
class dstriang_t : public triangle_t     // triangle for depth sorting
{
public:
  ~dstriang_t() ;
   dstriang_t() ;

   virtual dsrec_t* make_dsrec(const scene_t*) const ;
} ;

#endif

//***********************************************************************
```

FAKE HIDDEN LINE REMOVAL

This algorithm can be used on a raster device to display a wireframe scene of solid objects. This does not contradict what we said above. We must still draw the scene by filling the triangles. We can define the scene strictly with triangles initially. We must specify the original triangles such that each vertex is associated with either a move or a draw command, as we explain in Section 10.3.3 below.

We first do a fill with the background color, then draw the triangle's outline according to the commands associated with each vertex. The filling will erase all earlier lines that lie under the triangle. The result is as if we draw only its edges. The sequence of first filling and then drawing the outline is essential to prevent the polygon-filling algorithm from erasing the triangle's outline.

10.3.3 HIDDEN LINE REMOVAL

On plotters, it is not possible to erase a line by overdrawing it with the background color. The same is true for the so-called vector scan CRTs, a limited number of which are still in use. For both devices, a line once drawn cannot be undone or removed by covering it, so one cannot use the painter's algorithm. Vector scan CRTs have all but disappeared, but plotters will remain popular for a long time. On these devices, objects are drawn by drawing their edges as lines. One needs a different algorithm to solve the problem of removing hidden lines.

The preparatory work for the painter's algorithm, depth sorting, is essential for removing hidden lines. Another thing is also necessary: when specifying the scene's triangles, we must associate each of its vertices with either a move or a draw command. We can do this by augmenting the class triangle to contain not only the three pointers to the vertices, but also three codes. The code indicates whether one moves to that vertex or draws a line to that vertex.

As we have said, our objects must be described by triangles. Sometimes, however, the solid object's faces have more than three edges. Figure 10.21 shows how we can specify the hexagon $(a \ b \ c \ d \ e \ f)$ as four triangles:

$$(a\{0\} \ b\{1\} \ c\{1\})$$
$$(a\{0\} \ c\{0\} \ d\{1\})$$
$$(a\{0\} \ d\{0\} \ e\{1\})$$
$$(a\{1\} \ e\{0\} \ f\{1\})$$

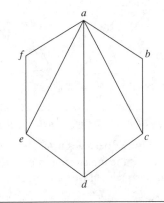

Figure 10.21   Hexagon composed of triangles

The letters in curly braces are the associated code; 0 means move, and 1 means draw. The drawing of each separate triangle begins with a move to the last vertex.

Triangle ($a\{0\}$ $b\{1\}$ $c\{1\}$) is drawn by:
1. move to last point (c)
2. move to a
3. draw to b
4. draw to c

Triangle ($a\{0\}$ $c\{0\}$ $d\{1\}$) is drawn by:
1. move to last point (d)
2. move to a
3. move to c
4. draw to d

The other triangles are drawn analogously. Together, these commands draw the hexagon without drawing the diagonal lines.

To draw a scene comprised of triangles, we begin with the array of ordered triangles as in the painter's algorithm. Instead of being filled, however, the triangle will be "hidden-line-drawn" (we will use the abbreviation h-draw). Doing an h-draw is a lengthy process that requires considerable computation. Except for this change, everything else is identical. Whenever we find a triangle with behind-counter 0, we h-draw it, step through its frontlist, and decrease the behind-counters of the triangles listed there by 1. We also set the behind-counter of this triangle to −1 in order not to h-draw it again. As a result, new 0's continue to appear and we repeat this process until no triangles are left.

Before we can explain the h-draw process, you must clearly understand how line segments and triangles may be related. Figure 10.22 shows a line from point a to point b and a triangle. There are five possible ways in which the triangle can hide the line:
1. the line is not hidden
2. point a is hidden, point b is not
3. point b is hidden, point a is not
4. the whole line is hidden
5. a portion of the line is hidden, the end points are not

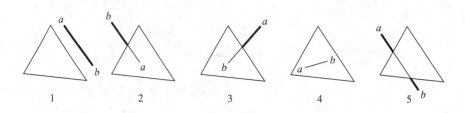

Figure 10.22   Five possible outcomes of hiding a line with a triangle

To perform h-draw, we need a routine that determines when a particular triangle hides a given line and computes the intersection point(s). For now, assume that we have this code so that you can become acquainted with the algorithm's main idea. We will give pseudocode for h-draw later.

When we h-draw a triangle, we decompose it into its three sides and process each side individually. The frontlist contains the triangles that might hide any of the three sides. We therefore give each of the three sides its own frontlist; these will originally be identical to the triangle's frontlist.

When we check a line against a triangle, it is possible to end up with two pieces of line (Case 5). We must check each of these pieces against the remaining triangles in the frontlist. Each check can increase the number of pieces by 1 and we must remember the result of each check. To do this, we use a stack on which we store all line segments that are to be checked. We initialize this stack with the three vertices of the triangle that is to be h-drawn and the associated commands move or draw. We also initialize a so-called "current point" at the start point of the first line segment. The line segment we will check against the triangles in the frontlist starts at the current point and ends at the point stored on top of the stack. Along with each point on the stack, we store its frontlist. We illustrate the stack for a triangle with vertices (a b c) and a frontlist consisting of the triangles 1, 2, and 3 (the notation is the same as in the last section).

The stack is initialized as:

current point		command	point	frontlist
c	stacktop:	dr	a	1 2 3
		dr	b	1 2 3
		dr	c	1 2 3

In this situation, we will check the line from point c (current point) to point a (top of stack) against the triangles 1, 2, and 3 before we draw it. (Actually, each stack element will only have a pointer to a frontlist, but for demonstration purposes we show the whole frontlist. The frontlists that are pointed to must be separate lists even though they are initially equal, because the individual frontlists will change.)

We now give the h-draw algorithm in pseudocode. Some explanations are necessary: "push" means that something is put on top of the stack, "pop" means that the top of the stack is assigned to something and then removed from the stack, and "command" and "list" always refer to the top of the stack.

H-draw first initializes the stack with the three vertices of the triangle to be h-drawn. It then checks the command and the frontlist; if the command is a move, no line can be hidden because no line is drawn, so the move is performed. If the frontlist is empty, there is no triangle in front of the line, so the command is always performed. Whenever a command is performed, the current point changes to the one on the top of the stack and the top of the stack is removed.

If the command is a draw and the frontlist is not empty, h-draw checks the line from the current point to the stack top against the first triangle in the frontlist. It does this by calling a routine (which we will write later). Whatever the result of this check, no more checks against this triangle will be made, so this triangle is immediately removed from the frontlist.

Depending on the check's five possible outcomes (see Figure 10.22), different actions occur.

In Case 1, nothing is done. We have already removed the initial triangle from the frontlist; the next check will be against another triangle.

In Case 2, the line intersects the triangle once and the triangle hides the current point. We want a move to the intersection, followed by a draw to the point currently on the top. The draw command is already on the top, so h-draw pushes a move to the intersection.

In Case 3, there is one intersection and the current point is not hidden. We want to draw to the intersection and then move to the top (even though the top is hidden, we need it to process the next line segment). H-draw therefore changes the command to move. Ahead of this move, there must be a draw to the intersection, so h-draw pushes a draw to the intersection. This draw can be hidden by the remaining triangles, so it receives the same frontlist as the former top.

In Case 4, the whole line is hidden, so h-draw changes the command to move in preparation for the next line check.

In Case 5, there are two intersections. Instead of drawing to the top, we can draw only to the intersection closer to the current point, followed by a move to the intersection farther from it, followed by a draw to the top. This last draw is already on the stack, so h-draw first pushes a move to the farther intersection and then a draw to the closer intersection. The draw must still be checked against the remaining triangles, so it receives the same frontlist as the previous top.

DESCRIPTION IN PSEUDOCODE

```
h-draw triangle (a,b,c):
{
    push c and command and frontlist of the triangle;
    push b and command and frontlist of the triangle;
    push a and command and frontlist of the triangle;
    current point = c;

    while (stack not empty)
        if (command == move or frontlist empty)
        {
            perform the command;
            current point = pop the stack;
        }
        else
        {
        check first triangle in frontlist against
```

```
                line from current point to top of stack;
                remove first triangle from frontlist;

                case 1                                  // nothing hidden
                no action;

                case 2              // start point hidden, end point not
                push move and intersection;

                case 3              // end point hidden, start point not
                change command to move;
                push draw and intersection and same frontlist as top;

                case 4                                  // completely hidden
                change command to move;

                case 5              // middle part hidden, end points not
                push move and farther intersection;
                push draw and closer intersection
                        and same frontlist as top
        }
    }
```

The Pen Plotter

There are two kinds of pen plotters. One is the *flatbed plotter*, in which the paper lies on a flat surface. In some constructions, it is held there by electrostatic force or by other means and does not move. The pen is held in a complicated mechanism that can move up-down and left-right. These plotters can deal with small to medium sized paper.

In another type of construction, the paper does not remain at rest on the flatbed, but can slide forward and backward (see Figure 10.A). This is achieved by two rollers that pinch the paper onto the bed and are rotated as necessary.

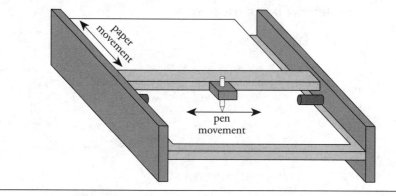

Figure 10.A   Flatbed plotter

The pen-holding mechanism moves only left and right. Each point on the paper can be reached through a combined movement of paper and pen holder. This mechanism is less complicated and more reliable than the first type of pen plotter. However, these plotters can handle only small paper because a big sheet cannot slide around on the bed very quickly. Flatbed plotters, especially the first kind, are quite accurate. In all constructions, however, there is a limit to the usable paper size.

The second kind of plotter is the *drum plotter*. A long strip of paper, which can be in a roll, is fed over a drum. Turning the drum moves the paper forward or backward along its length. The pen in the holder is moved sideways across the paper's width. Through combined movements, each point on the paper can be reached, as in a flatbed plotter of the second type. The drum plotters can partly overcome the limits in paper size in the above two constructions. The drawing can be of any desired length, but the width is limited to the drum's width. In big plotters, however, the drum can be several feet wide. A disadvantage is that the accuracy is somewhat lower than in a flatbed plotter.

The plotters are usually equipped with a carousel containing pens of several different colors and thicknesses from which the holding mechanism can choose. One can easily exchange the pens in the carousel by hand, so plotters can draw lines in a wide variety of colors and thicknesses. When moving to a certain point, the pen is lifted. When drawing, the pen is lowered.

What a pen plotter can do well and accurately is draw straight lines. That is all. Physically, a pen plotter is a vector device as opposed to raster devices such as dot matrix, ink jet, and laser printers. Curves are always approximated by short straight line segments. A plotter can fill areas with one solid color by drawing many parallel fill lines, but this is time-consuming. Plotters are usually equipped with software that lets them draw circles, ellipses, wedges, and rectangles and fill these either solidly or in various crosshatch patterns.

Plotters also have their own built-in character generator that allows them to write text when sent the proper string in ASCII. Often, the writing direction, size, and slant of the characters can be changed continuously to allow for all sorts of labeling.

A pen plotter's output quality can be matched by a low-end laser printer with about 300 dots per inch resolution. If it were not for the ability to produce a wide variety of colors, small pen plotters would soon be replaced by laser printers. Big pen plotters have the advantage over laser printers of a manageable paper size, which will keep them around for a long time.

To clarify the h-draw process, we examine a specific case, shown in Figure 10.23. Triangle 1 is to be h-drawn; it has triangles 2 and 3 in front. In the descriptions, the current point (*cur*) is at the left, then the command, then the point, and finally the frontlist (called *flist*). The first tableau is from initialization.

c	d	a	2	3	command == d, *flist* not empty.
	d	b	2	3	check line ca against 2, remove 2.
	d	c	2	3	case 5, intersections d and e:
					push m e, push d d and *flist*.

c	d	d	3	command == d, *flist* not empty.
	m	e		check line cd against 3, remove 3.
	d	a	3	case 3, intersection f:
	d	b	2 3	command = m, push d f and *flist*.
	d	c	2 3	

c	d	f		*flist* empty:
	m	d		perform draw f,
	m	e		cur = f, pop stack.
	d	a	3	
	d	b	2 3	
	d	c	2 3	

f	m	d		command == m:
	m	e		perform move d,
	d	a	3	cur = d, pop stack.
	d	b	2 3	
	d	c	2 3	

d	m	e		command == m:
	d	a	3	perform move e,
	d	b	2 3	cur = e, pop stack.
	d	c	2 3	

e	d	a	3	command == d, *flist* not empty.
	d	b	2 3	check line ea against 3, remove 3.
	d	c	2 3	case 1: no action.

e	d	a		*flist* empty:
	d	b	2 3	perform draw a,
	d	c	2 3	cur = a, pop stack.

a	d	b	2 3	command == d, *flist* not empty.
	d	c	2 3	check line ab against 2, remove 2.
				case 1: no action.

a	d	b	3	command == d, *flist* not empty.
	d	c	2 3	check line ab against 3, remove 3.
				case 1: no action.

a	d	b		*flist* empty:
	d	c	2 3	perform draw b,
				cur = b, pop stack.

b	d	c	2	3	command == d, *flist* not empty.
					check line bc against 2, remove 2.
					case 5, intersections g and h:
					push m h, push d g and *flist*.

b	d	g	3	command == d, *flist* not empty.
	m	h		check line bg against 3, remove 3.
	d	c	3	case 1: no action

b	d	g	*flist* empty:
	m	h	perform draw g,
	d	c	3	cur = g, pop stack

g	m	h	command == m:
	d	c	3	perform move h,
			cur = h, pop stack

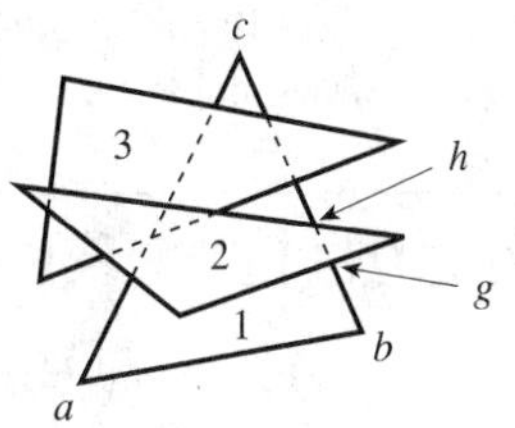

and so on.

Figure 10.23   Process of hidden line removal

We now outline a routine for finding which of the five cases applies, determining the intersections for cases 2, 3, and 5. For the current point and the point on top of the stack, we must determine if they are inside or outside the first triangle in the frontlist. We will not repeat how to do this, but we will describe what must be done depending on the outcomes of these two tests. We also suggest a possible formulation of this routine.

The routine must always test the line from the current point to the top of the stack against the first triangle in the frontlist on top of the stack. The routine will return three items: an integer for the case that applies and two floating point values for the intersections (if they exist). We have already seen the formulas for computing intersections.

When the routine tests the two points against the triangle, the following situations can arise:

1. Both points can be inside the triangle. It follows that the whole line is inside the triangle and is completely hidden. Return Case 4, both intersection arguments are empty.

2. One point is inside, the other outside. Return Case 2 or Case 3, depending on which point is inside. Next, test each triangle edge for an intersection with the line. For one of the edges, an intersection will exist; this is returned in the first intersection argument.

3. Both end points are outside the triangle. To distinguish between Cases 1 and 5, we test each triangle edge for an intersection with the line. If no intersections exist, the whole line is outside the triangle and is not hidden—return Case 1, both intersection arguments are empty. If intersections exist, there will be two and the line will traverse the triangle. Return Case 5. Determine which of the two intersections is closer and which farther from the current point; return the closer one in the first argument and the farther one in the second. The closer intersection is easily determined. Let $(cur_x \; cur_y)$ be the current point and $(a_x \; a_y)$ and $(b_x \; b_y)$ be the two intersections. Then:

If $abs(cur_x - a_x) < abs(cur_x - b_x)$ or $abs(cur_y - a_y) < abs(cur_y - b_y)$,
then $(a_x \ a_y)$ is closer, otherwise $(b_x \ b_y)$.

This is all that is required to do hidden surface and hidden line removal. We stress that all polygons must be triangles or quadrangles and that cyclic overlapping and penetrating surfaces are not allowed. Such cases can be handled with depth sorting, but the algorithms become conceptually much more complicated and computationally expensive. It is better to use the Z-buffer or subdivision methods (presented in Chapter 11), which can handle almost any imaginable case.

SUGGESTED READINGS

FVFH90 and HILL90 contain presentations of the essential ideas of depth sorting and the painter's algorithm. For further and more detailed reading about hidden line removal, refer to the literature listed in FVFH90, p. 666.

EXERCISES

To some extent, some of the exercises below reproduce code that is provided with this book. However, the fact that code is provided should not prevent the student from practicing the coding of basic concepts. Such coding is good exercise and helps one understand computer graphics.

SECTION 10.1

1. Define an input file describing a polygon mesh for a pyramid with a square base. Use world coordinates, such that the center of the base is at (0 0 0). Define the square base as two triangles. Be careful to specify all vertices in cw order. This will result in outward-pointing plane normals.

2. Write code to compute the plane coefficients for all triangles in Exercise 1, normalize them, and store them in the triangle records. Draw the pyramid as a wireframe with perspective projection by drawing all triangles of the pyramid. Each triangle is drawn by perspectively projecting all its vertices in world coordinates and drawing the projected triangle on the screen.

3. Write a main() function that reads the pyramid of Exercise 1, then produces a sequence of points that lie on a straight line through space, which passes near the top of the pyramid (do not pass exactly over the top!). Each point on that line is interpreted as the origin O of a view transformation (Chapter 5). Define the center of the pyramid's base (0 0 0) as the constant view reference point and define the vector (0 1 0) as view-up. For each of these definitions, construct a view transformation matrix, transform the pyramid by multiplying each vertex with this matrix, and project perspectively, assuming the projection center at the point (0 0 $-d$) in the new coordinate system. (Remember the original pyramid vertices!)

Draw the pyramid by drawing all its triangles as you practiced in Exercise 2. The sequence of pictures for different points on the line simulates an airplane flight over the pyramid.

SECTION 10.2

4. Add rotations about the x- and y-axes with fixed small angles and a frontface test to the code of Exercise 2. Rotate all vertices in the vertex list (overwrite the old vertices), recompute all plane coefficients, normalize them, and draw the pyramid as a wireframe. Draw only those triangles that pass the frontface test. Upon a keystroke, erase the old picture and repeat the above. This makes the pyramid rotate in space.

5. Instead of recomputing all plane coefficients from the rotated vertices, it is possible to compute the rotated plane coefficients from the old ones. Rotate each plane normal as if it were a point (d does not change in rotations around the origin). Once the plane coefficients are normalized, you need not normalize them again. Implement this method in the code of Exercise 4. (The vertices still must be rotated!)

6. Specify a cube as a polygon mesh in world coordinates with the cube's center at (0 0 0). Specify all sides as two triangles, with vertices cw. Do a view transformation of all vertices, but remember the old vertices. Compute all plane coefficients from the transformed vertices. Display the cube as a wireframe in perspective projection with backfaces removed.

7. Use the cube defined in Exercise 6. Program the view transformation for a viewpoint that is only a little off the current viewer's position and for a fixed view-up direction. Overwrite all vertices with the transformed vertices. Display the transformed cube with backfaces removed. Repeating this will show the cube from positions that correspond to a viewer's moving on a certain path in space.

8. Rewrite the provided functions `scene3_t::rotx()`, `roty()`, and `rotz()` so that they do not rotate the scene's objects about their own centroids, but about the scene's centroid. You have to add the member centroid to the `scene3_t` class, initialize it properly in the constructor, and update it properly when adding another object to the scene. For example, the scene's centroid could be the average of the centroids of all its objects.

SECTION 10.3

9. Practice establishing depth order by manually setting up the lists and counters for the triangles shown in Figure 10.24.

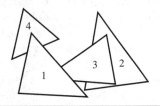

Figure 10.24   Exercise for depth sorting

10. Using the lists and counters you obtained in Exercise 9, practice using the painter's algorithm manually, as shown in the text.

11. Rewrite the function `dsscene_t::draw()`, to "draw" a scene using the painter's algorithm and "fake hidden line removal."
12. Write a function in C++ that takes a triangle and a line and determines which of the five cases of the triangle-line intersection results.
13. Using the triangles shown in Figure 10.25, practice the hidden line h-draw technique from the text.

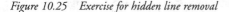

Figure 10.25   Exercise for hidden line removal

14. (Senior Project) Using the code for establishing the depth order as given in `dsscene_t::solid()`, implement the hidden line removal algorithm in C++. Add code for the h-draw process as described in the text.
15. Write a class template:

```
template <class V,class F> class mesh_t { ... } ;
```

    `V` is the type of vertex and `F` the type of facet for this mesh. The only change from `tmesh_t` is the facet pointer, `F* facet`. The member vertex should remain of type `vertex3_t**`. Write the member functions for `mesh_t` using those of `tmesh_t` as a guide, replacing `vertex3_t` with `V` and `triangle_t` with `F` in the proper places. Directly allocate `V` or `F` as required. Discard the functions `alloc_vertex()` and `alloc_facets()` and the class `tmesh_t`. You have to change the typecast in `scene3_t::solid()` to `mesh_t <vertex3_t, triangle_t>*`.
16. Use the class template to display a scene with backface removal, declare objects of type `mesh_t<vertex3_t,triangle_t>`, read them in, add them to a `scene3_t`, and call the scene's `solid()` function.
17. Change the typecast in the function `dsscene_t::solid()` to `mesh_t <vertex3_t,dstriang_t>`. Use the class template to display a scene with depth sorting, declare objects of type `mesh_t<vertex3_t,dstriang_t>`, read them in, add them to a `dsscene_t`, and call the scene's `solid()` function.
18. Discuss the runtime penalty of code reuse in rotating a `tmesh`: `point3_t::rotx()` etc. versus using a separately written `tmesh_rotx()`. (Consider the sin and cos computations!)
19. Speed up the overlap test in `Shape3d/dsrec.c` by adding a minmax test for the triangles' centers as described in the text.
20. Change `Shape3d/main.c` so that it accepts the data file to be displayed plus rotation and translation on the command line. Example:

```
    a.out ../Data/8pyr.dat 0 20 0 -1.5 0 0
```

11

HIDDEN LINES AND SURFACES

SCREEN SUBDIVISION AND DEPTH BUFFER METHODS

Chapter 11 is the second of three chapters that describe algorithms for hidden line or surface removal. This chapter covers two methods that are more general in scope and can handle cases beyond those of the last chapter.

11.0   **Introduction** tells how these methods differ from the previous ones and what limitations are imposed on them.

11.1   **Screen Subdivision Method (Warnock Algorithm)** is a "divide and conquer" technique that colors rectangular areas of the screen when it is determined that all should be painted identically. The method subdivides the screen systematically until this is true; at times, this reduces the area to a single pixel.

11.2   **Depth Buffer Methods** are conceptually simple, but require very much memory. They can handle all hidden surface problems, no matter how complicated the scene.

11.0   INTRODUCTION

The previous chapter introduced the important topic of hidden surface removal, but there are limitations to that chapter's methods. In this chapter, we describe two more general and powerful hidden surface removal methods: screen subdivision and depth buffer methods. These work only for raster displays and therefore cannot be used on vector devices, such as pen plotters. Both take advantage of the fact that a picture can be decomposed into its atomic parts, the pixels. At that level, the only graphics primitive the algorithms need is `setpix()`. There is no need to compute intersections of lines or polygons with other lines or polygons as in the depth sorting methods. We only have to test whether a given pixel is or is not within a certain polygon of the scene. If it is, the distance of this point from the screen or from the center of projection must be determined. This calculation is the only place where depth computation comes in. Finally, the single pixel is set with the proper color.

As we describe them here, both methods require that the scene's objects be bounded by planar polygons. We impose this restriction to stay within the intended scope of the book. (We can use the depth buffer method to display all sorts of scenes, even when objects are bounded by curved surfaces. In such cases, it is added as a postprocess to the rendering method.)

We could display a scene by computing and displaying every individual pixel. This will certainly work, but is costly. To reduce the cost, we could use the screen subdivision algorithm, which tries to avoid going that far in decomposing a picture. It does not use line and polygon primitives, only pixels and rectangles. We have not discussed rectangles before, but they are just a special case of polygons.

The algorithm does not need to draw a general polygon, but it must be able to determine whether a polygon in the scene overlaps with a rectangle or a pixel. We must determine whether two line segments intersect, but we do not need the intersection point itself. (Certain versions of the algorithm also determine and use the intersection points, but they should not be classified as pure screen subdivision methods.)

The screen subdivision algorithm can be varied slightly to draw only the outlines of polygons. In this case, it acts like a "fake" hidden line algorithm; that is, it still works only on raster displays.

Throughout this chapter, then, we will consider our spatial objects to have plane polygonal surfaces. There are no other restrictions on the scene's complexity.

11.1 SCREEN SUBDIVISION METHOD (WARNOCK ALGORITHM)

John Warnock first presented the *screen subdivision method* (WARN68, WARN69), which is often called the *Warnock algorithm*. It can be used to display scenes in which the objects are bounded by plane polygonal surfaces. The scenes can be of any complexity. In this respect, the algorithm is as powerful as the Z-buffer algorithm that we present later. It does not need a Z-buffer, but is more complicated. The version of the painter's algorithm presented in Chapter 10 excluded objects that penetrate each other or overlap cyclicly. There are no such restrictions here.

The polygons that describe the objects' surfaces can have any shape. However, we will consider only triangles. This is not a restriction because, as you have seen, we can decompose any polygon into triangles. The reason for this limitation to triangles is to systematize the data structure describing the objects and to have simpler overlap tests. If for some reason we do not want to split polygons into triangles, it is possible to implement a more general rectangle-polygon overlap test within the Warnock algorithm. However, this has nothing to do with the essential idea of the algorithm.

In the Warnock algorithm, the decision about a given area's color is not necessarily made at the pixel level. The algorithm tries to make the decision for as large an area as possible, in particular a rectangle containing many pixels. If the algorithm can determine that a whole rectangle is to be filled with the same color, it does so. This is less likely for bigger rectangles, more likely for smaller rectangles, and always possible for pixels.

The algorithm's basic form draws rectangles filled with one constant color. It starts out with a rectangle equal to the whole screen and checks whether it should be filled. If the rectangle is empty or if its contents belong to only one polygon, it is filled solidly with the background color or the color for that polygon. If the rectangle does not meet those conditions, it is subdivided into four smaller rectangles and checks are performed on each of these. The process may continue until the test rectangle becomes as small as a single pixel. At that point, a simple decision about the display is always possible.

We first use pseudocode to describe the basic version, without bothering to compute the intersections between rectangles and triangles. The pseudocode just finds out whether there is overlap. The polygons—in our case triangles—that are checked are the perspective projections of the scene's polygons onto the screen.

```
For a given rectangle do:

    If the rectangle is pixel size, check all triangles to see if they
    contain the pixel center.

        If no triangle contains the pixel center, set this pixel to
        the background color.

        If one or more triangles contain the pixel center, set the
        pixel to the color of the triangle closest to the screen at
        the pixel center.

    If the rectangle is bigger than pixel size, check all triangles
    for overlap with the rectangle.

        If no triangle of the scene overlaps, fill the rectangle with
        the background color.

        If a triangle surrounds the rectangle and is closer in depth
        than all other surrounding or overlapping triangles, fill the
        rectangle with this triangle's color.

        Otherwise, subdivide the rectangle.

end.
```

We see that a simple depth test is made either when a rectangle becomes as small as a pixel or at the rectangle's four corner points. We do not scan the whole screen pixelwise; whenever a rectangle is found to be of one color, it is displayed without being further subdivided.

The algorithm needs analytic criteria to determine whether a triangle overlaps with a given rectangle and, if so, whether the rectangle is completely contained in the triangle. We obtain the triangle vertices considered in the overlap tests through perspective transformations of the original three-dimensional triangle vertices and scaling to screen coordinates. The vertices are of floating point type. The perspective transformation is done only once at the outset of the algorithm. To explain the overlap tests, we assume the following triangle and rectangle coordinates:

Triangle vertices: $\quad P_1 = (x_1 \ y_1)$ (The z-values are ignored in overlap tests.)
$\quad\quad\quad\quad\quad\quad\quad\quad P_2 = (x_2 \ y_2)$
$\quad\quad\quad\quad\quad\quad\quad\quad P_3 = (x_3 \ y_3)$

Rectangle boundaries: $\quad l$ left boundary
$\quad\quad\quad\quad\quad\quad\quad\quad\quad r$ right boundary
$\quad\quad\quad\quad\quad\quad\quad\quad\quad b$ bottom boundary
$\quad\quad\quad\quad\quad\quad\quad\quad\quad t$ top boundary

We can use the minimax test to determine whether a triangle is wholly outside one of the rectangle boundaries. We apply this test first because it is the least expensive. We compute:

$$xmin = \min(x_1, x_2, x_3)$$
$$xmax = \max(x_1, x_2, x_3)$$
$$ymin = \min(y_1, y_2, y_3)$$
$$ymax = \max(y_1, y_2, y_3)$$

If any of the conditions below is true, there is no overlap:

xmax $< l$
xmin $> r$
ymax $< b$
ymin $> t$

The above test will determine that a triangle such as the one in Figure 11.1 is not overlapping the rectangle.

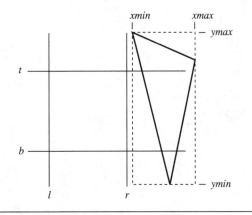

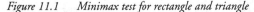

Figure 11.1   Minimax test for rectangle and triangle

Triangles that the above test does not remove can still be disjoint from the rectangle (an example is given in Figure 11.2.) If they are disjoint, we can avoid further subdivision. Thus, we must do more testing.

The next test to apply is an edge-rectangle intersection test. This test determines whether there is an intersection between a triangle edge and a rectangle. We express the triangle edge through the points $(x_1 \; y_1)$ and $(x_2 \; y_2)$ in parameterized form:

$$X = x_1 + u(x_2 - x_1)$$
$$Y = y_1 + u(y_2 - y_1)$$

Where this line intersects with the left boundary, l, we have $X = l$, from which it follows that $u = (l - x_1)/(x_2 - x_1)$. Accordingly we compute $Y = y_1 + (l - x_1)/(x_2 - x_1)*(y_2 - y_1)$. An intersection exists only if l is between x_1 and x_2 and the computed Y is between b and t. We do not need to compute u. The test for the right boundary, r, is analogous. We obtain very similar testing sequences for the top and bottom boundaries.

We can perform these four tests using only two divisions, four multiplications, and a few relational checks. To check the whole triangle for intersection with a rectangle, we must check all three edges. If there is an intersection, then there is overlap. Otherwise, we have one of three possible cases:

Case 1:
The triangle and rectangle are disjoint;
see Figure 11.2.

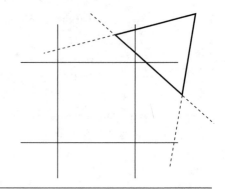

Figure 11.2   *Disjoint triangle and rectangle*

Case 2:
The triangle surrounds the rectangle;
see Figure 11.3.

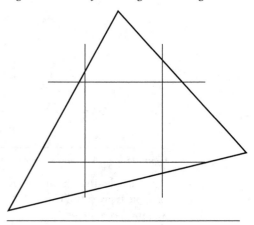

Figure 11.3   *Triangle contains rectangle*

Case 3:
The triangle is contained in the rectangle;
see Figure 11.4

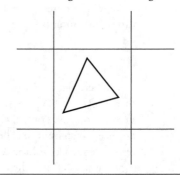

Figure 11.4   *Rectangle contains triangle*

We can distinguish between these three cases through general triangle-inside and rectangle-inside tests. If any corner of the rectangle is inside the triangle, the whole rectangle must be inside (Case 2). Otherwise, we test any triangle corner. If it is inside the rectangle, the whole triangle must be inside (Case 3). Otherwise, they are disjoint (Case 1).

Theoretically, we still miss the cases in which a triangle edge coincides with a rectangle boundary or a triangle vertex just touches a rectangle boundary or vice versa; see Figure 11.5. Because we work with floating point numbers, the likelihood of these cases is so small that we can ignore them.

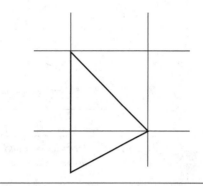

The algorithm also needs to determine a triangle's depth at a certain point. This depth must be computed as the intersection of a line parallel to the z-axis with the plane of the triangle's perspective transformation.

Figure 11.5   Hard-to-detect case

As we mentioned above, we perform a perspective transformation and scaling to screen coordinates of all object vertices before we start the overlap tests. The (*x* *y*)-values of the transformed vertices are used to determine overlap with rectangles on the screen; the z-values are used for the plane and depth computations. The structure of each triangle contains the coefficients of the plane through the transformed vertices to avoid repeating the computations.

If $ax + by + cz - d = 0$ is the equation of the "transformed" plane, the depth z at a point (*x* *y*) is:

$$z = (d - ax - by)/c$$

We can save the division by c in each depth computation by normalizing this plane equation to $c = 1$. With this, we mean that all coefficients are divided by c; c itself assumes the value 1.

When rectangles have been reduced to pixel size, we compute the depth value for all triangles that contain this pixel. The closest triangle is the one with the smallest z-value (lhs).

When a rectangle is not pixel size, we do the following. For all surrounding and all intersecting triangles, we compute the depth of their plane equations at the rectangle's four corner points. If one of the surrounding triangles has depth values that are smaller than all other depth values, this triangle is certainly closest to the screen.

This is a sufficient but not a necessary condition. In Figure 11.6, we see a screen and two triangles in heavy lines as viewed from above. The planes are shown in light lines. The depth is computed at the rectangle's corners, as the dotted lines indicate. We see only a two-dimensional projection of the situation, but it reveals the underlying problem. The surrounding triangle is closer than the intersecting triangle, but the algorithm cannot verify this, because point *b* is closer than point *a*. To determine this, the rectangle is subdivided. After the subdivision, shown in Figure 11.7, the depth situation is conclusive in the left part. In the right part, only one surrounding triangle exists, so both rectangles can be filled.

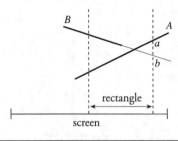
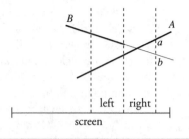

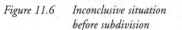

Figure 11.6   Inconclusive situation   Figure 11.7   Conclusive situation
before subdivision   after subdivision

IMPROVEMENTS TO THE ALGORITHM

We can avoid repeating checks for overlap by using linked lists. In languages such as C++, this is easy to program. We can reduce the number of triangles to be checked against each rectangle in the subdivision process by taking advantage of information acquired at an earlier level of the subdivision process. If a triangle surrounds a rectangle, it will also surround all the rectangle's parts. If a triangle is disjoint from a rectangle, it will be disjoint from all the rectangle's parts. For the subdivided rectangles, therefore, we need not derive this information again. How can we avoid this?

We maintain three global linked lists of triangles. One contains all disjoint triangles; we call it *dlist*. Another contains all surrounding triangles; we call it *slist*. The third contains all intersecting ones; we call it *ilist*. We must update these when descending or ascending in the subdivision process. When we descend to finer subdivisions, *slist* and *dlist* can only grow and *ilist* can only shrink. The opposite is true when we ascend from completed subdivisions.

It makes sense to remove the triangles from *ilist* physically and add them to *dlist* or *slist* when stepping to finer subdivisions. Because the triangles on *dlist* are not checked at all, this can significantly speed up the process for complicated scenes with many triangles.

Slist and *dlist* behave as first in–last out (FILO) stacks—what was put in first will be taken out last. When we process a rectangle, we first put a certain number, *d*, of triangles from *ilist* onto *dlist* and another number, *s*, from *ilist* onto *slist*. After this rectangle is filled, either directly or by further subdivisions, we return to *ilist* the first *s* triangles on top of *slist* and the first *d* triangles on top of *dlist* before we step up in the hierarchy. This allows us to shuffle the triangles between the lists efficiently. Only *ilist* does not behave as a stack. The elements to be taken from *ilist* can be anywhere within that list.

C++ has elegant ways to handle this. Subdividing a rectangle can be done by four recursive calls. Each recursive call has its own local pointers—*shold* points to the first triangle in *slist* and *dhold* to the first in *dlist* as they appear when we begin to process the rectangle. We always insert new triangles into the beginning of *slist* and *dlist*. Also, we always take triangles from the beginning of *slist* and *dlist*. Thus, when new triangles are inserted into *slist* or *dlist*, they push the ones already there further down. However, *shold* still points to the former first triangle. Before the processing of the rectangle finishes, we return elements from *dlist* to *ilist* until the one to which *shold* points is on the top. We do the same for *slist*.

At the beginning, when the whole screen is the first rectangle, *ilist* contains all the scene's frontface triangles and *dlist* and *slist* are empty. We will explain how the lists are handled for a general case when we discuss the subdivision process.

For a given rectangle, all triangles in *ilist* are checked for overlap. Surrounding triangles are moved to *slist*, disjoint ones to *dlist*. Then all plane equations in *slist* and *ilist* are checked for their depth at the four corners. If this rectangle can be filled and no further subdivisions are needed, all triangles moved to *dlist* or *slist* by this rectangle must be returned to the *ilist*. This guarantees that, after processing a rectangle, the lists will be in the same state as before. Otherwise, we subdivide and step down one level through a recursive call.

To explain this strategy, we use the following convention. We process the subdivisions of a given rectangle in the order 1, 2, 3, 4, as Figure 11.8 shows. The subdivisions of rectangle 2 are identified by 21, 22, 23, 24, so the highlighted rectangle in Figure 11.9 is 412. The original starting rectangle is identified by a space—it precedes all other identifications.

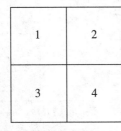

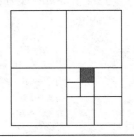

Figure 11.8   *Identification of the four subrectangles*

Figure 11.9   *Identification of the dark rectangle is 412*

The local pointers to the top of the *slist* and *dlist* at the start of the process are *shold* and *dhold*; we append the rectangle identification to the pointers. So, when we initially process rectangle 412, *shold* will be *shold412* and *dhold* will be *dhold412*. The lists are singly linked and terminated by NULL, here indicated by a 0. New elements are inserted in the front.

Figure 11.10 shows an example of *slist*. *Shold* points to its first element. After the triangles *f* and *g* have been inserted in the front, *shold* automatically points "further down," although it is never changed.

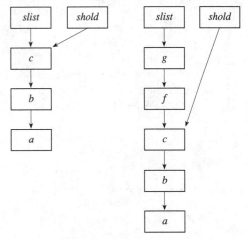

Figure 11.10   *Stack behavior of the lists*

Figure 11.11 shows the screen with three triangles *a*, *b*, and *c*. The lists at the start will be:

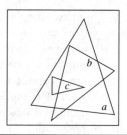

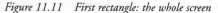

$$shold : 0$$
$$dhold : 0$$
$$ilist \rightarrow a \rightarrow b \rightarrow c \rightarrow 0$$
$$slist \rightarrow 0$$
$$dlist \rightarrow 0$$

Figure 11.11   First rectangle: the whole screen

Processing rectangle 1 will move triangles *b* and *c* to *dlist*, as these are now disjoint; see Figure 11.12.

$$shold1 : 0$$
$$dhold1 : 0$$
$$ilist \rightarrow a \rightarrow 0$$
$$slist \rightarrow 0$$
$$dlist \rightarrow b \rightarrow c \rightarrow 0$$

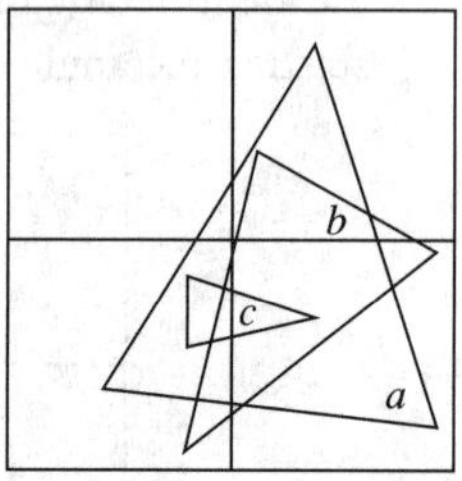

Figure 11.12   First subdivision

After processing rectangle 1, the lists will again be as before because the process returns elements starting from *slist* and *dlist* until it meets 0. We now skip rectangles 2 and 3. Processing rectangle 4 will not change the lists because all triangles are still intersecting (see Figure 11.13).

$$shold4 : 0$$
$$dhold4 : 0$$
$$ilist \rightarrow a \rightarrow b \rightarrow c \rightarrow 0$$
$$slist \rightarrow 0$$
$$dlist \rightarrow 0$$

The processing of rectangle 41 will move triangle *a* to the *slist*, as it is now surrounding; see Figure 11.13.

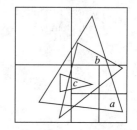

$$shold41 : 0$$
$$dhold41 : 0$$
$$ilist \rightarrow b \rightarrow c \rightarrow 0$$
$$slist \rightarrow a \rightarrow 0$$
$$dlist \rightarrow 0$$

Figure 11.13   Subdivision of rectangle 4

Figure 11.14 shows rectangle 41 with its four subdivisions magnified. When 412 is processed, it will move b to *slist* and c to *dlist*:

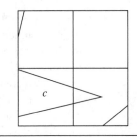

> *shold412 : a*
> *dhold412 : 0*
> *ilist* → 0
> *slist* → b → a → 0
> *dlist* → c → 0

Figure 11.14   Subdivision of rectangle 41

Rectangle 412 can now be filled, so no further subdivision is needed. After filling, the triangles moved to *slist* and *dlist* by 412 will be returned to *ilist*. Everything from the top of *slist* down to, but not including, a, and everything from the top of *dlist* down to, but not including, 0, is moved to *ilist*. Before rectangle 413 is processed, the lists will again look like this:

> *ilist* → b → c → 0
> *slist* → a → 0
> *dlist* → 0

Process 413 will use the information that a is surrounding. It moves b to *slist*, then subdivides. All its subdivisions will start with the lists:

> *ilist* → c → 0
> *slist* → b → a → 0
> *dlist* → 0

Process 4131 will not change the lists, because triangle c is still intersecting. Process 41313 will add c to *slist*:

> *shold41313 : b*
> *dhold41313 : 0*
> *ilist* → 0
> *slist* → c → b → a → 0
> *dlist* → 0

The process fills the rectangle, returns c to *ilist*, and ascends one step in the recursion.

We have shown some of these steps in detail and have assumed that the surrounding triangles are never closer than the intersecting ones; this has allowed us to move far down in the recursion to show the list-handling strategy. Of course, a rectangle may be filled while another triangle intersects it; this just shortens the subdivision process.

OO DESIGN AND CLASS SPECIFICATIONS

Tmeshes cannot be individually displayed with the Warnock algorithm because of possible mutual occlusions and intersections. All triangles of all the scene's tmeshes must be dealt with simultaneously. The same reasoning applies as that explained in the context of the painter's algorithm. We therefore design a class `wscene_t` whose `solid()` function displays all its tmeshes. The class is derived from `scene3_t`, but adds no data member. Its purpose is to redefine the function `solid()` to use the Warnock algorithm. The class `wscene_t` is initialized with a 3D window-viewport system and a light source. We can add tmeshes to it as with any scene.

```
//************************** File wscene.h **************************

#ifndef WSCENE_T
#define WSCENE_T

#include "../Shape3d/scene3.h"


class wscene_t : public scene3_t
{
public:
   wscene_t(const win_view3_t& wv,light_t* l) : scene3_t(wv,l) {}
   void solid() const ;                        // redefine solid filling
} ;

#endif

//********************************************************************
```

It should be clear from the above that the object's triangle and rectangle play an important role in implementing `wscene_t`. We therefore define the classes `warnrec_t` and `wrectangle_t`. `Warnrec_t` (Warnock record) represents a triangle and `wrectangle_t` (Warnock rectangle) a rectangle as they are used in the Warnock algorithm. `Warnrec_t` is derived from `dsrec_t` (the depth sorting record for a triangle) and therefore inherits several functions useful in overlap testing.

We add two members: a `wplane_t` and a link to the next triangle. A `wplane_t` (Warnock plane) is derived from `plane_t` with the addition of a member function for computing its depth at a given point. The reason for introducing `wplane_t` is only the OOP principle of not changing an existing class. `Warnrec_t` has a constructor that constructs it from a `scene_t*`, a `triangle_t`, and a link to the next warnrec. We provide a nonmember function, `movetolist()`, for moving a warnrec from one list to another, and two interface functions for handling the link. A destructor frees the whole allocated list.

```
//************************* File warnrec.h *************************

#ifndef WARNREC_T
#define WARNREC_T

#include "../Shape3d/point3.h"
#include "../Warn/wplane.h"
#include "../Shape3d/rgb.h"
#include "../Dsort/dsrec.h"

class warnrec_t : public dsrec_t                     // Warnock record
{
friend class wrectangle_t ;
friend void fill_or_subdivide(int,int,int,int) ;
public:
  ~warnrec_t() ;
  warnrec_t(const scene_t*,triangle_t*,warnrec_t*) ;

  warnrec_t*  givnext() const { return next; }
  warnrec_t*& setnext() { return next; }

private:
  wplane_t p ;          // plane through perspective transformed points
  warnrec_t* next ;
} ;

void movetolist(warnrec_t*&,warnrec_t*&) ;

#endif

//*******************************************************************
```

The class `wrectangle_t` carries the algorithm's heavy load—the overlap tests and filling itself recursively with colors of overlapping triangles. Its data members are simply four integers: the left, right, bottom, and top boundaries, given in absolute device coordinates. All overlap testing functions are member functions.

```
//************************* File wrectang.h *************************

#ifndef WRECTANGLE_T
#define WRECTANGLE_T
#include "../Shape2d/point.h"
#include "../Warn/warnrec.h"


class wrectangle_t
{
public:
  wrectangle_t(int,int,int,int) ;
```

```
      void fill(const warnrec_t*) const ;
      int operator ^ (const warnrec_t&) const ;                 // overlap test

   private:
      int l , r , b , t ;                        // absolute device coordinates

      int in(const point_t&) const ;
      point_t cen() const ;
      int minmax_overlap(const warnrec_t&) const ;
      int rect_edge_sec(const point_t&,const point_t&) const ;

   } ;


#endif

//***************************************************************************
```

Some comments on the implementation. The recursive screen subdivision, fill_or_subdivide(), is not a member function because it does not need to access any data members of wtriangle_t or wrectangle_t. All it needs are the global lists of the triangles and the rectangle boundaries, which must be passed as parameters anyway. During the subdivision process, the wtriangles are distributed among *ilist*, *slist*, and *dlist* and shuffled back and forth, as shown above.

The variables *shold* and *dhold* are set to the values of *slist* and *dlist* upon entry in fill_or_subdivide(). The subdivision first goes through *ilist* and determines the positions of its triangles with respect to a pixel (when the triangles are pixel size) or with respect to a rectangle (when rectangle size). Intersecting triangles are left in *ilist*, surrounding ones are moved to *slist*, and disjoint ones are moved to *dlist*.

If the rectangle is down to pixel size, all wtriangles are either surrounding or disjoint. Therefore, the function simply goes through *slist* and sets a pointer to the wtriangle that is closest in depth at the pixel center. The pixel is then set to the color of that triangle. If the pointer is NULL, the pixel is set to the background.

If the rectangle is not of pixel size, the process is more elaborate. The function tests the depth of all warnrecs (triangles) in *slist* and *ilist* at all four rectangle corners. For each corner, it holds the closest depth found so far and a pointer to the corresponding warnrec (these pointers all start with NULL). At the last corner, a variable, *pos*, also stores the position of the warnrec closest there, whether intersecting (SEC) or surrounding (SUR).

After all these warnrecs have been tested, the four pointers are checked for equality. If they are not equal, there is certainly no single surrounding triangle closest at all four corners and the pointers are not all NULL, so we must subdivide.

If the pointers are equal, they can be

1. pointing to no warnrec—all are NULL
2. pointing to a surrounding warnrec
3. pointing to an intersecting warnrec

The function distinguishes between these cases simply by testing the variable *pos*. This variable is initialized to DIS upon entering the function, signifying disjoint. If neither surrounding nor intersecting warnrecs exist, it is never changed. If *pos* has the value SUR, then a surrounding warnrec is closest at the last corner. As all pointers are equal, they all point to that same triangle. The reasoning is identical if *pos* has the value SEC (meaning intersecting). Depending on this value, the function fills either with the background, or with the color of the warnrec pointed to by the last pointer, or it subdivides.

After this the function restores *ilist* by returning to it all warnrecs that were distributed to *slist* and *dlist* in the process.

The function `fillrec()` initializes the pointer to the list of intersecting wtriangles and then calls the recursive subdivision. The overlap test is formulated as an overloaded operator. The implementation of the overlap tests and the recursive fill is not shown here—they proceed precisely as we explained in the text.

The proceeding of `wscene_t::solid()` is simpler than that of `dsscene_t::solid()`. A local pointer, `w`, to the linked list of `warnrecs` and a local counter for the lookup table entries are initialized to 0. Then, a loop walks through all tmeshes of the scene, calling each tmesh's function `setcolors()`. This sets the *rgb*-values in all frontface triangles to the computed intensities and, in case of a lookup table, also makes corresponding entries into it (we have explained this is Chapter 10). `Wscene_t::solid()` then tests each of the tmesh's triangles for frontface and, if it passes, inserts a warnrec, constructed from that triangle, into the list pointed to by `w`. After the list is created, a rectangle is constructed for the whole display and its function `fill()` is called with `w` as parameter. This draws the scene. Finally, the list of warnrecs is freed.

11.2 DEPTH BUFFER METHODS

Depth buffer methods are the most powerful and general techniques for hidden surface removal. There are several different implementations of this idea; the simplest ones need an enormous buffer space. Depth buffer methods can give a realistic display of even the most complex scenes, no matter whether objects are bounded by curved or planar surfaces and no matter whether objects mutually penetrate or occlude each other.

These methods use both the image and object space descriptions for their calculations and checking, and they compute the necessary information on a pixel by pixel basis. While these methods can handle objects with true curved surfaces, we confine ourselves to surfaces composed of planar polygons. (A later chapter will describe shading techniques that make these appear rounded.) We will discuss two versions of depth buffer methods. First, we mention some characteristics and prerequisites that are common to both.

The depth buffer methods for objects composed of planar polygons rely heavily on a modified polygon fill algorithm. The objects are most conveniently described by polygon meshes. They can be any shape, including concave. They can mutually penetrate and cyclicly occlude each other.

All polygons should be specified in a unique (cw or ccw) orientation to allow backface removal. This will speed up the depth buffer method. Although the method is operational without backface removal, we can cut the computing time in half with backface removal.

We will explain the depth buffer method for objects bounded by planar polygons and a perspective projection of the objects. (Applying the method to orthographic projection is actually a simplification.) To accomplish this, we use the perspective depth transformation, as we did in the Warnock algorithm and in Chapter 10.

When we look at a polygon in space, what we actually see is its projection. Its image on the screen is visible because the pixels are set to certain color values within the projection of this polygon's boundary. Several different polygons, even if completely disjoint in space, can have overlapping projections on the screen. In such a case, we see only the polygon that is closest to the screen. In other words, we set the pixels to the color of the polygon that is closest at this particular point. In essence, we must do this distance calculation for every pixel in the projection of a polygon.

However, we do not need the real distance (the real depth) of a polygon point from the screen; we can use the relative depth. The perspective depth transformation preserves the correct depth order, which is all we need. The relative depth is much easier to compute than the real depth.

Figure 11.15 shows three polygons in real-world space and three points on them that project to the same pixel in the view plane with a perspective projection. The perspective depth transformations of such points all lie on a line parallel to the z-axis. Their z-coordinate is their relative depth. The smallest relative depth corresponds to the smallest real-world depth.

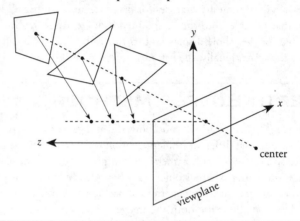

Figure 11.15   Relative depth values

11.2.1   THE Z-BUFFER ALGORITHM

The basic outline of the *Z-buffer algorithm* follows from the above. The perspective projection of a polygon is scanned with a polygon fill algorithm. For each pixel, we compute the distance from the view plane of the polygon point that projects onto this pixel; this distance is then stored in the Z-buffer (also called the depth buffer) for that pixel. This stored value will be compared to the depths of other polygon points that project onto this same pixel.

In the most straightforward case, the Z-buffer has as many storage cells as there are pixels on the screen. Each storage cell must be able to hold a depth value, which is a floating point number. Such a depth buffer will be much bigger than the whole frame buffer, a condition that may not be met in average graphics systems. A high-resolution graphics display of 1000×1000 pixels requires a Z-buffer of one million floating point numbers, each of which requires four bytes. However, there are versions of the algorithm that use a smaller Z-buffer; one of these will be described in the next subsection.

We must put into the Z-buffer the distance of the point of the polygon that is closest to the screen. As with all minimum-finding procedures, we initialize the whole Z-buffer with a number that is certain to be larger than any distance. We scan a polygon projection, then for each pixel we enter the distance of the corresponding polygon point if it is less than the number already in that Z-buffer location. At the same time, we set the frame buffer for that pixel to the color of that polygon point. When we conclude the process for all the polygons, only the depth of the closest one will survive in the Z-buffer and the color of this point will survive in the frame buffer. When we are finished, the frame buffer will correctly contain all visible parts of the scene.

In doing the implementation, we take advantage of the geometric properties of straight lines, planes, and perspective transformation to make the computations less extensive than they would be otherwise.

DESCRIPTION OF THE ALGORITHM

The objects we display with the Z-buffer method are specified as triangle meshes. (The method works for general polygons as well.) It is not necessary to display all meshes of the scene simultaneously, as in the screen subdivision method. The scene's individual triangles can be displayed in any order. Therefore, we display the scene mesh by mesh. Below, we describe the display of one mesh.

The mesh is specified in a 3D world coordinate system. The first step is the same transformation as in Section 11.1; we perspective-transform all frontface triangles of the mesh and then scale x and y to absolute device coordinates. This is very easy to do using existing code. We declare a convex polygon and put the triangle's three vertices in it. Then we call its solid() function with the containing scene as parameter. That function will clip the polygon and fill it with the current color. Because the scene's window-viewport system is a 3D type, the clipping will automatically occur in 3D space against the frustum. The resulting clipped vertex list will consist of the same type of vertices as are submitted to the clipper.

We now explain the Z-buffer filling of a single triangle from a triangle mesh. This is only slightly more complicated than normal polygon filling, as we explained in Chapter 2. In some sense, Z-buffer filling is simpler because the filling process is restricted to convex polygons. Here, we remind the reader that every solid polyhedron can be expressed as a triangle mesh. (Through clipping, a triangle can turn into a quadrangle or pentagon, but then it too is convex and the algorithm will run as well.)

Z-buffer polygon filling proceeds in the same manner as normal polygon filling with only this difference—for each pixel, the algorithm has to know its depth, that is, its distance from the transformed plane of that polygon and must compare it to the Z-buffer value.

This distance is measured along a line through the pixel and parallel to the z-axis. However, we do not have to compute it by intersecting this line with the plane. For each pixel in the filling process, we can derive the distance from the depth at the polygon vertices by simple increments, as mentioned above.

We scan the clipped and perspective-transformed polygon using the polygon fill algorithm of Chapter 2. For each new scan line, we update the two x-values where the scan line intersects with the polygon (there are only two because our polygons are convex) by adding the fixed amount dx. We also update the depth values, z, at the intersection points by adding the fixed amount dz. The first depth value at the beginning of an edge is simply the z-coordinate of that vertex.

When we draw the horizontal scan line from the start pixel to the end pixel, we take the depth value at the edge–scan line intersection as the depth of the first pixel. We take the depth value of the next edge intersection as the depth of the last pixel. The depth increment is then simply the difference of the two values divided by the number of pixels. (There is a way to save a little computation time when computing the depth increments. We explain it in an exercise.)

Every depth value is compared to the Z-buffer value for that pixel. If the pixel's depth is smaller than the Z-buffer value previously stored for this pixel, we replace the Z-buffer entry with the smaller value and set this pixel in the frame buffer to the color of the polygon. We fill the whole polygon in this manner.

OO DESIGN AND CLASS SPECIFICATIONS

If a scene is to be displayed with the Z-buffer method, we can display each of its tmeshes individually, ignoring the others. Even so, the whole scene must have one common Z-buffer that must be initialized only once for each solid filling of the scene. For this reason, we derive a class zscene_t (Z-buffer scene) from scene3_t. This class does not differ in data members from the base class. It redefines the virtual solid() function so that it allocates a Z-buffer before and deallocates it after displaying the scene's tmeshes. The other functions of zscene_t are simply inherited. We show the classes zscene_t and zbuf_t below:

```
//*********************** File zscene.h ************************

#ifndef ZSCENE_T
#define ZSCENE_T

#include "../Shape3d/scene3.h"


class zscene_t : public scene3_t
{
public:
   zscene_t(const win_view3_t& wv,light_t* l) ;
   void solid() const ;                          // redefine solid()
} ;

#endif

//******************************************************************
```

```
//*********************** File zbuf.h ************************

#ifndef ZBUF_T
#define ZBUF_T

//          Implementation of zbuf_t is in file zedge.c
```

```
class zbuf_t
{
public:
  ~zbuf_t() ;
  zbuf_t(int,int) ;
  float* operator [] (int i) { return f + i*cols; }
private:
  int rows ;
  int cols ;
  float* f ;
} ;

#endif

//*********************************************************************
```

It would not be a good design to add normal tmeshes to the zscene. One could write `zscene_t::solid()` so that it displays the tmeshes with the Z-buffer method, but then `zscene_t::solid()` would have to assume that each of its primitives is indeed a tmesh (there is no run-time-type checking in C++). This would make the software less flexible. The proper design is to derive a class `zmesh_t` from `tmesh_t`. It will not differ in data members from `tmesh_t`, but it redefines the `solid()` function of `tmesh_t` to display itself with the Z-buffer method. `Zmesh_t::solid()` will just walk through the list of primitives and call their respective `solid()` functions.

```
//*********************** File zmesh.h ************************

#ifndef ZMESH_T
#define ZMESH_T

#include "../Shape3d/tmesh.h"

class zmesh_t : public tmesh_t
{
public:
  ~zmesh_t() {}
  zmesh_t() ;
  zmesh_t(const zmesh_t&) ;
  prim_t* copy() const ;
  vertex3_t* alloc_vertex() const ;
} ;

#endif

//*********************************************************************
```

Now, let us make use of the power of OO programming. So far, no matter whether a vertex was 2D or 3D, it created the same type of two-dimensional edge using only its x- and y-coordinates. After all, an edge serves only for polygon filling, which proceeds in screen coordinates. The information that the z-coordinate of a 3D vertex provided was ignored. Now, however, we want to use this information for the depth tests. Therefore, we derive a new type of vertex from `vertex3_t` (`zvertex_t`) and give it a `create_edge()` function that creates an new type of edge designed for Z-buffer filling (`zedge_t`). The class `zvertex_t` adds no data members to the base class. It only redefines the virtual member functions `copy()` and `create_edge()`.

```
//*********************** File zvertex.h ***********************

#ifndef ZVERTEX_T
#define ZVERTEX_T

#include "../Shape3d/vertex3.h"


class zvertex_t : public vertex3_t
{
public:
  ~zvertex_t() {}
  zvertex_t() ;
  zvertex_t(const vertex3_t&) ;

  edge_t*   make_edge(const vertex_t&) const ;
  vertex_t* copy() const ;
  void operator = (const point3_t&) ;
} ;

#endif

//********************************************************************
```

The class `zedge_t` adds two data members to its base class. One is the depth value at the intersection with the scan line, z; the other is the increase in depth when progressing to the next scan line, `dz`. It redefines the two virtual member functions `update()` and `solidscan()`. Update() is now updating not only the x-value at the intersection with the scan line, but also the z-value. Solidscan() is basically identical to the `solidscan()` in the base class `edge_t`, in that it sets all pixels from the first to the second intersection. Here, however, the setting depends upon a check of the Z-buffer, as we described above.

```
//*********************** File zedge.h ***********************

#ifndef ZEDGE_T
#define ZEDGE_T

#include "../Shape2d/edge.h"
#include "../Shape3d/point3.h"
```

```
class zedge_t : public edge_t              // polygon edge for z-buffer
{
public:
  ~zedge_t() {}                            // edges are deleted singly
  zedge_t(const point3_t&,const point3_t&) ;

  void update() ;                          // redefine update
  void solidscan(double) ;                 // redefine solidscan
  double givz() const { return z; }

protected:
  double dz ,                    // depth value increase per scan line
         z  ;              // depth value at intersection with scan line
} ;

#endif

//********************************************************************
```

Examine `zedge_t::solidscan()` in `Zbuf/zedge.c` and you will see how the depth for an individual pixel is obtained in simple increments and how the comparison to the depth buffer is performed. You also see how the Z-buffer is made available to `solidscan()` through a global pointer that is static in this file. The pointer is initialized by the constructor of the Z-buffer. This constructor is called in `zscene_t::solid()` before the walk through the list of primitives. Its body is located in this file, which allows it to set the global `zbuf_t` pointer to the newly constructed Z-buffer. After displaying the scene, `zscene_t::solid()` frees the allocated memory.

The Z-buffer must be initialized with 1's, because the algorithm works only with depth values of the perspective transformation; these lie between -1 and 1, so 1 is the largest possible depth.

The Z-buffer algorithm is the simplest general-purpose hidden surface algorithm. Its only disadvantage is that it requires an enormous storage capacity for the buffer. Better graphics machines usually come with built-in Z-buffer and hardware support for the algorithm. The next section explains a way of using the algorithm without taking up so much buffer space.

11.2.2   SCAN LINE ALGORITHM

We can implement the scan line algorithm in several ways. We describe one of these. It uses a Z-buffer the size of one scan line. Other variations take better advantage of geometric properties of planes and therefore require less computation, but have more difficult logic, require the maintenance of more complex data structures, and are harder to program. The algorithm's name derives from the fact that it is most convenient to proceed along scan lines when processing individual pixels.

The Z-buffer is called a *scan line buffer*. The algorithm's logic is similar to that of the Z-buffer algorithm. (Also see NESP79, Section 24-4). We assume that the scene is described as one or more meshes of only convex polygons. Because we cannot proceed mesh by mesh, we must process all the scene's polygons simultaneously.

First, we clip all polygons against the given frustum. This will not change their convexity. Then, we do a perspective transformation of all vertices in the scene and scale the x- and y-coordinates to absolute screen coordinates. We should make these changes on copies of the original meshes.

Then, in going through the meshes, we put pointers to all the scene's polygons in one table, as Figure 11.16 shows. In that table, they must be ordered on the maximum y-value of each polygon. We call this the *polygon-table*. Figure 11.16 shows an example of this ordering.

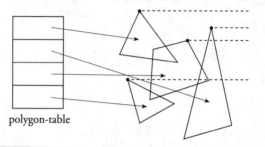

Figure 11.16   Order of the polygons

For this purpose, we use the structure `scanpol_t`, which is shown below. The polygon-table is an array of `scanpol_t`.

```
struct scanpol_t
{
    double    ymax ,                          // maximum y-value
              ymin ;                          // minimum y-value
    plane_t   p    ;             // transformed plane equation
    convex_t* pol  ;                    // pointer to polygon
} ;
```

The variables *ymax* and *ymin* contain the largest and smallest y-value of all polygon vertices, and p must contain the plane through the transformed vertices.

Once the polygon-table is created, the algorithm proceeds as follows. Two integers are maintained—*inpol* and *outpol*. These point into the table to the range of polygons that the current scan line intersects. On decreasing the scan line value by 1, we update *inpol* by looking for *ymax* values larger than the scan line value. We also update *outpol* by looking for *ymin* values larger than the scan line value. We do not have to search the entire table. Polygons that can be included are all below *inpol* and polygons that can be excluded are all between *inpol* and *outpol*. The logic of keeping this table is essentially the same as that described in Section 2.2.2.

For each scan line, the algorithm initializes the scan line buffer to all 1's, which is the maximum relative depth. It updates the pointers *inpol* and *outpol* in the polygon table. The currently intersected polygons are those in the index range from *outpol* through *inpol*.

For an individual polygon in that range, we do something that corresponds to processing a single scan line in the polygon fill algorithm. It is best accomplished as follows. Going through the list of polygon's vertices, we check the y-coordinates of two consecutive triples $(x_1 \ y_1 \ z_1)$

and $(x_2 \; y_2 \; z_2)$ against the scan line. If one is larger and the other smaller, this edge intersects, so we compute the x-value of the intersection and round to the nearest integer:

$$x = int\left(x_2 + (scan - y_2)\left(\frac{x_1 - x_2}{y_1 - y_2}\right)\right)$$

At the same time, we also compute the relative depth at this x-value from the z-coordinates at the two vertices:

$$z = z_2 + (scan - y_2)\left(\frac{z_1 - z_2}{y_1 - y_2}\right)$$

We will always find precisely two intersecting edges, because our polygons are convex. We might have to interchange these two x-values (together with their associated depths) to put them in ascending order. We also compute the depth increment:

$$dz = \frac{z_{beg} - z_{end}}{x_{beg} - x_{end}}$$

where x_{beg} is the first and x_{end} the second x-value after possible interchange and where the same holds for z_{beg} and z_{end}.

For all pixels from x_{beg} to x_{end}, the relative depth is computed. The first depth is z_{beg}. The others are obtained by adding the increment dz to this depth. For each pixel, the depth is compared to the depth already stored in that position of the scan line buffer. If the new value is smaller, it is entered into the scan line buffer at that position. If this occurs, we also set the frame buffer at the position of the scan line and the current x-value to the color derived from the currently intersected polygon.

The next intersecting polygon for that scan line is processed in the same way. When all polygons from *outpol* through *inpol* are processed, the frame buffer contains all visible parts of the scene for that scan line. This is repeated for all scan line values from the top to the bottom of the screen address range.

SUGGESTED READINGS

The Z-buffer algorithm with variants is presented in FVFH90, HILL90, and WATT89; in FVFH90 one can find another presentation of the Warnock algorithm.

EXERCISES

SECTION 11.1

1. Outline in pseudocode the basic idea of the Warnock algorithm.

   The Warnock algorithm fills either pixels or rectangular areas. Figure 11.17 shows how you can indicate this by hand. The small-size squares are pixels that are not to be further subdivided. The upper eight white pixels are filled as two 2×2 blocks, the lower eight as one 2×2 block and four individual pixels. Use this method in the following exercises.

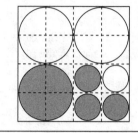

Figure 11.17   Rectangular blocks filled by the Warnock algorithm

2. Given the screen and the triangle definition in Figure 11.18, assume the background to be white and the triangle to be black. Perform the Warnock algorithm by hand and indicate in either black or white the areas that are filled as a whole.

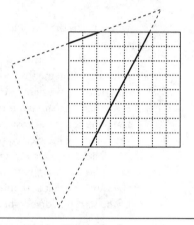

Figure 11.18   Exercise for the screen subdivision

In Figure 11.19, you see not only the filled areas as in Exercise 2, but also numbers that show the order in which the algorithm fills them.

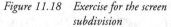

Figure 11.19   Subdivision and order of filling

3. Use the method of Figure 11.19 to indicate the areas and filling sequence for the triangle in Figure 11.20.

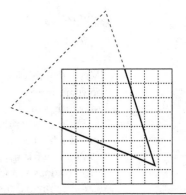

Figure 11.20   *Exercise for the filling sequence*

4. Consider Figure 11.21. How do the lists look when the algorithm is down to pixel (4,4)? How do they look at pixel (3,3)? How do they look at pixel (2,6)? (The small figures indicate how to number the triangles.)

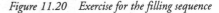

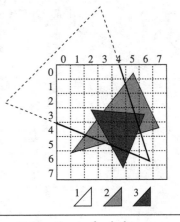

Figure 11.21   *Exercise for the list management*

SECTION 11.2

5. You can save a little computation time when computing the depth increment per pixel in `zedge_t::solidscan()`. Let $ax + by + cz - d = 0$ be the plane equation of a perspective-transformed polygon (this means a perspective depth transformation has been performed on the vertices and the x- and y-coordinates are scaled to absolute device coordinates). Then compute the depth increase from one pixel to the next as follows:
The depth z at a pixel center $(x\ y)$ is

$$z = \frac{d - ax - by}{c}$$

The depth at the next pixel center $(x+1\ y)$ is:

$$z + dz = \frac{d - a(x+1) - by}{c}$$

Subtracting the first from the second equation gives us the depth increment per pixel:

$$dz = -\frac{a}{c}$$

We see that this increment is independent of the point $(x\ y)$; it is constant for the entire polygon. If we normalize the transformed planes to $c = 1$, the depth increment is simply $-a$, which is the negative x-coefficient of the transformed and normalized plane equation. By implementing this, you can save the arithmetic operations for computing the depth increase dz. You can do this plane normalization after you have computed the illumination for that triangle. Do not forget, however, that in the case of reusing that same ztmesh after rotations and so forth, you have to renormalize its plane equations for proper illumination computations.

6. If the template introduced in Exercise 10.15 works on your platform, display a scene with the Z-buffer method as follows. Declare objects of type `mesh_t<zvertex_t, triangle_t>`, read them in, add them to a `zscene_t` and call the scene's `solid()` function. (On the input file such a mesh is just a normal triangle mesh.)

12

HIDDEN LINES AND SURFACES

SPECIAL CASES

In this third chapter on removing hidden lines and surfaces, we consider two special cases, both of which display mathematical functions of two independent variables. There are three sections.

12.0   **Introduction** gives some background information.
12.1   **Hidden Line Removal in Grid Surfaces** describes David P. Anderson's hidden line algorithm for displaying functions that are represented by their values on a set of grid points.
12.2   **Hidden Line Removal for Two-Dimensional Functions** explains how we can draw curves that represent a surface by drawing a sequence of lines at constant values of each independent variable. Doing the second set of curves is the difficult part.

12.0   INTRODUCTION

In mathematics and engineering, it is often useful to display a surface function of the form:

$$z = f(x, y)$$

In this notation the $(x\ y)$-plane is imagined to be horizontal and the z-values are heights above the plane; z then defines a surface in space. In computer graphics, the screen nearly always represents the $(x\ y)$-plane with the z-axis perpendicular to it. The above form could conflict either with our imagination or with this computer graphics coordinate convention, so we will switch y and z and express the function as:

$$y = f(x, z)$$

Here, the function is defined on the horizontal $(x\ z)$-plane in a left-handed coordinate system. It is essential for f to be a single-valued function of x and z, or else there will be two surfaces.

12.1   HIDDEN LINE REMOVAL IN GRID SURFACES

This section describes and develops a C++ implementation for the algorithm that David P. Anderson published in 1982 under sponsorship of the United States Army (ANDE82). We can best clarify its justification and use by citing from the report:

> Hidden line and hidden surface problems are often simpler when restricted to special classes of objects. An example is the class of grid surfaces, i.e. graphs of bivariate functions represented by their values on a set of grid points.
>
> Previous methods for drawing grid surfaces have achieved speed at the expense of exactness and generality. Butland's algorithm (BUTL79) is exact and linear-time but is restricted to parallel projection using a viewing direction whose projection on the xy-plane makes an angle with the x-axis which is a multiple of 45 degrees. The algorithm of Kubert, Szabo, and Gulieri (KSGU68) uses time of order $n^{1.5}$ and is not exact because segments which are partially hidden are not drawn at all. Williamson's algorithm (WILL72) can be used to draw x- or y-direction lines in the grid exactly, but not both . . . .

Anderson's algorithm is mostly used to draw terrain maps on a plotter. Such maps easily consist of up to 200,000 facets. The algorithm is exact, linear-time, and not restricted to certain projections or viewing directions. Its linear running time comes from using a *perimeter* and from processing the grid surface's facets against the perimeter in a certain *occlusion-compatible order*. Sorting and processing the facets simply by their distance from the projection's vanishing point would not guarantee a linear running time. They must also be processed adjacently so that the processed facet can be located quickly in the perimeter.

A *grid surface* interpolates among values defined only at the nodes of a rectangular mesh. Grid surfaces are used to display functions of two independent arguments defined on a plane, for example, $y = f(x,z)$ on the $(x\ z)$-plane. The function value corresponding to a certain argument $(x\ z)$ is $f(x,z)$, which is depicted as the height above the plane at point $(x\ z)$. The set of all function values over the function's definition area constitutes a surface in space. A three-dimensional figure is necessary to display such a function realistically. Relief surfaces are a good example, but modeling a relief surface by calculating many values of $f(x,z)$ is extremely expensive and time-consuming.

If only the function values for grid points in the $(x\ z)$-plane are computed or are otherwise available and if the adjacent points in space are connected by straight lines, we obtain a grid surface. In effect, we interpolate linearly between the available points. This grid surface is then projected onto a two-dimensional medium, either a piece of paper or a display screen. We sacrifice three-dimensionality for the sake of an easy, fast, and inexpensive picture. In most cases this simpler image makes sense because our visual system easily understands projections of three-dimensional objects onto two-dimensional media.

At the very least, we should remove hidden lines when projecting such a grid surface in order to accentuate the three-dimensional appearance. On a raster display, we can use the painter's algorithm to perform a "fake" hidden line removal, but a true hidden line removal algorithm will allow us to draw the grid surface with a plotter.

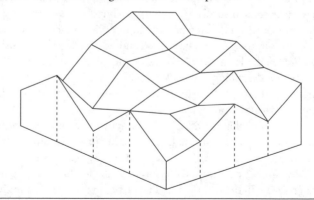

Figure 12.1   A grid surface

Figure 12.1 shows a typical grid surface. Some of its facets are partly or totally hidden. Drawing such a surface by hand is not difficult, but doing it in the computer requires us to determine whether a facet is hidden. To do this, we decompose the grid surface. It consists of the sum of all its facets, defined on a rectangular grid that is not necessarily spaced uniformly.

Each facet is the upper bound of a prism with a rectangular base in the $(x\ z)$-plane. Of course, in the general case, a grid surface's facets can also extend below the $(x\ z)$-plane, but we start with the simpler case of all positive values for $f(x,z)$. This is easier to visualize and we really do not lose generality.

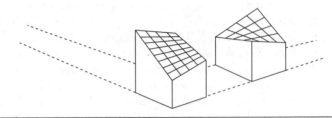

Figure 12.2   Two prisms of a grid surface

Figure 12.2 shows two isolated prisms from the front edge of the grid surface of Figure 12.1. The prism between them has been removed. As the cross lines indicate, the facets are usually not planar rectangles. We now investigate the conditions under which one facet can occlude another.

Whether or not a facet can occlude another depends on the point in space from which the surface is viewed. We let the eyepoint be at an arbitrary position above the surface, with its x- and z-coordinates lying within the grid surface's defined rectangular area. This is the most general approach we can take.

Figure 12.3 shows what we can see when viewing two prisms of a grid surface from straight above at a point between the prisms. The dots mark the grid points in the $(x\ z)$-plane, while dashed lines are hidden. If the prisms' vertical edges are extended downward, away from the eyepoint, their projections will converge to a single point in the drawing, or *van*, the *vanishing point*. This view is like looking down from an airplane onto a landscape of tall skyscrapers. The skyscraper comparison is not only good, but also extremely helpful in training our imagination. But there is a difference between our grid surface and the skyscrapers. The top facets of the prisms in the grid can be slanted and nonplanar, while the skyscrapers are usually topped by horizontal, planar facets. We have to remember this difference.

Before describing the construction of a grid surface, we must precisely define the grid surface in 3D space. To help the reader understand the C++ code, we use C++ language conventions whenever possible.

We assume that $x_0, \ldots, x_{cols-1}$ is a strictly increasing sequence of *cols* real numbers (in C++ we use the subscripts 0 through *cols*–1 rather than 1 through *cols*) and $z_0, \ldots, z_{rows-1}$ is another such sequence of *rows* real numbers. The values are not necessarily uniformly spaced. We use j to subscript the x-values and i to subscript the z-values. Every point with coordinates $(x_j\ 0\ z_i)$ is a *grid point* in the $(x\ z)$-plane. The planes that are vertical to the $(x\ z)$-plane and intersect it along the grid lines $x = x_j$ or $z = z_i$ are called *grid planes*. The rectangle in the $(x\ z)$-plane bounded by the lines $x = x_{j-1}, x = x_j, z = z_{i-1},$ and $z = z_i$ is called the *grid element (i,j)*. There are $(rows-1)*(cols-1)$ grid elements.

The function to be displayed is usually defined for all points in the $(x\ z)$-plane, no matter whether it is a mathematical function or a real-world terrain. Our intent is to obtain function values only at grid points. The function value at the grid point $(x_j\ z_i)$ is y_{ij}. To display the

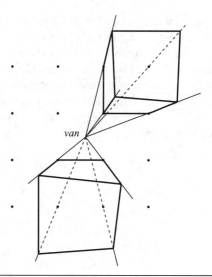

Figure 12.3   Top view of two prisms

function, we find the y_{ij} values, connect those that belong to horizontally adjacent grid points with straight lines, and do the same for the vertically adjacent grid points. This gives us a connected grid of straight lines in 3D space. The grid corresponds to replacing the function between the grid points with a bilinear combination of the function values at the four corner points of this grid element. The bilinear surface above grid element (i,j) is called *facet (i,j)*.

We will project the facet's boundary (its edges) onto the view plane and assume that this gives the facet's projection, even though this is not always correct. There are situations when a facet's projection is not bounded by the boundary's projection (although the facet's projection is always bounded by the convex hull of the boundary's projection). But if we do not make this assumption, the algorithm will be impractically complex. After all, the facets are only approximations of the true function value. They do yield a reasonably good image of the grid surface.

To display the grid surface, we project it onto the view plane using perspective projection. Because the surface can be viewed from any point in space, this leads to nine cases that correspond to nine different positions of the eyepoint's projection relative to the grid surface's subscripts. We explain this below.

As we introduced in Chapter 5, the point from which we view an object is called the *eyepoint* with coordinates $(E_x \ E_y \ E_z)$. To define the view unambiguously, we must also specify the view reference point $(R_x \ R_y \ R_z)$ and the view-up direction $(U_x \ U_y \ U_z)$. The view plane onto which we project is always normal to the viewing direction $(R_x{-}E_x \ R_y{-}E_y \ R_z{-}E_z)$. Once these entities are set, the view plane transformation matrix can be determined and the whole grid surface transformed and projected onto the view plane. This transforms it into a two-dimensional image.

In all our future explanations, we assume $E_y > 0$. In a real-world situation, this corresponds to viewing a terrain from *above* the ground. (To be completely general, we must allow $E_y < 0$, but this differs only by symmetry.) It is essential, however, that $E_y \neq 0$. If we project the eyepoint onto the plane $y = 0$, we get the point $(E_x \ 0 \ E_z)$, which we call *EP* (eyepoint projection). Below, we will make heavy use of this point. Depending on *EP*'s position in relation to the grid-surface boundaries, there are nine different ways of viewing the grid surface and the individual facets. See Figure 12.4.

If *EP* is inside the grid-surface boundaries (area 4), we say that we view the grid surface *face-on* (from above). The picture we see in such a case is like that in Figure 12.3. If *EP* is in the areas 1, 3, 5, or 7, we view the grid surface *edge-on*; if *EP* is in the areas 0, 2, 6, or 8, we view it *corner-on*, as in Figure 12.1.

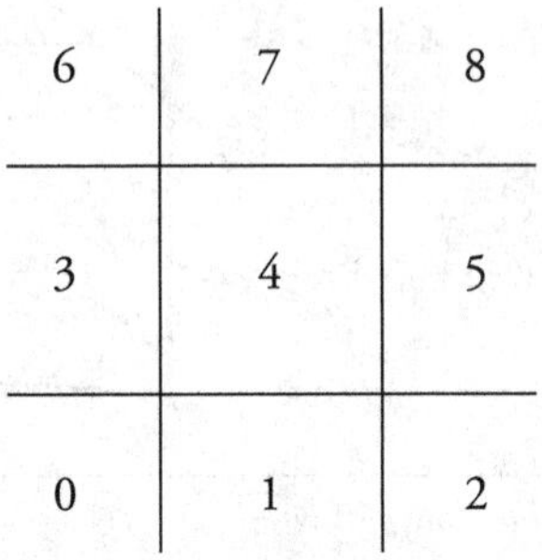

6	7	8
3	4	5
0	1	2

Figure 12.4   Nine different view cases

The vanishing point, *van*, is a point in the view plane. If the vertical edges of the prisms in the grid surface are drawn and if we project them onto the view plane, they converge at *van*. This is also the point where a line parallel to the y-axis and intersecting the eyepoint penetrates the view plane.

In Figure 12.5, the eyepoint's projection, *EP*, is inside the grid surface, which gives a face-on view. The line perpendicular to the viewing direction *R–E* indicates the view plane. The vanishing point is inside the projection of the grid surface onto the view plane.

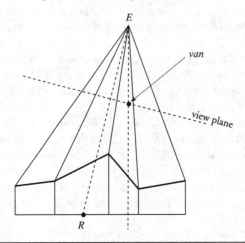

Figure 12.5   Face-on view

In Figure 12.6, the eyepoint's projection is outside the grid surface boundary, which gives a corner-on or an edge-on view. The vanishing point is outside the projection of the grid surface onto the view plane.

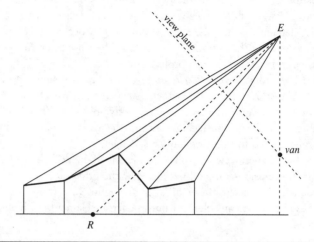

Figure 12.6   Edge-on or corner-on view

OCCLUSION-COMPATIBLE ORDER

From here on, when we talk about facets we mean the projections of the facets in the grid surface onto the view plane. When drawing the projection of the grid surface, we draw only the boundaries of facets that are not hidden by other facets. This is achieved by drawing the grid surface facet by facet in an *occlusion-compatible order*. That is, a facet that could be occluded by another facet is drawn only after that facet.

An important characteristic of grid surfaces is that, in whatever manner they are viewed, the facets can always be arranged in an occlusion-compatible order. This is because a grid surface is a one-valued mathematical function (the grid surface does not "double over"). Drawing grid surfaces differs in this respect from general hidden-line problems where an occlusion-compatible order of facets either does not exist or is expensive to find.

An occlusion-compatible order is a sequential order of the facets where if facet$_i$ can occlude facet$_j$, then $i < j$. Whenever a facet is drawn in an occlusion-compatible order, all facets that can occlude it will already have been drawn. We draw only the part of a facet not occluded by facets drawn so far.

We can determine whether a facet can occlude another in two different ways. One way is to relate the grid elements to the eyepoint projection, *EP*. Another is to relate the facet projections on the view plane to the vanishing point, *van*. These two methods are essentially identical; if a line starts at *EP* and penetrates some grid element, then the perspective projection of this line onto the view plane will start at *van* and will penetrate the projection of the facet of that grid element. The first method is easier to visualize. An order established for the grid elements is also valid for the facets. Grid element *A* can occlude grid element *B* if any straight line from *EP* that penetrates both elements penetrates *A* first. If no line from *EP* penetrates both elements, they have no relationship; any order can be considered occlusion-compatible.

Using *EP* and the grid elements, we can establish an occlusion-compatible order for the facets. Finding this order for a grid surface turns out to be easy. There are many different possible arrangements of the occlusion-compatible ordering. We will explain a simple one below. First, we show two different views of a grid surface (Figures 12.7 and 12.8) in which the grid elements are numbered 1 through 20 in occlusion-compatible order. (Because of the equivalence of the two methods, we will often use the term "element," which can stand for either grid element or facet projection.)

The orders have an *occlusion pivot*, or a pair of subscripts that indicate the area closest to *EP*. If *EP* is inside a grid element, the pivot consists of the subscripts of this element. If *EP* is outside the grid boundary, the respective pivot is either 0 or one higher than the highest subscript of the grid surface. We assume the row and column subscripts below to range from 1 through 5 and from 1 through 4 respectively.

In a face-on view, *EP* will be inside one of the grid elements. This element is certainly the first in occlusion-compatible order. For the other elements, we have indicated one possible ordering. The occlusion pivot is (3 3). Figure 12.7 shows a face-on view of a grid surface. Lines from *EP* to any element must penetrate elements with a lower number before a higher one.

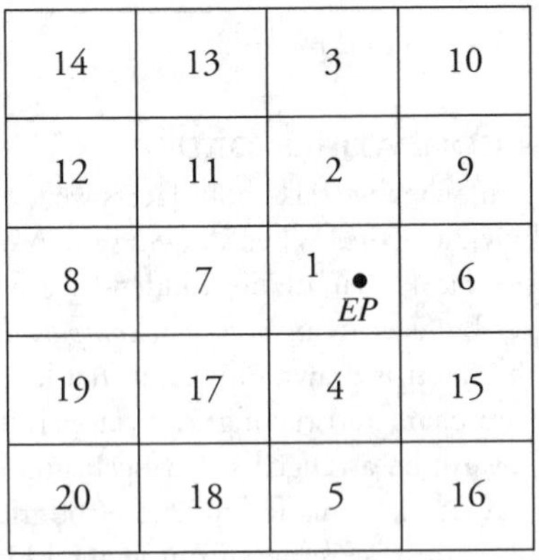

14	13	3	10
12	11	2	9
8	7	1 • *EP*	6
19	17	4	15
20	18	5	16

Figure 12.7   Occlusion-compatible order for EP

In Figure 12.8, *EP* is outside the grid surface, this time giving a corner-on view. The first element in occlusion-compatible order must be the corner element closest to *EP*. For the other elements, a possible ordering is indicated. The occlusion pivot is (0 0).

Figure 12.9 shows a traversal pattern leading to a valid order for any position of *EP*. Eight arrows point away from the occlusion pivot in the center. Following the arrows from their starting points in the order 1 through 8 sweeps over the grid elements in an occlusion-compatible order. At least one of the sweeps will always cover the grid surface, no matter where it is. In the face-on view of Figure 12.7, all eight sweeps cover the surface, and in the corner-on view of Figure 12.8, only sweep 5 covers the surface. If we know the pivot and the subscript boundaries, we can easily implement these sweeps with loops.

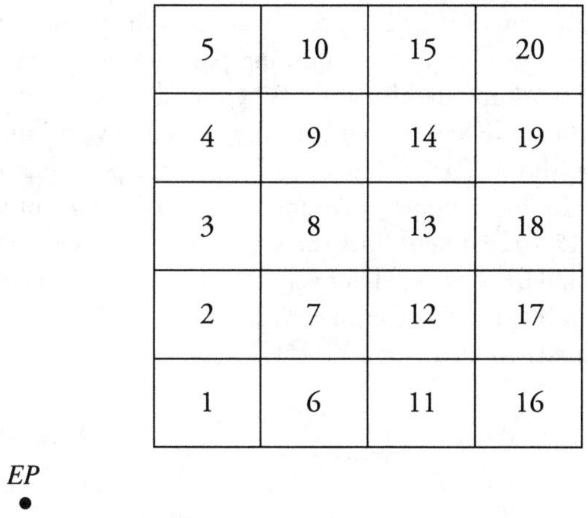

5	10	15	20
4	9	14	19
3	8	13	18
2	7	12	17
1	6	11	16

EP
•

Figure 12.8   Occlusion-compatible order for EP

This pattern also traverses facets in an *monotonic angle order*. Looking from *EP* at a point on an arrow and following the arrow never decreases its angle. The angle increases as we move counterclockwise. We reverse angle directions only when following a dotted line to start the next arrow. Therefore, it is not necessary to search the entire perimeter for the position where the next facet is to be entered. (See ANDE82, p. 18.)

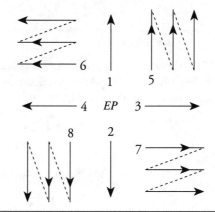

Figure 12.9   Traversal pattern

THE PERIMETER

When facets are drawn in occlusion-compatible order, those facets already drawn form a connected figure; no isolated facets are possible. The outside boundary of this figure is a polygonal outline, henceforth referred to as the *perimeter*. Whenever we draw a new facet whose vertices extend beyond the perimeter, the perimeter will be updated to include these vertices. The perimeter's importance is that, when we want to draw an edge of the facet, we never draw the part of the edge that lies within the perimeter (that part of the edge is hidden).

The initialization of the perimeter depends on the position of *EP* in relation to the grid surface or on the position of the vanishing point in relation to the projected grid surface. (These two relationships are identical.) When we display a perimeter, which consists of projected facet vertices, we have to show its relation to the vanishing point, *van*, not to *EP*. The next two figures show initialization and growth of the perimeter in a face-on view; position 4 in Figure 12.4. In this example, there are no facets occluding others.

In Figure 12.10, the light lines show the projection of the facets of a 3 × 4 grid surface. These lines should be considered not yet drawn. The facet that contains the vanishing point is drawn first; it forms the first perimeter, shown by the heavy outline. This outline is drawn when the perimeter is initialized.

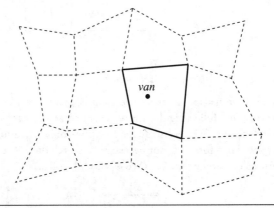

Figure 12.10   Initialization of perimeter

Figure 12.11 shows the perimeter three facets later. As each new facet extended beyond the perimeter, the perimeter was updated and new heavy lines were drawn. The current perimeter is the outer boundary of the heavy lines.

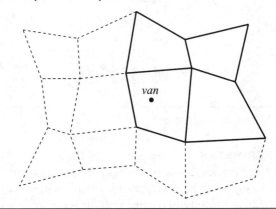

Figure 12.11   Perimeter after adding three facets

The next two figures show the perimeter's initialization and growth in an edge-on view. Here, some facets are occluding others.

In Figure 12.12, the vanishing point is outside the perimeter in front of the front edge. This gives an edge-on view, one of the positions 1, 3, 5, or 7 in Figure 12.4. Here, the perimeter is initialized with the sum of all front edges of the front facets.

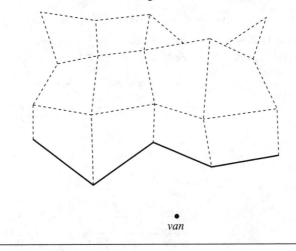

van

Figure 12.12   Initialization of perimeter

In Figure 12.13, the perimeter is shown three facets later in heavy lines. The first facet added was the one immediately opposite the vanishing point. Then came those behind that facet. As each facet extended beyond the perimeter, the perimeter was updated and new parts were drawn. Observe that the third facet is partly hidden behind the second.

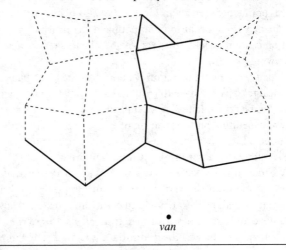

van

Figure 12.13   Perimeter after adding three facets

If a view is corner-on, the perimeter is initialized with the two front edges of the corner facet closest to the vanishing point and the front edges of all facets on the grid boundaries adjacent to that corner.

To understand the detail of a particular initialization in terms of the subscripts, refer to Figure 12.14. An *EP* position in area 5 (on the right of the grid surface) requires an initial perimeter consisting of the perspective projections of the points

$$\left(x[cols-1]\ \ y[i][cols-1]\ \ z[i]\right)\quad \text{for}\quad rows-1\ge i\ge 0$$

onto the view plane. Subscript i is decreasing, because we are looking from the right to the surface and going ccw through the points of the boundary.

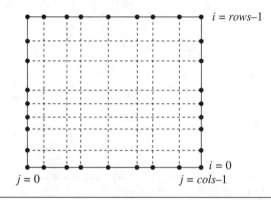

Figure 12.14   Grid point subscripts

When the viewing direction is not parallel to (or not nearly parallel to) the $(x\ z)$-plane, the images drawn have two important properties: they are always coherent and they are *star-convex* around *van*. The latter property means that if two image points lie on a ray from *van*, then all points between them on that ray also belong to the image. *Star-convexity* is a direct consequence of the occlusion-compatible order in which the drawing is done. If the viewing direction is not parallel to the $(x\ z)$-plane, the image has these two properties at every stage of the drawing process.

When the viewing direction is parallel to the $(x\ z)$-plane, we have a *horizontal view*. For numerical reasons, we have to treat a view as horizontal when the viewing direction is nearly parallel to the $(x\ z)$-plane. The occlusion-compatible order is that for an edge-on or a corner-on view, depending on the location of *EP*. The problem with these views is that it is numerically impossible to compute the vanishing point. But one can compute an approximation of *van* that allows the algorithm to run in the normal way.

We must now consider a new aspect. We associate an angle with every perimeter vertex by drawing a line from the vertex to the vanishing point and using a reference line such as a horizontal to determine the angle that this line makes. Below we show some perimeters in which the connecting lines are drawn from all vertices to the vanishing point. The perimeter's shape depends on the way the grid surface is viewed. The following figures show two different cases.

In a face-on view, the perimeter might look as it does in Figure 12.15 at any given moment. The vanishing point lies within the perimeter. If the perimeter is traversed ccw, the corresponding angles will monotonically increase.

Figure 12.15   Perimeter in face-on view

In an edge-on view, the perimeter might look as shown in Figure 12.16. *Van* lies outside the perimeter. The boundary nearest *van* is called the *inner perimeter*, while the other boundary is the *outer perimeter*. If the perimeter is traversed ccw, the corresponding angles will monotonically increase on the outer perimeter, but decrease monotonically on the inner perimeter. A corner-on perimeter looks similar to this one.

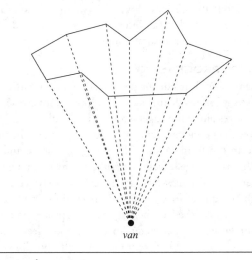

Figure 12.16   Perimeter in edge-on view

This monotonical change along the perimeter results from the star-convexity. If the vertex angles reversed direction while the perimeter vertices are traversed in consecutive order, then the vertices would describe a nonstar-convex shape. This property is called the *monotonicity of the vertex angles of the perimeter*. It is valid at all times while the perimeter is updated and has strong consequences for the algorithm's running time.

In a horizontal view, we compute an approximation for the vanishing point. This approximation lies in the direction of *van*, but not so far as to cause problems of floating point arithmetic over- or underflow. The angles will still differ enough to be distinguishable (see Figure 12.17). The algorithms for edge-on or corner-on processing can handle this case.

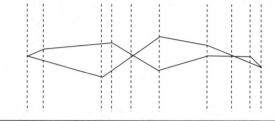

Figure 12.17   Horizontal view, edge-on perimeter

The angle defined above can be associated not only with the perimeter's vertices, but also with a facet's vertices. After all, perimeter vertices and facet vertices all are projected grid surface points. When we update the perimeter by a facet, we determine the biggest and smallest facet angles (the angles grow in ccw order around *van*), which we will call *Fmin* and *Fmax*. The "containing perimeter vertices" are the vertex with angle *Pmin*, which is just smaller than or equal to *Fmin*, and the vertex with angle *Pmax*, which is just larger than or equal to *Fmax*.

We can find all perimeter edges that intersect the facet edges by starting with *Pmin* and following the perimeter in a ccw direction until *Pmax*. This property results directly from the angle monotonicity. Without this ability, we would have to go through the entire perimeter to find perimeter edges that can intersect with the facet edges. This would give the algorithm a running time of at least quadratic order.

FACET PREPROCESSING

When a point is inside the perimeter boundary (inside the heavy lines of Figures 12.11 or 12.13), we say it is inside the perimeter. If the point crosses the perimeter boundary from in to out as it moves along the edge of a facet in the direction of increasing angles, we say that this edge leaves the perimeter. Conversely, an edge enters the perimeter if a point moving along it crosses from out to in. A single facet edge can leave and enter the perimeter several times. Whenever a facet edge leaves the perimeter, the perimeter is enlarged; we say it is updated.

When we add a new facet to the current perimeter, we must check all four facet edges against the perimeter for intersection. If we do this addition in occlusion-compatible order, one or two edges of the facet belong to a facet processed earlier. These edges have already been used in updating the perimeter, so they do not leave it. Consequently, they need not be checked—they are readily determined. It is also possible to determine just from the shape of the facet additional edges that cannot leave the perimeter. This, too, is easy to determine and we can save computation time by not submitting any of those edges to an intersection test. We call this *facet preprocessing*.

Below we explain how to preprocess a facet that is viewed edge-on and is checked against an outer perimeter. (For example, all three facets in Figure 12.13 are viewed edge-on.) We traverse the four facet vertices in the order of increasing angles and name them correspondingly F_0, F_1, F_2, and F_3.

Figures 12.18 through 12.21 show four possible cases. Keep in mind that we are moving ccw through the outer perimeter and the facet, or from right to left. The edge F_0–F_3, drawn each time as a heavy line, is closest to the viewer and is already contained in the perimeter (either by initialization or by being the far edge of a facet that precedes this one in occlusion-compatible order). Thus, the perimeter either runs above the heavy line or coincides with it.

Case 1: If the vertices F_1 and F_2 are both on the right of edge F_0–F_3, then the three other edges can leave the perimeter and must be checked against it.

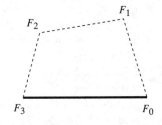

Figure 12.18   *The dotted edges could be outside the perimeter*

Case 2: If the vertices F_1 and F_2 are both on the left of edge F_0–F_3, then none of the other three edges leaves the perimeter, so this facet need not be checked at all.

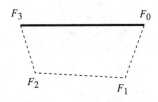

Figure 12.19   *The dotted edges are inside the perimeter*

Case 3: If F_1 is on the right and F_2 on the left, then only the edges F_0–F_1 and F_1–F_2 must be checked.

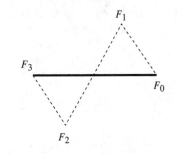

Figure 12.20   *Edge F_2–F_3 is inside the perimeter*

Case 4: If F_1 is on the left and F_2 on the right, then only the edges F_1–F_2 and F_2–F_3 must be checked.

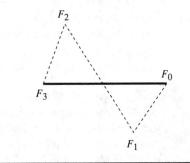

Figure 12.21   *Edge F_0–F_1 is inside the perimeter*

The cases can be distinguished by inserting the $(x\ y)$-coordinates of F_1 and F_2 into the equation of the line through F_0 and F_3 and checking the sign.

We now explain how to preprocess a corner-on facet, checked against an outer perimeter. There are only two different cases. We again number the vertices so that F_0 has the smallest and F_3 the largest angle (see Figures 12.22 and 12.23). The vertices F_0 and F_3 are already in the perimeter for reasons analogous to those mentioned above. Also, either F_1 or F_2 is already in the perimeter. Knowing the position of *EP* in relation to the grid surface allows us to determine which one it is. (See the code `perim_t::preproc_facet()`.) If F_1 is in the perimeter, we exchange the names of F_1 and F_2. As a result, F_0, F_2, and F_3 will be in the perimeter. (F_1 and F_2 are not necessarily in the order of increasing angles, but this is insignificant here.) The edges F_0–F_2 and F_2–F_3 are in the perimeter and are drawn by heavy lines.

We check F_1 against the two edges F_0–F_2 and F_2–F_3 to determine whether it is on the right or left of them.

Case 1 (Figure 12.22): F_1 is on the left of both edges. Neither the edge F_0–F_1 nor F_1–F_3 can leave the perimeter, so this facet need not be checked at all.

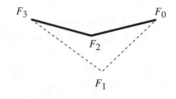

Figure 12.22   *The dotted edges are in the perimeter*

Cases 2, 3, and 4 (Figure 12.23): F_1 is on the right of one or both of the edges F_0–F_2 and F_2–F_3. Then both of the edges F_0–F_1 and F_1–F_3 can leave the perimeter and must be checked against it.

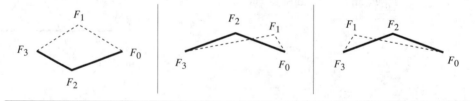

Figure 12.23   *The dotted edges could be outside the perimeter*

The last two cases in Figure 12.23 show that the heavy edges are forming a peak. If they form a valley as in the first case of the figure, then one edge can be completely contained in the perimeter and need not be checked. We can determine what shape the heavy edges form by testing whether F_3 is on the right or left of the edge F_0–F_2. It is questionable, however, whether this would speed up the computation.

THE PSEUDOANGLES

We have explained the reasons for having an angle associated with each perimeter vertex and facet vertex. But it is computationally expensive to work with real angles. This can be avoided by using a *pseudoangle*, which will maintain the angular order of all vertices with respect to *van*.

We define the pseudoangle as shown in Figure 12.24. At 0° the value is –3; at 90° it is –1; at 180° it is 1; and at 270° it is 3. The pseudoangle grows counterclockwise. At 315° there is a discontinuity; on the –45° line the value is –4, while at 315°–ε it is 4–ε for a very small ε. We must consider this discontinuity when comparing vertices' pseudoangles. We cannot directly compare the angle values when determining the relationship between two angles.

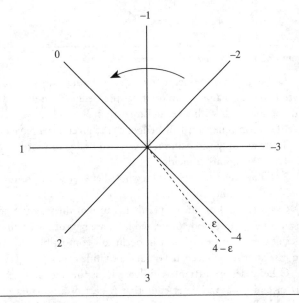

Figure 12.24   Pseudoangle

EDGE-PERIMETER PROCESSING

The task of comparing a facet's edge against the perimeter is at the heart of the algorithm. If the edge leaves the perimeter, the perimeter must be updated, and the updated part must be drawn. A facet's edges will be processed against the perimeter starting with the vertex with the smallest angle and ending with the vertex with the largest angle. This order implies that the first processed edge starts on or inside the perimeter and the last edge ends on or inside the perimeter. We will explain this process for an outer perimeter on which we move from right to left.

We use the abbreviations f-edge for facet edge, f-vertex for facet vertex, and p-edge and p-vertex for the perimeter. We can compare f-vertices to each other and to p-vertices. The terms smaller or larger refer to the pseudoangles of the compared vertices. When an f-edge is tested against the perimeter, we first must find the largest p-vertex smaller than or equal to the smaller f-vertex. The p-edge from that p-vertex to the next one is the rightmost one that can possibly intersect with the f-edge.

Figure 12.25 shows a section of the perimeter in heavy lines and an f-edge in light lines. The "vertical" lines indicate the angles, which grow from right to left. Clearly, no p-edge to the right of P_i can intersect with this f-edge. The p-edges starting at P_i and at P_{i+1} can intersect with this f-edge.

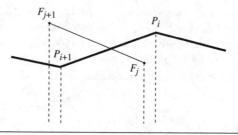

Figure 12.25   Facet-edge and perimeter

An f-edge can intersect many p-edges. In fact, any p-edge to the left of P_i that starts with a vertex smaller than F_{j+1} can intersect the f-edge. Therefore, we must test all p-edges until we find one that ends with a vertex larger than F_{j+1}. Then we advance to the next f-edge of that facet. This continues until all f-edges of the given facet have been processed.

There are only three different ways an f-edge can intersect with a p-edge:

1. Start points coincide.
2. The edges intersect somewhere between start points and end points.
3. End points coincide.

Cases 1 and 3 occur frequently because of the way the perimeter is constructed. Often, the far edges of an already processed facet are part of the perimeter, and coincide with the near edges of a facet processed next in occlusion-compatible order. Case 2 is the normal intersection case after some facets have started to hide others.

Other cases are extremely unlikely. It is theoretically possible that an f-edge happens to start or end on a perimeter edge that is part of a nonadjacent facet. These possibilities are negligible, however, because all floating arithmetic is done in double precision. (The probability is close to that of two random 52-bit long mantissas' being equal, which is about 10^{-16}.) Handling these cases in the algorithm is unduly complicated and is a waste of effort. If they do occur, we can easily eliminate them by changing the eyepoint slightly. This is justifiable because it will not create a perceivable difference in the picture. In these rare cases our algorithm will print a warning message and exit.

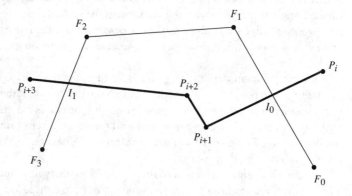

Figure 12.26   Updating the perimeter by a facet

Let us present another example to further clarify the edge-perimeter processing. Figure 12.26 shows a perimeter section with vertices P_i through P_{i+3} and an edge-on facet. The part of the facet that leaves the perimeter will be used to update it. This means that the vertices F_1 and F_2 and the intersection points I_0 and I_1 become p-vertices. The p-vertices P_{i+1} and P_{i+2} must be removed from the perimeter, however. (Because they are already drawn, they remain on the paper. Removal, here, refers to the perimeter's data structure.)

After we update that section of the perimeter, it looks as in Figure 12.27.

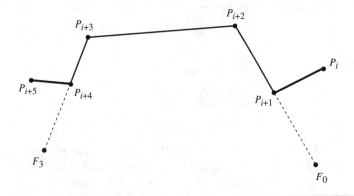

Figure 12.27   Perimeter after updating

We now describe the algorithm for processing a facet. At the beginning, the pointer *per* indicates the largest p-vertex smaller than or equal to the smallest f-vertex. A status variable representing the current position with respect to the perimeter is set to IN. Intersections with the perimeter must occur in pairs. We follow the edges of a facet ccw.

For any edge of a facet (not just the first one) we first check the status. If it is IN, then the edge starts inside or on the perimeter, which must be true for the first f-edge. If it is OUT, then the f-edge starts outside, so its start point is added to a list of new p-vertices. In the case of an edge-on facet, at most two edges can start outside and, in the case of a corner-on facet, at most one. We advance on the perimeter with the pointer *per* and check all p-edges against this f-edge until we find a p-vertex larger than the f-edge's left vertex (this is always the terminating condition for advancement on the perimeter). If an intersection is found, we check the status.

If the status is IN, the intersection is an exit point. The point is immediately added as a new vertex to the perimeter and *per* is advanced to it. The pointer "hold" is set to keep pointing to the new vertex. The status is set to OUT.

If the status is OUT, the intersection is an entry point. This point is immediately added as a new vertex to the perimeter and *per* is advanced to it. Furthermore, all points in the list of new p-vertices are added to the perimeter and all p-vertices between hold and *per* are removed from it. The list of new p-vertices is deleted and the status is set to IN.

Whenever the terminating condition for advancement on the perimeter is met (see above), we advance to the next f-edge of that facet and repeat the whole process just described. We do this until all edges of the facet have been processed. Even f-edges that are preprocessed as being inside the perimeter (they may not intersect) undergo the test in order to advance the perimeter pointer properly.

OO DESIGN AND CLASS SPECIFICATIONS

The code presented provides only for an outer perimeter. This is sufficient in most cases, because grid surfaces are most often used to render terrain maps, which cannot be seen from below. Readers who want to add an inner perimeter can derive everything by symmetry. They must then check every facet, one at a time, against both perimeters.

We do not limit ourselves to grid surfaces in which the x- and z-coordinates are equidistantly spaced. It does not require more storage if this is not the case. If the following data are contained in a file in the given order, they define a horizontal grid surface:

> number of rows (rows)
> row coordinates
> number of columns (cols)
> column coordinates
> row*column elevation values in row major form

We specify a grid surface by the class `gsurf_t`. It is a drawable primitive derived from `prim_t`. We can add a `gsurf_t` object to a scene, rotate it, translate it, and view-transform it.

The array of length *cols*, `xgrid`, stores the x-coordinates of the grid locations, while `zgrid`, the array of length *rows*, stores the z-coordinates. The array of length *rows*cols*, `surf`, stores the elevation values at the grid locations. The class contains only pointers and allocates the arrays dynamically. The surface points' 3D coordinates are then $(x[j]\ \ surf[i][j]\ \ z[i])$ for i from 0 to *rows*-1 and j from 0 to *cols*-1. We must store the full 3D points because once the surface rotates or otherwise changes, the grid property of the x- and z-coordinates is not fulfilled anymore. To save storage space, the surface points are of type `fpoint_t`, defined in `Frac/fpoint.h`, rather than `point3_t`. The type differs from `point3_t` in that the three coordinates are only single precision floating points.

The class `gsurf_t` contains a centroid about which rotations are performed. It contains the number of rows and of columns in order to perform explicitly the subscript arithmetic in the array of surface points. The class has a `plane_t` member that specifies its base plane, the plane in which the grid points lie. This plane is horizontal upon construction and is used in computing the pivot subscripts for the perimeter drawing. This design allows us to perform any desired transformation with the grid surface.

The class `gsurf_t` has two constructors. One constructs a `gsurf_t` object from a file, the other is a copy constructor. A destructor frees all allocated memory. The member functions are `draw()`, `copy()`, and functions for rotation, translation, and viewing transformation.

```
//********************* File gsurf.h *************************

#ifndef GSURF_T
#define GSURF_T

#include "../Frac/fpoint.h"
#include "../Shape3d/point3.h"
#include "../Shape2d/scene.h"
#include "../Shape3d/plane.h"
#include "../Grid/gpoint.h"
```

```
class gsurf_t : public prim_t
{
friend class gsurfiter_t ;
friend class perim_t ;
public:
  ~gsurf_t() ;
  gsurf_t(char*) ;
  gsurf_t(const gsurf_t&) ;

  void draw(const scene_t*) const ;
  prim_t* copy() const ;
  prim_t& rotx(double) ;
  prim_t& roty(double) ;
  prim_t& rotz(double) ;
  prim_t& translate(const point_t&) ;
  prim_t& viewtrans(const point_t&,const point_t&,const point_t&) ;

private:
  fpoint_t* surf ;                        // array of surface points
  float* xgrid ;                          // x-coordinates of grid
  float* zgrid ;                          // z-coordinates of grid
  int rows , cols ;
  point3_t cen ;                                      // centroid
  plane_t base ;                          // grid plane of surface
} ;


#endif

//*******************************************************************
```

The surface points can be considered a matrix-like arrangement of elevation values. Note that subscript j goes with the x-coordinates, that is, from left to right, while i goes with z. Small i-values correspond to the near part of the surface and large i-values to the far part. One must consider this when specifying a surface's file description because the top row in the file is read first and is associated with subscript 0. The array of values in the file cannot be considered as a map of height values seen from above; it must be flipped upside down.

The member function draw() first tests whether the surface is seen from the underside or horizontally. In these cases it exits with a message.

Because every change in the grid surface's orientation changes the vanishing point, this point must be computed before drawing the surface. The vanishing point is where a line through the eyepoint, or the center of projection, and normal to the surface's base plane penetrates the view plane $z = 0$. The static member in the first point of the grid point array is then set to the vanishing point.

Then draw() declares an object of type garray_t of the size *rows*cols* and projects all surface points perspectively onto $z = 0$. The member garray (see below) holds these projections. Each gpoint_t computes its own pseudoangle when it is constructed.

Next, draw() computes the row pivot, *pivi*, and column pivot, *pivj*. It uses the fact that *van*'s position relative to the grid's perspective projection onto the view plane is identical to the position of *EP* relative to the grid. We have already mentioned this in the section "Occlusion-compatible order." The position of *van* determines the pivot. Generally, the grid surface has an arbitrary orientation in space. However, the *x*- and *z*-coordinates of the grid points, contained in `xgrid` and `zgrid`, describe their position in the original, untransformed grid surface.

One approach would be to find the transformation that undoes the grid surface's arbitrary position and apply this transformation to the eyepoint's projection onto the base plane. Then one could compare the resulting point to the grid coordinates. It would not be easy, however, to find this transformation. We describe a simpler approach below.

The grid points form a rectangular grid in the base plane. We compute a vector, *vrow*, that runs parallel to the rows and a vector, *vcol*, that runs parallel to the grid's columns. Figure 12.28 shows the base plane and four corner points of the grid. The points *s*[ ] are surface points, while the points *g*[ ] are the corresponding grid points, obtained by projecting the surface points orthogonally onto the base plane.

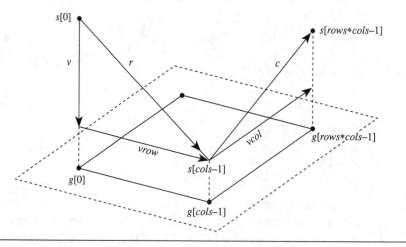

Figure 12.28   Finding vrow and vcol

Vector *v* is parallel to the grid plane normal, *norm*, and its length is the projection of *r* onto *norm*, or the dot product (*norm**r). Vector *r* is *s*[*cols*–1] – *s*[0]. Thus, *vrow* is obtained by vector subtraction: *vrow* = *r* – (*norm**r)*norm. By the same reasoning, *vcol* is obtained as *vcol* = *c* – (*norm**c)*norm.

Once we know *vrow* and *vcol*, we can determine the distance of the eyepoint's projection, *EP*, from the two lines through *g*[0] and parallel to these vectors. See Figure 12.29. The vector from *g*[0] to the eyepoint's projection is *vvan*. We find this vector with the same method that we used in finding *vrow* and *vcol*. Let *e* be the vector from *s*[0] to the eyepoint. Then *vvan* = *e* – (*norm**e)*norm. The distance, *distc*, is the dot product *vvan**vrow divided by the length of *vrow*. This length is simply *xgrid*[*cols*–1] – *xgrid*[0]. Analog reasoning gives the distance *distr*. After adding *xgrid*[0] to *distc* and *zgrid*[0] to *distr*, we can directly compare *distc* and *distr* to the grid point coordinates to find the grid interval containing the pivot.

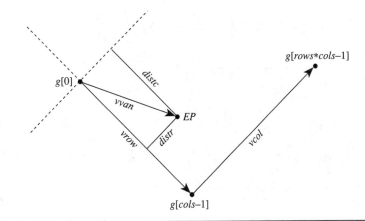

Figure 12.29   Finding distr and distc

When the eyepoint projection is very close (in the order of 0.001 or less) to one of the grid lines, numerical problems can occur in the edge-perimeter checking routine. In such cases, the program exits with the message that any of the viewing parameters should be changed slightly, whether the eyepoint or the view reference or both. The problem usually disappears after such a change.

Below, we specify classes representing projected surface points, an array of projected surface points, a perimeter, a perimeter point, and a facet. An *iterator* for the grid surface is defined, too, and described later. They are used by gsurf_t only so it can draw itself.

As mentioned above, draw() projects all of the surface's 3D points onto z = 0. We call the projected grid surface points gpoints. (Do not confuse them with grid points—we do not need a class for grid points.) They are specified in the class gpoint_t. A gpoint is a 2D point, derived from point_t, and has an additional data member that holds its pseudoangle. The vanishing point is a static data member in gpoint_t. This is the elegant way C++ offers for having common data available to all objects of a class without polluting the global name space and without having to pass it back and forth as a parameter. The constructor for gpoint_t automatically computes its pseudoangle. The class has an overloaded operator to compare gpoints to each other with respect to their pseudoangles.

```
//************************ File gpoint.h ************************

#ifndef GPOINT_T
#define GPOINT_T

#include "../Shape2d/point.h"

class gpoint_t : public point_t              // projected surface point
{
public:
    gpoint_t() ;
    gpoint_t(double,double) ;
```

```
      int operator < (const gpoint_t&) const ;         // angle comparison
      int operator > (const gpoint_t&) const ;
      int operator !=(const gpoint_t&) const ;
      void setvanpoint(point_t) ;

   private:
      static double vx , vy ;              // vanishing point coordinates
      double ang ;                         // angle around vanishing point
   } ;

   #endif

   //**********************************************************************
```

We need pseudoangle computations when we construct a gpoint. This occurs not only when the array of surface points is projected onto the viewplane, but also when new gpoints are created as edge-perimeter intersections. These, too, must have the static vanishing point data available.

Similar to the surface points in gsurf_t, the gpoints are held in a 2D array of size *rows* × *cols*. The array is represented by the class garray_t (gpoint array) and has an overloaded subscript operator for easy access to its elements.

```
   //*********************** File garray.h ***********************

   #ifndef GARRAY_T
   #define GARRAY_T

   #include "../Grid/gpoint.h"

   class garray_t                         // array of projected grid points
   {
   friend gsurfiter_t ;
   friend perim_t ;

   public:
      garray_t(int rows,int cols) : rows(rows) , cols(cols) ,
         g(new gpoint_t[rows*cols]) {}
      ~garray_t() { delete g; }

      gpoint_t* operator [] (int i) { return g + i*cols; }

   private:
      int rows ;
      int cols ;
      gpoint_t* g ;
   } ;

   #endif

   //**********************************************************************
```

A group of 2×2 adjacent gpoints in `garray_t` is a facet. A facet, therefore, consists of an array of four gpoints. An additional data member is the viewcase. We know from above that there are eight different viewcases. (The case "straight-on" occurs at most once in every drawing process and is used in initializing the perimeter. It cannot occur later in the drawing process.)

To construct a facet, one calls its constructor with `garray`, the array of gpoints, the subscripts of its lower left corner in `garray`, and the viewcase. The facet constructs itself from the gpoints with subscripts $[i][j]$, $[i{-}1][j]$, $[i{-}1][j{-}1]$, and $[i][j{-}1]$, taken in such an order that their pseudoangles are increasing; no angle testing is necessary. In edge-on cases, the angle order is clear from the subscripts. In corner-on cases, the smallest and largest angles are clear and the order of the two middle ones is insignificant, as one of them has already been processed against the perimeter by a former facet. We just have to distinguish between the eight different viewing cases (see Figure 12.25) and the proper arrangement becomes a simple matter.

A default constructor that initializes the viewcase to an impossible value is provided.

```
//*********************** File facet.h ***********************

#ifndef FACET_T
#define FACET_T

#include "../Grid/garray.h"
#include "../Grid/gpoint.h"

struct facet_t
{
    facet_t(const garray_t&,int,int,int) ;
    facet_t() ;                          // initialize to impossible value
    gpoint_t g[4] ;
    int viewcase ;
} ;

#endif

//*************************************************************************
```

The class `perim_t` represents the perimeter. It basically consists of a doubly linked list of perimeter points, `ppoint_t`. A perimeter point is derived from `gpoint_t` and has a forward and a backward link. Another structure that is needed only here is that of an edge formed by two gpoints. These two structures are therefore declared in the same file with `perim_t`.

In this algorithm, it is essential that every change to the perimeter (initialization or updating) must immediately be drawn on the output device.

The constructor `perim_t()` constructs a doubly linked list of the gpoints that form the first perimeter. Nine different initializations are possible, depending on the viewcase. The nine different initializations include one face-on case, four edge-on cases, and four corner-on cases. A face-on perimeter is a cyclicly closed doubly linked list. The others are doubly linked, too, but have a leftmost and a rightmost vertex.

There are a few special-purpose member functions. The function adjust_per_to()
points per to the perimeter point whose angle is smaller than or equal to a given gpoint.
Insert() inserts a given gpoint in the perimeter after the pointer "per" (in ccw direction)
and then advances *per* to this point. We also use this routine when we construct the first
perimeter. The function remove_insert() is another typical routine. It replaces all points
in the perimeter between "per" and "hold" with a given list of new gpoints, and then draws the
new part.

The overloaded operator += adds a new facet to the perimeter. It first tests the facet's
viewcase. If it has the value −1 (an impossible value), the operator does nothing and returns
FALSE. Otherwise, it initializes variables for the insertion process, adjusts the perimeter pointer,
preprocesses the facet to get the status of its edges, and then submits the edges individually to
the perimeter (two edges in corner-on cases, three in edge-on cases). Then it returns TRUE.

The other member functions have simple and obvious meanings.

```
//*************************** File perim.h ***************************

#ifndef PERIM_T
#define PERIM_T

#include "../Shape2d/win_view.h"
#include "../Grid/facet.h"
#include "../Grid/garray.h"

struct edge_t
{
    gpoint_t a , b ;                           // end points of edge
    int status ;                               // preprocessing status
    edge_t() {} ;
} ;


struct ppoint_t : public gpoint_t
{
    ppoint_t(gpoint_t g,ppoint_t* prev,ppoint_t* next) :
        gpoint_t(g) , prev(prev) , next(next) {}
    ~ppoint_t() { delete next; }
    ppoint_t* prev , *next ;
} ;


class perim_t
{
public:
    perim_t(const garray_t&,int,int,const win_view_t&) ;
    ~perim_t() ;
    int    operator += (const facet_t&) ;      // add facet to perimeter

private:
    ppoint_t* per ;
    const win_view_t &wv ;
```

```
   void    adjust_per_to            (const gpoint_t&) ;
   int     right_of_perimeter       (gpoint_t) ;
   void    remove_insert            (ppoint_t*,ppoint_t*) ;
   int     sect_edge_perim          (edge_t,gpoint_t*) ;
   void    insert                   (gpoint_t) ;
   void    check_against_perimeter  (edge_t) ;
   void    preproc_facet            (const facet_t&,edge_t*) ;
} ;


#endif

//**************************************************************
```

The facets must be taken from the projected grid surface, garray, and processed in occlusion-compatible order. Here is a beautiful example of an iterator class, a concept that C++ provides for such cases. We define an iterator class gsurfiter_t for gsurf_t. It is initialized with the grid surface and takes from it all the information it needs to fulfill its purpose. As with all iterators, it has a pointer to the object through which it iterates.

The iterator has a constructor and a member function next_facet() that returns the next facet in occlusion-compatible order. As soon as it determines the subscripts of the facet to be returned, it constructs that facet with its own constructor giving it the subscripts and the viewcase. That constructor produces the facet right away in the proper angle-order and next_facet() returns it. It could hardly be more convenient! When no more facets are to be returned, next_facet() returns a default facet, which has an impossible viewcase value. The viewcase is tested by the operator +=, which adds a facet to the perimeter.

The details of the iterator implementation are not very important, so we do not explain them. The interested reader can glean them from the code with the help of Figure 12.9. Basically, the iteration consists of eight loops, seven of which can be empty.

```
//********************** File gsurfite.h **********************

#ifndef GSURFITER_T
#define GSURFITER_T
#include "../Grid/garray.h"
#include "../Grid/facet.h"

class gsurfiter_t
{
public:
   gsurfiter_t(const garray_t&,int,int) ;
   facet_t next_facet() ;

private:
   const garray_t* g ;
   int rows    , cols    ,
       pivi    , pivj    ,
       upi     , upj     ,
       downi   , downj   ,
```

```
        upi1    , upj1    ,
        upi2    , downj2  ,
        downi3  , upj3    ,
        downi4  , downj4  ;
    } ;

#endif


//********************************************************************
```

The file `Grid/geometry.c` contains some free test functions from planar geometry, such as the intersection of two line segments. It is not shown here.

In the cases of a horizontal view or a view from underneath, the grid surface is not drawn. These cases are detected easily in `gsurf_t::draw()`. The normal of the base plane is checked. If its z-component is greater than zero, the surface points away from the viewer, who sees the underside. If the z-component is close to zero, one has a horizontal view. In both cases, the program exits with a message.

Figure 12.30 shows a sample grid surface of 15×15 points.

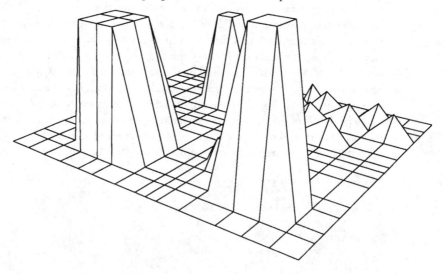

Figure 12.30   Grid surface drawn by the algorithm

12.2   HIDDEN LINE REMOVAL FOR TWO-DIMENSIONAL FUNCTIONS

Using the relatively simple floating horizon method, we can display a function defined on a 2D plane with hidden lines removed. This method can be implemented in a variety of ways and is restricted to raster displays.

We develop an algorithm that displays a 2D function by drawing the crosshatch lines in the surface as individual curves on the display. The algorithm is essentially identical to the one described in BUGI89, but there are a few differences. It is implemented in C++, it uses a simple straight line DDA rather than Bresenham's straight line DDA, it does not require a prerotation of the surface points, and it improves a minor shortcoming of that implementation.

We display the function by drawing two sets of space curves. One set of curves is intersections of $f(x,z)$ with planes of constant z-values; the other set is intersections of $f(x,z)$ with planes of constant x-values. On the screen we draw the perspective projections of these curves onto the plane $z = 0$. The effect is to display the surface as if it were crosshatched. Drawing these curves is simple; the difficulty is suppressing hidden lines. We develop the algorithm for this in steps.

12.2.1   UNIDIRECTIONAL HATCHING

When we draw the first set of curves, suppressing the hidden parts of the curves is easy. We assume that the first curves are the intersections of $f(x,z)$ with planes of constant z-values. If our viewing direction is toward the positive z-axis in a lefthanded system, it is easy to see that the planes with smaller z-values are closer to us.

The essential ideas behind the algorithm are:

1.   Draw the nearest curves before those farther away.

2.   Draw only those parts of each curve that are above or below anything drawn so far.

Figure 12.31 demonstrates these ideas. Curves 1 through 5 are drawn in that order. Whenever a curve dips below the upper horizon or rises above the lower horizon, it is not drawn; we draw only those parts above the upper or below the lower horizon. We update the respective horizon by the part drawn.

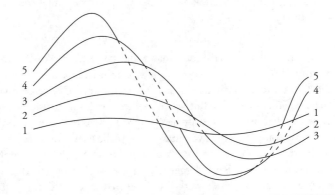

Figure 12.31   Basic idea of the floating horizon algorithm

On the left side of the display, we see the upper side of the surface; in the middle and on the right are parts of the underside.

We draw the curves that form the surface just by setting pixels on the raster display. We assume that the display has a width of *DWID* pixels and a height of *DHEI* pixels. Each pixel to be set is addressed by two integers, x_i and y_i; x_i ranges from 0 to $DWID-1$ and y_i from 0 to $DHEI-1$. The upper and lower horizons are kept in two integer arrays of length $DWID$, called upper and lower. Upper holds the greatest y_i values so far drawn and lower the smallest y_i values.

We restrict ourselves to drawing curves from left to right. The arguments and values of the function $f(x,z)$ are given in world coordinates. We must evaluate $y = f(x,z)$ for z = constant and an increasing x. We then rotate the obtained 3D points as specified, project them perspectively onto the screen, transform them to device coordinates, and connect the obtained points on the screen with straight lines.

Rotating the surface in space

The surfaces considered here are usually displayed in a slanted view. We could compute the function values on a more or less fine raster, store the obtained 3D points, and then rotate them into the desired position. But we do not do this, because for the display we do not evaluate the function on a raster. Instead, we evaluate it along a set of lines that run parallel to the x-axis and on another set of lines that run parallel to the z-axis. The number of evaluations along each line is much higher than the number of lines in either direction. When we display a function with hatch lines (or better hatch "curves"), the number of hatch lines should not be too high. But the individual hatch lines should be curves rather than polygonal lines, which necessitate a high number of function evaluations.

We achieve the rotation by individually rotating every computed point $p = (x \; f(x,z) \; z)$ of the surface before projecting it. Rotating p gives us the 3D point pr. The projection and transformation to absolute device coordinates is done by subjecting the point to the window-to-device transformation of the given window-viewport system, wv:

$$wv.win\_dev(pr)$$

This changes pr itself. Now we take the point's x- and y-coordinates, cast them to integers, and obtain:

$$xi = int(pr.x) \quad \text{and} \quad yi = int(pr.y)$$

This results in device coordinates that range from 0 to $DWID-1$ in xi and from 0 on the top to $DHEI-1$ on the bottom of the screen in yi. As explained in Chapter 2, the majority of absolute device coordinates have $y = 0$ at the top. Device configurations with $y = 0$ at the bottom sometimes exist. But we choose the predominant situation for our explanations. The presented algorithm can easily be changed to inverted screen coordinates.

After computing the two values xi and yi above, we compare yi to upper[xi]. If $yi <$ upper[xi], we set the pixel ($xi \; yi$) and update upper[xi] to yi. (A higher upper horizon means smaller y-coordinates!) If yi is not larger than upper[xi], we see whether $yi >$ lower[xi]. If so, we set pixel ($xi \; yi$) and update lower[xi] to yi. If neither condition is true, we do nothing.

To start the process, we initialize the upper (lower) horizon with numbers smaller (larger) than all those in later comparisons. All values in the array upper are set to 0 and all values in the array lower are set to $DHEI-1$. When a pixel is first checked, both horizons will be set to this pixel's y-value and the pixel will be set on the display.

When we draw a line from any point to any other on the display, then for every pixel to be set in the drawing process we check its y-value yi against the upper horizon upper[xi] and against the lower horizon lower[*xi*]. We can add this checking to a straight line DDA algorithm adapted for drawing floating horizons. We choose a simple straight line DDA for this purpose, because it is much simpler than Bresenham's DDA and because the additional comparisons would outweigh Bresenham's speed advantage.

A slight shortcoming of the DDA method is that gaps in the curves appear, particularly in those parts where the curve is almost vertical on the display and that are drawn downward with respect to the upper horizon. This is because after we test and set the first pixel, subsequent pixels with the same *x*-coordinate and higher *y*-coordinates cannot be set, as they lie below the upper horizon. The same applies to the lower horizon if the curve climbs upward steeply. We can somewhat mitigate (but not remove) this defect by drawing lines only upward. The DDA simply checks the line's start and end points and swaps them if necessary. This helps in most cases, because the functions are usually viewed from above, so lines below the lower horizon seldom occur. General solutions are possible, but require more testing and slow down the algorithm. They are not implemented here.

If we look toward the positive *z*-axis to view the surface, then we draw subsequent curves for increasing constant *z*-values. Curves drawn later will be farther away from us. Thus, we obtain a surface display hatched in one direction. This form of the algorithm is easy to program. Figure 12.32 shows the function:

$$f(x,z) = 0.7*\exp(4\log(\sin(1.7(x^2 + z^2)))) - x^2 - z^2)$$
$$+ 0.15*\sin(1.8*x + 0.3)*\cos(1.8*z - 0.3)$$

in the definition area $[-\pi\ \pi] \times [-\pi\ \pi]$. It is rotated by 28° about *y*, −37° about *x*, and displayed with 37 unidirectional hatch lines.

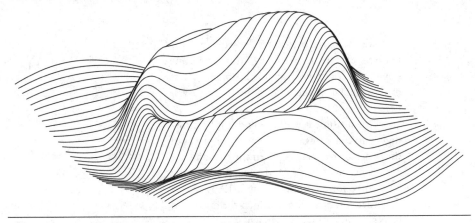

Figure 12.32   Surface drawn with unidirectional hatch

12.2.2   CROSSHATCHING

In Figure 12.32, we displayed the surface function by drawing the curves of intersections of $f(x,z)$ with planes of constant *z*-values. We want to further develop the algorithm to display the surface in a crosshatch manner, drawing curves of intersections of $f(x,z)$ with planes of constant *x*-values. Adding the second set of curves is not trivial, however.

It might seem that all we need to do is draw both sets of curves on top of each other, but this will not suppress all hidden lines. Figures 12.33 and 12.34 show two individual sets of curves. Figure 12.35 reflects the result of an overlay, and Figure 12.36 demonstrates the display that we want.

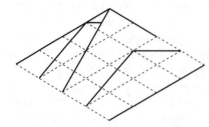

Figure 12.33   Curves of constant z

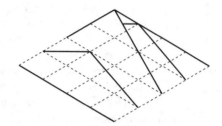

Figure 12.34   Curves of constant x

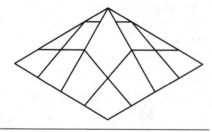

Figure 12.35   Overlay

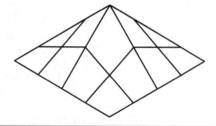

Figure 12.36   Correct display

We obtain the correct result by drawing the two sets of curves alternately, using the same upper and lower horizon for both. Both sets must be drawn in the order of increasing z-values.

One possible way of doing this is by drawing a curve at constant z, drawing all pieces of the constant x-curves between the first and the next constant z-curve, and then drawing the next curve for constant z. Figure 12.37 shows the order and direction in which the curve and pieces of curves must be drawn.

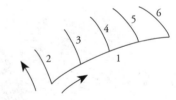

Figure 12.37   Drawing from left to right

Another possibility is to draw a curve at constant x and then draw the pieces of constant z-curves between the constant x-curve and the next constant x-curve. This is shown in Figure 12.38.

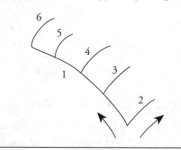

Figure 12.38   Drawing from right to left

IMPLEMENTATION

The algorithm assumes the function's definition area to be the square [−0.5 0.5] × [−0.5 0.5]. A function with a different definition area must scale the submitted argument from [−0.5 0.5] × [−0.5 0.5] to its own definition area. The definition area represents a square of size 1 × 1 in world coordinates. Where it appears on the screen depends on the specified window-viewport system. After rotating the definition area by 45° about y, its width will be roughly 1.41 times as wide as when unrotated. So as not to have too much of the display clipped away, one should consider this when specifying the window-viewport system.

The 2D function to be displayed is implemented in the file func.c. As explained above, the algorithm evaluates it for arguments that run equispaced along a grid of parallel lines through the definition area [−0.5 0.5] × [−0.5 0.5]. For a constant-z curve, the function is evaluated on 200 x-values equispaced from 0.5 to 0.5. For a constant-x curve, it is evaluated on 20 z-values equispaced between the given and the next constant-z value.

The 2D function used in our example has a definition area of [−π π] × [−π π] and transforms the passed arguments to this area.

The 2D function can be displayed as if rotated about y and x in this order. The function setrotation() in the file rotpoint.c computes the matrix for this rotation. The function rotate_xy() in the same file rotates individual surface points of the 2D function.

The function floathor() displays the 2D function. Its arguments are the number, *num*, of crosshatch curves in each direction (the same in x and in z), the rotation angles about x and y, the 2D function to be plotted, and the 3D window-viewport system. It draws constant z-curves through the whole x-extent, each followed by *num* constant-x curve pieces that reach from the just-used z-value to the next z-value. Drawing the constant-x curves is not repeated after the last constant-z curve.

Together with the function value at $(x\ z)$, each coordinate pair $(x\ z)$ forms a 3D-point $(x\ f(x,z)\ z)$. This point is rotated and then projected and transformed to screen coordinates. After computing two consecutive points in this manner, floathor() calls fhor_dda() to draw the connecting line. To avoid computing and transforming every point twice, the last computed point and its device coordinates are kept on local variables inside the loops. Fhor_dda() maintains the upper and lower horizons by doing all the testing as described above. Since the window-viewport system is 3D, the transformation to device coordinates does a perspective projection. One can obtain unidirectional hatching simply by commenting out the loop for the constant-x curves.

The main() routine sets a 3D window-viewport system and displays the 2D function for a varying number of rotation angles. Rotations are permitted only by positive angles smaller than 90° about y and by negative angles greater than −90° about x in this order. Through the y-rotation we obtain a corner-on view; through the x-rotation we can tilt the surface toward the viewer.

To allow arbitrary rotations of the surface, we must dynamically adapt to the viewing case the order of drawing the constant-z and constant-x curves. This requires adding case distinctions to the code and is an exercise. Figure 12.39 shows the same surface as Figure 12.32 in crosshatches.

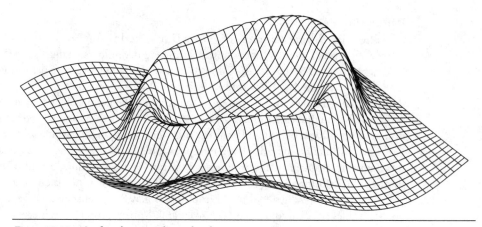

Figure 12.39   Surface drawn with crosshatch

EXERCISES

SECTION 12.1

1. See Figure 12.40. Process the facet (indicated by dotted lines) edge-on against the perimeter (indicated by solid lines). In all cases, draw the new perimeter by hand, or state whether this is impossible to do.

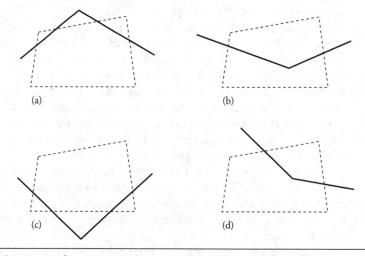

Figure 12.40   Exercise for perimeter updating

2. Construct a fractal grid surface by declaring an object of type `frect_t`, as developed in Chapter 9. Instead of drawing the fractal surface, write its data to a temporary file compatible with the grid surface description file explained in the text. (The fractal surface points can be accessed with the operator `[] []`.) Declare a grid surface, read the file, and display it using Anderson's algorithm.

3. Derive a class `hfrect_t` (hidden line fractal rectangle) from `frect_t` and give it the proper constructors and destructors. Make the display of the fractal surface developed in Exercise 2, a member function of `hfrect_t` by calling it `draw()`, thereby redefining the virtual function `draw()` of `frect_t`. A fractal surface of type `hfrect_t` will then use the hidden line method when drawing itself.

4. Display the fractal grid surface using "fake hidden line removal," as explained in Chapter 10. Do this by reversing the occlusion-compatible order developed in this chapter. Then draw the projections of the facets in the reversed order. Draw each facet as a polygon filled with the background color, then draw its outline with a different color.

SECTION 12.2

5. Draw in crosshatch the function $y = (\frac{1}{5})*\sin(x)*\cos(z) - (\frac{3}{2})*\cos(7a/4)*\exp(-a)$ with $a = (x-\pi)^2 + (z-\pi)^2$ displayed in the area $[0\ 2\pi] \times [0\ 2\pi]$. You have to scale the unit-interval to the given definition area. A display of this function in unidirectional hatch can be seen in ROGE85.

6. Currently all pixels to be set are tested against the horizons. This causes the terminal pixels of every line to be tested twice. One can increase the algorithm's speed by changing `fhor_dda()`. Eliminate the first pixel's testing (be careful about swapping the terminal points). When you draw one continuous curve, the individual lines are chained and each pixel tested only once. Each time you draw a new curve, first draw a `fhor_dda` line from the curve's starting pixel to itself.

7. (Senior project) If we just draw the constant-z and the constant-x curves in the given order, we can view only the surface from the negative z-axis. To view the surface from any other point, we must change the order. The simplest and most straightforward change is to keep track of the viewer's position (through rotations or view plane transformations) and to follow one of four different drawing orders. Just duplicate the code, change the orders in each code copy accordingly, and use the proper case when drawing. (Remember that we do not rotate or transform the surface, but each of its points when we draw.)

8. Views from straight above are still not possible. Why not?

9. (Senior project) Adapt the number of straight-line pieces used to draw one constant-x or constant-z curve to the extent of the curve in terms of pixels horizontally (not vertically) on the display. You can compute this extent from the given window-viewport system and the specified rotations. Compute the number of pieces so that each piece advances by two pixels horizontally.

13

SHADING
METHODS

In Chapter 13 we explain three methods often employed for shading polyhedral objects. The last two create the appearance of smoothness, even when a surface is composed of planar polygons.

13.0   Introduction outlines some factors that are important in creating realism.

13.1   Lambert Shading is the simplest shading method that takes light sources and illumination models into consideration. Objects appear faceted, not smoothly rounded.

13.2   Phong Shading is a technique for rendering the surfaces of displayed objects, making them appear smoothly rounded, creased, or peaked as desired.

13.3   Gouraud Shading is another technique for smooth rendering, but is less powerful than Phong shading.

13.0   INTRODUCTION

One of the major goals of computer graphics is to give an image visual realism, but producing images that look real is very difficult to achieve. The dictionary defines *rendering* as making a drawing in ways that bring out form and modeling. We want to render each part of our scenes to simulate real-world objects. But we cannot work only with individual objects; the objects within a scene interact. Light reflects from one object onto others. Objects cast shadows. They have textures, colors, and highlights, or they may be transparent. Models must be developed for each of these phenomena. Most important in this context is the interaction between light and an object's surfaces.

Shading an object reveals its form, helping to display the object realistically. In this chapter we discuss some well-known methods for shading. But we must first distinguish between the object's internal representation and the real-world solid object it is supposed to represent.

Consider objects with smooth, nonplanar surfaces. As discussed in Chapter 8, unless an object's surface has a simple mathematical description or can be assembled from one, we must describe its surface with parametric bicubic patches or the like. Rendering these is complicated and time-consuming.

It is not always necessary to use nonplanar surfaces, however. There are rendering methods that make a surface appear smoothly curved, even if it is not represented as smooth internally.

A typical example is illustrated in Figure 13.1. Internally, the object is just a prism with six faces. Using shading methods that we describe in this section, we can render this prism so that it looks like a cylinder in the display. In this chapter we consider only solid objects that are internally represented as solids bounded by planar polygons. Note the discrepancy between the seemingly smooth mantle of the cylinder and the polygonal edges of the top and bottom surfaces. The "smooth shading" methods discussed below are notorious for this effect.

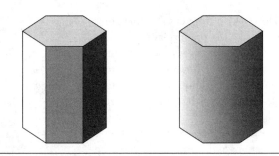

Figure 13.1   Internal representation of a solid and its smoothly shaded display

We will concentrate on shading techniques. Our objective is to make a surface composed of planar polygons appear smoothly curved.

13.1 LAMBERT SHADING

Lambert shading, also called *faceted shading*, does not achieve our goal of making a displayed object appear smooth, but studying it leads to two methods that do accomplish this goal. For each polygon that makes up the object's surface, we compute its surface normal and apply the illumination model to compute the surface's intensity. We then project the polygon and fill the projection with this intensity. The result will be a faceted object; that is, the object will look precisely as it is represented internally.

To come closer to a smooth appearance, we would have to increase the number of polygons that bound the object. This is feasible for uncomplicated objects such as a cone or a cylinder. For more complicated objects, the number of polygons is too great. Figure 13.2 shows the prism of Figure 13.1 with an increased number of vertical faces.

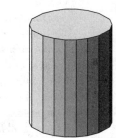

To make the appearance really smooth would require the polygons to be very narrow—of the order of a few pixels—which is impractical. The Lambert shading method never gives a smooth-looking surface.

Figure 13.2   Cylinder approximated by many flat facets

To display any "Lambert shaded" polyhedron, specify it as a triangle mesh with an *rgb*-color in a file, create a `tmesh_t` object from the file, and then display it with `Shape3d/tmesh_t::solid()` as shown in Chapter 10.

Before we describe two methods that do give smooth shading, we will disucss *vertex normals*, which are common to both. A vertex is the point where three or more of the object's plane faces meet. Mathematically, this point cannot have a normal. The concept of a vertex normal is just a practical expedient.

A vertex normal is the average of the normals of the polygons that surround this vertex. In Figure 13.3 the vertex *A* is surrounded by the polygons 1, 2, 3, and 4. The polygon's surface normals are shown as light arrows, the vertex normal at *A* as a heavy arrow.

The object is stored as a simple polygon mesh like the one explained in Section 10.1. The object's vertices are stored in the vertex table. The vertex structure is extended to contain not only the vertex's (*x y z*)-coordinates, but also the vertex normal.

The rendering process involves filling the projections of the surface's polygons by using the polygon-filling algorithm of Chapter 2. There is one essential difference, however. We do not just fill with a constant color, but with intensities that are computed separately for each pixel in the fill line. The part of the fill algorithm that actually draws a fill line needs to be replaced by a loop that sets each pixel individually.

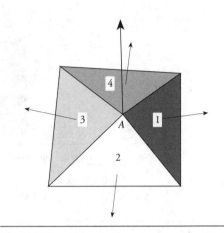

Figure 13.3   Concept of a vertex normal

13.2 PHONG SHADING

Here we describe a technique developed by Bui-Truong Phong, called *Phong shading* (PHON75). The objective of Phong shading is to display each of the object's surface polygons with an intensity that varies smoothly across it.

We must compute a normal for each pixel in the filling process. The normal is used to compute an intensity for this pixel. Computing a pixel's normal from the vertex normals is the essential idea of Phong shading.

For simplicity, let us use a triangle to explain this (see Figure 13.4). In a filling process we have to set all pixels on the indicated scan line that intersects at P_1 and P_2. The normal for P_1 is computed from the vertex normals at *A* and *B*. The normal for P_2 is computed from the normals at *C* and *B*. The normal for *P*, finally, is computed from those at P_1 and P_2. All these normals are easy to obtain. Let us concentrate on how we obtain the normal for P_1 from those at *A* and *B*. Here, we depart from the method traditionally used in Phong shading because it is not precise and leads to shading artifacts. Our method is precise, avoids the shading artifacts, and requires fewer operations.

Using the "member dot" syntax of C++, we can say that we want a normal "in between" *A.normal* and *B.normal* when we move along the edge from *A* to *B*. The "in between" normal should gradually rotate

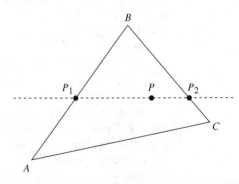

Figure 13.4   Deriving normal information for setting pixel P

from *A.normal* into *B.normal*. This is easy to accomplish. We observe that the cosine of the angle included by the two vectors *A.normal* and *B.normal* is the dot product:

$$\cos(\alpha) = A.normal * B.normal$$

We get α with an arccosine function. The filling algorithm knows the number of scan lines that the edge from A to B crosses, so α is divided by this number to give the angle ϕ. We then compute a three-dimensional rotation matrix that rotates by the angle ϕ. (The details of computing this matrix are irrelevant here.) We can then obtain the normals that correspond to the edge's intersections with successive scan lines by repeatedly multiplying *A.normal* by this matrix. The net result is a normal that varies along edge *AB*.

When the scan line from P_1 to P_2 is drawn, the normals of the two scan line intersections are taken and the number of pixels in that scan line, n, are computed. We use this information to compute a rotation matrix that rotates by $1/n$ of the angle between *P1.normal* and *P2.normal*. We then obtain the normals for the pixels by repeatedly multiplying *P1.normal* by this matrix.

Filling a polygon with the Phong method requires essentially the same preparation as filling with a constant color (see Chapter 2). Another requirement is that all faces of the object be specified as quadrangles. (We explain why later.) We create a linked list of the quadrangle's edges, sorted on decreasing *ymax*-values. The edge structure needed in Phong shading is the same as in normal polygon filling, but augmented by two additional entries—the rotation matrix for this edge, *rotmat*, and the normal at the intersection with the scan line.

The correct use of Phong shading to render various objects is not trivial. We discuss it in detail below. We take the cylinder of Figure 13.1 as a typical example. To achieve the display on the right, we have to smooth the intensities between adjoining mantle facets, but not between the mantle facets and the top or the bottom facets, or we would lose the sharp ridges at the top and the bottom.

Figure 13.5 shows the cylinder with some facets numbered and some vertices named. To make the ridge between facets 2 and 3 disappear after the filling process, the vertex normal at B must be the average of these two facets' normals. To make the ridge between 3 and 4 disappear, the vertex normal at C must be the average of these two. Similar reasoning applies to all other vertical edges of the cylinder's mantle.

On the other hand, one has to maintain the ridge between facets 1 and 2. One

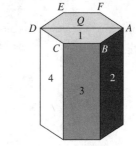

Figure 13.5   *Prism with vertices and faces numbered*

achieves this by drawing facet 1 with normals at A and B that are equal to the normal of facet 1. The same applies to all the cylinder's horizontal edges.

Now, the difficulty is that the cylinder's vertices must have two different normals and that the filling algorithm must somehow know the correct one to use when filling a particular quadrangle. When filling quadrangle 1, the normals at A, B, C, and D have to point upward; when filling a side quadrangle, the normals at all vertices must be averaged from the adjacent facets, which makes them point horizontally outward. But this problem is easily solved; a vertex will have only one vertex normal, but we specify each vertex twice.

Our data structure will specify the above cylinder not as one object, but as two separate ones. The first one will be only the mantle, the second one will be the top and the bottom plates. The vertices are specified twice, one set for each object. Neither of the objects "knows" of the other. We demonstrate this principle below. Let A, B, C, D, E, and F be the top vertices and $A1, B1, \ldots F1$ the corresponding bottom vertices, giving a vertex table of twelve vertices as shown below. The vertex coordinates are indicated just by the letters A, B, C, and so on. The first twelve are used for the mantle, the second twelve for the top and bottom plates.

vertex	coordinates	vertex	coordinates
$v[0]$	A	$v[12]$	A
$v[1]$	B	$v[13]$	B
$v[2]$	C	$v[14]$	C
$v[3]$	D	$v[15]$	D
$v[4]$	E	$v[16]$	E
$v[5]$	F	$v[17]$	F
$v[6]$	$A1$	$v[18]$	$A1$
$v[7]$	$B1$	$v[19]$	$B1$
$v[8]$	$C1$	$v[20]$	$C1$
$v[9]$	$D1$	$v[21]$	$D1$
$v[10]$	$E1$	$v[22]$	$E1$
$v[11]$	$F1$	$v[23]$	$F1$

The mantle consists of six quadrangles:

$q[2]$:   0   6   7   1
$q[3]$:   1   7   8   2
$q[4]$:   2   8   9   3
$q[5]$:   and so on
$q[6]$:   (some vertices are not visible in the figure)
$q[7]$:

The top plate consists of two quadrangles:

$q[0]$:   12   15   16   17   (not 0   3   4   5)
$q[1]$:   12   13   14   15   (not 0   1   2   3)

The bottom plate is constructed correspondingly. It is essential that the quadrangles of the top and bottom plate refer to vertices in the table that are different from those of the mantle, even though those vertices have identical coordinates in space. When computing the normal for vertex 1 (coordinates B), the algorithm will find that the quadrangles $q[2]$ and $q[3]$ share this vertex, but not $q[1]$. Thus, the normal for vertex 1 will be averaged from $q[2]$ and $q[3]$ only. When computing the vertex normal for vertex 13 (also coordinates B), however, the algorithm will find that only the quadrangle $q[1]$ has this vertex, so the normal will be that of $q[1]$.

In summary, the normals for the "mantle vertices" will point horizontally away from the cylinder, while the normals for the "top-and-bottom-plate-vertices" will point vertically upward or downward. In a sense, this double representation of some vertices fools the vertex normal algorithm into computing different normals for the different vertices.

We will now show more ways to use this technique. For example, to produce an object with a crease in the middle as in Figure 13.6, we define the object as two separate rooflike structures that coincide in the vertices *C* and *D*. See Figure 13.7.

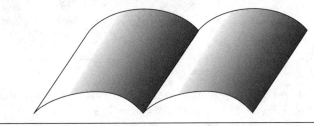

Figure 13.6   *Two smooth bumps*

When shading is done on these polygons, no smooth transition of intensities is to take place across the edge *CD*; a crease will appear. (Do not forget that the object's front and back outlines will look polygonal, not smooth as Figure 13.6 might suggest.)

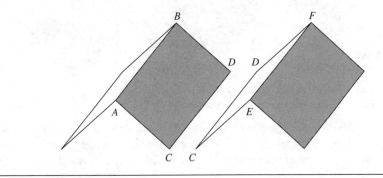

Figure 13.7   *Internal representation*

A typical problem that arises with Phong shading is flattening. If we want to display a wavelike, curved surface as in Figure 13.8, we would internally store a surface as shown in Figure 13.9.

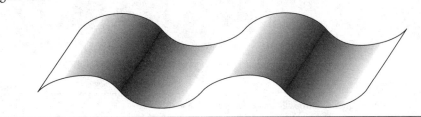

Figure 13.8   *Wavelike surface*

You might expect that the smoothing process will give us the wavelike shape. However, we will get a completely flat surface (except for the ends, which will be bent upward or downward with a polygonal outline in the front and back).

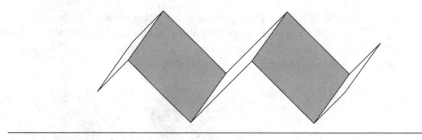

Figure 13.9   Internal representation

The reason for the flatness is that the vertex normals on the ridges and in the valleys are all parallel, as Figure 13.10 shows. The interpolation yields a constant pixel normal throughout the area from the leftmost ridge to the rightmost valley.

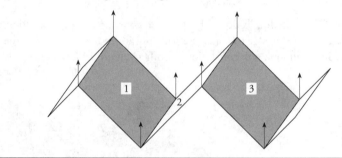
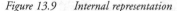

Figure 13.10   Identical vertex normals

We can solve this problem by introducing additional edges between each ridge and valley. Each of the polygons 1, 2, and 3 will be divided into two polygons by an edge, as Figure 13.11 shows. The vertex normals at the new vertices will be normal to the polygons 1, 2, and 3 respectively.

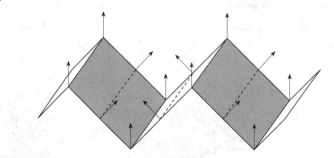
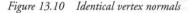

Figure 13.11   Introducing additional edges

Shading will now give a smooth wavelike surface. It is sometimes suggested that we replace each of the problematic polygons (1, 2, and 3 in our example) with three new ones instead of two, all in the same plane as the original one. Doing this creates a smooth wavelike surface (see for example ROGE85). The scheme we choose depends on the picture we want to produce.

The use of multiple vertices used in the cylinder example for inducing creases and peaks is not the only one. One can also introduce a pair of very narrow polygons on either side of the edge where there is to be a crease. These polygons must have the same slope as the originally adjacent polygons at the edge. The whole intensity interpolation will then take place within these narrow polygons; if they are narrower than a single pixel, the intensity interpolation is defeated. This method is a little more complicated. We will not pursue it further.

We must properly define the polygon mesh "by hand," compose the object of unrelated parts by repeatedly specifying the vertices, or split the polygons into several polygons when we specify the file that describes the polygon mesh.

We now present a further example that involves not only defining vertices in multiple ways, but also using triangles as facets.

We want to display a cone as shown in Figure 13.12. (We will not obtain a round bottom edge; instead, we will have a polygonal silhouette as on the cylinder in Figure 13.1.)

Figure 13.12   Ideal cone display

Internally, we represent the cone as a four-sided pyramid; see Figure 13.13. In practice, a six- or eight-sided pyramid would be much better, but the principle is the same. At E we want a sharp peak. The edges AE, BE, CE, and DE should be smoothed; at the bottom edges AB, BC, CD, and DA we want to maintain the creases. We specify the cone as two separate objects—the mantle and the bottom plate. This will guarantee the sharp crease at the bottom and the smoothing of the vertical edges.

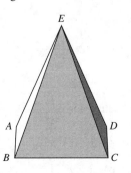

Figure 13.13   Internal representation of a cone

The mantle is defined as in Figure 13.14. We certainly do not want to smooth over the peak at E; we want to maintain a sharp point there. This can be achieved by using four top points $E_1, ..., E_4$ all identical to E in their coordinates. Only two adjacent facets share each E_i. In this way, the side facets are formally quadrangles in the data structure, but are shaped like triangles, since two of their vertices coincide. Figure 13.14 shows this.

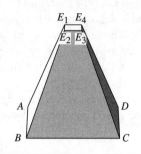

Figure 13.14   Representing the top by four coinciding points

The second part is the bottom plate, as Figure 13.15 shows. Its vertices should be listed clockwise when one looks at the bottom from below the pyramid. This will allow backface removal.

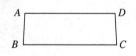

Figure 13.15   Bottom plate of the cone

While there are only five spatially different vertices, the cone consists of 12 vertices in the data structure. Observe that all five quadrangles list their vertices in clockwise order:

mantle vertices		bottom vertices	
$v[0]$:	A	$v[8]$:	A
$v[1]$:	B	$v[9]$:	B
$v[2]$:	C	$v[10]$:	C
$v[3]$:	D	$v[11]$:	D
$v[4]$:	E		
$v[5]$:	E		
$v[6]$:	E		
$v[7]$:	E		

mantle quadrangles				bottom quadrangle			
$q[0]$:	1	0	4	5			
$q[1]$:	2	1	5	6			
$q[2]$:	3	2	6	7			
$q[3]$:	0	3	7	4			

bottom quadrangle
$q[4]$:   0   1   2   3

When the vertex normal algorithm goes through all quadrangles of the mesh, it will find only two that share any of the top vertices E ($v[4]$ to $v[7]$). It will therefore assign a different vertex normal to each of these four peak vertices; see Figure 13.16. The top and bottom normals for each vertical edge are parallel.

Using quadrangles to represent triangles effectively constructs triangles that have two different vertex normals at the top end. This achieves a sharp peak at the top and smooths across the mantle edges without introducing shading artifacts.

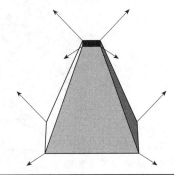

Figure 13.16   Four different top vertex normals

ARTIFACTS FROM USING TRIANGLES

The use of quadrangles instead of triangles in Phong shading is not a must, but leads to better results, as we now explain. Assume that we specify the above cone using four triangles for the mantle. The vertex normals at the bottom would be the same as in the cone above. On the top there would be four vertex normals, identical to the plane normals of the individual four triangles. Figure 13.17 shows two adjacent triangles of such a specification. Triangle 1 has the vertex normals a, c, and d, while triangle 2 has b, d, and e.

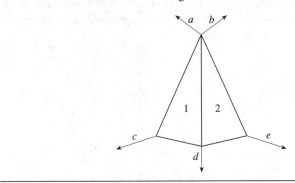

Figure 13.17   Cone constructed with triangles

Although this seems correct, it leads to abrupt changes in shading along the edges between the triangles. We can see why if we look at Figure 13.18. In this figure we are above the top of the cone and are looking straight down at it. (Only one half of the cone is shown.) We see the bottom vertex normal d pointing straight up in the figure. The top vertex normals a

and b are at an angle of 90°. At a point on the edge halfway between the top and the bottom, we show two normals—the normal ad, which is interpolated halfway between a and d, and the normal bd, which is interpolated halfway between b and d. Adjacent pixels close to this point and on different sides of the edge will have pixel normals almost identical to ad or bd. There is a gap of 45° between these two.

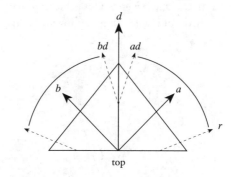

Figure 13.18   "Shading gaps" along edges

The figure also shows a normal, r, halfway between a and the bottom normal on the right. The arc from ad to r indicates that the normals along that height on the cone mantle will smoothly blend from ad to r. The arc from bd to the left indicates that similar things are true with the normals from bd along that arc. The gap along the edge will always be there, however. At the top the gap is 90° and gradually disappears toward the bottom. Such gaps form on all four edges of the cone. This causes abrupt changes in shading and thereby produces the impression of sharp ridges along the edges.

To avoid such artifacts, we give each triangle two vertex normals at the top—$a1$ and $a2$ for triangle 1, $b1$ and $b2$ for triangle 2. See Figure 13.19. They must be arranged so that $a2 = b1$, and so forth for all other top normals. In this figure the two triangles are separated spatially to make the drawing clearer, but they coincide along that edge in their coordinates.

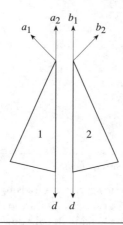

Figure 13.19   Using two top vertex normals

We achieve this in a simple manner by using quadrangles with collapsing top vertices instead of triangles. If the filling code handles quadrangles identically to triangles, why not use quadrangles throughout?

When we compute the plane equation of a quadrangle, we take from it three different vertices. Taking the first three vertices of a quadrangle when any two vertices may coincide will not guarantee that the three taken are different. We therefore adopt the rule that if two vertices of a quadrangle coincide, *the coinciding must be the last two.* All mantle quadrangles in the above figures were specified obeying this rule.

Coinciding vertices do not cause difficulties with other algorithms; polygon filling works with no problem. In depth sorting, a quadrangle is split into two triangles, which are tested separately against the triangles of the other split quadrangle. If two vertices coincide, one of the triangles will simply be empty.

NONUNIQUENESS OF PIXEL NORMALS

When we display the cone in different positions, we discover another problem—the method by which a pixel normal is interpolated from the vertex normals does not produce unique results. The interpolated pixel normal depends on the polygon's orientation on the screen. This problem is inherent in Phong shading and is more difficult to solve than those above, but FVFH p. 740 mentions some approaches to solving it.

We demonstrate this problem with an example. When we fill a mantle quadrangle that lies horizontally, we will not succeed in producing smoothly changing intensities.

Figure 13.20 shows this. The scan lines above the dotted line work with normals averaged from $n1$, $n2$, and $n4$; those below the dotted line work with normals averaged from $n1$, $n2$, and $n3$. At the peak on the left, these two different averages are used in adjacent scan lines. Consider only the left ends of the two scan lines just above and below the dotted line. The pixels of the upper scan line are influenced almost exclusively by $n4$, while those of the lower scan line are influenced by $n3$. These two normals are considerably different, so depending on the light position, these pixels can have very different intensities.

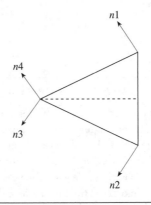

Figure 13.20 Shading artifact along dotted line

The differences gradually become smaller as we go to the right and they disappear entirely at the right end of the triangle. At the left, however, there will be a sharp ridge. This will occur whenever the peak vertex's y-coordinate is between the y-coordinates of the other two vertices (in absolute screen coordinates). The process of averaging the normals and thereby the intensities happens during the polygon filling. Therefore, the averaging has only a left-right direction.

Here we propose a solution not mentioned in other textbooks. If, in the above example, the interpolation of the normals occured in a vertical direction, the sharp ridge would disappear. It is certainly possible to fill a polygon with vertical scan lines instead of with horizontal ones. Filling with vertical scan lines or scan lines of 45° is the topic of the Chapter 2 Exercises for Section 2.3.

We now need a criterion for determining whether to fill horizontally or vertically:

1. Check the last two vertices of a quadrangle to see if they coincide.
2. If they do, see if the y-coordinate of the coinciding vertex is between the other two y-coordinates.
3. If so, then fill vertically; otherwise, fill horizontally.

This takes care of the above problem and many related ones. Unfortunately, some unsolved cases remain. Figure 13.21 shows one. The cone always has certain positions in which a triangle's projection will assume the indicated shape. Both horizontal and vertical filling will produce a sharp ridge, albeit in different directions, as the dotted lines indicate.

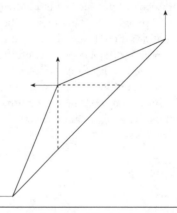

Figure 13.21   Shading artifacts can occur along dotted lines

To solve this problem, we could fill (or smooth) the polygon in a direction that connects the two triangle sides emanating from the peak. Filling with scan lines parallel to the triangle's base line (opposite the peak) will certainly always solve the problem. But this is impossible, unless we use 45° or 135° scan lines. If we provide for these two types of filling in addition to horizontal and vertical filling, we will achieve smooth shading in practically all positions. (One can still construct triangles that defeat all four directions of filling, but these are very long and narrow triangles that occur infrequently.)

By adding vertical and two slanted types of filling, we can obtain a higher quality Phong shading without increasing the algorithm's running time. Let us now develop the criterion to decide when to use which type of filling.

If a quadrangle has two coinciding vertices, we determine the slant of the opposite side (the side determined by the first two vertices). According to the list, then, the direction of the filling lines is:

$$-22.5° < \text{slant} \leq 22.5° \quad \text{horizontal}$$
$$22.5° < \text{slant} \leq 67.5° \quad 45°$$
$$67.5° < \text{slant} \leq 112.5° \quad \text{vertical}$$
$$112.5° < \text{slant} \leq 157.5° \quad 135°$$

A PRECISE SOLUTION

It is theoretically possible to proceed in the following way. Every point inside a convex polygon can be expressed as a convex combination of the vertices. We could compute the coefficients of the combination and use them to compute the normal at that point as a convex combination of the vertex normals. To find the coefficients, we would have to solve a linear system.

For each pixel, we would determine the point on the polygon corresponding to it in the projection, find the coefficients, compute the pixel normal as described above, and normalize it. This solution would correctly shade every polygon independent of the orientation and would be free of artifacts, but would also be slow. Phong shading is an intentional compromise between precision and speed. It therefore has inherent weaknesses that show as artifacts in shading (FVFH p. 740). The presented approach mitigates these and decreases the running time by using rotation matrices, quadrangles instead of triangles, and by filling with slanted scan lines when a quadrangle collapses to a triangle.

OO DESIGN AND CLASS SPECIFICATIONS

Using this solution, we proceed with the following requirements:

1. The vertices describing an object to be Phong shaded must have not only 3D coordinates, but also a vertex normal.
2. The object's individual facets are defined as quadrangles rather than as triangles.
3. If a quadrangle collapses to a triangle, the solid filling proceeds in one of four different directions: horizontal, vertical, slanted up, or slanted down.
4. The individual scan line in the filling performs an illumination computation for each pixel it sets.
5. The edges of the quadrangle must contain not only what a normal edge in polygon filling contains, but also a normal that is updated for every scan line and a rotation matrix that is used in updating.

We will use all existing classes and implementations and simply add the necessary members and functionality to achieve the purpose outlined above. At the heart of Phong shading is drawing one scan line with a pixel normal that changes gradually from the normal at the left edge intersection to the one at the right intersection.

We will take the class `edge_t`, used in polygon filling, and derive from it the class `pedge_t` (Phong edge). We add a member "normal," which holds the normal at the edge–scan line intersection. We also add the member "rotmat," which rotates the normal from one scan line to the next when the edge is updated. We redefine the virtual member function `edge_t::solidscan()` to use the normals at both ends of the scan line, as well as the light information, to compute the pixel illumination. We also redefine the virtual member function edge_t::update() to update not only the edge x-values at the intersection with the scan line, but also the normal.

How shall we achieve the filling with differently slanted fill lines? We know from before that whenever we are to fill a polygon with slanted fill lines, we can use horizontal polygon filling by applying it to a rotated polygon and rotating back the individual fill lines. We use this principle here. The function pedge_t::solidscan() will be implemented so that it executes one of four possible fill routines. We can determine which one it is when the four pedge_t for a quadrangle are constructed.

Before we show the class specifications, let us introduce another class. In Phong shading a vertex must have a vertex normal. Thus, we derive the class pvertex_t (Phong vertex) from vertex3_t and add a point3_t member that holds the vertex normal. From four pvertex_t a quadrangle (pquad_t) will be constructed and filled. Since filling can proceed in four different directions, we give the pvertex a static int member "tilt," which holds the information about how the quadrangle is tilted. The virtual member function vertex_t::create_edge() is redefined to create a pedge_t. When a pedge_t is created from two consecutive vertices, the tilt of the pquad is known and the type of fill line (horizontal, slanted, or so forth) is set.

Below is the class pedge_t, which is constructed from two pvertex_t. Three additional data members are the normal, the rotation matrix, and scan_pointer, a pointer to one of the four scan line functions. This pointer is initialized when the pedge_t is constructed from a pvertex_t pair.

The class pedge_t redefines only the virtual functions edge_t::solidscan() and edge_t::update(). Pedge_t::solidscan() now does Phong filling; we explain this below. Other member functions are the four scan line functions: scanh for horizontal, scanv for vertical, scanu for slanted up, and scand for slanted down.

```
//******************** File pedge.h ************************

#ifndef PEDGE_T
#define PEDGE_T

#include "../Shape2d/edge.h"
#include "../Phong/pvertex.h"
#include "../Phong/mat33.h"

class pedge_t : public edge_t    // polygon edge for Phong filling
{
public:
   ~pedge_t() {}                          // edges must be deleted singly
   pedge_t(const pvertex_t&,const pvertex_t&) ;

   void update() ;
   void solidscan(double) ;
   point3_t givnorm() const { return norm; }
```

```
private:
   point3_t norm ;
   mat33_t rotmat ;
   void (pedge_t::*scan_pointer)(double) ;
   void scanh(double) ;
   void scanv(double) ;
   void scanu(double) ;
   void scand(double) ;
} ;

#endif

//****************************************************************
```

A pvertex_t has a default constructor to allow us to declare an array of vertices, a copy constructor, and two constructors that just initialize its coordinates. Two additional data members are the normal and the tilt. The virtual function create_edge() is redefined to create a pedge_t (Phong edge). A pvertex_t can also copy itself through copy(). The functions such as rotx(), which are inherited from point3_t, must be redefined; when we rotate a Phong vertex, we must rotate not only its coordinates, but also its normal. Translation does not affect the vertex normal, so we simply inherit the translation. The functions givnorm() and setnorm() are used for obtaining or setting the normal.

```
//********************** File pvertex.h **********************

#ifndef PVERTEX_T
#define PVERTEX_T

#include "../Shape3d/vertex3.h"

class pvertex_t : public vertex3_t
{
public:
   ~pvertex_t() ;
   pvertex_t() ;
   pvertex_t(const pvertex_t&) ;
   pvertex_t(const vertex3_t&,const point3_t&) ;

   void rotx(double) ;
   void roty(double) ;
   void rotz(double) ;

   edge_t*     make_edge(const vertex_t&) const ;
   vertex_t*   copy() const ;
   point3_t    givnorm() const { return norm; }
   void        setnorm(const point3_t& n) { norm = n; }
   int         givtilt() const { return tilt; }
   void        settilt(int tilt) { this->tilt = tilt; }
```

```
private:
  point3_t norm ;
  static int tilt ;
} ;

#endif

//******************************************************************
```

An object to be Phong shaded consists of quadrangles rather than triangles. The class pquad_t describes a convex polygon with four vertices, so this class is derived from convex_t. It redefines the virtual function convex_t::solid() to display itself with Phong filling. We add the member function tilt(), which rotates the pquad by 0, –45, 45, or 90 degrees to help fill the polygon with the proper scan lines: horizontal, slanted up, slanted down, or vertical.

```
//********************** File pquad.h **********************

#ifndef PQUAD_T
#define PQUAD_T

#include "../Shape3d/scene3.h"
#include "../Shape2d/convex.h"

class pquad_t : public convex_t                    // Phong quadrangle
{
public:
  ~pquad_t() ;
  pquad_t() ;
  pquad_t(const pquad_t&) ;

  void solid(const scene_t*) const ;               // solid fill

private:
  pquad_t& tilt() ;
} ;

#endif

//******************************************************************
```

To Phong shade an object, we define it as a Phong mesh, which is essentially a triangle mesh. A Phong mesh is described by the class pmesh_t, derived from a triangle mesh, tmesh_t. There are no additional data members. The class pmesh_t has a destructor to free allocated memory, a default constructor, and a copy constructor. It has the function copy() to produce and return a copy of itself and the function read() to read itself from a file. Redefined are the virtual function alloc_vertex(), which now allocates and returns a Phong vertex, and alloc_facets(), which now allocates and returns an array of quadrangles.

```
//*********************** File pmesh.h ***********************

#ifndef PMESH_T
#define PMESH_T

#include "../Shape3d/tmesh.h"
#include "../Phong/pvertex.h"

class pmesh_t : public tmesh_t                        // phong mesh
{
public:
  ~pmesh_t() ;
  pmesh_t() ;
  pmesh_t(const pmesh_t&) ;
  prim_t* copy() const ;

  prim_t& read(char*) ;
  vertex3_t* alloc_vertex() const ;
  triangle_t* alloc_facets() const ;
} ;

#endif

//****************************************************************
```

The inherited member facet in a pmesh points to an array of quadrangles. A quadrang_t is derived from dstriang_t (depth sorting triangle), which is derived from triangle_t. No data members are added, but the array of integers, to which v now points, contains four subscripts instead of three.

A quadrang_t should not be confused with a pquad_t. A quadrang_t is a building block of pmesh containing the four subscripts into the vertex table of the mesh that describe a facet as demonstrated on page 472. On the other hand, a pquad_t is a convex polygon, derived from convex_t, that contains a linked list of vertices and is constructed only temporarily for the purpose of filling.

Deriving quadrang_t from dstriang_t and redefining make_dsrec() will allow us to add pmeshes to a depth sorting scene. We will say more about this later.

```
//*********************** File quadrang.h ***********************

#ifndef QUADRANG_T
#define QUADRANG_T

#include "../Dsort/dstriang.h"
#include "../Phong/pvertex.h"

class quadrang_t : public dstriang_t
{
public:
  ~quadrang_t() ;
```

```
    quadrang_t() ;

    vertex3_t& givd() { return *vertex[v[3]]; }
    void        draw(const scene_t*) const ;
    void        solid(const scene_t*) const ;
    dsrec_t*    make_dsrec(const scene_t*) const ;
    void        setcolor(light_t*,const rgb_t&,int&) ;
    void        read(ifstream&,vertex3_t**) ;
    void operator = (const triangle_t&) ;
} ;


#endif


//*******************************************************************
```

The data file describing a pmesh_t is essentially identical to that describing a tmesh, except that four subscripts are specified for each quadrangle. Of course, we must observe the multiple specification of vertices where creases and peaks are intended. Here is an example describing the cone in Color Plate 10 (the comments are not part of the data file):

```
0.9  0.6   0.3                              // rgb value of pmesh
18                                          // number of vertices
         0.0      0.45     0.0                   // vertex list
         0.0      0.45     0.0
         0.0      0.45     0.0
         0.0      0.45     0.0
         0.0      0.45     0.0
         0.0      0.45     0.0

         0.5     -0.45     0.0
         0.25    -0.45     0.433
        -0.25    -0.45     0.433
        -0.5     -0.45     0.0
        -0.25    -0.45    -0.433
         0.25    -0.45    -0.433

         0.5     -0.45     0.0
         0.25    -0.45     0.433
        -0.25    -0.45     0.433
        -0.5     -0.45     0.0
        -0.25    -0.45    -0.433
         0.25    -0.45    -0.433

    8                                       // number of quadrangles
         7     6     0     1                // quadrangle subscripts
         8     7     1     2
         9     8     2     3
        10     9     3     4
        11    10     4     5
         6    11     5     0
        12    13    14    15
        12    15    16    17
```

The function `pmesh_t::read()` reads a pmesh from the data file by first constructing a default pmesh and then calling its `read()` function. `Pmesh_t::read()` calls `tmesh_t::read()`, which reads all data. The member `vertex` will point to an array of `vertex3_t` pointers, which now point to `pvertices` constructed by `alloc_vertex()`. The member `facet` will point to an array of quadrangles constructed by `alloc_facets()`. We must add to the code the computation of the vertex normals, simply appending it after `tmesh_t::read()`.

Handling the illumination in the case of a lookup table environment is more complicated here than with faceted shading. `Main()` submits the *rgb*-values of each pmesh to `setcolmap()`, located in the file `pedge.c`, which contains the filling routines. If much parameter passing is to be avoided, all illumination computation must take place there, so the lookup table information must be available there. `Setcolmap()` creates 60 lookup table entries for each pmesh, from the lowest to the highest possible intensity under the given lighting parameters. It also stores the *rgb*-value of the pmesh in a table that increases by one entry for each pmesh. With these explanations, the strategy for computing the illumination that we explain below should become clear.

If we submit pmeshes to a 3D scene and call the scene's `solid()` function, it walks through the list of the pmeshes and calls each pmesh's function `setcolors()`, which is identical to `tmesh_t::setcolors()`. `Setcolors()` walks through all facets of the mesh and calls each facet's `setcolor()`. A facet (no matter whether a triangle or quadrangle) executes its own `setcolor()`. In our case all facets are quadrangles. A quadrangle's `setcolor()` sets only its own *rgb*-value to the pmesh's *rgb*-value, but does not make a lookup table entry.

The scene's function `solid()` then walks through the list of pmeshes again, calling each pmesh's function `solid()`. This executes a `tmesh_t::solid()` for each pmesh, because there is no redefinition of `tmesh_t::solid()`. `Tmesh_t::solid()` simply calls each facet's `solid()` if the facet is a frontface. Because all facets are now quadrangles, the `solid()` of a `quadrang_t` is executed.

`Quadrang_t::solid()` uses its *rgb*-value (identical to the pmesh's *rgb*-value) to set the global variable start in the file `pedge.c` before the filling process starts. As we said before, 60 lookup table entries were created by `main()` for each pmesh. The *rgb*-value for which such a range was made was stored in a global table in `pedge.c`. The quadrangle's *rgb*-value is searched in that table, and its entry location, multiplied by 60, gives the starting index in the lookup table for this quadrangle's colors. This value is stored in `start`.

After setting the `start` in `pedge.c`, `quadrang_t::solid()` constructs a convex polygon with four vertices (a `pquad_t` as introduced above) by adding to the `pquad_t` the four pvertices to which the `quadrang_t` points. Then it calls the pquad's `solid()`. (Observe the order in which the vertices are added to the pquad; if two vertices coincide, they must be the last two.) `Pquad_t::solid()` projects and scales its vertices using the given window-viewport system, then tilts itself if necessary, constructs a list of Phong edges, and calls the list's `fill()` with `solidscan` as parameter. `Solidscan()` is a virtual function of `edge_t` and is redefined in `pedge_t`; therefore run-time binding will bind the call to one of the four Phong filling routines.

`Pquad_t::solid()` does not clip against the 3D window. This clipping is a non-trivial addition to normal 3D clipping and is described in an exercise.

The class `plist_t` does not differ from its base class `elist_t` (convex polygon edge list); `plist_t` is only a different type and has its own constructor. This constructor checks the tilt of the given parameter, knowing that it is a `pvertex_t`. If the tilt is slanted, then the scan decrement and the scan value are initialized differently. We show `plist_t` below.

```
//*********************** File plist.h ***********************
#ifndef PLIST_T
#define PLIST_T

#include "../Shape2d/elist.h"

class plist_t : public elist_t
{
public:
    plist_t(vertex_t*) ;
} ;

#endif
//**********************************************************
```

We now explain how to fill a polygon with scan lines slanted down by 45°. The polygon is first rotated ccw by 45° and is then filled with horizontal scan lines. When each scan line is drawn, it is rotated cw by 45°. This last rotation needs to be done only to the starting point of the scan line. From then on, we simultaneously increase x and y by 1 to reach the next pixel. The horizontal filling of the rotated polygon proceeds in a 45° pixel raster; see Figure 13.22.

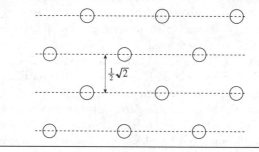

Figure 13.22   Slanted filling of a polygon

This implies that the distance between scan lines, `scan_decrement`, is not 1 but $\frac{1}{2}\sqrt{2}$. The starting value for *scan* must be the smallest multiple of $\frac{1}{2}\sqrt{2}$ larger than *ymax*, the largest y-value of the polygon. Let H be the value $\frac{1}{2}\sqrt{2}$. Then we compute *scan*'s starting value as:

$$scan = H*(\text{int}(ymax/H)+1)$$

Unfortunately, this works only if *ymax* is positive, because `int()` with a negative argument gives a result greater than the argument. Rotating the polygon, however, can bring *ymax* into the negative range. This does not impede the filling algorithm, but we must compute *scan* differently:

$$scan = H * \text{int}((ymax + 0.000001) / H)$$

The small value added to *ymax* assures that when *ymax* is exactly a negative integer value, *scan* will still be larger than *ymax*. These initializations are done in the `plist_t` constructor.

When constructing a `pedge_t`, we have a similar situation. The starting value for the edge–scan line intersection must be set so that, after the first updating, *x* has the precise intersection value. We ensure this by determining an amount proportional to the distance of the *y*-value from the next greater multiple of $\frac{1}{2}\sqrt{2}$. We then subtract this amount from the *x*-coordinate at the edge end point with the greater *y*-value. Here, again, we have to distinguish between positive and negative coordinate values. The initialization formulas for *x* are similar to those above. The value used to update *x* from one scan line to the next is now the negative inverse slope times $\frac{1}{2}\sqrt{2}$.

We show the constructor for a `pedge_t` below. First, it initializes all members inherited from `edge_t` by calling the base class constructor. Then it initializes the edge normal. Then it sets the pointer to the scan line function to one of four possible values, depending on the tilt of the polygon. If the tilt is slanted, it corrects the values of *x* and of *dx*, already set by the call of the base class constructor. The entity *ydif* expresses the number of steps per edge. The rotation matrix for updating the edge normal from one scan line to the next is also computed and the normal is corrected to its proper starting value.

```
pedge_t::pedge_t(const pvertex_t& a,const pvertex_t& b) :
    edge_t(a,b) , norm(a.givnorm())
{
    switch (a.givtilt())
    {
    case 2: scan_pointer = &pedge_t::scanh; break;
    case 0: scan_pointer = &pedge_t::scanv; break;
    case 1: scan_pointer = &pedge_t::scanu; break;
    case 3: scan_pointer = &pedge_t::scand; break;
    }

    float ydif = ymax - ymin ;
    float corr = ydif/(1-ymax+int(ymax)) ;      // correction for normal
    if (corr > 500) corr = 0;               // use identity matrix instead
    if (a.givtilt()%2)                               // if tilted fill
    {
        double s = (ymax >= 0)
                ?    HSR2*(int(ymax/HSR2) + 1)
                :    HSR2*int((ymax+0.00000001)/HSR2) ;
        x = a.givx() - (s - ymax)*dx;
        dx = dx*HSR2;
        ydif = ydif/HSR2;
        corr = corr/HSR2;
    }

    rotmat = ::rotmat(a.givnorm(),b.givnorm(),ydif);
    norm *= ::rotmat(b.givnorm(),a.givnorm(),corr);     // start value
}
```

Getting from one pixel to the next in the various scan line functions is very simple—we increase or decrease one or both of the pixel coordinates.

The illumination computation from pixel normal and lighting parameters is straightforward in a true-color environment (Tiga and Xwin24). In a lookup table environment (Xwin8), the range of color entries for this quadrangle begins in the global variable start. After a pixel's intensity is computed through the dot product of the light direction and the pixel normal, it corresponds to one of the colors in the range beginning at start. Multiplying this dot product by 60 and adding it to start gives the proper lookup table location.

This lookup table management can accommodate up to four Phong shaded meshes. For a higher number of meshes, we must reduce the size of the individual ranges in the lookup table.

The above shading does not compute soft highlights, as explained in Section 8.4.

The class mat33_t is simply a 3×3 matrix of doubles. Its implementation overloads the operator [] and *= to multiply a matrix by a point3_t. It also defines a function rotmat (point3_t, point3_t, n). This function computes a 3×3 rotation matrix, which rotates a given vector into another given vector in n steps.

DISPLAYING PHONG MESHES WITH DEPTH SORTING

Phong shading a mesh does not depend on the order in which the mesh's individual facets are shaded. This property allows correct Phong shaded rendering of more than one object or of concave objects in a scene by displaying their facets in a depth sorted order. We can accomplish this by adding the pmeshes to a dsscene_t (depth sorting scene) instead of to a normal 3D scene. We can add them with no problem because they are derived from tmesh_t. The dsscene will walk through all its meshes (and whatever is derived from them), check all facets, and if they pass the frontface test, create from them an array of depth sorting records. The depth sorting records are of type dsrec_t in the depth sorting algorithm of Chapter 10. They are created by the dstriangle's function make_dsrec(). Dstriangles are the triangles of which a dsmesh consists. They are identical to a triangle, but have one additional virtual member function—make_dsrec().

We can easily expand this concept to include quadrangles. When we add pmeshes to a dsscene, the facets through which dsscene walks will be quadrangles, derived from dstriang_t. Our first step is to redefine make_dsrec() in quadrang_t to create and return a depth sorting record called dsrec4_t for a quadrangle. We derive this record from dsrec_t so it inherits that class's functionality. Now that it represents a quadrangle rather than a triangle, it must contain one more point. A dsrec_t basically contains the triangle's vertices, projected and scaled to screen coordinates, in the array trans. Therefore, the constructor for dsrec4_t needs to append only the quadrangle's fourth point to the array. Thus, it simply calls the base class constructor, which enters the first three points. Then it adds, projects, and scales the fourth point. (With some foresight, we allocated the array trans in dsrec_t with a length of four.) Here is the class dsrec4_t:

```
//************************* File dsrec4.h *************************

#ifndef DSREC4_T
#define DSREC4_T

#include "../Dsort/dsrec.h"

class dsrec4_t : public dsrec_t
{
public:
  ~dsrec4_t() ;
   dsrec4_t() ;
   dsrec4_t(const scene_t*,dstriang_t*) ;

   point_t givd() const { return trans[3]; } //  return fourth point
   int operator ^ (const dsrec_t&) const;  // redefined overlap test


} ;

#endif

//**********************************************************************
```

A virtual overloaded operator performs the overlap test in dsrec_t. We must now redefine it to work for quadrangles, but we hardly need any coding. The operator in dsrec4_t simply decomposes the two quadrangles to be tested into four triangles, constructs a dsrec_t for each triangle, and "crosswise" tests these for overlap by using the dsrec_t overlap operator. This is a strikingly nice example of code reuse, so we show it below:

```
int dsrec4_t::operator ^ (const dsrec_t& t) const       // overlap test
{
   dsrec_t a( giva(),  givb(),  givc()) ;
   dsrec_t b( giva(),  givc(),  givd()) ;
   dsrec_t c(t.giva(),t.givb(),t.givc()) ;
   dsrec_t d(t.giva(),t.givc(),((dsrec4_t&)t).givd());

   return (a^c || a^d || b^c || b^d);
}
```

If any test results in overlap, the testing ends. The successful test will produce a common point in the static base class member common, which is used in the depth comparison. The operator for the depth test need not be redefined.

13.3   GOURAUD SHADING

Another technique to achieve smooth shading was developed by Gouraud (GOUR71). Here, too, the basic idea is to fill the projections of the polygons with intensities that vary continuously and blend smoothly into each other across the edges of adjoining polygons.

In this method, instead of computing each pixel's normal and from that its intensity, the pixel's intensity is directly interpolated from the intensities at the vertices. We explain this with the help of Figure 13.23.

The principle is simpler than in Phong shading. Using the vertex normals at the vertices A, B, and C, we compute the intensities at the vertices using any illumination model and store them in the same data structure as the vertices. We then compute each pixel's intensity with linear interpolation from the intensities at the vertices.

The intensity at P_1 is derived linearly from those at A and B. The intensity at P_2 is derived linearly from those at C and B. Finally, the intensity at P is obtained from those at P_1 and P_2.

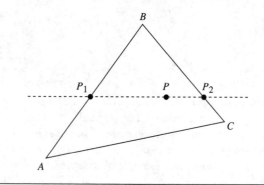

Figure 13.23   *Deriving intensity information for setting pixel P*

The intensity at P_1 can be expressed by the formula:

$$I_{P1} = sI_A + (1-s)I_B \qquad s = P_1B / AB$$

in which s is the length from P_1 to B divided by the length of the whole edge. There is an easier way to compute I_{P1}, however. Knowing I_A, I_B, and the number of scan lines that the edge AB intersects, we can compute the intensity increment per scan line. Then, going from A to B, we obtain the intensity for any point P_1 on the edge by repeatedly adding this increment to I_A. We handle the edge BC analogously.

When we have the intensities at P_1 and P_2, we obtain the intensity at P by linear interpolation. We first figure out how many pixels there are in the scan line from P_1 to P_2. Then we divide $I_{P2}-I_{P1}$ by this number. The result is the increment that we repeatedly add to I_{P1} when filling the scan line.

We must compute the vertex normal once in order to find the vertex intensity; then the vertex intensity, not the normal, is stored in the vertex data structure. The data structure for a vertex is:

```
struct vertex3_t
{
  point3_t cor ;                              // vertex coordinates
  rgb_t rgb ;                                 // vertex intensity
} ;
```

The edge structure is that for normal polygon filling, augmented by an entry for the intensity at the edge–scan line intersection and an intensity increase per scan line. We would, of course, implement this edge with a derivation.

```
struct edge_t                                        // polygon edge
{
  double ymax ,                      // larger of the edge's y-values
         ymin ,                      // smaller of the edge's y-values
         dx   ,                          // x-increase per scan line
         x    ;         // intersection x-value of edge and scan line
  rgb_t rgb  ,          // intensity at edge-scan line intersection
        drgb ;              // intensity increase per scan line
  edge_t* next ;                             // pointer to next edge
} ;
```

Gouraud shading is used in the same manner as Phong shading. The object is defined by quadrangles; the smoothing process can be defeated by repeatedly specifying vertices, quadrangles must be split to obtain a wavelike surface, and so on. The problems with artificial ridges when shading quadrangles with coinciding vertices exist here as well.

While Phong shading handles specular highlights excellently, Gouraud shading does them poorly. We elaborate on this below.

Imagine a scene in which the light source, the object, or the viewer slowly changes its position. As long as the viewing direction (indicated by the eye) is close to the reflection direction (how close depends on the surface's shininess), a highlight will be produced around the pyramid vertex (see Figure 13.24).

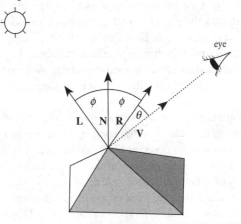

Figure 13.24   Pyramid with highlight at the top

When positions change (for example, when the light source moves), these two directions separate more and more. The highlight becomes weaker and may disappear instead of just changing its location on the surface. In Figure 13.25, the angle θ has become so big that Phong's illumination model will compute an essentially 0 specular reflection for that vertex. In both Figures 13.24 and 13.25, the object is shown as it is stored internally; the display will, of course, be a smooth cone.

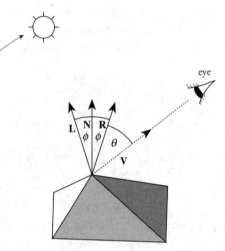

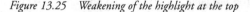

Figure 13.25   Weakening of the highlight at the top

The term Phong illumination used above refers to the illumination model for computing soft highlights, not to the shading technique. Do not confuse Phong shading with Phong illumination.

We assume that the other vertices do not have a specular reflection, because their normals are not in a reflecting position. The intensity interpolation will therefore not produce a highlight anywhere. This is in stark contrast to what happens on a smooth shiny object in reality. When the light source moves as shown, the specular reflection on the object really moves slightly toward the viewer. Moving the object itself or the position of the viewpoint has the same effect as moving the light source.

With Gouraud shading, if a vertex is exactly in the proper position, a highlight will appear on the smoothed object at the location corresponding to that vertex. Further position changes will cause the highlight to disappear; it may reappear at a position corresponding to a different vertex.

We summarize this behavior as follows. On a Gouraud shaded object, specular highlights do not move; they can only disappear and reappear at a different location. This effect is especially pronounced for objects of high shininess and in animation.

With low shininess, it is possible that the highlight at one vertex is still present, though dimmer, while the highlight at another vertex begins to appear. This effect can easily include several vertices if they are close together. This gives an oversized and irregularly shaped highlight. This phenomenon, typical of Gouraud shaded objects, frequently occurs with that method.

Another failure of highlights from Gouraud shading is that the size of the highlight does not vary with the object's shininess.

SUMMARY

Both methods have the disadvantage that objects will have polygonal silhouettes and outlines. Phong shading is more expensive in terms of processor time, but it yields smoothly shaded objects that look better than Gouraud shaded ones, especially for highlights. Phong shading is widely used for smooth shading.

SUGGESTED READINGS

An explanation of (traditional) Phong shading, and its shortcomings and strategies to overcome these, is given in FVFH90 p. 734 ff. BUGI89, HILL90, and WATT89 all contain presentations of the shading methods in this chapter.

EXERCISES

SECTION 13.1

1. Use the procedure `fracrect()` implemented in the exercises for Chapter 9 to generate a fractal grid surface. Draw the facets of the grid surface in occlusion-compatible order as filled polygons. The facets are nonplanar quadrangles, so split every quadrangle into two triangles to obtain unique surface normals. Illuminate the triangles with the Lambert shading method.

SECTION 13.2

2. Figure 13.26 shows the usual way of computing the in-between normals in Phong shading. Show that this method of computation does not give the precise in-between normals and requires more operations than the one we presented. Count in terms of multiplications. One division is equivalent to two multiplications, one square root is equivalent to twelve multiplications, one cosine or arccosine is equivalent to fifteen multiplications. One rotation matrix computation is equivalent to 75 multiplications.

    Assume that the normals at the scan line intersection are as shown in Figure 13.26. Show that adding the constant vector $(N_{P2}-N_{P1})/npix$ to N_{P1} to obtain all in-between normals gives normals as shown in the figure ($npix$ is the number of pixels in the scan line). These normals are not all of the same length and therefore must be normalized after each addition to compute the pixel illumination.

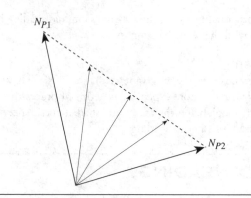

Figure 13.26   Traditional way of normal interpolation

3. Rewrite the function `illum()` in `pedge.c` to include the computation of a soft high-light. Take the vector from the eyepoint to the point (pixel) being illuminated as constant (0 0 1). This obviates the need to compute this point's coordinates. Now you can compute the reflection of this vector about the normal at the point (the pixel), test it against the direction to the light source, and compute a highlight as explained in Chapter 8.

4. In `pmesh_t::solid()`, we can clip the `pquad_t` before filling it. This is not a trivial process. The 3D clipping will compute only the coordinates of newly added vertices, but will not change their vertex normals. Remember the unclipped pquad—let its vertices be v_0, ... v_3, its vertex normals n_0, ... n_3. The clipped polygon has up to six vertices: w_0, ... w_k. They lie in the same plane as the v_i. Walk through the list of the clipped polygon and correct the normals in the following way. For each w_i, check whether it is identical to some v_j. If so, the normal is correct. If not, express the w_i as

$$w_i = a*v_0 + b*v_1 + c*v_2 + d*v_3$$

To find a, b, c, and d, you must solve a 4×4 linear system. The fastest solution is to use Gaussian elimination. Then set the normal of w_i to

$$a*n_0 + b*n_1 + c*n_2 + d*n_3$$

and normalize.

5. If the `template<class V, class F> class mesh_t`, as explained in Chapter 10, works on your computing platform, you can declare a

```
template<class V, class F> class pmesh_t
```

derived from `mesh_t<class V, class F>` and use it in Phong shading. The derived class `pmesh_t` is necessary because, in addition to reading the `mesh_t` from the file, code needs to be executed to compute the vertex normals. Everything else is inherited from the base. With this template in place, declare pmeshes with `pmesh_t<pvertex_t, quadrang_t>`, read them from the file, add them to a dsscene, and call the scene's function `solid()`.

SECTION 13.3

6. Implement the Gouraud shading technique. Reuse as much code as possible.

14

RAY CASTING

14.0 INTRODUCTION

Ray casting refers to the technique of shooting rays into a scene without bouncing them off the objects they hit. In effect, this produces scenes with only nonreflecting objects. On the other hand, *ray tracing* is the technique of bouncing a ray off the object it hits (if the object has total or partial reflectivity) or refracting the ray into and through the object (if the object is transparent). In these cases, the ray's trace might have to be pursued through many reflection and/or refraction steps. This is certainly the more general and powerful technique.

In the quest for visual realism, ray tracing plays an important role. It handles scenes in which the object's surfaces have specular reflectivity or are transparent, refracting the light that passes through them. Such scenes are displayed very realistically. Objects with dull, nonreflecting, or only partially reflecting surfaces are displayed with less visual realism.

Techniques that produce more visual realism in scenes with nonreflecting objects have been developed (for example, radiosity techniques), but they do poorly on those scenes in which ray tracing is strong.

Ray tracing is computation-intensive, but can use an arbitrary degree of computational parallelism, limited only by the number of available processors. This can speed up the operation; there are also other techniques to accelerate the procedure. Ray tracing is the most versatile rendering technique in computer graphics and is used frequently in solids modeling.

This chapter develops a powerful ray caster, starting with simple scenes and arriving at arbitrarily complex scenes. We expand this ray caster to a ray tracer in Chapter 15. We do not implement speed-up techniques, because of the book's limited space. We will, however, explain them at the end of Chapter 15. Chapter 16 adds flat and solid textures.

There is a wealth of literature about ray casting and tracing, but it is difficult reading. To present all aspects of ray tracing would require a whole book in itself. Rather than do this, we present something digestible that gradually builds up your understanding to a point from which you can advance independently.

In this chapter, we are trying to gradually develop the reader's understanding of ray tracing. We therefore present two preliminary ray casters. This should give you the opportunity to code the algorithms of this chapter on your own and follow the principle of the code's gradual changes.

The first stage is a ray caster for a simple scene of several spheres. It is nearly the simplest possible case, and every student should be able to code it alone. Because it includes smoothly shaded surfaces, shadows, and an arbitrary number of spheres of arbitrary colors it can nevertheless provide for a satisfying coding experience in computer graphics.

The second stage is a ray caster that includes arbitrary rotation of solids and their Boolean combinations of unlimited complexity. To make it meaningful, we have to introduce nonspherical solids. Its power is limited only by the number of solids added to it. We restrict the explanations to ellipsoids and cylinders, but class modules for all other primitive solids are found in Appendix B. We can add these to the stage two implementation. This stage involves introducing the concept of a linked "hitlist." Coding this from the ground up is advisable only for a student who plans to attain a full understanding of ray tracing.

The third and final stage is attained by adding reflection, refraction, and texturing, and is explained in Chapter 15.

14.1 THE BASIC PRINCIPLE

Every visual impression we have of the world around us comes to us through light rays that emanate from what we see. As Chapter 8 explained, visible objects emit light, which they either produce themselves or receive from elsewhere and reflect or refract toward us. Whenever a light ray reaches our eyes, we recognize something in the direction of the ray.

Our field of vision is the area in front of us that we see. Its shape can be approximated with an ellipse that is somewhat more wide than high. (This is probably the reason why most visual displays, such as pictures, TV screens, movie projections, use a rectangular shape that is wider than it is high.)

The information in the field of vision is conveyed to us through an infinity of light rays that come from every point in the field to our eyes. Our internal visual system gives us the impression of a continuous picture. However, the information that our brain receives is not continuous, but is *rasterized* through the receptors in the retina. The rasterization is certainly very fine, but not equally fine in all areas.

In explaining this matter, it is simpler to consider the field of vision for one eye only. (Our two eyes receive different pictures, as they are at different locations.) We can consider the picture we see as composed of a finite number of points, each of which sends one light ray into our eye. This assumption is a simplification. In reality, an infinite amount of light rays from any given point reach the opening of our pupil. However, the cornea and lens focus all of these back together onto one point on the retina, so assuming one ray from each point is close to reality.

Below, we often use the more general term ray tracing, meaning both casting and tracing. In ray tracing, we simulate the above process in a somewhat crude way. We try to collect the light rays that come toward us from a scene onto a "retina"—the computer screen. One difference between reality and our simulation is in the geometry of the projection. In reality, the rays coming from the picture converge to one point (the lens) between picture and the receptor (the retina), but in our simulation, the rays converge to one point (the eyepoint) on the other side of the receptor (the screen). This is a mere geometric difference—it produces identical projections.

We consider the point to which the rays converge in our simulation to be in front of the screen; the scene is behind the screen. We call the point of convergence the *eyepoint*. We consider the rays that converge to the eyepoint as passing through the screen, such that there is precisely one ray per pixel and it passes through the pixel's center. Although every point in the scene sends rays in all directions, only those rays that pass through a pixel center and through the eyepoint are seen. Only as many points in the scene as there are pixels on the screen lie in such a position in space that one of the light rays emanating from them passes through a pixel center and the eyepoint. Figure 14.1 demonstrates this concept, showing three light rays coming from three points on the vase and converging on the eyepoint.

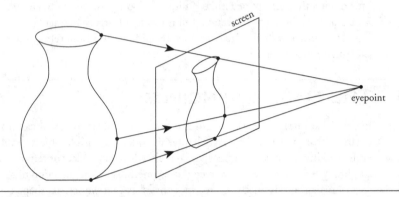

Figure 14.1   Geometry of projection in ray tracing

The way we find these points in the scene describes the basic idea of ray tracing and gives it the name. For each pixel on the screen, we know that there is one ray going through its center and reaching the eyepoint. We can find where this ray comes from by tracing the ray's path backwards.

This is essentially the method of ray tracing: for every pixel on the screen, we compute a straight line through the eyepoint and pixel center and check whether it hits any of the scene's objects. If it does, we have traced backwards to determine the path of the light ray coming from this point and going through that pixel center to the eyepoint. We now give that pixel the color of the point that the straight line has hit. If the line hits no point on the object, it corresponds to a ray coming from the background (sky or whatever) and we color that pixel correspondingly. We call this straight line a *ray*.

This is the basic method that we refine below. It allows us to investigate only such light rays that really hit the eyepoint, and of those finitely many, one per pixel. What happens in reality is impossible to simulate. We would have to send out light rays from all point sources in the scene in all directions, follow and reflect them whenever they hit a shiny surface, and continue to follow each of the reflected rays. If a ray hits a diffusely reflecting surface, we would have to spread it out into countless weaker rays emanating from this point and follow each of these. Each ray will eventually fly off into space, be absorbed in the dull surface of a completely nonreflecting object, or (and these are the rays we see) end up in the eyepoint. If it reaches the eyepoint through a pixel center, we consider it. The overwhelming majority of rays would be followed in vain. That is why we trace rays in the opposite direction.

14.2   A FIRST EXAMPLE

Let us first define some of the nomenclature used in this and the next chapter. *Solid primitives* that cannot be further decomposed mathematically and for which an equation is solved to find intersections with a ray are simply called *solids* and sometimes *primitives*. Later, we introduce the term *composed solid*, which is an entity composed from solids. (We avoid the word "object," because it has another, more general meaning in C++. However, when we use it, we mean a composed solid.)

We begin the explanation of ray casting with a simple nonreflecting solid. The simplest solid to ray trace is a sphere, so we use one in this first example. We position ourselves, that is, the eyepoint, on the negative z-axis at $(0 \ \ 0 \ \ -d)$ and look in the direction of the origin. We put the screen somewhere in front of us, normal to the z-axis. Later, we will see that it does not matter how far away we put it (it does not even have to be between the eyepoint and the object).

We define all scenes in world coordinates. The sphere is defined by specifying its center and its radius. Eyepoint, screen position, sphere position, and radius all are specified in world coordinates.

The reader must be aware that ray casting and tracing deal intensely with spatial geometry. We now introduce one of its geometric concepts and data structures—the *ray*. A ray is more than just a vector. It is an entity that has a starting point in space and a direction in which it progresses, expressed by a vector. The rays that we produce start at the eyepoint and go through the center of a pixel. Below, we show a preliminary structure for a ray to help in developing the mathematics. It will be overridden later by a class specification. A ray, too, is specified in world coordinates.

```
typedef struct
{
    point3_t s ;                        // start point
    point3_t d ;                        // direction
} ray_t ;
```

We specify points on a given ray in parametric form:

```
x = ray.s.x + u*ray.d.x
y = ray.s.y + u*ray.d.y
z = ray.s.z + u*ray.d.z
```

As the parameter u increases, the point $(x \ \ y \ \ z)$ moves along the ray through space. We can say that we look along the ray in the direction of increasing u-values. For $u = 0$, the point $(x \ \ y \ \ z)$ equals the starting point, *ray.s*. For negative u-values, the point $(x \ \ y \ \ z)$ is behind us.

In this example, the sphere has its center at $(c_x \ \ c_y \ \ c_z) = (0.1 \ \ 0.3 \ \ 0.8)$ with radius $r = 0.4$; the eyepoint is at $(0 \ \ 0 \ \ -3)$.

We now shoot rays through every pixel $(x_s \ \ y_s)$ on the screen, where x_s and y_s are in absolute device coordinates. These must be transformed to world coordinates in order to determine the geometry of the rays. Figure 14.2 shows this arrangement from above. The horizontal line is the screen. The extent of the sphere on the screen is proportional to the size the screen assumes in the scene. This extent is the set of all intersections of the screen with lines from the sphere to the eyepoint. Geometrically speaking, the extent is the intersection of the screen plane with the cone determined by the sphere and eyepoint. In Figure 14.2, it extends over roughly one third of the screen's width.

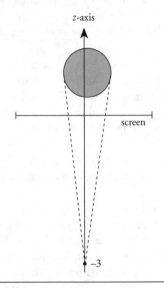

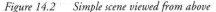

Figure 14.2   Simple scene viewed from above

It is essential that the screen be vertical to the z-axis. We assume that the screen center is at (0 0 0) in world coordinates. It follows that all z-coordinates on the screen are 0. We define the right end of the screen at the x-coordinate 1 and the left end at the x-coordinate –1. Now everything is in place to determine the transformation from absolute screen to world coordinates.

By screen, we do not necessarily mean a whole CRT monitor. It could be only a rectangular part of a CRT display, such as an X-window. If our screen has a pixel range of 0 to 639 from left to right, then x_s = 0 corresponds to –1, and x_s = 639 corresponds to +1. This gives us the transformation:

$$x_{world} = (x_s - 320)/320$$

We assume a pixel range in y from 0 at the top to 399 at the bottom and a square pixel ratio. The transformation is then:

$$y_{world} = (200 - y_s)/320$$

The denominator is 320 in both expressions because only the pixel *extent* in y is smaller than in x; the pixel distance is the same. Also, the y's are measured from the top of the screen; positive y's are downward.

Now, when we shoot a ray from the eyepoint through the center of pixel (x_s y_s), we first transform x_s and y_s to world coordinates. This gives us the point in world coordinates through which the ray goes. It is:

$$x = (x_s - 320)/320 \qquad y = (200 - y_s)/320 \qquad z = 0$$

The ray start point is:

$$ray.s = (0 \quad 0 \quad -3)$$

The *ray direction* is the difference between the point on the screen and the start point:

$$ray.d.x = (x_s - 320)/320 - 0$$
$$ray.d.y = (200 - y_s)/320 - 0$$
$$ray.d.z = 0 - (-3)$$

We make it a rule always to normalize every vector that we create to 1, so we must normalize *ray.d*.

Now we are ready to check this ray for intersection with the sphere. The equation of a sphere surface is:

$$(x - c_x)^2 + (y - c_y)^2 + (z - c_z)^2 - r^2 = 0$$

where $(c_x \; c_y \; c_z)$ is the center and r the radius. If a ray intersects a sphere's surface, there must be a point on the ray that fulfills the sphere's equation. All points on the ray are expressed by:

$$x = s_x + u*d_x$$
$$y = s_y + u*d_y$$
$$z = s_z + u*d_z$$

This is the same parametric expression of the ray, but we have abbreviated *ray.s.x* by s_x, *ray.d.x* by d_x and so on.

Now we must insert the expressions for x, y, and z into the sphere equation to find u. Computations are simpler if we translate ray and sphere together so that the sphere's center is at the origin. This means we check for an intersection with a sphere at $(0 \; 0 \; 0)$. Such a spherical surface is expressed by:

$$x^2 + y^2 + z^2 = r^2$$

A ray's translation involves only its start point—the direction does not change. We compute the translated start point s_t:

$$s_{tx} = s_x - c_x$$
$$s_{ty} = s_y - c_y$$
$$s_{tz} = s_z - c_z$$

An intersection point with the sphere at $(0 \; 0 \; 0)$ fulfills the equation:

$$(s_{tx} + u*d_x)^2 + (s_{ty} + u*d_y)^2 + (s_{tz} + u*d_z)^2 = r^2$$

The only unknown is u. We expand this expression, order on powers of u, and obtain:

$$a_2*u^2 + a_1*u + a_0 = 0$$

with

$$a_2 = d_x{}^2 + d_y{}^2 + d_z{}^2 \qquad (=1, \text{ see below})$$

$$a_1 = 2*(d_x * s_{tx} + d_y * s_{ty} + d_z * s_{tz})$$

$$a_0 = s_{tx}{}^2 + s_{ty}{}^2 + s_{tz}{}^2 - r^2$$

This is a quadratic equation in u that we solve with the formula:

$$u = \frac{-a_1 \pm \sqrt{a_1{}^2 - 4a_2 a_0}}{2a_2}$$

We can simplify the computation by dropping the factor 2 when computing a_1, so we redefine a_1 as:

$$a_1 = d_x * s_{tx} + d_y * s_{ty} + d_z * s_{tz}$$

In the formula we then have to write $2*a_1$ instead of a_1. We get:

$$u = \frac{-2a_1 \pm \sqrt{4a_1{}^2 - 4a_2 a_0}}{2a_2}$$

We see now that the factor 2 cancels out. Also, as the ray is normalized, a_2 equals 1. The formula simply becomes:

$$u = -a_1 \pm \sqrt{a_1{}^2 - a_0}$$

The value of a_2 need not be computed. The formula yields 0, 1, or 2 solutions for u, depending on the value of $a_1{}^2 - a_0$. If this value is negative, we have no solutions—the ray misses the sphere. If it is 0, we have precisely one solution—the ray grazes the sphere. If it is positive, we have two solutions—the ray penetrates the sphere.

Cases in which the ray grazes or just barely hits the sphere we consider as misses. This simplifies things without having any effect on the resulting picture and it allows us to deal with only two cases:

1. A hit of the sphere yields two intersection values. The first intersection occurs when the ray enters the sphere; the second one occurs when it exits.

2. A miss of the sphere.

Solving for u requires a time-consuming square root computation. Once we have a_1 and a_0, however, we can perform an inexpensive check to exclude some cases in which no intersection is possible from further consideration.

We use Figure 14.3 to explain the geometry involved. The start point of the ray, r_s, has the coordinates $(s_{tx}\ s_{ty}\ s_{tz})$. The ray direction is r_d. Let S be the distance from the center to r_s, that is: $S^2 = s_{tx}{}^2 + s_{ty}{}^2 + s_{tz}{}^2$. Then the length of the heavy line, L, is S minus the radius: $L = S - r$. If $L > 0$, it follows that $S > r$, which implies that $S^2 - r^2 > 0$. That is, $s_{tx}{}^2 + s_{ty}{}^2 + s_{tz}{}^2 - r^2 > 0$. However, the expression on the left of the greater sign is a_0. In the same way, it follows from $L < 0$ that $a_0 < 0$. This shows that the signs of L and a_0 are equivalent.

If $a_0 > 0$, then $L > 0$, and the ray starts outside the sphere. The value of a_1 is the dot product of the vector from $(0\ 0\ 0)$ to r_s with r_d. If this is positive, the ray direction is more or less parallel to vector r_s and points at most by 90 degrees off to the side. It never points toward the sphere.

If a ray starts outside and points away from the sphere, there cannot be an intersection with the sphere and we stop further testing. In summary, if $a_0 > 0$ and $a_1 > 0$, there is no intersection.

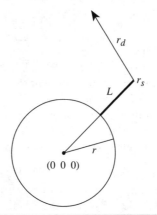

Figure 14.3   Pretesting for possible intersections

If the two conditions above are not fulfilled, we continue and check whether $a_1^2 - a_0$ is greater than some small positive number. If this is not true, we have missed the sphere. As the sphere is the only object in our scene, this means that the ray hits the background. In this case we set the pixel $(x_s\ y_s)$ to the color we want for the background, for example, blue.

If the condition is met, however, the ray does hit the sphere. The smaller of the two u-values, u_{en}, corresponds to the point where the ray enters the sphere and the larger one, u_{ex}, is where it exits. We consider the sphere a solid object, so we use only the entry point. The fact that the ray has an entry and an exit point is of only theoretical value now. Later on, when we use Boolean coordinates, we will make much use of both intersections.

If u_{en} is smaller than some small value, say 0.001, our ray starts on or close to the sphere surface and goes into the sphere. We consider such cases as no hits.

Only the ray's entry point is visible. We call it the *hit point*. This point is computed by inserting u_{en} into the three equations of the untranslated ray:

$$hit.x = s_x + u_{en} * d_x$$
$$hit.y = s_y + u_{en} * d_y$$
$$hit.z = s_z + u_{en} * d_z$$

We could now simply set the pixel $(x_s\ y_s)$ to the sphere color. This would give us a correct picture, but a very bland one. In ray tracing, it is easy to give the sphere a shaded appearance because we are displaying it pixelwise.

As we learned in earlier chapters, we can use Lambert's Law and other shading concepts to obtain shading. We have to assume a certain amount of ambient light ($I_{ar}\ I_{ag}\ I_{ab}$) and a point light source with intensity ($I_{pr}\ I_{pg}\ I_{pb}$) somewhere in the scene.

We give the sphere a certain color in terms of its *rgb*-components. The contribution of the ambient light is obtained by multiplying these components pairwise with the ambient light values. To find the point light's contribution we have to know the incident angle—the angle between the surface normal and the direction to the light source. The normal on a sphere surface is simply the direction from the center to the surface point:

$$nor.x = hit.x - c_x$$

$$nor.y = hit.y - c_y$$

$$nor.z = hit.z - c_z$$

We assume for simplicity that the light source is infinitely far away. Hence, the direction to the light source is the same for every point in space. (Later, we will use light sources at finite distances. There is little difference in the treatment of these two cases.) We specify the direction to the light source with the vector (*lit.x lit.y lit.z*). After normalizing the normal and the direction to the light source, we compute the dot product of these two vectors:

$$lam = nor.x * lit.x + nor.y * lit.y + nor.z * lit.z$$

If this is negative, the normal is pointing away from the light source. This means that the hit point is in the shadowed part of the sphere. For such a point, we make the point light contribution 0 and the illumination of that pixel will depend only on the ambient light.

If *lam* is positive, we multiply the point light intensities with *lam*, multiply the result pairwise with the sphere *rgb*-values, and then add them to the ambient light contribution.

The intensity of the pixel is then:

$$I_r = r * I_{ar} + r * lam * I_{pr}$$

$$I_g = g * I_{ag} + g * lam * I_{pg}$$

$$I_b = b * I_{ab} + b * lam * I_{pb}$$

This completes the tracing for this ray. We repeat this for every pixel on the screen.

Here is an example of the computations for the above scene (a single sphere) for the pixel (307 123). We take the sphere color to be (*rgb*) = (0.8 0.5 0.1)—an orange color. Assume gray ambient light of intensity (0.4 0.4 0.4) and a point light source of intensity (0.9 0.9 0.9) in the direction (−0.597 0.717 0.358). (This vector is already normalized.)

Start point:

$$s = (0\ \ 0\ \ -3)$$

Sphere center and radius:

$$(0.1\ \ 0.3\ \ 0.8)\qquad 0.4$$

Pixel screen coordinates:

$$(x_s\ \ y_s) = (307\ \ 123)$$

Pixel world coordinates:

$$(x\ \ y) = ((307 - 320)/320\ \ (200 - 123)/320) = (-0.04062\ \ 0.24062)$$

The ray:

$$ray.s = (0 \quad 0 \quad -3)$$

$$ray.d = (-0.04062 \quad 0.24062 \quad 3)$$

normalized:

$$ray.d = (-0.01349 \quad 0.07994 \quad 0.99671)$$

Translated start point of ray:

$$s_t = (0-0.1 \quad 0-0.3 \quad -3-0.8) = (-0.1 \quad -0.3 \quad -3.8) \qquad \text{..... (i)}$$

The quadratic equation intersection test:

$$a_1 = (-0.01349)*(-0.1) + (0.07994)*(-0.3) +$$
$$(0.99671)*(-3.8) = -3.81013 \qquad \text{..... (ii)}$$

$$a_0 = (-0.1)^2 + (-0.3)^2 + (-3.8)^2 - (0.4)^2 = 14.38 \qquad \text{..... (iii)}$$

$(a_1 > 0$ and $a_0 > 0)$ is not true, ray may intersect, so continue,

$$a_1{}^2 - a_0 = (-3.81013)^2 - (14.38)$$
$$= 0.13709 > 0.0001, \text{ intersection of sphere}$$

Intersection values:

$$u = -(-3.81013) \pm \sqrt{3.81013^2 - 14.38} = 4.18038, \ 3.43987$$

$$u_{en} = 3.43987, \ u_{ex} = 4.18038 \qquad \text{..... (iv)}$$

$$u_{en} > 0.001, \text{ so continue.}$$

The hit point:

$$hit = (0 + 3.43987*(-0.01349)$$
$$0 + 3.43987*(0.07994)$$
$$-3 + 3.43987*(0.99671)) \qquad \text{..... (v)}$$
$$= (-0.04642 \quad 0.27499 \quad 0.42855)$$

The normal at the hit point:

$$n = (-0.04642 - 0.1 \quad 0.27499 - 0.3 \quad 0.42855 - 0.8)$$
$$= (-0.14642 \quad -0.02501 \quad -0.37145)$$

normalized: ..... (vi)

$$n = (-0.36605 \quad -0.062525 \quad -0.92862)$$

The dot product of normal at the hit point and light source direction:

$$lam = (-0.36605)*(-0.597)$$
$$+ (-0.062525)*(0.717)$$
$$+ (-0.92862)*(-0.358) \qquad \text{..... (vii)}$$
$$= 0.50614$$

This is positive, so the hit point is illuminated with intensities of:

$$I_r = 0.8*(0.4+0.50614*0.9) = 0.684$$
$$I_g = 0.5*(0.4+0.50614*0.9) = 0.427$$
$$I_b = 0.1*(0.4+0.50614*0.9) = 0.085$$

..... (viii)

If we have a 24-bit frame buffer, we can now directly compute the *rgb*-values and set the pixel. If we have to work with a lookup table, we must find the entry number that matches this *rgb*-value most closely and set the pixel to that number.

The order of computations for various pixels is not critical. They can even be done simultaneously if several processors are available.

14.3   A PRELIMINARY IMPLEMENTATION

Here, we show a preliminary implementation that should be used for practicing; except for some class specifications, it is not provided on diskette. The general OO design and final implementation will be explained later. However, we use the final class specifications, except where indicated.

This preliminary ray caster differs from the final one in one essential feature—solid primitives cannot be combined with each other (added, subtracted, or intersected) to form more complex objects. All solid primitives added to a scene are linked into one linear list, from which they will be traced. The final design uses a linked list of trees.

Let us express a point or vector in space with the class point3_t, developed in Chapter 6. However, we need more functionality, as will become clear later. Rather than reopening an implemented class in order to add members, we use inheritance and add the functionality to the derived class. We must add functions that compute the reflection and refraction vectors. Only the prototypes are shown in the specification. The other added functions are just constructors. The class is called rpoint_t (for ray trace–point). We add two prototypes of nonmember operators to the .h file for point-matrix multiplication.

```
//*************************** File rpoint.h ************************

#ifndef RPOINT_T
#define RPOINT_T

#include <stdio.h>
#include "../Shape3d/point3.h"

class mat33_t ;

class rpoint_t : public point3_t
{
public:
   rpoint_t() ;
   rpoint_t(double,double,double) ;
   rpoint_t(const rpoint_t&) ;
```

```
      rpoint_t(FILE*) ;
      rpoint_t(const point3_t&) ;

      void givxyz(double&,double&,double&) const ;
      point3_t reflec(const point3_t&) const ;
      point3_t refrac(const point3_t&,double) const ;
      void operator = (const rpoint_t&) ;
   } ;

   rpoint_t operator* (const rpoint_t&,const mat33_t&) ; // point*matrix
   rpoint_t operator* (const mat33_t&,const rpoint_t&) ; // matrix*point

   #endif

   //***********************************************************************
```

The next class is the ray. It consists of two `rpoint_t`: the starting point and the direction vector.

```
   //*********************** File ray.h ***************************

   #ifndef RAY_T
   #define RAY_T

   #include "../Raytrace/rpoint.h"


   struct ray_t
   {
      rpoint_t s ,                              // starting point of ray
               d ;                              // direction vector of ray
      ray_t() : s(0,0,0) , d(0,0,0) {}
      ray_t(const rpoint_t& s,const rpoint_t& d) : s(s) , d(d) {}
      rpoint_t operator () (const double u) const
      { return s + d*u; }
   } ;

   #endif

   //***********************************************************************
```

Colors are again expressed using the primaries red, green, and blue. We can use the class `rgb_t` introduced in Chapter 9, but we need more functionality. We derive the class `rgb1_t` from `rgb_t`, adding only member functions.

```
//************************* File rgb1.h *************************

#ifndef RGB1_T
#define RGB1_T

#include <stdio.h>
#include <iostream.h>
#include "../Shape3d/rgb.h"

class rgb1_t : public rgb_t
{
public:
   rgb1_t() ;
   rgb1_t(double,double,double) ;
   rgb1_t(const rgb_t&) ;
   rgb1_t(FILE*) ;
                        // operators and functions not defined in rgb_t
   rgb1_t operator +=(const rgb1_t&) ;
   rgb1_t operator *=(const rgb1_t&) ;
   rgb1_t operator ^ (double) const ;              // rgb power double
   void   read(ifstream&) ;
   void   write(ofstream&) ;                   // write as 3 shorts
   void   write3char(ofstream&) ;              // write as 3 characters
   void   finish_read() ;
   void   finish_write(ofstream&) ;
   void   givrgb(double&,double&,double&) const ;
} ;


#endif


//***************************************************************
```

Next, we introduce the class that specifies a texture. By *texture* we mean the material composition of a solid primitive at a given point. This texture contributes to the appearance of a solid's surface, but is not identical to its color.

To understand the concept of texture, think of a white sphere with black latitudinal stripes. If this sphere is in a completely dark room, it will look black everywhere. In a room with only red light, the white parts will look red and the stripes black. By itself, the sphere possesses the texture "white with black stripes," independent of what light strikes it. This texture works together with the given light to produce certain colors on the surface. The "white" parts diffusely reflect all incoming wavelengths equally, while the "black" parts consume all incoming wavelengths.

Thus, color is the result of the interaction of light and the texture exposed to it. It is only this texture that is expressed by the class texture_t, not the color. Texture also contains the specular and the refractive coefficients constituting a texture. We will use these later.

Below is an abstraction that we use for the preliminary ray caster (it is not a class specification of the final design).

This abstraction is the class presolid_t (preliminary solid). The type presphere_t and whatever solid primitive goes into the preliminary ray caster are derived from it. In this design, we link all of a scene's solid primitives into a list. The class therefore has a member `presolid_t* next`.

The member `cen` is the center of the primitive. `Tex` is a pointer to a function that returns its texture. These members are in the base class because every solid primitive has a center and a texture. The class has two virtual functions. `Intersect()` computes the *u*-values of the intersections with a given ray and returns the number of intersections. This number is zero if the primitive is not intersected, two if it is intersected and convex, and up to four for a concave primitive such as a torus—but it is always even! (We do not allow a ray to graze a primitive.) `Normal()` returns the normal at the hit point on the primitive.

```
//************************ presolid.h ************************
// preliminary

#ifndef PRESOLID_T
#define PRESOLID_T

#include "../Raytrace/rpoint.h"
#include "../Raytrace/texture.h"
#include "../Raytrace/ray.h"

class presolid_t
{
public:
    presolid_t(rpoint_t,texture_t(*)(),presolid_t*) ;
    ~presolid_t() ;
    virtual int intersect (const ray_t&,double*) ;
    virtual rpoint_t normal (const rpoint_t&) const ;

protected:
    rpoint_t  cen ;                              // center
    texture_t(*tex)() ;                   // texture function
    presolid_t* next ;                    // link to next solid
} ;

#endif

//*******************************************************************
```

The sphere is derived from `presolid_t`, so it inherits the solid's center and texture. What is particular to a sphere, the radius, is specified in the sphere class. Other solids will have other particular data, such as axes or matrices. A sphere also redefines the virtual functions `intersect()` and `normal()`.

Do not consider all this overkill, just because ray tracing a sphere is very simple. We will need this apparatus when describing and ray tracing other solids and more complicated scenes. It would be beneficial for the reader to understand this concept before moving on to the final design.

The function `intersect()` finds the intersections of a sphere and a ray, `normal()` returns the surface normal at a given point of a sphere. It speeds up computations to add the precomputed square of the radius and its inverse to `presphere_t`.

The radius is certainly a typical or essential property of a sphere. Other solids have other essential properties; an ellipsoid, for example, has three diameters. However, a solid's center can not really be considered an essential property. It does not describe the solid's size, shape, or actual extent, but only its location or position in space. As in real life, one can put the same solid in several different positions. We consider only the properties that describe a solid's permanent size or shape to be essential, as these are its constituent parts. They are also unique to it; only one solid is described by one radius alone—the sphere.

This is the reason we make the radius a member of the sphere, but not the center. All solid primitives have a center, so we let them inherit it from the base class `presolid_t`. By the same token, we make data for speeding up solid-specific computations, such as the sphere's inverse radius members. These do not exist for other solids. For example, the solid's ellipsoid and cylinder, which will be introduced in the next section, have axes but no radius.

```
//************************* presphere.h *************************
// preliminary

#ifndef PRESPHERE_T
#define PRESPHERE_T
#include "presolid.h"
#include "../Raytrace/rpoint.h"
#include "../Raytrace/ray.h"

class presphere_t : public presolid_t
{
public:
   presphere_t(double,rpoint_t,texture_t (*)(),presolid_t*) ;
   int intersect (const ray_t&,double) ;
   rpoint_t normal (const rpoint_t&) const ;

private:
   double r ;                                  // radius
   double rinv ;                        // inverse radius
   double rsqu ;                        // square of radius
} ;

#endif

//****************************************************************
```

We use the presphere to show one implementation example of a solid. In the code, we use numbers to refer to the places in the sample computation of the sphere-ray intersection above.

A few additional explanations are in order. In `intersect()`, we save computation time by using the precomputed r^2, which is stored as a data member. In `normal()`, we subtract the sphere's center from the hit point to find the normal. This vector is easy to normalize by multipying it by the inverse radius. We save computation time by storing the inverse of the radius as a data member.

The function `presphere_t()` constructs a sphere by setting radius, center, and a pointer to a texture function. Several spheres are defined by repeatedly calling `presphere_t()` and linking the data so created into a singly linked list terminated by NULL.

```
//************************ presphere.c ************************
// preliminary

#include <stdio.h>
#include <math.h>
#include "presphere.h"

presphere_t::presphere_t(              // initialize a sphere
   double      r      ,                        // radius
   rpoint_t    cen    ,                        // center
   texture_t (*tex)() ,                 // texture function
   presolid_t*    next ) :              // link to next solid
   r(r) , rsqu(r*r) , rinv(1/r) ,
   presolid_t(cen,tex,next) {}

int presphere_t::intersect(const ray_t& r,double* u)
{
   rpoint_t s = r.s - cen ;           // translate start point (i)
   double a0 = s*s - rsqu ,                    // (iii)
          a1 = s*r.d ;                         //  (ii)
   if (a0 > 0 && a1 > 0) return 0;   // start outside, point away

   double dis = a1*a1 - a0 ;
   if (dis < 0.00001) return 0;              // check intersection

   dis = sqrt(dis);
   if (-a1 + dis < 0) return 0;

   u[0] = -a1-dis;                                    // (iv)
   u[1] = -a1+dis;
   return 2;
}

rpoint_t presphere_t::normal(const rpoint_t& hit) const
{
   return (hit - cen)*rinv;                          // (vi)
}

//***************************************************************
```

Tracing a ray against a scene involves traversing the list and calling each solid's intersection function for the given ray. If the function returns 0, we miss that sphere; if it returns 2, we check the smaller of the returned values, $u[0]$, against the u-value that we keep locally. If the returned value is larger, we ignore it; otherwise, we replace the local u-value with it and remember the pointer to that solid.

The function that does this is `trace()`. It first sets the parameter u to a very high value and the local pointer solid to NULL. When it finds an intersection and a $u[0]$ smaller than u, then u and the solid are updated. If the solid still has its initial value, NULL, after reaching the end of the list, we have not hit any sphere. Otherwise, it points to the nearest of all spheres that are hit.

Observe that `trace()` does not use the class `presphere_t`, but only `presolid_t`; it does not need to know to what actual solid the pointer solid points. Inside the if statement, it calls the intersection function of the solid to which this pointer points.

If two u-values are returned, both are positive. (It could theoretically happen that `intersect()` returns a negative $u[0]$ and a positive $u[1]$, but this means that the ray starts inside the sphere; see Figure 14.4. For the present, we do not allow such scenes.)

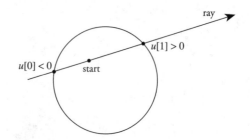

Figure 14.4   Ray starting inside a sphere

```
//************************** trace.c ***************************
// preliminary

#include "presolid.h"
#include "../Raytrace/ray.h"

presolid_t* trace(presolid_t* all,ray_t ray,double* uu)
{
   presolid_t* solid = 0 ;
   double u[2] ;

   *uu = 10000;
   for (presolid_t* cur = all; cur; cur = cur->next)
     if (cur->intersect(ray,u) && u[0] < *uu)
     {
        *uu = u[0]; solid = cur;             // update uu and solid
     }
   return solid;
}

//*************************************************************
```

In `textures.c` below, three texture functions are defined that have no arguments. They return just constant colors, independent of the hit point. In the final design, the texture functions will have three parameters (pointer to the solid hit, hit point, and incident angle of the ray that hits the solid).

```
//*********************** textures.c ************************
// preliminary

#include "../Raytrace/texture.h"

texture_t green_cyan()
{
    return texture_t(0.2,0.8,0.5,0,0);
}

texture_t yellow()
{
    return texture_t(0.9,0.8,0,0,0);
}

texture_t grey_blue()
{
    return texture_t(0.3,0.3,1.0,0,0);
}
//****************************************************************
```

For the definition of the scene, we also need ambient light and one or more point light sources. These we specify in a linked list of `light_t`, for which we use the class `light_t` of `Shape3d`.

We employ the rule that the first element in the list is the ambient light, because there is always exactly one ambient light. For the ambient light, the position is ignored. The following elements in the list are point light sources.

The function `illum()` is called with a pointer to the list of all solids, a pointer to the solid that is hit, the hit point and a pointer to the light sources. After obtaining the texture-*rgb* of the solid, `illum()` computes the illumination. It obtains the ambient light through the first value of the light pointer.

Then it advances the light pointer to obtain the point light data. A ray from the hit point to the light source is formed and normalized (`ray_to_light`). The normal to the solid is obtained by calling that solid's normal function. The dot product of `ray_to_light.d` and the normal gives us the factor of the point–light intensity. If this product is negative, the surface points away from the light source and so is in its own shadow; in this case, the point light contribution is 0.

CHECKING FOR SHADOW OF OTHER SOLIDS

In this context, let us explain checking for shadows. If the above dot product is positive, the surface at the hit point points toward the light. Whether point light reaches the hit point depends on if other solids in the scene are between the hit point and the light source. This is easy to check. We already have `ray_to_light`. We trace it against all solids in the scene and check whether the returned pointer is 0. If it is not, some other solid occludes the light, the hit point is in the shadow, and we make the point light contribution 0.

If the pointer is NULL, point light does strike the hit point and its contribution is added to the ambient light. Walking through the whole list of point light sources, we sum up all contributions. After the loop, the result is multiplied by the sphere's *rgb*-values.

```
//************************ illum.c ****************************
// preliminary

#include "../Raytrace/rpoint.h"
#include "../Raytrace/ray.h"
#include "../Shape3d/light.h"
#include "../Raytrace/texture.h"
#include "presolid.h"

presolid_t* trace() ;

rgb1_t illum(
   presolid_t*  all ,                    // list of all solids
   presolid_t*  solid ,
   rpoint_t     hit ,
   light_t*     light )
{
   rgb1_t   ambient = light->rgb ;          // get ambient light
   rpoint_t nor = presolid->normal(hit) ;
   rgb1_t   rgb = presolid->texture().rgb ;
   ray_t    ray_to_light(hit,rpoint_t()) ;

   for (light_t* l = light->givnext(); l; l = l->givnext())
   {                         // walk through all point light sources
      double dum , uplight ;

      ray_to_light.d = (light->givpos() - hit).normalize();

      uplight = nor*ray_to_light.d;                    // (vii)
      if (uplight < 0.001)        // surface faces away from light
         uplight = 0;
      if (uplight && trace(all,ray_to_light,&dum))      // shadow
         uplight = 0;

      ambient += light->givrgb()*uplight;
   }

   rgb *= ambient;
   return rgb.trim_to_1();
}

//*****************************************************************
```

Main() creates a linked list of three solids (spheres in this example); see Figure 14.5. Then, main() enters a double loop for all pixels on the screen. For each created ray, main() calls trace() and, if some solid is hit, it computes the hit point. It then calls illum() to find the illumination of the hit point. Finally, it sets the pixel to the closest color in the lookup table.

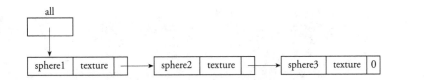

Figure 14.5   Linked list of solids

```
//*********************** File main.c **************************

#include "../Raytrace/rpoint.h"
#include "../Raytrace/ray.h"
#include "../Shape3d/light.h"
#include "../Raytrace/texture.h"
#include "../Raytrace/rgb1.h"
#include "presolid.h"

texture_t green_cyan() ,
          yellow()      ,
          grey_blue()  ;
rgb1_t    illum()      ;
presolid_t* trace()    ;

void main()
{
   light_t* light =
      new light_t(rpoint_t( 0.0,0.0, 0.0),rgb1_t(0.4,0.4,0.4),
      new light_t(rpoint_t(-5.0,7.0,-3.0),rgb1_t(0.9,0.9,0.9), NULL));

   presolid_t* all =
    new presphere_t(0.4 ,rpoint_t( 0.1,0.3,0.8),green_cyan,
    new presphere_t(0.25,rpoint_t(-0.1,0.2,0.5),yellow,
    new presphere_t(0.22,rpoint_t(-0.2,0.0,0.2),grey_blue, NULL)));

   for (int x = 0; x < 640; x++)
      for (int y = 0; y < 399; y++)
      {
         presolid_t* solid ;
         rgb1_t rgb ;
         double u ;

         ray_t ray(rpoint_t(0,0,-3),              // start is eyepoint
                   rpoint_t( (x-320)/320.0,         // ray direction
                            (200-y)/320.0,
                              3
                          ).normalize()
                  ) ;
         if (solid = trace(all,ray,&u))
         {                    // solid not NULL, some solid was hit
            rpoint_t hit ;

            hit = ray.s + ray.d*u;                        // (v)
```

```
                rgb = illum(all,                    // all primitives
                            solid,                   // primitive hit
                            hit,                     // hit point
                            light);                  // light sources
            }
            else                                     // nothing was hit
                rgb = rgb1_t(0,0,1);                 // set blue

            setpixv(x,y,rgb);
        }
    delete light_t;                                  //cleanup
    delete solid_t;
}


//**************************************************************
```

We have made use of the function setpixv(), which sets the pixel (x y) to the color *rgb* given in normalized values. More powerful graphics workstations have a 24-bit or 32-bit frame buffer. There, the *rgb*-value can be transformed into its representation as a 24-bit or a 32-bit color, consisting of 1 byte each for red, green, and blue. This color is then stored in the corresponding pixel location. For example, on the Number Nine #9GXi true color graphics board, the command for setting the pixel would be put_pixel(val,x,y), where val is a 32-bit hex number containing the *rgb*-values.

Less expensive workstations have only an 8-bit deep frame buffer. Values stored in this buffer are addresses into a so-called color map, a programmable table that associates an 8-bit pixel value with a particular *rgb*-value; see Section 8.4. Finding the best possible entries for the *rgb*-values created when a given scene is ray traced is nontrivial.

Adding another solid primitive to the scene, such as a cylinder, involves writing a class specification and implementation for it and deriving the class from presolid_t. The only change to existing code is in main() where the new solid must be constructed and linked into the list. No other changes are necessary. The exercises give you some help on this.

14.4 ROTATION AND TRANSLATION OF SOLIDS

Now, we start to rotate and position the primitives arbitrarily and combine them in any desired way.

To intersect an arbitrarily positioned solid with a ray, we use the following approach. We first translate solid and ray together so that the solid's center is at (0 0 0). We then rotate solid and ray to align the solid with the coordinate axes. Next, we scale solid and ray so that the solid becomes a *unit-solid* of the same type.

A unit-solid is a solid of the same type, axis-aligned, centered at the origin and of unit size. For example, a unit-sphere is a sphere of radius 1, centered at (0 0 0); a unit-cylinder is a cylinder along the *y*-axis with radius 1 and height 2, one half of the cylinder is above the *xz*-plane, the other half below. A unit-cylinder could, of course, be aligned with another axis, but this is simply our convention. Similarly, every solid has a clearly defined unit-representation, described in Appendix B.

Finally, we intersect the ray that has undergone all these transformations with the unit-solid. Such an intersection is much easier to compute than the intersection of an arbitrary ray with an arbitrary solid. The net result is that, after the transformations, the ray is still arbitrary and no more complicated than initially, but the solid is reduced to one of the unit-types that we define in our ray caster.

We need to make two very important points:

1. By intersecting the transformed ray with the unit-solid, we obtain the u-values for entry and exit. Inserting those in the transformed ray gives us the intersection-point coordinates (on the unit-solid, of course). However, inserting those in the original ray gives us the intersection-point coordinates on the original solid! The reason is that all transformations we do to ray and solid (translation, rotations, scaling) are (geometrically) linear. We omit the mathematical details.

2. All transformations are done only to the ray. It is pointless to do them to the solid, as we know that it will be transformed into the unit-solid.

It is easiest to think in terms of a real solid, such as an ellipsoid, rather than an abstract, shapeless one. While we will use an ellipsoid, it is important to keep in mind that the underlying principles are of general applicability.

THE ELLIPSOID

We will explain how to specify an ellipsoid, how to intersect it with a ray, and how to compute its normal. The code for this is in `Raytrace/ellipsoi.c`.

An ellipsoid is somewhat like an egg, but, while a egg usually is thicker on one end, an ellipsoid is absolutely regular. How is an ellipsoid specified?

We obtain an arbitrary ellipsoid by starting with a unit sphere with center at (0 0 0) and radius 1. This sphere is first scaled by the so-called *half-axes* (*a.x a.y a.z*), which transforms it into an ellipsoid of diameter 2**a.x* in *x*, 2**a.y* in *y*, and 2**a.z* in *z*. This initial ellipsoid is still aligned with the coordinate axes, so we then rotate it by the angles (*r.x r.y r.z*)—the order of the rotations is critical—and finally translate it by (*c.x c.y c.z*).

If we have an ellipsoid with axes (*a.x a.y a.z*) and with center at (*c.x c.y c.z*), which is rotated about its center by the angles (*r.x r.y r.z*) (in this order), we know how this ellipsoid was obtained from the unit sphere. We also know how to transform it back into the unit sphere—we just do the above transformations in reverse order.

We explain the mathematics in two stages that we call "from unit to arbitrary" and "from arbitrary to unit."

"From unit to arbitrary": to make an ellipsoid out of a unit sphere, one performs the above transformations to each point of the unit sphere. The scaling and the rotations are done by multiplying with 3×3 matrices. The translation is done directly by adding the translation amount.

Scaling by the axes is done with a 3×3 scaling matrix:

$$\mathbf{A} = \begin{pmatrix} a.x & 0 & 0 \\ 0 & a.y & 0 \\ 0 & 0 & a.z \end{pmatrix}$$

Rotation by $(r.x \; r.y \; r.z)$ is done with three 3×3 rotation matrices. Using the abbreviations:

$$\cos(r.x) = cx \qquad \sin(r.x) = sx$$
$$\cos(r.y) = cy \qquad \sin(r.y) = sy$$
$$\cos(r.z) = cz \qquad \sin(r.z) = sz$$

the three matrices are:

$$\mathbf{R}_x = \begin{pmatrix} 1 & 0 & 0 \\ 0 & cx & sx \\ 0 & -sx & cx \end{pmatrix} \qquad \mathbf{R}_y = \begin{pmatrix} cy & 0 & sy \\ 0 & 1 & 0 \\ -sy & 0 & cy \end{pmatrix} \qquad \mathbf{R}_z = \begin{pmatrix} cz & sz & 0 \\ -sz & cz & 0 \\ 0 & 0 & 1 \end{pmatrix}$$

Translation is done with:

$$x = x + c.x \qquad y = y + c.y \qquad z = z + c.z$$

If each point $(x \; y \; z)$ on the unit sphere is subjected to the four matrix multiplications and translation, the sphere becomes the ellipsoid. The four matrices can be multiplied into a single matrix. We call this the *unit-to-arbitrary matrix*:

$$\begin{pmatrix} A & \mathbf{R}_x & \mathbf{R}_y & \mathbf{R}_z \end{pmatrix}$$

ELLIPSOID INTERSECTION

Now we have to go back the other way—"from arbitrary to unit." Consider the ellipsoid's transformation back into the unit sphere. We transform the ray at the same time by doing the above transformations in reverse order. The explanation is illustrated with some drawings.

Drawings can only show a two-dimensional projection of the process. We do not see the ellipsoid's extent in the z-direction, nor can we demonstrate rotations about the x- or the y-axis. We therefore consider only a rotation about the z-axis. Figure 14.6 shows an arbitrary ellipsoid and a ray. We assume that the longer axis has length 2, while the shorter one has length 1.

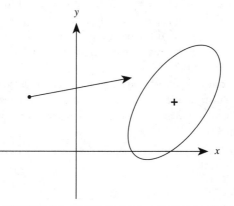

Figure 14.6   Arbitrary ray and arbitrary ellipsoid

The translation:

$$x = x - c.x \qquad y = y - c.y \qquad z = z - c.z$$

will put the ellipsoid's center at (0 0 0). Ray and ellipsoid both move. See Figure 14.7.

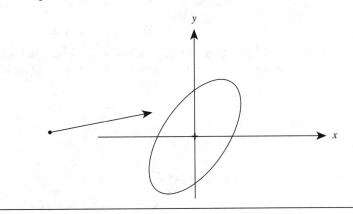

Figure 14.7   After translation

We now multiply by the inverse of the unit-to-arbitrary matrix:

$$\left(\mathbf{R}_z^{-1} \ \ \mathbf{R}_y^{-1} \ \ \mathbf{R}_x^{-1} \ \ \mathbf{A}^{-1} \right)$$

This matrix is easy to compute. (The inverse of a rotation matrix is just its transpose.) The product of $\mathbf{R}_z^{-1} \ \mathbf{R}_y^{-1} \ \mathbf{R}_x^{-1}$ is:

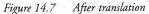

$$\begin{pmatrix} cy*cz & -sx*sy*cz - cx*sz & -cx*sy*cz + sx*sz \\ cy*sz & -sx*sy*sz + cx*cz & -cx*sy*sz - sx*cz \\ sy & sx*cy & cx*cy \end{pmatrix}$$

The rotation gives us an ellipsoid whose axes are along the coordinate axes. In Figure 14.8, we see that ellipsoid and ray have both been rotated about the origin in a clockwise sense.

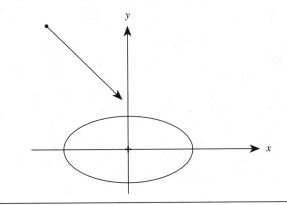

Figure 14.8   After rotation

Now we scale by the inverse axes. The inverse of **A** is:

$$\mathbf{A}^{-1} = \begin{pmatrix} 1/a.x & 0 & 0 \\ 0 & 1/a.y & 0 \\ 0 & 0 & 1/a.z \end{pmatrix}$$

Scaling with $\mathbf{A}^{-1}$ transforms the ellipsoid into a unit sphere. In Figure 14.9, scaling for the example requires scaling only in the x-direction by a factor of 0.5, reducing the ellipsoid's x-extent to 1.

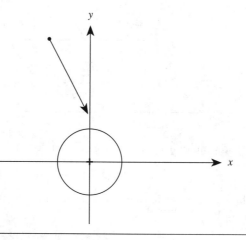

Figure 14.9   After scaling

The arbitrary-to-unit matrix is the product of the inverse rotation matrices and $\mathbf{A}^{-1}$, which is:

$$\begin{pmatrix} cy*cz/a.x & (-sx*sy*cz - cx*sz)/a.y & (-cx*sy*cz + sx*sz)/a.z \\ cy*sz/a.x & (-sx*sy*sz + cx*cz)/a.y & (-cx*sy*sz - sx*cz)/a.z \\ sy/a.x & sx*cy/a.y & cx*cy/a.z \end{pmatrix}$$

We call this matrix **T**. As the figures illustrate, if every point on the ellipsoid is subjected to translation and then multiplied by **T**, the ellipsoid turns into a unit sphere.

We do this transformation only to the ray, because it is unnecessary for the ellipsoid, as we know that it will turn into a unit sphere. Therefore, the reader need think about only the transformation that the ray undergoes. While translation and rotation do not change the length of a ray, scaling does.

Here is how we transform the ray. We translate a ray by translating only its start point, as Figure 14.6 shows. The direction vector does not change under a translation. In C++ notation with an overloaded operator -= this is:

```
ray.s -= c;
```

Rotation and scaling must be done to both start point and direction vector. Rotation and scaling are composed into **T**, so we can perform this in one matrix multiplication. In C++ notation, using an overloaded operator * for the vector-matrix multiplication and *t* for **T**, this is:

```
ray.s = ray.s*t;
ray.d = ray.d*t;
```

After we transform the ray, we intersect it with the unit sphere. This intersection is identical in principle to that shown in the file `sphere.c`, with two differences. The transformed ray does not have the length 1, so the quadratic equation shown for the sphere intersection does not simplify and must be computed fully. Also, the sphere radius is now equal to 1.

ELLIPSOID NORMAL

We now compute the normal on any point of the ellipsoid. We do this specifically, because normal computations differ considerably between solids. We illustrate this geometrically and explain it through an example using a two-dimensional ellipse. We omit a mathematical proof.

Our sample ellipse is centered at (0 0 0) and parallel to the coordinate axes. Its *x*-axis is 2 and its *y*-axis is 1. The normal is obtained at point *v*. The vectors used in our explanations start at (0 0 0), meaning we can use the terms *point* and *vector* interchangeably.

By connecting the center with *v*, we obtain the vector *v*, but this is not normal to the ellipse at *v*. If we divide all *x*-coordinates by two, we scale the ellipse to a unit circle. Scaling *v* similarly will transform it to the vector *v'*. While *v'* is normal to the circle, it is not normal to the ellipse at *v*.

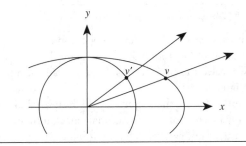

Figure 14.10   Scaling v to v'

Thus, one does not obtain the ellipse normal by using the scaling that transforms the circle into the ellipse. This is true for the following reason: Scaling the circle by a factor of two in the *x*-direction reduces the slope of the connecting line from the center to the surface point; the slope is divided by two. At the same time, the value of the tangent to the ellipse is reduced by the same factor. It is not hard to show that the tangent at every point on the circle is divided by two in this process; see Figure 14.11. When a line's slope is divided by two, the slope of its normal is multiplied by two.

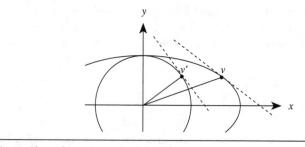

Figure 14.11   Slopes change inversely to the scaling

When we scale the circle into the ellipse, if we scale the circle normal along with it, its slope will be divided by two, when actually it should be multiplied by two. This tells us how to obtain the ellipse normal from the circle normal—we scale the circle normal by $\frac{1}{2}$. The point v' becomes the point v'', therefore the vector v'' has twice the slope of the vector v'. This then gives the ellipse normal, as Figure 14.12 shows. In the figure, we have translated the vector v'' to the point v to show that the vector is normal to the ellipse.

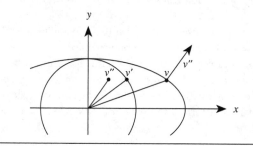

Figure 14.12   Normals, too, change inversely to the scaling

In summary, we did the following operations:

1. We scaled the vector v by $\frac{1}{2}$ to obtain the circle normal at the scaled point.
2. We scaled the circle normal by $\frac{1}{2}$ to transform it into the ellipse normal at the original point.

In general, we scale the vector v by the reciprocal of the square of the axis.

We apply this to a three-dimensional ellipsoid by scaling all axes, not just x. The original ellipsoid is usually not parallel to the coordinate axes, so to center and align it, we first translate by the center, then do an arbitrary-to-unit rotation. However, we transform only the hit point, not the ellipsoid itself. After scaling with the reciprocals of the squares of the axes, we have the normal at the hit point of the centered and axis-aligned ellipsoid. We must now backrotate with a unit-to-arbitrary rotation. (The normal need not be translated back to the arbitrary ellipsoid.)

This process is described with these matrix multiplications:

$$\left(\mathbf{R}_z^{-1} \mathbf{R}_y^{-1} \mathbf{R}_x^{-1} \mathbf{A}^{-1} \quad \mathbf{A}^{-1} \mathbf{R}_x \quad \mathbf{R}_y \quad \mathbf{R}_z \right)$$

The first four matrices are the arbitrary-to-unit matrix $\mathbf{T}$. The last four are not the unit-to-arbitrary matrix $\mathbf{T}^{-1}$, because the axes are inverted. Instead, they are simply the transpose of $\mathbf{T}$. We can accomplish the whole operation (except for the initial translation) by multiplying with one matrix:

$$\mathbf{C} = \mathbf{T} \ \mathbf{T}^T$$

This is the characteristic matrix of the ellipsoid. We can easily obtain and store it to help compute the normal. The name derives from the fact that an arbitrary ellipsoid (actually every conic) can be expressed as a quadratic form using this matrix (except for the translation):

$$(x \quad y \quad z) \ \mathbf{C} \begin{pmatrix} x \\ y \\ z \end{pmatrix} = 0$$

The resulting normal v'' is not of length 1, even though the normal to the sphere v' is. Therefore, it must be normalized.

THE CYLINDER

We show how to specify a cylinder, how to intersect it with a ray, and how to find its normal. This involves principles not used in the case of an ellipsoid.

A unit-cylinder is defined by the quadratic equation:

$$x^2 + z^2 = 1$$

This cylinder is upright, centered around the y-axis, and has radius 1. It has a circular cross-section and is infinitely long. Thus, we cut it off with two horizontal planes at the heights -1 and $+1$. We can obtain from this any arbitrary cylinder—even one with an elliptic cross section—by scaling, rotating, and translating. However, we cannot obtain a cylinder whose ends are slanted. There are other easy ways to obtain such a cylinder.

The intersection of a ray with an arbitrary cylinder is found by translating, rotating, and scaling the ray as explained for the ellipsoid, then intersecting it with the unit cylinder. The intersection and normal have to be found only for this unit cylinder. We show this in Figure 14.13.

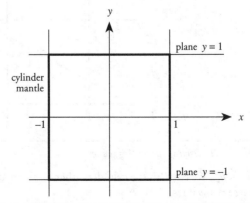

Figure 14.13   Unit cylinder cross section

CYLINDER INTERSECTION

The general principles are shown in Figures 14.14 through 14.17. By "ray" we refer to the transformed ray with start point $(s_x\ s_y\ s_z)$ and direction $(d_x\ d_y\ d_z)$. We find the intersections' u-values by solving this quadratic equation:

$$a_2 * u^2 + a_1 * u + a_0 = 0$$

where

$$a_2 = dx^2 + dz^2$$
$$a_1 = sx * dx + sz * dz$$
$$a_0 = sx^2 + sz^2 - 1$$

If real solutions exist, they are u_{en} and u_{ex} $(u_{en} < u_{ex})$. At u_{en} we enter the mantle of the cylinder, and at u_{ex} we leave it. We also find the intersections with the two cutting planes, which we call p_{en} and p_{ex} $(p_{en} < p_{ex})$. At p_{en} we enter the space between the two planes, and at p_{ex} we leave it. We quit the computation whenever both values are negative. See Figure 14.14.

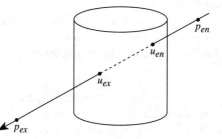

Figure 14.14   Intersecting the cylinder mantle

Figure 14.15 shows the same situation as 14.14, but in a projection parallel to the cutting planes. We compute u_{en} = maximum (u_{en}, p_{en}), which makes u_{en} the larger entry value. We also compute u_{ex} = minimum (u_{ex}, p_{ex}), which makes u_{ex} the smaller exit value.

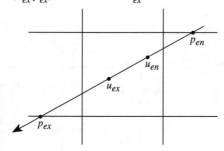

Figure 14.15   Intersecting the cutting planes

If $u_{en} < u_{ex}$, we have hit the cylinder either on the mantle or on the cutting planes and we return these two values.

Figure 14.16 shows a case in which the larger entry value is p_{en}. The cylinder is hit at the upper cutting plane.

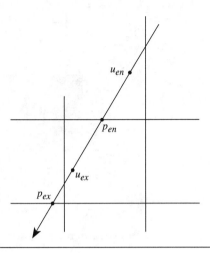

Figure 14.16   Hitting the cylinder at the cutting plane

Figure 14.17 shows a case in which the cylinder is not hit. Here the smaller exit, p_{ex}, is smaller than the larger entry, u_{en}.

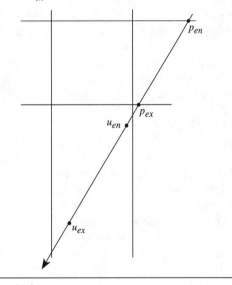

Figure 14.17   Missing the cylinder

An inexpensive test that saves computation time involves checking the ray start and direction with respect to the planes. When the ray starts on or above the top plane and goes parallel or upward, there is no intersection. It is similar at the bottom plane; see Figure 14.18. These conditions are tested in the intersection routine, using values that, for numerical reasons, will also exclude rays that start on the top plane or above and go just slightly downward. The test at the bottom plane is analogous.

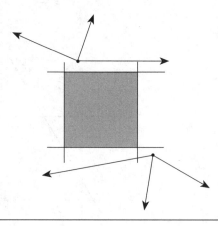

Figure 14.18   Pretesting for possible intersections

This test excludes rays almost parallel to the planes, as well, but only if they start outside or on the planes. (If they start inside, they can hit the cylinder.) We handle these cases by assigning $-\infty$ to p_{en} and $+\infty$ to p_{ex} to avoid dividing by a very small number or zero.

In analogy to a similar test with a sphere, we can exclude the case where the ray starts outside the cylinder mantle and points away from it. The ray starts outside if $sx^2 + sz^2 > 1$, which is equivalent to $a_0 > 0$. It faces away from the mantle if $sx*dx + sz*dz > 0$, which is equivalent to $a_1 > 0$.

The principle of comparing the largest of several entry values to the smallest of several exit values, which determines whether an intersection exists, is generally applicable to all solids with convex surfaces. We will make more use of it later.

CYLINDER NORMAL

This is a relatively simple computation. We do an arbitrary-to-unit transformation of the hit point on the cylinder to obtain the hit point on the unit cylinder. Then we test whether the hit point is on one of the planes or on the mantle. If it is on the top plane, the normal is (0 1 0). If the hit point is on the bottom plane, the normal is (0 −1 0). If the hit point is on the mantle, the normal is the vector from (0 0 0) to the hit point; the y-coordinate is set to 0, because all mantle normals are horizontal.

This normal has length 1 in all cases. If it is normal to the mantle, we have to scale it with the inverse axes (the cylinder's cross section could be elliptical) and then rotate it back to the rotational position of the original cylinder. This transformation is done with the transpose of t. We must then normalize.

The two plane normals are much easier to find. On the unit cylinder, they are (0 1 0) and (0 −1 0). We rotate these back to the original cylinder. Doing this with *rot* instead of t avoids scaling and maintains the length of the vectors—we do not need to normalize. Multiplying (0 1 0) or (0 −1 0) by the transpose of *rot* gives just the second column of the matrix. Thus, we precompute and store these two normals as private data.

To locate the hit point, we test its y-coordinate. If this is very close to 1, we consider the hit point to be on the top plane. If it is very close to −1, we consider it to be on the bottom plane. In all other cases, it is on the mantle.

14.5 BOOLEAN COMBINATIONS

The above class specifications for `presolid_t` and `presphere_t` were preliminary. All others are those of the final OO design. When we designed `presolid_t`, we knowingly made some simplifications to help implement a simple ray caster for educational and practicing purposes.

When we add the feature of Boolean operations on solids, it becomes necessary that the virtual intersection routine return a linked list with certain information. We therefore redesign the class specification for a solid.

14.5.1 DEFINITIONS

Much of the ray casting's power and versatility comes from the fact that Boolean combinations of solids produce composed solids of unlimited complexity. Practically every imaginable shape can be so constructed. While this is difficult mathematically, no mathematics is needed at all in ray casting. This section explains how this construction is done.

The Boolean operations that we will use are union, intersection, and difference. They are defined by the set operations of the same names. Figure 14.19 shows a cone and a cylinder separated in space. In Figure 14.20, they have been moved so they touch each other. In Figure 14.21, they penetrate each other. To produce Boolean combinations, we allow such mutual penetration of solids, even though this is impossible with real solids.

From now on, we will use the word "solid" in a general sense. It can mean either a primitive solid (one that is not further subdivided) or a composed solid. By the latter, we mean a Boolean combination of solids. Observe the sense of recursion in this definition. Later, we will give the word additional meaning.

The union of two solids is the set of points that belong to either solid. The three figures below show the union of the cone and the cylinder.

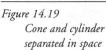

Figure 14.19
  Cone and cylinder
  separated in space

Figure 14.20
  Cone and cylinder
  touching each other

Figure 14.21
  Cone and cylinder
  penetrating each other

The union of the two solids of Figure 14.21 is shown more realistically in Figure 14.22 (with "hidden lines removed").

The intersection of two solids is the set of points that belong to both solids. When solids do not penetrate each other, their intersection is empty. The intersections of the solids in Figures 14.19 and 14.20 are empty, but the intersection in Figure 14.21 is not and is shown in Figure 14.23.

The difference of solid A minus solid B is the set of those points that belong to A but not to B. Figure 14.24 shows a cone partially penetrating a cylinder from the side. Figure 14.25 shows the difference of cone minus cylinder. The resulting solid is the cone without the part that the cylinder penetrates.

We now explain how the union, intersection, and difference of two solids can be intersected with a ray. We assume for the present that each is a convex solid that has two intersections with the ray. Later, each solid can itself be a Boolean combination of unlimited complexity.

Our example takes two spheres that overlap in space. Their projections are two overlapping circles, A and B. The possible intersections are two pairs of u-values, A_1 A_2 and $B_1 B_2$. There are nine possible cases in order of increasing u-values.

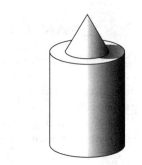

Figure 14.22   Union of cone and cylinder

Figure 14.23   Intersection of cone and cylinder

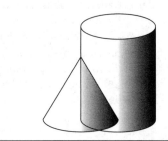

Figure 14.24   Cone and cylinder positioned for subtraction

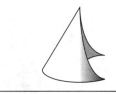

Figure 14.25   Cone minus cylinder

```
0:
1:   A₁    A₂
2:   B₁    B₂
3:   A₁    A₂    B₁    B₁
4:   A₁    B₁    A₂    B₂
5:   A₁    B₁    B₂    A₂
6:   B₁    A₁    A₂    B₂
7:   B₁    A₁    B₂    A₂
8:   B₁    B₂    A₁    A₂
```

Figure 14.26 illustrates these. For each of the nine cases, a ray is shown, labelled with the case number.

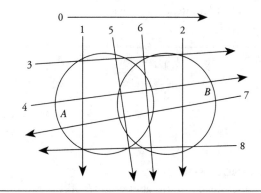

Figure 14.26   Nine cases of intersecting two convex solids

We give tables for each of the various Boolean combinations of solids A and B. Read the tables by columns that are headed by the case number. The letters constitute the intersections. The intersections always come in pairs and there can never be more than four intersections, the sum of the number of possible intersections with the solids.

UNION

The intersections with the union are shown in Figure 14.27 and its corresponding table. Observe that there can be four intersections with the ray; this is because the union of the two spheres is concave. The construction of the table is obvious if we compare with Figure 14.26.

	0	1	2	3	4	5	6	7	8
entry		A_1	B_1	A_1	A_1	A_1	B_1	B_1	B_1
exit		A_2	B_2	A_2					B_2
entry				B_1					A_1
exit				B_2	B_2	A_2	B_2	A_2	A_2

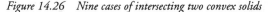

Figure 14.27   Union of two spheres

INTERSECTION

The intersection of the two spheres is convex, so there can be at most two intersections with the ray. These are shown in Figure 14.28.

	0	1	2	3	4	5	6	7	8
entry						B_1	B_1	A_1	A_1
exit						A_2	B_2	A_2	B_2

Figure 14.28   Intersection of two spheres

DIFFERENCE A–B

B can be subtracted from A only where it overlaps with A. The resulting solid is concave, so there can be four intersections with the ray. $A–B$ is shown in Figure 14.29.

	0	1	2	3	4	5	6	7	8
entry		A_1		A_1	A_1	A_1	B_2	A_1	
exit		A_2		A_2	B_1	B_1	A_2	A_2	
entry						B_2			
exit						A_2			

Figure 14.29   *Difference of two spheres*

DIFFERENCE B–A

This is analogous to the above case. $B–A$ is shown in Figure 14.30.

	0	1	2	3	4	5	6	7	8
entry			B_1	B_1	A_2		B_1	B_1	B_1
exit			B_2	B_2	B_2		A_1	A_1	B_2
entry							A_2		
exit							B_2		

Figure 14.30   *Difference of two spheres*

14.5.2 COMBINATIONS OF HIGHER ORDER

We have just defined the combinations of two primitive solids. We now develop the Boolean combinations of more complicated solids. Generally, they must be defined and implemented only for two operands. We obtain combinations of more than two solids by repeating the operations to the results of previous operations. For example, we can combine a solid A with a solid B in three different ways.

When a ray intersects any solid A, there will always be an even number of intersection values where the ray alternately enters and exits A. We order these on increasing size. They are shown in Figure 14.31 plotted on the straight line A, called a *Roth diagram*, ROTH82. The same ray may also intersect the second solid B. Its intersection values are plotted on a second straight line labelled B. We call these lines the *hit lists* of the solids.

Think of these lines as a succession of events as the ray alternately enters and exits the solid. The heavy sections indicate the times inside and the light sections the times outside the solids.

The lines labelled $A+B$, $A*B$, and $A–B$ represent the resulting Boolean combinations of A and B. For the union, it is a logical OR of the heavy sections of A and B. For the intersection, it is a logical AND. For the difference, $A–B$, one subtracts the heavy sections of B from the heavy sections of A.

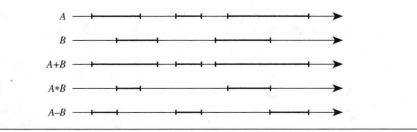

Figure 14.31   Roth diagrams

We obtain the Boolean combination of two hit lists through a simple algorithm. We use three flags, one for *A*, one for *B*, and one for the result. These are named *flaga*, *flagb*, and *flagc*, respectively. The flags are set to 0 (outside) or 1 (inside). Each starts with 0. We move along the lines *A* and *B* in parallel, from left to right. Whenever we hit a point on these lines, we flip the corresponding flag. Then we determine the value of the Boolean combination of *flaga* and *flagb*. If it is different from the current value of *flagc*, we flip *flagc* and enter the current point on *A* or *B* into the result. This continues until no points are left on *A* and *B*.

The table below shows the flag settings for the three operations.

State of		State of *flagc* for		
flaga	*flagb*	$A+B$	$A*B$	$A-B$
0	0	0	0	0
0	1	1	0	0
1	0	1	0	1
1	1	1	1	0

As an example of the algorithm, we derive the result for the Boolean intersection of the lines shown previously. The *flagc* setting should be taken from the table. We show the lines *A* and *B* and their intersection again in Figure 14.32.

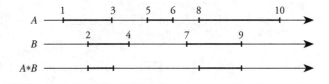

Figure 14.32   Example: Determining the intersection

	flaga	*flagb*	*flagc*	Effect on *flagc*:	
initial settings:	0	0	0		
point 1:	1	0	0	no change	no entry
point 2:	1	1	1	change	enter 2
point 3:	0	1	0	change	enter 3
point 4:	0	0	0	no change	no entry
point 5:	1	0	0	no change	no entry
point 6:	0	0	0	no change	no entry
point 7:	0	1	0	no change	no entry
point 8:	1	1	1	change	enter 8
point 9:	1	0	0	change	enter 9
point 10:	0	0	0	no change	no entry

The final result is (2 3 8 9).

14.5.3 INTERSECTING A COMPOSED SOLID

Intersecting a solid means producing its hit list. How do we intersect a ray with a composition of two arbitrary solids, which in turn are compositions of arbitrary solids, and so on? All the intersection routine needs to do is correctly compose the hit lists of two arbitrary solids and return the resulting hit list. To obtain the two arbitrary hit lists, the routine simply calls itself recursively for the two children of the solid.

The hit lists are implemented as linked lists. Each list element contains the u-value of the intersection and some other information that will be needed later.

Composing ("weaving") two hit lists into their Boolean combination means changing the links in the lists to thread them into one, while removing those elements that are skipped (such as 1, 4, 5, 6, 7, and 10 in the above example). The memory of these elements is freed. The resulting hit list contains 2, 3, 8, and 9, and is shown in Figure 14.33. The links are drawn so that the positions of the elements reflect the ordering of the u-values from smaller to greater.

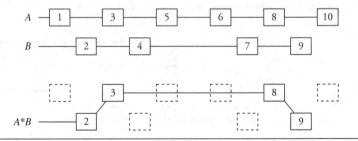

Figure 14.33   Weaving two hit lists

The resulting hit list can contain hit-pairs with both u-values negative, even when none of the argument hit lists has such a pair. Such pairs are discarded and their memory is freed.

A *solid* is an entity consisting of a Boolean combination and pointers to its two children, which are also solids. The function `intersect()` intersects a solid by intersecting its left child, then its right child, then weaving the resulting hit lists into one and returning it.

As an example, we create the solid shown in Figure 14.34. It consists of the union of two boxes, one of which is rotated by 45°. Then a cylinder is subtracted, producing the hole in the center.

Figure 14.35 shows a side view and a ray. The horizontal rectangle is the cylinder. The dotted outline is the box that is rotated by 45°. All intersection points are numbered. At point 2, both boxes are entered simultaneously.

We can view a solid as a binary tree that has solids as children; see Figure 14.36. Leaf nodes are solid primitives—a special kind of solid. In the drawing on the right, we use the same numbers as in Figure 14.35. In the nodes, we see the Boolean operation. The hit lists start at the node to which they belong and are drawn downward. The hit lists of the two boxes are composed with union to produce the list pointing down from the +node. The cylinder hit list is then subtracted, and the result is the list which points down from the −node. This last hit list is finally returned by intersect().

This is a very powerful and versatile method of defining solids if additional information is given in the tree's nodes. A tree node contains not only the Boolean operation, but also a rotation matrix, a center, and a texture function. This information has the following significance.

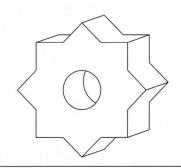

Figure 14.34   Composition of solids

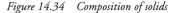

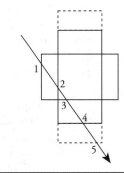

Figure 14.35   Ray intersecting two boxes and a cylinder

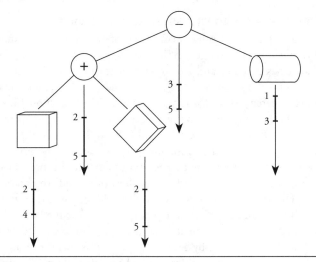

Figure 14.36   Tree representation of composed solid

The position (rotation and center) specified in a node pertains to the whole solid rooted in that node. A rotation about the y-axis, for example, specified in the minus-node of Figure 14.36, rotates the whole solid about y. A rotation about the x-axis in the plus-node rotates the joined boxes, but not the cylinder. Every position in a node is relative to the position in the node above. This makes the composing of more complicated solids very easy.

The texture specified in a solid pertains to the whole solid represented by that node, even if the children specify different textures, because they will be overridden. The reason for this design is that one solid should have one texture throughout—this is a natural and reasonable model of reality. A solid that changes the material it consists of somewhere inside itself actually represents different solids joined together. The implementation developed below does allow the user to deviate from this principle. There is no overriding the children's textures if a solid specifies NULL as its own texture. In many cases, however, this produces unrealistic pictures.

We show how to define the above solid. The solid "box" is a primitive defined as an axis-parallel unit cube. We define a box for the leftmost node with equal x- and y-axes, a short z-axis (to make it flat), center at (0 0 0), and no rotation. We define a box of the same size and center for the next node and specify a rotation of 45° about z. We define a unit cylinder, upright, of a certain diameter and height, center at (0 0 0), and a rotation of 90° about the x-axis to align it with the z-axis. The definition and positioning of the primitive solids are now complete.

We specify a union for the node connecting the boxes and a difference for the topmost node together with whatever positioning we want for the whole solid. This aspect is discussed later.

When a solid is intersected, `intersect()` returns the hit list. This consists of a linked list of "secinf" structures. An individual element of that list contains the intersection u-value, a pointer to the primitive solid intersected at this u-value, a pointer to the solid in which the applicable texture function is specified, and a link to the next element. We define the classes `solid` and `secinf` below.

OO DESIGN AND CLASS SPECIFICATIONS

The fact that a solid is composed of two other solids should be reflected as closely as possible in its class design. The definition of the class `solid_t` is similar to `presolid_t` in that it has a center and a pointer to a texture function. It also has the virtual functions `intersect()` and `normal()`. They have the same meaning as before. However, it has a much different constructor that we will explain in Section 14.5.4.

One new member is `op`, which contains the Boolean operation on the children, and uses 0 for union, 1 for intersection, and 2 for difference. Other new members are the rotation matrix `rot`, the virtual function `position()`, the function `weave()`, the function `set_rot_cen()` for setting rotation matrix and center during the initialization process, and `givrot()` and `givcen()` to allow other code to obtain its center and rotation.

The function `weave()` "weaves" two hit lists into their Boolean combination. Given the two hit lists and the Boolean operation, it returns the "woven" hit list. The "woven" hit list never contains more elements than the argument lists together, but it can contain fewer.

`Weave()` is used by `intersect()`. It is useful to realize that when a solid specifies a Boolean intersection or difference and the left child returns an empty hit list, the right one need not be intersected—the result is always an empty hit list. When specifying Boolean intersections, commutativity allows us to save even more computation time. We specify the solid whose intersections are easier to find as the left child and the computation-intensive one as the right child. The solid's intersection function will then be executed less often.

```
//*********************** File solid.h ************************

#ifndef SOLID_T
#define SOLID_T


#include "../Raytrace/mat33.h"
#include "../Raytrace/rpoint.h"
#include "../Raytrace/texture.h"
#include "../Raytrace/ray.h"
#include "../Raytrace/secinf.h"

typedef int op_t ;

class solid_t                                    // composed solid
{
public:
   texture_t (*tex)(solid_t*,const rpoint_t&,double) ;
   solid_t(rpoint_t,rpoint_t,op_t,char*,solid_t*,solid_t*) ;
   virtual  secinf_t*  intersect  (const ray_t&) ;
   virtual  rpoint_t   normal     (const rpoint_t&) const ;
   virtual  void       position   (const mat33_t&,const rpoint_t&) ;
   virtual  ~solid_t() ;
   mat33_t  givrot() const { return rot; }
   rpoint_t givcen() const { return cen; }

protected:
   mat33_t rot ;
   rpoint_t cen ;
   void set_rot_cen(const mat33_t&,const rpoint_t&) ;

private:
   solid_t* left , * right ;
   secinf_t* weave(secinf_t*,op_t,secinf_t*) const ;
   op_t op ;
} ;

#endif

//***************************************************************
```

The class `secinf_t` has the members we described above. When intersecting a ray with a composed solid, the call `intersect()` returns the solid's hit list—a list of `secinf_t` elements. The first element in the hit list gives us the closest intersection u-value, from which we compute the hit point. The pointer to the solid primitive that is intersected (`secsolid`) gives us access to its normal function. The texture specified at the intersection point can be different from that defined in the solid primitive if overridden in the parent solid. The solid that did the overriding contains the applicable texture, and `texsolid` will point to it. It is important to know not just the texture, but also the solid for which it is specified, because most non-trivial textures need the position coordinates of the solid for which they are specified. We will say more about this in Chapter 16.

```
//*********************** File secinf.h ***********************

#ifndef SECINF_T
#define SECINF_T

struct solid_t ;

struct secinf_t                                // intersection record
{
   secinf_t(solid_t* solid,double u,secinf_t* next) :
      secsolid(solid) , texsolid(solid) , u(u) , next(next) {}
   ~secinf_t() { delete next; }

   solid_t*   secsolid ;                        // intersected solid
   solid_t*   texsolid ;                 // solid containing texture
   double     u       ;
   secinf_t*  next    ;
} ;

#endif

//***********************************************************************
```

14.5.4 DEFINING A SCENE

You should understand the term *solid* as follows. A solid is an entity that consists of solids composed in some fixed way; it moves as a whole and has one texture throughout. On the other hand, a scene usually consists of several disjoint solids that are unrelated in terms of position and texture.

A basic design principle of our ray caster (and ray tracer) is that individual solids must be disjoint entities. They must not penetrate each other. While penetration is allowed for the purpose of doing Boolean combinations, once we define the diverse solids in the scene, they must be positioned as in reality where penetration is not possible. If this is not observed and two disjoint solids penetrate each other, the result will be a composite not intended by the user.

Suppose we want something that looks like the penetration of two different objects? The "no-penetration" rule need not pose an obstacle in our quest for realistic pictures. The simple and natural solution is to define one solid as a subtraction of the two so there is no penetration. There will be no difference in the appearance, whether the solids penetrate or not.

When solids are transparent, however, abiding by this rule is essential. A noticeable and unexpected difference in appearance results when it is violated. We will cover this later.

The advantage of this design principle is that it tremendously increases the ray tracer's simplicity and clarity. Simplicity and clarity are a primary purpose of any teaching endeavor. It is hard to imagine scenes which cannot be modeled because of the no-penetration principle.

Disjoint solids are represented as trees with separate roots. All roots are linked in one linear list, as are the solids in the preliminary ray caster. A pointer points to the first element in the list. We implement this in the function trace(), which walks through a list of roots. For each root, we obtain the hit list and retain it or replace it with another as we progress through the roots. This process retains only that hit list whose closest *u*-value is smallest. The hit list returned by trace after traversing all roots contains the intersections of only one composed solid—the closest one.

To carry this out, we define the structure disjoint_t.

```
//*********************** File disjoint.h ***********************

#ifndef DISJOINT_T
#define DISJOINT_T

#include "../Raytrace/solid.h"


struct disjoint_t                    // root of disjoint combined object
{
   solid_t* solid ;
   disjoint_t *next ;

   disjoint_t(solid_t* c,disjoint_t* d) :
      solid(c) , next(d) {}
   ~disjoint_t()
   {
      delete solid; delete next;
   }
} ;

#endif

//*************************************************************************
```

DEFINITION AND CONSTRUCTION OF A RAY TRACE SCENE

A *ray trace scene* consists of a linked list of composed solids, a pointer to the list of light sources, and some additional specifications whose implementations we explain in the next chapter. These specifications are not entirely new: the eyepoint from where the scene is observed (eye), the view reference point (ref), the view-up direction (vup), the size of the display in pixels (dwid and dhei), and the peripheral angle that the display extends when seen from the eyepoint (peri_ang).

All this is specified in the class rtscene_t (ray trace scene). This class has very little in common with previously defined scene-classes, so we do not derive it from any of those. Member functions are a constructor that constructs a scene from a file that describes the scene (we explain scene files below); display() executes the ray tracing process; traceall()

casts a single ray against the list of disjoint objects and returns the closest pair in the hit list; illum() takes the hit list and ray and computes the illumination of the first object in the hit list, returning an *rgb*-value.

```
//*********************** File rtscene.h ***********************

#ifndef RTSCENE_T
#define RTSCENE_T


#include "../Shape3d/light.h"
#include "../Raytrace/rgb1.h"
#include "../Raytrace/disjoint.h"
#include "../Raytrace/rpoint.h"
#include "../Raytrace/secinf.h"
#include "../Raytrace/ray.h"


class rtscene_t                                // ray trace scene
{
public:
  ~rtscene_t() ;
  rtscene_t(char* scenefile) ;
  void display() ;                             // display the scene
  void makep6(char*) ;                         // produce p6 format file

private:
  disjoint_t* all ;                            // list of all objects
  light_t* light ;                        // list of all light sources
  rpoint_t eye ,                                      // eyepoint
           ref ,                            // view reference point
           vup ;                            // view-up direction
  int dwid , dhei ;             // display-width and -height in pixels
  double peri_ang ;                         // peripheral view angle

  secinf_t* traceall(const ray_t&) ;
  rgb1_t illum(const ray_t&,secinf_t*) ;
} ;

#endif

//*******************************************************************
```

Constructing an rtscene_t consists of setting the viewing parameters, the pointers to the light sources, and constructing the linked list of composed solids. The last one is a non-trivial but one-time process.

Each node in the list of composed solids points to a tree that describes the solid. We must construct and link together all these trees before ray tracing begins. The member all will point to the first node. Let us first look at the construction.

THE SCENE FILE

To make specifying a ray trace scene easy, we specify it through a scene file, which is simply a text file. For example, we could specify a scene consisting only of the above solid by writing this scene file:

```
light    -40 60 -40      0.4 0.4 0.4
amb        0  0  0       0.6 0.6 0.6

eye        0  1.0  -10
ref        0  0  0
vup        0  1  0
dis      1024  768
per       12

(
   (  box(0.5 0.5 0.2)      0 0 0     0 0 0     NULL
      +    0 0 5     0 0 0     NULL
      box(0.5 0.5 0.2)      0 0 45    0 0 0     NULL
   )
   -  0 -40 0    0 0 0     silver
   cylinder(0.3 0.3 0.3)    90 0 0    0 0 0     NULL
)
```

The file starts by specifying the light sources. These end with the word amb, which specifies the ambient light. Then come the viewing parameters, such as eyepoint (eye), reference point (ref), view-up (vup), display width and height (dis), and peripheral angle (per) in any order. After this come the primitive or combined solids. The number triples in parentheses are the axes of the given solid. Then come rotation and center, in this order. All tokens are separated by white space. A NULL indicates that no texture is specified for the solid or for the whole composition. We combine two solids by listing the operation, rotation, center, and texture between the two solids and enclosing it all in parentheses. We see that a rotation of (0 –40 0), a center of (0 0 0), and a common texture silver are specified at the minus-node, that is, for the whole gear wheel. Silver must be an existing function in the ray tracer. For simple color settings, including reflection and refraction, we could define the texture in the scene file by specifying the coefficients. However, more elaborate texture functions require a texture-specific code to be executed at run time. We cannot read in such a function. Therefore, we specify it by indicating the name of an existing texture function.

The scene file can contain comments identical to those used in a C++ program (but only one pair of / * ... * / per line). We explain how the scene file is parsed in the comments below about the implementation.

POSITIONING THE COMPOSED SOLIDS

We now explain the positioning of the solid primitives in a composed solid. This positioning is necessary because the user specifies a composed solid by specifying its two constituent parts' spatial positions relative to the parent node. This corresponds to the construction of complicated solids from simpler ones. Two primitives can be composed by specifying their position in relation to the parent, which is assumed to be unrotated and centered at the origin.

However, the parent can then be positioned as a whole and composed with other composed solids. That composition can again be positioned, and so on. The positioning of a solid pertains to all its subparts. The absolute position of the lowest element in a composed solid is therefore an accumulation of all positions above that element.

When intersecting a solid with a ray, all positioning information could be accumulated while descending down to the primitive solids. Only these primitive solids are ultimately intersected by a ray. The accumulated rotation and center could then be used to perform the ray's arbitrary-to-unit transformation before calculating the intersections. However, this would be a waste of computational effort because the accumulation result is constant for each primitive solid. "Positioning" means computing the accumulated position in absolute coordinates for each primitive solid and storing it in its `rot` and `cen` members. We illustrate this below.

We explain the function `position()` by assuming an existing solid that contains positional information in all nodes (similar to Figure 14.36 above). This solid appears in Figure 14.37 with unrelated information omitted. Before `position()` traverses it, all positional information is relative to the node above. After the traversal by `position()`, all positional information is in absolute terms of the scene's coordinate system.

For example, the rotation matrix in the leaf for the right box accumulates to

$$\left(rotmat(0 \ \ 0 \ \ 45) * rotmat(0 \ \ 0 \ \ 5) * rotmat(0 \ \ -40 \ \ 0)\right)^T$$

$$= rotmat^T(0 \ \ -40 \ \ 0) * rotmat^T(0 \ \ 0 \ \ 5) * rotmat^T(0 \ \ 0 \ \ 45)$$

where $rotmat^T(x \ \ y \ \ z)$ means the transpose of the rotation matrix for rotation about x, y, and z. (The user specifies a solid by rotating it into position in terms of the unit-to-arbitrary positioning, but we need the arbitrary-to-unit matrix, which is the transpose.)

The center in this leaf becomes

$$\left((0 \ \ 0 \ \ 0) * rotmat^T(0 \ \ 0 \ \ 5) + (0 \ \ 0 \ \ 0.1)\right) * rotmat^T(0 \ \ -40 \ \ 0) + (0.2 \ \ 0 \ \ 0)$$

The rotation matrices and centers in a tree's nodes can be set in the following way. We use the matrix **G**, initialized to identity. When we descend to the next node, the relative rotation matrix we meet there is multiplied into **G** and the matrix in the node is set to **G**. The center is

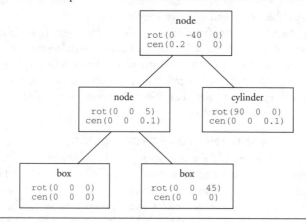

Figure 14.37   Positional information in the nodes

updated in an analog way; see the explanations above. The relative rotation matrices in the nodes do not yet exist because the user specifies the rotations only by setting three angles, as you can see in the scene file above. These angles are stored in the first three positions of the member `rot`. Computing the *a*-to-*u* matrix from those, multiplying that matrix by the accumulated matrix, and setting the center is repetitive code, which is done with a call to the member function `set_rot_cen()`.

COMMENTS ABOUT IMPLEMENTING SOLID_T

Let us first explain the constructor. The arguments `rot` and `cen` are `rpoint_t`. The rotation matrix `solid_t::rot` is initialized with the three rotation angles from the scene file. All other elements are zero. The center `solid_t::cen` is initialized with the numbers read from the scene file. The argument `tex` is a string describing an implemented texture function. `Distribute_texture()` compares it against all implemented texture functions and returns a pointer to the designated one. The member `solid_t::op` is initialized using the character scanned in from the scene file. In the case of ' ' (space) `op` is assigned −1, for '+' 0, for '*' 1, and otherwise 2. The last two arguments are the pointers to the two children.

`Solid_t::intersect()` calls `intersect()` for the two children and then calls `weave()` for the two obtained hit lists and the operator. The woven hit list is returned. If the member `tex` in the composed solid is not NULL, then overriding the texture pointers in the hit list is intended, so all `texsolid` members in the hit list are changed to `this` (= pointer to the solid itself). C++ allows us to formulate it in a very short and elegant way, which is worth showing:

```
secinf_t* solid_t::intersect(const ray_t& ray)
{
    secinf_t* a = left->intersect(ray) ;
    secinf_t* b = (a || !op) ? right->intersect(ray) : 0 ;
    secinf_t* c = weave(a,op,b);

    if (tex)
        for (a = c; a; a = a->next)
            a->texsolid = this;

    return c;
}
```

The member function `solid_t::normal()` is only a dummy to be redefined by the normals of derived solids.

`Solid_t::position(mat33_t r, rpoint_t c)` sets a node's members `rot` and `cen` by calling `set_rot_mat(r,c)`, which accumulates them by `r` and `c`. It then sets the children's matrix and center by calling their position member functions with this node's updated `rot` and `cen`. The positioning of a primitive, however, is different. That is why `position()` is virtual and is redefined when we implement a primitive solid. A primitive has no children—no further calls will occur. Its positioning will accumulate rotation and center as in the node above, but will also compute the transformation matrix by incorporating axes or other private data. This results in the transformation matrix to which the intersecting ray is subjected.

COMMENTS ABOUT IMPLEMENTING RTSCENE_T

We can understand all routines in the implementation of this class, except the function `rtscene_t::illum()`, on the basis of the present state of the development.

`Rtscene_t::rtscene_t()` is called with a file name as argument and constructs the scene. In this context, we explain the code for parsing the scene file, because it is essentially the constructor of the ray trace scene. The scene file must be of the form shown above. We scan the parameters' values with numerical conversions. The names of primitive solids and textures are *strings*. To produce the corresponding function calls in our code, we use two distributing functions that test the strings for equality with the names of the known solids or textures, and then call the corresponding constructors for the solids or set pointers to the corresponding texture functions. Compare these explanations to the following code: `rtscene_t::rtscene_t(char* filename)`.

The scene file is first stripped of comments through a call to `preproc()`. The stripped file is then processed. The parser reads the light sources and viewing parameters. Then it analyzes the scene by calling `maketree()`. Here is how `maketree()` operates:

1. When it meets a text string, it is the name of a primitive solid. `Makesolid()` eats it into `prim`, skips the opening parenthesis, eats the string up to the closing parenthesis into args, and skips the parenthesis. Then it calls the constructor `rpoint_t(f)` twice with the file as argument, which eats six numbers and provides the rotation and center for this primitive. Then it eats the texture string into `texture`. Then it calls `distribute_prim()` with all these arguments. This calls the constructor for the specified primitive and returns a pointer to it. `Makesolid()` returns this pointer.

2. Presence of an opening parenthesis instead of a text string marks the beginning of a Boolean combination. `Makesolid()` skips the parenthesis and calls `makesolid()`, assigning the pointer returned by this call to the local `solid_t* left`. This eats the entire solid, which starts here off the file and stops at the Boolean operator.

   Then the Boolean operator (+, *, or –) is eaten into `op`, followed by `rpoint_t(f)` twice and a text scan, which eats six numbers and the texture string. (Ignore for a moment the line "`if (op[0] == ')') return left;`" in the code.) These give rotation, center, and texture.

   What follows is eaten by a recursive call to `makesolid()`, assigning whatever it returns to a local `solid_t* right`. Then the closing parenthesis is skipped, a solid is constructed with all the above arguments, and a pointer to it is returned.

3. When the end of file is met, `makesolid()` returns NULL.

If a closing parenthesis is met instead of a Boolean operator, the user has specified one parenthesis pair too many. Consequently, `makesolid()` is one level too deep in the recursion. The pointer to the left subtree that has already been produced is returned. This makes the scanner tolerant of superfluous parenthesis pairs surrounding primitives or solids.

The scanning process stops when the level of parenthesis pairs is down to zero. This corresponds to scanning one disjoint solid. However, the scene file can contain more solids, which we find with additional calls to `makesolid()`.

This is a simple and lean parser that takes spaces, tabs, or CR/LF as white space to permit a clearly arranged scene file. However, it does no error recovery and will usually crash if the file is syntactically incorrect.

`Distribute_prim()` and `distribute_texture()`, the two functions which were mentioned above, are in the file `Raytrace/distribu.c`. `Distribute_prim()` calls one of the individual constructors after checking the string `prim` against the implemented primitives. All solid-constructors have the arguments `args`, `rot`, `cen`, and `tex`. `Args` is the string scanned in from the scene file that contains the arguments for this primitive constructor. They are easily scanned off the string using `sscanf()`. When a new primitive or a new texture function is implemented, the corresponding statements must be added to the above codes and the functions recompiled.

`Rtscene_t::traceall()` is the routine that traces a ray against all solids in the scene. It walks through the list and calls each solid's intersection function. It discards intersection pairs whose starting *u*-value is not greater than zero. Of all obtained hit lists, it returns only the one with the smallest *u*-value.

`Rtscene_t::display()` creates a ray for each pixel on the screen and calls `traceall()` with this ray as argument. The returned hit list and the ray are submitted to `illum()`, which computes the illumination of the object hit. Then the forementioned pixel is set to this illumination.

The sequence in which the individual pixels are illuminated is immaterial. The code takes advantage of this and first covers the whole display with a coarse raster of illuminated rectangles. This allows the creator of a scene to see very early an approximate picture. Positions and colors of objects and shadows can usually be verified at this point. It is not necessary to wait long before a pixelwise scan reaches a certain area of interest. The raster of subsequent scans over the display becomes finer by factors of two until pixel size is reached.

The *rgb*-values obtained in one scan are written to a file. In the next, finer scan, these are not computed again, but simply read in from the file. A new, larger file is written that contains all the new values. This continues until pixel size is reached. This saves some computation time, but the main reason for the file approach is the computation of an optimal lookup table setting. On a true color graphics board, such as the #9GXi, which we used in the PC version, no lookup table computation or file handling is needed. On all machines with less than 24-bit frame buffers, such lookup table management is necessary.

To compute an optimal color map (meaning a lookup table) arrangement, all *rgb*-values ever created for a scene must be known. In other words, the whole scene must be traced before the color map is computed. If the *rgb*-values were not written to a file, we would have to recreate them in order to set the proper frame buffer entry for each. (Remember that no *rgb*-values are entered into the frame buffer, only addresses into the lookup table.) The lookup table manager is in the file `Raytrace/colormap.c`. A short explanation is in Appendix B.

`Rtscene_t::illum()` consists of three parts. Part One computes the hit point's illumination using only the diffuse reflectivity of its texture-value. Part Two adds the contribution from specular reflection. Part Three adds the contribution from refraction. We explain only Part One here. Parts Two and Three are explained in the next chapter.

Part One obtains the hit point's normal. The situation here is different from that of the preliminary ray caster in the following way. Hit information is now obtained from the woven hit list. Although hit points still alternately enter and exit the composite solid in pairs, the two points of a pair do not necessarily belong to the same solid. A hit point can be an entry to a composed solid and at the same time the exit of another primitive or composed solid. The normals at such points can therefore point either way. They must be turned around if they do not point opposite the ray's direction. To do this, we compute the cosine of the incident angle, *cia*, which is the dot product of the ray direction and the surface normal. If this product is positive, the surface normal is not pointing in the correct direction, therefore `illum()` turns it around.

Then `illum()` goes into a loop through all point light sources. For each, it generates a ray to the light source and computes the contribution of intensity according to Lambert's law, which uses the cosine of the incident angle. It adds all these together. Inside this loop is the checking for shadows.

Here is a part that traces the ray to the light source through a transparent solid to create tinted shadows. Also inside this loop is the creation of soft highlights if specular reflectivity is above zero. These last two features must be in the loop because they depend on the number of point light sources. We will say more about this in the next chapter.

MORE SOLID PRIMITIVES

Here we show the class `sphere_t`, derived from `solid_t`. It differs from `presphere_t` in the return type of the member function `intersect()` and in the constructor. It may serve as a template for all other solid primitives the user wants to implement.

```
//*********************** File sphere.h ***********************

#ifndef SPHERE_T
#define SPHERE_T

#include "../Raytrace/solid.h"
#include "../Raytrace/rpoint.h"
#include "../Raytrace/ray.h"
#include "../Raytrace/secinf.h"

class sphere_t : public solid_t
{
public:
    sphere_t(char*,rpoint_t,rpoint_t,char*) ;
    void        position    (const mat33_t&,const rpoint_t&) ;
    secinf_t*   intersect    (const ray_t&) ;
    rpoint_t    normal       (const rpoint_t&) const ;

private:
    double r ;                                    // radius
    double rinv ;                                 // inverse radius
    double rsqu ;                                 // square of radius
} ;

#endif

//*******************************************************************
```

Introducing more solid primitives consists simply of defining their individual class modules. All new primitives are derived from `solid_t`. One has to give them their own constructors and to specify the three virtual member functions `intersect()`, `normal()`, and `position()` according to the particularities of the primitive. In so far, it is just more of the same. In Appendix B, you can find the classes:

bground_t	dodhedron_t	prism6_t
board_t	ellspiral_t	tethedron_t
box_t	halfspace_t	torus_t
cone_t		

We provide source code for these because it is not available in other books on computer graphics or ray tracing. Some are difficult to code, for instance, the cone, because its basic shape is concave, the dodecahedron, because the derivation of the different plane equations is time-consuming, and the torus, because no textbook presents a correct transformation of the parametric ray description into a quartic equation for the parameter u.

EXAMPLE OF A SCENE FILE

Below, we define a *pipe tee* or *plumber's tee*. We define it as the difference of two plain tees, the smaller representing the space inside the walls of the pipe tee. The second has a somewhat smaller diameter than the first and its cylinders are a little longer to guarantee proper subtraction of the inner space. See Figure 14.38 for this.

Every plain tee is the union of a vertical and horizontal cylinder. The horizontal cylinders have their centers at (0 0 0), the vertical ones are on the y-axis with their lower ends exactly at (0 0 0). No rotations are specified for the two tees and no textures for any cylinder or tee. Only the composite object has an arbitrary rotation, center, and texture, specified in the "–" node. A plumber's tee can be seen in the scene "everything."

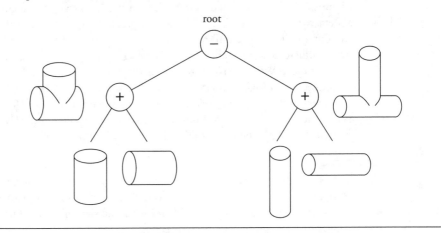

Figure 14.38   Composition of a plumber's tee

We can create an `rtscene_t` object with the file "plumber's tee" as argument and call its display function. The file for plumber's tee is:

```
900    650

((
   cylinder(0.5 0.625 0.5)   0 0 0    0 0.625 0   NULL
   +    0 0 0   0 0 0   NULL
   cylinder(0.5 1.125 0.5)   0 0 90    0 0 0   NULL
)
-   -30 30 7   0 -0.188 0   yellow
(
   cylinder(0.425 0.75 0.425)   0 0 0    0 0.75 0   NULL
   +    0 0 0   0 0 0   NULL
   cylinder(0.425 1.19 0.425)   0 0 90    0 0 0   NULL
))
```

EXERCISES

SECTION 14.3

1. Use the provided code for the classes `ellipsoid_t` and `cylinder_t` as a guide for writing class specifications and implementations for an ellipsoid and a cylinder. Write them in the spirit of the preliminary ray caster—derive it from `presolid_t`, `intersect()` returns an integer, the primitives are linked into a linear list.

SECTION 14.4

2. Write a class `pyramid4_t`, derived from `solid_t`, that specifies a four-sided pyramid of height h and base side length s. The unit pyramid is sitting on the $(x\ z)$-plane, the center is at $(0\ 0\ 0)$, the height is 1, and the base side length is 1.
3. Write a class `prism8_t`, derived from `solid_t`, that specifies a regular eight-sided prism with outer radius r and height h. The unit prism is centered around the y-axis, the height is 2, and the outer radius is 1. Use the class `prism6_t` as a guide.
4. Write a class `octahedron_t`, derived from `solid_t`, that specifies an octahedron with outer radius r. The unit octahedron has its center at $(0\ 0\ 0)$ and its six vertices on the coordinate axes at distance 1 from the origin.
5. (Senior project) Write a class `revol_t`, derived from `solid_t`, that specifies a shape of revolution. It is upright, centered around the y-axis, and its height is 1. Its base is on the $(x\ z)$-plane and its top is at $y = 1$. The shape is given by an array of 100 or so doubles that specify the surface's distance from the y-axis at equidistant intervals. Use the method given in [BIER83] where the solid is defined as a composite of stacked cone segments.

SECTION 14.5

6. Write a member function `rtscene_t::changeview()` that changes the viewing parameters `eye`, `ref`, `vup`, and `peri_ang` so that subsequent calls to `rtscene_t::display()` would create a scene viewed with the new parameters. No changes to the object positions are necessary.
7. Write a scene file that displays a planar cut through the "plumber's tee" so one can look inside (cut through with a halfspace). Specify the textures so that the inside has a different color from the outside.

15

Ray Tracing

15.0 **Introduction** outlines what is discussed in the chapter, which adds the treatment of reflection and refraction to the ray casting of Chapter 14. This gives us *ray tracing*.

15.1 **Reflection** explains how to model and ray trace reflective objects.

15.2 **Refraction and Transparency** explains how to model and ray trace transparent objects.

15.3 **Implementation** explains the code.

15.4 **Ray Tracing from an Arbitrary Point in Space** explains a simple way of tracing rays so that the scene is displayed as if viewed from an arbitrary point.

15.5 **Speeding Up Ray Tracing** discusses a way to limit the number of intersection tests performed for each ray.

15.6 **Distributed Ray Tracing** explains the term and briefly discusses additional improvements to ray traced images that we can obtain by this method.

15.0 INTRODUCTION

Reflection and refraction are phenomena that ray tracing models very well, even though the models used are far simpler than reality. They can achieve a high degree of visual realism. More precise models require more computation time, but, as the power of graphics workstations increases, even these complicated models are affordable. We describe and give code for a fairly precise model of reflection and refraction. It provides a solid understanding of the basics and is good preparation for the more difficult models.

15.1 REFLECTION

Until now, when a ray's path was traced back from the eyepoint, the trace ended when the ray hit an object. The ray was assumed to start on the object's surface. This is not true in reality. Actually, the ray that is traced back is one of the many rays that emanate from that surface point because of diffuse reflectivity. Light that reaches this surface point from other points in the scene is to some extent bounced off in all directions, retaining only those wavelengths that are allowed by the diffuse reflectivity. Light rays from all over the scene hit this point and so contribute to the one ray that reaches our eye. It would be impossible to trace all those rays.

This impossibility is one reason why we consider the ray to start on the object's surface. The other reason is that we can determine the ray's color without further tracing. Knowing the composition and intensity of the light striking the point and the diffuse reflectivity factors is enough.

Objects that have shiny, mirrorlike surfaces act upon the incoming light in a different way. A light ray that strikes such a surface rebounds, sometimes completely. It is not scattered in all directions; rather, it rebounds along a very precise path, the path of the reflection vector. Another characteristic of specular reflection is that the composition of the light hardly changes in the process. When this ray reaches our eye, its color is the color of its original source. We described reflection in general and the computation of the reflection vector in Section 8.4. We made this code a member function of `rpoint_t` in Chapter 14. It computes the reflection of an incoming vector "hit" about itself, while it plays the role of the surface normal:

```
rpoint_t rpoint_t::reflec(const rpoint_t& hit) const
{           // reflection of (infacing) hit about (outfacing) *this
    return hit - *this*2*(*this*hit);
}
```

How can we model such objects? When the traced ray hits a shiny object, we cannot yet determine the color of the ray. The color is that of the reflected ray, which, in the ideal case, is precisely one ray. It becomes not only possible but also necessary to trace this ray further. An example will clarify this. Figure 15.1 shows a scene consisting of two completely shiny spheres hovering over a black and white checkerboard. The background is blue.

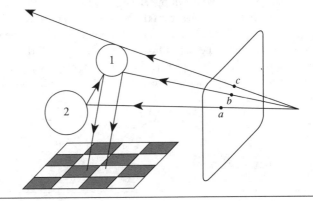

Figure 15.1   Scene with reflecting solids

The figure shows three cases. The ray's trace through pixel *a* bounces off sphere 2 and then off sphere 1 before hitting the checkerboard in a black square. This means that a ray coming from that black square bounces off the spheres two times before reaching the eyepoint through pixel *a*. Pixel *a*, therefore, is black.

Similarly, using less precise language, the ray through *b* bounces off sphere 1 and hits the checkerboard in a white square, so pixel *b* is white. The ray through *c* bounces off sphere 1 to hit the background, so pixel *c* is blue.

Here is the method we use: Whenever the ray hits a reflective object, we trace the reflected ray. (Such a ray is called *secondary*.) The tracing stops when a diffuse object is hit (or after a maximum number of reflections). The pixel's color is the color of the point where the tracing ends.

The coding is easy. The function that determines a ray's color is `illum()`. It returns *rgb*-values, using the hit point's diffuse reflectivity factors and the intensity of light hitting the point. We now include a second way to determine the *rgb*-value, implemented in the second part of `illum()`. When the hit point has specular reflectivity, `illum()` finds the ray's *rgb*-value by tracing the ray's reflection vector and calling `illum()` for the hit point of the reflection vector. Recursion allows arbitrary reflection depths.

We have assumed above that specular reflection is perfect, but this is rarely true. Most reflective objects behave somewhere between diffuse and specular reflectivity. A light ray hitting such an object is reflected mostly along the reflection ray, but it also scatters somewhat. The reflected rays form a cone with its tip at the hit point and centered along the ideal reflection vector. The cone's narrowness is a measure of the specular reflectivity or shininess of the surface.

When a reflected ray is scattered in different directions, not all the parts have the same energy or intensity. Usually, the closer they are to the reflection vector, the stronger they are (but there are exceptions to this). Sometimes the total energy of the cone of scattered rays is equal to the energy of the incoming ray; sometimes the cone's energy has been reduced. The reduction can occur if the surface absorbs some of the energy or if a part of the incoming ray continues through the object in the case of transparency.

The incident angle of the light ray often plays a role in this energy distribution. In Figure 15.2, the ray's energy is shown by its length. The different reflection behaviors are illustrated. The incident light ray comes from the left. The reflection vector is at the right. The left picture shows a nearly perfect reflector; very little light departs from the reflection vector. The middle picture shows almost perfect diffuse reflection with a little "bump" in the direction of the reflection vector. The right picture shows what is called an *off-specular peak*, when the surface reflects most of the light along a vector other than the reflection vector. This is explained more fully in FVFH90.

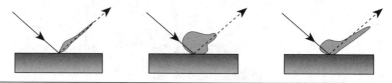

Figure 15.2   Different reflection behaviors

It is too costly to simulate all these behaviors in ray tracing, but we can approximate some of these phenomena with feasible models.

NEARLY PERFECT SPECULAR REFLECTION

We first discuss a nearly perfect specular reflector. If the object has no color of its own and is not transparent, we have the simplest case—a mirror. We can model it by following a secondary ray in the direction of the reflection vector and using the color that it returns.

Handling the dependency of reflection on the incident angle requires a knowledge of what is happening to the light that is not reflected. If the object is opaque, we have a surface with diffuse as well as specular reflection. It is possible for an object to have its own color and still be a nearly perfect reflector, as with polished gold and silver and nontransparent colored glass. Their reflections are sharp, though tainted with the color of the material. The more the light is reflected in a specular manner, the less it is reflected diffusely, and vice versa. How the amount of specular reflection depends on the incident angle is shown in Figure 8.33.

About 50% of a light ray that hits polished gold straight on will be reflected specularly. The remainder is diffusely scattered with a reduced blue component giving a yellowish hue. In tracing a ray that hits such a surface, we give the ray a color that consists of 50% of the yellowish *rgb*-combination typical for gold and 50% of the color that the reflected ray returns. When the ray hits at a 60° incident angle, the ratio will be 65% gold-*rgb* and 35% of the reflection ray's color.

This is the essence of our model. The texture function for such a material computes the specular reflectivity factor, *spec*, using the known incident angle. This is returned together with the *rgb*-values typical for the material. The function `illum()` modifies the *rgb*-intensities, depending on ambient and point light, and obtains the *rgb*-values of the reflected ray. These are added, weighted by (1–*spec*) and (*spec*) respectively.

IMPERFECT SPECULAR REFLECTION

In such reflection, the impinging light ray is scattered in a more or less narrow cone around the reflection vector. Because the reflection is not precise, a whole cone of light rays is reflected to the eyepoint. All the colors in these rays contribute to the color of the ray that reaches us. When we trace the ray backwards and reach the hit point, we should trace a whole cone of reflection rays and combine their colors to determine the ray's color.

Reflections on such surfaces cannot be sharp. The wider the reflection cone, the fuzzier the reflection. This is an inherent weakness of ray tracing. Fuzzy reflections cannot be modeled, except at a very high cost.

Most real-world objects are fuzzy reflectors. They often have a good portion of diffuse reflectivity, as well. Ray tracing tries to model this by deriving most of the ray's color from diffuse reflectivity and only a small part from tracing a single reflected ray. The results are not very good. The "fakeness" of the picture becomes obvious on close examination; although they are very faint, the reflections on the object are still sharp. A costly remedy is to shoot out a sample of rays that lie somewhere randomly in the reflection cone and combine their returned *rgb*-values. A related approach is cone tracing.

The above model also does not consider that the specular reflectivity varies not only with the incident angle, but also with the wavelength of the light and other properties. FVFH90 contains much more information and has references to the literature.

At the other end of the spectrum, there is specular reflection that is far from perfect. The specular reflection cones are so wide that the reflection is practically diffuse. This, as we know, is handled satisfactorily in ray tracing.

SOFT HIGHLIGHTS

Highlights occur at those points on a surface where a ray coming from a point (or almost point) light source is reflected before reaching the eyepoint. With an ideal point light source and an ideal reflector, there is precisely one such point—*the highlight point*. As most objects in the real world are fuzzy reflectors, they have so-called *soft* or *fuzzy highlights*.

Fuzzy reflectors scatter incoming light into a reflection cone. Therefore, some rays from the light source that do not precisely hit the highlight point are still reflected toward the eyepoint. This causes an area around the highlight point to reflect rays from the same light source to the eyepoint. Because rays that are reflected less precisely usually have less energy, the points farther from the highlight point appear weaker. This gives the appearance of a soft highlight; the fuzzier the reflector, the larger and fuzzier the highlight.

Because real-world light sources are never point sources, but are distributed sources such as windows, lamps, and even the sun, they also contribute to soft highlights. This alone would produce a highlight of nonzero area on even the most perfect reflector. On fuzzy reflectors, it enhances the fuzziness of the highlight. It is obvious, then, that highlights are almost always fuzzy.

Because highlights contribute much to visual realism and are easy to produce, they should be added to a scene. They are produced with the principle explained in Section 8.4. They are best computed when we check for shadows. If the hit point is not in shadow, we compute the reflection vector, r, of the traced ray. We test this against the vector pointing to the light source, l. If they are identical, we have hit the highlight point precisely. If they differ by a small angle, we are close to it. In these cases, we add some of the point light intensity to the rgb-values computed for the hit point. The greater the deviation angle between these two vectors, the less we add. One models this by raising the cosine of the included angle, dot (l,r), to a high power and multiplying it by the point light intensity before adding it to the rgb of the surface.

Exponent values around 100 give very fuzzy highlights; values of 1000 or higher make them smaller without making them really sharp.

15.2   REFRACTION AND TRANSPARENCY

These two are intimately related and must be treated together. Ray tracing can handle them quite well. Light rays penetrate a transparent object when they hit it; at the same time, their direction and color change. The change in direction is due to refraction, while the change in color results from the absorption of certain color components while passing through the object. Part Three of `illum()` handles this case.

15.2.1   REFRACTION

When light passes from a medium of a given refractive index into a medium of a different refractive index, its direction changes at the transition. The amount of change of direction depends on the angle with which the ray hits the transition plane and on the ratio of the two refractive indices. At the transition point, there is a common normal N to the transition plane, which extends in both directions; see Figure 15.3. The angle of the light ray with the normal inside material a is θ_a. Inside material b, it is θ_b. According to Snell's law, these two angles fulfill the relation:

$$\frac{\sin \theta_a}{\sin \theta_b} = \frac{n_b}{n_a}$$

Here, n_a and n_b are the refractive indices of materials a and b. It does not matter in which direction the light travels. A more dense transparent medium almost always has a higher index of refraction; in our description we sometimes refer to the density of a medium, even when it would be more precise to use the term *refraction index*.

We explain the computation of the refraction vector using the method of Heckbert and Hanrahan as presented in FVFH90, p. 757, and adding a few steps.

In Figure 15.3, unit vector I lies on the incident ray and points away from the point of incidence, O. Unit vector R lies on the refracted ray and also points away from O. N and $-N$ are unit vectors normal to the surface between materials a and b. (These normals coincide.)

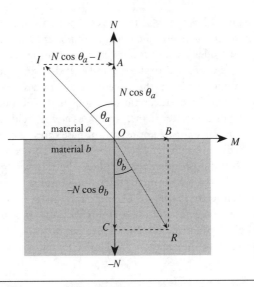

Figure 15.3   Geometry for computing the reflection vector

Project I onto N to produce point A. The distance from O to A is $\cos\theta_a$, while the distance from the end point of I to A is $\sin\theta_a$. The vector from O to A is therefore $N*\cos\theta_a$, and the vector from the end point of I to A is $N*\cos\theta_a - I$. If we scale this vector by $1/\sin\theta_a$, we obtain a unit vector that is normal to N and in the plane of N and I. Call this vector M and let it start from O. We then have

$$M = \frac{N*\cos\theta_a - I}{\sin\theta_a}$$

By the same reasoning, the distance from O to B is $\sin\theta_b$ and the distance from O to C is $\cos\theta_b$. Multiplying vector M by $\sin\theta_b$ gives the vector from O to B, while the vector from O to C is $-N*\cos\theta_b$. By vector addition, we have

$$R = M*\sin\theta_b - N*\cos\theta_b$$

Inserting the expression for M leads to:

$$R = (N*\cos\theta_a - I)*\frac{\sin\theta_b}{\sin\theta_a} - N*\cos\theta_b$$

If we let $f = \dfrac{\sin\theta_b}{\sin\theta_a} = \dfrac{n_a}{n_b}$, we can write:

$$R = N*(\cos\theta_a * f - \cos\theta_b) - I*f$$

Since I is known, we can compute $\cos\theta_a = \mathrm{dot}(I,N)$. We can also compute $\cos\theta_b$ as:

$$\cos\theta_b = \sqrt{1 - \sin^2\theta_b} = \sqrt{1 - (f*\sin\theta_a)^2} = \sqrt{1 - f^2 *(1 - \cos^2\theta_a)}$$

We now have:

$$R = N*\left(f*\mathrm{dot}(I,N) - \sqrt{1 - f^2 *\left(1 - \mathrm{dot}(I,N)^2\right)}\right) - f*I$$

In Figure 15.4, the light ray is penetrating from a thinner into a denser medium. This bends it toward the denser medium. The quotient f in this case is less than 1. It follows that the radicand under the root is not negative, assuring the existence of the refraction vector R.

Let us now reverse the roles of I and R. If the light comes from the direction of R and goes into the thinner medium, the same drawing applies and we can obtain I from R using the reciprocal of f. However, certain directions of R will not lead to a refraction vector I. The quotient f will be greater than 1 and, for certain incident angles of R, the radicand will be negative. No refraction vector exists. In these cases, the light ray does not penetrate into the thinner medium, but is reflected back into the denser medium. This is called *total internal reflection*. It is this phenomenon that keeps light traveling inside an optical glass fiber.

The code for computing the refraction vector is straightforward. It checks the sign of the radicand before attempting to compute the square root. If the sign is negative, a reflection vector is computed. The incident and refraction vector both face in the direction of the ray ("down light"). We made this code a member function of `rpoint_t`. It computes the refraction vector of an incoming vector "hit" about itself, while it plays the role of the surface normal:

```
rpoint_t rpoint_t::refrac(const rpoint_t& hit,double eta) const
{        // refraction of (infacing) hit about (outfacing) *this
    double d = *this*hit ;
    double s = 1 - eta*eta*(1-d*d) ;

    if (s < 0)
        return (*this).reflec(hit);    // total internal reflection
    else
        return hit*eta - *this*(d*eta + sqrt(s));
}
```

A ray that reaches the eyepoint through a pixel center after passing through a transparent object can be traced back like any other ray. We follow a ray through the pixel center; if a transparent object is hit, we compute the refraction ray. We follow this ray to the next intersection. At this point, it either leaves the object or is bounced back through internal reflection. See Figure 15.4. The same process is repeated if the ray is internally reflected.

After 20 reflections, we assume that the ray leaves the object instead of bouncing back. The number 20 is an arbitrary choice. The idea behind it is that, after a large number of internal reflections, the ray has become practically random. There is no calculable difference in the randomness after this large number of internal reflections. We make the ray leave by continuing it in the same direction after the last hit.

This method of handling refraction is a rough simplification of reality. Refraction is actually different for the different wavelengths in the light ray. (White light passing through a glass prism is refracted into a whole band of rainbow

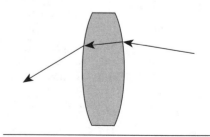

Figure 15.4   Refraction on entry and exit

colors. In physics, refraction is used to analyze the composition of light.) Large optical lenses have problems because of this property. Telescopes operating with lenses ("refractors") can hardly go beyond a four-foot lens diameter. Reflecting mirrors ("reflectors") must be used instead.

15.2.2 TRANSPARENCY

When an object is transparent, such as water or glass, our model assumes that it has no diffuse reflectivity. Although this is not entirely correct, it is very close to reality. When such an object seems to have some color, it is the result of altering the composition of light passing through it, plus a small amount of diffuse reflection. Both processes change the light in very similar ways. Green glass, for example, reduces the red and blue components of light passing through it more than it reduces the green. Whatever we see through green glass will therefore have a greenish tint. It may also diffusely reflect a little of the incoming light, reducing the red and blue components more than the green. The results of both optical effects are very similar.

An illumination model becomes simpler if one assumes no diffuse reflectivity for transparent objects. Our model will interpret the texture's given rgb-values as transparency factors, with 1 being the highest and 0 the lowest. Components of (1 1 1) describe an ideally transparent medium. Light green glass might be described by (0.9 1 0.9). Describing a transparent object in this way accords with how we describe a nontransparent one of the same hue. A slightly greenish object is also described by (0.9 1 0.9).

When we look through a transparent object, we see objects behind it. The light emanating from objects behind the transparent one reaches our eyes after passing through it, possibly being altered in the process. We will model this as follows. When a ray hits a transparent object, we refract it and let it go on through the object and out of it (maybe after some internal reflections). The ray returns an rgb-value from the object behind. We modify this rgb-value by multiplying each component by the respective transparency factor. An ideally transparent medium would not change them. Greenish glass or water with rgb = (0.85 0.99 0.85) would reduce the red and blue components, but would reduce the green only very slightly. A whitish object with rgb = (0.95 0.95 0.95) seen through that medium would then look greenish:

$$(0.95*0.85 \quad 0.95*0.99 \quad 0.95*0.85) = (0.806 \quad 0.941 \quad 0.806)$$

Observe that when the light passes through an object, the intensity of each of its components decreases. (An ideally transparent material does not exist, although optical glass-fiber comes very close.) The amount by which the light diminishes depends on the distance it travels inside the transparent material. The rgb-transparency factors are therefore interpreted as factors per unit of distance. We can obtain the distance traveled at no additional cost. We follow the refraction vector until it hits the surface again from the inside. Every vector we generate is normalized to length 1. Thus, the distance traveled is given by the parameter u of the intersection. If internal reflection occurs, we accumulate the u-values until the refraction ray leaves the object. The diminishing factors are determined by taking the transparency factors to the power of the distance t: (r^t g^t b^t). These multiply the rgb-values of the objects behind.

DEPENDENCY ON THE COORDINATE SCALE

An object's transparency depends on the scale of the user coordinates because the accumulated travel distance inside a transparent object is obtained in user coordinates. The light travels farther through a transparent object if the scale is large than it does if the scale is small. If we render the same scene in large-scale and in small-scale coordinates, a transparent object will look darker in the first scene than it does in the second.

We should achieve the right transparency by choosing the right coordinate scale, not by changing the transparency factors. We should choose the factors so that a transparent object of thickness 1 before a white background will exhibit the same hue as a nontransparent object with these factors as *rgb*-values.

This dependency on the coordinate scale is not a flaw in the model, but corresponds to reality. There is no sense in trying to find a different model that somehow eliminates it.

15.2.3 HANDLING OF TRANSPARENT OBJECTS

All solids that are disjoint, no matter whether they are transparent or opaque, should be specified individually and positioned accordingly; they should not penetrate each other. The function `traceall()` returns only the intersections for the closest disjoint object. If we let opaque disjoint objects penetrate each other, they would have the appearance of a Boolean union, even though the intersections of the farther one are discarded.

However, this is not true if one of the objects is transparent. If an opaque object penetrates into a transparent one (both being disjoint), it will not be visible on the inside. For example, sticking a pencil through a glass sphere will make the part of the pencil inside the sphere invisible. The pencil's intersection pair that is inside the sphere starts farther on the ray than the sphere's intersection pair, so the pencil's pair is discarded.

A ray that hits a transparent object penetrates it and travels inside until it hits again. That second hit is assumed to be an intersection with the same transparent object. Thus, the ray tracer can properly handle the ray as it leaves the transparent object; the refraction coefficient is inverted and internal reflection can occur.

The design of a ray tracer that allows the ray to hit another (maybe transparent) object while inside a transparent one is much more complex. A ray would have to carry along a list of pointers to the objects it penetrates and update it with each intersection. This still leaves the question unanswered which of these objects the ray is really inside of, which transparency and refraction factors to apply, and so on. For more about this, see FVFH90, p. 754f.

Our approach is simpler, but it still creates the scene described above. The glass sphere is simply specified as sphere minus pencil, where the subtracted pencil has a slightly larger diameter than the one we actually stick through it. It is enough if the subtracted diameter is larger by 10^{-4} or so; this prevents the sphere and pencil from touching.

Our approach is not only simpler, but also more realistic. Some reflection will show why we must not deviate from the nonpenetration rule. If two objects penetrate each other, what material actually exists at locations that are inside both? Does this material belong to the first object, the second one, or an alloy of both? No two objects can be in the same space at the same time. A penetration creates an impossibility, and we cannot really model impossibilities.

By treating disjoint objects as disjoint, the code avoids these problems, even if penetration should accidentally occur. The user can override this mechanism by specifying a Boolean combination of two penetrating objects and giving each a different texture. This is acceptable as long as none of the textures are transparent. (If one of the textures is transparent, the ray tracer could invert the notions of inside and outside and wrong illuminations could result.)

We model a combination of two lenses of different refraction (often built in camera optics) by specifying them as disjoint objects that are very close together, but do not touch; see Figure 15.5. A ray leaving the first will do so with the inverse of the first refraction coefficient, which is *lens1/air*. It enters the second lens with the coefficient *air/lens2*. As the path traveled in air is very short, there will be essentially no offset of the ray and the resulting refraction will be identical to *lens1/air * air/lens2 = lens1/lens2*. (This model actually corresponds to reality, because no matter how precisely the lenses are constructed, there will be a gap in between.)

A liquid such as water can actually touch another refractive object. We model such a situation by specifying the water as a solid with a proper refraction coefficient and putting it close to the other object leaving a little gap. The resulting mixed refraction will be accurate and the very thin airspace will not be noticeable.

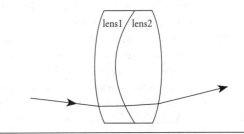

Figure 15.5   Combination of objects of different refractions

15.3 IMPLEMENTATION

Reflection and refraction are implemented entirely within `rtscene_t::illum()`.

Reflection is easy. If the texture at the hit point has a specular reflectivity greater than zero, we find the reflection vector of the ray direction about the normal. The hit point plus this vector is the reflection ray. (For additional safety, we move the ray's start point a little off the surface.) `Traceall()` is called for this ray and returns its hit list. Then `illum()` is called for this ray and its hit list. Whatever *rgb*-value it returns is weighted with the specular reflectivity factor and added to the *rgb*-value.

Refraction is not so easy. The first consideration is how to handle shadows. Transparent objects can produce something similar to a shadow if their translucency is not too high. The physical reality is much too complicated to be handled by ray tracing, but we can produce a weak shadow that becomes darker with decreasing translucency. When checking for a shadow, we trace the ray to the light source through transparent objects without refraction.

We do this by checking the texture of the object that was hit. If it is transparent, we compute the *way length* through the object as the difference of the two *u*-values (our rays are normalized!). We also compute the total way length, which is simply the second *u*-value. The total way length is needed to determine whether the point light source has been reached. Also, we raise the transparency factors of the penetrated object to the power of the way length.

Then we start a new ray at the exit point with the same direction. If the next object hit is again transparent, we compute the way length and add it to the former one. We do the same for the total way length, raising again the transparency factors to the power of the way length again and multiplying them by the former factors.

We do this until we hit a nontransparent object or until the total way length becomes greater than the distance to the light source. (The process will certainly stop when we hit the background, which is nontransparent.) In the first case, we have a total shadow, in the second case a reduced shadow. The latter is computed by modifying the *rgb*-values of the point that is being checked for shadow with the accumulated factors. The shadow takes on the tint of the transparent object or objects that lie between it and the light source. This testing is embedded in the normal checking for shadows. Details can be found in the code.

The second consideration is refraction. (A reminder: a refraction value of zero means the object is not transparent; a value greater than zero means the object is transparent. In the latter case, the value is interpreted as the refractivity factor. A value of 1 means no refraction, smaller values mean increased refraction.) If the texture at the hit point has a refraction value greater than zero, the ray's refraction vector is computed; call it *frac1*. This vector plus the hit point gives the entry ray. Its start point is backed off a little from the surface in the direction of the refraction ray to ensure that both intersections will be positive. After tracing the ray, we take the second element in the hit list, which is the exit point from the same object. We then use the inverse refraction coefficient to compute the refraction vector of *frac1*; call it *frac2*. This vector plus the exit point is the exit ray. However, this computation may result in internal reflection. To find if this is so, we check the dot product of *frac2* and the inward pointing normal at the exit point.

If this product is negative, the exit ray refracts out of the object. We move its start point a little bit off the surface, trace it, and obtain its illumination through a call to `illum()`. If the dot product is positive, we have internal reflection and the ray remains inside the object; we continue as above, again backing off a little before shooting into the composed solid. Eventually, at most after 20 internal reflections, we will arbitrarily leave the object.

As long as the ray remains inside the object we accumulate the distances traveled. Upon leaving, the object's transparency coefficients are raised to the power of the accumulated distance and used to modify the illumination obtained from tracing the exit ray. This gives the objects behind the transparent object a tinted appearance.

We mentioned earlier that the scale of the user coordinates determines the darkness or lightness of translucent objects. This applies to the shadows of translucent objects as well. Frequently, such objects will look too dark or too light, even if the hue or tint is right. This should be corrected by changing the scale of the whole scene file. If this is too complicated, a quick fix is possible. Before using the accumulated distance as an exponent for the transparency factors, we scale it by a number, *transcale*, found empirically for a particular scene. Of course, this requires recompiling the source code.

15.4   RAY TRACING FROM AN ARBITRARY POINT IN SPACE

A useful addition to our ray tracer is the option to view a given scene from any point in space without changing the scene. Below, we present a method that is far superior to the view plane transformation method of Chapter 5. It does not obviate view plane transformations, because it is applicable only to ray tracing.

ADVANTAGES

Doing the view change with the view plane transformation is not really straightforward. We would have to compute the view plane transformation matrix *vpt* and pass it to the constructor `rtscene_t()` that sets up the trees for the composed objects. When constructing the nodes and primitives in these trees, *vpt* must be multiplied into each of their transformation or rotation matrices and their centers. We would also have to apply *vpt* to all light sources.

The method that we present is not "intrusive" in the sense that it changes the objects' positioning information. It is absolutely independent from the way the objects are stored and can be added to any ray tracer later on. Its main advantage is in animation.

If a fixed scene is to be displayed in motion as seen from a moving point in space, the *vpt*-method would have to recompute *vpt* for every new frame and recompute all rotation and transformation matrices and light sources. If we speed up with the BSP-method (see Section 15.5), we would have to recompute the BSP-tree. Only after all these changes can the raytracing of the scene begin. The presented method, however, does not require any of these recomputations. The number of computations for initializing a primary ray is not increased.

EXPLANATION

The point from which one views the scene is specified by the user and called the *eyepoint*.

$$eye = (eye.x \quad eye.y \quad eye.z)$$

The user also specifies the *view reference point*, the point onto which one focuses the view.

$$ref = (ref.x \quad ref.y \quad ref.z)$$

Usually, it is a point in or close to the scene.

From those two points, we determine the *view vector*, *V*, which points from the eye in the direction of *ref*. Its coordinates are $(V.x \quad V.y \quad V.z)$, computed by $V = ref - eye$. We normalize this vector and obtain *v*.

We look at *ref* from the eyepoint through the screen. We imagine the screen to be in front of us, between the eyepoint and the view reference point, and normal to the view vector. We produce a ray traced view of the scene on the screen by shooting rays from the eyepoint through each pixel of the screen. The view vector penetrates the screen in its center.

The user must set a third item in order to specify the view unambiguously. This is the *view-up vector*, *vup*, which determines which direction will be up on the screen. The projection of *vup* onto the screen will be the *y*-axis in the screen.

The angle, α, that spans the rays from the eyepoint through the screen should be about 20° from left to right. We call this the *peripheral angle*. (This is the angle of a natural field of view for a human being. A larger angle would produce a distorted scene.) If we assume a constant peripheral angle, the distance of the screen from the eye is not important because the rays that are shot out from the eye through each pixel on the screen are the same, no matter how great the distance from the eye to the screen.

If we assume the screen to be at a distance of 1 in world coordinates from the eye, the screen's half-width, *wid*, is:

$$wid = \tan(\alpha / 2)$$

If the screen width in pixels is *dwid*, then the distance in world coordinates between adjacent pixels on the screen, *step*, is

$$step = wid(dwid / 2) = \tan(\alpha / 2) / (dwid / 2)$$

We now express the *x*-axis on the screen in world coordinates. This axis is normal to *vup* and *v*. Therefore, we can determine it as a cross product of these two vectors:

$$X = vup \times v$$

(Here we assume a left-handed coordinate system. The resulting vector *X* points to the right in the screen.)

A precaution: this cross product will be (0 0 0) if *vup* is parallel to *v*. Further computations will stall because the null vector cannot be normalized.

The *y*-axis in the screen is normal to *v* and *X*. Therefore, we can again find it as a cross product:

$$Y = v \times X$$

The center, *O*, of the screen is easy to determine. It is at a distance of 1 from the eyepoint, eye:

$$O = eye + v \qquad\qquad (v \text{ is normalized})$$

We normalize *X* and *Y* and obtain *x* and *y*. The vector that brings us from one pixel in the screen to its neighbor in the *x*-direction is *deltx*:

$$deltx = x * step$$

Analogously, if we assume a square pixel ratio, the vector that brings us from one pixel to its neighbor in the *y*-direction is *delty*:

$$delty = y * step$$

We determine the coordinates of the top left point in the screen, *S*, by adding to *O* the proper number of steps in the *x*- and *y*-directions:

$$S = O - dwid / 2 * deltx - dhei / 2 * delty$$

where *dhei* is the screen height in pixels. The above computations are done only once when setting up the scene.

The direction of the ray from the eyepoint through the pixel (*x y*) can now be determined. Keeping in mind that *deltx* and *delty* are vectors, not scalars, we have, using C++ notation with our overloaded operators:

$$ray.d = S + deltx * x + delty * y - eye$$

The ray direction for a pixel can be found by incrementing the previous ray direction by *deltx* or *delty*; these never change throughout the scene. Only three additions are needed.

When an arbitrary viewer position is allowed, the user must have a way to specify the arbitrary view in the scene file. The scene file definition and the parser that reads and interprets it were explained in Section 14.5.

CONCLUSION

One problem in ray tracing occurs if the start points of secondary rays lie slightly inside the objects from which they start, due to numerical roundoff. In this situation, the first intersection the ray finds is with the same object; it is also an intersection from the inside. This can lead to wrong results, such as unwanted shadows and even infinite loops. Several strategies have been devised to solve this problem; see HAIN89.

This ray tracer avoids the problem. All objects are solid, and their intersections with the ray come in pairs (two, four, or six, etc). Also, intersections are retained or discarded in pairs. If the larger u-value of a pair is smaller or equal to zero at a solid intersection, the whole pair is discarded. If the smaller u-value of a pair is smaller or equal zero after the final weaving, that pair is discarded as well. (These cases can happen when starting inside or into a composed solid or off its surface from slightly inside.)

This guarantees that for rays that start on an object's surface and point away from it, this intersection pair is discarded. If a ray starts on the surface penetrating into a solid, which happens only when it penetrates transparent ones, we retain the pair because we back a little off the surface before shooting the ray.

The eyepoint must be outside all objects. That is, all primary rays start outside the objects of the scene. An eyepoint inside a solid object makes no sense. If we want to look out from within a transparent solid (for example water), it is a different matter. We just surround the eyepoint with a little sphere that we subtract from the solid; the result is an eyepoint that is outside! As all rays start from the center of that little sphere, they hit the solid straight on, so no refraction occurs. There will be only one refraction upon leaving the water and the effect is exactly as if the eyepoint were submerged in the water.

15.5 SPEEDING UP RAY TRACING

There are several methods for speeding up raytracing. A good overview of these is presented in ARKI89. We present only one of those without giving code. This is the *binary space partitioning* method. Several variants exist.

The most straightforward one consists of first enclosing the whole scene (without the background) in one axis parallel box. Then the following principle is applied: The box is checked for the number of primitive solids whose surfaces intersect the box volume. If there are more than two (or another fixed low number), the box is divided in half between left and right by a vertical plane. The two resulting halves are tested again for the number of intersecting primitives. If the number is higher than two in a subbox, that box is divided in half between bottom and top by a horizontal plane. The test is then repeated on those two halves. If there are more than two in one of those subboxes, that one is divided in half between front and back by a vertical plane.

This cycle of halving the box first in the x-direction, then of halving the results in the y-direction, and then of halving these results in the z-direction is repeated until every box is intersected by at most two (or the chosen number of) primitives or until it has reached a size limit.

While this partitioning proceeds, a *binary space partitioning* tree (BSP-tree) is constructed. It is a binary tree whose nodes represent a partition in the x- or y- or z-direction, depending on the depth. The root is x, the next level y, and the next z, after which this pattern repeats. The dividing planes that form the partition can each be expressed with one single number. The leaves of the tree represent the resulting subboxes, sometimes called *voxels*. Although this last term is usually restricted to octrees, we prefer to use it here instead of "subbox." Each voxel is sufficiently described by two 3D points that give the coordinates of two diagonally opposed corners. In addition to these points, a leaf node also contains a linked list of pointers to those primitives that it intersects.

Below, we show an example of this. It will show only a two-dimensional scene, a two-dimensional partition, and the corresponding BSP-tree. The three-dimensional case is an easy extension of this, but is not easy to draw. In Figure 15.6, we see the whole scene enclosed in a box with dimensions [−1 +1] in x and [−.8 +.8] in y. The six primitives are numbered from 1 through 6. Sphere 1 intersects with two voxels, sphere 5 with three. In this example, the coordinates of the successive x-divisions are 0, 0.5, and 0.75, while those of y are 0, 0.4, and 0.2.

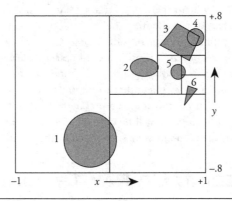

Figure 15.6   Binary partitioning of a scene

Figure 15.7 shows the resulting BSP-tree. We have entered the coordinate of the dividing plane in each node and indicated the dividing direction. In the leaves, we do not show the voxel coordinates, only the numbers of the primitives with which that voxel intersects.

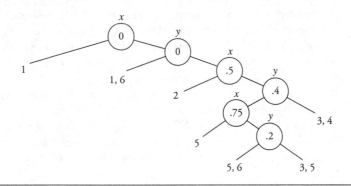

Figure 15.7   Binary partitioning tree

Shooting a ray into the scene is now done in a different manner. A ray that starts from the eyepoint is first checked for intersection with the big box. Once the intersection point is found, one moves along that ray a tiny bit to the point R in order to penetrate into the first voxel. The voxel containing the point R is "located" in the BSP-tree by starting at the root and descending either left or right, depending on how the number in the node compares with the coordinates of R. In the first node, one compares $R.x$ to the number in the node; in the next node, one compares $R.y$ to the number and finally $R.z$. Continuing like this, one reaches the voxel containing R.

The ray can intersect only the primitives listed in that voxel. We later describe what to do with those. One now has to find the next voxel along the ray. For this, one computes the exit point of ray and voxel, then proceeds again a little bit to find the new point R. The voxel is located using the same method as above. In this way, one penetrates through all voxels until the ray leaves the big box. Figure 15.8 shows a ray, and the penetrated voxels shaded. We see that the primitives 2, 3, 4, and 5 cannot possibly be intersected. Their intersection routines will not be executed (see below).

If a ray starts at some other point in the scene, one has to locate the voxel that contains the start point. The primitives in it are the first that can be intersected. From here on, one proceeds as above.

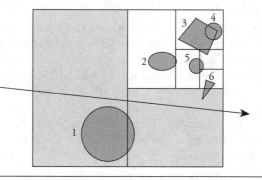

Figure 15.8   Ray penetrating the scene

JOINING BSP AND BOOLEAN COMBINATIONS

We now suggest how to join the BSP-tree speed-up scheme with our method of producing Boolean combinations of solids. While pursuing a ray through the voxels, we flag all those primitive solids that are listed in the voxels as possible intersections. We must add this flag as an additional data member to all primitives. The flag setting is the preprocess for every ray-scene intersection test.

We also have to change the intersection routines with primitives. Each routine first checks the flag. If the flag is not set, the routine immediately returns an empty hit list, because no intersection is possible. Otherwise, it computes the ray-primitive intersections and returns those, if any. In both cases, it resets the flag. With these changes in place, a ray is traced against the scene by first doing a preprocessing step (only flag setting) and then calling `traceall()`.

The setting up of the BSP-tree is done only once per scene. For this, one needs routines that test a given voxel and primitive for intersection. Such routines are easy to write for a box and a sphere; for other primitives, they become quite complicated. They are therefore often replaced by routines that compute a bounding box or sphere for the primitive and test only that box or sphere for intersection with the voxel. This is better than nothing, but not precise and can indicate a voxel intersection where a tight routine would not indicate one.

This speeds up ray tracing, because if a scene contains a large number of objects, only a tiny fraction of those will really be tested for intersections with any given ray. The saved time easily outweighs the additional time for setting up the tree and preprocessing the ray. You can find more about this in ARKI89.

15.6   DISTRIBUTED RAY TRACING

Instead of shooting just one ray per pixel into the scene, in distributed ray tracing we shoot several. This principle can be applied not only to primary rays, but also to all other rays: reflected rays, refracted rays, and rays to the light sources for shadow testing. Shooting several rays is also called *super sampling*. Super sampling increases the running time of the ray tracer enormously, but what are the advantages?

ANTIALIASING

Super sampling is a way to achieve antialiasing. Aliasing in ray tracing is most conspicuous in the stairsteps that we see when a straight edge of an object is just slightly slanted with respect to the display raster. We explain this in more detail with an example below; see Figure 15.9. There, we assume the edge of a red object to be almost horizontal against a green background. The squares are adjacent pixels on the display. With normal sampling, we shoot only one ray per pixel center, which appears as a dot in the center of the square. Depending on whether this ray hits the object or the background, the pixel will either be red or green. In the rightmost three pixels (shaded), the edge is above the pixel center. These pixels are red. All other pixels are green.

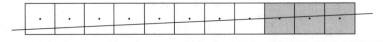

Figure 15.9   Stairstep on a raster display

Instead of a slanted boundary, we see a horizontal one with stairsteps. In a still picture produced on a high-resolution display, the stairsteps might not be very noticeable. However, if this picture is only one in a sequence of frames for animation, the stairsteps become very disturbing. Figure 15.10 shows the situation after a slight upward movement of the red object. What changes is only the number of red pixels. Instead of an upward movement of the boundary, we see the stairstep move to the left. Such a "strange" or "other" effect is called an alias.

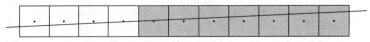

Figure 15.10   Stairstep has moved to the left

This movement of one or several stairsteps along edges becomes an overly conspicuous and disturbing side effect in animated pictures. The reason for the stairsteps is that we color a pixel either red or green when actually neither color is correct. We cannot subdivide a pixel! We can mitigate the problem, however, if we give the pixel a color in between red and green, depending on the ratio of the colors that it covers.

Super sampling can bring us closer to this goal. Instead of shooting only one ray through the center, we shoot, say, five rays that are distributed throughout the pixel area either in a regular or random way. Figure 15.11 shows the first approach. The pixel's color is computed as an average of the color values returned by the five rays. Consequently, it will be either red, one of four different yellows, or green. The color changes between pixels will become smoother and less abrupt, even though the number of stairsteps increases. But even this might not be good enough for the human visual system, with its amazing capability to pick up any regularities.

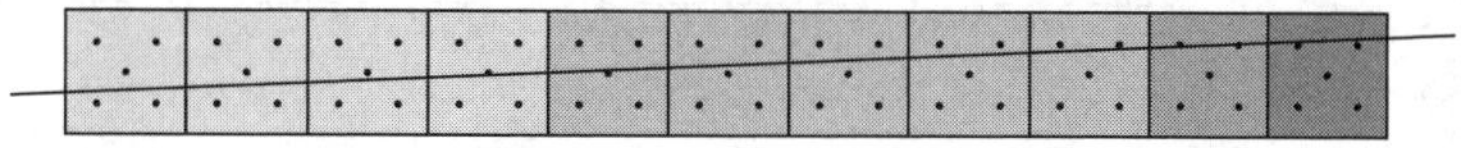

Figure 15.11   Sampling each pixel at five points

We can improve on the above method by distributing the five rays in a random way throughout the pixel area. This is called *stochastic super sampling*. Although there are still only six different colors per pixel in the boundary area, the changes from one to the next will not occur in a regular way, either within one frame or from frame to frame. Consequently, they will hardly be perceptible.

Because one does not know what object one will hit or not hit when shooting a ray, one must do super sampling for every pixel in the frame in order to suppress aliases. There are methods for deciding during the super sampling whether or not to take more samples for this pixel. Another method is to sample only once per pixel, but rather than shooting the ray strictly through the pixel center, one "jitters" it by a random amount about that point. It is impossible to describe all these methods here. We refer the reader to FVFH90 and GLAS89, where more references can be found.

PENUMBRAS

Another advantage offered by super sampling is the ability to produce more natural-looking shadows. In the real world, shadows are rarely sharp like the ones our ray tracer produces, but fuzzy. These halfshadows are called *penumbras*. The principle for shadow creation is the same as the one we have learned, but instead of testing only one ray per light source, we test many. First, we compute the exact direction to the light source, then we shoot out, say, five rays in directions that differ from the exact one by little, random amounts. Depending on how many of those do not hit any other object, we set a shadow of varying intensity.

FUZZY REFLECTIONS

As you have read above, most reflectors are not perfect. To model an imperfect specular reflector, we can again employ the method of super sampling. We compute the precise direction of the reflection vector. Then we shoot out several rays that differ by little, random amounts from the exact direction. The *rgb*-values returned by these are weighted into one *rgb*-value, which is used instead of the one value returned by a single ray.

To come a little closer to reality, we would have to shoot a great number of reflection rays. The amount of deviation from the exact direction can model the perfection of the reflector; nearly perfect reflectors will have little deviation, and fuzzier ones will have more deviation. Unfortunately, this causes an explosion in computation time.

Other effects one can achieve with super sampling are motion blur and depth of field simulation. We only mention these here and refer the reader to GLAS89.

SUGGESTED READINGS

RAYT89 is a good source of information for readers with advanced knowledge of ray tracing; it provides many additional literature references. A good introduction can be found in HILL90.

EXERCISES

SECTION 15.6

1. Implement stochastic super sampling to achieve antialiasing. Shoot five rays per pixel that are distributed randomly inside the pixel area. Average the returned *rgb*-values and set the pixel to this value. You have to add one inner loop to the ray tracing loops in `rtscene_t::display()`. The running time will increase fivefold.

2. Improve on Exercise 1 to reduce the running time. Shoot out only two randomly distributed rays for every pixel. If their returned *rgb*-values differ, shoot out the remaining three.

3. We can obtain penumbras by changing `rtscene_t::illum()`. In the first part of `illum()` is a loop that walks through all point light sources. From the hit point, it shoots out a single ray toward each light source and tests it against all objects in the scene. Make the following change: shoot out five rays toward the light source that scatter randomly about the precise ray to the light source. Depending on how many of these strike some object decrease the contribution of this light source accordingly.

4. We can obtain penumbras by changing the scene file alone: Instead of specifying individual point light sources, specify them in groups. Each group consists of five or so point light sources that are positioned closely together. Specify a scene file to test this method.

16

TEXTURING

This chapter presents methods for giving images a realistic appearance by adding patterns or textures to surfaces. There are four sections.

16.0   **Introduction** outlines the chapter.
16.1   **Surface Texturing** reviews parametric surface descriptions as a means of establishing a one-to-one relation between the object's surface and the texture to be mapped. It then covers pasting a predefined flat texture onto a surface.
16.2   **Bump Mapping** explains how to give a smooth surface an uneven appearance.
16.3   **Solid Texturing** explains how to generate textures, such as granite and marble. The technique is to define a three-dimensional texture and then "carve" an object from it.

16.0   INTRODUCTION

Real-world objects seldom have one constant color and perfect smoothness as we have assumed until now. Usually, there are variations in color and often in smoothness. Two techniques have been developed in computer graphics to give the appearance of natural colors and texture. One technique is *surface texturing*, the other is *solid texturing*. In the first, the texture is defined on a flat area; this area is then pasted onto the object. In the second, the texture is defined in 3D space; the object is "carved" out of it.

Surfaces can be rendered in a variety of ways. One can draw polygons (depth sorting, Phong shading), draw rectangles or pixels of constant color (recursive screen subdivision), and compute and set individual pixels (ray tracing). Only when the Cartesian coordinates of the surface points are available, as in ray tracing, can texturing be feasibly applied.

We first describe surface texturing. We use this when a surface should exhibit a certain pattern or picture that is defined separately as a two-dimensional entity. We map the pattern or picture onto the surface, comparable to pasting wallpaper on a wall or painting something on the surface. The weakness of this method is that a 2D pattern cannot be mapped onto a curved surface whithout distorting it. Inconsistencies or discontinuities in the pattern become apparent when one maps around corners or poles of an object. This problem is solved through solid texturing.

Related to surface texturing is the technique of normal perturbation which we call *bump mapping*. This roughens or disturbs an object's surface to give it a more realistic appearance. It is a mathematically complicated process and is computationally costly.

In solid texturing, a texture is defined in three-dimensional space and the object is carved out of it. This technique does not have the weaknesses of surface texturing because the texture value is a function of position in three-dimensional space. The mathematical process is not difficult and the results are very good, but the implementation requires considerable memory and defining the solid texture can be a challenge. Creating solid textures is an interesting area of research that is marginally related to computer graphics.

16.1   SURFACE TEXTURING

The most versatile rendering technique that we have discussed is ray tracing. For every pixel, we find a hit point. This is a point on the surface of an object expressed in Cartesian coordinates $(x\ y\ z)$. Information is now available about the mathematical nature of the surface (is it spherical, conic, flat, toroidal, bicubic, etc.?). From the previous chapters, we know how to compute the illumination at this point; it depends on the surface's texture-properties at the point.

In order to map a separately defined flat texture onto the surface, we must know where the hit point lies in relation to the object's surface as a two-dimensional entity: in the middle, on the edge, etc. Then we can look at the corresponding point in the separately defined texture and take the value there as the texture at the hit point. Surface texture mapping relies on such a one-to-one relation between the spatial coordinates $(x\ y\ z)$ of a surface point and the corresponding two-dimensional position in the surface.

Parametric surface descriptions (called explicit descriptions) yield a 3D point for every parameter pair $(u\ v)$. Three parametric formulas (one for x, one for y, and one for z) describe the whole surface of the three-dimensional object. Such descriptions will serve to establish the one-to-one relationship mentioned above. Because first-time readers usually have problems understanding this concept, we base the following discussion on two examples: a sphere and a torus.

16.1.1   DESCRIBING A SURFACE PARAMETRICALLY

A SPHERE

The surface of a sphere with radius R and center at the origin in a lhs is described by three equations in the parameters u and v:

$$x = R*\cos(2\pi u)*\sin(\pi v)$$
$$y = R*\cos(\pi v)$$
$$z = R*\sin(2\pi u)*\sin(\pi v)$$

.... (1)

It will help to compare this to a globe of the earth (see Figure 16.1). The variable u-curves are horizontal circles with the y-axis as their center; these are circles of latitude. For example, holding v at 0.5 will keep the corresponding sin terms in the equations for x and z constant at 1; y will assume the value 0. Varying u from 0 to 1 lets the point $(x\ y\ z)$ travel in a full circle of radius R around the origin at a height of $y = 0$ (the sphere's equator). The direction of motion is ccw when we look down from the positive y-axis. Other values of v produce a y different from 0, and the variable u-curves will be smaller circles at the height of y. They will be circles of latitude between the equator and the poles. The variable v-curves are semicircles of longitude running from the north to the south pole when v varies from 0 to 1.

When the pair $(u\ v)$ varies through the rectangle $[0\ 1] \times (0\ 1)$, the point $(x\ y\ z)$ varies through the sphere surface. (Observe that the second interval is open: v does not assume the values 0 or 1.) Different $(u\ v)$-pairs in this range will produce different surface points, ultimately producing every point on the surface except for the poles. This is a one-to-one relationship between $(x\ y\ z)$ and $(u\ v)$. The poles can be defined separately.

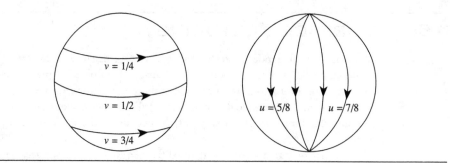

Figure 16.1   Variable u-curves and variable v-curves

A TORUS

A unit-torus (center at (0 0 0), horizontal, large radius 1, circular cross section of radius *r*) is shown in Figure 16.2.

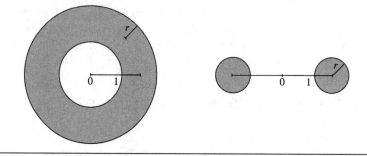

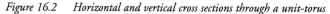

Figure 16.2   Horizontal and vertical cross sections through a unit-torus

The parametric description of the unit-torus surface is:

$$x = (1 + r * \cos(2\pi v)) * \cos(2\pi u)$$
$$y = r * \sin(2\pi v)$$
$$z = (1 + r * \cos(2\pi v)) * \sin(2\pi u)$$

.... (2)

Figure 16.3 shows the variable parameter curves. The variable *u*-curves are horizontal circles that go ccw around the *y*-axis when we look down from the positive *y*-axis. The variable *v*-curves are vertical circles. We can imagine a variable *v*-curve as the intersection of a vertical half-plane starting at the *y*-axis with the torus surface. A point moves upward on it on the outside of the torus as *v* increases.

The equations in (2) give us the one-to-one relation between the Cartesian coordinates (*x* *y* *z*) of a point on the torus surface and the surface parameters (*u* *v*). We do not have to provide separate treatment for poles.

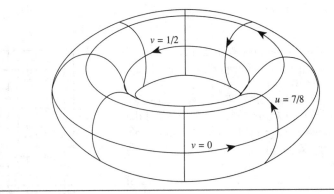

Figure 16.3   Variable u-curves and variable v-curves

16.1.2 THE MAPPING FUNCTION

The texture that we map onto either of these surfaces is defined by a function `texmap(u,v)` whose arguments *u* and *v* range through [0 1] × [0 1], the parameter square. For a given (*u v*)-pair, `texmap()` returns texture information that we can interpret as needed. It could be an *rgb*-value, or simply black-white, or an entire texture consisting of *rgb* and specular and refraction coefficients.

There are basically two possible ways in which `texmap()` finds the texture value to return. One is that `texmap()` computes the value. In this case, not much memory is needed and the implementation is easy for simple, regular textures. For more complicated textures that involve irregularities and randomness, the code of `texmap()` will be more complicated.

The other way is for `texmap()` to use a texture-map, a two-dimensional array of values that is stored in memory. In this case, `texmap(u,v)` will look up the value at the point in the texture-map that corresponds to *u* and *v*. Any two-dimensional picture, say a page with text or a photograph, can serve as the texture-map. In the simplest case, when the texture-map contains only black-and-white information, it is called a *bit map*. The texture-map is either scanned in, created by another computer program (for example a fractal close-up or a cloud), or created manually with a paint program.

If `texmap()` computes the return value rather than looking it up in a texture-map, the computation will use *u*- and *v*-values in the parameter square. If it takes the return value from a texture-map, `texmap()` must stretch or compress the texture-map to fit into the parameter square. This is a trivial scaling operation, because texture-maps are rectangular in shape, so they are easily stored as two-dimensional arrays.

In either case, even if the value is computed, we can for the sake of simplicity assume a rectangular texture-map from which the value is taken. Each point in it corresponds to precisely one (*u v*)-pair and hence to precisely one point on the surface. No matter what the shape of the surface (sphere, torus, or something else), the texture-map corresponds one-to-one to it through the parametric surface description.

Our first example uses a sphere and the texture-map shown in Figure 16.4. Its domain [0 1] × [0 1] covers the spherical surface, except for the poles. We define the surface value for $(u\ 0)$ to be the north pole and the surface value for $(u\ 1)$ to be the south pole for any u. This gives a relation between texture-map and sphere that is one-to-one except for the poles. The texture is a grid of heavy straight black lines, intersecting at right angles with a white background. We can easily compute it on the fly.

We map this texture onto the sphere by giving the point $(x(u,v)\ y(u,v)\ z(u,v))$ on the sphere the texture-value of the point $(u\ v)$ in the map. The result is shown in Figure 16.5. This is not an unfamiliar pattern for a sphere, but we must be aware that a strong distortion actually takes place; the entire lowest horizontal line of the texture-rectangle is mapped onto one single point, the north pole of the sphere, while the highest horizontal line is mapped onto the south pole, which is invisible in this picture.

Whenever we map a texture-map onto a whole sphere a distortion of the texture around the sphere's "poles" will occur. We can avoid only the distortion by not mapping anything onto the neighborhood of the poles. Usually it is sufficient to map onto only part of the sphere, because only part is visible. This sometimes allows us to avoid the poles.

Not all surfaces have poles, so the problem of poles does not always exist. The torus is a good example; the mantle of a cylinder is another.

Figure 16.6 shows the same texture when mapped onto a torus. Observe that there is no "polar" distortion because there are no poles.

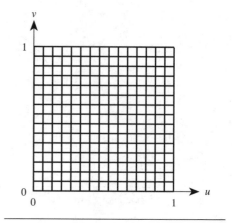

Figure 16.4   Rectangular grid as a texture map

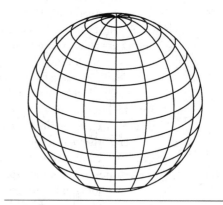

Figure 16.5   Rectangular grid mapped onto a sphere

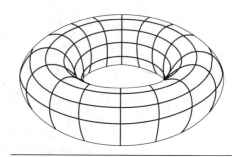

Figure 16.6   Rectangular grid mapped onto a torus

16.1.3 EXAMPLES OF MAPPING FUNCTIONS

Consider a sphere as a first example. A hit point on an arbitrary sphere surface has the Cartesian coordinates (*hit.x hit.y hit.z*). To find the texture for this point, we first have to find the (*u v*) parameter pair that leads to (*hit.x hit.y hit.z*) in the parametric sphere description. Below, we show how to solve the three parameter equations for *u* and *v*.

The equations in (1) describe a sphere with radius *R*, centered at (0 0 0); the arbitrary sphere may have a different center and may be rotated. Although rotations have no effect on a sphere's shape, they are visible if the sphere has a texture. Therefore, we first subtract the sphere's center from the hit point, then multiply it by the sphere's composed rotation matrix. This transforms it to the hit point (*x y z*) on the centered and axisparallel sphere with radius *R*.

We need only the first two equations of (1) to extract *u* and *v*:

$$v = \text{acos}(y / R) / \pi$$
$$u = \text{acos}(x / (\sin(v * \pi) * R)) / (2\pi)$$

We obtain the value of *v* by computing $d = \text{acos}(y/R)$ and $v = d/\pi$. If *v* equals 0 or 1, we set *u* to any value between 0 and 1. Otherwise, we compute $d = \sin(d)*R$ and $u = \text{acos}(x/d)/(2\pi)$. If $z/d < 0$ we change *u* to 1−*u*. We must then find the value of the texture-rectangle at (*u v*) by calling `texmap(u,v)`. The texture value that is returned is assigned to the hit point (*hit.x hit.y hit.z*).

We proceed similarly for a torus. The parameter equations in (2) describe a unit-torus, while the arbitrary torus can have any position in space. We first center the hit point on the torus by subtracting the torus's center; we then rotate and scale it by multiplying it by the transformation matrix. This transforms it to the corresponding hit point on the unit-torus: (*x y z*).

Again, we need only the first two equations of (2) to extract *u* and *v*:

$$v = \text{asin}(y / r) / (2\pi)$$
$$u = \text{acos}(x / (1 + r * \cos(2\pi v))) / (2\pi)$$

First we find *v*. We compute the angle $d = \text{asin}(y/r)$. If $x^2 + z^2 < 1$ (the point (*x y z*) is on the inside of the torus), we change *d* to $\pi−d$. If $d < 0$ now, we change *d* to $2\pi+d$. We get $v = d/(2\pi)$. Then we compute $d = 1 + r*\cos(d)$ and $u = \text{acos}(x/d)/(2\pi)$. If $z/d < 0$, we change *u* to 1−*u*.

The next step is the same as for the sphere—we find the value of the texture-rectangle at (*u v*) by calling `texmap(u,v)`, assigning the texture value to the hit point (*hit.x hit.y hit.z*).

Our next example is the mantle of a cylinder. Although we have not presented a parameter representation for it, we can easily create one. The mapping process requires a one-to-one relation between the texture-map and the surface onto which it is mapped. We construct this by removing the cutting planes from the mantle, cutting it open lengthwise, and flattening it out so it will become a rectangle. The surface of a unit-cylinder becomes a rectangle of width 2π and height 2. We must now determine where a given hit point lies in relation to the cutting line.

The hit point (*hit.x hit.y hit.z*) of an arbitrary cylinder is first translated by the cylinder's center and then multiplied by the transformation matrix. This transforms it to the hit point (*x y z*) on the unit-cylinder. We relate its *y*-coordinate to *v* by $v = (y+1)/2$. The ccw angular position, α, of the hit point with respect to a horizontal circle will give us a value between 0 and 2π. If we let the *x*-axis be the start and end of this circle, α can be related to *u* by $u = \alpha/(2\pi)$.

We find α by computing $\alpha = \operatorname{asin}(z)$. If $x < 0$, we change α to $\pi - \alpha$. If $\alpha < 0$ now, we change α to $2\pi + \alpha$. Then we use (*u v*) to find the texture value of the hit point, as above. An implementation example appears in the file `cylmaps.c` below.

Mapping onto a planar surface is the simplest case of all. If the surface onto which we are mapping is a rectangle, such as the side of a box, its relation to the texture-rectangle is so trivial that we do not demonstrate it.

If the surface is a nonquadrilateral polygon or is bounded by a curve (circle, ellipse, cubic), we map by mapping onto a rectangle big enough to contain the surface. Those parts of the texture-map that correspond to areas outside the surface are simply ignored.

In all these cases, the texture-map may be mapped onto only part of the surface. Conversely, only part of the texture-map may be mapped onto the surface. This is accomplished by adding weights to the parameters *u* and *v* and/or scaling them with factors different from 1. If after such scaling a (*u v*) pair is outside the texture-map, a default texture must be assigned to the corresponding hit point.

As an example we map the letter E, specified as a black-and-white bit map, onto part of a spherical surface. The bit map is shown in Figure 16.7. The part onto which we map it is described by the parameter range $[0.68\ 0.93] \times [0.13\ 0.5]$. This part is shown in Figure 16.8.

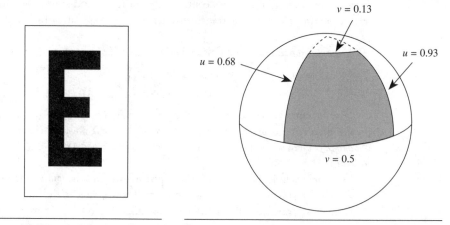

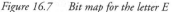

Figure 16.7   Bit map for the letter E   *Figure 16.8   Mapping area*

If (*u v*) is in this range, we map (*u v*) on the sphere to ($u_1\ v_1$) on the bit map with:

$$u_1 = \frac{u - 0.68}{0.93 - 0.68} \qquad v_1 = \frac{v - 0.13}{0.5 - 0.13}$$

These two numbers are between 0 and 1 and are used as normalized subscripts into the bit map. By multiplying v_1 with the number of rows in the bit map, we obtain the row index; likewise, by multiplying u_1 by the number of columns in the bit map, we obtain the column index. With these subscripts, we access the corresponding element of the bit map and get either black or white. Assigning this color to the corresponding point on the sphere surface produces the mapping shown in Figure 16.9.

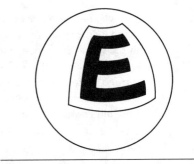

Figure 16.9   Letter E mapped onto the sphere

OO DESIGN AND CLASS SPECIFICATIONS

Whether the map used is a bit map (black/white) or an *rgb*-map (*rgb*-values) or a texture-map (full texture values), the principle is the same in all cases.

The class we provide is `rgbmap_t`, which represents a map of *rgb*-values. The constructor builds the map in memory by reading a file given in the `.ppm` format, see KALE92. The memory for the map is allocated dynamically. Data members of the class are the map's width and height and a pointer to its beginning. The class has a member function `value()`, which returns the value of the map that corresponds to a coordinate pair in the range $[0\ 1] \times [0\ 1]$.

In order to process other file formats, one should add an additional parameter to the constructor that specifies the file format. Then one must add additional code to the implementation to read that file format. All graphics file formats are described in KALE92.

```
//*********************** File rgbmap.h ***********************

#ifndef RGBMAP_T
#define RGBMAP_T

#include "../Raytrace/rgb1.h"
#include "../Raytrace/charrgb.h"

class rgbmap_t
{
public:
    rgbmap_t(char*) ;
    ~rgbmap_t() ;
    rgb1_t value(double,double) ;

private:
    int wid ;                       // size of rgbmap is wid*hei*3 char
    int hei ;
    unsigned char* t ;
} ;


#endif

//*****************************************************************
```

We find the value corresponding to the parameter pair by using the width and height to compute the offset into the map as a character array. This offset is multiplied by three because, in the .ppm file format, width and height specify the map size in character triples.

One example of cylinder mapping follows. It maps a texture around a cylinder. The cylinder's top and bottom plane receive constant colors. The end of the code demonstrates how a texture is composed from *rgb*-values obtained from the map and some added specular reflectivity. The function constructs a static local variable of type rgbmap_t from a file given in the .ppm format. The static keyword causes the construction to occur only once.

```
//*********************** File cylmaps.c ***************************

#include <math.h>
#include "../Raytrace/texture.h"
#include "../Raytrace/solid.h"
#include "../Raytrace/rpoint.h"
#include "../Raytrace/cylinder.h"
#include "../Raytrace/rgbmap.h"
#include "../Shape2d/const.h"

texture_t cylindermap1(solid_t* c,const rpoint_t& hit,double)
{
    static rgbmap_t rgbmap("../Maps/akina.ppm") ;
    rpoint_t h = (hit - c->givcen())*((cylinder_t*)c)->givtrans() ;

    if (h.givy() > 0.999 || h.givy() < -0.999)
        return texture_t(0.6,0.7,0.7,0.2,0);

    double lon , u , v ;
    if (fabs(h.givx()) < 0.00001)           // longitude angle 0 .. 2*PI
        lon = h.givz() > 0 ? PIHALF : -PIHALF;
    else
        lon = atan(h.givz()/h.givx());
    if (h.givx() < -0.00001) lon += PI;
    lon += PIHALF;
    u = lon/TWOPI;                           // 0 .. 1
    v = (h.givy() + 1)/2;

    return texture_t(rgbmap.value(u,v),0.2,0);
}

texture_t cylindermap2(solid_t* c,const rpoint_t& hit,double)
{
    static rgbmap_t rgbmap("../Maps/atext.ppm") ;
    rpoint_t h = (hit - c->givcen())*((cylinder_t*)c)->givtrans() ;

    if (h.givy() > 0.999 || h.givy() < -0.999)
        return texture_t(0.6,0.7,0.7,0.2,0);

    double lon , u , v ;
    if (fabs(h.givx()) < 0.00001)           // longitude angle 0 .. 2*PI
        lon = h.givz() > 0 ? PIHALF : -PIHALF;
```

```
    else
        lon = atan(h.givz()/h.givx());
    if (h.givx() < -0.00001) lon += PI;
    lon += PIHALF;
    u = lon/TWOPI;                                    // 0 .. 1
    v = (h.givy() + 1)/2;

    return texture_t(rgbmap.value(u,v),0.2,0);
}

//******************************************************************
```

16.2 BUMP MAPPING

Bump mapping is another way to obtain realism in the surface. The procedure we describe is Blinn's method of *surface normal perturbation*; see BLIN78. The general idea is easy to grasp. Blinn's article explains it well.

Consider an orange. As a first approximation, it is a sphere. It would be more realistic to create it from bicubic patches to allow deviation from a perfect spherical shape. However, it would still have a perfectly smooth surface, while we want a surface with many little irregular bumps. Blinn's approach consists of finding an independent function that defines a bumpy surface. More generally, the function can describe a regular or irregular surface. This is called a *bump map*. This bump map is then patched onto any surface.

Assume for now that we can define an orange peel surface, or perhaps an even more rugged one. (We later discuss how we do this.) The bump map might look like the one in Figure 16.10.

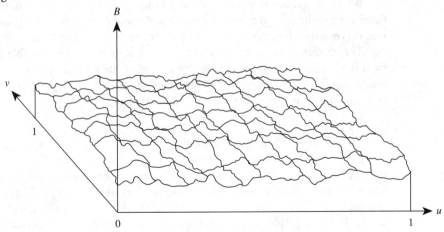

Figure 16.10 Bump map

We are to patch this bump map onto the smooth surface as if we were pasting on real orange peels. First we develop the mathematics to do the "pasting," then we return to the problem of defining the bump map itself. The bump map function has the two arguments u and v: $B(u,v)$. It is not vector-valued but scalar-valued, meaning $B(u,v)$ returns just a number.

We describe the surface onto which we map parametrically. Examples are a sphere, a torus, a cylinder mantle, or a composite of bicubic patches:

$$S(u,v) = \big(x(u,v) \quad y(u,v) \quad z(u,v)\big)$$

Figure 16.11 shows a smooth surface on the left and the same surface with the added bump map on the right.

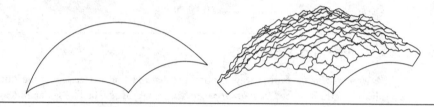

Figure 16.11   Pasting a bump map onto a surface

The return value of $B()$ is added to the value of the surface S in the direction of the normal to S. In effect, we perturb the smooth surface perpendicularly by amounts given by $B(u,v)$. Adding B to S in this way creates a new surface, S'. Below, we develop the mathematical formalism for adding the bump map.

16.2.1 FORMALISM OF NORMAL PERTURBATION

Depending on how the surface onto which we bump map is rendered, we obtain a point on the surface and its normal in different ways.

When the surface is given in implicit form, as in ray tracing, we have the hit point's Cartesian coordinates ($hit.x$ $hit.y$ $hit.z$). We center and transform the hit point to (x y z) and find the corresponding parameter pair (u v), as shown in Section 16.1.

The normal, n, at the point (x y z) or (u v) is in most cases available geometrically or from the implicit surface description. If no implicit surface description is available (as with bicubic patches), we compute the normal from the parametric description. We find it as the cross product of the partial derivatives $S_u(u,v)$ and $S_v(u,v)$:

$$N = S_v \times S_u$$

We normalize N to length 1 and call it n.

Figure 16.12 shows the two partial derivatives and the normal on a parametric torus surface. The cross product in the above order results in an outward pointing normal in a left-handed system. When we really have to find the normal as a cross product, we must preserve this order. (While we can express the normal as the above cross product, we need not find the normal in this way. The torus is an example of a surface in which we can find the normal more easily by geometric means; see Appendix B.)

On the right, we see part of a torus surface and the partial derivatives S_u and S_v at point P. They lie in a plane tangent to S at this point. Computing the cross product in the above order yields a normal vector N that points out of the surface as shown.

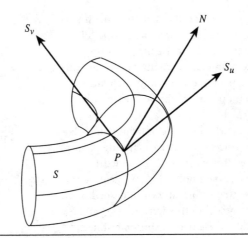

Figure 16.12   Torus normal as cross product of partial derivatives

We add the bump map B to the surface S in the direction of n by adding $B(u,v)*n$ to the point $S(u,v)$. This creates the new surface, S':

$$S'(u,v) = S(u,v) + B(u,v)*n \qquad \ldots\ldots (2)$$

We now need to compute N', the normal to S', in order to render S'. This normal is the cross product of the vectors $S'_u(u,v)$ and $S'_v(u,v)$:

$$S'_u(u,v) = S_u(u,v) + B_u(u,v)*n + B(u,v)*n_u$$
$$S'_v(u,v) = S_v(u,v) + B_v(u,v)*n + B(u,v)*n_v \qquad \ldots\ldots (3)$$

Observe that we have applied the rule for differentiating a product, as n is itself a vector-valued function of u and v. The vectors n_u and n_v depend on the curvature of the surface S. Normally, this curvature is so small that $|n_u|$ and $|n_v|$ are negligible. We commit only a small error in discarding the terms $B(u,v)*n_u$ and $B(u,v)*n_v$.

As we continue this, we will omit the arguments (u,v) for the vector-valued functions S, S_u, and S_v and for the scalar-valued function B. This simplification gives:

$$S'_u \approx S_u + B_u*n \qquad \text{and} \qquad S'_v \approx S_v + B_v*n$$

The normal to S' at (u,v) is now $N' \bullet S'_v \times S'_u$.
We compute $N' \bullet S_v \times S_u + B_u*S_v \times n + B_v*n \times S_u + B_v*B_u*n \times n$.
Keep in mind that B_u and B_v are scalars. We can move these to the left of their respective terms, but we must not change the order of the cross products. Because $S_v \times S_u = N$ and $n \times n = (0\ \ 0\ \ 0)$, we have

$$N' \approx N + B_u*S_v \times n + B_v*n \times S_u \qquad \ldots\ldots (4)$$

We see that N', the perturbed surface normal, uses the partial derivatives of the bump map function and the partial derivatives of the surface function. After normalizing N' to n', we use it to compute the illumination at this point.

Be sure to realize that when we use this method in connection with ray tracing, we do not actually move the hit point away from the surface by the amount $B(u,v)*n$. This amount is

added only to define the new, perturbed surface formally, and to derive the normal of the
perturbed surface. If we use the perturbed normal in the illumination computation, the surface will appear like the bump map although
the actual hit points still lie on the smooth surface!

A geometric view of N' is helpful in visualizing the process of bump mapping. Figure
16.13 gives this view. N' is obtained by perturbing the surface normal N. We achieve this
by adding two vectors, shown in dashed lines,
which are parallel to the derivatives S_u and S_v.
The length of these two vectors determines the
perturbation of N. Another geometric explanation can be found in BLIN78.

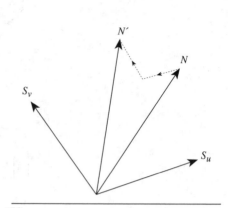

Figure 16.13   Geometric view of N'

16.2.2 MAPPING THE BUMP MAP

Suppose that the parameter pair $(u\ v)$ corresponds to a given point on the surface onto which
we map. We need the two partial derivatives $S_u(u,v)$ and $S_v(u,v)$ at the point, so we take the
partial derivatives of the parametric surface description $S(u,v)$. For a sphere, using the parameterization in 16.1.1, they are:

$$\left(S_u x \ \ S_u y \ \ S_u z\right) = \begin{pmatrix} -R*\sin(2\pi u)*\sin(\pi v)*2\pi \\ 0 \\ R*\cos(2\pi u)*\sin(\pi v)*2\pi \end{pmatrix}$$

$$\left(S_v x \ \ S_v y \ \ S_v z\right) = \begin{pmatrix} R*\cos(2\pi u)*\cos(\pi v)*\pi \\ -R*\sin(\pi v)*\pi \\ R*\sin(2\pi u)*\cos(\pi v)*\pi \end{pmatrix}$$

In some cases (for example bicubic patches) this is the only way of finding the derivatives.
Often, however, the derivatives can be obtained more simply by geometric means using the
implicit description of the centered and axis-aligned unit solid together with the Cartesian
coordinates of the surface point. We explain this for a sphere and a torus. In both cases, one
computes the perturbed normal at the point $(x\ y\ z)$ on the unit solid that corresponds to the
original hit point on the arbitrary solid.

For a sphere, let $(x\ y\ z)$ be the point on the surface corresponding to $(u\ v)$. Then:

$$\left(S_u x \ \ S_u y \ \ S_u z\right) = \left(-z \ \ 0 \ \ x\right)$$
$$\left(S_v x \ \ S_v y \ \ S_v z\right) = \left(xy \ \ -x^2 - z^2 \ \ yz\right)$$

We obtain the first expression by projecting a unit sphere onto the (x z)-plane. Since all u-derivatives are tangents to the sphere and are parallel to the (x z)-plane, their slopes do not change in the projection. They are negative inverses of the line from the center to (x y z). We obtain the second expression by calculating a cross product of the normal at the hit point with the u-derivative.

For a torus, let (x y z) be the point on the surface corresponding to (u v) in the parameterization given in 16.1.1. Then:

$$\left(S_u x \quad S_u y \quad S_u z\right) = \left(-z \quad 0 \quad x\right)$$

$$\left(S_v x \quad S_v y \quad S_v z\right) = \left(-xy \quad x^2 + z^2 - \sqrt{x^2 + z^2} \quad -yz\right)$$

After obtaining the partial derivatives, we normalize them. We obtain the (u v)-pair corresponding to (x y z) as shown in Section 16.1.3 and find the respective distortion values in the bump map at (u v). We multiply the partial derivatives by the distortion values and add them to the normal at the point (x y z), thereby perturbing it. Then we normalize it. This gives us the perturbed normal at (x y z), which we must transform back into the arbitrary position by multiplying it with the solid's transformation matrix. Finally, we use the normal to compute the illumination.

16.2.3 DEFINITION OF A BUMP MAP

How can we define a bump map function? We initialize a two-dimensional array, tab, of floating point numbers with values. The size of the array depends on the resolution we desire. We define a function bump() whose parameters u and v range through [0 1) × [0 1). For reasons that will become clear, we have to allow arguments slightly outside this range. If the argument is outside this range, it is taken modulo the range; see the first four lines of the function bump().

```
#define SIZE 64
static float tab[SIZE][SIZE] ;
static double d = 0.5/SIZE ;

double bump(double u,double v) const          // linear interpolation
{
    int l = int(u*SIZE) ,                               // left
        r = (l+1)%SIZE ,                                // right
        b = int(v*SIZE) ,                               // bottom
        t = (b+1)%SIZE ;                                // top

    double fx = u*SIZE - l ,
        fy = v*SIZE - b ;

    return (1-fy)*((1-fx)*tab[b][l] + fx*tab[b][r])
        + fy *((1-fx)*tab[t][l] + fx*tab[t][r]) ;
}
```

The arguments are scaled by the array size and truncated to produce subscripts. At a grid point ($i/SIZE$ $j/SIZE$) with integers i and j the function returns the value `tab[i][j]`. At other points, the function returns a bilinear interpolation of the surrounding grid point values. The function `bump()` basically models a bilinear grid surface, consisting of nonplanar squares separated by sharp ridges.

Figure 16.14 shows a grid-surface with randomly spaced bumps that are equally high and not smooth. It is defined on a 26×26 table with a random number generator. One can make the grid finer, change the density of the bumps, and give the bumps a random height.

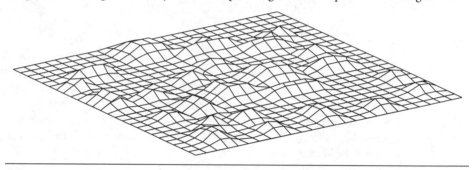

Figure 16.14   Surface with random bumps

Instead of producing a bilinear grid-surface, we could do bicubic interpolation between the grid points. This would give us a surface with smooth bumps. We could then use the partial derivatives of this surface. However, this approach is expensive.

The formulas show that what we need for the normal perturbation is not the bump map itself, but its two partial derivatives. As long as these are smooth, we will have a smooth bump map. We can create smoothly changing partial derivatives from the bilinear grid-surface by approximating them with central differences along u or v with an increment equal to the distance between grid points, that is, $1/SIZE$.

The following functions return these central differences. (The Appendix A explains how to approximate derivatives with central differences.)

```
double gradu(double u, double v)
{
    return bump(u+d,v)-bump(u-d,v);
}

double gradv(double u, double v)
{
    return bump(u,v+d)-bump(u,v-d);
}
```

Here, we have used central differences to approximate the derivatives. However, this can cause array subscripts of -1 or $SIZE$, which are out of range. Thus, we do modulo arithmetic in `bump()`, which amounts to a cyclic repetition of the array.

Another very efficient way to create bump maps is to draw a sample of the bump map by hand. When we draw with a black-and-white paint program, we are actually filling a frame buffer with bits. Hence, our drawing fills some area of the frame buffer with a design of our choice. We can consider this area as the array defining the bump map. The 1-bits are the high values and the 0-bits are the low (or vice versa). We then interpolate these table entries bilinearly and compute the derivatives as shown above.

16.3 SOLID TEXTURING

16.3.1 CHARACTERISTICS OF NATURAL TEXTURES

Man-made materials such as glass, metal, porcelain, and plastic are mostly uniform in their texture and show no variety unless special efforts are made in the production process.

On the other hand, most natural materials consist of a conglomerate of different substances. These mixtures can range from very fine to very coarse. The substances vary in density, color, translucency, shininess, and so forth. Wood varies internally in hardness, density, and color in a semiregular arrangement, due to its year-rings. Rocks show as great a variety. Some rocks, such as obsidian, are glasslike with a uniform appearance; others, such as granite or marble, have inclusions and veins of different colors.

It is an interesting challenge to develop techniques for modeling such nonuniform natural materials. Such objects are very common, and rendering them well adds greatly to a scene's liveliness and realism.

Objects made of natural material are nearly always cut from a single piece. Often, the main objective is to show the material's texture. Elegant furniture will often display the grain of the wood—this may even be enhanced through staining and varnishing. Marble or granite tabletops, tiles, or stairways are made from these materials only to show the texture.

16.3.2 SIMULATION OF NATURAL TEXTURES

Simulating the actual combinations of these different types of matter is difficult because the forces causing certain combinations are very complex and not always understood. We can, however, try to simulate with simple models.

To clarify this point, consider the structure of wood. When a growing tree adds more wood around the circumference at different rates during the year, it produces darker and lighter parts. We could say the darker and lighter wood forms concentric pipes along the trunk of the tree. The deviations from that concept are what make wood really look like wood; this is difficult to render. One deviation is that the tree trunk is not straight, but bent and warped in irregular ways. Another is that the pipes are not round. Third is that their thicknesses vary from year to year, even around the tree trunk in the same year. Fourth is that branches with their own ring patterns are encircled by and enclosed in the growing trunk, the knots. There are certainly more sources of irregularities, even some of which we are not aware because of their subtlety. Together they produce the familiar wood texture.

Consider granite as another example. Granite has conglomerations of crystals with brighter and darker colors at random positions. Crystals of one kind usually tend to form clusters of various sizes that are distributed randomly. However, there are different types of granite. Understanding how the conglomerations are arranged lets us formulate some rules that seem to be obeyed. When we implement these rules, we model a granite structure.

Whether in wood, granite, or marble, a degree of randomness always overlays the arrangement. The randomness permeates the whole solid texture and it changes gradually from one point to another. Sudden changes do not occur. (For example, if the distortion of the year-rings from a true circle happened abruptly, we would see broken year-rings.) The veins in marble preserve a certain continuity, even when they change drastically. This means we cannot just apply the rules of the model to obtain a color at points in space and then distort it by random numbers. The neighbors of a point must show continuity.

16.3.3 SPATIAL RANDOM NOISE

We need a distribution of random values at discrete locations in space to represent densities, colors, and the like. At locations between these values, we need values that represent smooth transitions from one random value to the next. Such a distribution is called *spatial random noise.*

We can implement this by creating a three-dimension lattice of random numbers. At a lattice point, the value is the number stored there. We interpolate the values in between from the surrounding lattice points. A linear interpolation of the eight closest lattice points gives a reasonable smooth variation through space. Cubic interpolation of the surrounding 64 lattice points gives an even smoother variation, see PERL85 and FVFH90, p. 1015. We will show how to implement a 3D B-spline interpolation. With this approach the value of the texture is a function of position in 3D space.

IMPLEMENTATION

Implementing a spatial lattice requires a lot of memory, making it worthwhile to use the smallest possible memory unit for the individual lattice element. If we need only densities or gray values, one byte, giving 256 different values is sufficient. If color-*rgb* values are needed, however, then three bytes are required per lattice element. A lattice of 100 elements on each side then uses three megabytes of memory.

As an example, consider an object that is carved out of a material whose texture ranges from black to gray to white, distributed like spatial random noise. Only those parts of the texture that lie on the object's surface are visible. We can think of the object as being "inside" the texture. A ray hits only at a surface point. For this point, we compute the texture value and set the pixel color accordingly.

Two problems are immediately evident. The first is that the texture's fineness is directly related to the scale of the object's world coordinates. A small object with a diameter of 0.5 will fit into a single lattice cube; it will then show hardly any variation. However, this is easily solved by upscaling the hit point coordinates.

The second problem is the finite size of the whole lattice. Upscaling the hit point coordinates to give finer texture may bring the point outside the lattice. We solve this problem through modular arithmetic. Unfortunately, modular arithmetic will not work correctly if the lattice coordinates contain a change in sign, so all lattice points must be greater than or equal to zero. This is guaranteed if we treat the lattice as a 3D array and if array subscripts ranging from zero upward are the coordinates of lattice points. The lattice will be entirely in the positive octant.

To carve the solid from the lattice, we must shift the solid into the positive octant by adding numbers to the hit point coordinates. The numbers must be chosen large enough to make sure that every solid will be entirely in it. Numbers too large do not matter, because modular arithmetic will always bring the coordinate back into the lattice.

We must consider yet another problem. Through the modular arithmetic, we can obtain an almost infinitely large lattice. Still, we cannot texture a solid with the lattice value at the actual coordinates of the hit point. If we move the solid inside the texture, the solid would change its texture while moving through the standing lattice. We do not want this, especially if we do animation! Therefore, we must determine the texture of a centered solid that is rotated to its unit position. We can easily accomplish this by translating the hit point by the solid's center and rotating it with the solid's arbitrary-to-unit rotation matrix. The centered and rotated solid is then shifted into the lattice by a fixed amount. Doing this guarantees that the lattice-texture "follows" all the solid's movements.

Observe that the hit point will be multiplied by the rotation matrix, rather than the transformation matrix. The latter would scale it to a point on the unit solid. As a result the growth or shrinkage of the textured solid would grow or shrink the texture as well. However, that contradicts the principle that the solid is being carved out of the material. A large solid should exhibit a finer texture in relation to its size than a small one when textured with the same material.

Geometrically, we imagine a lattice as a 3D array, although we do not implement it as such. We will implement it through a class with a constructor for dynamic memory allocation and will have initialization and member functions to operate on the lattice. We treat the allocated memory as if it were a 3D array, although we have to do subscript arithmetic explicitly because of the dynamic size. The spatial coordinates of the lattice point with integer subscripts i, j, and k are $(i\ j\ k)$.

Our geometrical convention for a 3D lattice is that the first array subscript correspond to the x-coordinate, increasing from left to right. The second subscript corresponds to the y-coordinate, increasing from bottom to top. The third subscript corresponds to z, increasing from near to far. We call the eight lattice points that are adjacent in the x-, y- and z-directions an *8-cube*. Below, we also need the cube consisting of $4 \times 4 \times 4$ adjacent points, the *64-cube*.

Linear interpolation in the lattice requires that we first determine the 8-cube that contains a given point $(x\ y\ z)$. We call the two x-coordinates of the 8-cube l and r for left and right; the y-coordinates b and t for bottom and top; the z-coordinates n and f for near and far. We obtain l, b, and n by truncating the values of x, y, and z to integers. Then the integers are reduced modulo the size of the lattice. By adding 1 to each of l, b, and n, we obtain r, t, and f. These we reduce again, as the 8-cube might straddle the boundary of the lattice. The 8-cube is shown in Figure 16.15. The distances from $(x\ y\ z)$ to the left, bottom, and frontface constitute its relative position inside the cube.

We show how to do a 3D linear interpolation for the position (x y z) from the eight cube corners. First, we compute the relative position of (x y z) within the cube. Subtracting l, b, and n from x, y, and z respectively gives us the position (fx fy fz) within the cube. We have $0 \le (fx, fy, fz) < 1$.

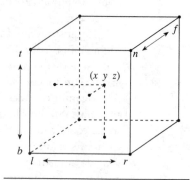

We begin the interpolation by first interpolating the cube's four left-to-right corner pairs with $(1-fx)$ and fx as the respective weights. We take the resulting four values as two pairs and interpolate them bottom-to-top with the weights $(1-fy)$ and fy. The resulting two values are interpolated front-to-back with the weights $(1-fz)$ and fz. The demonstration code below should clarify the concept.

Figure 16.15   Position of a point inside an 8-cube

```
//*************************************************************

#include "../Shape3d/point3.h"
#define SIZE 20
unsigned char lat[SIZE][SIZE][SIZE] ;

double linpol(const point3_t& p)
{
    int    l = int(p.givx()) %SIZE ,                    // left
           r = (l+1)           %SIZE ,                   // right
           b = int(p.givy()) %SIZE ,                    // bottom
           t = (b+1)           %SIZE ,                   // top
           n = int(p.givz()) %SIZE ,                    // near
           f = (n+1)           %SIZE ;                   // far
    double fx = p.givx() - int(p.givx()) ,
           fy = p.givy() - int(p.givy()) ,
           fz = p.givz() - int(p.givz()) ;
            // 3D linear interpolation of eight lattice points
    return (1-fz)*((1-fy)*((1-fx)*lat[l][b][n] + fx*lat[r][b][n])
             + fy *((1-fx)*lat[l][t][n] + fx*lat[r][t][n]))
         + fz *((1-fy)*((1-fx)*lat[l][b][f] + fx*lat[r][b][f])
             + fy *((1-fx)*lat[l][t][f] + fx*lat[r][t][f])) ;
}


//*************************************************************
```

Linear interpolation does not give smooth transitions across cube boundaries. However, the discontinuities are not very noticeable. The resulting noise pattern is adequate for creating textures.

Let us now look at cubic interpolation. We are explicit about it because it cannot be found in other textbooks and is difficult for beginning students. The source code is the function `charlat_t::cubpol()` in `Raytrace/charlat.c`.

Cubic interpolation in an 8-cube is done by using the 64-cube in which this 8-cube is centered. The lattice-subscripts are obtained as above, but one must subtract 1 from the lower subscript and add 1 to the higher one to get four subscripts in each coordinate.

We first interpolate in the x-direction, then in the y-direction, and finally in the z-direction. Each interpolation uses four values. In going through the 64-cube in the x-, or y-, or z-directions, we find four lattice points. We consider these to be values at the equispaced arguments -1, 0, 1, and 2 for a one-dimensional polynomial interpolation in that direction. (The relative position values (fx fy fz) are between 0 and 1 and relate to the central 8-cube.) We first do 16 interpolations from left to right through the 64-cube at fx. We take the resulting 16 values as four groups of four vertically aligned values. We interpolate these from bottom to top at fy. The four values that result are interpolated from front to back at fz.

In each of the interpolations we may use a cubic Newton-Gregory polynomial, a Catmull-Rom polynomial, or a uniform cubic B-spline. By changing the formula in the function `cubic()` (in the file `charlat.c`), we can have any of these. Since the interpolating polynomials are different for different 8-cubes, there will be practically invisible discontinuities at the transitions from one to the next. These discontinuities are in the first derivative with Newton-Gregory, in the second with Catmull-Rom, and in the third with B-splines. The first two methods have the disadvantage that interpolation values greater or smaller than those of the lattice points can result. If these exceed the color range, we must truncate them to avoid severe color discontinuities.

B-spline approximation has neither of these problems and produces a very smooth pattern. We therefore use it in the code.

16.3.4 MARBLE

There are endless varieties and kinds of marble. Only a few types have been successfully modeled so far. We present and explain the kind that is penetrated by relatively regular veins of darker or lighter color, as done by Perlin, PERL85; also see FVFH90, p. 1046ff.

We use a *turbulence texture* to create this marble texture. This texture is based on a 3D random noise. *Turbulence* itself is a certain type of random noise, which is created by summing up noise values of increasing frequencies and decreasing intensities. The frequency of a given noise function can be increased by multiplying the argument (x y z) by the same factor in all three coordinates.

If, for example, we multiply the hit point by two before interpolating it, the resulting noise pattern will be twice as fine because the point moves through the lattice twice as quickly. This leads, of course, to a more rapid repetition of the lattice through the modulo arithmetic. The turbulence used by Perlin sums up the noise values for frequencies that double with each summation term. We do not increase the fineness of the noise terms after they become smaller than pixel size; such a fine variation would not be visible. For a "normally" scaled original noise pattern (approximately 50 to 100 pixels per noise variation) four or five terms give enough turbulence. We implement turbulence through the function `turb()` using cubic interpolation for the noise and summing only four terms.

The weights of the terms have the ratios 8:4:2:1 and sum to 1. `Turb()` returns double values ranging from 0 to 255.

The marble design itself has distorted layers of darker color running vertically through it. Disregard the lattice and the noise for now and define the texture at a point $(x\ y\ z)$ as $(\sin(x) + 1)/2$. Observe that y and z are not used. This definition has values ranging from 0 to 1 with a period of 2π. Displaying 0 as black and 1 as white with gray between, $(\sin(x) + 1)/2$ defines vertical layers that run parallel to the $(y\ z)$-plane. The transitions are gradual from black to white to black. The layers are at a distance of 2π from each other. Going from left to right through space, we alternately enter black and white areas. Parallel to the $(y\ z)$-plane, there is no variation.

If we distort these layers by adding `turb(x,y,z)` to the argument of `sin()`, we obtain something that resembles marble. The argument for `turb()` involves all three coordinates. This causes the distortions of the sine-waves along paths parallel to the x-axis to differ when these paths differ in y and z. This gives layers that are bent and gnarly, wider in some places and narrower in others.

It is essential that the magnitude and fineness of the distorting turbulence be correct. We accomplish this by multiplying `turb()` by a factor to set the magnitude and by multiplying the argument of `turb()` by a factor to set the fineness. If the magnitude of the turbulence is too great, the layers break up, becoming loops and knots; they will not look like veins. Exaggerating the fineness leads to veins that oscillate too much and might obscure the presence of veins completely.

OO DESIGN AND CLASS SPECIFICATIONS

Lattices require huge amounts of memory. (This is why lattices and solid textures cannot be implemented in DOS applications.) To save memory in at least a moderate way we use only a single character per lattice point. The class `charlat_t` represents a 3D lattice of unsigned characters.

The constructor is given the size of the lattice and allocates the memory on the free store. It initializes every lattice point with a random value between 0 and 255. The function `charlat_t::cubpol()` interpolates cubically for a given point, while `charlat_t::turb()` computes a turbulence at a given point using cubic interpolation.

```
//*********************** File charlat.h ***********************

#ifndef CHARLAT_T
#define CHARLAT_T

#include "../Raytrace/rpoint.h"

class f_t {                         // for overloaded operator [] [] []
   long f ;
   unsigned char* lat ;
   int size ;
public:
   f_t(int f,unsigned char* lat,int size) :
      f(f*size*size) , lat(lat) , size(size) {}
   unsigned char* operator[] (int i) const
   {return lat + f + i*size;}
} ;
```

```
class charlat_t
{
   unsigned char* lat ;
   int size ;
public:
   charlat_t(int) ;                                // constructor
   ~charlat_t() {delete lat;}
   double cubpol(const rpoint_t&) const ;
   double turb(const rpoint_t&) const ;
   f_t operator[] (int i) const
   {return f_t(i,lat,size);}
} ;


#endif

//*******************************************************************
```

The texture function `marble()` is short, so we show it here to accompany the explanations. Marble is created using the technique explained above. The function declares a static local lattice of unsigned characters of the desired size. It shifts the hit point to the center and rotates it by the rotation matrix of the solid to which it belongs.

The function uses a sin wave of period $\pi/10$ for the layers. The argument of the sin function is distorted using the turbulence function specified in the lattice. That distortion varies from 0 to 36. (`Cubpol()` and `turb()` return values between 0 and 255, because they are member functions of a character lattice.) The argument for `turb()` is the hit point times 2.7. We found all these numbers empirically. Experimentating with different numbers helps one develop a feeling for this process.

```
//*********************** File marble.c ***********************

#include <math.h>
#include "../Raytrace/charlat.h"
#include "../Raytrace/solid.h"


texture_t marble(solid_t* s,const rpoint_t& hit,double)
{
   static charlat_t lat(50) ;
   rpoint_t h = (hit - s->givcen())*s->givrot() ;
   rpoint_t fhit(h*2.7) ;

   double d = (sin(10*h.givx() + lat.turb(fhit)/7) + 1)/2 ;
   return texture_t(rgb_t(d,d,d)*0.8 + rgb_t(0.1,0.1,0.1),0,0);
}

//*******************************************************************
```

16.3.5 GRANITE

Granite comes in many different varieties. The most characteristic feature of all granites is that they contain randomly shaped clusters of crystals of different sizes and colors. A conglomeration of crystal-shaped bodies can be produced by a nonsmooth transition between the lattice values. A nonsmooth transition is achieved by a step function. We now clarify the concept of a step function on a two-dimensional lattice.

We assume two values in each lattice point: a *color value*, v, and a *weight*, w. Consider the square formed by four adjacent lattice points; an arbitrary point $(x\ y)$ is inside with both coordinates between 0 and 1. We do not want to give $(x\ y)$ a color value that is intermediate between the four lattice values, but instead precisely one of those values. Our decision about assigning $(x\ y)$ a color value is based on the weights of the lattice points.

If we were simply to give $(x\ y)$ the color of the closest grid point, we would divide the square into four smaller squares. In the 3D lattice, this would create regularly shaped cubes with constant color values surrounding the individual lattice points. We avoid this if we base the choice between lattice values on the ratio of their weights.

For example, we base the decision between left and right at the bottom of the square on x and the weights w_{lb} and w_{rb}. To compare the weights to x, we must divide them by their sum, $w_{lb} + w_{rb}$, to normalize. That is, we assign to x the left value if $x < w_{lb}/(w_{lb} + w_{rb})$. Otherwise, we assign the right value. We can see that in the case of equal weights, the left half of the line would be assigned the left value and the right half the right value—the line is divided in half.

At the top of the square, we base the decision on x and the weights w_{lt} and w_{rt}. For the arbitrary point $(x\ y)$ between bottom and top, we base the decision on a weighted sum of the bottom and top ratios with the weights $1-y$ and y respectively. We set:

$$b = w_{lb}/(w_{lb} + w_{rb}) \qquad \text{the normalized bottom left weight}$$
$$t = w_{lt}/(w_{lt} + w_{rt}) \qquad \text{the normalized top left weight}$$

and we choose left if $x < b*(1-y) + t*y$.

We make the decision between bottom and top analogously. Figure 16.16 shows a square of four lattice points with weights at the corners. The color values are not shown. The combination of left-right and bottom-top decisions causes the indicated partition of the square. In each partition, the color values are constant and equal to the color value in the lattice point. They are shown by the gray values of the areas.

Figure 16.17 shows the effect of such partitions in a larger portion of a 2D lattice. The areas with equal gray values are bounded by straight lines and are irregular in shape.

The result of such partitions in a 3D lattice are irregularly shaped concave or convex solids bounded by planes. The weight ratios determine their sizes and shapes and the color values determine their colors. Within each irregular solid, the color value is constant. In this way, one can approximate the crystalline structure of granite.

The lattice we choose has a weight value and a color value per lattice point and is represented by the class `rgblat_t`. The weight is an unsigned character, while the color is expressed by a `charrgb_t`, which consists of three unsigned characters. The step-interpolation in the lattice is done with a member function.

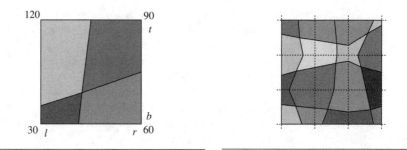

Figure 16.16   Step function based on weight ratios   Figure 16.17   Irregular partitions in a 2D lattice

In natural granite, there is a correlation between the color, size, and frequency of the crystals. We could probably simulate this by correlating the weights and values in the lattice points, but we use a different method to simulate the tendency of crystals with equal color values to form small clusters at random locations.

We use a member function cluster(), which is given a random lattice point. It assigns a certain color value to this point and then randomly grabs neighboring lattice points, giving them the same color value. This creates a cluster of points with the same color. (The weights are ignored in this process.) We also want to achieve clusters that are neither regularly round nor lacking in compactness, which would make them look fuzzy and too spread out. They should randomly be somewhere between these extremes.

Up to a distance of two, the neighbors of a given lattice point can be specified by number triples (i j k) in which the components have the values -2, -1, 0, 1, or 2. Index i stands for left-right, j for up-down, and k for near-far. One can produce these triples with a random number generator. If we let the numbers -1, 0, and $+1$ occur more frequently than -2 and $+2$, the adjacent neighbors will be chosen more frequently than the farther ones. This creates more compact clusters. (Theoretically, such a cluster can grow to a size of 125 points—a regular $5 \times 5 \times 5$ cube. Such a cube is undesirable, because it is too rectangular, so we discard triples in which all numbers are -2 or $+2$. This prevents the corners of the cube from being chosen, creating a more round cluster.) The function triple() below creates these triples.

The function cluster() calls triple() up to 250 times. This exceeds the number of 116 possible neighbors. If a call grabs a neighbor that is not yet a member of the cluster, we decrease the number of possible calls by two. If the grabbed neighbor is already a member of the cluster, this triple is wasted, but we decrease the number of calls only by one to have more chances for grabbing new neighbors. Not decreasing it at all can cause infinite loops. This cluster function creates relatively compact, randomly shaped clusters. Using fewer than 250 possible triple calls per cluster increases the frequency of smaller clusters. We could also make this number random. We vary the colors a little from cluster to cluster, but not within a cluster.

We interpolate between lattice points in the discontinuous manner described above. This gives sharp transitions from cluster areas to the surrounding material, which shows some small-scale crystalline structure itself. If the initial lattice values vary only a little, the surrounding material is more uniform in color. Preparing this lattice is time-consuming, but it is done only once. After its creation, the texturing goes as quickly as with any other solid texture.

The technique we describe is only one of many ways to create clusters, and the cluster method is only one of many ways to create granite. Mainly, we want to show the versatility of the lattice approach.

OO DESIGN AND CLASS SPECIFICATIONS

The class rgblat_t represents a lattice of *rgb*-values. To save on memory, we do not use the type rgb_t, which consists of three doubles but the structures charrgb_t and latpoint_t. Charrgb_t consists of three unsigned characters and latpoint_t consists of one unsigned character and a charrgb_t.

The constructor for the *rgb*-lattice is given the size and allocates the memory on the free store. It initializes every lattice point to a random weight between 1 and 255 (no zero weights are allowed) and a random color value that varies slightly in a narrow range. This represents the more or less uniform surrounding material of the clusters. Then it creates 1400 clusters of dark color, 1000 clusters of lighter color and 1000 clusters of an in-between color. The number of clusters must be found empirically and depends on the size of the lattice. Decreasing the number of dark clusters, for example, immediately appears as a rarification of the dark specks in the granite. Increasing the size of the lattice without increasing the number of clusters also rarifies the clusters.

The color of the clusters is not constant, but varies more or less within a certain range. We can set the variation and range through the factor of the random call and the added weight. The variation of the individual red, green, or blue components can be influenced separately. For this, see the code Raytrace/rgblat.c.

```
//*************************** File rgblat.h *********************

#ifndef RGBLAT_T
#define RGBLAT_T

#include "../Raytrace/charrgb.h"
#include "../Raytrace/rpoint.h"

struct latpoint_t
{
   unsigned char w ;                                    // weight
   charrgb_t  v ;                                  // color value
} ;

class rgblat_t
{
   latpoint_t* lat ;
   int size ;
   void cluster(int,charrgb_t) ;
public:
   rgblat_t(int) ;                                   // constructor
   ~rgblat_t() {delete lat;}
   charrgb_t steppol(const point_t&) const ;
} ;

#endif

//*****************************************************************
```

It is certainly worthwhile to develop a language for defining these parameters and an input mechanism for setting the parameters without the need to recompile. This would allow to test a wide variety of settings to find good granite or other textures. The provided code does not implement this. Changing the settings requires recompilation.

The function granite() is short, so we show it here to accompany the explanations. The function declares a static local lattice of type rgblat_t of the desired size. This initializes it with random clusters as described above. The hit point to be textured is shifted to the center and rotated by the rotation matrix of the solid to which it belongs. Then it is translated into the positive quadrant by adding the point (10,10,10). Finally, it is scaled, which sets the fineness of the granite texture.

```
//********************* File granite.c ****************************

texture_t granite(solid_t* s,rpoint_t hit,double)
{
    static rgblat_t lat(80) ;
    rpoint_t h = (hit - s->givcen())*s->givrot() ;

    h = (h + rpoint_t(10,10,10))*50;              // shift and refine
    charrgb_t c = lat.steppol(h) ;
    return texture_t(c.r/255.0,c.g/255.0,c.b/255.0,0.2,0);
}


//*****************************************************************
```

AVOIDING TEXTURE REPETITION

When texturing a large flat area, for example a tabletop, we cannot avoid repeating the lattice. Simply increasing the lattice size beyond $100 \times 100 \times 100$ is not feasible because of the memory requirements. The modulo arithmetic will take care of the repetition. Unfortunately, the repetitions are perceptible and disturbing because the human visual system is extremely sensitive to regularities.

There is a simple method for avoiding the regularities. It consists of carving the flat area out of the lattice in a slightly slanted way. The difficulty is that the lattice itself cannot be rotated. The object can be rotated, but the texture specified for it would follow that movement. The trick is to define the texture, not for the object itself, but for a node on a higher level than the object. If that node is rotated slightly, the texture will follow it; the object, however, is rotated back by the same amount, so it still has its original position and the texture is applied to it in a slanted manner.

We show this through the scene file description of a flat box. Instead of defining:

```
box(2 0.1 1.5) 0 0 0   0 0 0   marble
```

we specify:

```
(
    box(2 0.1 1.5) 0 0 4   0 0 0   NULL
  - 0 0 -4   0 0 0   marble
    sphere(1)      0 0 0   10 0 0   NULL
)
```

Observe that we need a "dummy" primitive in order to establish a higher level node. We choose a sphere because it is easy to check for intersection. The sphere is subtracted from the box, but is so far to the right that it does not change the box.

SURFACE TEXTURING VERSUS SOLID TEXTURING

The question is often posed, why bother defining a 3D texture in a lattice when one can simply scan a natural granite, marble, or wood map and paste it on the object with surface texturing? The latter method is fine only if one pastes onto a completely flat surface. But if the texture is to be exposed in more than one dimension, a mapped surface texture would show inconsistencies. Wood is a perfect example. If a wooden tabletop shows its surface as well as its front side, the wood texture will look different in these two areas. In the surface, the wood grain would run lengthwise, while in the front side we would look directly into the year-rings. The change in pattern is even more complicated in a wooden sphere or torus. The situation is identical with marble, granite, and other natural textures. Solid texturing is the only way to produce a correct texture.

SUGGESTED READINGS

Additional information on solid texturing and further literature references (for mathematically oriented readers) is available in FVFH90. WATT89 has a good and detailed introduction to flat and solid texturing.

EXERCISES

SECTION 16.3

1. (Senior project or thesis) Develop a specification language to define a parameter setting for defining of marble or granite. Provide an input mechanism that reads a file specified in this language and sets the parameters accordingly. With these tools, test a variety of settings to find good marble or granite textures.

2. (Senior project or thesis) Develop a wood texture. Define the wood texture inside a fine lattice by producing year-rings and setting the lattice points on the year-rings to a darker color. Distort the rings slightly to avoid exact roundness; change the distance between year-rings and their thickness slightly and randomly to avoid regularity. Introduce slight artifacts and irregularities in the nonyear-ring material. (This lattice can be cyclicly repeated, but only in a "lengthwise" direction.)

17

ANIMATION

This chapter explains how conventional animated pictures are made, how the computer can assist in this, and how to animate computer-produced pictures.

17.0   **Introduction** defines what is meant by animation, how computers relate to it, and how a sequence of still pictures can appear as smooth motion.

17.1   **Devices for Producing Animation** shows the different processes for exhibiting animated pictures on movie screens and CRTs.

17.2   **Computer-Assisted Animation** tells how the laborious procedures needed for conventional animation can be simplified by generating "in-between" pictures with a computer.

17.3   **Real-Time Animation** describes ways to add animation to computer graphics; sprites and lookup table changes are two such procedures. Animation for flight simulation is an important application that requires sophisticated hardware.

17.4   **Frame-by-Frame Animation** can produce complex moving pictures on simple computers, but not in real time. The individual pictures are displayed with a device other than the computer.

17.0   INTRODUCTION

Long associated with cartoons and sometimes rising to higher art forms, animation seems quite the opposite of mathematics and logic. At first glance, it appears to be something that depends on intuition and feelings. The computer can play an important role in these productions, but there has been much reluctance to accept it. Today, however, the movie industry uses computers extensively in doing animation, and computer-generated scenes are common in television, particularly in commercials and cartoons.

Our study of animation in relation to computer graphics must begin with a look at conventional animation methods. We first define animation, investigate why animation is possible at all, examine some ways in which the computer assists the animator, and finally see how we can add animation to computer graphics.

Animation essentially means to make something "come alive." The term also means the technique of producing moving pictures. Animation is not necessarily just movement, although "movement is the essence of animation" (HALA74). Animation can also involve a change of shape or color. What role can the computer play in animating pictures? How can we add animation to computer graphics? In other words, how can we use a computer to produce pictures that move rather than just stand still?

Animation works because of human physiology, so this is where we begin.

When we see a movie on a TV screen or in the theater, we perceive smooth and continuous motion. This movement is really an illusion achieved with a rapidly displayed sequence of still pictures that differ only slightly from one to the next.

A real object moving through our field of vision excites a sequence of light-sensitive cells in the eye. These cells lie on the path of the object's projection onto the retina. Strictly speaking, in terms of the excited cells, there is a jerky change—a *digitization*—because there are only a finite number of discrete cells; we are not really provided with a continuously moving impulse. The brain's visual processes create the sensation of continuous motion.

Our optical perception system has developed the ability to cope with a lot of jerkiness in the impulses. Each blink of the eye interrupts the optical impulses for a short time without disturbing our vision. Obstacles between the moving object and our eyes, changing light levels, and shadows passing over the moving object all create discontinuity. We "see around" these things, however, with an ability to integrate jerky optical signals into a perception of smooth motion.

This ability is so fully developed that we cannot see jerkiness under a certain threshold even if we try. Nobody is able to see a neon lamp flicker, although it does so 60 times per second. The integration effect implies that we cannot see a picture that does not last long enough, even if it is completely different from the images before and after. The picture is integrated out of existence by the overwhelming presence of the images that come before and after.

What is the limit in jerkiness? When do the separate scenes appear as distinct images? We percieve continuous motion when we see pictures taken of an object every 1/30 of a second. These pictures can be hand-drawn or can be photographs taken in a rapid sequence. We can actually present as few as twenty pictures per second before the motion seems somewhat jerky.

Interestingly, the smoothing or integrating effect does not occur with equal facility for impulses received on different areas of the retina. You might have observed that you can see the flicker of a CRT screen displaying a still picture when you look at it from the corner of your eye rather than straight on.

17.1 DEVICES FOR PRODUCING ANIMATION

Two very different kinds of devices produce moving pictures—CRT screens, whose pixels are rapidly changed, and conventional movie projectors. (Recently, small liquid crystal displays that are fast enough to serve as TV displays have appeared on the market, but we will not consider these.) We look at the film projector technique first.

A *film projector* produces images by shining a white light beam through a transparent medium onto which the picture is painted with transparent dyes. On passing through the dyes, the light is robbed of certain wavelengths (a subtractive process) and the remaining colors hit the screen, producing the picture that is then reflected to our eyes. The projector holds each picture frame for a while and then exchanges it quickly for the next one; during the change, the light is temporarily blocked off. About 100,000 individual pictures are stored on the film for an hourlong movie. Creating this many individual pictures takes much, much longer than the time needed to display them.

A video movie uses a *CRT*. The CRT is used both for television and for computer graphics; technically, there is no difference between a graphics monitor and a TV monitor. You already know how images are produced on this device. Animation on a CRT screen requires a rapid sequence of different images, at least 20 per second. While the display tubes are the same for TV and computer graphics, there is a basic difference in the way the information is provided to the display circuitry for each of them.

If the CRT is used as a *graphics monitor*, the image is always held in a frame buffer. This buffer tells the circuitry what color to put into each of the hundreds of thousands of pixels that compose the screen. To change the picture, we must change the contents of the frame buffer.

This proves to be a speed bottleneck. The frame buffer is comparable to one frame of movie film, while the display circuitry is analogous to the film projector. Animation on a graphics CRT monitor actually means producing new contents for the frame buffer at very high speed.

Several techniques have been developed to overcome the speed bottleneck. A common one is to work with more than one frame buffer. While one buffer is being displayed, the graphics system fills the other with a new picture. Then the memory area to be scanned by the circuitry is changed to the other frame buffer simply by changing a base address in the CRT controller. Changing the base address takes essentially no time, so the displayed picture changes at once. The viewer is never aware of the frame buffer's changing.

Another technique uses memory areas besides the frame buffer to hold parts of the image. As the frame buffer is scanned, the scan jumps to the other area, then back again to the frame buffer. This method is used to display cursors, sprites, and related objects.

Even so, it is still a major problem to create or change the contents of the frame buffers fast enough for animation. It can be done with conventional hardware for very simple pictures and with extremely fast hardware for more complicated pictures, such as that used for flight simulation. A computer graphics system is generally not well adapted to produce animation.

If the CRT is used as a *TV monitor*, there is no counterpart to a frame buffer that holds the picture information. The process starts at the video camera, which transforms the scene into an electronic signal. The receiver portion of the TV set obtains the signal continuously from the air, transforms it through hardware into RGB intensities and synchronization pulses, and feeds these to the display circuitry. There is no fixed relation between the picture information and a particular pixel location on the screen, except indirectly through horizontal and vertical synchronization. The major difference is that the TV signal is analog, while the graphics information is digital. The signals for a whole line of the display are one continuous stream. No memory has to be scanned, created, or changed to make the display. Therefore, there is no speed bottleneck. The signal can easily carry the information for 30 different pictures per second. (We are omitting details of interlacing, phase alternation, and so on.)

The essential point is that even a TV monitor creates only still pictures, although in rapid sequence. No picture ever moves in and of itself.

The *video recorder* can record TV information. It stores individual pictures on a magnetic tape. The signals for one field—between two vertical sync signals—are recorded as they come from the air onto the tape as one track—a slanted path of magnetization across the tape. The frames for a video recorder can also be produced directly with a video camera.

Thirty frames per second can easily be recorded and a tape of reasonable length can contain the information for several hours of animation. When playing back a videotape, the TV set reads the signal off the tape, transforms it, and feeds it to the display circuitry, just as if it received the signal from the air.

Producing a videotape with a video camera is a much faster process than producing a film. It is becoming increasingly popular because no chemical development is involved. However, the quality is still not equal to that of film.

We see that film plus film projector and video camera plus CRT are the two major devices for producing animation for movies and television. Where does computer graphics come in?

17.2 COMPUTER-ASSISTED ANIMATION

When we speak of animated movies, we mean animation with drawn pictures, not movies staged with actors in real-world scenes. For several decades, Walt Disney movies have been a prototype. Today, there are countless animated cartoons on TV and many animated TV commercials. The techniques involved have evolved rapidly, using the most up-to-date equipment to make their production fast and economical. The newest tool in this area is the computer with its graphic capabilities.

CONVENTIONAL ANIMATION

When creating an animated movie, someone first writes a script for the story. From the script, a series of pictures is drawn to show important moments in the story. This series of pictures is called the *storyboard*. A TV commercial might have about 15 different pictures.

Once the storyboard is created, the actual animation process begins. It involves producing hundreds or thousands of individual pictures, called *frames*, which then must be individually filmed or recorded on videotape. The process of producing all these frames can be mechanized in different ways; computer graphics is the most recent. Computers have a potential here that has barely begun to be tapped.

No matter how much we mechanize, the intervention of the human artist, the animator, will always be a considerable and costly part of the animation. The first step is the same as it was several decades ago. With the help of the storyboard, the most experienced and skilled animators draw *key frames*. These frames are selected for their central role in the motion because of their importance as anchors, their extreme positions in the movement, their typifying the character's postures and expressions, or for their special visual effects. The key frames are spread timewise throughout the development of motion between pictures in the storyboard. They are not close enough together to be used as the actual animation frames.

The final animation is achieved by filling the gaps between adjacent key frames with in-between frames. How many need to be drawn to fill the gap depends on how far apart the key frames are in time. In-between frames are easier to produce than key frames and in conventional animation they were drawn by the less skilled and less expensive apprentice animators. Today they can be drawn by the computer! Figures 17.1 through 17.4 represent a sequence of animation frames.

   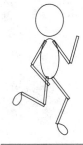

Figure 17.1   *Figure 17.2*   *Figure 17.3*   *Figure 17.4*

Sequence of animation frames

COMPUTER GENERATED IN-BETWEEN FRAMES

You will better understand how this process can be mechanized if you first look at some conventional techniques used to facilitate it. A common technique is to decompose an animation picture into several parts that can move more or less independently. These parts are drawn individually on a clear plastic material that are called *cels* (short for cellulose). The individual cels can be overlaid to produce the whole picture and then filmed or video recorded as one frame. For example, when the animation character tilts its head or lifts an arm, the change can be produced by appropriately moving the individual cels that show the head and the arm. Consecutive in-between frames differ only slightly from each other so often several in-between frames can often be created this way. Figure 17.5 shows eight cels containing movable parts of the cartoon character above.

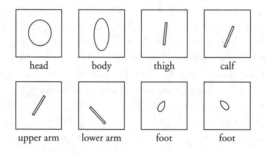

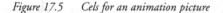

Figure 17.5   Cels for an animation picture

There are always parts in the picture that have to be drawn anew in each in-between frame, such as facial expressions, but the amount of hand drawing can be drastically reduced with this method. It takes advantage of the fact that not everything in a picture changes from one in-between frame to the next. If the character is talking, it may be enough to have just mouth and hand movements, making no change to the rest of the picture. This greatly increases the speed of production.

It is now possible to enter a key frame into a computer by using an animation paint system, a specialized version of those we will discuss in the next chapter. A graphics tablet allows us just to trace the key frame. The animation paint system composes the picture as sequences of strokes. A *stroke* is a straight or curved line portion of the drawing. While the stroke is being displayed, the system creates a sequence of number pairs and stores them internally. These number pairs are the coordinates of the points through which the stroke goes. Strokes stored in this manner can be handled mathematically by the computer; they can be translated, rotated, or changed in size.

The animator enters the key frame by drawing all of its strokes. (Actually the entire key frame does not have to be entered. Something resembling the above cel technique is possible, letting the animator work "celwise" and later overlay the cels.) The animator then enters the next cel in the same manner. It is important that it be drawn with the same strokes, which now, of course, are somewhat different. The graphics system must know how the strokes in the two cels correspond.

Some systems allow the user more freedom; the number of strokes can be different in the two cels. In such a case, the system will divide the strokes into shorter ones to match them.

If the animator tells the computer how many in-between frames to produce, the computer will do an interpolation to turn all the strokes of the first frame gradually into the strokes of the second frame. It will choose an interpolation step size to produce the desired number of in-between frames.

To transform one stroke into another gradually, the computer must progressively transform the points of one stroke into those of the next. To do this, it is necessary that both strokes consist of the same number of points. However, the user cannot determine the number of points in the stroke. The number of points in corresponding strokes may differ even if the strokes outwardly look identical.

The system can solve this problem. It determines which stroke has fewer points and then adds to them to make the numbers equal. Figure 17.6 will help explain this. On the left, we see a stroke in the first cel and on the right the corresponding stroke in the second cel. The first stroke consists of 11 points, the second only of 7. The system finds that it must add four points to the second stroke. There are six intervals in the second stroke, more than the points to be added. Special techniques are used to distribute the added points within the intervals. The inserted points are shown as circles.

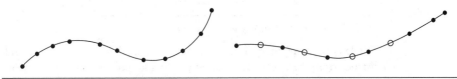

Figure 17.6   Adding points to a stroke

If there were more points to be inserted than intervals, the system would insert two points per interval at positions 1/3 and 2/3 among the original points until the excess points were accommodated, and then only one point per interval. This is not difficult because the portions between the points are always straight lines. Without going into too much detail, you can see that the system tries to distribute the inserted points as equally as possible. More about this in THAL86, for example.

Once the number of points in two corresponding strokes is equal, the points can be interpolated. The simplest form of this, *linear interpolation*, may result in jerky and unnatural motion between key frames. *Curvilinear interpolation*, if done properly, will give smooth motion. We could define two Bezier curves, one for each end of the stroke. In a user-friendly system, these are easy to specify interactively with a mouse or its equivalent. These curves connect the corresponding end points of the two strokes and thereby specify the paths these end points take from one key frame to the next. The computer will compute intermediate end points between the first stroke and the next stroke. For the other points on the strokes, the system will compute in-between curves along which they will be interpolated. The mathematics is simplified by having the user define the curves through their end points and the slopes at the ends instead of the four control points. Figure 17.7 shows this.

The two user-defined curves are curve 1 and curve 2. The strokes each have four points. We can see that the slopes at the inner points of the stroke change gradually. The closer a point is to an end point, the more its slope resembles that of the end point. The situation is somewhat exaggerated in the figure to make the concept clear. As the slopes are in-between, the curves will also be in-between. For each in-between frame, four new stroke points will be computed at intervals along these curves and connected by straight lines. Therefore, the first stroke gradually changes into the second stroke.

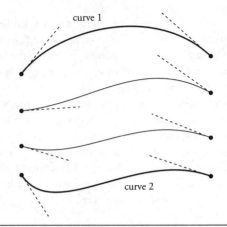

Figure 17.7   Gradually changing one curve into another

To determine the interpolated slope at an intermediate point, the system has to compute its distance from the end points. Slopes can be interpolated by treating them as normalized vectors, using a variant on the mathematics presented for Bezier curves to represent them in terms of slopes at their ends.

There is another problem in addition to obtaining smooth curves for the in-between points. We must avoid jerkiness in time. To make the motion slow, we just ask for many in-between frames. To make it fast, we request only a few. Still, there can be sudden changes in speed, jerkiness in time, at the key frames.

If we want the motion to speed up or slow down gradually, or if we just want to have better control over the speed, we must be able to specify where an in-between frame should be created along the in-between path. This can be done when we use curvilinear interpolation. We know from Chapter 6 that the path along a curve can be described by a parameter moving from 0 to 1 and that the points corresponding to equidistant parameter values are not necessarily equally spaced on the curve.

Figure 17.8 shows a Bezier curve shaped by manually pulling the slopes attached to the end points as indicated by the dotted lines (more about this in Chapter 18). The points on the curve correspond to parameter steps of 0.1. We see that those points are almost equidistant as long as the Bezier curve is smooth and not extreme in any way.

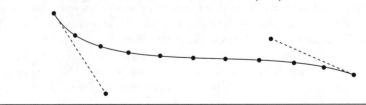

Figure 17.8   Points corresponding to parameter steps of 0.1

If we force the curve into sharper turns, for example, by pulling the slopes very hard, the points will be crowded together in the areas of sharp curvature, even though these correspond to equidistant parameter values (see Figure 17.9). Usually such sharp turns are not desired. If they are present, the motion will be slower there.

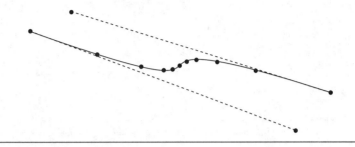

Figure 17.9   Crowding of equidistant parameter values

In Figure 17.10, we see the same curve as in Figure 17.8, but the points that correspond to successive parameter values occur at decreasing distances. It is easy to specify and implement this through a *bias number* that can crowd the points either to the left or right.

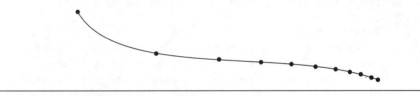
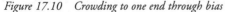

Figure 17.10   Crowding to one end through bias

In short, it is possible to give the animator control over the speed of the motion between two key frames. One could even have the computer specify the distance ratios interactively by clicking on a scale.

Another technique (REEV81) uses *moving point constraints*; the animator explicitly specifies each point along the path rather than paths along Bezier curves.

Look at Figure 17.11. The two heavy lines are the corresponding strokes of two key frames. The strokes' end points are connected by a sequence of points, the same number for each sequence. These are the "moving points." The system will figure out transformations (translations, rotations, and scaling) that gradually transform the stroke of key frame 1 into that of key frame 2, so that the end points move along these "moving points" and the inner points move along paths implied by these transformations. With this technique, the animator has even more control over the time intervals.

In a color movie, the frames all have to be colored in. This was another very time-consuming task in traditional animation, but it can be done by the computer. To fill an area outlined by a boundary, for example by solid lines, the computer uses a *seed fill*. This is very useful in paint systems. All the computer needs to know is the *seed point*, a start point within the area to be filled. If the animator provides the corresponding seeds in both key frames, the in-between seed points will always be inside the in-between areas, so the system can automatically color all in-between frames.

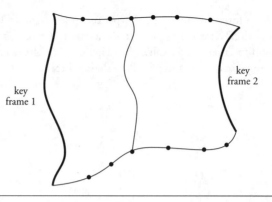

Figure 17.11   Transformation of a stroke along "moving points"

The animator can always manually insert or delete lines or make small changes and touch-ups in the in-between frames to accommodate details that the automation cannot easily do.

In animation systems, user friendliness, ease of entry, and speed are critical. With experience, natural-looking animations can be produced in a fraction of the time and with much less human effort than that needed for conventional animation.

DRAWBACKS

This kind of animation is strictly two-dimensional. Therefore, there are some things the system cannot do. All objects and characters are flat, not spatial. They do not have a front and back. It is not possible to turn an object around gradually, because new lines, formerly invisible, will appear and others will disappear. A pairwise correspondence between lines in adjacent key frames does not exist. The animator can overcome the problem by doing more touch-ups.

17.3   REAL-TIME ANIMATION

The previous section showed how computer graphics can assist hand-drawn animation. In several applications, the computer creates all frames of an animation sequence. One type is real-time animation.

Real-time animation may be the ultimate in computer graphics. It is the production of pictures that move directly on the screen, comparable to a moving TV picture. The best-known applications are computer games and flight simulation.

Consider computer games. The growing capacity and speed of computer chips allow real-time animation in software for games with a simple pictorial environment and background. We see an increasing number of games that are created only in software with "off the shelf" hardware. Special-purpose hardware, sprites, for example, can create games with more sophisticated pictorial environments and backgrounds.

COMPUTER GAMES IN SOFTWARE

Consider a software version of a well-known computer game—PacMan. The pictorial content is simple: a stationary maze and five moving objects. Whenever a picture is as simple as this, real-time animation is no problem. PacMan can be run on a desktop computer such as the Macintosh in black and white. The Motorola 68000 processor can update the picture in the frame buffer fast enough that the motion appears smooth. We refer to a specific machine only to make the example more concrete; the explanation below applies to any hardware.

To achieve speed, we employ at least two frame buffers; we will call them A and B. The technique is sometimes called *page flipping* or *ping-ponging*. We assume that A is currently being displayed and that B is being drawn in response to the user's input. Both frame buffers contain a copy of the stationary maze. The four ghosts and the PacMan are in constant motion. We will omit programming details, such as keeping track of the current positions of the five objects, reading the mouse or joystick input, producing the proper sounds, and so on.

Redrawing B involves first erasing all five figures by overdrawing them with little rectangles in the background color. Then all five objects are redrawn into the frame buffer at their new positions, done by copying templates. The smallest amount of motion is only one or two pixels and depends on the object and the situation. We know that the ghosts have to be able to move faster than the PacMan in order to produce excitement, so we must have the option to move by different amounts from frame to frame.

Drawing a template into the frame buffer can be time-consuming if the template has to be shifted by just a few pixels, because some parts of the template would cross word or byte boundaries. Therefore, many templates are provided, depending on the position in relation to the word or byte boundaries; these are called *offset templates*. If the four ghosts are all different, we might need up to 16×4 different ghost templates, but we always can copy them starting at word boundaries and save time.

For the PacMan we might need even more templates because its mouth points in one of four possible directions, the direction in which it moves. For each of these we need a different template and a set that is offset from word (or byte) boundaries. The opening and closing of the mouth itself is not really an additional burden because the offset templates can be prepared with different mouth apertures. Vertical movements do not need offset templates, so here we need only to have templates that achieve the mouth movement. Figure 17.12 shows two PacMan templates. The PacMan on the right is shifted by two pixels in relation to the byte boundaries, and the mouth is a little more closed.

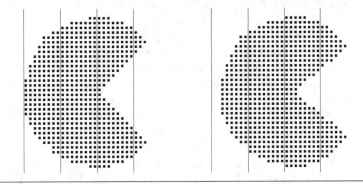

Figure 17.12   Two PacMan templates

The display is switched from *A* to *B* as soon as the copying is completed. Then the new situation is redrawn in the *A* buffer. We could wait for a vertical sync signal before switching the display, but this would cause a delay, so we switch on the fly whenever a new picture is ready. This can produce a little jerk in an object if the switch occurs exactly when the beam is halfway through drawing this object, but the gain in speed is worth this trade-off.

Such a program should be written in assembly language because a lot of low-level bit manipulation is involved. Most game programs for desktop computers are written in assembly.

GRAPHIC COMPUTER GAMES IN HARDWARE

The hardware versions of these games work with chips that support one or several sprites, for example, the Video Display Processors TMS9118, TMS9228, and so forth from Texas Instruments, the 6566/6567 chip used in the Commodore 64, or the "Denise" chip used in the Amiga.

A *sprite* is a little object whose pattern is positioned relative to a set of Cartesian (*x*,*y*)-coordinates. The position can be controlled to a resolution of one pixel, and the sprite is moved by changing only positional information. For this reason, the graphics information defining the sprite can remain in fixed RAM locations. This considerably reduces the software needed for this type of animated graphics.

It is essential to know that the sprite appears on the screen without being stored in the frame buffer. When the sprite appears on the screen, it covers whatever would otherwise be displayed there, but does not destroy it in the frame buffer. Thus, when the sprite moves, the background reappears automatically. The frame buffer often contains only a static background picture that does not need to be changed. To fully understand this, you must understand the principle of a bit-mapped graphics display. We explained this in Chapter 2, but we will repeat it briefly.

When a frame buffer is scanned to put its picture onto the CRT display, hardware produces each of the addresses of all the frame buffer's memory cells for every display cycle. This hardware also produces the signals for horizontal and vertical synchronization that keep the monitor circuitry in alignment. The different chips that do this may be an intelligent graphics coprocessor, a CRT controller or a sprite supporting chip. We will call it a *video display processor,* or *VDP.*

We will assume a somewhat simplified system that is not like any specific hardware, although our description will be closest to the sprite handling done in the Commodore 64 (see COMM82). Assume that the frame buffer consists of 320×200 pixels. (In the Commodore, there is actually characterwise display management even in bit-mapped mode, but we ignore this.)

The VDP has two internal registers that hold the *x*- and *y*-addresses of a certain location on the screen expressed as an (*x*,*y*)-coordinate pair. This address is the starting location on the screen for a sprite. We call it the *sprite x-address* and the *sprite y-address.* After producing the addresses of one horizontal scan line, the VDP always checks the sprite *y*-address. If this *y*-address equals that of the scan line, the first raster line of the sprite is included in the scan line. To do this, the VDP checks a certain location in RAM, usually at the end of the video memory, which contains a *sprite pointer,* the starting address of the sprite description. This points to the sprite description in a bit map. It is like the bit map for a character, but is usually larger in size. The 6566/6567 chip from Commodore works with descriptions that are 63 bytes long, corresponding to bit maps of 24 × 21 bits. Commodore's name for a sprite is a movable object (MOB).

When the scan line y-value is equal to the sprite y-address, certain internal counters and comparisons start working. In principle, this is what is done. At some place during the scan line, the current x-position of the frame buffer scan will be equal to the sprite x-address. At that point, instead of producing the frame buffer address corresponding to pixel $(x\ y)$, the VDP will produce the sprite starting address that it found when checking the RAM at the end of the video memory. That sprite starting address is updated appropriately (3 is added in the case of the Commodore because the sprite is 3 bytes = 24 bits wide). The net result is that the contents of the sprite description rather than the frame buffer are sent to the display circuitry.

Figure 17.13 shows this schematically. On the left is RAM memory, partly used as frame buffer and partly as sprite pointers and sprite descriptions. On the right are some registers of a sprite-supporting chip. This holds the sprite addresses that define locations in the frame buffer (that is, on the screen) along with color registers. The essential idea of the technique is that the chip scans either the frame buffer or the sprite description.

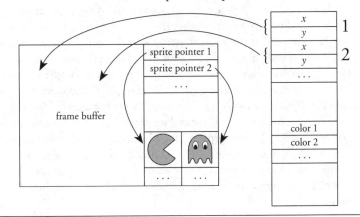

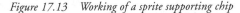

Figure 17.13   Working of a sprite supporting chip

The content of the sprite description is also checked before being sent to the display circuitry. When a bit in this description is 1, the specified sprite color is sent out; when the bit is 0, the frame buffer information corresponding to this location is sent out. This makes the sprite transparent where it is uncolored. The sprite color is held in a separate register. In order to have several sprites, the chip must provide for more of these register pairs, color registers, and associated checks.

The programmer can define the starting address of the sprite description, the sprite description itself, and the sprite color. Where the programmer puts the sprite description is up to him or her. Creating a sprite involves writing bit maps into the RAM areas pointed to by the sprite pointers. The 6566/6567 checks up to eight sprite pointers per scan line and therefore can have the parts of eight different sprites on one scan line. To move the sprites, we write into the register pairs that contain their screen positions, changing them during vertical blanking, that is, between two frames. When the next frame is displayed, the sprites will be at those positions.

The 6566/6567 is a hardware device that also handles collision detection between sprites and between a sprite and objects specified in the foreground color. The chips of the TMS9118 family also do this. A collision occurs whenever two nontransparent bits of two or more different sprites happen to be displayed at the same position. The chip then produces an interrupt that the programmer can use.

These chips also allow the programmer to define priorities for the sprites. These priorities specify which of several different sprite colors will be displayed if they overlap. The programmer can change the shape of a sprite by writing into its RAM area description or by using different sprite descriptions (see below). In the 6566/6567 chip, one sprite is one constant color, but different sprites can have different colors. In certain display modes, an individual sprite can have up to three different colors (plus transparent), but we will not go into these details.

This property permits all sorts of sophisticated programming. For example, changing the sprite pointer between frames and having several slightly different sprite descriptions allows us to change the sprite itself, as well as just move it. Changing the sprite $(x\ y)$-address at the time of a horizontal scan line interrupt allows more than eight sprites on the screen simultaneously, but only at different vertical positions.

Remember that the above description gives only the basic principle of displaying an object that is actually not in the frame buffer. The exact process is more complicated and varies for different hardware. A full understanding requires familiarity with the specific hardware. The interested reader should consult, for example, the product descriptions for the TMS9118 chip family, as COMM82 does not really contain a chip description.

The current direction is to produce chips that expand on the principle to an even greater extent. Graphics display chips will soon be available and architectures are being designed that will operate without frame buffers, collecting the information for the display from various distributed sources, including video cameras. This will provide for displays that show a TV-like picture, intermixing moving objects and traditional graphics that are now produced with frame buffers.

LOOKUP TABLE ANIMATION

Lookup table animation is a completely different sort of animation. We have learned how a lookup table is used to relate colors to the numbers in the frame buffer. By changing the lookup table values, we can have animation. For example, we assume a frame buffer of depth four, that is, four bits per pixel; this means that the value in a frame buffer location can be a number between 0 and 15. We assume a lookup table of 12 bits overall width, four bits for each primary, and a length of 16, corresponding to the range of values possible in the frame buffer. Each primary can be specified in 16 different intensities and we can have at most 16 different colors on the screen at the same time. Figure 17.14 shows a schematic for the example.

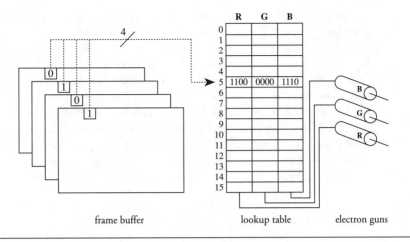

Figure 17.14   Example for a lookup table arrangement

When the CRT controller produces a frame buffer address to be displayed, the content of this address is used as an address into the lookup table. If the content of the frame buffer location is 6, then location 6 in the lookup table is addressed. The table contains intensities for the three primaries. Suppose these are 14 for red, 13 for green, and 1 for blue. The contents of the three addressed entries in the table are read out, transformed into analog intensities, and fed to the electron guns for the respective primaries. The given pixel would therefore look yellow on the display.

It is possible to change the color of that pixel without making a change in the frame buffer. The main processor can, for example, write 0 into location 6 of the red table. Our pixel will immediately become green. At the same time, all other pixels with a 6 in their frame buffer locations will immediately turn green, because they all obtain their color from location 6 in the table!

Now we can see how the lookup table technique can produce animation. We use a very simple example—moving a blue ball across the screen from left to right. To achieve this, we draw 10 instances of the ball on the screen, all in different colors. Actually, we should say we draw them in different numbers; what color these numbers represent is determined later. Figure 17.15 shows this.

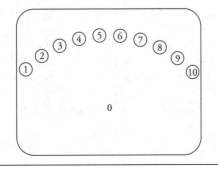

Figure 17.15   Lookup table animation

In the frame buffer, the background pixels all consist of 0's and the balls are drawn as filled polygons with buffer values of 1 through 10. The balls' colors depend on the lookup table entries, but that is not important because we will change them. First, we make the background and all balls look black. We do this by filling the lookup table positions 0 to 10 with 0's. Nothing will appear on the screen. In order to make the first ball appear on the screen with a blue color, we enter the intensities (0,0,15) into position 1 of the table. Now, we want to make ball 1 black and ball 2 blue. To do this, put (0,0,0) into position 1 and (0,0,15) into position 2. This is repeated for all consecutive balls and a single ball appears to move across the screen. Below is a C code segment that does this. It makes the balls appear in blue one after the other and finally leaves the last one as blue on the screen. The procedure setlook(r,g,b,pos) enters the specified intensities into the table at the position pos.

```
for (i = 0; i < 11; i++)              // make everything black
   setlook(0,0,0,i);

setlook(0,0,15,1);                    // display first ball

for (i = 2; i < 11; i++)
{
   setlook(0,0,0,i-1);               // reset one ball and
   setlook(0,0,15,i)                 // display the next
}
```

By writing the proper loops, we can make the ball bounce back and forth endlessly. The speed of this animation depends solely on the speed with which entries in the lookup table are made. If one entry were made per vertical blanking, then the above 10 positions can be produced in one-third of a second. If that motion is too fast, we insert pauses between the lookup table changes.

The object can be of arbitrary complexity. Fifteen is the maximum number of different positions that we can animate with this technique if we have a lookup table adequate for 16 simultaneous colors, because one color must be saved for the background. However, if we have a system with a larger lookup table—256 is common—we have much more potential and we can move several objects of different colors individually.

The above motion would not appear very smooth, because the steps between the individual frames are much too great. Smoothing it requires smaller steps, but then the different ball positions can overlap and the problem becomes more complicated. An exercise goes into this.

Lookup table animation is very popular. Practically all desktop computers with color screens have a demonstration portfolio of impressive pictures. Many of them are animated with this technique. The Neochrome paint system running on the Atari ST lets the user define colors directly in the lookup table by clicking the mouse. The user can produce lookup table animation automatically by specifying a range through which the colors will cycle.

Displaying Colors Beyond the Frame Buffer Limit

The lookup table technique allows us to create a huge palette of colors, but only a fraction of these can be displayed at the same time on the screen. This number is given by the length of the lookup table. If the depth of the frame buffer is n, this number is 2^n.

Some demonstration programs and color paint systems show more colors on the screen at one time than are possible based on the depth of the frame buffer! This is achieved by fast changes in the lookup table during the display.

Assume a frame buffer of size 320×200 with 4 bits per pixel and a lookup table of 16 entries with 9 bits each. With this, we can display 16 colors from a palette of 512. Here is a way to put more than 16 colors onto the screen simultaneously—maybe even all 512. The example does not try to produce a certain picture; it shows only the principle.

We fill the frame buffer so that we have all numbers from 0 to 15 in 10 adjacent scan lines. Normally, these lines will display all 16 colors that we have encoded into the lookup table. We assume further that we have an interrupt with every horizontal sync pulse of the CRT controller indicating the end of one scan line. As soon as this interrupt occurs we have about 15 microseconds to change some entries in the lookup table. The timing of this action is critical; it must be finished before the end of the horizontal blanking, a time when the lookup table is not accessed. If the interrupt routine manages to change at least one entry in this time, we will have a new color in the next scan line, because the phosphors in the scan line above are still "glowing" and will do so for the duration of a complete frame. This gives us a total of 17 colors. If we continue like this, we can produce 25 different colors on these scan lines.

Usually, there will be enough time to change more than one entry, and the numbers in the frame buffer and lookup table will be carefully prepared to produce a certain picture. Of course, the interrupt routine has to know which scan line is being displayed to produce the correct change in the table. At the end of the frame, the lookup table must be reset to the original values so that the process can be repeated in the next frame. However, the vertical retrace lasts long enough that this is no problem.

"Extra" Colors on the Amiga

The Commodore Amiga uses another interesting technique to display all colors of its palette on the screen at the same time. We will only sketch the principle. For full technical details, consult the Amiga ROM Kernel Reference Manual.

The frame buffer has a variable depth that the programmer can set in order to save memory when a large color range or high resolution is not needed. The greatest depth is five bit planes; correspondingly, the color lookup table has a length of 32. Its width is 12 bits, four for each primary. This results in a palette of 4096 colors, of which 32 can be on the screen simultaneously.

However, the machine can be set to a specific mode, the *hold and modify* (*HAM*) *mode*. In this mode, it uses memory equivalent to a 320×200 resolution with six bits per

(continued)

pixel. Of these six bits, only four are used to define a color. The remaining two are called HAM bits and can have the following settings: 00, 01, 10, and 11. These are interpreted as follows:

00:    Use the four color bits to address the lookup table.
01:    Hold the color setting from the last pixel and use the color bits to modify the red component.
10:    Hold the color setting from the last pixel and use the color bits to modify the green component.
11:    Hold the color setting from the last pixel and use the color bits to modify the blue component.

The last used intensities of the primaries are held in a register. When a HAM-00 pixel is displayed, the register is filled from the lookup table. In the other cases, the four color bits replace either the red, green, or blue component in the register and define the pixel color. In this way, the Amiga can achieve a color change from one pixel to the next (from left to right) by any amount, as long as this change is limited to one primary. It is possible to change to any possible color of the palette within the space of three pixels. There is no difficulty in having all 4096 colors on the screen simultaneously. Abrupt changes are not possible, but with careful setting, the "smears" can be very inconspicuous and fine, gradual color changes can be displayed.

Software has recently been developed that fills the frame buffer in HAM mode with a digitized color picture and sets the HAM pixel values automatically.

FLIGHT SIMULATION

This is an important application of animated computer graphics. We will give a short sketch, although computer graphics is only one aspect of it. Fast computers can simulate an aircraft's response to the movements the pilot makes at the controls for acceleration, deceleration, change of direction, and so on. These reactions were formerly displayed to the pilot in a mock cockpit packed with meters and gauges. Later, the display of a filmed landscape was added to simulate what would be seen through the cockpit windows, but this was not very satisfactory.

Today, it is possible to display a landscape that changes according to the movements of the aircraft. Typically, the cockpit windows can be simulated by three or four CRT displays, each of which displays a part of the landscape so as to give the impression of one continuous picture. In Figure 17.16, we are looking down at a typical arrangement of three CRT displays and the pilot. The display is derived from a terrain map that is stored in a database and contains the topology of the terrain over which the training and testing flights take place. This terrain consists of such structures as mountains, valleys, lakes, rivers, roads, building clusters, and the airport.

The graphics display processors used for this are usually custom made. They can do the necessary three-dimensional transformations of data points, the projections of the display, the filling of polygons, and so forth very rapidly in hardware. Silicon technology has improved so

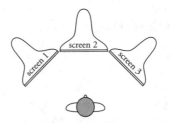

Figure 17.16   Several displays for flight simulation

much that even mass-produced general graphics processors can do polygon fill for convex polygons in hardware.

With all this speed, it is possible to display pictures composed of a reasonable number of filled polygons rapidly enough to achieve real-time animation. Of course, the picture has to correspond to what the pilot would see from the window of the real aircraft. This depends on the aircraft's location, tilt, angle, and speed.

The aircraft's reaction to control movements depends on many parameters: its shape, the design of the fins and wings, the position of the fins, its current speed, inertia, the thrust from the engines, and so on. The simulation involved is so complicated that it can only be solved numerically. Only the fastest array processors that have as much parallelism as possible are able to do this simulation in real time.

This is all very costly, but the benefits make it worthwhile. One can carry out many tests of a new airplane that exists only on the drawing board by entering all these parameters into the simulator. The optical display that simulates a real flight over a real landscape makes it a very valuable testing and training tool.

Let us look at the graphics component a little more closely. We assume that the display consists of three screens, simulating three cockpit windows. To achieve a "connected" real-time display, the main simulator that knows about the aircraft's position has to convey it to the three graphics processors. Each processor knows the direction of its window and will use whatever data of the terrain map it needs to produce its correct display. The three processors can work in parallel. The landscape displays must be programmed so that a variable amount of detail from the database is used, depending on the distance from certain objects. This means that more detail is used as the distance decreases, but the width of the field also decreases. Otherwise, this could become a speed bottleneck. The proper organization of the database plays a role. Figure 17.17 shows three such screens as they would look to the pilot. The scene shows a horizon, some hills, a street, fields, and a farm building. The aircraft is moving in a curve to the right with a corresponding tilt of the wing.

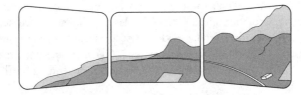

Figure 17.17   Landscape displayed on several screens

17.4   FRAME-BY-FRAME ANIMATION

Another type of animation is *frame-by-frame animation*. This sort of animation can be created with modest graphics hardware, even with a desktop computer. We also need a videotape recorder or a movie camera with single-frame exposure and a darkroom.

Actually, whenever we are animating very sophisticated computer graphics, we must resort to this type of animation. We know that, even on fast hardware, producing smoothly shaded surfaces, depth sorting, drawing texture-mapped objects, ray tracing scenes with reflections, and the like takes time. Generating a single frame in the buffer is so complex that real-time animation is not possible. Still, we have seen such animated pictures on graphics monitors and on TV. With our current knowledge, we can generate a single frame containing such a picture. This is just a general computer graphics task, but how can we produce animation? We consider this below.

RECORDING ON FILM OR VIDEOTAPE

Whenever a single picture is finished in the frame buffer, it can be displayed and then filmed or videotaped as a single frame. Even though this might take days, the entire sequence of frames can eventually be produced. Then we display them in rapid succession. This sort of animation is used primarily to produce TV commercials and, increasingly, movies.

This approach has several problems. There is the interim production of an optical picture on film, with a possibility of additional noise or disturbance. Over longer periods of time, the brightness of the monitor can undergo slight changes, as can the light level of the room. Such changes can be aggravated by the filming itself, so they may be perceivable when it is played back. It is necessary to have a room with stable light conditions.

We could completely avoid producing an interim optical picture by recording the content of the frame buffer directly as one magnetic track on videotape. However, here too we are confronted with difficulties.

The signal stored on a videotape is identical to the color TV broadcast signal. This is a complicated composition of several different kinds of information: luminance, hue, saturation, horizontal sync pulses, color reference burst, vertical blanking, and reference black level. It is called the *NTSC composite video signal*. One TV frame is composed of two interlaced fields. Each field consists of 262.5 horizontal scan lines and the whole TV frame consists of 525 interlaced scan lines. (However, only about 500 scan lines are displayed on the screen to allow time for vertical retrace.) The composite TV signal carries 60 fields per second, which corresponds to 30 frames. (The precise field rate is 59.94 Hz.)

Today's videotape recorders are of the helical type. The magnetic reading and writing heads are located on a spinning cylinder around which the magnetic tape is pulled in a slanted track. The rotation speed of the cylinder and the tape speed depend on the type of machine.

The majority of today's video recorders record one field per video track. The cylinder that carries the read and write head rotates at 60 rpm (older types rotate faster). The tape is wound more or less completely around the cylinder, depending on the type of recorder (see Figure 17.18).

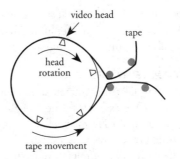

Figure 17.18   Read and write head in a VCR

While the cylinder rotates, the tape is pulled over it in a slanted path and a video track is read or written in a slanted path across the tape, as in Figure 17.19. The audio signals are recorded on a special audio track by other heads. A pulse for each frame is also recorded. Some devices can later add and read a binary time code for each field. This time code is added in the video track and does not affect the signal. This is important in videotape editing for finding and identifying individual fields. For more on this subject, see ANDE84, for example.

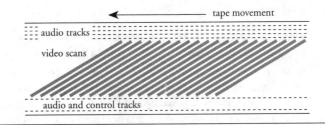
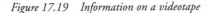

Figure 17.19   Information on a videotape

The best quality video recording is achieved with recorders of the C type in which the tape is wound almost all the way around the cylinder, as shown in Figure 17.18. These recorders use one-inch-wide tape. Recording on a video cassette recorder (in which the tape is not operated on an open reel, but is enclosed in a cassette and is only 3/4 inch or 1/2 inch wide) usually produces lower picture quality.

In our application, we want to record a single frame stored in the frame buffer of a graphics system. The output from the frame buffer to the monitor is done in a variety of ways. If it is just an RGB signal consisting of three separate signals for red, green, and blue with sync pulses on the green, then it has to be transformed into the NTSC standard to be recordable on videotape. Graphics boards in the middle price range can produce an NTSC composite video output. A so-called *genlock feature* is needed to tie the frame buffer's scan rate to the recording rate. Another thing that the circuitry has to account for is that a frame buffer can have a various number of scan lines, while the NTSC frame always has 525.

It is very likely that we will soon see devices that record the video information digitally. A step in this direction is RGB video cameras, which store the information in RGB code rather than NTSC composite. Red, green, and blue intensities, and the horizontal sync signals are stored for each scan line. To play back such a tape requires either an RGB monitor or a converter to produce the NTSC signal for an ordinary TV screen. At present, video recording is mostly analog; only the time code is digital.

STORING FRAMES IN MEMORY

We can see complicated animated scenes on computer graphics screens for low-priced desktop computers. One example is the "Juggling Robot" on the Amiga computer. In this particular case, the individual frame is a fairly complicated scene generated by ray tracing. The robot consists of many spheres that are partially overlapping, but not reflecting. The robot juggles three spheres that are completely reflecting. All the spheres cast shadows on the ground. Although scenes consisting of spheres are the simplest case of ray tracing, it is absolutely impossible to produce this picture in 1/20 of a second.

The animation in this case actually is frame by frame animation. It consists of 20 frames, which give about one second of animation. These frames are displayed in cyclic order by changing the starting address of the area to be scanned during the vertical blanking time; the display then repeats. It is like page flipping with more than two frame buffers. On computers with a large enough memory, several frames can be pregenerated and stored. With a resolution of 320×200 in color mode, one frame requires 32K bytes. The whole animation can be stored in 640K bytes.

INTERACTIVENESS IN PAINT AND DRAW APPLICATIONS

In paint and draw programs or in CAD/CAM applications, there is also real-time animation on the screen. Examples are rubber band lines, growing rectangles, ellipses that change in shape with the movement of the input device, and so on. This really is animated graphics. The animation in these cases is achieved by rapidly drawing, erasing, and then redrawing the graphics primitive in question. Here, animation is not the primary objective. It is merely a requirement for giving the fast response desired to keep the shape of the graphics primitive in synchronization with the user's action. Paint and draw programs are described in Chapter 18.

EXERCISES

1. Write a program that produces lookup table animation. The animation consists of a sphere that moves across the screen from left to right and back, repeating this in an endless loop. Draw individual spheres in consecutive colors such that the spheres just touch each other; see Figure 17.20.

Figure 17.20   Exercise for lookup table animation

2. Produce the same animation as in Exercise 1, but achieve a smoother motion by overlapping the individual spheres by half the diameter; see Figure 17.21.

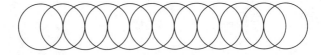

Figure 17.21   Lookup table animation for overlapping objects

You can achieve this using only the two shapes shown in Figure 17.22.

Figure 17.22   The two shapes needed for Exercise 2

3. Write a program that produces a three-dimensional rotating pie chart (see Figure 17.23).

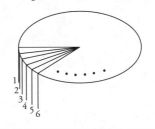

Figure 17.23   Three-dimensional rotating pie chart

Hint: a three-dimensional pie chart that seems to rotate around its center can be drawn by computing points on the circumference of an ellipse, then drawing straight lines from the center of the ellipse to the points on the circumference, with each line having a different color. If you do not have enough colors, draw groups of consecutive lines in the same color. From the end points of lines drawn within the front half of the pie, draw vertical lines of constant length with the same color as the line (see Figure 17.24).

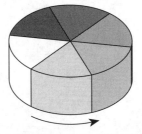

Figure 17.24   Lines of constant color in the pie chart

Motion is achieved by setting a group of consecutive lines to the same color, adding lines in the succeeding direction to the group, and removing lines from the group at the other end. The motion is smoother if your system allows many different colors.

18

Principles of Interaction and Graphics Standards

This last chapter focuses on clarifying basic principles of interaction with the user and on introducing standards in computer graphics.

18.0   **Introduction** points out the importance of considering the user's needs in system development and examines some of those needs.

18.1   **Principles of Interaction** explains the basic principles for categorizing graphics applications.

18.2   **Graphics Standards** discusses several important graphics systems (GKS, X Window System, PHIGS, PostScript) that have become official or de facto standards.

18.3   **Uses and Techniques of Printers** describes these most important hard-copy devices for output of computer graphics. We also explain some common raster-printing techniques.

18.0   INTRODUCTION

Most of this book has dealt with algorithms and programming considerations for creating graphics on the screen. At the same time, it is equally important for you, as the builder of an application that incorporates graphics, to be acutely aware of the user's needs. The person who will actually sit at the terminal and use the application that you create is the most important component of the whole system.

In Chapter 1, we explained the importance of a graphics interface, considered how the operating system can be accessed more flexibly through graphics, and described a number of graphics applications with user-computer interaction.

In the past, the designers of systems have too often overlooked the problems users face, particularly new users. Program developers have a tendency to use terse, non-mnemonic abbreviations in their command structures. While a short version of a command saves a lot of typing, it does prolong the learning curve and causes users to relearn much if they access the package infrequently.

Graphics can change this. Pictures can supplement or even replace words, producing significantly better recognition of what the command is supposed to do. Often, the operation is speedier when the user can point to an object on the screen, rather than typing in its name. For example, moving a picture or block of text is simpler when a pointing device is used to define the item and to designate the new location. When the results of the move are immediately shown on the screen after the user drags an object with the pointer, the user is more in control and feels a part of the system, not just a passive participant. This instant feedback is also important to let users know immediately when they have asked for something they do not really want. (This implies the necessity of having an UNDO function whenever the results could be catastrophic.)

18.1 PRINCIPLES OF INTERACTION

18.1.1 GRAPHICS PACKAGES

A graphics package is a set of routines that generate graphics primitives of various complexity on a display and perform other graphics-related actions. The routines, number, names, and actions vary between packages. When implemented on some hardware, the routines can be used to create graphics without worrying about the hardware's particularities.

For example, the five functions `color()`, `setpix()`, `line_t::draw()`, `polygon_t::solid()`, and `circle_t::solid()` in Chapters 2 and 3 can be considered a very simple graphics package. (The first two are completely hardware-dependent and therefore are not coded in this book.) Once the functions are implemented on some hardware with graphics capabilities and a C++ language environment, anyone with a little programming knowledge can write a program in C++ in which these functions are called. Running this program will create a picture.

Creating a picture in this way means operating in *batch mode*. In many environments, it is the only way to produce graphics. For example, suppose we draw the outline of a house, as in Figure 18.1. (The numbers are the screen-coordinates of the vertices and are not part of the picture.) The following C++ code segment would draw the house. (We assume that there is a function `line_t::draw()` without arguments that simply draws in device coordinates.)

```
#include "../Shape2d/line.h"

line_t(100,130,100, 70).draw();
line_t(100, 70,150, 20).draw();
line_t(150, 20,200, 70).draw();
line_t(200, 70,200,130).draw();
line_t(200,130,100,130).draw();
```

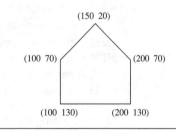

Figure 18.1   Outline of a house

Operating in batch mode is not user-friendly, especially not with such a simple graphics package. One reason is that too few graphics primitives are available; another is that the vertices must be given in absolute screen coordinates; no user-specified scale is possible. (Here, we purposely understate the possibilities to make the point. The default window specification will automatically use device coordinates.) The third and most important reason is the lack of interaction: the user must transform the idea of the picture into numbers to write the code. There is no pictorial feedback. Only by compiling and running the code can the result be seen. If not satisfied with the picture, one must make adjustments by going back into the program, changing the numbers, compiling and running it again. This may have to happen several times.

The package's first deficiency can be overcome by adding more functions, for example, to set the thickness and style of lines (dotted, dashed, bold, draw XOR mode), or to draw hatched polygons, circles, and so forth. The second one can be overcome by providing for user coordinates through windows and viewports. Even with these added functions, however, this package allows pictures to be created in batch mode only.

To make creating a picture more user-friendly, one must change the user's mode of operation from batch to *interactive*. This requires two things. One is adding a function to the package that provides for *graphical input*, the other is writing an *interactive graphics application* using the package. Below, we elaborate on both of these terms.

The basic difference between the batch mode and interactive applications is interactiveness. An interactive application makes it unnecessary for the user to have programming knowledge. The user can create pictures of various complexity by painting, drawing, resizing, recoloring, shading, touching up, moving parts around, recombining parts, and changing existing portions of a picture.

18.1.2 GRAPHICAL INPUT

First, we clarify the term *graphical input*. Every input, even the keyboard, can be made graphical or graphics-related. You may have worked with programs that let you move a rectangle-shaped cursor on the screen by hitting the arrow keys or other keys. Such cursor movement is graphics-related, but very crude because the cursor is large and jumps in large steps. For graphics we need a fine "crosshair" cursor and a fine, pixelwise movement. While we could achieve this with the keyboard, the ideal device for such input is the mouse. Below, we talk about user input in more detail.

GENERAL CONCEPTS OF INTERACTIVE INPUT

One proven method of obtaining input from an external device, such as a mouse or keyboard, is to use *interrupts*. In this technique, the device sends a signal when it wants to send data. The computer's central processor is designed so that when this signal is on the interrupt line, its current activity stops (though any instruction in progress is completed). Thus, the system knows immediately when an external device needs to be serviced and, after saving the machine's current state, it carries out the servicing task. Additional interrupts can be received during this servicing; if the new request is of higher priority, the current action stops and the new servicing begins. When that is finished, the system handles the first interrupt, then finally returns to the original task. Successive interrupts can be stacked up along with the data they are sending. Keyboards and mice operate with interrupts. We will not pursue further this important topic except to say that the computer can have several levels of interrupts and can disable (ignore) interrupts that are below a certain level. Handling a number of requests simultaneously usually involves establishing queues of requests and data.

THE MOUSE

In a graphics environment, the mouse has become the standard input device, although several others can do the same job. Every graphic-oriented operating system provides for mouse operation. In such a system, the mouse pointer or cursor can move on the screen to follow the mouse movements and to handle the signals produced when the user clicks the buttons. The cursor's current position on the screen is interpreted as the current mouse position.

By constantly checking the position, the system can automatically start certain actions whenever the cursor enters or leaves certain screen areas. Other actions can be triggered by checking the position only when a button is clicked or released. The button method is used to point at certain things on the screen, for example at options in a drop-down-menu or at one of several displayed geometric figures.

In such a system, there are routines available for checking the current position and the status of the buttons. These routines can provide functions for graphical input in a graphics package. We consider a mouse with at least one button and describe it in more detail in a sidebar.

The Mouse

The mouse is a small input device that one hand can work and that has one or more push buttons. The mouse may operate mechanically or optically. The mechanical mouse contains a rubber-coated steel ball that slightly protrudes at the bottom. Pushing the mouse around on the table surface rotates the steel ball. The ball's movement rotates two little capstan wheels whose axes are at 90° to each other (see Figure 18.A).

The axes of the capstan wheels have small disks with openings. Their rotation causes an infrared light beam to be interrupted. This sends signals to the computer. The capstan wheels are arranged so that one of them is rotated by a vertical mouse movement and the other by a horizontal movement. Other directions rotate both wheels. The schematic is shown in Figure 18.B.

The mouse sends separate signals for horizontal and vertical movement, as well as other signals that help the computer determine the direction of the movement and depression or release of the mouse buttons. For further details, you should study IMAC85 and the appropriate chip descriptions.

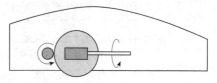

Figure 18.A   Cross-section, mechanical mouse

The optical mouse can be moved on any smooth surface that has some light-dark pattern, for example on a paper with fine raster lines. A light source inside the mouse shines onto the surface to make the light-dark pattern recognizable. The mouse's movement makes the pattern move under some light-sensitive cells, producing signals that are sent to the computer. The optical mouse has no moving parts and so is not subject to mechanical wear.

Each signal sent to the computer is received by an I/O chip, for example, a Zilog Z8530 Serial Communications

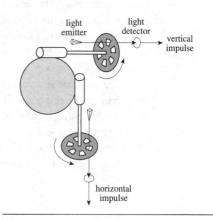

Figure 18.B   Schematic of impulse generation

(continued)

Controller or a Synertek SY6522 Versatile Interface Adapter, which are very common in microcomputers. The chip transforms this signal to an interrupt for the processor. Thus, the processor receives interrupts for vertical and horizontal movement and for mouse buttons. All the processor needs to do when receiving such an interrupt is to check the status of the I/O chip and increase or decrease counters for these movements.

In addition, the processor checks these counters once per vertical retrace—that is, 60 or so times per second—and resets them to zero. The information obtained is the mouse's relative movement since the last retrace. This is basically a combination of interrupt and polled operation.

The mouse is amazingly simple, user-friendly, and versatile. Still, it is a relative-motion device; it does not report its absolute location, like a stylus on a graphics tablet, only how far and in which direction it is moving. Even the direction is relative to the mouse. If it is accidentally held upside down, an up movement on the table results in a down movement of the cursor; left/right is also reversed. The mouse is not as accurate as a stylus. It is very difficult, if not impossible, to trace a given drawing or curve with the mouse in order to enter it into the computer, for this would require holding the mouse perfectly parallel to its starting position during the whole tracing process. On the other hand, you can master normal mouse operations with little practice in just a matter of a few minutes. This property and its low price make it one of the most popular input devices in computer graphics.

OTHER INPUT DEVICES

A number of other devices can also send the system information that is translated to the movement of a cursor on the screen. A *trackball* is something like an upside-down mouse, where a large ball is rotated directly by hand. *Joysticks* are widely used in computer games. Moving the joystick activates two potentiometers. An early device was two thumb wheels that changed two potentiometers.

A *digitizer tablet* (also called a *digitizer board*) works somewhat differently. The position of a stylus relative to the edges of the tablet generates signals that reflect its absolute x- and y-coordinates. There are many ways to generate these signals, including sensing the voltage difference between embedded wires in a matrix arrangement, interrupting optical rays that cross at the stylus position, and using acoustical methods. A special advantage of a digitizing tablet is that one can trace a drawing that overlays the tablet, or pick key points from it. A digitizer-type device can be made a part of the bezel around the computer screen. If this device works by interrupting optical or acoustical rays, the user can activate it by pointing with a finger. There are three-dimensional versions that use the same techniques as a tablet.

Even the keys on the keyboard can be used to indicate a position on the screen. Arrow keys can be programmed to move the cursor a certain distance in the direction of the arrow. This is never as convenient or as quick as the other devices.

ADDING INPUT TO THE GRAPHICS PACKAGE

We now assume that we have a graphical input function, `sample_mouse()`, which we can add to the package. It assigns the current position of the mouse in absolute device coordinates to its two arguments and returns an integer indicating the button's current status in a snapshot action. The prototype of this function is:

```
int sample_mouse(int *x,int *y) ;
```

There is no such function in the provided software, but it could easily be implemented using the class `mouse_t`. To implement it in a DOS environment, use the `int86()` system call as shown in the function `mouse_t::test_button()` in the file `Shape2d/mouse.c`. In an X Window environment, use the function `poll_mouse()` in the file `Xglib/xglib.c`. The current position is reflected by a cursor on the screen that follows all mouse movements. Such a function is hardware-dependent; this book therefore does not present code for it. All nontrivial graphics packages provide this and other, more sophisticated, functions for graphical input. With a graphical input function available, we can write an interactive program.

18.1.3 INTERACTIVE APPLICATIONS

There is an essential difference between batch mode and interactive mode. While the code of a draw program in batch mode reflects the picture, the code of an interactive draw program does not, because the picture is determined only at run time. To explain the basic strategies of interactive mode, we show code that allows the user to draw the house (or any other shape) in Figure 18.1 interactively.

We assume that the mouse has two buttons. The left one is represented by the values 2 (down) and 0 (up), the right one by 1 (down) and 0 (up). `Sample_mouse()` returns their combined status as a binary number: 0 means both up, 1 means left up, right down, 2 means left down, right up, and 3 means both down. The "mouse routines" of graphics packages very often return button positions in this manner.

Our design is the following: clicking the left button enters the current position for the start point of a straight line. Clicking the left or right button enters the position for the end point and draws the line on the screen. Ending with the left button loops the line back to start again, while ending with the right one stops the line drawing process.

Let us explain the logic. The loop:

```
while (sample_mouse(&x1,&y1) != 2);
```

keeps sampling the mouse until the left button is pressed. Other buttons or combinations do not end the sampling. When it ends, x_1 and y_1 have the last mouse position.

After this, the program must wait until both bottons are up because the user cannot release the button fast enough. If the code samples for the end point right away, the button might still be down and the same or similar mouse position will be entered for the end point. Thus, we loop until the button value is 0 and receive the position values in dummy variables. Then we sample for the end point with a loop that ends when either button is pressed:

```
while (button = sample_mouse(&x1,&y1),
       button != 2 && button != 1);
```

All this is repeated in a loop that ends when the right button is pressed. Then the program stops. Due to the loop logic, we have to wait for both buttons to be up at the beginning. (We assume that there is a function line_t::draw() without arguments that simply draws in device coordinates.) Here is the code:

```
#define BOTH   3
#define LEFT   2
#define RIGHT  1
#define NONE   0
{                                        // draw individual disjoint lines
   int button = NONE ;

   while (button != RIGHT)
   {
      int x1 , y1 , x2 , y2 , dum ;
      while (sample_mouse(&dum,&dum)  != NONE);
      while (sample_mouse(&x1,&y1)    != LEFT);
      while (sample_mouse(&dum,&dum)  != NONE);
      while (button = sample_mouse(&x2,&y2),
             button != LEFT && button != RIGHT);
      line_t(x1,y1,x2,y2).draw();                      // draw the line
   }
}
```

This is much more user-friendly because the user only has to run this program in order to draw, and need not program anything! Let us think about improvements, however. Above, all vertices of the house must be clicked twice, even though one line's end point is the start point of the next. We change the loop so that the lines are drawn in a chained form, as long as the left button is pressed. The chain ends with the right button:

```
{                                        // lines are chained together
   int x1 , x2 , y1 , y2 , dum ;
   int button = NONE ;

   while (sample_mouse(&x1,&y1) != LEFT);        // get start point

   while (button != RIGHT)                  // right button ends it
   {
      while (sample_mouse(&dum,&dum) != NONE);
      while (button = sample_mouse(&x2,&y2),     // get end point
             button != LEFT && button != RIGHT);
      line_t(x1,y1,x2,y2).draw;
      x1 = x2;               // end point becomes next start point
      y1 = y2;
   }
}
```

This little program could be called a *rudimentary paint program*. We could further improve it by showing the lines on the screen with their start point fixed and the end point moving in real time with the cursor, as long as no button is pressed. Pressing a button fixes the line in place and starts the next one or ends the whole process, depending on which button is pressed. This very common technique is called *rubber banding*. We do not elaborate on this.

We have explained the essentials of interactive drawing to introduce the reader to the inner workings of an interactive graphical program. Certainly, there is much more to it, such as drop-down menu management, bit-blit, and double buffering, which we cannot cover in this book.

ADDING GRAPHICAL EDITING

What our above "paint program" cannot do is interactively change the created picture. Once we have drawn a line, there is no way to remove or change it interactively. Such changes are called *graphical editing*. Adding such a capability to the program requires considerably more sophistication. To explain graphical editing, let us look at two important types of applications: paint programs and draw programs.

PAINT PROGRAMS

A paint program is an application for interactively creating a picture on the screen. Using the principles outlined above, it consists of the routines of a graphics package. A commercial paint program differs only in the number of features but not in principle from what we have presented. We may add a "bit-blit" feature (a shortened version of the expression "Bit Block Transfer", usually supported by DMA "blitter" chips). This feature copies a rectangular area of the frame buffer to some other rectangular area in several modes, such as SET, XOR, OR, and so forth. If we also add a flood-fill algorithm and a character generator (Section 4.3.), we can use the package to implement a full paint program.

It is typical of paint programs to create pictures only in the frame buffer. Once a line is drawn, the program does not remember what it did and is not able to identify the drawn line on the screen. For example, after drawing the house in Figure 18.1, the user cannot "grab" a vertex such as the gable and lower or raise it, pulling the two connecting lines along, even though the user has not exited the program. Changes must be made by erasing and redrawing the affected parts.

A paint program such as ours does not create an internal record of the picture. That is, it does not store the end points of drawn lines or the coordinates of other primitives internally in some data structure. The graphics package on which we base it also does not store this information; the command `line_t(x1,y1,x2,y2).draw()` only draws, but nothing else. Such an application and such packages are said to work in *immediate mode*. Examples for paint programs are Neochrome and Degas on the Atari. Examples for graphics packages in immediate mode include the one we outlined above, X Windows, PostScript, and the GEM routines on the Atari.

DRAW PROGRAMS

A draw program is an application for interactively creating a picture on the screen and editing it on the level of the graphics primitives. The user can identify primitives or objects on the screen, for example by pointing at them, and then change them by: scaling, rotating, changing their style, copying, moving, or deleting them. After drawing the house in Figure 18.1, the user could "grab" the gable and drag it to a different location. The two connecting lines will follow.

Consequently, a draw program is more complicated than a paint program. To turn our above example into a draw program, we would need not only to draw the line according to the user input, but also to store its endpoints in some data structure. We could use other mouse input to find coordinates in the data structure that are close enough to the point on which the user clicked. Through this, we could identify a primitive that was already drawn. This would allow our program to remove and redraw that primitive. Writing a draw program using only an immediate mode graphics package is difficult because the details are more complicated than that.

It would be convenient if the command that we issue for drawing the line, `line_t(x1,y1,x2,y2).draw()`, would also store the endpoints automatically. Some graphics packages do provide such primitives (for example, those based on the PHIGS or GKS standard), not only for lines, but for circles, polygons, and so forth. Writing a draw program would be much easier using such a package. A graphics package or an application that retains the geometric data of the interactively created primitives is said to work in *retained mode*. Examples of draw programs in retained mode are Adobe Illustrator and Aldus FreeHand on either the Macintosh or PC-compatible computers.

We will see that the GKS standard can group primitives into so-called *segments*. GKS provides functions that return the primitive's segment number and identifier when the user selects a primitive on the screen. The application can then simply use functions that deal with that segment to transform it as a whole. GKS can group only on one level; segments cannot be nested. PHIGS, on the other hand, allows arbitrarily complex objects.

We have elaborated on this distinction because it is essential. Students whose specialty is computer graphics will seldom be completely familiar with a particular application. Their knowledge must be of a different kind and must go much deeper. They must understand the principles of a graphics package, as well as the concepts and strategies of writing an interactive application. As developers, they use the routines of a certain graphics package to write the application.

18.2 GRAPHICS STANDARDS

Every aspect of computers, both software and hardware, can benefit if there are *standards*. When standards exist and are adhered to, system users are assured that components work well together and can move more easily from one installation or application to another. Users also have a better way to compare the performance and features of competing products. Unfortunately, standards are very hard to agree on and often become outdated quickly. Graphics standards are no exception.

Several graphics routine packages have been developed over time to promulgate graphics standards. They are not based on any particular hardware or written in a particular programming language. Their intent is to acknowledge methods and techniques that have proved useful to workers in the field, to unify their diverse efforts, and to increase their effectiveness by providing a common graphics language.

It is unfortunate that standardization in computer graphics has not been very successful. A major reason is that the field is developing rapidly. It is impossible to standardize something that is not a stable entity; new hardware and software develop so quickly as to defy significant efforts for standardization. Still, it is important to examine some of the attempts. The discussion below illustrates how standards are affected by advances in hardware.

A graphics standard would provide functions for certain graphics primitives and graphics-related actions, define ways of organizing the picture, and introduce certain notions and nomenclature.

The graphics standards presented below are defined as a number of routines with well-defined parameters and actions. Their creators hope that there will be implementations on a variety of hardware and in diverse major programming languages and that non-standard techniques will not be used.

18.2.1 GKS

The GKS (Graphical Kernel System) is an important effort to develop a standard. It was started in the mid-seventies. Hence, it is characterized by an underrepresentation of raster graphics features. Raster graphics was only patched into GKS. Consequently, references to it are sparse in the GKS description (see HDGS83). GKS does not allow the full use of raster graphics capabilities. It is a retained mode, object-level, geometric graphics package. It updates the screen whenever an editing operation makes it necessary.

LANGUAGE BINDING

Any GKS implementation must be written in and the functions must be accessible from some programming language. For example, it might be convenient for a given procedure to return a parameter as Boolean. If the language in which the system is implemented does not have the type Boolean, the required information must be returned differently, perhaps as 0 for false and 1 for true. For another example, decisions must be made as to how a procedure should convey the four possible directions of text alignment: up, down, left, and right. What numbers are to be associated with each direction?

Because it would be beneficial for all implementers to follow the conventions, the GKS description contains *language binding*, which sets these guidelines for FORTRAN. Recently, ISO has developed GKS language bindings for the C language.

LOGICAL WORKSTATIONS

GKS introduces the concept of the *logical workstation*. Graphical input and output devices have their own capabilities, which can be very different from one another. GKS tries to treat them all similarly. Workstations are classified into nine different types; a graphical input and output device will always fit into one of these categories. Every device of the same type can then be handled in the same way. This requires the particular installation to have individual device drivers that interpret the GKS commands. For example, the line type of a line might be interpreted on a plotter as a certain pen, on a color CRT as a certain color, and on a vector scan CRT as a white or a dot-dash line. This is determined by the individual device driver while GKS generates the same command.

GKS can assign attributes, such as a particular viewport setting for an individual workstation. An image sent to that workstation will be displayed there at a different location than when sent to another workstation assigned a different viewport setting. GKS provides many routines to exploit this idea in terms of windows, viewports, line types, fill types for polygons, and so forth.

LOGICAL INPUT DEVICES

Input devices are the following:
1. *locator* inputs an $(x\ y)$ position
2. *stroke* inputs a sequence of $(x\ y)$ positions
3. *pick* identifies a displayed object
4. *choice* selects from a set of alternatives
5. *valuator* inputs a scalar value
6. *string* inputs a string of characters

We give examples for some physical devices typical of the late 1970s that realize the above logical devices. The following examples below are not the only possibilities:

The locator can be realized by a stylus on a tablet, a keyboard-driven cursor, or a thumbwheel-driven cursor.

The stroke can be most effectively realized by a stylus on a tablet.

The pick can be realized on a vector scan CRT by a light pen and, less reliably, on a raster CRT with a light pen. On a raster CRT, the pick is best realized with a screen cursor driven by stylus, keyboard, or mouse.

The choice can be realized by checking the status of several buttons.

The valuator can be realized by thumbwheels.

The string can be realized by a keyboard.

GKS purposely does not specify the relation between a physical device and the logical device. Any physical device that can input an $(x\ y)$ position can be a locator. The language binding and the drivers of the specific implementation take care of associating the physical device with the logical device.

Today, there are new physical devices. The mouse did not exist when GKS was defined, but it falls readily into either locator or stroke and, as we will see, can be used for pick and choice. The digitizer board is still a valuable input device. Light pens are disappearing, as they do not work very well with raster displays. Thumbwheels were frequently used as locators or valuators, but they are harder to operate than a mouse or stylus and can be so easily simulated by these that there is now little justification for them. The classes pick and choice are similarly handled. In the spirit of GKS, the type of application of an input device puts it into one of the six classes; the actual hardware is not important.

GRAPHICS PRIMITIVES

GKS has six main primitives:
1. `polyline(int n, float x[], float y[])`
2. `polymarker(int n, float x[], float y[])`
3. `fill_area(int n, float x[], float y[])`
4. `text(float x, float y, char *string)`
5. `cell_array(float xl, float yl, float xh, float yh,`
   `int n, int m, int ca[n][m])`
6. `generalized_drawing_primitive(int n, float x[],`
   `float y[], int id, int il, int ia[])`

The last two have been added later and apply to raster devices and other hardware.

We have used C notation to show these functions. In the first three primitives, x and y are arrays giving the n points $(x[0]\ y[0])$ to $(x[n-1]\ y[n-1])$. Observe that these are two-dimensional Cartesian coordinates. They are specified in world coordinates determined by the functions `set_window()` and `set_viewport()`, which work precisely as we described in Chapter 4.

`Polyline()` draws $n-1$ line segments joining adjacent points, starting with the first and ending with the last. The type or color of the line can be set by calling another procedure before calling `polyline`.

`Polymarker()` draws a marker at each of the n point positions. The type of marker is determined by a separate call. Line segments between the markers are not drawn.

`Fill_area()` draws a filled polygon whose vertices are given by n points. The polygon is automatically closed back to the first from the last point. The fill pattern for the interior is set by a separate call.

`Text()` accepts a string of arbitrary length and its start position $(x\ y)$ in world coordinates. This string is written as text into the picture. Many different attributes of the text, such as writing direction or size of the characters, can be specified by separate calls.

The cell array primitive accepts two points in user coordinates $(x_l\ y_l)$ and $(x_h\ y_h)$ that specify the lower left and top right corners of a rectangular area into which the array, `int ca[n][m]`, is mapped. The entries of `ca[n][m]` are lookup table positions. The rectangular area is divided into n cells in x-direction and m cells in y-direction. The cell (i,j) is then filled with the color `ca[i][j]`. Consult HDGS83 for more detail.

The generalized drawing primitive (GDP) is the mechanism that GKS provides to make use of the hardware capabilities of certain special workstations. These capabilities include drawing circles, ellipses, and even spline curves. The `id` parameter specifies the type of GDP to be performed. It is used by the individual device driver, which invokes the built-in general primitives. The parameters x and y are arrays of points to specify a set of screen positions that the GDP can use. Again, see HDGS83 for more detail.

All primitives are automatically clipped against the given window and viewport if clipping is enabled.

MODES OF INTERACTION

All logical devices can be used in three modes: REQUEST, SAMPLE, and EVENT. These can be implemented by three different sets of calls in C.

In REQUEST mode, a device is read only upon some action by the user. Assume that a stylus is used as a locator on a particular workstation. When the graphics system software executes the routine `request_locator(ws,dv,&st,&nt,&x,&y)`, it will go into a wait state until the user presses the stylus button. Only then is the position of the stylus read and entered into the parameters x and y. `Ws` specifies the workstation at which the request is to be executed, `dv` is the device number of the locator, and `st` is the status. `Nt` returns the number of the viewport that the locator is in. (This makes sense when several viewports exist on the screen.) The software can now use the values obtained by the call, for example, to draw a line to the point $(x\ y)$.

`Request_pick(ws,dv,&st,&seg,&pickid)` is used to determine the element at which the user points with the pick device. The first three arguments are the same as above. This function will again wait until the user has pressed the button and then read the device's coordinates. On a raster scan workstation, these might be the position of a stylus or of a mouse-driven cursor. After obtaining the position, the function checks all lines in the picture to find one that is close enough to that position (see Figure 18.2 below). Seg will be assigned the number of the segment to which this line belongs. If this line has a pick identifier associated with it, pickid will be assigned this value. This provides for an even closer identification within the segment.

In SAMPLE mode a device is read immediately without waiting for a trigger; it is similar to sample_mouse() in Section 18.1.3.

The third type is the EVENT mode. If a device is in this mode, any inputs from it are put in a queue. There is only one queue for all classes. This queue is checked by the procedure await_event(timeout,&ws,&class,&dv). If it is not empty, the procedure removes the oldest event from the queue and returns its information: workstation number, device class, and device number that did the input. If the queue is empty, the program waits at most timeout seconds and then goes on; class is assigned zero. It is critical that the program not be suspended indefinitely (as when it is in REQUEST mode) when no input comes.

After EVENT, subsequent statements in the program check the parameter class to find which input device produced the event. If the device is the desired one, the information is obtained by get_locator(), for example. If the event is from another device, it is either ignored or some other action is performed. The application can be written so that the user can control several input devices at the same time.

The next two figures illustrate some actions in GKS.

Figure 18.2 shows three lines in a raster display and a mouse-driven cross-hair cursor. When a button is clicked, the package determines the cursor's distance from each of the three lines. As the cursor is closest to line *AB*, this line is chosen. Thus, the mouse-driven cursor acts as a pick. Formerly, on vector scan displays, such picks were done by light pens.

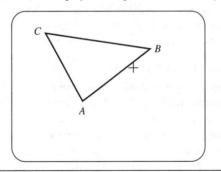

Figure 18.2   Cursor used in picking the line AB

Figure 18.3 shows the mouse-driven cursor choosing the word "yellow" from a menu. On the left side of the screen, we see a bar representing numbers between 0 and 100 that indicate the intensity of the chosen color. By touching this with the cursor, we can prompt the display of the corresponding number on the screen. The number changes with the cursor's movement, and the user clicks the button when the desired number is indicated.

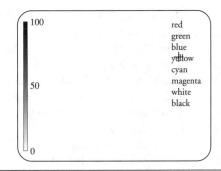

Figure 18.3   Cursor used in choosing from a menu

In selecting a word from the menu, the cursor acts as a choice device. Such choices were formerly made with light pens from the screen or by pressing certain buttons. When used on the number bar, the cursor acts as a valuator, for which thumbwheels were formerly used.

Output devices are not classified in GKS. Vector scan CRTs play too big a role within GKS considering the fact that they are disappearing, and being supplanted by raster scan displays. In hard-copy output, the line plotter acts as a vector device. Large line plotters will certainly be around for quite a while, but small ones are being supplanted by raster printers—dot matrix, ink jet, and laser printers. GKS does not deal with these sufficiently.

SEGMENTATION

GKS routines are available for opening, identifying, or closing segments. The segments can be given attributes and assigned to particular workstations so that certain attributes are in effect only at those workstations. Every graphic primitive created after a segment is opened belongs to that segment. This permits primitives to be grouped in various segments, but segments cannot be nested or edited. Once a segment is closed it can be changed only by deleting and recreating it.

METAFILES

Since GKS works in retained mode, it provides routines for saving the drawings on external files, called *metafiles*. For further reference, see EKPF84.

GKS has recently been extended to GKS-3D [INTE88], which includes 3D viewing functions. A shortcoming is that it does not allow a hierarchy of segments—a consequence of the hardware situation at the time of its first development. Another shortcoming is that it still does not sufficiently use the full capabilities of raster displays.

18.2.2 PHIGS

PHIGS (Programmers Hierarchical Interactive Graphics System) is a retained mode, object-level, geometric graphics package. It supports a structure hierarchy that is absent in GKS. It operates in either 2D or 3D world coordinates.

The PHIGS approach is more modern and has been developed under the regulations of the American National Standards Institute. It tries to overcome the shortcomings of older device-independent graphics systems, such as poor utilization of advanced hardware and inefficient data structures.

Many of the GKS concepts are repeated in PHIGS: it has the same graphics primitives and logical input devices as GKS; it works with the same three modes of interaction: RE-QUEST, SAMPLE, and EVENT; and it maintains the concept of logical workstations.

The principal ways in which PHIGS differs from GKS are PHIGS' 3D graphics primitives and its more sophisticated and editable data structures. The `polyline()` and `fill_area()` primitives, for example, can be specified with number triples as well as with number pairs, which enables spatial objects to be described. Language bindings for PHIGS are specified in FORTRAN, C, and Ada.

We will focus on the data structures of PHIGS. PHIGS describes simple, uncomposed objects by *structures*. Objects composed of other simple or composed objects are described by *structure networks*; below, we simply call them *networks*. They describe composed objects similar to those described in a scene file in Chapter 14, but there are differences. A node in a network can have an arbitrary number of subnetworks or structures. If these are identical, they can be represented by only one network or structure that is referred to repeatedly.

We obtain a graph analogy of a PHIGS network by allowing a tree to have more than two children per node and also to "have the same child several times." This tree turns into a *directed acyclic graph*, DAG.

A structure contains *structure elements*, which can be a graphics primitive, an attribute, a view selection, a transformation element (which is a 4×4 transformation matrix), or a pointer to another structure. This last is called an *execute element*. When a structure has such pointers, it becomes a network. One can edit structures by inserting elements into or deleting elements from structures or networks at any time.

The example below explains the structure concept; it is adopted from the article ABBU86, which describes a PHIGS implementation in Pascal, but is changed in some ways. The lunar vehicle in Figure 18.4 is a three-dimensional object. It consists of a frame and four wheels. These are subobjects, pointed to by execute elements in the object CAR. The highest level is an object ROOT, chosen to allow the positioning of the vehicle as a whole.

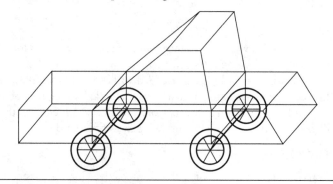

Figure 18.4   Object represented in a PHIGS structure network

Figure 18.5 shows the directed acyclic graph that represents the network that implements the CAR object. CAR has five children. One of them is the structure FRAME, while the other four are the network WHEEL four times. WHEEL itself has two children, which are the structure TIRE two times (the inner and outer radii).

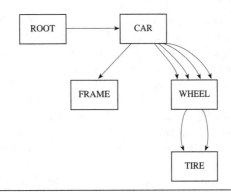

Figure 18.5   PHIGS structure network

Implementing the network packs additional information into the structures; see Figure 18.6. CAR consists of FRAME and WHEELS. FRAME consists of the body drawn in normal color and the two axles drawn in black or any other color when displayed on a color device. The structure WHEEL is defined only once, but is referenced four times, which makes the network a DAG.

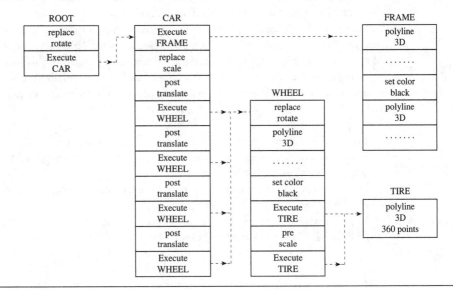

Figure 18.6   Structure network implementation

DISPLAY TRAVERSAL OF THE NETWORK

Displaying the object described by a network requires traversal of the network. As the network is traversed, transformations are accumulated and reset according to the elements as they are encountered. The same is true for display attributes.

Transformation elements have an additional parameter that describes the mode of the transformation: REPLACE when this transformation is not accumulated to the other transformations encountered so far, but "starts a new one;" PRECONCAT when it is accumulated by multiplying it on the left; and POSTCONCAT analogously. (In this text, we have the vector on the left when multiplying with a matrix, so we explain the above example in this sense. If an implementation does such multiplications the other way around, pre- and postconcatention must be reversed.) In Figure 18.6 the modes are indicated in the transformation elements.

The WHEEL is displayed at four different positions, because the four execute elements are preceded by translation matrices. These are in postconcat mode, which means each must be specified in relation to the preceding one. Therefore, the preceding scaling need not be respecified.

WHEEL executes TIRE twice. Between the first and the second execution, a scaling transformation in preconcat mode makes the second circle smaller than the first. This avoids the shear effect that results when scaling is done after a rotation.

When encountered during traversal, attributes such as color stay in force until they are changed by the next attribute element or until traversal returns to a higher level. In this case, the attributes at the higher level are resumed. We now explain the traversal algorithm in pseudocode.

A given structure, $struc$, (plus all its children) is traversed by the call $traverse(struc)$. Children (plus all their children) are traversed simply by recursive calls. The matrix $glob$, global to $traverse()$, is used to transform primitives—all their coordinates are multiplied by $glob$. $Traverse()$ maintains a local matrix, $save$, for saving $glob$ and another, acc, for accumulating the transformations specified in this structure.

At the start, the entry value of $glob$ is saved and acc is initialized to identity. Then the structure is traversed and one of the following actions is taken when an element is encountered:

1. In case of a primitive element, the element is displayed using $glob$.
2. In case of a transformation element in replace mode, acc is replaced with the element and $glob$ updated to $acc*save$.
3. In case of a transformation element in pre- or postconcat mode, acc is multiplied by the element as specified and $glob$ is updated to $acc*save$.
4. In case of an execute element, the element is executed by a recursive call.
   At the end, $glob$ is restored to its entry value.

```
//************* Pseudocode for network traversal **************

matrix_t glob = ident ;                              // 4x4 matrix

void traverse(element *struc)
{
    mat_type acc  = ident ,
             save = glob ;                   // save entry value
```

```
for (all elements in struc)
switch (element)
{
    case prim:                                   // primitive
        display(prim,glob); break;        // display using glob

    case replace:                    // replace mode transformation
        acc = replace; glob = acc*save; break;

    case precat:              // premultiply mode transformation
        acc = precat*acc;  glob = acc*save; break;

    case postcat:              // postmultiply mode transformation
        acc = acc*postcat; glob = acc*save; break;

    case exec:                                   // execute element
        traverse(exec);                        // traverse child
}
glob = save;
}

//*************************************************************
```

PHIGS provides pick routines that allow the user to identify a primitive interactively. When the user points the cursor or similar device to a primitive in order to pick it, the routine returns the path from the structure's root down to that element. This path consists of the structure id, the number of the execute element in the structure that points to the next lower structure, the type of element (line, polygon, execute element, and so forth) and the id of that element for all structures in the path.

PHIGS also has routines that allow editing of structures. This includes changing a transformation matrix, an attribute, coordinates of a primitive, deleting or adding elements, structures, and so on. Every time the structure of an object is edited, a redisplay and consequently a traversal of the structure is necessary. How the data structures are programmed, how interactive editing is done in detail, and so forth depends on the implementation.

The basic characteristics of PHIGS are apparent from the above example. Its main strength is the flexible and powerful data structure that can precisely reflect the hierarchy of elements in a picture. However, this data structure can also be a burden, especially in an application that already maintains internal detailed descriptions of the objects (for reasons such as stress analysis or other physical computations). The information for display could be derived from that description. That means that complex data structures are duplicated.

An extension to PHIGS is being developed. PHIGS+ attacks the problem of full raster graphics utilization. Using B-splines and other cubic curves and patches allows parametric curves and surfaces to be defined. Thus, it is possible to render smooth shapes such as airplane wings, car bodies, and many smooth mechanical parts using the techniques of Gouraud and Phong shading. It includes shading, lighting, depth cueing, and direct color specifications. All these features depend on the display's capability to produce fine, gradual color changes. For a description of PHIGS and PHIGS+ see PHIG88.

18.2.3 THE X WINDOW SYSTEM

An emerging de facto standard is the X Window System, called X for short. Developed at Massachusetts Institute of Technology, it is currently supported by a broad range of hardware and software manufacturers. Its capabilities go far beyond those of a graphics package. It can be characterized as a network transparent windowing system.

X consists of a library of function calls, Xlib, that is written in the C language and available as source code at no cost. Writing an X application consists of writing a program that calls these functions. An application will call functions that create windows on the display, define graphics contexts, colormaps, fonts, etc. Through function calls, windows can be changed in size, moved and destroyed, or text and graphics primitives can be displayed in them. Events can be solicited from windows, such as the mouse pointer has entered or exited the window, a mouse button has been pressed, a key on the keyboard has been struck, or a portion of the window has been exposed through the movement or disappearance of another window. Events are obtained by an application through reading its event queue. The application then has to react properly to the event.

In X one has to distinguish between the machine on which the application is running, the Xhost, and the machine on which the display occurs, the Display or Server. Xhost and Server communicate with each other through the network using the Xprotocol. The Server software running on the Display is machine dependent. It is immaterial how it is written, as long as it reacts in the prescribed way to Xprotocol requests. An application can display on many different Servers simultaneously and many different applications can display on the same Server simultaneously. X also provides for inter-application communication.

The Server keeps track of what is happening on its display (keyboard hits, mouse button presses, mouse pointer entering or exiting windows) and sends reports of those events to all applications on the network that have solicited them.

X AS A GRAPHICS PACKAGE

X's graphics primitives are simpler than those of GKS or PHIGS. There are no commands for specifying a world-coordinate system, segments, polylines, and so forth. The primitives and other graphics-related functions are not easy for an untrained user to program. The user must understand many parameters and global variables and set them properly to make the functions work.

Among them are functions for:

1. setting the drawing color
2. drawing filled polygons, rectangles, arcs
3. setting a pixel
4. sampling the mouse pointer
5. reading and setting the lookup table
6. creating and destroying a window on the display
7. and many others

Sampling the mouse pointer returns its $(x\ y)$ coordinates as integers relative to the upper left corner of the window soliciting the event. One can interpret this as if the window were the display and $(x\ y)$ were absolute device coordinates of that display. Lines and polygons are always clipped to the boundaries of the window in which they are displayed. We must distinguish between X's windows and those used in GKS and PHIGS, introduced in Chapter 4. The latter are specifications of world coordinate systems. Windows in X are display areas on the screen that represent a whole display in the sense of GKS or PHIGS. As a graphics package, X must be termed as operating in immediate mode.

USING THE X WINDOW SYSTEM

There are several X applications available that must be installed on the Display together with the Server software and must be started up together with it. One of these is Xterm. It brings up a window that receives input from the keyboard and allows the starting of login processes. Usually the user will log in through such an Xterm or equivalent window to any machine on the network. Another application that is started up simultaneously is the X Window manager. It puts itself between any other application (including Xterm) and the Server and "filters" almost all communication between these. It allows the user to interactively move or resize the windows, iconize them, have scroll bars, and so on. It can be set to customize the user's windows.

A set of functions that makes the writing of X applications easier are the Xt Intrinsics. They consist mostly of "convenience functions" that group functions of Xlib together to allow X programming on a higher level. More recently one further step was taken by the Open Software Foundation with the Motif functions. These allow an even higher level of X programming using Xt Intrinsics' "widgets" and "gadgets," graphics objects such as push buttons, menu bars, scroll bars, frames, borders, or text display areas. Their behavior can be controlled by callback functions. Although written in C, the Motif software is organized in an OO fashion.

Once the basic principles of X are understood, programming in it is straightforward. The only difficulty is the overwhelming number of different functions available. A student of the author has developed a library of functions, Xglib, that simplify the calls to the appropriate X graphics primitives. It is used successfully in all graphics classes at the author's university to produce graphics in batch mode and allows problem-free portability between all the diverse graphics machines that run X. It is provided with this book.

X differs significantly from other windowing systems. One difference is that it is a public domain system—everyone is free to use it. For this reason, many manufacturers have quickly implemented it. Another major difference is that X is compatible with networks. It allows programs executing on one machine in a network to display their output and take their input from other machines in the network, completely transparent to the user. It can be considered the state of the art in window systems and provides excellent portability in computer graphics. As a graphics package, however, it is not as powerful as the other systems.

18.2.4 PostScript

PostScript is not only a graphics standard, but also a graphics package and a programming language. It is called a *page description language* (PDL). As a graphics package, it works in immediate mode and is two-dimensional. It is designed to describe a two-dimensional graphic in precisely the way it will appear as hard copy. It "runs" not on a computer, but on a laser printer or laser film recorder. (Versions that run on a computer with CRT display have been developed, called Display PostScript.) Implementations on black-and-white laser printers for

8.5" × 11" paper work with a resolution of 300 to 600 dots per inch and require a drawing memory (frame buffer) of one to four megabytes.

We will limit our description of PostScript to its main characteristics. A PostScript program is not compiled but is interpreted, producing graphics in batch mode. Its graphics routines include:

1. straight lines
2. circular and elliptic arcs, Bezier curves
3. polygons
4. polygon and area fill
5. clipping against any closed path
6. two-dimensional transformations
7. text
8. images (bit maps)
9. screens

A PostScript program does not have windows and viewports. By default, it works in "absolute printer" coordinates, which are 1/72 of an inch (the standard "point" in the printing industry). However, it can easily be programmed to work in a user-specified coordinate system. In connection with the other capabilities, this property achieves the equivalent of windows and viewports. All coordinates and arithmetic are in floating point.

As a programming language, PostScript is almost as powerful as Pascal or C, but more difficult. Variables can be introduced, procedures can be defined and called with parameters, and conditional statements, loops, and even global and local variables can be programmed.

SCREENS

The language has some unique features. One of these is the capability to produce *screens*. PostScript screens resemble those used on all commercial printing presses to achieve gray levels (halftones). PostScript allows the precise definition of screens in terms of fineness ("frequency"), screen angle, and shape of the screen spots.

Look at a black-white reproduction of a photograph in a newspaper with a magnifying glass. You will see round dots of varying sizes, in a raster of about 60 per inch and tilted 45 degrees. PostScript calls them *spots*. Their centers are fixed in the raster, but they can be so large that neighboring spots merge, producing a completely black area, and they can vanish, leaving a totally white area.

Figure 18.7 shows a screen in which the gray intensity decreases from left to right. The leftmost spots have actually disappeared, but the figure still shows their positions. The screen angle is 45°. PostScript uses such screens to produce gray levels.

The laser printer on which PostScript runs is a raster device that can only produce little dots in a very fine raster. We call these the *atomic dots*. We will say more about laser printers below. It is important to realize that the spots themselves are com-

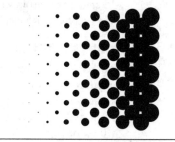

Figure 18.7   A screen in PostScript

posed of atomic dots. In PostScript, one can write a *spot function* that defines precisely where the individual atomic dots go in forming spots of various sizes.

The words *spot* and *dot* are used rather loosely in the literature. "Dots per inch" (dpi) sometimes refers to the screen frequency (spots) and sometimes to the laser printer resolution (atomic dots). Assuming a frequency of 60 spots per inch and a laser printer resolution of 300 dpi, one can figure out that the area of one spot covers about 5 × 5 = 25 atomic dots. From this, it follows that there are only 25 spots differing in gray value! Using a screen of frequency 100 will reduce this to only nine. There is a trade-off between the sharpness of the picture (related to the screen frequency) and the number of gray gradations. Students often have difficulty understanding this.

Another unique feature of PostScript is its powerful character-generating capability. Every desired character font can be loaded into the interpreter. PostScript can produce the characters of the given font in any desired size, tilt, and spacing, and can screen (shade) them with any desired gray level or pattern. Their outlines can even be used as paths against which to clip other primitives.

Learning the language and programming efficiently in it is not easy. The programmer has to develop a good understanding of the internal run-time stack through which all procedure parameters are passed. Another difficulty is the strict reverse polish notation that permeates all language features. PostScript's name is derived from this.

The syntax rules are very simple. A program consists of tokens separated by white space, as in C. The following sample program gives the idea. It draws a straight line from the point (301.5 450) to (560 500) on an 8.5" × 11" sheet of paper.

```
0.5 setgray
301.5 450 moveto
560 500 lineto
stroke
showpage
```

All identifiers (setgray, moveto, and so forth) are procedures that take their parameters from the run-time stack. As the interpreter goes through this program, it puts 0.5 on the stack and calls setgray; setgray takes the top of the stack as its parameter so that the gray for all following draw commands is set to 0.5 (halfway between black and white). The stack is again empty.

Then the interpreter puts 301.5 and 450 on the stack and calls moveto; moveto takes these numbers from the stack and moves the cursor position to (301.5 450). The same happens with 560 500 lineto. This creates an internal "path," consisting of one straight line stored in the interpreter's memory.

When stroke is called, it takes this path and produces its rasterization into the frame buffer. (The rasterization is, in the simplest case, a Bresenham straight line. Usually, however, the line has thickness and is "screened" so that the process is more complicated.) The path is deleted by stroke, so PostScript is still an immediate mode graphics package. Finally, showpage activates the laser printer and puts the buffer content onto the paper.

PostScript's main importance is as resident software in laser printers and laser film recorders. Draw programs often transform the retained description of the picture into a corresponding PostScript program and send it to a laser printer. The interpreter residing in the printer produces this picture on the paper. In principle, laser film recorders do the same, except that the medium "printed" on is a film and is larger in size.

PostScript is notoriously slow. Several "clones" have been developed that are comparable in quality and run much faster. Nevertheless, PostScript has become the de facto standard in the printing industry. Within a few years, all printing development will go directly onto film electronically without "human" intervention. This rapid change is due mostly to the advance in laser printer technology and PostScript's foresight and power, which make the computer such a useful tool in printing.

The best reference and learning tool for PostScript remains the three volumes from Adobe, POST87.

18.2.5 OTHER STANDARDS

We now mention some other standards whose fuller description would go beyond the scope of the book.

IGES (Initial Graphics Exchange Specification) is a graphic image storage and transfer standard, specifically of interest to users of CAD/CAM systems. Its main purpose is to enable a complete description of annotated drawings and engineering information on parts and assemblies. It differs considerably from GKS and PHIGS in that it includes about 50 more graphics primitives, such as conic arcs, surfaces of revolution, several types of finite elements, B-spline curves, and B-spline surfaces.

VDM (Virtual Device Metafile) is a proposed graphic image storage and transfer standard that is designed for maximum compatibility with GKS.

VDI (Virtual Device Interface) is intended as a companion document for the VDM standard.

NAPLPS (North American Presentation Level Protocol Syntax) is a graphics device interface standard with a special focus on videotex and teletext terminals.

18.3   USES AND TECHNIQUES OF PRINTERS

Hard-copy output is essential for the full utilization of computer graphics. Printers, especially raster printers, constitute the most important device for such output. In addition to raster printers, there are *nonraster printers*, also called *formed character printers*. We first look at these; many basic construction principles are the same. These printers are not particularly useful in computer graphics and even outside computer graphics they are gradually being supplanted by raster printers.

18.3.1 FORMED CHARACTER PRINTERS

Daisy wheel printers work on the same principle as typewriters. Typewriters have a hard rubber platen over which the paper rolls. A character is printed on the paper when a metal type (the formed character) strikes against an inked ribbon, transferring ink to the paper and leaving the shape of the type on the paper in excellent quality. We can drive the mechanics of a typewriter with a motor and control the stream of letters to be typed with a computer—then we have a letter font printer.

A daisy wheel printer is called this because the type characters are arranged at the ends of radials of a very lightweight plastic wheel that looks like a daisy. The wheel is rotated to bring into printing position the desired letter, which is then knocked onto the ribbon and paper by a little hammer. Other formed character printers arrange the types in different ways: on a rotating chain, on a golf ball-size print head, or on variations of the daisy arrangement.

Formed character printers produce good-looking letters, but they need a separate type for every possible character. This becomes an insurmountable task when printout is required in a complicated writing system, such as Chinese or Japanese. Nor can such a printer produce good graphics.

18.3.2 DOT-MATRIX PRINTERS

This kind of printer also has a platen, but has only a single print head consisting of a vertical column of pins. Striking a pin against the ribbon onto the paper produces a single dot. Letters are formed as dot matrices defined in a character generator. While the head moves across the paper, the pins strike at just the right times to form every possible dot matrix. Figures 18.8 through 18.12 show how a print head with seven pins produces a T.

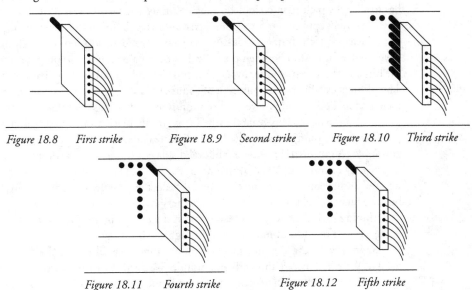

Figure 18.8   First strike   *Figure 18.9   Second strike*   *Figure 18.10   Third strike*

Figure 18.11   Fourth strike   *Figure 18.12   Fifth strike*

In text mode, the computer sends ASCII codes to the printer, which has its own character generators. The character generators consist of a ROM area in which the bit matrices for several different fonts of characters are stored. Many of the newer dot-matrix printers also have a RAM area in which the user can store other bit maps and can direct the printer to use these instead of the ROM area. In text mode, the printer advances the paper to the next line after one line is completed.

Practically all the newer dot-matrix printers can be switched to graphics mode. In this mode, the printer's basic operation is much different. The codes sent to it from the computer are not interpreted as ASCII codes, but directly as bit patterns. A common technique is to set the transmission protocol so that the computer sends and the printer receives eight-bit bytes.

A second difference in graphics mode is that the bit pattern is not used to address the character generator, but to set the configuration of the pins for a particular strike. The printers usually have more than seven pins; less expensive ones have eight or nine. In the latter case, only the upper eight pins would be used in graphics mode. Each byte accounts for one column of dots. The printer stores all the bytes for one line in a buffer before it prints so that it can sweep across the page at a fixed speed.

The third difference is that the printer automatically sets the paper advance so that the uppermost dot in one line is adjacent to the lowest dot in the previous line. The printer can thus cover the whole paper area with a raster of dots.

The ratio of the horizontal to the vertical distance between raster dots is not necessarily 1:1. There are wide differences between competing products. Many printers can be set to have larger or smaller horizontal dot spacing by changing the number of horizontal microsteps between two consecutive pin pulses. The vertical distance between pins cannot be changed. Some printers can be set to advance the paper by only half a vertical dot distance, which gives a very dense raster that helps in producing graphics.

Essentially, any rasterized picture can be produced on these printers. The computer just has to slice the picture into eight-bit long columns and send the resulting bit patterns row by row. The usual application for a dot matrix output is to dump the contents of a frame buffer onto the paper. If the frame buffer stores just a black-and-white picture with 1 bit per pixel, we have a 1:1 relationship between pixels and dots. All a screen dump program must do is read the bits out of the frame buffer in the proper order and send these 8-bit patterns to the printer. The printers usually have a resolution of about 600 dots across the width of the paper, or often increased to 1200 through several resolution steps. An average-size frame buffer can easily be dumped to the dot-matrix printer only if it is strictly black and white without gray levels.

The task of dumping a picture becomes more demanding if the frame buffer stores it with gray levels. A dot-matrix printer is a bilevel display; it can only strike or not strike a pin. It has no capacity to produce dots of different gray levels. When the picture is stored as gray levels, we could still represent one pixel by one dot on the printer by setting a threshold number below which a pixel is considered black. Otherwise, it is white. There are many strategies for determining such thresholds, all belonging in the area of image processing. In any case, such strategies lead to a loss of information through the loss of gray levels.

Suppose we want to represent a continuous tone, also called a *halftone image*, on a bilevel display. We will illustrate this with an example. We assume that the picture is stored with four bits per pixel, resulting in 16 gray levels; the frame buffer size is 320×200. The printer can produce 640 dots across the paper with a raster ratio of approximately 1:1. One technique to produce a halftone printout is called *dithering*. In our example, we represent each pixel with a matrix of 2×2 dots on the printer, called a *dither matrix*. Five dither matrices are used, as Figure 18.13 shows.

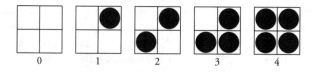

Figure 18.13   2 × 2 dither matrices

Using dither matrices causes a variable density for the population of dots on the paper, resulting in apparent gray levels through the merging effects of our perception. The picture requires twice as many dots in both directions. It becomes twice as large, but will still fit on the paper, because the printer can produce 640 dots horizontally. Only five gray levels are preserved with these dither matrices. We have to print several different gray levels on the display with the same dither matrix. For example, we could apply this grouping:

gray level 0–3	matrix 4
gray level 4–7	matrix 3
gray level 8–10	matrix 2
gray level 11–13	matrix 1
gray level 14–15	matrix 0

The lowest gray levels correspond to black and the highest to white on the display. The sizes of the groups of gray levels should not be equal. You need to experiment; the difference in apparent grayness on paper may be large between matrices 3 and 4, but small between matrices 0 and 1. Making the difference correspond to the appearance on the screen requires trial and error. It is not possible to predict what grouping will be best.

To preserve all 16 gray levels, we have to use 4×4 dither matrices that actually allow for 17 gray levels. Figure 18.14 shows the first five of these.

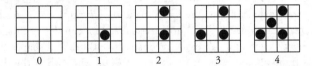

Figure 18.14   4 × 4 dither matrices

The others are obtained by executing the generating pattern to the right:

The numbers indicate the positions in which new dots are added to the matrix, so matrix 3 has dots in positions 1, 2, and 3. As we need only 16 gray levels, we will not use one of the matrices, for example, matrix 15. Now the picture will require

$$\begin{pmatrix} 16 & 8 & 2 & 10 \\ 12 & 4 & 14 & 6 \\ 3 & 11 & 1 & 9 \\ 15 & 7 & 13 & 5 \end{pmatrix}$$

1280 points horizontally. It probably will not fit onto the paper unless the printer can be set to produce 1280 points in one row. If the vertical paper feed can be set to 1/2 dot distance, as mentioned above, we again have a square dot ratio and can fit the image on the paper.

The individual dither matrices contain the dots in a very disordered and unsymmetrical layout. This is intentional. The dot layout must be designed so that in areas of identical intensity, no conspicuous patterns appear on the printout. If the four-dot dither matrix were designed as in Figure 18.15, an area of this intensity would show horizontal lines.

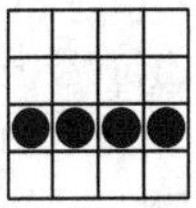

Figure 18.15   Too regular arrangement in dither matrix

Printing each pixel as a dither matrix will soon cause a problem. Assume that the frame buffer is of the size 640 × 400 with a depth of four and that we want to preserve all 16 gray levels. We would need to print 2560 dots across the page. Printers cannot do this. However, there is a solution. The basic idea is that we print not each pixel, but each array of 2 × 2 pixels as a 4 × 4 dither matrix. Internally, we compute the average gray level of the four pixels of a 2 × 2 array by adding all gray levels and dividing by four. This will give us a real number between 0 and 15. After rounding to the nearest integer, we have the average gray level of this 2 × 2 pixel array. This array is now printed by the corresponding dither matrix (see Figure 18.16).

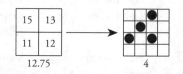

Figure 18.16   2 × 2 pixel area represented by 4 × 4 dither matrix

Printing with 16 gray levels gives reasonably smooth-looking output. If the original picture in the frame buffer has even more gray levels, we can preserve them in the printing by using larger dither matrices. 6 × 6 matrices allow 37 different levels and can be used if 32 gray levels are stored in the frame buffer. Of course, we are trading resolution for gray levels. Up to a certain extent, more gray levels make the output look better to the human eye, even with decreased resolution. The human visual system can derive much information from changing intensity levels and can easily reconstruct outlines and shapes that are somewhat blurred, so this trade-off increases printout quality. This ends when the dither matrices become so big that they are individually recognizable as squares. Matrices of 8 × 8 are usually too large. For more about dither matrices, see FOLE84.

18.3.3 INK-JET PRINTERS

Ink-jet technology uses an ink-jet head that has a number of vertically or otherwise arranged nozzles. This head sweeps across the paper much like the dot-matrix print head, but instead of striking pins against a ribbon onto the paper, little ink droplets are shot out from the nozzles against the paper. Each nozzle is connected by a tiny channel to a separate ink chamber, which is surrounded by piezocrystals. Those give a little jerk when an electric impulse of about 80 volts is applied. This pulsing shoots out the ink drop.

Another technique, developed by Hewlett-Packard, is free of any mechanically moving parts. Each ink channel is surrounded close to its nozzle by a material with high electric resistance. When a very short but extremely high pulse of current is applied to this area, the heat causes the ink to boil into a gas bubble. The sudden pressure is sufficient to push out one droplet through the nozzle. The bubble disappears within a fraction of a millisecond and capillary forces form another meniscus of ink on the nozzle surface, thereby pulling more ink toward the nozzle. These ink-jet heads have the nozzles arranged in a circle around the main ink feeder channel.

No ribbon is necessary in ink-jet printers, and the speed is about the same as that of a dot-matrix printer. Letters, numbers, and other shapes are again formed in a raster of dots. High-quality heads have more than 30 nozzles over a vertical distance of 3 to 4 mm and can produce printout that the eye cannot distinguish from formed characters.

One of the important advantages of these printers is their quietness compared to the noisy dot-matrix printers—a very valuable quality in offices. Another advantage is that there is practically no wear on the head. Still, the technological trend seems to go in the direction of jet heads that are thrown away once the ink supply is exhausted.

Some problems with this technology are gradually being overcome. A notorious one was the sensitivity of the jet heads. The nozzles easily became clogged when the printer was not in use. Replacing the main ink feeder tank could be messy. Furthermore, most types still require special paper.

Another promising new development is *thermo jet technology*. This works with a special ink called plastic or solid ink. This is not ink in the common sense, but a material that is liquid only at a certain high temperature and solid at room temperature. During operation, the material in the ink-jet heads and reservoirs is heated to this high point and droplets can be ejected toward the paper, where they immediately solidify. This solves the nozzle-clogging problem.

Because it offers certain advantages, ink-jet technology is still a strong competitor to other raster printer technologies, even if the quality of the latter is increasing. For example, the dots produced by the impacting pins in a dot-matrix printer have a minimum size, as a pin cannot be made arbitrarily thin, but the dots formed from individual ink drops can be much smaller. The mechanical parts of both dot-matrix and ink-jet printers, including paper transport, rubber platen, and so on, are certainly much simpler than those of laser printers, which we describe next.

18.3.4 LASER PRINTERS

These printers are becoming more and more popular as the technology advances and their prices come down. We only sketch the technical background and use simplified terms.

Inside the printer is a cylindrical drum whose width is about the width of the paper. This drum is coated with a photoelectric substance, a material that develops a positive or negative charge when hit by light. A laser beam is directed at the drum. Wherever this beam hits the drum, it will charge it with electrons, thus drawing an electrostatic latent image on the drum.

After this image is drawn, the drum passes over a reservoir of black powder that is attracted by the electrostatic charge. This so-called *toner* sticks to the drum surface only where the surface is charged. The drum now carries the picture in the form of black particles. The paper is charged with a very high potential and brought into contact with the drum, causing the powder to jump onto the paper. The powder is then fused to the paper by feeding it over heated rollers. This part of the process is identical to that of a copying machine.

The basic difference between a copying machine and a laser printer is the way the electrostatic latent image is formed on the drum. A laser source emits a laser beam in a fixed direction, but with varying intensity. This beam is deflected by a rotating mirror (see Figure 18.17). The mirror usually has eight or 16 facets; it is simplified in the drawing.

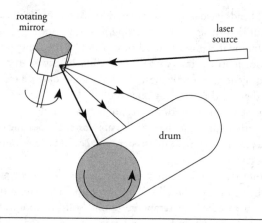

Figure 18.17   Principle of a laser printer

The rotating mirror sweeps the beam across the width of the drum in horizontal scan lines. At the same time, the drum slowly rotates in small steps so that the scan lines are parallel across its entire surface. Thus, the beam can draw a rasterized picture by being turned on and off at the proper moments. The beam movement is independent of the picture and is always the same.

Laser printers usually have their own processor and memory. The cheaper ones usually print with a resolution of 300 dots per inch. They have internal character generators in ROM, which they scan in much the same way as a CRT controller scans the character generator in text mode to put the characters onto the screen. In this mode, the printer can be driven by receiving only ASCII codes from the computer and the printing speed can be several pages per minute. If the printer has little software and memory, the output of graphics can be very time-consuming. The computer must drive them the same way it drives a dot-matrix printer, that is, by sending the whole picture as a bit map. With such a high resolution, this requires a lot of data and creating a printout in this way can easily take hours.

The more advanced printers have an internal memory of one to two megabytes in which they can store the rasterized image for an 8.5" × 11" page with 300 dots per inch. They also have internal software—a PDL interpreter such as PostScript. In this case the computer sends the text of a program that describes the image on the page. The resident interpreter runs that program, thereby producing the hard copy. Doubling the resolution to 600 dots per inch requires a fourfold increase in internal memory and a faster processor; four times as many "pixels" must be set for any shape, whether a letter or graphic primitive.

Low-end laser printers are still much more expensive than dot-matrix printers, but we can expect a significant price drop within the next decade, making them more affordable.

18.3.5 COLOR PRINTERS

Dot-matrix, ink-jet, and laser printers can be made to print in color. They achieve this by repeating a basic black-and-white printing process four times on the same paper with the four primaries—cyan, magenta, yellow, and black. All colors can be produced by a proper mixture of these (see Section 8.3.5).

A color dot-matrix printer is equipped with a ribbon that consists of four parallel strips in the four colors. The driver program sends the print head over the same line of print four times while activating a different color each time. The task involves decoding a given pixel or an array of pixels into its color components, transforming from RGB into CMYK, choosing the proper dither matrices, and sending the proper bit patterns columnwise to the printer. This is called *color dithering.*

We will explain this with an example. Assume a display of 640×400 pixels represented in a frame buffer of the same size and a depth of eight bits per pixel. The colors on the display are determined through a lookup table with eight bits per RGB primary. We assume that the printer is able to produce 640 dots across the paper width. If we print with 4×4 dither matrices, we can preserve 17 intensity levels on the printout. We group the pixels into 4×4 blocks and print each block as four dither matrices, one for each printer primary. Assuming a print head of eight pins, it is advantageous to prepare a memory area large enough to hold the result of the analysis of a strip of 640×8 pixels. Such a strip contains 160×2 of these pixel blocks.

We must first analyze the colors. Sometimes, a lookup table can only be written to but not read from by the main processor. If this is the case, then whenever a lookup table entry is made, the processor must also write a copy to an array. We look up the intensities of all three RGB primaries of each 4×4 pixel block and average and round to obtain the average RGB values of this group: $(r\ g\ b)$. We transform these into normalized values between 0 and 1 and then into CMYK values using the formula:

$$c = \max(rgb) - r$$
$$m = \max(rgb) - g$$
$$y = \max(rgb) - b$$
$$k = 1 - \max(rgb)$$

We store the *cmyk* values for each of the 160×2 pixel blocks in order not to have to read the pixels and lookup table several times. Then we determine through tables which dither matrices to use for the different printer primaries.

Let us look only at the cyan primary, as all the others are analogous.

The cyan table *TC* will be an array of 18 numbers, something like this:

TC[0]	0.0000
TC[1]	0.1200
TC[2]	0.2280
TC[3]	0.3252
...	
TC[16]	0.9777
TC[17]	1.0000

If $TC[i] < c < TC[i+1]$, we use dither matrix [16−i]. Observe that the numbers are not equally spaced. The length of the subintervals decreases by a factor of 0.9 from one to the next in this example. This is an attempt to accomodate the fact that there is only a small intensity difference between dither matrices 15 and 16, but a larger one between dither matrices 0 and 1. This 0.9 factor may not be the best choice—some experimenting is necessary to find a good distribution, and the distributions for different primaries might not be the same. We take this into account by having separate tables for the primaries.

We need to complete a whole row of printout for each primary, so we take the c-values of block (1,1) and (2,1), determine their dither matrices, and print out the leftmost column of each, which gives the first eight-pin column for cyan on the printer. Then we do the same for the second column, and so forth. After the entire cyan row is printed, we repeat the same process for magenta, then yellow, and finally black, without moving the paper. This gives one row of color printout. We repeat the above process for the remaining rows of the picture.

Experiments suggest that it is advantageous not to use the same dither matrices for different primaries. This increases the likelihood that color dots are more randomly spread around and makes the formation of patterns of any sort less probable. There are many ways to define a particular dither matrix. Figure 18.18 shows four different dither matrices with four dots obtained by rotating the original one by 90°. For more information about this, see KUBO85.

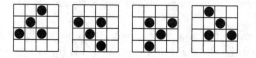

Figure 18.18   Changing dither matrices through rotation

Color ink-jet printers basically follow the same principle of dithering to achieve halftones, except that different ink-jet heads are needed for the various primaries.

The Hewlett-Packard ink-jet printer we described above works with the thermo jet principle; it is a color ink-jet printer. So is the Pixelmaster printer, operating with solid ink technology. Both have four jet heads, one for each of the primaries cyan, magenta, yellow, and black. The Pixelmaster has eight nozzles on each print head and produces a resolution of 240 dots per inch.

Color laser printers, driven by a PDL, work on the same basic principle as black-and-white laser printers. The paper is imprinted four times, halftones are achieved through screening, and the screens for the four primaries are tilted by the angles 0°, 22.5°, 45°, and 67.5°. They are about four times as expensive as their black-and-white counterparts.

A LOOK TO THE FUTURE

It is hard to be certain about printing hardware developments. Dot-matrix printers will certainly continue to be very common for a long time, because they are a time-proven and mature technology.

Although laser printers seem very promising, other technologies could take the lead. Instead of using a laser beam to create the electrostatic latent image, there could be a dense array of light-emitting diodes across the whole width of the drum, which could be switched on and off at the proper moments while the drum slowly rotates.

It is possible to use ion beams rather than light. With these, the drum surface does not have to be light sensitive. It can be of a less fragile material in order to withstand more pressure. This allows the toner powder that has been deposited on the paper to be simply pressed in under high pressure; no heat is needed. These last two technologies have the clear advantage of fewer moving parts.

SUGGESTED READINGS

For further reading about standards I recommend FVFH90 and, of course, the standard descriptions like the X Window System series from O'Reilly & Assoc. Inc. Detailed information on GKS can be found in HDGS83.

EXERCISES

In the exercises below, you must have a way to read a pixel in the frame buffer.

SECTION 18.1

How is the cursor moved to follow the movements of the mouse? The system is continually informed of the mouse's movements. When the mouse moves, the system blanks out the old cursor before displaying the new one. If this updating occurs only at every vertical blanking signal, the motion on the screen will still be a good animation, because the redrawing occurs 60 times per second. (If you move the mouse rapidly enough, you can observe the cursor in discontinuous positions.)

1. Write a function `void xorcursor(int x, int y)` that draws a cross-hair cursor in the frame buffer in XOR mode such that the center is at location $(x\ y)$. The size of the cursor is nine pixels horizontally and nine pixels vertically.
2. Write a function `void xorline(int x, int y)` that draws a straight line in the frame buffer in XOR mode using the simple straight line DDA of Chapter 2.

Rubber banding is a very popular and user-friendly way to draw straight lines in paint-and-draw-systems. In the following exercise, you will develop a rubber band-drawing routine. You will be XORing pixels in the frame buffer. In a black-white display, pixel values can be 0 and 1. You change the pixel value x to $1-x$. If you have eight bits per pixel, you could for example change x to $255-x$. In both cases, two consecutive changes bring the pixels' value back to the original value.

3. Write a function `void rline()` that takes the position of the mouse upon a left button click as the starting point of a line. As long as the left button is held down the function draws a line in XOR mode to the new mouse position. Upon the mouse's movement, the old line is removed by redrawing it in XOR mode, and then a line to the new position is drawn in XOR mode. When the left button is released, the last line is drawn in SET mode.

APPENDIX A

MATHEMATICAL REFRESHER

This appendix develops the mathematics useful in computer graphics more fully than the summary in Chapter 1. The order of topics is the same as in that chapter.

A.1 COORDINATE SYSTEMS

The position of a point in a plane or in space is given by its coordinates. In a Cartesian system these are the distances from two perpendicular axes (from three mutually perpendicular axes in space). Figures A.1 and A.2 show some examples:

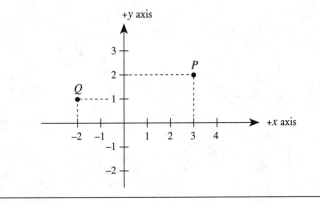

Figure A.1   Points in Cartesian coordinate system

In Figure A.1, point P is at $x = 3$, $y = 2$. We represent P as the number pair (3 2); by convention, the x-coordinate is given first. Similarly, $Q = (-2 \ 1)$ and, in Figure A.2, $R = (30 \ -4)$. Observe that the scale factors (units/distance) can be varied and they need not be the same along the different axes. The origin O is the point (0 0) in two dimensions (2D).

In three-dimensions (3D), while Cartesian axes are always perpendicular to each other, there are two possible orientations. If the x-axis is to the right and the y-axis is upward, the z-axis can point away from the viewer in a left-handed system (lhs), or toward the viewer in a right-handed system (rhs). These terms come from the fact that one can orient the thumb, forefinger, and middle finger of the left hand along the positive x-axis, the positive y-axis, and the positive z-axis respectively if it is a lhs. If it is a rhs, the right hand allows a corresponding alignment of the fingers (see Figure A.3). We will use a lhs most often in this book.

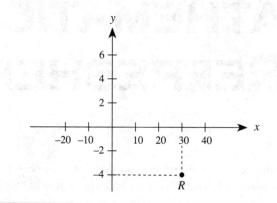

Figure A.2   Different scaling for x and y

A point in 3D is given by the number triple $(x \ y \ z)$ where these are the distances from the respective axes. The origin in 3D is $(0 \ 0 \ 0)$.

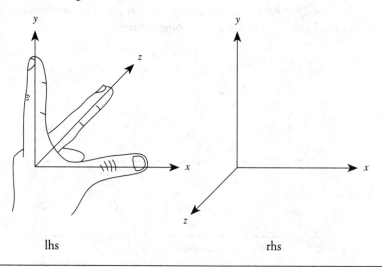

lhs   rhs

Figure A.3   Hand model for left-handed system

By using the Pythagorean theorem, it is easy to compute the distance d from $P_1 = (x_1 \ y_1)$ to $P_2 = (x_2 \ y_2)$:

$$d = \sqrt{(x_2 - x_1)^2 + (y_2 - y_1)^2}$$

In Figure A.1, the distance from P to Q is $(5^2 + 1^2)^{1/2} = 5.09902$. In three dimensions the distance is

$$d = \sqrt{(x_2 - x_1)^2 + (y_2 - y_1)^2 + (z_2 - z_1)^2}$$

Many other coordinate systems are possible. We will sometimes use polar coordinates where the position is specified as $(r \ \theta)$ with r being the distance from a chosen origin and θ the counterclockwise (ccw) angle from a chosen reference line (see Figure A.4).

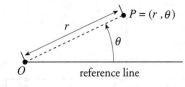

Figure A.4   Polar coordinates

A.2   INTERVAL NOTATION

In one-dimensional space we express a closed interval with square brackets and an open interval with parentheses. The interval $(0 \ 1)$ consists of all real numbers x such that $0 < x < 1$. Observe that the endpoints are excluded. The interval $[0 \ 1)$ consists of the same numbers as before but includes the number 0.

Two-dimensional intervals are rectangular areas in 2D and are expressed as Cartesian products of 1D intervals. The area $[0 \ 1) \times [0 \ 1)$ consists of all number pairs $(x \ y)$ with $0 \leq x < 1$ and $0 \leq y < 1$.

A.3   ROTATIONS

Rotating a point by a given angle is a common operation. Rotating a point by θ (measured ccw) is equivalent to rotating the axes by θ in a clockwise (cw) direction. The formulas are easier to derive from the latter. We will use Figure A.5 to derive them.

From Figure A.5, it is apparent that:

$$x = ON = OP \cos \alpha$$
$$y = NP = OP \sin \alpha$$
$$x' = ON' = OP \cos(\alpha + \theta)$$
$$y' = N'P = OP \sin(\alpha + \theta)$$

Since:

$$\cos(\alpha + \theta) = \cos \alpha \cos \theta - \sin \alpha \sin \theta$$
$$\sin(\alpha + \theta) = \sin \alpha \cos \theta + \cos \alpha \sin \theta$$

it follows that:

$$x' = x \cos \theta - y \sin \theta$$
$$y' = y \cos \theta + x \sin \theta$$

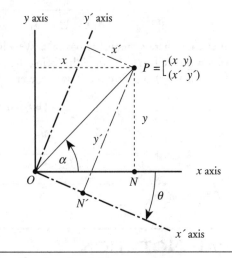

Figure A.5   Geometry of rotation about origin

A.4   ANALYTIC GEOMETRY

Analytic geometry is the representation of geometric figures through algebraic equations. We are most interested in straight lines, planes, and simple curves given by conic sections, especially circles and ellipses.

The equation of a straight line is a relation between y and x that gives the y-coordinate when an x-coordinate is specified (or the reverse). There are several forms, three of which involve the slope of the line, or the increase in the y-value due to a corresponding change in the x-value. The slope is constant for a line so any two points P_1 and P_2 define the slope:

$$\text{Slope} = \frac{y_2 - y_1}{x_2 - x_1}$$

We then have these forms:

Two-point: $\dfrac{y - y_1}{x - x_1} = \dfrac{y_2 - y_1}{x_2 - x_1}, \quad x_2 \neq x_1$

Point-slope: $\dfrac{y_2 - y_1}{x_2 - x_1} = m, \quad x_2 \neq x_1, \quad \text{where } m = \text{slope}$

Slope-intercept: $y = mx + b$, where b is value of y at $x = 0$.

The slope is also the tangent of the angle between the x-axis and the line. Two parallel lines have the same slope because both make the same angle with the x-axis. For two perpendicular lines, $m_1 = -1/m_2$ as Figure A.6 demonstrates:

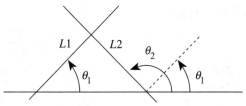

Figure A.6   Slope of perpendicular lines

It is clear that $\theta_2 = \theta_1 + 90°$, so:

$$m_2 = \tan\theta_2 = \tan(\theta_1 + 90\circ) = -\cot\theta_1 = \frac{-1}{\tan\theta_1} = \frac{-1}{m_1}$$

(If one of the lines is vertical so that the slope is undefined, the development requires taking limits.)

In addition to the above forms, there is the general form for a straight line:

$Ax + By - C = 0$, with A and B not both equal to zero.

For $B \neq 0$, the slope $m = -A/B$ and the intercept $b = C/B$. An equation with only first powers of the variables is called a linear equation and extends to linear equations in more than two variables.

$Ax + By + Cz - D = 0$ defines a plane. If $D = 0$, the plane goes through the origin. If $Ax_1 + By_1 + Cz_1 - D = 0$, the plane contains $P_1 = (x_1\ y_1\ z_1)$.

We will use Figure A.7 to develop the equation for the distance of a point from a line. $P_1 = (x_1\ y_1)$ is a point not on the line $L = Ax + By - C = 0$ and $P_2 = (x_2\ y_2)$ is the intersection of L with L', a line that is perpendicular to L through P_1. The equation for L' is $Bx - Ay - C' = 0$ from previous relationships.

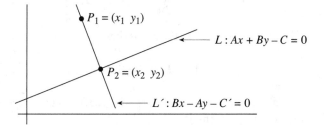

Figure A.7   Distance of point P_1 from line L

Since P_2 is on both L and L', its coordinates satisfy both line equations:

$$L:\quad Ax_2 + By_2 - C = 0$$
$$L':\quad Bx_2 - Ay_2 - C' = 0$$

Eliminating y_2 gives:

$$x_2 = \frac{AC + BC'}{A^2 + B^2}$$

Eliminating x_2 gives:

$$y_2 = -\frac{AC' - BC}{A^2 + B^2}$$

P_1 is also on L', so $C' = -Ay_1 + Bx_1$. Substituting for C' in the above equations for x_2 and y_2, we have:

$$x_2 = \frac{AC + B(-Ay_1 + Bx_1)}{A^2 + B^2}$$

$$y_2 = \frac{A(Ay_1 - Bx_1) + BC}{A^2 + B^2}$$

This gives:

$$x_1 - x_2 = \frac{x_1(A^2 + B^2) - AC + B(Ay_1 - Bx_1)}{A^2 + B^2}$$

$$= \frac{A(Ax_1 + By_1 - C)}{A^2 + B^2} = AW$$

and

$$y_1 - y_2 = \frac{y_1(A^2 + B^2) - A(Ay_1 - Bx_1) - BC}{A^2 + B^2}$$

$$= \frac{B(Ax_1 + By_1 - C)}{A^2 + B^2} = BW$$

where W represents the common factor

$$\frac{Ax_1 + By_1 - C}{A^2 + B^2}$$

The distance of P_1 from the line is then:

$$\sqrt{A^2W^2 + B^2W^2} = |W|\sqrt{A^2 + B^2} = \frac{|Ax_1 + By_1 - C|}{\sqrt{A^2 + B^2}}$$

The distance d from the point $P_1 = (x_1\ y_1\ z_1)$ to a plane defined by $Ax + By + Cz - D = 0$ is given by a similar formula:

$$d = \frac{|Ax_1 + By_1 + Cz_1 - D|}{\sqrt{A^2 + B^2 + C^2}}$$

This formula is more readily developed by using vectors (see texts on vector algebra).

Formulas for curves can also be expressed by parametric equations. If $y = f(x)$, there is a lack of symmetry because we must think of y as dependent on the independent variable x. While we may be able to invert this to give x as a function of y, it is often preferable to rewrite the function as two functions of a separate independent variable u that we call the parameter: $x = X(u)$ and $y = Y(u)$. Now, as u varies, both x and y assume new values and trace out the curve. For a straight line between $(x_1 \ y_1)$ and $(x_2 \ y_2)$, if

$$x = x_1 + u(x_2 - x_1) \quad \text{and} \quad y = y_1 + u(y_2 - y_1)$$

then, as u varies from 0 to 1, points on the line are generated between the two ends. The equation $u = 0$ gives the point $(x_1 \ y_1)$, $u = 1$ gives $(x_2 \ y_2)$, and intermediate values give other points at distances from the beginning that are equal to the fraction u times the length of the line. Points outside the line segment are generated by values of u outside the range [0,1].

The three parametric equations $x = X(u)$, $y = Y(u)$, and $z = Z(u)$ generate points on a space curve.

Conic sections are curves formed by the intersection of a plane and a cone and have equations that are quadratic in x and y. The general second-order equation:

$$ax^2 + bxy + cy^2 + dx + ey + f = 0$$

describes any of the conics; which one depends on the value of $b^2 - 4ac$, called the discriminant, *DISC*. If:

> *DISC* = 0, the curve is a parabola
> *DISC* < 0, the curve is an ellipse
> *DISC* > 0, the curve is a hyperbola

Rotating the points of a conic about the origin does not change the value of the discriminant, nor does the sum of a and b change.

A circle is described parametrically by the equations

$$x = r\cos\theta, \quad y = r\sin\theta$$

where θ is the parameter.

Using different values for r in the two equations generates an ellipse.

A.5   ALGEBRA

The solution of a quadratic equation in one variable $(ax^2 + bx + c = 0)$ is conveniently found through the quadratic formula:

$$x = \frac{-b \pm \sqrt{b^2 - 4ac}}{2a}$$

Nonlinear equations of the form $f(x) = 0$ can be solved by Newton's method. This is a technique for successively improving the accuracy of estimating the solution using the formula:

$$x_{n+1} = x_n - \frac{f(x_n)}{f'(x_n)}$$

where f' is the derivative of f.

EXAMPLE

Suppose

$$f(x) = x^2 - 2\sin x = 0$$
$$f'(x) = 2x - 2\cos x.$$

A sketch of $f(x)$ indicates a solution near $x = 1.3$. When $x_0 = 1.3$, $f(1.3) = -0.23712$, $f'(x) = 2.06500$, and $x_1 = 1.41483$. Continuing, $x_2 = 1.404500$, $x_3 = 1.404415$, and so on.

A system of linear equations can be solved simultaneously by elimination or, equivalently, through the ratios of determinants, known as Cramer's rule. For three equations:

$$a_1 x + b_1 y + c_1 z = d_1$$
$$a_2 x + b_2 y + c_2 z = d_2$$
$$a_3 x + b_3 y + c_3 z = d_3$$

$$x = \frac{\begin{vmatrix} d_1 & b_1 & c_1 \\ d_2 & b_2 & c_2 \\ d_3 & b_3 & c_3 \end{vmatrix}}{\begin{vmatrix} a_1 & b_1 & c_1 \\ a_2 & b_2 & c_2 \\ a_3 & b_3 & c_3 \end{vmatrix}}, \quad y = \frac{\begin{vmatrix} a_1 & d_1 & c_1 \\ a_2 & d_2 & c_2 \\ a_3 & d_3 & c_3 \end{vmatrix}}{\begin{vmatrix} a_1 & b_1 & c_1 \\ a_2 & b_2 & c_2 \\ a_3 & b_3 & c_3 \end{vmatrix}}, \quad z = \frac{\begin{vmatrix} a_1 & b_1 & d_1 \\ a_2 & b_2 & d_2 \\ a_3 & b_3 & d_3 \end{vmatrix}}{\begin{vmatrix} a_1 & b_1 & c_1 \\ a_2 & b_2 & c_2 \\ a_3 & b_3 & c_3 \end{vmatrix}}.$$

The vertical bars represent determinants. Observe that the denominator determinant is the same in all three expressions. A similar arrangement solves a set of n equations. Computing the determinant is explained below under matrices.

A.6   PLANES

A plane $Ax + By + Cz - D = 0$ can be defined by three noncollinear points P_1, P_2, P_3 or by two nonparallel vectors. It separates all of space into two halves. The vector $n = (A\ B\ C)$ is normal to the plane. When we put the start of this vector in the plane, the side it points to is called the positive side of space. Figure A.8 illustrates this.

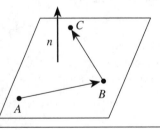

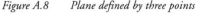

Figure A.8   Plane defined by three points

We often normalize plane equations by dividing every component by $\sqrt{A^2 + B^2 + C^2}$. We then express the divided components by lowercase letters. The normalized plane equation is then:

$$ax + by + cz - d = 0$$

In a normalized plane equation the length of the plane normal n is 1 and the coefficient d is equal to the distance of the plane from the origin.

A.7 VECTORS

A vector is a compound quantity; it has both magnitude and direction. This means that it can be pictured as a directed line segment whose length represents the magnitude and whose orientation (an arrow is placed on the far end) represents the direction. Two vectors with the same magnitude and direction are equal. Normally a vector is considered to be a free vector that can be moved parallel to itself so equal vectors can be superimposed. Vectors are also represented as a number pair where the values are the x- and y-coordinates of the end point when the start point is at the origin of Cartesian axes. These numbers are called the components of the vector.

Two vectors are added graphically by drawing the second vector starting at the end point of the first. One vector is subtracted from a second by adding its negative, which is the vector in the opposite direction with the same length. See Figure A.9 for examples.

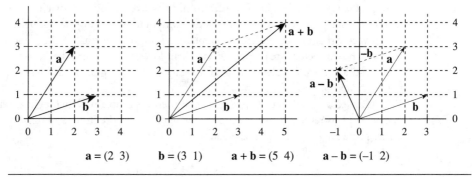

$$\mathbf{a} = (2\ \ 3) \qquad \mathbf{b} = (3\ \ 1) \qquad \mathbf{a} + \mathbf{b} = (5\ \ 4) \qquad \mathbf{a} - \mathbf{b} = (-1\ \ 2)$$

Figure A.9   Vector addition and subtraction

Vectors are often written using boldface lowercase letters, as we have done in the figure.

An alternate (and preferred) way to add or subtract vectors is to add or subtract the components:

$$\text{If } \mathbf{v}_1 = (x_1\ \ y_1) \text{ and } \mathbf{v}_2 = (x_2\ \ y_2), \text{ then:}$$

$$\mathbf{v}_1 + \mathbf{v}_2 = (x_1 + x_2\ \ y_1 + y_2), \ \mathbf{v}_1 - \mathbf{v}_2 = (x_1 - x_2\ \ y_1 - y_2)$$

The length or magnitude of a vector is written with bars: $|\mathbf{v}|$, and $|\mathbf{v}| = \sqrt{x^2 + y^2}$ when $\mathbf{v} = (x\ \ y)$. This is exactly the length of the vector when drawn in the Cartesian plane. Normalizing a vector means making its length unity without changing its direction. To normalize vector $\mathbf{v}$, divide each component by $|\mathbf{v}|$.

When working with vectors, ordinary numbers are called scalars to distinguish them. Multiplying a vector by a scalar multiplies its length. In terms of components, if $\mathbf{v} = (x\ \ y)$, $c\mathbf{v} = (cx\ \ cy)$.

In three dimensions, a vector is defined by three components:

$$\mathbf{v} = \left(x\ \ y\ \ z\right)$$

Two vectors can be multiplied together and there are two kinds of products. We will use these products only for vectors in space, therefore we explain them here.

The dot product is a scalar, also called the scalar product. Another name is the inner product. It is computed by adding the products of the corresponding components:

$$\mathbf{v}_1\ \mathbf{v}_2 = x_1 x_2 + y_1 y_2 + z_1 z_2$$

but this is equivalent:

$$\mathbf{v}_1\ \mathbf{v}_2 = \left|\mathbf{v}_1\right|\left|\mathbf{v}_2\right| \cos\theta$$

where θ is the angle between $\mathbf{v}_1$ and $\mathbf{v}_2$.

The second kind of vector product is the cross product, also called the vector product or the outer product. It is a vector and is computed by:

$$\mathbf{v}_1 \times \mathbf{v}_2 = \left(y_1 z_2 - z_1 y_2\ \ \ z_1 x_2 - x_1 z_2\ \ \ x_1 y_2 - y_1 x_2\right)$$

The resulting vector is perpendicular to $\mathbf{v}_1$ and $\mathbf{v}_2$. Its direction is such that $\mathbf{v}_1$, $\mathbf{v}_2$ and the cross product, when taken in that order, form a rhs in a rhs and a lhs in a lhs. The cross product is not necessarily of unit length, so in most computations it must be normalized.

A vector that is perpendicular to a plane is said to be normal to the plane.

When two vectors are perpendicular, their dot product is zero (because cos 90° = 0). The cross product of two parallel vectors is the vector (0 0 0). These conditions are used to test for perpendicular or parallel vectors.

As an example of vector arithmetic, consider this problem. When light enters a transparent object, it is refracted (its direction is changed) when the indices of refraction are not the same. The change of direction is given by the relation:

$$\sin a' = \left(\frac{\mu}{\mu'}\right)\sin a$$

where a and a' are the angles between the vector normal to the surface and the entering and leaving rays, and μ and μ' are the refractive indices (see Figure A.10).

We wish to determine the components of $\mathbf{L}'$, given $\mathbf{L}$ (a unit vector pointing to the light source), $\mathbf{n}$ (a unit vector normal to the surface), and the values of μ and μ'. We draw the line from Q to R parallel to $\mathbf{L}$ and through the end point of $-\mathbf{n}$. It is clear that angle $c = 180° - a$, and, because they are the internal angles of triangle PQR, that $a' + b + c = 180°$. From these relations, angle $b = a - a'$. From the law of sines we have:

$$\frac{d}{1} = \frac{\sin a'}{\sin(a - a')} \quad \text{where } d = \text{ length of } QR.$$

We then get $\mathbf{L}'$ by vector addition: $\mathbf{L}' = -\mathbf{n} - d\mathbf{L}$. Ordinarily we would normalize $\mathbf{L}'$ by dividing by its length.

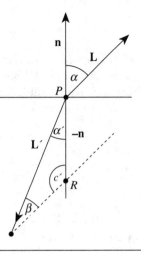

Figure A.10   Geometry of light refraction

A.8   MATRICES

A matrix is another compound quantity composed of components or elements arranged as a rectangular array, so it has rows and columns. A matrix of r rows and c columns is said to be $r \times c$ in size. A matrix is often represented as an uppercase letter in boldface, while its components are represented as the same lowercase letter with two subscripts, the first indicating the row and the second the column. The matrix is also represented as the general element enclosed in square brackets:

$$\mathbf{A} = \begin{pmatrix} a_{11} & a_{12} & a_{13} \\ a_{21} & a_{22} & a_{23} \\ a_{31} & a_{32} & a_{33} \end{pmatrix} = [a_{ij}]$$

In the above, $\mathbf{A}$ is 3×3. A matrix is square if the number of rows equals the number of columns. Matrices do not have to be square, but most matrices used in computer graphics are square. Two matrices of the same size can be added or subtracted:

$$\mathbf{C} = \mathbf{A} + \mathbf{B} = [a_{ij} + b_{ij}] = [c_{ij}]$$
$$\mathbf{D} = \mathbf{A} - \mathbf{B} = [a_{ij} - b_{ij}] = [d_{ij}]$$

If a matrix is multiplied by a scalar, each of its elements is multiplied by the scalar: $c\mathbf{A} = [ca_{ij}]$.

Two matrices can be multiplied if they are conformable for multiplication, meaning that the number of columns of the first equals the number of rows of the second. When $\mathbf{A}$ is $r \times c$ and $\mathbf{B}$ is $c \times t$, the product $\mathbf{E} = \mathbf{A}\,\mathbf{B}$ is $r \times t$. Its elements are:

$$e_{ij} = \sum_{k=1}^{c} a_{ik}b_{kj}, \quad i = 1\ldots r, \quad j = 1\ldots t$$

which is the sum of products of elements in row i of **A** times those in column j of **B** taken in pairs as we move across the rows and down the columns. The order of the factors (**A** and **B**) cannot be interchanged in matrix multiplication.

EXAMPLE

$$\text{Let } \mathbf{A} = \begin{pmatrix} 3 & 2 & 4 \\ -1 & 1 & 0 \\ 3 & 0 & 1 \end{pmatrix} \quad \text{and } \mathbf{B} = \begin{pmatrix} 1 & 3 & 1 \\ 2 & 2 & 0 \\ -2 & 0 & 2 \end{pmatrix}$$

$$3\mathbf{A} = \begin{pmatrix} 9 & 6 & 12 \\ -3 & 3 & 0 \\ 9 & 0 & 3 \end{pmatrix}$$

$$\mathbf{A} + \mathbf{B} = \begin{pmatrix} 4 & 5 & 5 \\ 1 & 3 & 0 \\ 1 & 0 & 3 \end{pmatrix} \quad \mathbf{A} - \mathbf{B} = \begin{pmatrix} 2 & -1 & 3 \\ -3 & -1 & 0 \\ 5 & 0 & -1 \end{pmatrix}$$

For $\mathbf{E} = \mathbf{A}\,\mathbf{B}$, here are some typical elements:

$$e_{31} = a_{31}b_{11} + a_{32}b_{21} + a_{33}b_{31}$$
$$= (3)(1) + (0)(2) + (1)(-2) = 3 + 0 - 2 = 1$$
$$e_{23} = (-1)(1) + (1)(0) + (0)(2) = -1 + 0 + 0 = -1$$
$$e_{33} = (3)(1) + (0)(0) + (1)(2) = 3 + 0 + 2 = 5$$

Completing for all rows and columns gives:

$$\mathbf{E} = \begin{pmatrix} -1 & 13 & 11 \\ 1 & -1 & -1 \\ 1 & 9 & 5 \end{pmatrix}$$

If the components of a vector are written in a row, the vector can be thought of as a special case of a matrix, one with only one row. Similarly, writing the elements in a column makes the vector another special case of a matrix. When vectors are so written, they are called row vectors or column vectors. These two forms can make the vector conformable for multiplication, so multiplication of vectors and matrices is defined. A superscript T is sometimes used to designate a column vector, so if the components of **v** are 3, −1, and 4:

$$\mathbf{v} = \begin{pmatrix} 3 & -1 & 4 \end{pmatrix} \quad \text{and} \quad \mathbf{v}^T = \begin{pmatrix} 3 \\ -1 \\ 4 \end{pmatrix}$$

EXAMPLE

Using $\mathbf{A}$ and $\mathbf{v}$ as defined above,

$$\mathbf{A}\,\mathbf{v}^T = \begin{pmatrix} 23 \\ -4 \\ 13 \end{pmatrix} \qquad \mathbf{v}\,\mathbf{A} = \begin{pmatrix} 22 & 5 & 16 \end{pmatrix}$$

This means that $\mathbf{v}\,\mathbf{v}^T$ forms the dot product of $\mathbf{v}$ with itself, according to the rules for matrix multiplication.

Since the rows of a matrix are, in effect, row vectors, we can think of a matrix as a column of row vectors or, conversely, as a row of column vectors.

A.9 TENSOR PRODUCTS

A tensor product can be described as a matrix multiplication in which the first matrix is a column vector $(c_i)^T$ and the second a row vector (r_j). The result is a matrix (m_{ij}) with as many rows as the number of elements in the first vector and as many columns as the number of elements in the second vector.

The elements in (m_{ij}) are $m_{ij} = c_i * r_j$.

EXAMPLE

$$\begin{pmatrix} -2 \\ 3 \\ 1 \end{pmatrix} * \begin{pmatrix} 3 & 4 & 5 \end{pmatrix} = \begin{pmatrix} -6 & -8 & -10 \\ 9 & 12 & 15 \\ 3 & 4 & 5 \end{pmatrix}$$

A.10 SYSTEMS OF LINEAR EQUATIONS

A system of linear equations can be written in matrix form. For example, this set of three equations:

$$4x_1 - 3x_2 + 2x_3 = -1$$
$$x_1 + 2x_2 - x_3 = 7$$
$$2x_1 + x_2 + x_3 = 2$$

is the same as $\mathbf{A}\,\mathbf{x}^T = \mathbf{b}^T$, where

$$\mathbf{A} = \begin{pmatrix} 4 & -3 & 2 \\ 1 & 2 & -1 \\ 2 & 1 & 1 \end{pmatrix}, \quad \mathbf{x}^T = \begin{pmatrix} x_1 \\ x_2 \\ x_3 \end{pmatrix}, \quad \mathbf{b}^T = \begin{pmatrix} -1 \\ 7 \\ 2 \end{pmatrix}$$

Solving a system of n equations is usually done by elimination if n is greater than 3. Systems of this magnitude occur rarely in Computer Graphics—one example is the computation of an interpolating spline curve. See numerical analysis books such as GEWH84. For a system up to size 3 it is more convenient to use Cramer's rule.

The matrices that we use in this book are always square. A square matrix has some important properties. When all elements on the main diagonal are unity and all others are zero, the matrix is called the identity matrix and the symbol $\mathbf{I}$ is used. In this case, when $\mathbf{A}$ is the same size,

$$\mathbf{I}\,\mathbf{A} = \mathbf{A}\,\mathbf{I} = \mathbf{A}$$

which is an exception to the rule that matrix multiplication is noncommutative.

Every matrix $\mathbf{A}$ has a so called transpose, written $\mathbf{A}^T$. The elements t_{ij} of the transpose are obtained by $t_{ij} = a_{ji}$.

EXAMPLE

$$\mathbf{A} = \begin{pmatrix} 4 & -3 & 2 \\ 1 & 2 & -1 \\ 2 & 1 & 1 \end{pmatrix} \qquad \mathbf{A}^T = \begin{pmatrix} 4 & 1 & 2 \\ -3 & 2 & 1 \\ 2 & -1 & 1 \end{pmatrix}$$

Except for certain pathological cases, a square matrix has an inverse, written $\mathbf{A}^{-1}$, and:

$$\mathbf{A}\,\mathbf{A}^{-1} = \mathbf{A}^{-1}\mathbf{A} = \mathbf{I},$$

another exception to the noncommutative rule. We don't elaborate on how to find the inverse of a matrix.

A square matrix has a determinant, a scalar quantity that is often represented by magnitude bars. The evaluation of determinants of sizes bigger than 3×3 is complicated. We show below the evaluation of determinants of sizes 2×2 and 3×3:

$$\begin{vmatrix} a_{11} & a_{12} \\ a_{21} & a_{22} \end{vmatrix} = a_{11}a_{22} - a_{21}a_{12}$$

$$\begin{vmatrix} a_{11} & a_{12} & a_{13} \\ a_{21} & a_{22} & a_{23} \\ a_{31} & a_{32} & a_{33} \end{vmatrix} = \begin{array}{l} a_{11}a_{22}a_{33} + a_{21}a_{32}a_{13} + a_{31}a_{12}a_{23} \\ -a_{11}a_{32}a_{23} - a_{21}a_{12}a_{33} - a_{31}a_{22}a_{13} \end{array}$$

This example will clarify, where $\mathbf{A}$ is the same matrix as before:

$$\det(A) = \begin{vmatrix} 4 & -3 & 2 \\ 1 & 2 & -1 \\ 2 & 1 & 1 \end{vmatrix} = \begin{array}{l} 4*2*1 + 1*1*2 + 2*(-3)*(-1) \\ -4*1*(-1) - 1*(-3)*1 - 2*2*2 \end{array}$$

$$= 8 + 2 + 6 + 4 + 3 - 8 = 15$$

A.11 DERIVATIVES

The need for calculus is relatively modest in computer graphics; we use only formulas for derivatives. The important standard formulas are just tabulated. These assume that u is the independent variable: $x = x(u)$, $y = y(u)$. They use the notation $x' = dx/du$, $y' = dy/du$:

$$\frac{du}{du} = 1 \qquad \frac{dx}{dx} = 1 \qquad \frac{dy}{dy} = 1$$

$$\frac{d(x+y)}{du} = x' + y'$$

$$\frac{dy}{dx} = \left(\frac{dy}{du}\right)\left(\frac{du}{dx}\right) = \frac{y'}{x'}$$

$$dx^n = n\left(x^{n-1}\right)x'$$

$$d(\sin x) = (\cos x)x'$$

$$d(\cos x) = -(\sin x)x'$$

Derivatives can be approximated by central differences:

A.12 COMPLEX NUMBERS

Complex numbers are another type of compound quantity, being composed of a real part and an imaginary part. They occur quite naturally in solving quadratic equations where $\sqrt{b^2 - 4ac}$ requires taking the square root of a negative quantity. If we represent $\sqrt{-1} = i$, a complex number can be written as $a + ib$. This can be plotted on the complex plane, known as an Argand diagram, where the real axis is drawn horizontally and the imaginary axis vertically. This indicates that a complex number can also be represented by the number pair $(a\ b)$, which is equivalent to a vector from the origin to the point $(a\ b)$.

The operations of addition and subtraction are exactly equivalent to the same operations with vectors. However, multiplication and division are defined differently.

Let

$$z = (a\ b),$$

$$z_1 = (a_1\ b_1),$$

$$z_2 = (a_2\ b_2).$$

Then we have

$$\alpha * (a\ b) = (\alpha a\ \ \alpha b) \qquad (\alpha \text{ is a real number})$$

$$z_1 * z_2 = (a_1 a_2 - b_1 b_2 \quad a_1 b_2 + a_2 b_1)$$

$$z_1 / z_2 = \frac{(a_1 a_2 + b_1 b_2 \quad a_1 b_2 - a_2 b_1)}{a_2^2 + b_2^2}$$

The magnitude of a complex number is obtained exactly as with a two-component vector:

$$|z| = \sqrt{a^2 + b^2}$$

The distance between the random numbers z_1 and z_2 in the complex plane is

$$d = \sqrt{(a_1 - a_2)^2 + (b_1 - b_2)^2}$$

We will often use the square root of a complex number. A complex number $(a\ b)$ can be written in exponential form: $(a\ b) = re^{i\phi}$, which is $(r*\cos\phi\ \ r*\sin\phi)$ according to Euler's formula. In this expression $r = \sqrt{a^2 + b^2}$. It follows that

$$\sqrt{(a\ b)} = \sqrt{r}e^{\frac{i\phi}{2}} = \pm\left(\sqrt{r}*\cos\left(\tfrac{\phi}{2}\right)\ \ \sqrt{r}*\sin\left(\tfrac{\phi}{2}\right)\right)$$

The trigonometric formulas for the half-angle are:

$$\cos(\phi/2) = \sqrt{\tfrac{1}{2}(1 + \cos\phi)} \quad \text{and} \quad \sin(\phi/2) = \sqrt{\tfrac{1}{2}(1 - \cos\phi)}$$

Putting those into the expression for $\sqrt{(a\ b)}$ and multiplying by r within the radical, we get

$$\pm\left(\sqrt{\tfrac{1}{2}(r + r*\cos\phi)}\ \ \sqrt{\tfrac{1}{2}(r - r*\cos\phi)}\right)$$

Since $a = r*\cos\phi$ we have:

$$\sqrt{(a\ b)} = \pm\left(\sqrt{\tfrac{1}{2}(r + a)}\ \ \sqrt{\tfrac{1}{2}(r - a)}\right)$$

The deficiency of this formula is that it computes the same square roots for $(a\ b)$ and $(a\ -b)$ although they are not identical. This is corrected by making the imaginary part negative if $b < 0$ and positive if $b \geq 0$.

A.13 BINARY NUMBERS

Computers store all values as binary numbers. These use 2 as a base and are composed of bits that may be either 0 or 1. (Actually, the values are one of two voltage states that we interpret as 0 or 1.) The bits in a binary number have a place value just as the digits in our usual base 10 numbers do, but in a binary quantity each bit to the left represents the next power of 2 rather than a power of 10. For example, 1101 is:

$$
\begin{array}{llllll}
\text{bits:} & 1 & 1 & 0 & 1 \\
\text{weight:} & 2^3 & 2^2 & 2^1 & 2^0 \\
\text{value:} & 8 & +4 & +0 & +1 & = 13 \text{ as a base 10 number}
\end{array}
$$

Shifting to the right (losing the rightmost bit in the process) divides the number by two while a left shift (filling in at the right with 0) doubles it:

right shift: $1101_2 \rightarrow 110_2 = 6_{10}$

left shift: $\quad 1101_2 \rightarrow 11010_2 = 26_{10}$

(When numbers of different bases are used together, it is customary to show the base as a subscript.) The division above is integer division so the fractional part is lost. Since the computer's registers can do shifts on their contents quite readily, doubling or halving is a fast operation.

Two binary numbers are added by adding each corresponding bit. The addition table is simple: 0+0 = 0, 1+0 = 1, 1+1 = 10, with the 1 here carried over to the next set of bits, so we also need 1+1+1 = 11. Here is an example:

```
      1  1  1        1  ← carries
      1  1  0  1  0  0  1
   +  1  0  1  1  0  0  1
   ─────────────────────
sum   1  1  0  0  0  1  0
```

The other operations of subtraction, multiplication, and division are similar to those in base 10 arithmetic, but we will not use them in the book. We will need the logical operations of AND, OR, and XOR. These tables show the results:

AND	0	1		OR	0	1		XOR	0	1
0	0	0		0	0	1		0	0	1
1	0	1		1	1	1		1	1	0

With AND, both bits must be 1 for the result to be a 1; with OR, the result is 1 if either or both bits are 1; with XOR, the result is a 1 if either is a 1 but not both. With multiple bit quantities, the operations are performed on each pair of corresponding bits.

A.14 RANDOM NUMBERS

A true random number is a value that cannot be predicted or computed in advance. We might get a random number by drawing values from a mixed pool of numbers or by throwing dice. In a computer, pseudorandom numbers are computed by an algorithm that gives results resembling true random numbers and pass one or more tests for randomness. A simple scheme is to multiply a seed number by another (carefully chosen) value and taking several digits from the middle of the product. Often this value is used as the seed for getting the next one.

There are other techniques but the method is less important than the concept.

APPENDIX B

SPATIAL GEOMETRY OF SOLIDS

This appendix explains the implementations of the solids provided for this book, except for sphere, ellipsoid, and cylinder, which are explained in Chapter 14.

B.1   THE CONE

The cone is a common conic solid. We reduce an arbitrary cone to a unit-cone, which is described below:

The quadratic equation:

$$x^2 - y^2 + z^2 = 0$$

describes the so called mantle. It extends to $+\infty$ and $-\infty$, its slope is 45° and the cross section is circular. We call the solid contained by the mantle the mantle-body; see Figure B.1. To obtain a unit-cone we cut it off with the planes $y = 0$ and $y = -1$; see the darker shaded portion in the figure. This unit-cone is upright and centered around the y-axis. The vertex is at (0 0 0). Any arbitrary cone—even one with elliptic cross section—can be derived from this one by scaling, rotation and translation. However, these operations will not create a cone that is cut off at a slant. (Other ways exist to do that.)

The intersection of a ray with an arbitrary cone is found by subjecting the ray to the same operations that are applied to the arbitrary cone and then intersecting it with the unit-cone. We now explain the intersection and normal for the unit-cone.

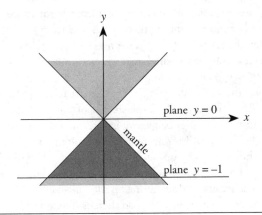

Figure B.1   Vertical cross section through unit cone

B.2   UNIT-CONE RAY INTERSECTION

The general principle for finding the intersections is related to that used for the cylinder. But care must be taken, as the mantle-body is infinitely large and concave. It is critically important to distinguish between the mantle-body and the unit-cone that we are modeling. To test for the intersection with the mantle we solve the quadratic equation:

$$a_2 * u^2 + a_1 * u + a_0 = 0$$

with

$$a_2 = d_x^2 - d_y^2 + d_z^2$$
$$a_1 = s_x * d_x - s_y * d_y + s_z * d_z$$
$$a_0 = s_x^2 - s_y^2 + s_z^2$$

We compute

$$dis = \sqrt{a_1^2 - a_2 * a_0}$$

and

$$u_1 = (-a_1 - dis) / a_2$$
$$u_2 = (-a_1 + dis) / a_2$$

if they are real.

Whether $u_1 < u_2$ depends on a_2. The smaller of u_1 and u_2 is not necessarily an entry to and the larger not necessarily an exit from the mantle-body! We also compute the two ray-plane intersections, which are p_{en} and p_{ex} ($p_{en} < p_{ex}$).

Now we test the slope of the ray to find whether it is between $+45°$ and $-45°$ ("flat"), or outside this range ("steep"). A ray is "flat" if $d_y < \sqrt{d_x^2 + d_z^2}$. This translates to $d_x^2 - d_y^2 + d_z^2 > 0$, equivalent to $a_2 > 0$. The ray is steep if $a_2 < 0$. (We ignore the case $a_2 = 0$ which is not likely.

This requires a special treatment of the quadratic equation. One can avoid it by setting a_2 to a small number and continuing the normal operation.)

When the ray is flat ($a_2 > 0$), the mantle-body behaves like a convex object: the smaller of the u-values is an entry, the larger an exit, and $u_1 < u_2$. As with a cylinder we compute $u_1 = \max(u_1, p_{en})$ and $u_2 = \min(u_2, p_{ex})$.

When the ray is steep ($a_2 < 0$), the situation is more complicated. The mantle-body behaves like a concave object: the smaller of the u-values is an exit, the larger an entry, and $u_1 > u_2$. In the examples below, we ignore whether the entry and exit values are negative or positive (behind us or in front of us when looking in the direction of the ray). We distinguish between the cases "steep upwardly" and "steep downwardly."

A ray steep upwardly always exits the mantle-body at $u = u_2$ and enters at $u = u_1$; u_1 is meaningless because it does not lie on the unit-cone. This is demonstrated in Figure B.2.

In the code we set u_1 to p_{en}, so there is only one entry: p_{en}. Also $u_2 < p_{ex}$ is always true, so u_2 is the smaller exit.

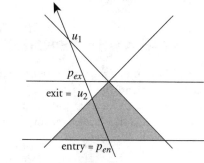

Figure B.2   *Ray intersecting unit cone steep upwardly*

A ray steep downwardly always exits the mantle-body at $u = u_2$ and enters at $u = u_1$; u_2 is meaningless because it does not lie on the unit-cone. This is demonstrated in Figure B.3.

In the code we set u_2 to p_{ex}, so there is only one exit: p_{ex}. Also, $u_1 > p_{en}$ is always true, so u_1 is the larger entry.

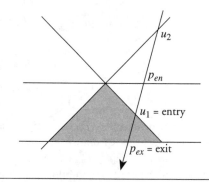

Figure B.3   *Ray intersecting unit cone steep downwardly*

Finally, we test for $u_1 < u_2$. If this is true, the ray hits the cone and we return these two values if they are not both negative. If $u_1 > u_2$ the ray misses the cone.

Here, too, we can preclude cases from further testing: when the ray starts on or above the top plane and points parallel or upward, or on or below the bottom plane and points parallel or downward. Rays parallel to the planes and starting inside the planes must be treated separately to avoid division by zero or a very small number, as with the cylinder.

We can also sift out cases in which the ray starts outside the mantle-body and points in such a direction that a hit is impossible. The formulation for this condition is more complicated; we omit the details.

B.3   CONE NORMAL

We subject the hit point on the original cone to an arbitrary-to-unit transformation to obtain the hit point on the unit cone. If its y-coordinate is close to -1, the hit point is on the bottom plane, otherwise it is on the cone mantle. In the first case the normal is (0 -1 0). This vector is rotated back to the original cone by multiplying it by the transpose of the rotation matrix rot. This results in the second column of the matrix. We precompute and store this normal in the private member bot.

In the second case it is the vector from (0 0 0) to the hit point with the y-coordinate made positive. This changes its slope from -1 to $+1$. This vector must be scaled by the inverse axes because the mantle of the arbitrary cone might have a different slant and the cross section might be elliptic. Then it must be backrotated to the original cone. We do this by multiplication by t^T. Afterwards the vector is normalized.

B.4   THE BACKGROUND

If the ray hits a solid, illum() obtains an *rgb*-value by invoking the texture function for the object hit, subjecting this value to further change through interaction with light sources, and other factors. Illum() should do this consistently.

Defining the background as a primitive of the scene guarantees that at least one object is always hit when tracing a ray. So it allows consistent behavior of illum() in all cases and also provides the opportunity to define non-trivial background textures.

Its intersections with the ray are defined to always exist when a test is made. Two identical hit points (entry and exit), which are large constants, are returned. This guarantees that any other object in the scene will be closer than the background if it is hit. The normal at any hit point of the background is set to (0 0 0). It then follows that in testing for a shadow at the hit point, the dot product of normal and vector to the light source will be zero. Consequently, only the ambient light plays a role when computing the background illumination.

B.5   THE HALFSPACE

A halfspace is the simplest possible primitive. It consists of one plane and the space on the negative side of it. This makes the normal point away from it. As the unit-halfspace we take the $(x\ z)$-plane and the space below. Its center is the origin. The halfspace can be positioned arbitrarily in space by specifying rotation and center.

To display a halfspace as such makes no sense, but it is very useful in Boolean combinations. For example, to view a cross section of any object, one intersects it with a halfspace. Arbitrary polyhedra can be formed as intersections of halfspaces.

A ray is intersected with the arbitrarily positioned halfspace. If the ray is not parallel to the plane, we compute the intersection value and determine whether it is an entry or exit. If it is an entry, we set the exit u-value to a large positive number. If an exit, we set the entry u-value to a large negative number. (Remember that it is our principle to always return pairs of intersection values for every primitive.)

If the ray is parallel to the plane and the ray starts outside, we return intersection values of zero. If the ray starts inside, we return a large negative number as the entry and a large positive number as the exit.

B.6   THE BOARD

We model only boards that are rectangular with specified extents in the local x- and z-directions. A board is infinitely thin, so its local y-extent is zero. It can have an arbitrary position in space.

An arbitrary board is reduced to a unit-board with center at $(0\ 0\ 0)$ and with x- and z-axes equal to 1. It extends from -1 to $+1$ in x and from -1 to $+1$ in z.

There are two things out of the ordinary. When transforming the ray, there is no scaling by y, as the board has no thickness—all boards are equal in terms of y. Also, the principle of returning pairs of intersection values is preserved—when the board is hit, two equal hit-values are returned. In other respects the intersection of the transformed ray with the unit board is straightforward.

B.7   THE BOX

The arbitrary box is reduced to a unit cube. This unit-cube is centered at $(0\ 0\ 0)$ and bounded by the planes $x = \pm1$ (left and right), $y = \pm1$ (top and bottom) and by $z = \pm1$ (near and far). These planes are specified so that their normals point outward. The transformed ray is intersected with these six planes. This gives us six hit values, of which three are entry and three are exit points. A hit point is an entry point if the dot product of ray-direction and plane-normal is negative; otherwise it is an exit point.

We use the same principle as for the cylinder-ray intersection. We find the smallest exit value, u_{ex}, and the largest entry value, u_{en}. If $u_{en} < u_{ex}$ then these two are the intersection values with the ray, otherwise the ray misses the unit cube.

We must test whether the ray is parallel to any of the planes. If this is the case and if the ray runs outside the plane against which it is tested, there is no intersection; the function returns zero. This can be found by testing the ray start-point:

$$ray.s.x < -1 \;\|\; 1 < ray.s.x$$
$$\| \; ray.s.y < -1 \;\|\; 1 < ray.s.y$$
$$\| \; ray.s.z < -1 \;\|\; 1 < ray.s.z$$

If the parallel ray runs inside, nothing is computed and u_{en}, u_{ex} maintain their settings at $-\infty$ and $+\infty$ respectively. After all planes are tested (and no 0 has been returned), u_{en} and u_{ex} must have been set, because no ray can be parallel to all six planes.

The six normals are precomputed in position(). After finding on which plane the hit point lies, that plane's normal is returned. One finds the plane by checking whether the x-, y-, or z-coordinate of the transformed hit point is close to ± 1.

B.8   THE TETRAHEDRON

The tetrahedron is one of Plato's solids. It is bounded by four equilateral triangles. A unit-tetrahedron has its bottom plane horizontal and its center at the origin. It has the front edge of the bottom triangle parallel to the x-axis. It is scaled so that the distance from the origin to any vertex is 1.

To get the coordinates of the planes that hold the faces of the unit-tetrahedron, we look down from the positive y-axis at a correctly positioned but unscaled tetrahedron. Figure B.4 shows this. $V1$, $V2$, and $V3$ are the vertices of the bottom triangle. The projections onto the $(x\ z)$-plane of the three lines connecting the origin with the vertices of the bottom triangle make angles of 120°. The third connecting line coincides with the z-axis. Setting $c = \cos(30°)$ and $s = \sin(30°)$, we can specify the coordinates of these three vertices as

$$V1 = \begin{pmatrix} c & y & -s \end{pmatrix} \qquad V2 = \begin{pmatrix} -c & y & -s \end{pmatrix} \qquad V3 = \begin{pmatrix} 0 & y & 1 \end{pmatrix}$$

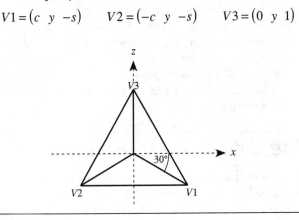

Figure B.4   Unit tetrahedron seen from above

The fourth vertex that points directly toward us has the coordinates $V0 = \begin{pmatrix} 0 & \alpha & 0 \end{pmatrix}$. The coefficients y and α are unknown in these relations. Taking the vertices as vectors from the origin, the dot products between any two of them must be equal, as they are at equal angles with each other and of equal length.

The equal lengths of $V0$ and $V1$ give the relation: $\alpha^2 = c^2 + y^2 + s^2$. The dot products of any two normals are equal, so we get:

$$\text{dot}(V1, V2) = -c^2 + y^2 + s^2 = y * \alpha = \text{dot}(V1, V0)$$

Squaring the above equation and substituting the value for α leads to:

$$\left(-c^2 + y^2 + s^2\right)^2 = y^2 * \left(c^2 + y^2 + s^2\right)$$

Inserting $\sin(30°) = \frac{1}{2}$ and $\cos(30°) = \frac{1}{2}\sqrt{3}$ leads to:

$$\left(y^2 - \tfrac{1}{2}\right)^2 = y^2 * \left(1 + y^2\right)$$

from which we obtain: $y^2 = \frac{1}{8}$. We take $y = -\frac{1}{4}\sqrt{2}$. It follows that $\alpha = \frac{3}{4}\sqrt{2}$. By inverting all signs in the vectors $V0$ through $V3$, we obtain the surface normals of the opposite planes. After normalizing them the y-coordinates of the three side-normals are 0.333333. It follows that, if we put the bottom vertices at a distance of 1 from the origin, their y-coordinates must be 0.333333. Therefore, the bottom plane has a distance of 0.333333 from the origin and so do all other planes. This gives the tetrahedron an inner radius of 1/3 and an outer radius of 1. The resulting plane equations are shown in the constructor `tethedron_t()`.

In finding the intersection of an arbitrary tetrahedron with an arbitrary ray there is no advantage in transforming the ray and then intersecting it with the unit tetrahedron. (The reason is that the plane equations even of a unit-tetrahedron are not "simple"—like those of a unit box.) So we intersect the ray directly with the arbitrary object.

We define the arbitrary tetrahedron by scaling, rotating and translating the planes of the unit tetrahedron to the arbitrary location and storing the coefficients of these four planes. We use a structure consisting of an array of four planes and the radius for this. The definition of the four planes and their transformation to arbitrary positions is done in `position()`.

The intersections are found as we did with the box. We intersect all planes with the ray. For each intersection value we determine whether it is an entry or exit by checking the sign of the dot product of the ray direction with the plane normal. Then we compare the largest entry and the smallest exit values.

The normal at a given hit point is found by inserting the point into the four plane equations and seeing if the result is zero. The point must lie in one of the planes. We then return the normal of that plane.

B.9   THE DODECAHEDRON

This is another of Plato's solids. It is bounded by 12 planes that form regular pentagons. A unit-dodecahedron is positioned so that its center is at (0 0 0), its top and bottom planes are horizontal and turned about y so that one vertex of the top pentagon points in the direction of the z-axis. We call this vertex V.

Figure B.5 shows it looking down from the positive y-axis. Two surface normals are indicated, $n1$ and $n2$. Their projections onto the $(x\ z)$-plane make an angle of 72°. They are therefore at angles of 54° with the x-axis and of 36° with the z-axis. It follows that their x- and z-coordinates are in the ratio of $\cos(54°)$ to $\sin(54°)$. The third surface normal that is used in our computations points straight toward us, $n3$. It cannot be seen in the figure.

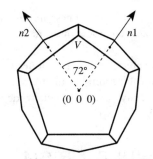

Figure B.5   Unit dodecahedron seen from above

Proceeding in a fashion similar to the tetrahedron, we set $c = \cos(54°)$ and $s = \sin(54°)$ and express the three normals as follows:

$$n1 = \begin{pmatrix} c & y & s \end{pmatrix} \qquad n2 = \begin{pmatrix} -c & y & s \end{pmatrix} \qquad n3 = \begin{pmatrix} 0 & \alpha & 0 \end{pmatrix}$$

The coefficients y and α are unknown. The normals are of equal length and at equal angles with each other. The equal lengths of $n1$ and $n3$ give us the relation $\alpha^2 = c^2 + y^2 + s^2$. The dot products of any two normals must be equal, so we get:

$$\text{dot}(n1, n2) = -c^2 + y^2 + s^2 = y*\alpha = \text{dot}(n1, n3)$$

Squaring the above equation and inserting the value for α leads to:

$$\left(-c^2 + y^2 + s^2\right)^2 = y^2 * \left(c^2 + y^2 + s^2\right)$$

from which we get:

$$y^2 = \frac{\left(s^2 - c^2\right)^2}{3c^2 - s^2}$$

Inserting $\sin(54°) = \frac{1}{4}\left(\sqrt{5}+1\right)$ and $\cos(54°) = \frac{1}{4}\sqrt{10 - 2\sqrt{5}}$ we get the numerator:

$$\left(s^2 - c^2\right)^2 = \frac{6 - 2\sqrt{5}}{16}$$

and the denominator:

$$3c^2 - s^2 = \frac{3 - \sqrt{5}}{2}$$

This fraction evaluates to $y^2 = \frac{1}{4}$ giving $y = \frac{1}{2}$. The normals therefore are:

$$n1 = \begin{pmatrix} c & \frac{1}{2} & s \end{pmatrix} \qquad n2 = \begin{pmatrix} -c & \frac{1}{2} & s \end{pmatrix} \qquad n3 = \begin{pmatrix} 0 & \frac{1}{2}\sqrt{5} & 0 \end{pmatrix}$$

The x- and z-coordinates of the other normals are $\cos(18°)$ and $\sin(18°)$ respectively. We define a unit-dodecahedron by making the distance of all planes from the origin (the inner radius) equal to 0.794655. This leads to an outer radius of 1.

The top and bottom normals are vertical, the five upward pointing normals have $y = 0.5$. Because of symmetry, the five lower normals are obtained from the upper ones by inverting the signs of the y- and z-coordinates. These are still unnormalized vectors; we normalize them and set their signs so that they point outward. The resulting plane equations are shown in the constructor.

Intersecting the object with a ray is done the same as with the tetrahedron: not transforming the ray to the unit-position, but intersecting it directly with the arbitrary object. All functions in the file `dodhedron.c` are actually identical to those in `tethedron.c` except that the loops run to 12.

B.10   THE SIX-SIDED PRISM

All prisms are easy to define. Consider an example of a regular six-sided prism. The unit prism is upright and centered around the y-axis; its base is a regular hexagon. We define it with an inner radius of 1 and a height of 1. This gives it an overall length from top to bottom of 2. It has a total of eight planes counting the ends. We omit the details of deriving the plane equations. The intersections are found by intersecting the arbitrary prism with the arbitrary ray. It is essentially the same code as above, except that all loops run to 8.

B.11   THE TORUS

A torus—also called an anchor ring—is shaped like a doughnut or innertube. Figure B.6 shows two cross sections. It is described by a "big radius" R, a horizontal "small radius" r, and a vertical "small radius" v. The vertical cross section is an ellipse if v and r are unequal. We do not consider a torus with a true elliptic cross section, for example a slanted ellipse, nor do we consider a torus with an elliptical horizontal cross section.

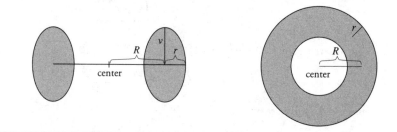

Figure B.6   Vertical and horizontal torus cross sections

B.11.1   THE TORUS INTERSECTION

When we intersect an arbitrarily positioned torus with arbitrary axes R, r, and v, we first translate it to put its center at the origin and rotate it to make it horizontal. Then we scale by $\frac{1}{R}$ in the x- and z-coordinates and by $\frac{r}{R*v}$ in the y-coordinate. This leads to a torus with R equal to 1 and a circular cross section of radius $\frac{r}{R}$. We call this a unit-torus. (Observe that the small radius is variable.) The transformations are done by applying the arbitrary-to-unit transformation matrix to the ray and then intersecting it with the unit-torus.

The unit-torus is expressed by this equation (r is the small radius):

$$\left(x^2 + y^2 + z^2 - \left(1 + r^2\right)\right)^2 = 4\left(r^2 - y^2\right)$$

With $(s_x\ s_y\ s_z)$ being the startpoint of a ray and $(d_x\ d_y\ d_z)$ the direction, a point $(x\ y\ z)$ on the ray becomes:

$$x = s_x + u * d_x$$
$$y = s_y + u * d_y$$
$$z = s_z + u * d_z$$

Inserting this in the torus equation, expanding and ordering on powers of u results in a quartic equation in u:

$$a_4 * u^4 + a_3 * u^3 + a_2 * u^2 + a_1 * u + a_0 = 0$$

To express the coefficients we use

$$t_2 = d_x^2 + d_y^2 + d_z^2$$
$$t_1 = d_x * s_x + d_y * s_y + d_z * s_z$$
$$t_0 = s_x^2 + s_y^2 + s_z^2 - \left(1 + r^2\right)$$

and obtain

$$a_4 = t_2 * t_2$$
$$a_3 = 4 * t_2 * t_1$$
$$a_2 = 4 * t_1 * t_1 + 2 * t_2 * t_0 + 4 * d_y^2$$
$$a_1 = 4 * t_1 * t_0 + 8 * d_y * s_y$$
$$a_0 = t_0 * t_0 - 4 * \left(r^2 - s_y^2\right)$$

We make the highest order coefficient equal to 1 by dividing by a_4. This gives the equation:

$$u^4 + a * u^3 + b * u^2 + c * u + d = 0$$

The four solutions can be obtained analytically without the need for complex arithmetic. (Complex solutions always occur in conjugate complex pairs.) The computations are tedious but straightforward.

One first finds a zero of the so-called resolvent cubic equation: $x^3 + p * x^2 + q * x + r = 0$ in which

$$p = -b$$
$$q = a * c - 4 * d$$
$$r = d * \left(4 * b - a^2\right) - c^2$$

The cubic is first reduced by the substitution $x = y - p/3$ which leads to the cubic equation

$$y^3 + 3*A*y + 2*B = 0$$

$$\text{with } A = \frac{3q - p^2}{9} \quad \text{and } B = \frac{2p^3 - 9pq + 27r}{54}$$

This is solved using Cardano's formula. A cubic equation always has a real root. (This is the only root we are interested in.) It is, by Cardano's formula:

$$y = \sqrt[3]{-B + \sqrt{D}} + \sqrt[3]{-B - \sqrt{D}} \quad \text{with } D = B^2 + A^3$$

When D is greater than or equal to zero, both cube radicands are real, so we compute their real cube roots and add them.

When D is smaller than zero, the cube radicands are conjugate complex numbers. It follows that their cube roots are conjugate complex numbers, too. Adding them cancels the imaginary parts and results in two times the real part of any one of the cube roots.

The cube root of a complex number is easily computed in the complex plane using polar coordinates. We express the complex number as

$$(r, \phi)$$

where r is the distance from the origin and ϕ is the angle made with the positive real axis.

Then the cube root of the complex number is

$$\left(r^{\frac{1}{3}}, \frac{\phi}{3}\right)$$

What is needed for solving the cubic, then, is a function that returns the real part of the cube root of any complex number: `realcbrt()`, see below. For this function we need the cube root of any real number. Some math libraries have the function `cbrt()`. If it is not available, one can compute it using the functions `log()` and `exp()`.

Having found the root, y, of the resolvent cubic equation, you may find the roots of the quartic by computing:

$$R = \sqrt{\frac{a^2}{4} - b + y}$$

$$g = \frac{a^2}{2} - b - y$$

$$h = \frac{a*(b - a^2/4) - 2*c}{R}$$

If $g - h > 0$ we get two real roots:

$$x_0 = \frac{-a/2 - R + \sqrt{g - h}}{2} \qquad x_1 = \frac{-a/2 - R - \sqrt{g - h}}{2}$$

If $g + h > 0$ we get two more real roots:

$$x_2 = \frac{-a/2 + R + \sqrt{g + h}}{2} \qquad x_3 = \frac{-a/2 + R - \sqrt{g + h}}{2}$$

Theoretically, the radicand in the equation for R is never negative, but roundoff errors can bring it slightly below zero. This can be avoided by using higher precision arithmetic, for example long double. The code contains such a portion which is commented out.

When computing the coefficients for the quartic in intersect(), we not only normalize them to $a_4 = 1$ but also scale them: a_3 by $\frac{1}{2}$, a_2 by $\frac{1}{4}$, a_1 by $\frac{1}{8}$, and a_0 by $\frac{1}{16}$. This requires no additional operations and produces a quartic whose roots are scaled by $\frac{1}{2}$. Therefore no division by two is needed when computing the $x[i]$. The scaling has a smoothing effect on the coefficients and makes the computations slightly more stable.

The ray is first tested to see if it starts above the torus and points up, or below the torus and points down. In these cases there cannot be an intersection—we can return 0 right away.

B.11.2 THE TORUS NORMAL

We first translate the hit point on the arbitrary torus and multiply by the arbitrary-to-unit matrix so that it lies on the unit-torus. Intersecting the unit-torus with a vertical plane defined by y-axis and hit point gives the situation shown in Figure B.7. The normal at the hit point lies in this plane. It is the vector from the center of the small circle $(c.x \; 0 \; c.z)$ to the hit point. That center is at a distance of 1 from the origin in the direction of the hit point's projection onto the $(x \; z)$-plane. The projection is simply $(hit.x \; 0 \; hit.z)$. Normalizing the vector from $(0 \; 0 \; 0)$ to the projection gives us $(c.x \; 0 \; c.z)$. The normal on the unit-torus is then $(hit.x–c.x \;\; hit.y \;\; hit.z–c.z)$.

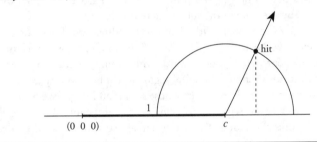

Figure B.7   *Geometry of torus normal*

Applying the same reasoning as used to find the ellipsoid normal, this vector is converted to the normal on the elliptic cross section by scaling its y-coordinate with the factor $\frac{r}{v}$. It must then be rotated back to the arbitrary position.

Scaling and rotating back is done by multiplying the vector by the transpose of the arbitrary-to-unit matrix. In addition to rotating, this scales the x- and z-coordinates by $\frac{1}{R}$ and the y-coordinate by $\frac{r}{R*v}$. In terms of the change in slope for y, it is the same as scaling y alone by $\frac{r}{v}$. This is followed with a normalization.

The constructor computes the small radius of the unit-torus and its square. Position() computes the transformation matrix. When computing the scaling factor for y, we must remember that r is already normalized.

B.12   THE ELLIPTIC SPIRAL

The elliptic spiral is an example of how unusual and interesting looking solids can be implemented relatively simply.

This object is created by taking an ellipsoid, wrapping a ribbon around it from the top down to the bottom to give a spiral, and then considering only the ribbon itself as the object. We introduce it to show the usefulness and power of parametric patterns, and how they can be defined.

We first find the intersection with the ellipsoid; this is done by intersecting the transformed ray with the unit-sphere. The ribbon pattern is specified on the unit-sphere. This makes the computation considerably easier. The entry point on the sphere is checked to see if it lies on the ribbon.

We will need the longitudinal and latitudinal coordinates of a point $(x \ y \ z)$ on a sphere. The latitude is $\arcsin(y) + \pi/2$. This gives an angular coordinate from 0 at the south pole to π at the north pole. This number is scaled to range from 0 to 10. The scaling is determined by the number of spiraling turns of the ribbon (here it is 10).

The longitude is found by computing $\alpha = \arcsin(z)$ if x is positive and $\alpha = \pi - \arcsin(z)$ if x is negative. If α is negative we change it to $2\pi + \alpha$. This gives a full circle angular coordinate α that ranges from 0 at the right "horizon" of the sphere to 2π after a full circle around the y-axis. This is scaled to range from 0 to 1. The scaling is determined by the number of different ribbons spiraling down the sphere (here it is 1).

Points on the sphere with identical latitudinal coordinates lie on a horizontal circle around the sphere. Points with identical sums of their longitudinal and latitudinal coordinates lie on a spiral segment that tilts downwards while going counterclockwise around the sphere. After one full turn the end of the spiral segment will be lower by exactly one unit latitude.

If we consider those points whose sum is an integer, we have ten spiral segments. But the end of each spiral segment coincides with the beginning of the next, so that these points describe one continuous spiral that circles 10 times ccw while descending down the unit-sphere.

This is the basis for defining the spiral band. The width of this band is, of course, zero. Considering all points whose sum differs from a whole number by at most a certain amount gives a band of finite width.

We first check the entry point to the sphere. If it belongs to the ribbon, we have found two spiral intersection points: these are coinciding entry and exit points. We then check the exit point of the sphere; if it belongs to the ribbon, two more spiral coinciding intersections have been found. The number of intersections can be zero, two, or four, because the spiral is a concave object. The spiral itself has no "body," it is infinitely thin like the board introduced above. The normal is simply the ellipsoid normal.

B.13   SURFACES OF REVOLUTION

Defining a curve in the $(x \ y)$-plane and rotating it about the y-axis produces a so-called surface of revolution. Many real world objects have such surfaces: bottles, cups, glasses, vases, lamp stands and lamp shades, even certain buildings like a minaret tower or a lighthouse.

Only for very simple defining curves is there an equation for the surface of revolution. A slanted straight line, for example, produces a cone surface. But in the majority of cases an implicit form for the surface does not exist. To intersect a ray with such a surface is difficult. We show how to obtain an equation for the parameter value u where the ray intersects with the surface.

There is no analytical advantage in doing the rotation about the y-axis rather than the x- or z-axis. The last two rotations can define the object as well. It is only that we are used to seeing such objects as upright. In this spirit we assume the defining curve given in the $(x\ y)$-plane by $x = f(y)$, the ray is given by

$$x = sx + u * dx$$
$$y = sy + u * dy$$
$$z = sz + u * dz$$

The three-dimensional intersection problem can be transformed into a two-dimensional one. Understanding this transformation requires some spatial imagination capability because it is not simply a projection of the kind we are used to. We should rather call it a rotational projection.

Imagine the surface and a ray that does not intersect the y-axis. For any given u-value we take the corresponding point on the ray and imagine a plane through this point and the y-axis. The intersection of this plane with the surface is the defining curve. When we now advance along the straight line the plane determined by point and y-axis will more or less rotate about the y-axis. Its intersection with the surface will always be the same defining curve, it is constant in the plane, but the point on the straight line will move whithin the rotating plane. Starting on the straight line on one end infinitely far away and going to the other end will correspond to a 180 degree rotation of the plane. All intersection points of straight line and surface with the plane that have accumulated on that rotation are considered the rotational projection of these points onto the plane.

The path of the point within the plane can be expressed by the parameter u of the ray. Wherever this path intersects the defining curve, the ray intersects the surface of revolution.

We can display the rotational projection in a two-dimensional drawing in x and y. To prevent confusion we call the three spatial coordinates x_{sp}, y_{sp}, and z_{sp}. The positive x-axis in the projection corresponds to the $(x_{sp}\ z_{sp})$-plane in space (actually that part only over which the rotation swept), its y-axis is still identical to the y_{sp}-axis in space. Any point along the straight line in space is given by the parameterization:

$$x_{sp} = sx + u * dx$$
$$y_{sp} = sy + u * dy$$
$$z_{sp} = sz + u * dz$$

The x-coordinate of a point on the path is the distance of the corresponding point in space from the y_{sp}-axis. This is

$$x = \sqrt{x_{sp}^2 + z_{sp}^2} = \sqrt{(sx + u * dx)^2 + (sz + u * dz)^2}$$

The *y*-coordinate of a point on the path is the distance of the corresponding point in space from the $(x_{sp} \; z_{sp})$-plane. This is

$$y = y_{sp} = sy + u*dy$$

The path intersects the curve $x = f(y)$ at those *u*-values for which

$$\sqrt{(sx + u*dx)^2 + (sz + u*dz)^2} = f(sy + u*dy)$$

is fulfilled. Squaring both sides and moving all terms to the left gives us the desired equation for *u*:

$$(sx + u*dx)^2 - (f(sy + u*dy))^2 + (sz + u*dz)^2 = 0$$

If the defining curve is a cubic polynomial, we get a 6th degree polynomial in *u*. If it is a sin function or the like we get a transcendental equation. We see that in most cases the zeroes must be found by iterative methods. You will have to use a root finder from some math library if you want to attack such problems.

B.14   THE LOOKUP TABLE MANAGER

IMPLEMENTATION BY DR. CLINT STALEY

When working in a lookup table environment, like Xwin8, only 256 different colors can be displayed on the screen at any given time. Ray tracing, however, generally produces a different color for every pixel, computed as an *rgb*-value; far more colors than the graphics hardware can display. What is stored in the frame buffer for that pixel location is an address into the lookup table. The *rgb*-value computed for a pixel must be transformed into the lookup table address which optimally represents this *rgb*-value. How good the optimal representations are depends on the setting of the lookup table. If, for example, only 256 or fewer different *rgb*-values are produced by the ray tracer (no matter the number of pixels), then a lookup table setting is possible in which a precisely matching *rgb* entry can be found for every pixel. In general, however, the lookup table must be set to contain a best compromise.

A best compromise strategy can be sketched in plain language as follows: *rgb*-values are computed that are in or close to clusters of frequently occurring or similar *rgb*-values of the picture (even if no *rgb*-value of the picture exactly corresponds to it). Altogether 256 representing *rgb*-values are computed and entered into the table. Consequently, more frequent *rgb*-values or denser clusters of *rgb*-values in the picture will have closer matches in the table than rare and isolated *rgb*-values.

In order to compute and enter the best matching *rgb*-values, all pixel *rgb*-values must be known. Therefore, only after the whole picture is ray traced can an optimal lookup table be set. In an Xwin8 environment the ray tracer must make at least two passes. (The code in `Raytrace/display.c` makes more than two passes for a different reason: To provide a course overview of the picture which gradually becomes finer as the raytracing proceeds.) In the first pass the *rgb*-values of all pixels are written onto a file (to avoid a second raytracing) and posted to the lookup table manager (LTM). After the raytracing ends the LTM computes the best lookup table setting. Subsequently, all *rgb*-values are read in from the file and submitted to the LTM which now finds the best matching LT entry; this one is entered into the frame buffer. See the code in `Raytrace/display.c` under the `#ifdef` "Xwin8" directive.

Below is a precise description of the algorithm provided by Dr. Staley.

The LTM module is an implementation of the algorithm described by Paul Heckbert in HECK82. The algorithm is standard to many color mapping systems.

Assuming that colors are represented as *rgb*-values with components between 0 and 255, then we may view the space of all colors as a cube, with each of the three dimensions of the cube representing red, green, and blue, respectively. The "corner points" of this cube would be:

(0	0	0)	or black
(0	0	255)	or blue
(0	255	0)	or green
(255	0	0)	or red
(0	255	255)	or cyan
(255	0	255)	or magenta
(255	255	0)	or yellow
(255	255	255)	or white

Each color is a point within this cube. For each color point in the cube, we count the number of pixels in the image that have that color. This number is the "weight" at that color point.

We divide the cube into two halves, cutting perpendicular to one of the axes. We choose a division point such that the total weight of points in each of the two halves is as close to equal as possible. We then repeat this process recursively for each of the two halves, dividing them evenly (by weight) into smaller parallelepipeds. We divide across a different dimension each time, to keep the pieces as close to cubical as possible. We continue to divide until we have as many pieces as there are colors in the color map, say 256. We then assign every color within a piece to a single entry in the color map, which may be the "center" color of the piece, or may be chosen to be the color within the piece that is the center of mass, using the weights of the color points.

BIBLIOGRAPHY

ABBU86   Abi-Ezzi S, Bunshaft A: "An Implementer's View of PHIGS." In *IEEE Computer Graphics and Applications*, February 1986.

ANDE82   Anderson DP: "Hidden Line Elimination in Projected Grid Surfaces." *MRC Technical Summary Report #2447*. Madison: Mathematics Research Center, University of Wisconsin, December 1982.

ANDE84   Anderson GH: *Video Editing and Post Production: A Professional Guide*. White Plains, NY: Knowledge Industry Publications, 1984.

ARKI89   Arvo J, Kirk D: "A Survey of Raytracing Acceleration Techniques." In *An Introduction to Raytracing*, edited by Andrew S. Glassner, 201. San Diego: Academic Press Inc., 1989.

BASL88   Barnsley MF, Sloan AD: "A Better Way to Compress Images." *Byte* (January 1988).

BARS88   Barsky B: *Computer Graphics and Geometric Modeling Using Beta-splines*. New York: Springer-Verlag, 1988.

BEUR37   Besicovitch AS, Ursell HD: "Sets of Fractional Dimensions (V): On Dimensional Members of Some Continuous Curves." *Journal of the London Mathematical Society* 12 (1937): 18–25.

BIER83   Bier EA: "Solidviews, An Interactive Three-Dimensional Illustrator." BS & MS thesis, Department of Electrical Engineering & Computer Science, MIT, May 1983.

BLNE76   Blinn JF, Newell ME: "Texture and Reflection in Computer Generated Images." *Communications of the ACM* 19, 10 (1976): 542–547.

BLIN78   Blinn JF: "Simulation of Wrinkled Surfaces." *Computer Graphics* 12, 3 (1978): 286–292.

BRES77   Bresenham JE: "A Linear Algorithm for Incremental Digital Display of Circular Arcs." *Communications of the ACM* 20, 2 (February 1977): 100–106.

BRON74   Brons R: "Linguistic Methods for the Description of a Straight Line on a Grid." *Computer Graphics and Image Processing* 3 (1974): 48–62.

BRON85   Brons R: "Theoretical and Linguistic Methods for Describing Straight Lines." In *Fundamental Algorithms for Computer Graphics*, Nato ASI Series, vol. F17. New York: Springer-Verlag, 1985.

BUGI89   Burger P, Gillies D: *Interactive Computer Graphics*. Reading, MA: Addison-Wesley, 1989.

BUTL79   Butland J: "Surface Drawing Made Simple." *Computer-aided Design* 11.1 (January 1979): 19–22.

CAD184   CADAM: *The CADAM System Training Handbook and Procedure Guide*. CADAM, 1984.

CAD284   CADAM: *CADAM 3-D Handbook*. CADAM, 1984.

CAPI85   Castle CMA, Pitteway MLV: "An Application of Euclid's Algorithm to Drawing Straight Lines." In *Fundamental Algorithms for Computer Graphics*. Nato ASI Series, vol. F17. New York: Springer-Verlag, 1985.

CATM74   Catmull E: "A Subdivision Algorithm for Computer Display of Curved Surfaces." Technical Report, Computer Science Department, University of Utah, December 1974.

CATM75   Catmull E: "Computer Display of Curved Surfaces." In *Computer Graphics Pattern Recognition Data Structure*, 11, Proceedings from IEEE Conference, May 1975.

CLAR80   Clark JH: "A VLSI Geometry Processor for Graphics." *Computer* 12, (July 1980): 7.

CLRI80   Cohen E, Lyche T, Riesenfeld RF: "Discrete B-Splines and Subdivision Techniques in Computer Aided Geometric Design and Computer Graphics." *Computer Graphics and Image Processing*, vol. 14, (1980): 87–111.

COHE69   Cohen D: "On Linear Difference Curves." *Computer Display Review*. Watertown, Mass.: Keydata Corporation, 1969. (This review is now published periodically by GML Associates, 594 Marrett Rd., Lexington, Mass. Articles on graphics techniques are contained in volume 4.)

COMM82 Commodore Business Machines: *Commodore 64 Programmer's Reference Guide*. Commodore Business Machines and Howard W. Sams, 1982.

COTO82   Cook RL, Torrance KE: "A Reflectance Model for Computer Graphics." *ACM Transactions on Graphics* (January 1982): 7–24.

COXM72   Cox MG: "The Numerical Evaluation of B-splines." *J. Inst. Maths. Applics*. 10 (1972): 130–149.

CROW87   Crow F: "Displays on Display. The Origins of the Teapot." *IEEE CG&A* (1987): 8.

CUGS83   Curry J, Garnett L, Sullivan D: "On the Iteration of Rational Functions: Computer Experiments with Newton's Method." *Commun. Math. Phys*. 91 (1983): 267–277.

CUNN90   Cunningham S: "3D Viewing and Rotation Using Orthonormal Bases," in *Graphics Gems* vol. 1, 516, edited by Andrew Glassner. Boston: Academic Press Inc., 1990.

CUSC47   Curry HB, Schoenberg IJ: "On Spline Distributions and their Limits: the Polya Distribution Functions." *Bull. Amer. Math. Soc*. 53, Abstract 380t (1947): 109.

DEBO72   deBoor C: "On Calculating with B-Splines." *J. Approx. Theory* 6 (1972): 50–62.

DEBO78   deBoor C: *A Practical Guide to Splines*. New York: Springer-Verlag, 1978.

DOHU82   Douady A, Hubbard JH: "Iteration de Polynomes Quadratic Complexes." *CRAS* (Paris), 294, (1982): 123–126.

EKPF84   Enderle G, Kansy K, Pfaff G: *Computer Graphics Programming, GKS — the Graphics Standard*. New York: Springer-Verlag, 1984.

EKPE93   Ellzey M, Kreinovich V, Pena J: "Fast Rotation of a 3D Image About an Arbitrary Line." In *Computer & Graphics*, vol 17, no. 2, Pergamon Press, (1993): 121–126.

FATO19   Fatou P: "Sur les Equations Fonctionelles." *Bull. Soc. Math. Fr*. 47 (1919): 161–271; 48: 33–94, 208–314.

FIMO87   Fichter W, Morf M, eds.: *VLSI CAD Tools and Applications*. Kluwer Academic Publishers, 1987.

FOLE84   Foley JD, Van Dam A: *Fundamentals of Interactive Computer Graphics*. Reading, MA: Addison-Wesley, 1982.

FVFH90   Foley JD, Van Dam A, Feiner S, Hughes J: *Computer Graphics, Principles and Practice*, second edition. Reading, MA: Addison-Wesley Publishing Company, 1990.

FREE70   Freeman H: "Boundary Encoding and Processing." In *Picture Processing and Psychopictorics*, edited by Lipkin BS and Rosenfeld A, 241–266. New York: Academic Press, 1970.

GEWH89 Gerald CF, Wheatley PO: *Applied Numerical Analysis*. Reading, MA: Addison-Wesley Publishing Company, 1989.

GILO78   Giloi WK: *Interactive Computer Graphics*. Englewood Cliffs, New Jersey: Prentice-Hall, 1978.

GORI74   Gordon WJ, Riesenfeld RF: "B-Spline Curves and Surfaces." In *Computer-Aided Geometric Design*, edited by Barnhill RE and Riesenfeld RF. New York: Academic Press, 1974.

GOUR71   Gouraud H: "Continuous Shading of Curved Surfaces." *IEEE Trans. on Computers* (June 1971): 623–629.

HAIN89   Haines E: "Essential Ray Tracing Algorithms." In *An Introduction to Raytracing*, edited by Andrew S. Glassner, 46. San Diego: Academic Press Inc., 1989.

HARR83   Harrington S: *Computer Graphics, A Programming Approach*. New York: McGraw-Hill, 1983.

HDGS83   Hopgood FRA, Duce DA, Gallop JR, Sutcliffe DC: *Introduction to the Graphical Kernel System (GKS)*. London: Academic Press, 1983.

HEBA86   Hearn D, Baker P: *Computer Graphics*. Englewood Cliffs, New Jersey: Prentice-Hall, 1986.

HECK82   Heckbert P: SIGGRAPH Proceedings 1982, 297–307.

HILL90   Hill FS Jr.: *Computer Graphics*. New York: MacMillan Publishing Co., 1990.

HORN76   Horn BKP: "Circle Generators for Display Devices." *Computer Graphics and Image Processing* 5 (1976): 280–288.

HUKA84   Hung SHY, Kasvand T: "On the Chord Property and its Equivalences." Proceedings 7th International Conference on Pattern Recognition, Montreal, 1984: 116–119.

IMAC85   *Inside Macintosh, Volume III.* Reading, MA: Addison-Wesley, 1985.

INTE88   International Standards Organization: *International Standard Information Processing Systems—Computer Graphics—Graphical Kernel System for Three Dimensions (GKS-3D) Functional Description,* ISO Document Number 8805:1988(E). New York: American National Standards Institute, 1988.

JOLH73   Jordan BW, Lennon WJ, Holm BC: "An Improved Algorithm for the Generation of Non-parametric Curves." *IEEE Trans.,* C-22, 12 (December 1973): 1052–1060.

JULI18   Julia G: "Sur l'Iteration de Fonctions Rationnelles." *Journal de Math.* Pure et Appl. 8 (1918): 47–245.

KALE92   Kay DC, Levine JR: *Graphics File Formats.* Windcrest/McGraw-Hill, 1992.

KAPP85   Kappel MR: "An Ellipse-Drawing Algorithm for Raster Displays." In *Fundamental Algorithms for Computer Graphics.* Nato ASI Series, vol. F17. New York: Springer-Verlag, 1985.

KAYD79   Kay DG: "Transparency, Refraction and Ray Tracing for Computer-Synthesized Images." Master's thesis, Cornell University, 1979.

KDGD79   Kay DG, Greenberg D: "Transparency for Computer Synthesized Images." *Computer Graphics* 13 (1979): 158–164.

KSGU68   Kubert BR, Szabo J, Guliery S: "The Perspective Representation of Functions of Two Variables." *JACM* 15,2 (April 1968): 193–204.

KUBO85   Kubo S: "Continuous Color Presentation Using a Low-cost Ink Jet Printer." In *Frontiers in Computer Graphics,* edited by Kunii TL, 344–353. Tokyo: Springer-Verlag, 1985.

LCWB80   Lane JM, Carpenter LC, Whitted T, Blinn JF: "Scan Line Methods for Displaying Parametrically Defined Surfaces." *Communications of the ACM* 23 (January 1980): 23–34.

LIBA83   Liang YD, Barsky BA: "An Analysis and Algorithm for Polygon Clipping." *CACM* 26,11 (November 1983): 868–877, and *Corrigendum CACM* 27,2 (February 1984): 151.

LIBA84   Liang YD, Barsky BA: "A New Concept and Method for Line Clipping." *ACM Transactions on Graphics* 3, 1 (January 1984): 1–22.

MAND69   Mandelbrot BB: "Computer Experiments with Fractional Gaussian Noises." *Water Resources Research* 5 (1969): 228.

MAND71   Mandelbrot BB: "A Fast Fractional Gaussian Noise Generator." *Water Resources Research* 7 (1971): 543–553.

MAND75   Mandelbrot BB: "Stochastic Models for the Earth's Relief, the Shape and the Fractal Dimension of the Coastlines, and the Number-Area Rule for Islands." *Proc. Nat. Acad. Sci. USA* 72 (1975): 3825–3828.

MAND77   Mandelbrot BB: *Fractals: Form, Chance, and Dimension.* San Francisco: W. H. Freeman, 1977.

MAND82   Mandelbrot BB: *The Fractal Geometry of Nature.* New York: W. H. Freeman, 1982.

MARO82   Maron MJ: *Numerical Analysis: A Practical Approach.* New York: Macmillan, 1982.

MIEL91   Mielke B: *Integrated Computer Graphics.* New York: West Publishing Company, 1991.

MORT85   Mortenson ME: *Geometric Modeling.* New York: John Wiley & Sons, 1985.

MUUS87   Muuss MJ: "Understanding the Preparation and Analysis of Solid Models." In *Techniques for Computer Graphics,* edited by Rogers DF and Earnshaw RA. New York: Springer-Verlag, 1987.

NESP79   Newman WM, Sproull RF: *Principles of Interactive Computer Graphics.* New York: McGraw-Hill, 1979.

NILN87   Nicholl TM, Lee DT, Nicholl RA: "An Efficient New Algorithm for 2-D Line Clipping: Its Development and Analysis." SIGGRAPH 87: 253–262.

NNSA72 Newell NE, Newell RG, Sancha TL: "A Solution to the Hidden Surface Problem." Proceedings from ACM Annual Conference Boston (August 1972): 443–450.

NYEX92 Nye A: *Xlib Programming Manual*, vol 1. Sebastopol, CA: O'Reilly & Assoc. Inc., 1992.

PERI86 Peitgen HO, Richter PH: *The Beauty of Fractals*. New York: Springer-Verlag, 1986.

PESA88 Peitgen HO, Saupe D: *The Science of Fractal Images*. New York: Springer-Verlag, 1988.

PHIG88 PHIGS+ Committee, Andries van Dam, chair: "PHIGS+ Functional Description, Revision 3.0." *Computer Graphics*, 22(3), (July 1988): 125–218.

PHON75 Phong Bui-Tuong: "Illumination for Computer Generated Images." *Communications of the ACM*, 18, 6 (June 1975): 311–317.

PITT67 Pitteway MLV: "Algorithm for Drawing Ellipses or Hyperbolae with a Digital Plotter." *Comput. J.* 10, 3 (November 1967): 282–289.

RAST85 Conrac Corporation: *Raster Graphics Handbook*. New York: Van Nostrand Reinhold, 1985.

RAYT89 Glassner AS (Editor): *An Introduction to Raytracing*. San Diego: Academic Press Inc., 1989.

REEV81 Reeves WT: "In-betweening for Computer Animation Utilizing Moving Point Constraints." Proceedings from ACM SIGGRAPH Conference (1981): 263–269.

RICH61 Richardson LF: "The Problem of Contiguity: An Appendix of Statistics of Deadly Quarrels." *General Systems Yearbook* 6 (1961): 134–187.

ROAD90 Rogers DF, Adams JA: *Mathematical Elements for Computer Graphics*, second ed. San Francisco: McGraw-Hill Publishing Co., 1990.

ROGE85 Rogers DF: *Procedural Elements for Computer Graphics*. New York: McGraw-Hill, 1985.

ROTH82 Roth SD: "Ray Casting for Modeling Solids." *Comput. Graph. Image Processing*, 18(2), (February 1982): 109–144.

SCHO67 Schoenberg IJ: "On Spline Functions." In *Inequalities*, edited by Shisha O, 114, 157, 255–291. New York: Academic Press, 1967.

SCHO73 Schoenberg IJ: "Cardinal Spline Interpolation." CBMS 12, Philadelphia: SIAM, 1973.

SPSU68 Sproull RF, Sutherland IE: "A Clipping Divider," AFIPS Conference Proceedings 33 (1968): FJCC, 765.

SUTH63 Sutherland IE: "Sketchpad: A Man-Machine Graphical Communication System." SJCC 1963. Baltimore, MD: Spartan Books, 329.

SWBA86 Sweeney AJ, Bartels RH: "Ray Tracing Free-Form B-Spline Surfaces." *IEEE Computer Graphics and Applications*, 6 (Feb 1986): 41–49.

TARA80 Taramon SK, ed.: *Meeting Today's Productivity Challenge*. Society of Manufacturing Engineers, 1980.

TEXA86 *TMS34010 User's Guide*. Texas Instruments, 1986.

THAL86 Thalmann D, Magnenat-Thalmann N: *Computer Animation, Theory and Practice*. New York: Springer-Verlag, 1986.

VOSS85 Voss RF: "Random Fractal Forgeries." Course notes 15 of the twelfth annual ACM SIGGRAPH conference. San Francisco, 1985.

WARN68 Warnock JE: *A Hidden Line Algorithm for Halftone Picture Representation*. University of Utah Computer Science Dept. Rep., TR 4-5 (May 1968): NTIS AD 761 995.

WARN69 Warnock JE: *A Hidden Surface Algorithm for Computer-Generated Halftone Pictures*. University of Utah Computer Science Dept. Rep., TR 4-15 (June 1969): NTIS AD 753 671.

WATT89 Watt A: *Fundamentals of Three-dimensional Computer Graphics*. Menlo Park, California: Addison-Wesley, 1989.

WEIL80 Weiler K: "Polygon Comparison Using a Graph Representation." SIGGRAPH 80, 10–18.

WILL72 Williamson H: *Algorithm 420—hidden-line plotting program* (J6). CACM 15,2 (February 1972): 100–103.

INDEX